FAIRMOUNT TEMPLE LIBRARY

In Honor of

INDIA'S
BENE ISRAEL

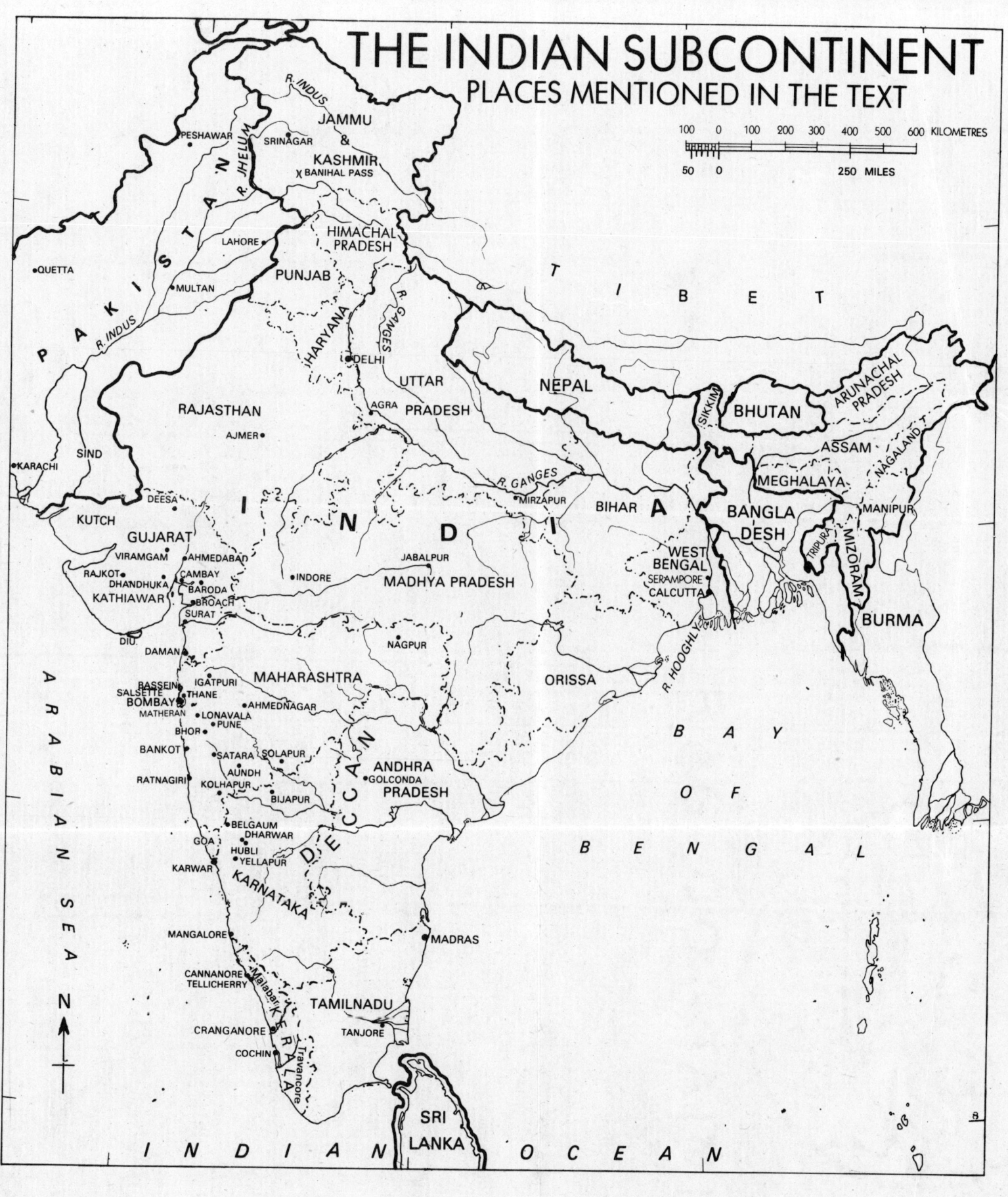

SHIRLEY BERRY ISENBERG

INDIA'S BENE ISRAEL

A Comprehensive Inquiry and Sourcebook

JUDAH L. MAGNES MUSEUM
BERKELEY, CALIFORNIA

India's Bene Israel is published in separate editions
simultaneously in India and the United States respectively, by

POPULAR PRAKASHAN PVT. LTD.,
35-C Pandit Madan Mohan Malviya Marg,
Tardeo, Bombay 400 034, India.
(3331)

JUDAH L. MAGNES MUSEUM
2911 Russell Street
Berkeley, California, USA

Publication of the American edition was assisted by :
ANJALI AND DONALD MORRIS
IN MEMORY OF MR LORRIE MORRIS

Copyright © 1988 by SHIRLEY B. ISENBERG

All rights reserved. No part of this work, including text, maps,
photographs, block prints, etc., may be reproduced or transmitted
in any form or by any means, electronic or mechanical,
including photocopying and recording, or any information
storage and retrieval system, without permission in writing from the author.

ISBN : 0-943376-27-0

Library of Congress Catalogue Card :

10 9 8 7 6 5 4 3 2 1

PRINTED IN INDIA

by Rekha Printers Pvt. Ltd. A — 102/1 Okhla Industrial Estate Phase II, New Delhi 110020
and published by Ramdas G. Bhatkal for Popular Prakashan Pvt. Ltd.,
35-C Pandit Madan Mohan Malviya Marg, Tardeo Bombay 400 034.

To
MY HUSBAND ARTUR
who shares with me my love of India

Preface

The genesis of this volume goes back to the author's having been commissioned by an Indian publisher to write a brief introduction to Judaism together with a general survey of the three Jewish communities[1] of India, as part of a series on "Cultural and Religious Patterns in India", intended primarily for Indian readers. To inform India about its own unique Jewish communities is desirable in itself, the more so since during the past three decades their numbers have dwindled to such an extent that they may never again constitute the vibrant communities which once they were.[2] There has long been a very real and basic need for a thorough and comprehensive study of these three communities. The present volume is devoted to the largest of the three, the Bene Israel.

As research progressed, it became clear to me that an approach based exclusively upon the concepts and methodology of anthropology would be quite inadequate ; properly to be understood and appreciated, the Bene Israel had to be placed within the context of their own history, with more emphasis on the latter than is usually allotted in an anthropological study. This meant setting out upon a lengthy trail of historical detection. The result now before the reader is thus a synthesis of anthropology and historiography.

Bits and pieces of information (including some misinformation) about India's three Jewish communities are as numerous as they are widely scattered; no one has, so far, taken the trouble of gathering the relevant extant material in one place. The observation applies with equal force to the three communities taken together and — on an interdisciplinary level — to any one of them taken by itself. In a sense, the present volume serves as a kind of source-book on the subject of the Bene Israel. On the assumption that it will be read not only within India, but outside as well, it includes explanations of Indian historical background, definitions of Indian terms, etc. It also contains, as necessary background information, explanations and definitions of certain relevant terms and events of the religion and history of the Jewish people, for the benefit of readers who may not be familiar with these matters.

II

India, herself the cradle of several great religions, has for centuries been hospitable to Judaism, Christianity and Islam, all of which originated in the Middle East, in that chronological order. And it is most likely that devotees of these religions made their appearance in India in the same order. These religions took root and became part of the rich fabric of Indian civilization. Of the three, the story of Judaism and of the Jews of India is the one least known within India, while outside India — and this is true even among other Jewish groups — the very fact of the existence of Jews of India is often completely or nearly unknown. This ignorance may be due, in part, to the relatively small number of Indian Jews who, even at their most populous period, during the 1940s, totalled not more than 30,000 souls.[3] The so-called Cochin Jews of what today is the Indian state of Kerala and the Bene Israel of Maharashtra are remarkable and especially worthy of note because, unlike Jews in most other parts of the world, they were allowed to live in peace and harmony in India for many centuries, perhaps for two millenia or even more; because they have retained their essential Judaism; and because they still pose a challenge to the historian as regards the facts of their origins in India. Of particular interest to students of Jewish history : there is not only the impressive fact that Indian Jews were never victimized by anti-semitism,[4] but also that there existed for centuries on Indian soil, in Kerala, the rare phenomenon of a privileged, highly honored, respected and largely autonomous Jewish community,[5] and of Jews (the Bene Israel) whose origins might conceivably go back to the lost tribes of Israel. Soon, however, owing to large-scale emigration to Israel, the number of Jews remaining in India may sink into insignificance. Each of the three main Jewish communities of India has its own different history and way of life. All of this should be documented as fully as possible before it is too late. The writing of the present book should be viewed as a step in that direction.

III

The three separate Jewish communities of India are : (1) the Bene Israel (maximal population 20,000 in1951), whose center is the Konkan[6] area of Maharashtra; (2) the Cochin Jews of Kerala (maximal population 3,000 in the 1940s); and (3) much more recently arrived in India, the so-called Iraqi or Baghdadi Jews (maximal population 6,500 in the 1940s) who, preceded by individuals during the late 18th century, came to India from Iraq as an immigrant community in the early years of the 19th century, settling mostly in Bombay and in Calcutta.[7] The Bene Israel community was, and remains, the largest of the three groups, greatly outnumbering the other two put together. Bene Israel history has not yet been adequately researched. As a prerequisite for a hoped-for probe in great depth into the records of the past, the sundry pieces of known information on the subject should be sorted out, discussed under one cover; full bibliographic details of all that has so far appeared in print need to be gathered and recorded. The present attempt to do so will, it is hoped, provide the necessary perspective and encourage others to carry the search further. While research into the past of the Cochin Jews has been by no means exhaustive, and much archaeological, archival and folkloristic work still needs to be done, Cochin Jewry has always been a more manageable unit to study than have the Bene Israel — more uniform, concentrated within a tiny area, and better known to the world outside India through wider contacts, extending over a much longer period of time. The Iraqi Jewish community in India is relatively of very recent origin, a fact which limits the quantum and scope of relevant material. To state such a truism is, however, not at all tantamount to saying that volumes could not be written about the Iraqi Jewish community. Indeed, two substantial accounts of this community were recently published, one in 1974, the other in 1975.[8]

Just what were the factors which enabled the Indian Jewish communities — different from each other as they were, and located in different parts of India — to thrive unmolested and in an uninterrupted state of amity and accord with their non-Jewish Indian neighbours? No other Jewish group in the diaspora has enjoyed such a blessing, continuing throughout the vicissitudes of so many centuries, and involving so many changes of government. Some contributing factors apply to India as a whole, irrespective of time or of the particular regime which happened to be in power. These characteristics are especially significant because they are either unique to India, or seem to operate more intensively in that country than anywhere else. They include : India's ability to absorb and to accommodate an unparalleled variety of different peoples with their differing ways of life — a diversity of languages, religions, costumes and customs, from the most primitive to the most modern, from the most religious to the most scientific. Sometimes people of widely different cultures are found living in the closest proximity. No group seems shocked that other groups should be living differently from itself. The caste system (see below pp. 16-17, n. 48) perpetuated differences, but there was room for all, not only for non-caste Hindus, but also for every conceivable non-Hindu group. The Jews of India were an infinitesimally small minority, and with India's multitude of differing groups, there was never any inclination to single out or to discriminate against the Jews as a people different and apart. Each of the three Indian Jewish communities has its own respective history, neighbors, and other life contexts providing each group with its own characteristic form of Indian experience and sense of belonging.

IV

As already indicated, the present writer has made a conscious effort to pull together available strands of information about the Bene Israel, their past and their present, from the extant literature, in print and sometimes in manuscript. Equally important information has emerged from numerous intensive interviews conducted by the author with individual members of the Bene Israel community—both with Bene Israel persons who have remained in India as well as with many Bene Israel after they had emigrated to Israel. In preparation for this book, research and interviews began in 1968 and continued, intermittently, for more than a decade.

The extant literature may be briefly described as follows: a number of more or less sketchily written articles of the journalistic variety; articles in the official gazetteers and census reports of the Konkan area; 19th century missionary journals, books and reports; a very few university theses, focusing on limited specific aspects; references to the Bene Israel in the writings of pre-20th century travellers; the studies of Benjamin J. Israel; and the writings of Walter J. Fischel, Haeem Samuel Kehimkar, Joan G. Roland, Shellim Samuel and Schifra Strizower.

A lengthy, well-written account of the Bene Israel appeared in the 31 August and 7 September 1888 issues of *The Jewish Chronicle* (London), contributed by Haeem Samuel Kehimkar, himself a member of the Bene Israel community. Kehimkar expanded the subject matter of these two articles into the manuscript of a full-size book, *The History of the Bene-Israel of India.* Although the manuscript was completed in 1897, it was not published until forty years later, in 1937.[9] Long out of print, it still remains *the* classic book on the subject. In it Kehimkar presented a copious record of Bene Israel traditions and depicted Bene Israel lifestyles of the 19th century. Some of his comments and analyses may be naive; his attempts to fit Biblical quotes to Bene Israel customs, or to theories of the community's origins, may fail to carry conviction; a few statements may be contradictory. Yet none of these criticisms can gainsay the fact that Kehimkar's book preserves a wealth of information which, but for his labors, would have been lost to posterity. The value of the book is greatly enhanced by the 51 photographs illustrating the features and dress styles of Bene Israel individuals of diverse backgrounds (rural, urban, civilian and military). The photographs were added by Dr. Immanuel Olsvanger, a man who, inter-alia was a Sanskrit scholar and who, while in Bombay, learned of the existence of Kehimkar's manuscript, appreciated its great importance, and, with the permission of the author's son, Joseph Kehimkar, arranged to have it printed and published in Tel Aviv in 1937, 28 years after the author's death.[10]

Shellim Samuel, a Bene Israel and an advocate by profession, has taught and written on the subjects of civics and economics. In his book, *The Treatise on the Origin and Early History of the Beni-Israel of Maharashtra State,*[11] he musters a great deal of possibly relevant data, from ancient through medieval times, to weigh various speculations concerning Bene Israel origins and early history.

Dr. Schifra Strizower, in her book, *The Children of Israel : the Bene Israel of Bombay*,[12] concentrates on the Bene Israel within the city of Bombay in modern times, having done most of her fieldwork in Bombay during 1954/55. She is a social anthropologist and writes perceptively on those sociological aspects on which she focuses, with, however, too little attention to the community's Indian context *per se*, and apparently with too narrow a range of respondents. Even so, her observations on certain internal and external Bene Israel relationships are both pertinent and cogent.

Another useful book, which provides even more information about the Cochin Jews than about the Bene Israel, is that by the Rev. J. Henry Lord, *The Jews in India and the Far East*[13] — mainly because of its footnotes, bibliographies and population tables. But our earliest *substantial* information about the Bene Israel comes from various writings and lectures of the Rev. John Wilson during the second quarter of the 19th century.[14]

The late Professor Walter J. Fischel, Professor of Semitic Languages and Literature at the University of California at Berkeley from 1945 unitl his untimely death in 1973, unearthed massive documentation on the activities of important individual Jews whose paths took them to the Indian subcontinent from the early Middle Ages until almost the beginning of the 20th century. Some of these Jews stayed in India only for relatively brief sojourns, some for several years, while a few remained for the rest of their lives. But most of them had come from outside India and, except for a few Pardesi Cochin Jews, left India without establishing legitimate families which would remain permanently in the subcontinent, forming part of an Indian Jewish community. Fischel's accounts of these individuals are to be found in a number of articles written by him in English (see Bibliography) as well as in his book (written in Hebrew), *Ha-Yehudim B'Hodu* (The Jews in India, Their Contribution to the Economic and Political Life).[15] Even in this book Professor Fischel's focus is on individual Jews (as defined above), with relatively few comments on India's Jewish *communities* as such. In this respect the title of Dr Fischel's book is somewhat misleading, even with its subtitle. Although his subject matter is both important and interesting, his book is only tangentially relevant to the scope of the present work. In what follows, therefore, only some of Dr Fischel's characters are dealt with, and they too only when they have a bearing on the background of one or another of the Indian Jewish communities.[16]

Professor Joan Roland's lengthy article, *A Decade of Vitality : Bene Israel Communal Development, 1917-1927*[17] is a valuable mine of information, showing the forces which were at play within the Bene Israel community and recording a full description of the activities of the Bene Israel Conference and of the All India Israelite League, thereby making the reader aware of many hitherto unexplored details about the Bene Israel community during the decade concerned. Dr Joan Roland is Professor of History at Pace University, New York City. During the summers of 1977, 1978 and 1980 she did research in Bombay into details of Bene Israel and of Baghdadi-Jewish public life, their journals, institutions and organization in Bombay, covering the late 19th century onwards.

Benjamin J. Israel (Wargharkar), a Bene Israel of Bombay, has done careful research into several aspects of Bene Israel history. An Introduction and six articles by him about the Bene Israel have been published under the title *The Bene Israel of India : Some Studies*, Orient Longman Ltd., Bombay, 1984.[18] B.J. Israel had an M.A. in Philosophy. For ten years he served as Secretary of the Bombay Public Service Commission. After his retirement he began his studies in depth about his community, combining an objective, scholarly approach with his deep interest in and knowledge of the Bene Israel community, even while usually not involving himself actively in Bene Israel affairs.

ACKNOWLEDGMENTS

The present writer is very appreciative of her several discussions and communications with Dr. Joan Roland, always helpful and stimulating. Many thanks are also due to Dr. Raymond K. Renford, the author of a comprehensive book (see Bibliography) *The Non-Official British in India to 1920*, about the lay-British presence in India (i.e. businessmen, planters, missionaries, etc.). Dr Renford furnished me with copies of many old newspaper items, documents, letters, etc. of relevance to the subject of this book, which he had gathered from his own researches in England's India Office Library, The British Library, and in India itself.

I owe a debt of gratitude to Professor B. Anderson, Librarian (now retired), Bombay University Library, for his kind assistance in locating and providing me with copies of many relevant passages from the extant literature.

Of the greatest importance to my study of the Bene Israel has been the assistance of Benjamin J. Israel. Over a period of many years he generously shared with me a wealth of information relating to the Bene Israel and to historical details of their background, and he has brought to my notice dozens of written references, always with meticulous citation and documentation of sources — all these have been of inestimable value to me in the preparation of my book.

My sincere thanks also go to the very many members of the Bene Israel community who have spent numerous hours patiently answering hundreds of probing questions and reminiscing about life, past and present, in the community.

I am also very appreciative of an unsolicited gift from Tamara Rubins, New York City, New York, in memory of her late husband, Dr Jack Rubins — both of them very dear friends of mine — which has enabled me to cover some of the considerable expenses related to the preparation of this book. Similarly, I wish to express my gratitude to the Jerusalem Centre for Anthropological Studies for its generous financial support.

I am grateful also to the copyright owners concerned for having granted me the required permission to quote from various books and articles in the course of this work.

To my husband, Artur Isenberg, whose wide knowledge of India complements my own special interests, my deepest appreciation and thanks. His wise substantive ideas and his keen editorial advice with respect to the entire manuscript have vastly improved the quality of this book.

* * * * * * * * * *

Before beginning the story of the Bene Israel, a brief further comment on the book's format may be useful.

Specifically Indian, Jewish or other terms are usually, but not always, defined when and where first mentioned in the text. Wherever definition of an Indian term would be unwieldy if included within the body of the book, it appears in the Glossary (as does also a repetition of those definitions already provided within the text).

In order to make readily available to the reader the actual substance of significant, new, or unusual information, a great deal of space is devoted to verbatim quotations (or, where necessary, to literal translations into English) of often quite lengthy passages from a wide variety of original sources, many of which are rare and not readily available. Some of these quotations have been referred to in the literature, but have either not been quoted verbatim, or else have been cited without adequate context. Many of the quotations in this book have been selected with the purpose of indicating relevant nuances, which often throw different or additional light on the subject and thus afford the reader a much more adequate basis for drawing conclusions. They are intended to permit a fuller appreciation of the overall picture.

As for the Appendices and for the abundance of notes found at the end of each chapter, most of them are meant to provide the interested reader with background (usually about India) going beyond, but not entirely irrelevant to, the immediate subject at hand — because they provide pointers for further research. Since research in depth about the Bene Israel has hitherto been so neglected, this book deliberately includes material that may at times, and to some readers, seem tangential, if not superfluous. Such a detail, however, may turn out to be exactly the clue needed to set another reader off on a trail of discovery which would help fill lacunae in our present knowledge of Bene Israel history.

When reading this book one must bear in mind that it was written in order to help fill definitely felt needs of today's interested anthropologists and historians. As such, it is designed to :

(a) provide a *comprehensive, documented* account of the Bene Israel in India, with special attention to their *Indian context* and background, and to *culture-change* as such;
(b) serve as a *source-book* on the Bene Israel in India; and
(c) point the way to *future in-depth research*, especially aimed at unearthing data about the Bene Israel in pre-British India.

All three of these aims are so inter-dependent that it is necessary to deal with all of them within the cover of a single book.

Jerusalem
January, 1985   SHIRLEY B. ISENBERG

Preface xiii

NOTES

1. Throughout this book the word "community" is used in its common Indian-English meaning, i.e. relating to the overall Indian patterning of society into traditionally endogamous groups. It refers not only to endogamous Hindu sub-caste (*jati*) groupings (see below, pp. 16-17, n. 48), but applies as well to endogamous groups of outcastes, of tribal peoples, of adherents of non-Hindu religions, and to their traditionally endogamous sub-groupings (if any).

2. The publisher, the late Sri Madurai Narasimha Rao of Seshachalam and Company, Madras and Hyderabad, is responsible for the present author's decision to delve deeply into the subject of this volume on the Bene Israel. It was his initiative to include the Jews of India (even though they are such a tiny minority) in planning his series on *Cultural and Religious Patterns in India*. Later, his patience and appreciation of the urgent priority to probe carefully beyond the scope of a mere survey set the present author on the path of research-in-depth which led to this present volume. The fruits of this research had not yet been gathered completely when Sri M.N. Rao died suddenly early in 1978.

    Originally, Meera (Mendrekar) Mahadevan (see below, p. 211) was to have collaborated with the present author in writing about the Bene Israel, from her perspective as a Bene Israel woman (although she married a non-Jew, their only child, a son, was brought up as a Jew), and as an author in her own right. She too felt very keenly that no one had adequately written about the Bene Israel. However, her total involvement in the creation and development of a network of Mobile Creches for underprivileged families — and then her untimely death — kept her from contributing her own chapters to this volume, although many discussions between her and the present author are reflected in its contents.

3. This figure is the usual estimate, the peak years having been the mid-1940s. The Government of India official decennial census figure for 1941 was 22,480 and for 1951 was 26,512.

4. Except in Cranganore and later in Cochin; and both of these episodes of anti-Semitism were propagated by foreigners.

5. Isaac Ben Zvi in his, *The Exiled and the Redeemed*, lists ten "Attempts at Jewish political sovereignty". None of them lasted anywhere nearly as long as did the Jewish community at Cranganore (which is one of the ten attempts)—located in today's state of Kerala—and which enjoyed a highly privileged autonomous position beginning around the year 1000 A.D., and lasting for at least five hundred years. Cf. *The Exiled and the Redeemed*, subtitled *The Strange Jewish Tribes of the Diaspora*, translated from the original Hebrew by Isaac A. Abbady; Valentine, Mitchell and Company, Ltd., London, 1958, 334 pages; see pp. 284-306. The terms of the royal grant as inscribed on the famous Copper Plates, now in the Pardesi Synagogue in Cochin, are seen by B. J. Israel (in his *The Bene Israel of India, Some Studies*, Orient Longman, Bombay, 1984, p.37) as "the conferment of the kind of feudatory privileges which Indian rulers were wont to bestow on their nobles, falling far short of sovereignty, somewhat resembling the rights belonging to feudal barons in medieval Europe".

6. The Konkan forms part of the western coastal strip of India, stretching from c. 60 miles north of Bombay (at the Maharashtra-Gujarat border) southward until Goa. It faces the Arabian Sea and extends inland for some 40 to 50 miles. The Konkan area is divided into Thana, Kulaba (formerly called Kolaba, and very recently officially named "Raigad District"), and Ratnagiri Districts.

7. In the 1960s another group called attention to itself under the name of "The United Tribal Jews of North East India" (including the Indian states of Manipur, Assam and Mizoram). Its members are sometimes simply called "Manipuri Jews". Their physical features are East Asian, and they claim that their ancestors were Jews of Kaifeng in the province of Honan in China, who fled thence, sojourning in caves in Indo-China, and later in the hills of Burma, in the 18th century migrating to Manipur and Mizoram (as other groups from Burma have done). They claim that they brought with them certain practises and artifacts of the Jewish religion which missionaries, beginning in 1834 (or 1854?), destroyed when they converted these people to Christianity. Since the establishment of the State of Israel, members of this group have been making concerted efforts to learn about Judaism and to become practising Jews.

xiv *India's Bene Israel*

Additionally, there has been recent revival of interest in reported similarities to some Jewish customs as practised by certain Pathan tribes in the Northwest Frontier of India.

8. *The Jews of Calcutta : the Autobiography of a Community, 1798-1972,* by Flower Elias and Judith Elias Cooper; published by the Jewish Association of Calcutta, Calcutta 700 001, 1974. *On the Banks of the Ganges : the Sojourn of Jews in Calcutta,* by Rabbi Ezekiel N. Musleah;The Christopher Publishing House, North Quincy, Massachusetts, U.S.A., 1975; 568 pages.

9. The President of the First Bene Israel Conference (1917), in his Presidential Address, suggested that efforts should be made to publish the *History of the Bene Israel* which H.S. Kehimkar had written. But nothing further was done about it by the Bene Israel community itself.

10. Hayeem Samuel Kehimkar : *The History of the Bene Israel of India;* copyright by Dr Immanuel Olsvanger, Jerusalem; published by Dayag Press, Ltd. Tel Aviv, 1937; viii, 290 pages, plus 25 pages of 51 photographs.

I was intrigued by the first of two entries under "Kehimkar, Hayeem Samuel" in the *National Union Catalog of Pre-1956 Imprints,* Volume 291, page 536; Mansell Information Publishing Ltd., London and American Library Association, Chicago, 1973. This is a verbatim copy of the entry concerned :

"Kehimkar, Hayeem Samuel
  History of the Bene Israel of India [Marathi]
  Bombay, Prakash, [1927]
  300 p. illus. 18 cm.
  1. Beni Israel. I.ti.
  NK 0069620 OCH"

OCH is the code for the library of Hebrew Union College, Cincinnati. Upon examining xerox copy of this entire volume, I found the entry to be in error. The person responsible was probably misled by the full-page photograph of Hayeem S. Kehimkar which appears as the frontispiece. The book's Preface (in Marathi) clearly states that the book is *dedicated to* Kehimkar posthumously. It is, in fact, an authorized Marathi translation of Paul Goodman's *A History of the Jews,* first published (in English) by J.M. Dent and Sons, London in 1911; being one of many Judaic writings which have been translated into Marathi for furthering the Jewish education of those Bene Israel who felt more comfortable reading in Marathi rather than in English or in other languages. The exact translation of the Marathi title page reads as follows :

  The History of the People of Israel
  The translation of the book written in English by Mr. Paul Goodman.
  Publisher : Saul Jacob,
  Secretary, "Aitz Hayyim" Prayer Hall, Bombay.
  (The publisher has reserved all the rights to himself.)
  Printer : V.V. Atitkar, B.A.
  Samartha Bharat Printing Press, 35 Sadashiv Peth, Poona City.
  The year 1927.

The Marathi word "Lok" used in the title means "people", and is *not* the Marathi equivalent of "Bene" which (in Hebrew) means "children of". In lines 3 and 5 above the Marathi word is "Prakashak" (and *not* "Prakash"). "Prakashak" means "publisher" and is not the name of *a* publisher. What is involved here is more than error in translation. The entire entry as such is a mistake. I have brought this error in cataloguing to the attention of the publishers of the *National Union Catalog of Pre-1956 Imprints,* and to the Librarian of Hebrew Union College in Cincinnati.

11. Shellim Samuel : *A Treatise on the Origin and Early History of the Beni-Israel of Maharashtra State ;* copyright reserved by the author; printed by Iyer and Iyer Private Ltd., Bombay, 1963; 187 pages. Maharashtra is the modern Indian state of which the Konkan (the native area of the Bene Israel) is a part.

12. Schifra Strizower : *The Children of Israel : the Bene Israel of Bombay ;* Basil Blackwell, Pavilion Series, Social Anthropology; Oxford, 1971; xiv, 176 pages.

13. Rev. J. Henry Lord : *The Jews in India and the Far East.* a reprint of articles contributed to *Church and Synagogue,* together with appendices; printed at the Mission Press, Kolhapur, 1907;

  120 pages plus 17 pages of appendices.
14. See below, Appendix 5.
15. Walter J. Fischel : *Ha-Yehudim B'Hodu, Ḥelkam b'Ḥayim ha-Kalkaleeim v'ha-M'deeneeim* (The Jews in India, Their Contribution to the Economic and Political Life); publication of the Ben Zvi Institute, Hebrew University, Jerusalem, 1960; 215 pages.
16. However, two of Fischel's articles, namely, *The Literary Activities of the Bene Israel in India* and *The Haggadah Shel Pesach in Marathi of the Bene Israel* (cf. Bibliography below), do relate to the Bene Israel community as such.
17. Published in *Jews in India*, edited by Thomas A. Timberg, Advent Books Inc., New York, 1986, pp. 285-347.
18. B.J. Israel's *The Bene Israel of India : Some Studies* contains the following articles :
    (a) *The Jews of India*, previously published by E. Kolet for the Centre for Jewish and Inter-faith Studies, Jewish Welfare Association, New Delhi, 1982; 55 pages.
    (b) *Religious Evolution Among the Bene Israel of India Since 1750*, previously published by the author; printed by G.G. Pathare, Popular Press Private Ltd., Bombay 1963; 22 pages.
    (c) "The Jewish Population of Kulaba District, Maharashtra, India : 1961 and 1971" : hitherto unpublished.
    (d) "Bene Israel Surnames and Their Village Links" : hitherto unpublished.
    (e) "Age of Marriage Among the Bene Israel : Some Statistics of 1881" : hitherto unpublished.
    (f) *Khan Bahadur Jacob Bapuji Israel, A Personal Sketch*; previously printed for private circulation, Bombay 1960; 50 pages.

Contents

PREFACE   VII

PART I
BEGINNINGS

1. Traditions and Theories of Origin   3
2. Historical Data of Likely Relevance to Bene Israel Early Development   19
3. Earliest Known Documentation on the Bene Israel   33
4. Earliest Contacts between the Cochin Jews and the Bene Israel   40
5. The Bene Israel in the 18th Century   49

PART II
THE BENE ISRAEL IN THE 19TH CENTURY : DEVELOPMENT OF THEIR RELIGIOUS AND COMMUNITY LIFE

6. The Influence of Cochin Jews   59
7. The Influence of Christian Missionaries   65
8. Arts and Letters   91
9. Caste – Like Patterns   98
10. Typical Features of Bene Israel Jewish Life   111
11. Life – Cycle Rituals   127
12. Bene Israel Synagogues   148
13. Bene Israel Names   154
14. 19th Century Bene Israel Occupations   160
15. Home Life   165
16. Haeem Samuel Kehimkar and the Israelite School   169
17. Bene Israel in Konkan Towns   173
18. Bene Israel Beyond the Konkan   176
19. At the Turn of the Century   193

PART III
THE BENE ISRAEL IN THE 20TH CENTURY

20. 20th Century Bene Israel Occupations   199
21. Bene Israel Individuals of Distinction   208
22. Bene Israel Village Life in the 20th Century   213
23. Bene Israel Life-Styles in Bombay   224

24.	Bene Israel Places of Worship in the 20th Century	232
25.	Bene Israel Publications of the 20th Century	238
26.	The Bene Israel Conference and the All-India Israelite League	243
27.	Bene Israel in India's Independence Struggle	247
28.	Education	257
29.	Some Community Activities and Inter-relationships	263
30.	Emigration to Israel	268
31.	The Jews Remaining in India	274
32.	Monument to Bene Israel Ancestors at Navgaon	277
33.	Demographic Data	279
	AFTERWORD	307
	APPENDICES	
1.	Garcia de Orta	309
2a.	The Ashtamkar *Sanad*	311
2b.	*Sanad* of 1840	312
2c.	*Sanad* of 1770	313
3a.	Discussion as to Date of Samaji Hassaji's Release from Prison-of-war	314
3b.	Excerpts from Cadell's *History of the Bombay Army*	320
4.	From a "Review of the Travels of Rabbi David D'Beth Hillel"	325
5.	From *The Oriental Christian Spectator*	327
6.	Solomon Reinemann on the Bene Israel	339
7.	The Hebrew-Marathi *Haggadoth* of the Bene Israel	350
8.	List of Bene Israel Publications, from *The Bene Israel Annual And Year Book*, Volume III	355
9.	B.J. Israel's *List of Bene Israel Surnames and Their Village Links*	368
	GLOSSARY AND HISTORICAL NOTES FOR INDIAN TERMS USED IN THIS BOOK	375
	GLOSSARY AND NOTES FOR JEWISH TERMS USED IN THIS BOOK	382
	BIBLIOGRAPHY	391
	INDEX	403

LIST OF STATISTICAL TABLES

1.	Schedule of the Native Free Schools, 1829	66
2.	Occupations or Means of Livelihood of Jews of Bombay City in 1872 and 1931	201
3.	Sources of Income for Indian Jews in the 1940s.	204
4.	Jewish Employees at the Manchester Mill, Bombay in 1943	205
5.	Population of Bombay Island in 1812, According to Religion	280
6.	Bombay Census of 1833, According to Religion	280
7.	Bene Israel Population in 1838	280
8.	The Jewish Population of the Indian Subcontinent in 1837 and 1941	282
9.	Literacy Among the Bene Israel, 1946-7	283
10.	Religions in Kolaba District in 1961 and 1971, Percentage-wise	284

11.	Number of Jews of Different Ages Present in Bombay and Its Different Divisions and Sections on the Night of the 1st February, 1864 (Table XLI)	286
12a.	The Jews of the Bombay Presidency Proper, 1881, 1891 and 1901	288
12b.	The Jews of Sind : 1881, 1891 and 1901	289
12c.	The Jews of Aden in 1901	289
12d.	The Jews of the Feudatory States in 1881, 1891 and 1901	289
13a.	Details of Jewish Population of Kolaba District	290
13b.	Details of Jewish Population of Poona District	290
13c.	Details of Jewish Population of Thana District	290
13d.	Details of Jewish Population of Bombay City	291
13e.	Jewish Population of the City of Bombay in 1864, 1872, 1881, 1891 and 1901	291
14.	Total Jewish Population of India for 1881, 1891, 1901 and 1941	292
15.	Jewish Population in India States-wise for 1951, 1961, 1971 and 1981	294
16.	Decennial Summary of Total Jewish Population for All India 1881-1981	296
17.	Chronological Summary of Total Jewish Population of Bombay, 1814-1971	297
18.	Chronological Summary of Total Jewish Population for Kolaba District, 1881-1961	297
19.	Location of Indian Jews on the Subcontinent in 1941	298
20.	Number of Bene Israel Residents as of 1945-47 in Some Places of Kolaba District	299
21a.	Religions of Bombay State 1921-51 Percentage-wise	300
21b.	Jewish Population in Bombay State, 1921-51	300
22.	Jewish Population of Maharashtra State 1961 and 1971, according to Districts	301
23.	Annual Jewish Emigration to Israel, from 1948 to 1984	302
24.	Number of Immigrants and Tourists Settling in Israel Who Were Born in India or Pakistan	303

LIST OF PHOTOGRAPHS

The photographs included in this volume were not intended to constitute an adequate range of Bene Israel-related illustrations. Thirteen of them, however, have never before appeared in any Bene Israel-related publication. About half of the book's chapters have at least one photograph illustrative of something mentioned therein. The order in which the photos appear generally follows the sequence of the chapters, although a given photo may, and often does, relate to more than one chapter. It is hoped that through one or another of the photographs, readers will be helped to visualize some details mentioned in this book which hitherto may have been unfamiliar to them. With this in mind, some of the captions are deliberately longer than the usual printed legend accompanying a photograph.

1. HAEEM SAMUEL KEHIMKAR. Photo reprinted from Kehimkar's *History of the Bene Israel of India,* published by Immanuel Olsvanger, Tel Aviv, 1937. Haeem David Haeems, a grandson of H.S. Kehimkar, has identified this picture as being a photograph of an original portrait painted by a Bene Israel artist whose surname was Talkar, and who married a Janjira Princess and converted to Islam, taking the name Fayizee Rahmin. The same artist also painted a portrait of H.D. Haeems'

maternal grandmother.

2. Portrait of the REV. JOHN WILSON D.D., F.R.S., engraved by Joseph Brown from a photograph by Moffett, as published in George Smith's book *The Life of John Wilson,* John Murray, Albemarle St., London, 1878. (See Chapter 7.)

3. BENE ISRAEL OIL-PRESS. We see here Mr. Avaskar and his young son in Alibag in 1985 operating one of the last Bene Israel oil-presses. (See pp. 55-56, n. 18.) Now the Avaskar family lives in Israel. Photo, courtesy of Joseph Guedj, formerly Director of ORT India.

4. A Bene Israel MALIDA PLATTER, in celebration of a joyous occasion, as prepared in Israel 1986. It contains: a confection composed of rice flakes, powdered sugar, almonds, grated coconut, raisins, cardamom and nutmeg; a fragrant plant, in this case roses; and five different kinds of fruit, in this instance banana, pear, apple, orange and several dates. The dates do not show in this photograph, they are behind the roses. (See p. 114.) Photo, courtesy of Jacob Benjamin.

5. BETH-EL SYNAGOGUE in Ashtami. This Bene Israel Synagogue was founded in 1882. The building is a simple, village-type house, with tile roof and lattice-enclosed verandah. Photo. courtesy of the photographs Archive of the Ethnography Department of the Israel Museum, Jerusalem.

6. MEZUZAH, made of brass. This particular style of *mezuzah* is used on the doorposts of many synagogues and homes of Bene Israel in India. (See pp. 14 n.6; 165; and 227.)

7. JEWISH RITUAL ITEMS from a Bene Israel synagogue: two varieties of prayer shawl *(talith)*; a silver cup for *kiddush* wine; and a set of phylacteries *(t'filin)*. (See pp. 121 and 388.)

8. BENE ISRAEL FAMILY, photo taken at the turn of the century. Notice the women's long-sleeve blouses, the characteristic way of covering the head with the *sari,* and the fact that the woman on the far right draped her *sari* over her chest and left shoulder (Maharashtrian style) while the other women (in Gujarati style), did not drape their *saris* across the chest, kept their left shoulder and arm free, and after covering the head with the *sari* from the back, let a considerable length of the *sari* fall from the right shoulder and hang loosely in front. Notice also the three different kinds of men's head-wear (the two turbans being of Gujarati style), and the several different styles of men's jackets. (See pp. 166-7.) Photo, courtesy of the Photographs Archive of the Ethnography Department of the Israel Museum, Jerusalem.

9. FAMILY photo, taken in 1910, showing David Haeems (the youngest son of H.S. Kehimkar), his wife Hannahbai, their son Samuel, and baby daughter Esther. Photo, courtesy of H.D. Haeems.

10. Part of a BENE ISRAEL FAMILY IN CHEUL, 1980. Notice the mother's (at right) glass bangles between two gold bangles, and her *Laccha* (neck-lace) (longer than the silver choker, and barely visible) showing one gold bead between black beads. (See p.145 n.25.) Photo, courtesy of Carmel Berkson.

11. BACKYARD OF A BENE ISRAEL FAMILY IN CHEUL, 1980. Note the lush vegetation, coconut palms, and water wheel. (See Chapter 22.) Photo, courtesy of Carmel Berkson.

12. A corner of a BENE ISRAEL KITCHEN IN PEN. The water pots, with their slightly rounded bottoms stock one on top of another, with the lowest being supported on a special stand. Flat-bottomed cooking pots too are sometimes placed one on top of another, using only one flame to cook the contents of 2 or 3 pots

simultaneously. Notice the large grinding stone and pestle (roller) located on the floor beneath the cabinet door, and the trunk (to the right of it) for storage. (See p. 165.) Photo, courtesy of the Photographs Archive of the Ethnography Department of the Israel Museum, Jerusalem.

13. An All-Marathi page from the Bene Israel *HEBREW-MARATHI HAGGADAH OF 1846* showing the platter of symbolic items for the Passover Seder table: egg, bitter herbs, shank bone of a lamb, parsley, and discs of unleavened bread which, in this *Haggadah* are differentiated respectively by 1, 2 and 3 protuberances (illustrating the Bene Israel's unusual way of differentiating these three *matzot*). The three cups, illustrated at the bottom of the page, contain respectively: salt, sour lime juice (into which the bitter herb is to be dipped), and a thick sweet date-syrup (which serves the same purpose as the mixture of honey, chopped apples and nuts on an Ashkenazi Seder table). (See pp. 92-3 and pp. 350-1.)

14. FRONT PAGE OF THE JULY-AUGUST 1924 ISSUE OF "THE ISRAELITE" The translation of its Marathi Table of Contents is as follows:

Sabbath Song	p. 105
Bravery and Cleverness of Women	p. 106
One Lamentable Death	p. 109
Diseases of Small Children	p. 110
A Few Words Worth Contemplation	p. 113
Synagogue Building Fund	p. 113
Tiferet Israel Synagogue – Receipt of Donation	p. 114
General Thoughts	p. 116
Polite Apology for a Mistake	p. 119
Garland of Good Advice	p. 120
Family Ceremonies	p. 120

    (See pp. 239-40).

15. Delhi's only Synagogue : The JUDAH HYAM HALL. (See pp. 187-8.)

16. THE JEWISH CEMETERY IN NEW DELHI. Note the coffin lid being used as a marker for a recent burial (See p. 141 and p. 186.)

17. Preparing for the MEHNDI (pre-wedding) CEREMONY, Bombay 1984. Notice the whole coconut and the uncooked rice in the typically Indian winnowing fan (symbolizing fertility); a plate of sweets; the henna *(mehndi)* paste is in the shallow pan covered by a crocheted doily; the typically Indian oil-lamp, already lit, stands on the floor; the groom, wearing a skull cap, and barefoot, is seated on a chair which has been covered with a white sheet, and soon the floral wedding "crown", the *sherra,* will be put on his head; all persons in the photo are wearing western-style clothes, except the woman on the far right who is wearing a *sari*. This function took place in a room located above the Tiferet Israel Synagogue. (See p. 134.) Photo, courtesy of the Photographs Archive of the Ethnography Department of the Israel Museum, Jerusalem.

18. CAPTAIN AARON JOSEPH, M.B.B.S., son of Dr. Joseph Benjamin of Ahmedabad. (See p. 184.) In World War I he served as Medical Officer under British General Edmund Allenby, in Mesopotamia, Egypt and Palestine. He entered Jerusalem with General Allenby in 1917. Later he was bombed and shell-shocked in the fighting at Kantara. He died in 1924. This picture was taken in 1916. Photo, courtesy of Moses A. Joseph.

19. BENJAMIN J. ISRAEL (WARGHARKAR), August 1906 – January 1987 :

remembered for his pioneering scholarly research concerning the Bene Israel community.

20. THE MONUMENT AT NAVGAON, dedicated to the memory of the shipwrecked ancestors of the Bene Israel. (See Chapter 32.) Photo, courtesy of Carmel Berkson.

MAPS

1. The Indian Subcontinent — facing page 56
2. Villages of Kulaba District Possibly Linked with Bene Israel Surnames — facing page 160
3. Bombay Peninsula (Greater Bombay) — facing page 224

INDIA'S
BENE ISRAEL

1

2

3

4

5

7

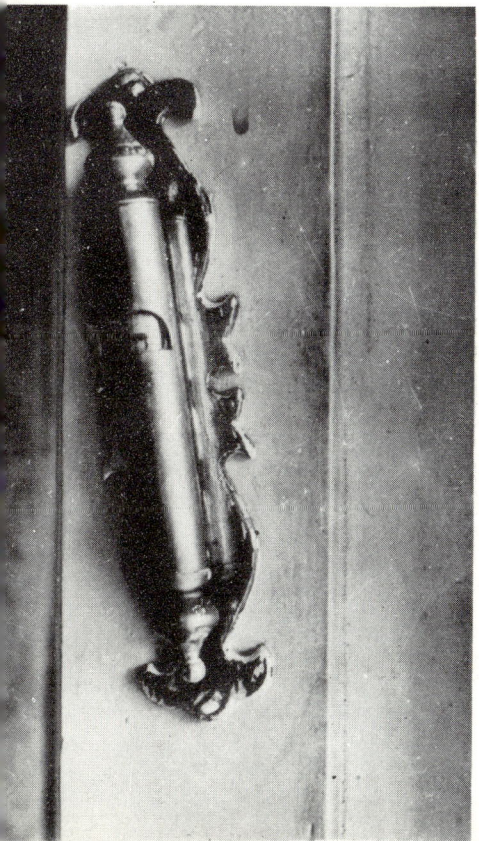

8

9

10

11

12

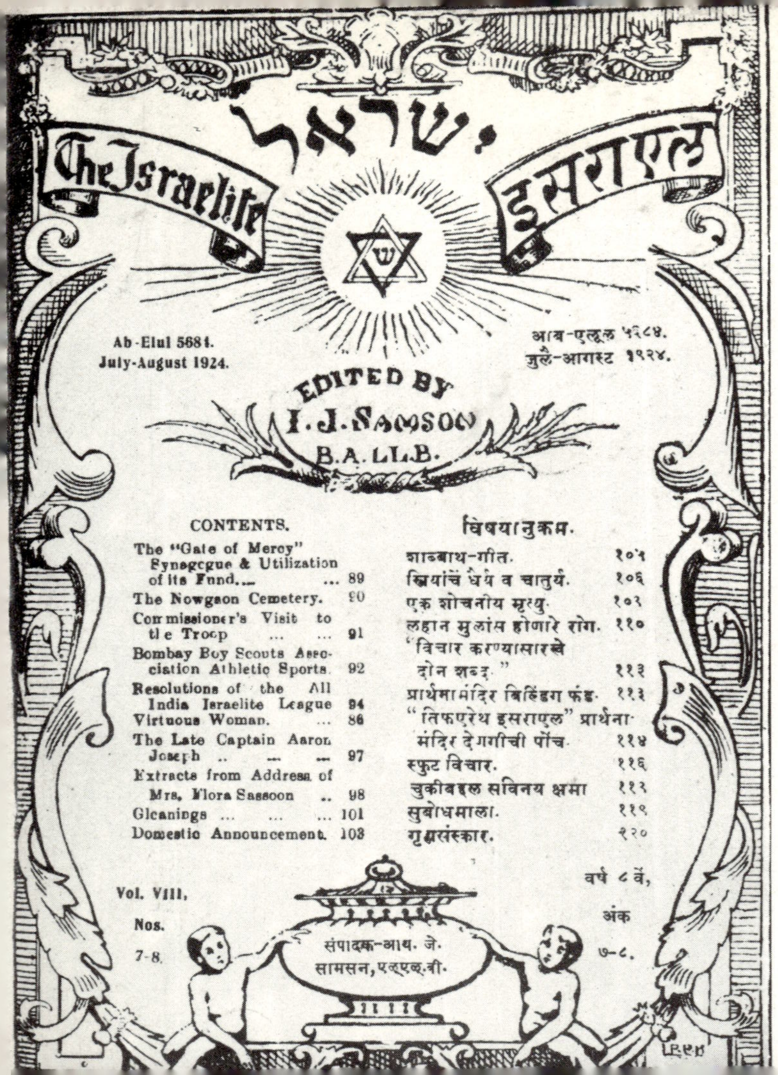

The Israelite — ישראל — इसराएल

Ab-Elul 5684.
July-August 1924.

आब-एलूल ५६८४.
जुलै-आगस्ट १९२४.

EDITED BY
I. J. SAMSON
B.A. LL.B.

CONTENTS.

The "Gate of Mercy" Synagogue & Utilization of its Fund...	89
The Nowgaon Cemetery.	90
Commissioner's Visit to the Troop	91
Bombay Boy Scouts Association Athletic Sports.	92
Resolutions of the All India Israelite League	94
Virtuous Woman. ...	96
The Late Captain Aaron Joseph	97
Extracts from Address of Mrs. Flora Sassoon ..	98
Gleanings	101
Domestic Announcement.	103

विषयानुक्रम.

शाब्बाथ-गीत.	१०१
स्त्रियांचें धैर्य व चातुर्य.	१०६
एक शोचनीय मृत्यु.	१०७
लहान मुलांस होणारे रोग.	११०
"विचार करण्यासारखे दोन शब्द."	११३
प्रार्थनामंदिर बिल्डिंग फंड.	११३
"तिफएरेथ इसराएल" प्रार्थनामंदिर देणगीची पोंच.	११४
स्फुट विचार.	११६
चुकीबद्दल सविनय क्षमा	११९
सुबोधमाला.	११९
गृहसंस्कार.	१२०

Vol. VIII,
Nos.
7-8.

वर्ष ८ वें,
अंक
७-८.

संपादक-आय. जे. सामसन, एलएल.बी.

13

14

सुचना

ज्येष्ठ पुत्र अथवा कन्या बापाची अगर आईची असतील त्यांहीं या पवदाचे तारखेचे दिवशीं उपास केला पाहिजे.

पवदाचे तारखेचे तिसरे प्रहरीं मेज तयार करावें असें कीं जितके लोकांस मान करवेल तितके करावे. मध्ये येक तबक ठेऊन त्यामध्यें तीन भाकऱ्या लगत ठेवाव्या. त्यांत येकांत मिठ दुसऱ्यांत खजूराच्या शिरा तिसऱ्यात आंबटरस असें ठेवावे. त्यांवरताचवर तीन शेदारीमच्या भाकरीं ठेवाव्या असा कीं वर कोहेन मध्यें लेवी आणि खाली इस्राएल आणि समोरचे दोन बाजूस एकीकडे करपास दुसरी कडे त्याचे समोर मारोर ठेवावा. आणि दुस त्या दोन बाजूस येकीकडे सजेरोवा दुसरीकडे त्याचे समोर उकडलेलें अंडें ठेवावे. भांड्यांत द्राक्षारस भरून ठेवावा. असा कीं मेजावरील सर्वांस पुरेल आणि येक येकास एक एक गलास वेगळे ठेवावें आणि तें तबक साफ कापडानें झाकून संतोषाने ईश्वर प्रार्थनेस जावें.

पदार्थाने भरलेलें तबक.

हे खाली राहू पदार्थ वेगळाले तबकाचे समजण्या करितां दाखविले आहेत.

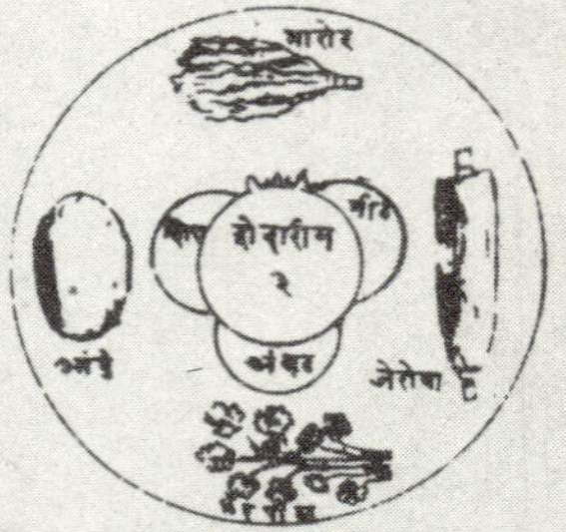

जे खाली वेगळाले हे पदार्थ दाखविले आहे ते ते वर तुकांत त्या प्रमाणे ठेविले आहेत त्या प्रमाणे ते तबकांत ठेऊन ते तबक साफ कापडानें झाकून ते मेजावर ठेवावें

15

16

# PART ONE
Beginnings

Chapter 1
Traditions and Theories of Origin

It is important to separate *theories* of origin from what little was known to the Bene Israel themselves as part of their *tradition* before people began to theorize. The "pristine" Bene Israel traditions were told to Christian missionaries early in the 19th century. "Their ancestors, they say, came to the coast of India from a country to the northward, about 1600 years ago" wrote the Rev. Dr John Wilson in his *Lands of the Bible*.[1] The tradition is that their ship had been wrecked off the Konkan coast, leaving only fourteen survivors, seven men and seven women, who reached the shores of Navgaon, a village which is located near two small rocky islands, Henery and Kenery. Navgaon lies next to the village of Kehim and is very near Alibag, a town about thirty miles south of Bombay.[2] Many bodies of the drowned were washed ashore, and the survivors buried these in two elongated mounds still visible at Navgaon today. The northerly mound is said to contain the bodies of the male dead, the southerly one those of the females.[3] All the possessions, including religious articles, belonging to the survivors were lost in the shipwreck. The survivors somehow managed to settle in the area and became farmers and oilpressers, completely out of touch with Jews elsewhere. Bene Israel tradition also remembers one David Rahabi, a Jew who suddenly appeared among them, some say about the year 1000 A.D., others say about 1400, while still others put the date as late as about 1600. In the Bible the word "Rahab" is occasionally used to refer to Egypt: perhaps David Rahabi's family, or he himself came from Egypt. Be that as it may, he was convinced that the Bene Israel were really Jews, because:

(1) They observed the Sabbath (*Exodus* 35 : 2 & 3; *Deuteronomy* 5 : 12-15). To this day the rural Bene Israel are known as "Shanwar Telis"[4] (Saturday Oilmen) because they abstain from work on Saturdays. There are in the same area "Shukrewar Telis" (Friday Oilmen) who are Muslim, and "Somwar Telis" (Monday Oilmen) who are Hindus of the *sudra*[5] caste. But only the "Shanwar Telis" did *no* manner of work on their day of rest; neither did they kindle any fire, nor cook any food on that day. This fact alone suggests a Jewish origin, since it is the sacred duty of Jews to observe Saturday as a complete day of rest.

(2) Although they did not possess any book or scroll of the *Torah*, and did not know any of the Hebrew liturgy, they did pronounce in Hebrew the opening sentence of the *Shema*, the fundamental tenet of the Jewish faith: "Hear, O Israel, the Lord our God is one" (*Deuteronomy* 6 : 4).[6] They repeated the formula at every rite of passage and on every occasion for prayer.

(3) They circumcised all their male infants on the eighth day after birth (*Genesis* 17 : 7-14). Although the Muslims in the same area also practised circumcision, they performed the rite at a much later date in the life of the child.

(4) They refused to eat any fish except those with fins and scales (*Leviticus* 11 : 9 & 10).

4   Beginnings

We cannot be sure just where Bene Israel "pristine" tradition ends and where theorizing begins, i.e. theorizing on the part of non-Jewish as well as of Jewish individuals with a knowledge of the Bible and of other Jewish and non-Jewish writings. All agree, however, that David Rahabi proceeded to re-Judaize the Bene Israel.

According to Kehimkar, a fifth Jewish trait (which David Rahabi may or may not have recognized as such) among the Bene Israel was their observance of certain Jewish holidays prescribed in the Bible. This was analysed by Kehimkar as follows:

> It will be seen that all of the fasts and feasts which the original ancestors of the Bene Israel observed, have purely Marathi[7] names, and were invariably called *San*, which means a "holiday" .... The other holidays[8] which date from the time of the religious revival by David Rahabi, have received their names in Hindustani[9] as it was spoken by David Rahabi with the ancestors of the Bene Israel.[10]

The holidays of "pristine" tradition, i.e. those with Marathi names, are described by Kehimkar (p. 22) as follows:

Marathi Name	Hebrew Name[11]	English Name
a) Naviacha San	Rosh Hashana	New Year
b) Darfalnicha San	Yom Kippur	Day of Atonement
c) Shila San[12]	Simhat Kohen	Merry-making day of the priest
d) Khiriacha San	Hag He-asif	Feast of the Ingathering
e) Holicha San	Purim	Feast of Esther
f) Anashi Dhakacha San	Pessah	Passover

It is disturbing, though necessary to note that in Kehimkar's earlier writing, *A Sketch of the History of Beni-Israel and the Appeal for Their Education*,[13] he listed (p.9) the 9th-of-Av Fast, commemorating the destruction of the First Temple, as one of the holidays with a Marathi name, namely *Birdiacha San*. It also appears thus in Joseph Ezekiel's article on the Bene Israel in the 1903 edition of Funk and Wagnall's *Jewish Encyclopedia'*, Volume III, p.18. However, in Kehimkar's later work, *The History of the Bene Israel of India* (p. 22, from which the above list has been copied) *Birdiacha San* does not appear. Instead, Kehimkar added it to his list of Hindustani-named holidays[14] referring to it as *Birdiacha Roja* (not *San*). It so happens that the 9th-of-Av Fast was one of four fast days officially discontinued after the construction of the Second Temple, being reinstated only *after* the destruction of the Second Temple. Kehimkar's switch from *Birdiacha San* to *Birdiacha Roja* makes one wonder whether he dropped it from the Marathi list because it conflicted with his theory that

> the ancestors of the Bene Israel observed before the religious revival in India only those fasts and feasts which were in vogue in Palestine during the time of the Second Temple. The four fasts of National Mourning, however, were only introduced among the Bene Israel after the religious revival[15]

and that the Bene Israel ancestors had left their homeland circa 175 B.C., i.e. before the destruction in 70 A.D. of the Second Temple. Also, the holiday called *Shila San* does not appear at all in Kehimkar's earlier work; it is found neither in his list of Marathi-named holidays, nor in his Hindustani list. The suffixes *-acha* and *-cha* are Marathi, signifying "of" or "pertaining to". To be consistent about a category of Hindustani-named holidays, the Hindustani suffix -*ka* should replace the Marathi -*acha* or -*cha*. While this basis for differentiating between "pristine" and "later" observances remains suspect, we do see in these holiday names an amalgamation of both Marathi and Hindustani (Muslim) influences. In any case, however, judging from Kehimkar's description of the unique traditional ways in which the Bene Israel were wont to observe the above mentioned holidays, the latter must have formed part and parcel of Bene Israel religious life long before the Bene Israel adopted additional Jewish holidays together with all the customary Jewish observances for the above-listed Biblically-prescribed[16] annual holidays. According to Kehimkar (pp. 17-21) the Bene Israel's own traditional modes of observance for these holidays (or analogous dates) were as follows :

1. *Naviacha San* (*Numbers* 29 : 1; *Leviticus* 23 : 24) : The Bene Israel believed that each individual was put on trial by God on this day. This is the one Jewish holiday which, both in Israel and in the diaspora, is celebrated for two days. According to Kehimkar (p. 17.) the Bene Israel, however, observed only one day.[17]
2. *Darfalnicha San* (*Numbers* 29 : 7) in Marathi means "holiday of the closing of the doors". On this day the Bene Israel sat fasting inside their houses with doors closed and locked. On the preceding day they bathed first in warm, then in cold water; ate at about 5 p.m., then fasted until 7 p.m. of the following day. During their fast they did not touch people of other religions,[18] and they dressed all in white (as did the High Priest in the Temple at Jerusalem on Yom Kippur, and as do several other Jewish communities on Yom Kippur even today). This was the day when God decided upon a verdict of condemnation or pardon for each person for the coming year.
3. *Shila San* is a holiday unique to the Bene Israel, falling on the day after Yom Kippur (See below, p. 120). The Bene Israel celebrated this day as one of rejoicing; and probably only later did they connect it with the rejoicing of the High Priest who, in the days of the Temple, rejoiced after he had performed well all the complicated rituals and services of the Day of Atonement. On *Shila San* the Bene Israel visited, entertained friends and relatives, and gave alms to the poor.
4. *Khiriacha San* : The Bene Israel observed this holiday on the third day of the new year (which coincides with the Fast of Gedaliah). Their observance consisted of burning incense, reciting the *Shema* over an offering made of *khir* (basic ingredients: rice or wheat, milk or coconut milk, sugar, cardamom), and then partaking of the concoction. But, for some inexplicable reason, the Bene Israel did not traditionally observe any holiday which we might really equate with the Biblical instructions for celebrating the holiday of *Succoth* (*Exodus* 23 : 16; *Leviticus* 23 : 39-43) the Feast of Tabernacles (also known in Hebrew as *Hag He-   although Kehimkar seems arbitrarily to have done so.[19] *Succoth* actually occurs two weeks after the first day of the new year and is a harvest festival.[19] Nor did they celebrate anything reminiscent of the festival of *Shavuot*, the ingathering of the first fruits, Pentecost (*Exodus* 14 : 22; *Deuteronomy* 16 : 10 – 12).
5. *Holicha San* : Originally the Bene Israel did not relate this holiday to the story of Purim (as recorded in the *Book of Esther*), although *Holicha San* coincided in date with that Jewish holiday. *Holicha San* also coincides with the popular Hindu holiday called *Holi*, not only in time of year, but also in name. The Bene Israel fasted on the preceding day, and feasted on the day itself, paralleling the Purim custom among other Jews.
6. *Anashi Dhakacha San*, in Marathi literally means "the holiday of the closing of the *anas*", a special clay pot for containing a sour liquid, a kind of yoghurt culture. The Bene Israel abstained from using this substance, as well as from using all other forms

of leaven, during the eight [20] days of this holiday, as prescribed for Passover in *Exodus* 12:15, 17, 18; and 23:15. However, the Bene Israel did not know the reason for this abstention, nor were they familiar with the Passover story as such (i.e. with the exodus of the Jews from Egypt).

An important feature of Bene Israel tradition was, and continues to be, the practice of making special offerings. Since the destruction of the Second Temple, no other Jewish community has so consistently continued to observe this kind of ritual because the prerequisites—Temple, altar, and the formal services of the *Cohanim* (priests) and Levites (Temple servants)—were no longer extant. Particularly the *Book of Leviticus* enumerates in detail many prescribed offerings for different occasions. Although the Bene Israel observed by no means all of those Biblical requisites which might have been feasible in their Indian environment, it still remains a remarkable coincidence that so many of the offerings customary among the Bene Israel are analogous in purpose, meaning, format and detail to the Biblical prescriptions. While it is true that there are some adaptations to local conditions, there remains a definite resemblance to Biblical prescriptions, a matter which will be discussed in greater detail below (p. 116).

The above-mentioned holidays and offerings all have parallels in the Bible and it is important to remember that none of these observances originated in post-Biblical times.

In the first half of the 19th century Christian missionaries and certain other Europeans began theorizing about Bene Israel origins, suggesting descent from Jews of the early Babylonian-Persian diaspora; from Yemenite Jewish settlements; from those Jews who were persecuted by the Prophet Mohammed; or from still other sources. Later, in the light of their study of the Bible, of other Jewish literature, of ancient historical sources relating to India, the Middle East, etc., some members of the Bene Israel community itself, including H.S. Kehimkar, D.J. Samson, and Shellim Samuel, put forth still other arguments and theories of their own.

Kehimkar believes that since

> the Bene Israel were ignorant until a recent date of the Feast of the Dedication of the Second Temple (Hannukah) introduced in commemoration of the cleansing of the Temple on the 25th Kislev—165 B.C., that they were ignorant of the overthrow of the Second Temple by Titus the Roman Emperor 70 years after Christ; that they did not keep the four fast days of national mourning which were abolished at the time of the Second Temple, and that they keep up to the present day a distinction between the real descendants of Israel and those who are the offspring of alien women, in accordance with the dictates of the sages Ezra and Nehemiah,[21] all go to prove that the ancestors of the Bene Israel must have left their mother country, we believe to have been the province of Galilee, before the time of the invasion of Antiochus Epiphanes, 175 B.C.[22]

He holds that some time after the era of Ezra (5th century B.C.) they were probably heading for the seaport of Cheul (a few miles south of Navgaon) which he says was then an important trade emporium.[23]

Kehimkar also presses the point that the *malida*, i.e. ritual offerings in the observances of the Bene Israel,[24] apart from their emphasis on the Prophet Elijah, are remarkably similar to the particular form of observances maintained in the Kingdom of Israel after its separation from the Kingdom of Judah and from the Temple in Jerusalem, uninfluenced by the later adaptations which evolved in the mainstream of Judaism as a result, first, of the Babylonian captivity (586 B.C.), and, thereafter, of the destruction of the Second Temple (70 A.D.). But emphasis upon ritual offerings has no place among Jews of Arab lands, and this fact is a strong argument against the possibility of Bene Israel origins from any of those communities which stem from the dispersed inhabitants of the Kingdom of *Judah*, the eponym of the words "Judean" ("Yehudi" in Hebrew) or "Jew". The Bene Israel of India did not use the appellation "Yehudi", although in the 19th century they began to refer to themselves or to be referred to, in English, as "Jew Caste", and were listed as "Jews" in official censuses. The words "Bene Israel" literally mean "Children of Israel". Kehimkar believes that their having been called "Bene Israel", rather than "Yehudim", was a fortunate asset to the community during the period of Muslim supremacy in the Konkan (see below pp. 11 and 49). The Rev. Lord[25] and others suggest that the appellation might have been deliberately adopted by the community at just that period, taking into consideration Muslim attitudes about Jews. It seems that in several passages of the *Koran* where the Jews are called "Yehudim", they are being berated for having corrupted their sacred trust from Allah, beginning in Biblical times, and for not having accepted Islam in the Prophet Mohammed's day. On the other hand, sometimes (but not always) when the *Koran* refers to the Jews as the "Children of Israel" or as "people of the Scripture", it reflects a more positive attitude toward these people — because Allah had made a covenant with them, had given them the commandments, etc.

H.G. Reissner has effectively argued the case for a possible connection between the expulsion of the Banu Israil from Hejaz (under the Prophet Mohammed's successor Omar) and the arrival of the Bene Israel in India. Reissner equates the Hebrew term *am ha-aretz* with the Arabic word *umma*, meaning the large mass of a people. The Koran speaks of the *"ummiyyun* who know not the Book", i.e. the Banu Israil. On the other hand, a *Yahud* (Jew) in the Koran was the educated, urban, mercantile Jew, accursed by Allah. The Banu Israil were the illiterate, non-urbanized, non-mercantile Jews—those who were Jews by birth only. The Banu Israil were ignorant of "the Mosaic Law in accordance with principles laid down in the (Babylonian) *Talmud"*. But they too refused to accept Islam and in 640 A.D. were "sent north into Syria"—i.e. north of the Hejaz. Perhaps a portion of these Banu Israil eventually fled by sea from the northern country (possibly through the port of Akaba) and finally reached and settled in the Konkan on the west coast of India.[26]

The Rev. Wilson believed that the original Bene Israel had come from Yemen circa 6th century A.D.[27] Others think Bene Israel ancestors were Yemenite Jewish voyagers who came to the western shores of India later during the Middle Ages. But, Yemenite Jews were conversant with both the *Babylonian Talmud* and the *Jerusalem Talmud* (compiled between the 3rd and 5th centuries A.D.) Would the influence of these basic Jewish treatises have been entirely erased from Bene Israel memory, even if the actual writings had been lost in a shipwreck? Why should the Bene Israel have remembered only precepts from the *Torah* and no teaching and traditions from post-Biblical times? Or, did the supposed Jewish Yemenite ancestors of the Bene Israel arrive in the Konkan before the Talmudic period? Jews were living in Yemen at least as early as the beginning of the 2nd century of the Christian era. And, presumably, there was some trade and travel from South Arabia via the sea to the Western Coast of India—taking advantage of the seasonal prevailing winds—even before the Arabs who came by sea began pillaging not so far north of the Konkan in 636 A.D. (see below, p. 25). However, the few similarities between Bene Israel and Yemeni Jewish liturgy and customs need not be traceable to any Yemeni ancestry. These can be accounted for by the fact that during the 19th century at some Bene Israel synagogues and prayer halls a Yemeni and not a Cochini *hazan* (cantor) officiated and thus introduced some Yemeni practices.

8   Beginnings

Another theory is that the Bene Israel ancestors came to India, by sea, from Persia, fleeing from early Islamic persecution there. Or, Jews may have arrived in pre-Islamic times since there had been very early intercourse with Konkan ports from Persia as well as from South Arabia.

D.J. Samson, in a series of three articles entitled "The Bene Israel: Why, Where and Whence", published in 1917 in the Bene Israel periodical *The Israelite*,[28] argues that

> the ancestors of the Bene Israel came to India through the ports of Elath and Ezion-Geber, at the head of the Gulf of Akaba, between 740 and 500 B.C., by sea from Palestine in order to escape persecution.[29]

He adds that because "Reuben" is such a common name among the Bene Israel, perhaps their ancestors were of the tribe of Reuben; and that, in order to escape Assyrian captivity, they had fled southward along the Dead Sea to the Gulf of Akaba port and thence to India.

We do not know whether, at the time of their discovery by David Rahabi, the Bene Israel already gave prominence to the Prophet Elijah[30] in their ceremonies connected with vows and offerings. Kehimkar does not say so explicitly. If the particular forms of emphasis on the Prophet Elijah did exist among the Bene Israel at the time of their discovery by David Rahabi, this focus on Elijah might tend to substantiate the theory that they came to India in the 8th century B.C., suggesting Bene Israel origins in time and place not too far removed from the lifetime of this awesome prophet.

In 1917 D.J. Samson was of the opinion that

> an exact solution of the question is well-nigh impossible; nevertheless it will be possible to arrive at a more or less correct view as science advances, and we are in a position (a) to examine with the help of experts, the anthropometric data relating to the Bene Israel that have been collected and will have been collected, (b) to examine with the assistance of geological and antiquarian experts the mounds at Navgaon, which are reputed to be the resting places of the shipwrecked forefathers of the Bene Israel, with a view to see whether they will deliver up any coins, vessels, weapons or other articles, which might by their date and their original home indicate the probable time when, and the place from which, the ancestors of the Bene Israel came, and (c) to examine the traditions, old ceremonies, customs, and other facts with the help of philology and comparative history of religions.[31]
>
> I would therefore earnestly appeal to all my brethren to collect such old traditions, customs and phrases and publish them for the benefit of those who will be in a position to investigate this subject.[32]

Would that all of these sound recommendations had been pursued with strict academic methodology and objectivity![33]

The hypothesis of Shellim Samuel, in 1963, also favours an 8th century B.C. date. But, instead of D.J. Samson's choice of the tribe of Reuben, Shellim Samuel sees it in "the country to the north", the Upper Galilee section of the troubled Kingdom of Israel, and believes that the ancestors of the Bene Israel were of Asher and Zebulon, then in close contact with the famous sea-faring peoples of the coast, and who lived in an area famous for its oil-pressing industry (the latter fact having been previously noted by Kehimkar). Shellim Samuel suggests a time even earlier than the destruction of the First Temple in 721 B.C., i.e. during the reign of King Ahaz in Judah and the days of the Prophet Hosea in Israel, for the time of the Bene Israel shipwreck off the coast of Navgaon. In his

Traditions and Theories of Origin 9

Treatise on the Origin and Early History of the Bene-Israel of Maharashtra State [34] he postulates that Ophir (the Sophir [35] of Josephus) is the same place as Surparaka in Sanskrit writings [36] (i.e. today's Sopara) situated some 37 miles north of Navgaon; that, on the eastern shore of the Mediterranean Sea, members of the tribes of Asher and Zebulon [37] participated in ship-building and sea-faring together with the coastal people of Hiram's kingdom; that the trade which King Solomon had with Ophir [38] (setting out from the port of Ezion-Geber on the Red Sea's Gulf of Eilat-Akaba) later developed sufficiently to warrant having Jewish factors remain in Ophir; that certain members of the tribes of Asher and Zebulon, because of their experience in ship-building, sea-faring and maritime trade, might well have been en route with their families in order to settle in India when they were shipwrecked off Navgaon.

If we accept, for the time being, that Ophir was identical with Surparaka, we still do not know for sure just where that ancient Indian port was located. Max Müller places it at the mouth of the Indus River. [39] The geographers Al Mas'udi [40] of Baghdad (10th century) and Al Idrisi [41] (born in Morocco toward the end of the 11th century) locate Subara (Sopara) on the Gujarat coast near Cambay.

An Indian geographer, Dr. S. Muzafer Ali, places Surparaka near Cambay which is much closer to Bombay than is the mouth of the Indus River.

Surparaka (or Suryaraka) is evidently the western coastal plain drained by the river Surya which runs parallel to the coast from north to south and enters the sea near Bassein. It approximately coincides with the Thana district of Maharashtra.[42]

Some scholars doubt that Ophir can be connected with Surparaka primarily because in King Solomon's time (965 – 928 B.C.) there was no known great Indian trading power which might have participated in overseas trade from this area. If the Biblical Ophir was indeed in India, and if Solomon traded with India, who were the rulers at Ophir during that period? What can archaeological excavations along India's west coast tell us about that period? Several scholars feel that excavations at the mouth of the Surya River (as well as at Cranganore in Kerala) are likely to turn up evidence of contacts and trade which thus far is only speculative.[43]

Even if there were no direct routes at that time to distant lands, Indian products and contacts must have spread far and wide either overland, or by sea hugging the coastlines (or both) from earliest times, in a series of perhaps small stages of progression.

The Rev. Lord, in his *Jews in the Far East* (p. 45) succinctly sums up his considerations about Bene Israel origins in this manner:

> The tradition of the hailing of the Bene-Israel "from northern parts" could of course have been used with peculiarly strict accuracy of their coming from or through Afghanistan and Baluchistan; with comparative accuracy of their coming from Mesopotamia or Persia; and of their coming from Arabia or the Red Sea only in the sense that in hugging the coasts in voyaging to India, if they did so, they would be arriving from the north. We candidly own that we cannot with our respected, and now venerable author, Mr. Haeem S. Kehimkar, believe that the reference in this tradition is to the northern provinces of Palestine.

Irrespective of their land of origin, if we bear in mind the fact that the Indian caste system did not acquire its rigidity until about the 5th century A.D., and if the Bene Israel Jewish ancestors arrived in India before the 5th century A.D., then Rev. Lord's proposition, as follows, seems plausible.

> To the unbiased observer the Bene-Israel suggest themselves as the descendants of Hebrews who at their first introduction into India must have made somewhat free alliances with the women of the land ...... and thus an infiltration of Indian blood into their community would have taken place at an early stage of their sojourn in India.
>
> This was doubtless soon succeeded by a rigid practice of allowing marriage only with members of their own body—a rule which the example and the influence of the Hindu caste system around them would have tended to encourage, and to which they have doubtless ever since most strictly adhered. ("Bene-Israel", *Hastings Encyclopaedia of Religion and Ethics*, Vol. II, p. 470.)

It is clear that the descendants of the first Bene Israel ancestors, wherever they came from, dispersed in several Konkan villages, and for centuries remained isolated from Jewish life elsewhere. Then, according to Bene Israel tradition, a David Rahabi discovered this vestigial Jewish community living in the Konkan, and proceeded to enlighten its members about the full and proper observances of Judaism as it had evolved through post-Biblical Midrashic and Talmudic interpretations. These teachings by David Rahabi and the Jewish observances adopted by the Bene Israel at that time will henceforth be referred to as "the first Bene Israel religious revival" as distinct from the religious revival initiated by the several Jewish teachers from Cochin during the first half of the 19th century. (See below, pp. 59 – 63). According to Kehimkar, Rahabi

> taught Hebrew reading and writing, without translation, to three Bene-Israel young men from the Jhiratkar, Shapurkar and Rajpurkar families. Thenceforth all ceremonies were performed in accordance with authorized Hebrew ritual, and the irregular repetition of the *Kiryath* [recitation of] *Shema* was done away with; the *Ketuba* (marriage bond) [contract] was also introduced about this time. David Rahabi alone had a copy of the liturgy and scriptures; consequently, every prayer that was required to be said at the time of ceremonies was read from the manuscripts which his disciples had copied from his book. Unfortunately David Rahabi was, it is said, killed by a local chief two or three years after the commencement of his good work amongst the Bene-Israel, and it is said that his grave is in the village called Sarul near Alibag.[44]

From David Rahabi's three young disciples there arose three families of hereditary officiating priests called *kajis*. Kehimkar writes that

> though their headquarters were chiefly at Alibag, Revdanda, Ambepur, Panwell and Murud, they went wherever their services were required to perform the rites and ceremonies of the people, and also to manage and settle communal disputes, etc., with the help of some influential men in the community of the place. For all these functions *kajis* received fees, as well as their travelling and other expenses .... The *Kaji* received special honour and was accorded precedence in every ceremony and festivity. He was entitled to a double share in feasts, given on the occasion of the birth, marriage, death, vow, etc.[45] .... The performance of the rites and ceremonies of Regimental Bene Israel was made by a person nominated by them (the *Kajis*), and styled *Mulnaji* .... *Kajis* were exempted from paying the house tax and cattle toll and were entitled to receive gratuitous labour when required. Under the British Government, the Bene-Israel *Kaji* in Bombay was employed in succession on a monthly salary to administer the oath to the Bene-Israel in courts; but for the last 30 or 40 years the appointment has been dispensed with.[46]

Traditions and Theories of Origin 11

Since the word *kadi* or *kaji* is a Muslim term (designating a judge), it must be noted here that, apart from the very early scattered presence of Muslim traders on the Konkan coast, the first substantial Muslim penetration and actual rule in the area took place only in the early 14th century. Why use this Muslim term for the person who was to officiate over the newly introduced Jewish ritual? Was it because David Rahabi himself spoke Arabic? (See below, p. 14, n. 9.) The word *kaji* as used among the Bene Israel denotes a person performing the dual function of judge and of priest, judging in civil cases, as well as performing all the Jewish religious rites and ceremonies. Strizower thinks that

> it is likely that Rahabi chose for training those who *already* [emphasis supplied] held authority in the community, and that this training lent further prestige to the *Kaji* office. In any case, the term *Kaji* has not been in use in other Jewish communities.[47]

On the one hand, the Bene Israel adoption of the word and of the office of *kaji* might have taken place no earlier than the 14th century. On the other hand, however, usage of Muslim terms need not necessarily imply that, by any other previous name, the *role* of *kaji* among the Bene Israel—and, for that matter, the existence in the area of the Bene Israel community itself—were related to the coming of Islam to the area; the role may have existed under another name in pre-Muslim days. It could, rather, be an example of addition to, or replacement of local terms by words brought in by relatively recent newcomers to a given region. At any rate, it was most likely during the centuries (14th – 17th) of Muslim dominance of the area that the Bene Israel began to imitate and/or adapt many details of Muslim custom, probably as a form of social up-grading.

Before listing the chronological specifics of documented history, we should deal with the suggestion which has occurred to several people (non Bene Israel) that Bene Israel origins do not go very far back in time and might be traced to Jewish merchants (either from outside India or from Cochin) who had converted to Judaism some local inhabitants with whom they had contact. They argue that most probably these converts had been local servants who worked for Jewish merchants, as well as some of the latter's concubines and the children born to them. Those who prefer the theory of conversion to Judaism by Jewish merchants (whether before or during the British Raj) clearly ignore a number of very basic facts, namely that

1. the Bene Israel heartland villages not only comprise, or are very close to, coastal ports or former ports which have since become silted up (such as Panvel and Roha Asthami), but also many villages which are located considerably inland (see map of Bene Israel ancestral villages);
2. the original and traditional occupation of the Bene Israel was oil-pressing and, as oil-pressers, only a few Bene Israel families dwelt in any given village; and
3. within caste-bound India, where sub-groups (both of caste[48] and of out-caste society) were associated with occupational functions and were inter-dependent upon each other, a newcomer to a particular village could not easily or quickly take over such an ancient and important function as oil-pressing.

How then is one to account for the actual diffusion of the Bene Israel throughout *so many* Konkan villages, whether or not one assumes Bene Israel conversion to Judaism through the auspices of some wandering Jew, merchant or otherwise? Three alternative possibilities come to mind :

1. A foreign Jewish merchant (or several Jewish merchants) at a Konkan port (or ports)

converted to Judaism his/their local servants in order to simplify his/their *kosher* housekeeping while in India, and also converted his/their local concubines so that their progeny would be Jewish. (From the converts' point of view, there might have been the attractions of a higher standard of living and of a higher social status, the elimination of caste restrictions, and the emphasis in Judaism on caste-free social justice and ethics.) Yet, we would have to postulate that, some time after their conversion, the converts and their children returned to their respective native villages,[49] where all of them just happened to take up the occupation of oil-pressing, or, by coincidence, just happened to belong to the group which did oil-pressing in each of many different villages.

2. A wandering Jew appeared in a given Konkan village and converted a family of oil-pressers. But, since Jews do not usually proselytize, here again, if this did happen, it could have been in order to assure *kosher* housekeeping for the wandering Jews concerned.[50] In order to pursue this alternative further one must also postulate that these converted oil-pressers later converted only oil-pressers of other villages. This latter might have taken place, for instance, within the context of the Indian practice of selecting marriage partners only from among one's own sub-caste (*jati*), but from a village other than one's own village. And thus Judaism may have reached oil-pressers in additional villages. We must remember that Jews are/were sometimes not the only oil-pressers in Konkan villages; there are Hindu and Muslim oil-pressers too. But the Bene Israel were the main oil-pressers in many areas of the Konkan before the 19th century (see below, p. 17, n. 52).

3. or, a small group of Jews, or of "partial" Jews, who already were experienced oil-pressers, appeared from outside India (or at least from beyond the Konkan), offered their skills to the local inhabitants, and somehow found a place for themselves among them, with each of several Konkan villages absorbing a few members of the group. This is something quite different from conversion to Judaism separately of each oil-pressing family in each village. Conceivably the stranded band, especially if they indeed did come from the Galilee, were not only succored by the people who found them, but might have been brought to the attention of the then ruler of the area; and when asked what skills they had, because of their familiarity with oil-pressing, were settled individually in a number of different villages. I submit that this would have taken place no later than the 16th century (because of the evidence in the Ashtamkar Sanad—see below, p. 33 and also Appendix 2a) and, I can see no reason why it might not have occurred much earlier than the 16th century,[51] even before the destruction of the Second Temple in Jerusalem.

Some intermarriage with the local inhabitants must have taken place, in order to account for those aspects of Bene Israel physical resemblance to their neighbours. Such intermarriage, as well as acceptance in a village occupation could have occurred much more easily, and on a large scale, in an era before caste barriers had become rigid, i.e. before the Gupta Period, some time before the 5th century A.D. However, this does not preclude the possibility of intermarriage and village absorption having taken place even after the 5th century A.D.[52]

Alternative (1) is absurd. Of alternatives (2) and (3), the latter would fit in with the Bene Israel tradition of a shipwreck and of having come from a country to the north. The "wandering Jew" element may have come into the picture in the form of David Rahabi, who in turn instructed the first three *kajis* in Judaism, and urged them to go from village to village and to revive what little Judaism had survived among Bene Israel families. Most probably Jewish merchants had, from antiquity onwards, confined themselves to

Traditions and Theories of Origin   13

the port areas of the Konkan coast, and never set foot in any village away from the coastline. The David Rahabi of Bene Israel tradition must have been quite an exception, if indeed he encountered the Bene Israel in their more inland villages rather than within, or very close to, a port area. If he did travel inland, it should be pointed out that he probably did not venture very far, since the three families from which he appointed *kajis* all lived in *seacoast* towns (or perhaps these were only villages in those days). From B. J. Israel's article "Bene Israel Surnames and Their Village Links", and also from Map 2 we see that the Jhiratkar family stems from Zirad, the Shahpurkar family from Shahapur, and that both of these places are located in Alibag Taluka. The Rajpurkar family stems from Rajpuri which is located in Murud Mahal. Both Alibag Taluka and Murud Mahal lie along the coast, the most likely area for contact with Jews coming from outside the Konkan.

NOTES

1. Rev. Dr John Wilson : *Lands of the Bible*, William Whyte and Company, Edinburgh, 1847, Volume II, p. 667.
2. There is a frequently mentioned tradition of origin of the Chitpavan (Konkanasth) Brahmins of Maharashtra which is worth noting here because of some similarity to the origin legend of the Bene Israel, namely that the bodies of some shipwrecked persons (sometimes the number given is fourteen, sometimes another figure is cited) were discovered by Parasuram (as incarnation of the Hindu god Vishnu) on the Konkan coast; were brought to life, or were revived by him as they lay on the funeral pyre (*chita*) which had been erected for them; and they were converted into, or ultimately became, a distinct and important subcaste of Brahmins. The frequency of gray-green eyes among Chitpavans (otherwise very uncommon in this region) suggests foreign ancestry. But how long ago this intrusion happened is as vague as is the advent of the Bene Israel, or of their first introduction to Judaism. That two such different Maharashtrian communities, as the Chitpavans and the Bene Israel, in their origin legends share a common element of persons shipwrecked off the Konkan coast suggests the following speculations; (a) the two communities may actually have had a common origin; or (b) since shipwrecks off the Konkan coast were not unusual, the presence of this element in the legends of both communities could very easily have been due to mere coincidence; or (c) one community has copied elements of legend from the other.

    One legend, still told *among the Bene Israel,* specifically connects Bene Israel and Chitpavan origins by relating that from the same shipwreck which brought the few surviving Bene Israel ancestors to Navgaon there were also several others washed ashore, drowned; the latter were piled in a heap on the shore by a local Brahmin who then set fire to the pyre. The heat from this fire revived nine persons on the pyre who had not really been dead to begin with. The Brahmin subsequently converted these nine persons to Hinduism and called them Chitpavan Brahmins. (After the caste system had become firmly established in India, conversion to the Brahmin caste would not have been possible, at least in theory. One had to be the child of a Brahmin father and mother in order to have Brahmin status. So, the event in the above legend, if true, must have occurred before the 5th century A.D. (See above, p. 12 and below p. 16, n. 48.)
3. At Navgaon, adjacent to these mounds (but separate from them) there is a regular Bene Isreal burial ground. Here, the seemingly earliest burial markers are very like those in local Muslim graveyards; low brick and mortar constructions without any inscription. These are situated closest to the traditional mounds. Of the tombstones with decipherable inscriptions, one written both in Hebrew and in Marathi marks the grave of one Moses Ben Joseph Belkar who died at the age of 71. According to the inscription's Marathi date, i.e. "Shake 1740", the year indicated is 1818 A.D. Its Hebrew date, i.e. "Hay, Tov, Ayin, Het", indicates the year 5,478 according to the Hebrew calendar, or 1718 A.   For further discussion of this date, see below, p. 35   The

Navgaon mounds and cemetery were long ago entrusted to the care of the first Bene Israel synagogue, the Gate of Mercy Synagogue in Bombay. Throughout the 20th century various Bene Israel institutions have perennially recommended proper protection and preservation of "this ancient landmark of the Bene Israel advent to India". Because of insufficient funds, only temporary and very inadequate measures were taken in the matter. But, finally in 1974 a serious fund raising campaign was undertaken, and work was begun toward the construction of a proper monument and protective wall enclosure. (See below, pp. 277-278)

4. *Til* is the word for sesamum, or sesame. In the Konkan sesame seeds are among the principal seeds pressed for their oil content. "*Tili* or *Teli*, the oil-presser, means either one who presses oil, or one who handles sesamum." (G.S. Ghurye : *Caste, Class and Occupation*, Popular Book Depot, Bombay, 1961, p. 31.)

5. See below, p. 16   n.48

6. Before the formalization of a fixed liturgy for prayer, the *Shema* consisted of only this one verse, i.e. *Deuteronomy* 6:4, as part of the Temple Service, but no one seems to have suggested this fact as a possible clue to Bene Israel origins. One might argue that perhaps the Bene Israel knew only this one verse because they had left the Galilee before additional verses had been incorporated into the service and before additional verses were learned by the common man. In the course of time *Deuteronomy* 6:4–9 and 11:18-21 were added to the Temple Service. Much later a third portion, i.e. *Numbers* 15:37–41, was added as part of the *Shema* prayer and remains as such in synagogue liturgy to this day, to be recited morning and evening. Being of early Biblical origin, the *Shema* is older than other Jewish prayers. The text inside the *Mezuzah* case contains only the first two portions (i.e. *Deuteronomy* 6:4-9 and 11:13-21), always written on parchment, in 22 lines according to the same rules as for inscribing the *Torah* and *Tefillim*. (See Glossary of Jewish Terms.) But, until their second religious revival, which began late in the 18th century, the Bene Israel did not know about the universal Jewish custom of fastening a *Mezuzah* on every Jewish doorpost or gate, nor did they bind *Tefillim* on head and left arm as prescribed in *Deuteronomy* 6:8 & 9.

Marathi, the language (with Sanskrit roots) of the majority of the population living in the Konkan area, as well as of virtually all Maharashtra.

8. See below, pp. 117-118

9. The language called *Hindustani* was the bazaar and army version of *Urdu*. The letter was developed by Muslims in India, a form of *Hindi* with a considerable admixture of Persian and Arabic word-roots. Urdu is written in Arabic script, as is Hindustani. (In British days the Roman script was sometimes used for Hindustani.) Hindi and Marathi, both based on Sanskrit roots, are written in the Devanagri script.

It must be remembered that Islam came to the Konkan and to the Deccan through entirely different and earlier waves of Muslim conquest, immigration and conversions than those which influenced North India–the original Muslims in the Konkan and Deccan had come by way of Basra and Sind, overseas from the Arabian peninsula, and from East Africa. Traders were the earliest to come.

In private correspondence with the present author, B.J. Israel has written that although Urdu had become a common language in the North, it

was in the Deccan Sultanates that Urdu developed into a literary language – in the North it was Persian. Urdu was prevalent in the Konkan *before* the Moghuls came South. So, if David Rahabi communicated with the Bene Israel in Hindustani, it could have been as early as 1300 or 1400 A.D. Actually, to my mind, all this is futile speculation, based on the presumption (for which there is no basis but legend) that a David Rahabi established the institution of *Kaji* and gave it its name; that he instituted some additional festivals and gave them Muslim names, etc.

To the present writer it seems likely that the Bene Israel might have communicated with David Rahabi through Arabic with the help of their friendly Muslim neighbors in the Konkan. If David Rahabi had come from any Levantine background, he would have spoken Arabic.

10. Haeem Samuel Kehimkar : *The History of the Bene Israel of India;* pp. 22, 23.

Traditions and Theories of Origin   15

11. See Glossary of Jewish Terms for descriptions and times of year of these regular Jewish holidays. Before their religious revival, the Bene Israel had calculated their Jewish holidays according to the local Indian lunar calendar.

12. *Shila* means "stale" in Marathi. The sweets and other foods used in celebrating this holiday had to be prepared two days in advance (no cooking was allowed on Yom Kippur). Hence they were stale by the time they were used.

13. Haeem Samuel Kehimkar : *A Sketch of the History of the Beni-Israel and an Appeal for Their Education;* printed at the Education Society's Press, Byculla, Bombay, 1892, 38 pages.
14. See below, pp. 117 – 118
15. Kehimkar : *History*, p. 23. Here the words "religious revival" refer to the instruction in Judaism which David Rahabi gave to the Bene Israel.
16. With the exception of *Shila San*, all the rest have Biblical counterparts.
17. It is interesting to note that today the Jews in New Delhi meet as a full congregation only on the first day of *Rosh Hashonah*, most men taking off from work only one, rather than two days; this applies not only to the local Indian Jews, but also to most foreign Jews who are stationed in Delhi. The orthodox Bene Israel synagogues of Bombay, Poona (Pune) and Ahmedabad hold *Rosh Hashonah* services on two days.
18. This custom among the Bene Israel was, no doubt, due to the influence of Hindu ideas that defilement results from touching members of certain "unclean" communities.
19. Kehimkar, *History* : "(4) On the evening of the fourth of Tishree they observed a feast of harvest in-gathering, and called it Khiricha San. (p.17) ....This feast they observed by mistake a fortnight before the feast of Tabernacles (p.18) ......(6) On the 15th of Tishree falls the Feast of Tabernacles, and it continues until the 23rd of that month. This feast was totally forgotten by the Bene-Israel, but the Feast of Harvest In-gathering, which was to be solemnized during this week, was, as stated above, through a mistake, observed a fortnight before the proper time. Owing to their forlorn and depressed condition, the early Bene-Israel colonizers probably could not afford to erect booths, which is a peculiarity of this Feast. (*Numbers* 29 : 12-39.)"
20. Though the Bible specifies seven days for Passover, seven days are observed only in Israel, whereas eight days are celebrated by Jews in the diaspora.
21. See Glossary of Indian Terms and also below, pp.104-107about the *gora* and *kala* subdivisions of the Bene Israel.
22. Kehimkar, *History*, p. 12.
23. See below, pp. 23-24
24. See below, pp. 111-115
25. Rev. J. Henry Lord : *The Jews of India and the Far East*, printed at the Mission Press, Kolhapur, 1907, pp. 9 – 10.
26. H.G. Reissner : "The Ummi Prophet and the Banu Israil of the Qur' an" in *The Muslim World*, a quarterly review of history, culture, religions and the Christian Mission in Islam, edited by Edwin E. Calverly, the Hartford Seminary Foundation, Hartford, 1949, Vol. 39, pp. 276 – 81.
27. Rev John Wilson : "The Bene Israel of Bombay", an article in *The Indian Antiquary*, November, 1874, pp. 321 – 3).
28. *The Israelite*, Vol. I, no. 4, April 1917, pp. 66 – 70; no. 5, May 1917, pp. 86 – 9; and no. 6, June 1917; pp. 108 – 13).
29. Ibid., Vol. I, no. 4, April 1917, p. 68.
30. See below, pp. 111-114
31. *The Israelite*, Vol. I, no. 4, April 1917, p. 66.
32. Ibid., no. 6, June 1917, p. 113.
33. In 1906 D.J. Samson had collected notes on the Bene Israel for the compiler of the *Gazetteer of Bombay City and Island* (see *The Israelite*, Vol. I, no. 4, April 1917, p. 66). Shellim Samuel, in a way, did follow up on some of D.J. Samson's theories of origin, and did do some research into the ancient and medieval literary sources, as may be seen from his book *A Treatise on the Origin and Early History of the Beni-Israel of Maharashtra State.* An American anthropologist, Mrs.

Beginnings

Lee Ranadive, collected some blood samples of the Bene Israel; she also wanted to excavate the Navgaon mounds, but could not obtain the community's permission to do so.

34. Shellim Samuel; Ibid, pp. 108, 118, 123.
35. F. Max Müller, in his *Lectures on the Science of Language*, Longmans, Green and Co., London, 1882, Vol. I, p. 235, footnote 34, says that "In Coptic *Sofir* is the name for India". (But medieval writers, when referring to Ethiopia, sometimes referred to Ethiopia as "Middle India" or as "Second India".)
36. Surparaka is mentioned in Vedic and in Puranic contexts. The references indicate that it was an important city from about 1500 B.C. to 1300 A.D. Vedic context indicates a time not much later than 1500 B.C., while the Puranic Age began several centuries after King Solomon.
37. Cf. *Genesis* 49 : 13 : "Zebulon shall dwell at the margins of the seas; and he shall be at the haven of ships; and his border shall be near to Zidon." Also, *Judges*, 5 : 17 : "..........Asher remained on the seashore and abode near its bays".
38. Cf. *I Kings*, 9 : 26, 27, 28 : "And King Solomon made a ship in Ezyon-Geber, which is near Eloth, on the shore of the Red Sea, in the land of Edom. And Hiram sent in the ship his servants, seamen, that had knowledge of the sea, with the servants of Solomon. And they came to Ophir, and fetched from there gold, four hundred and twenty talents, and brought it to King Solomon." Also, 10 : 11 : "And also the ship of Hiram, that fetched gold from Ophir, brought in from Ophir in great abundance sandalwood and precious stones." And 10 : 22 : "For the king had a Tharshish ship at sea with the ship of Hiram : once in three years the Tharshish ship used to come home, laden with gold and silver, ivory and apes and peacocks."
39. F. Max. Müller, Ibid, p. 234.
40. Elliot and Dowson : "Early Arab Geographers", from *The History of India As Told by Its Own Historians, The Muhammadan Period;* the Posthumous Papers of the late Sir H.M. Elliot, edited by Prof. John Dowson, Susil Gupta (India) Ltd., Calcutta, 2nd edition 1956, p. 31.
41. Ibid., p. 118.
42. S. Muzafer Ali : *The Geography of the Puranas*, People's Publishing House, New Delhi, 1966, 234 pages; this reference is from pp. 147 – 8.
43. The great Indus Valley Civilization had already crumbled more than 500 years before King Solomon's time.
44. Kehimkar : *History*, p. 41.
45. This is reminiscent of the Hindu custom of special feasting of Brahmins on similar occasions, as well as upon completion of a meritorious deed for the benefit of others.
46. Kehimkar : op. cit., pp. 250-1.
47. Strizower : *The Children of Israel* : *the Bene Israel of Bombay*, Basil Blackwell Ltd., Oxford, c 1971, pp. 38-9 reprinted by permission of the publisher. See too p. 49 note 6 of the same book.
48. Hindu caste rules became rigid around the 5th century A.D. The Constitution of independent India forbids specific forms of caste discrimination which are contrary to democratic principles.

Hindus belong either to one of the four main caste groupings, which are called *varnas*, or to non-caste (i.e. outcaste) Hindu society. The four *varnas*, in order of highest rank, are :

Brahmin, the priestly caste;
Kshatriya, warriors, nobility and administrators;
Vaishya, merchants and some cultivators;
Sudra, some cultivators, some artisans, and some serving people.

According to the strict tradition, any Hindu who does not belong to one of these four *varnas* is an "outcaste" and is "untouchable". These are usually landless labourers doing the most menial work. Touching, or taking water from, or eating food with or prepared by, an untouchable has been traditionally considered to be polluting to "caste Hindus" (i.e. to a member of one of the four *varnas*). In this sense, all non-Hindus were also considered to be untouchable. In modern, democratic India all peoples mix at work, in restaurants, in public transport, in schools and colleges—and customs based on untouchability are dying.

Each of the four *varnas* are divided into many hereditary, endogamous sub-castes which are called *jatis*. (In English, the term "caste" is often used interchangeably with *"jati"*.) *Jati* is the main term of social identity throughout India. Even non – *varna* peoples in India have organized themselves into hereditary, endogamous *jatis*. Each *jati* has a name, which today is sometimes used as a family surname; and even today many male members of a given *jati* still follow the specific occupation traditional for that *jati*.

Muslims, Christians and Jews, who have lived in India for centuries, also follow the *jati* system and have, on their own, evolved into subgroups which do not usually intermarry with each other, even though their respective religions stress equality and the right to marry anyone within their own religion.

49. As in many countries, but particularly in India, many villagers, especially of the lower classes, are attracted to towns or cities; leave their native village; work in a metropolis, sending their earnings back to their families in the village; and themselves returning to their native place only for holidays and rites of passage. They may, however, retire to their native place in old age.

50. This need for strictly *kosher* housekeeping as a motivation to proselytize is not as farfetched as it may seem at first. We know of Jewish merchants and travellers in the Middle Ages who did their best to maintain their orthodox Jewish rituals and way of life even while on journeys of several years' duration to the far ends of the earth. The far-flung dispersion of Jewish settlements in the diaspora could, and did, offer them aid and comfort in this respect. They tried to maintain *kashrut* even when not near a Jewish settlement. S.D. Goitein, in his *Letters of Medieval Jewish Traders* (Princeton University Press, 1973; translated from the Arabic with introductions and notes by S.D. Goitein) mentions (on pp. 176, 177 and 190) instances of Jewish merchants importing from home for themselves such things as *kosher* wine for *kiddush*, or wheat (when they were in a rice-eating country) since, according to their own ritual, rice could not be substituted for wheat when making a certain blessing, etc. etc. India, with its pervasive vegetarianism, did make it somewhat easier for the Jews to maintain *kashrut* by simply becoming strictly vegetarian, thus eliminating the entire complicated *kashrut* regimen which forbids the mixing of meat meals with milk products.

Actually, there is a 20th century example of conversion of local household servants in the conversions to Judaism by the White Jews of Cochin of some of their own household servants.

51. An inscription belonging to the 1st-2nd century A.D. has been found in Govardhana (south of the Tapti River, roughly parallel with Surat and not far north of Sopara—see above, p. 9) which specifically mentions *an oil-pressers' guild* existing even in those early days and seemingly as important as the guild of irrigation engineers, the potters' guild, and the weavers' guild—all four being mentioned on the same inscription. (See Gairola, *Western Indian Guilds and International Trade in Ancient India, c. 1st-2nd centuries A.D.*, pp. 4, 5.)

52. Village surveys of today sometimes distinguish between "domanial" castes, made up of people who have lived in a given village since its origin and who own land (many Bene Israel villagers owned their own land), and "immigrant" castes, some of which may have resided in a given village for only one or two generations. We do know that the *jati* make-up of residence in India's villages has not been static over the centuries. Generally speaking, intrusion of newcomers to a village was more likely if the newcomers were introducing a completely new service or occupation such as e.g. in modern times, the services of a photographer or of a tractor-mechanic, whom together with his family, the villagers might want to integrate into their midst, and who would then service several surrounding villages also. But, even in oil-pressing, new families of *jatis*, new to a village, have been known to settle down in a village which hitherto had been traditionally serviced by oil-pressers of other *jatis*. According to the 1883 *Gazetteer of the Bombay Presidency, Volume XI, Kolaba and Janjira Districts*, the Hindu oil-pressers then resident in these districts were themselves not indigenous to these districts, but were comparatively recent migrants from inland; Khoja (Muslim) oil-pressers now of the Konkan had originated from Gujarat, etc. So, too, the Bene Israel oil-pressers might not have been indigenous to the Konkan and could have come in as Jews from elsewhere. The same *Gazetteer* says that

> most oil-pressers and oil-sellers are Beni-Israels, [although] Maratha *Telis* are found in Nandgaon and Mandla .... They (the Maratha *Telis*) are said to have come in the beginning of the present century from the Deccan, and are now permanent residents. They press oil out of *til* (sesame) and from *karanj* and *undi* berries.........Their state and prospects are poor. (p. 412)

18 *Beginnings*

Since the Bene Israel oil-pressers antedated the Maratha (i.e. Hindu) *Telis* who came into Kolaba and Janjira Districts only at the beginning of the 19th century, the Bene Israel must have been the *main* oil-pressers here at least in the 18th century.

Chapter 2
Historical Data of Likely Relevance to Bene Israel Early Development

Several references to India are found in the huge body of *Responsa Literature*,[1] some dating back to early centuries of the present era. But the most consequential link of Jews to India must have been the many Jewish merchants who came in person to India to trade even in the early Middle Ages. Jewish merchants had broken the Syrian trade monopoly when, between the 5th and 6th centuries A.D., they increasingly replaced their Syrian competitors, especially in the commerce between Europe and the East. Hebrew was the *lingua franca* of Jews, who were scattered all over the then known world. Their common knowledge of Hebrew afforded the Jews a communications network throughout Europe where, as elsewhere, the local Jews also spoke the language of whatever area they inhabited. Thus they had an advantage over the Syrian merchants who had no such Arabic (or Aramaic)-knowing communities resident in Europe to assist them as reliable, easily available interpreters in their European trade.[2] The Jew had access to both Muslim and Christian spheres of influence.

Until the rise of Venice in the 10th century, Jewish merchants called Radhanites held almost a monopoly on the trade between Europe and the East. They might well have served as a possible instrument in the early development both of the Bene Israel and of the Cochin Jewish communities.

The only known contemporary reference to Rādhānites is that of a provincial postmaster in the Eastern Caliphate, one Ibn Khurdādhbe, 'Ubaydallah b. 'Abdallah, who died in 912 A.D. He is the author of a book on the geography of the then known world. This book, entitled, *Kitab al-masalik wa'l-mamalik*[3] or *The Book of the Roads and the Kingdoms*, contains a section called "The Routes of the Jewish merchants called Rādānites".[4] The author details four principal routes, partly on land and partly by sea, from "the land of the Franks" to "Sind, Hind (India), and China."

Although the place of origin of the Rādhānites and other specifics about their identity are unknown, some scholars believe that their headquarters were in France, may be in one of the ports on the Rhone River.[5] However, the most convincing, and the most recent argument as to the identity of the Rādhānites is that presented by Moshe Gil in his paper "The Rādhānite Merchants and the Land of Rādhān".[6] Gil connects these merchants with the administrative district of Rādhān on the eastern shore of the Tigris River. This district included what is now the eastern part of Baghdad as well as several places mentioned in Gaonic *Responsa* (Jukha, Mada, Nahrwan, Kilwadha). Rādhānites, i.e. one Gaon from Jukha followed by a Gaon from Kilwadha, led the *yeshiva* in

Pumbedita from 788-98 A.D. For the first three centuries of Islam the largest Jewish concentration in the entire Diaspora centered on the Jewish spiritual academies of Pumbedita, Sura, and of the Exilarch of Baghdad. Gil suggests that even though the name "Rādhānite" is not found in Jewish sources, the Jews of Rādhān district might have been designated as

> Rādhānite Jews, at least by their non-Jewish neighbours .... They [the Rādhānite Jewish merchants] were no association, nor organization, nor group, they only had in common their country of origin. The very fact that Ibn Khurdādhbe refers to otherwise generally known routes, open to anybody, as "routes of the Jewish merchants" is evidence of their unrivaled position in the international trade of that period.[7]

Gil believes that the early Rādhānite Jewish merchants were the progenitors of the Jewish magnates in Baghdad of the 10th century.

Even if the Rādhānite Jewish merchants were not native to "the land of the Franks", it would not have detracted from their importance to Europe. We know that during the reigns of Charlemagne (768-814 A.D.) and of Louis the Pious (814-840 A.D.) many Carolingian charters were issued, granting extraordinary preferential treatment and protection to Jewish merchants. As traders, or as curious travellers accompanying them, the Jews were the logical transmitters to Europe of many aspects of Arab and other Eastern cultures, then far in advance of anything known to Europe (outside the Iberian peninsula.) In noting prices and in making calculations the Rādhānites must have used and spread the knowledge of several numbering systems. It is quite possible that they were instrumental in bringing the East Indian numerals (incorrectly if widely known as "Arabic numerals") to Europe. A manuscript of Abraham ben Meir Ibn Ezra (1092-1167 A.D.), a roving Spanish-Jewish scholar and writer, mentions a Jew who was sent by the Caliph Es-Saffah (750-55 A.D.) on a mission to bring back to the Caliph one who knew the Indian numerals and astronomical writings.[8]

Jewish merchants not only had the unique advantage of connections and access via their co-religionists throughout the known world; their trade was facilitated also by the fine system of communications which had been established throughout the Caliphate Empire. One route of the Rādhānites hugged the entire coastline of India; another entered Bactria (just west and extending slightly north of what is now the Indian state of Jammu and Kashmir). Bactria, also known as Balkhi, Balhi, or Valhi (of the *Mahabharata*), was the seat of Greek power after the conquest of this area by Alexander the Great. Much later, Balkhi became an important link in Jewish trade between Europe and China. A community of Jews lived in Balkhi and one of its members, Rabbi Hiwi al-Balkhi (c. 875 A.D.), was known to have been a Bible critic and writer, an adversary of Babylon's Saadia Gaon. At least some Jews must have entered India from Balkhi[9] via Kashmir, bringing their Jewish culture with them. We know from the work of Abu Rihan al-Biruni (970-1039 A.D.) that

> Kashmir[10] is a valley surrounded by lofty inaccessible hills and broad deserts.........- The servants of the Government are always on the alert, and watch the passes and strongholds of the country. They do not allow strangers to enter the country, except by ones and twos. This prohibition extends *even* to Jews and Hindus, how then can anyone else gain admittance? The principal entrance is at Birahan, halfway between the Sind and the Jhelum.[11] [Emphasis supplied.]

This statement seems to take entirely for granted the coming and going of Jews in that part of the world. Such Jews, no doubt, were mainly merchants coming from or going to peninsular India through the Banihal Pass or the route of Indus River tributaries (the Sind or the Jhelum Rivers), thence toward the sea; or inland through the Punjab. By whatever route Jewish merchants may have entered India, there certainly must have been more than just a handful of them, beginning at least as early as the 9th century. Conceivably, they had more influence than we can document today in shaping Jewish communities in India.

More to the south, on the Indian coast of the Arabian Sea, the Muslims first invaded the mouth of the Indus River in 711 A.D. Later, in the 9th century, the Eastern Caliphate crossed the Indus (up to what is now northwest Gujarat), but maintained its hegemony only for a short time. However, the Indus Valley again became subject to the Eastern Caliphate for some decades in the 11th century. Rabinowitz argues that

> During the whole period of the activity of the Radanites, therefore, this important station [Sind] on their long route was an integral part of the Eastern Caliphate, through the length and breadth of which ... the Jews spread themselves. Even, therefore, if there were no direct evidence of the existence of Jewish communities in India during this period, it could confidently be assumed on this ground alone, since there was nothing to prevent the Jews from extending their residence to the confines of the Caliphate.[12]

Through the Rādhānites and through the extension of the Eastern Caliphate, movements of Jews probing further southward might well have been expedited in such a way as to have made possible the "discovery" of the Bene Israel coinciding roughly in time with the Bene Israel tradition of their first Jewish revival "about 1000 years ago".

Even after Mediterranean trade had been closed to Jewish merchants, their trade beyond the Mediterranean continued (but now no longer as a monopoly, because by then many Muslim merchants were also engaged in this trade) until first the Portuguese, and thereafter other European powers usurped and dominated the trade with the East. We do know of about one *thousand* Jewish merchants who traded in the East during this period. We know them by name from a particular source, the Cairo *Geniza*.[13] The Cairo *Geniza* documents, however, have relatively little to do with those who were actually the majority of Jewish traders of that time, i.e. those who came from Baghdad and from Persia. Naturally, their papers would not turn up in Cairo. But *Genizot* in Baghdad and in Persia must hold (or must have held) comparably precious archival information, very likely including information relating to Indian Jewish communities.

A very rich collection of letters, written in Arabic and in Hebrew by Jewish merchants, was among the items found in the Cairo *Geniza*. Professor Shelomo D. Goitein, who made an analytical study of these letters, found about 400 documents from this collection which relate to trade with India. In Goitein's book, *Letters of Medieval Jewish Traders* (pp. 175-229), he reproduces in his chapter on India eleven of the "India Letters" while another five "India Letters" occur elsewhere in the book. The earliest letter is dated 1097 A.D., the latest being dated 1226 A.D. In none of these is any mention made of Indian Jewish communities as such. However, in one letter, labeled No. 45 by Professor Goitein, written about 1204 A.D., the writer of the letter explicitly notes that "the congregations in Aden and in India often asked me to lead them in prayers."[14] But, since we know that many Jewish merchants were trading with India in those days, it is conceivable that a "Jewish congregation in India" might have consisted exclusively of foreign Jewish merchants, i.e. there might not necessarily have been any indigenous Jewish members in their congregation. On the other hand, we do know that these merchants came very close to places of Indian Jewish settlement, and not only of the so-called Cochin Jews. The writer of one letter (No. 9, written in 1145 A.D.) said, "I had previously written to you at Tana."[15] Thana (Goitein has spelled it "Tana") happens to be adjacent to the Bene Israel heartland. Professor Goitein, before his death in February 1985, was planning to publish a separate book devoted to "the India letters" alone.[16] He had assured the present writer orally that none of these letters makes any mention of indigenous Jewish communities.[17]

During this period, however, there must have been children born of unions of Indian women with Jewish foreign merchants. Surely this offspring is among the forebears of many Indian Jews. Two questions arise :

(1) Were the children of such unions assigned at that period in history to full-fledged membership in the Indian Jewish community? Goitein touched only tangentially upon this aspect when he wrote about one Abraham ben Yiju, the Tunisian Jewish merchant who lived on the Malabar Coast for at least 17 years in the 12th century :

> His [Yiju's] wife certainly was an "outsider", not as usual a cousin or other more remote relative. Nowhere, not even here [i.e. in Letter No. 41, a very relevant letter written by Yiju] is a reference made to her in his letters.........the probably beautiful, Indian slave girl Ashu whom Abraham Yiju manumitted in Mangalore on October 7, 1132, with so much ado, might have become his wife and the mother of his children. Now returning to the West and the social climate of his youth, he hoped that at least his daughter would marry into the family .... This wish was fulfilled .... She married her cousin, the writer of Letter No. 75 in the summer of 1156.[18]

In this case the concern is with the acceptance by the family back home of an Indian wife or of the progeny of such an intermarriage. The question about the status *within* the Jewish community inside India remains unanswered.[19]

(2) During this period, did the Jewish foreign merchants *in the Konkan too* have social and sexual relations with the forebears of the present Bene Israel community?

A fair percentage of the Jewish traders who came to the west coast of India during the Middle Ages hailed from Yemen. Professor Goitein informs us that,

> When Islamic seafaring became ousted from the [Mediterranean] sea by European competition, the Jews of that area turned to the India trade. The twelfth century C.E.[20] was the great epoch for the involvement of Yemenite Jews in those undertakings.......... When, as from the thirteenth century C.E. the trade was monopolized by the great Karim, our sources on it become scarce.[21]

Several persons, the Rev. John Wilson among them, have suggested a Yemenite connection in Bene Israel ancestry. Kehimkar has taken great pains to try to counter this suggestion (see pp. 23, 33-4, 47-50, 58-9, and 61-2 of his *History of the Bene Israel of India*.) All we can say is that it is rather likely that Yemenite Jews did reach the Konkan coast during the Middle Ages, but that, unfortunately, no records or letters written by or about Yemenite Jewish traders on the Konkan coast have so far come to light.

Let us now consider what little information we do have about the early presence of Jews on the Konkan coast.

Medieval sources, Al Idrisi[22] and Al Biruni, mention Tana as being directly south of Subara (Sopora; probably on or near the site of the ancient port of Surparaka). Al Biruni names Tana as the capital of the Konkan.[23] Today there is the modern town of Thana (with many Bene Israel inhabitants), about 21 miles north-east of Bombay. However, further south on the Konkan coast and more intriguing is the town of Saimur.

Unfortunately, no systematic study has ever been made of *Indian* writings (as distinct from the writings of geographers, historians, travelers, scholars and traders who were *not* native to India) looking for mention of Jews in India. Some of the early non-Indian writers have mentioned Jews in places along the Malabar coast, but Al Kazwini (of Persia) is probably the only medieval writer who has mentioned Jews anywhere near the vicinity of what is now Bombay. About 1263 A.D. he wrote concerning the city of Saimur :

> Saimur : A city of Hind near the confines of Sind......... There are Musulmans, Christians, *Jews*, and Fire-worshippers [Parsis] there.......... In the city there are mosques, Christian churches, *synagogues,* and fire temples......... This information has been derived from Mis' ar bin Muhalhil, author of the "Ajaibu-l buldan", who travelled into various countries and recorded their wonders [24] [emphases supplied].

The Mis'ar bin Muhalhil to whom he refers, and from whom he obtained this information, actually travelled to China and to India in 942 A.D. There must have been quite a sizeable community of Jews to have warranted more than one synagogue in Saimur at that time! Is it likely that the foreign merchant colony had already assumed such large proportions as to constitute an actual community in residence? Had an indigenous Jewish community merged with them? Or did an indigenous Jewish community exist there separate from them? The important point is that Saimur has been quite convincingly identified with Cheul of the Konkan. [25] It is located only ten miles from Navgaon, the traditional place of arrival of the Bene Israel shipwrecked ancestors. While the 10th century synagogues in Saimur may well have been established not by Bene Israel, but by early foreign Jewish traders, they may or may not have been associated with, or absorbed by, the local Bene Israel. At any rate it is natural to ask : what happened later to those Jews who had synagogues at Cheul in the 10th century?

Jew's from Cheul may have brought news of the Bene Israel to Maimonides, a possibility which has been suggested by the following data : From Cairo in the year 1199 or 1200 the famous physician and rabbi, Moses Maimonides, wrote a letter to the Rabbis of Lunel in Southern France explaining that most Jewish communities of that day were "dead to spiritual aims" and that, as for Palestine, Syria and Yemen–

> Only lately some well-to-do men came forward and purchased three copies of my code which they distributed through messengers in these countries, one for each country. Thus the horizon for these Jews was widened and the religious life in all communities *as far as India* revived. *The Jews of India know nothing of the Torah, and of the laws none save the Sabbath and circumcision* [emphases supplied].[26]

It is very doubtful that this statement referred to the Jews of Cranganore (later known as Cochin Jews) because the existence of the important Jewish community at Cranganore (Shingli) and of their special trade and other privileges make it more likely that they were, in those days, in contact with outside Jewry. We have good reason to believe that even in those days they were much more knowledgeable and more observant as Jews than described as above by Maimonides. (And, it is therefore very surprising that no mention of them occurs in any of the Cairo *Geniza* letters from Jewish merchants who traded in South India.) Some think that the David Rahabi of Bene Israel tradition might have been Maimonides' own younger brother David, who travelled extensively as a merchant dealing in precious stones.

Goitein reproduces a letter from Maimonides' brother David. This letter, No. 42,[27] was written in 1170 A.D. by David while on his way to India. He never returned from this journey. It is believed that he was drowned in the Indian Ocean. One must, however, be cautious about the medieval use of the term "India", since "Middle India" or "Second India" were terms used to designate Ethiopia in those days.

To return to our study of Cheul : we would like to be able to substantiate the statement of Dr. Gerson Da Cunha who, in his monograph entitled *Notes on the History and Antiquities of Chaul and Bassein*, states that "the Bene Israel have settled in Chaul and its vicinity from time immemorial."[28] However, as far as is known to the present writer, factual documentation for Da Cunha's assertion is lacking. But there *is* inferential evidence which links the Bene Israel to Cheul *before* the 18th century. To begin with, Cheulkar (meaning "belonging to Cheul" or "from Cheul") is a Bene Israel family surname;[29] and the history of Cheul extends far back into ancient times. This Bene Israel surname tie to Cheul opens up at least a possibility of a Bene Israel presence there at a very early date. To follow up on this clue let us outline some of the history of the Cheul area, and see how it may relate to the Bene Israel.

Rev. Lord, in his article on the Bene-Israel in the *Hastings Encyclopaedia of Religion and Ethics* blames the silting-up of Cheul Creek and "the caprices of local misrule at one period" for "closing this ancient port to foreign trade." He goes on to say :

> and this perhaps may have been the means of cutting off the Bene-Israel from further opportunities of contact with their people elsewhere; for they present the appearance of a community who, having up to a certain point preserved intercourse with the main body of their nation, were at some stage in their history separated from the same, and left to develop in their own independent way." (p. 470)

There is a considerable Muslim population in the Konkan and the Bene Israel have absorbed many Muslim customs. As yet we have no evidence that the coming of Islam to the *Konkan* followed the same pattern as its introduction in Kerala.

> Arab traders do not seem to have been trading with the Konkan coast as they did on the Kerala coast which is rather surprising .... Muslim religion thus came in the wake of Muslim conquest and almost all the Muslims in Maharashtra are converted Muslims.[30]

The fabulous wealth of India attracted conquest from outside. But the Muslim invaders who conquered the northwest coasts of India and thence proceeded inland were not the Turks, Mongols, Persians and Afghans who invaded India via the north. An Arab expedition from the sea is known to have pillaged the coast of Kutch, the northernmost part of today's Gujarat State and to have appeared also at Broach and Tanah[31] (adjacent to today's Bombay) as early as 636 A.D. Thereafter, Islam penetrated into Gujarat and southwards, including penetration into the Konkan. The area was annexed to the Muslim Sultanate of Delhi only in 1297 and did not long remain under this

Historical Data of Likely Relevance to Bene Israel

northern hegemony. Eventually, several local Muslim dynasties arose. According to the 1964 revised edition of the 1883 *Kolaba District Gazetteer* (pp. 72 & 73), certain Konkan ports, including Cheul, were in Deccani Muslim hands since 1318 A.D. In the 14th century, the large Muslim Bahmani Kingdom ruled the Deccan and the central section of the west coast of India. In the late 15th century, the Bahmani Kingdom was broken up into the five Muslim Sultanates of Ahmednagar, Bijapur, Berar, Bidar and Golkonda. Ahmednagar and Bijapur dominated the Konkan.

From the end of the 15th century, Abyssinian [32] Muslims, known as *Hubshis* or *Sidis*, who had originally come by sea as mercenaries [33] to the local Muslim Sultanates, held sway over Janjira, though they themselves were under the Ahmednagar Sultanate. Their leader bore the title "Nawab of Janjira" and ruled over the port of Upper Cheul and over the fortress of the territory of Janjira (about 44 miles south of Bombay). The Sidi Nawabs held this foothold in the Konkan even while they themselves were under Ahmednagar, Bijapur, and then the Moghuls. This Sidi foothold retained its supremacy until the British took over the Konkan in 1818. Many Bene Israel were living within the Sidi territory and it is thought that the Sidis identified the Bene Israel with the "Banu Israel" of the Koran, and for that reason treated them well.

Very early in the 16th century the Sidis allowed the newly arrived Portuguese expeditions to engage in the spice trade and to settle in the region of Lower Cheul, [34] where the Portuguese first set up a modest factory (see below, p. 47, note 16) for their traders. Soon, however, the Portuguese built an extensive fort for themselves there, and then took over control of shipping and other powers. But, because the Sidis had not originally resisted them and had granted them residential privileges, the Portuguese refrained from forcibly converting the local population to Catholicism– bothering neither Hindus, Muslims, nor Bene Israel living in that Sidi territory. [35] This was in marked contrast to the cruel behaviour which the Portuguese displayed elsewhere in their enclaves and territories on the west coast of India, especially in Goa. [36] As yet the present author is aware of no Portuguese records which make mention of the Bene Israel or of Shanwar Telis. However, it is known that there were many Marranos [37] among the Portuguese who had come to the Konkan. If any Marrano had had any real contact with the Bene Israel, he would have recognized the Jewish traits of that community. [38]

In his book, *The Bene Israel of India, Some Studies*, on page 65, B.J. Israel states:

> In Bombay City and the Island of Salsette thousands of conversions to Roman Catholicism were made by the Portuguese. Even in the Kulaba District the Portuguese forced the Christian religion on numbers of Hindus. But they seemed to have left the Bene Israel alone.

Even though the British military were well aware and appreciative of the Bene Israel "caste" among their Native Troops during the 18th century, the community was relatively insignificant to Europeans until 1813 when Christian missionaries were first permitted inside British territories in India. These were missionaries of various Protestant denominations and they focused much of their attention on the Bene Israel (see below, pp. 65–90). The Portuguese concentrated on converting Hindus to Catholicism. If the Bene Israel had been noticed at all by the Portuguese (perhaps in such places as Cheul and Bombay where considerable numbers of Bene Israel were living), the Portuguese probably assumed that they belonged to a sect of Muslims (as others also are known to have assumed). In any case, however, scholars who are already working in Portuguese archives, and especially among the archives of the Portuguese Inquisition in

Goa, should be enlisted to be on the lookout for, and to report from their research, findings of any remarks about or indicating the presence of indigenous Indian Jews.

At the beginning of the 17th century, the Moghuls annexed the Ahmednagar Sultanate. This was actually only a formality, the Moghul suzereignty involving only nominal control. Most of the Ahmednagar Sultanate was in reality being ruled by Malik Amber, the Abyssinian (Sidi) serving as the Ahmednagar Sultanate's Prime Minister (see below, p.33) until his death in 1626. And even after 1626, the Sidi viceroys of Janjira continued to protect the Muslim pilgrim traffic to Jidda against the merchants-turned-pirates who plied the entire west coast, making forays mainly against the Portuguese who had usurped the traditional trade of these merchants. The Portuguese, in turn, conducted punitive raids inland, where the pirates usually went to hide. This caused havoc in the villages. The Sidis, on their part, from time to time, ravaged the Kolaba coast in raids against the Marathas.[39] In the face of all these dangers, many villagers, Bene Israel included, fled eastward for safety, cleared the jungle, and established themselves in new villages. This would account for the location of some (but not necessarily all) "traditional" Bene Israel villages located inland. More could be learned about Bene Israel settlement in these inland villages through research into the history of the origins of these villages as such.

The Moghuls, even at the zenith of their power, never really held sway over the Konkan (except for Upper Cheul, which Emperor Akbar held from 1600 until 1615 when it was regained by Malik Amber), notwithstanding the Moghul annexation of the Ahmednager and Bijapur Sultanates. By the end of the 17th century the Konkan, except for Janjira, had already become the preserve of the Moghul's great rival, the Marathas.

In 1659 Shivaji (1627-80), the founder of the great Maratha Power,[40] captured Danda-Rajpuri.[41] The chapter devoted to Janjira State in the *Bombay Presidency Gazetteer of 1883*[42] notes that *before* the Maratha incursions there were said to have been 120 Bene Israel families (a very large cluster in terms of Bene Israel settlement patterns) living in the immediate vicinity (i.e. in Panchaitan or Diva Borlai) of Danda-Rajpuri alone. In 1667 the Marathas took possession of the entire Konkan coast except for Cheul. In 1672 they destroyed the port of Lower Cheul and four years later they conquered Upper Cheul. Cheulkar, Dandekar and Rajpurkar are all very well-known traditional Bene Israel surnames, based on places of origin which were in Janjira State. However, Revdandkar (after the new name "Revdanda" given by the Marathas to Cheul after Lower Cheul was finally surrendered to them by the Portuguese as late as 1793) is *not* a traditional Bene Israel surname. Their traditional surnames alone indicate that the Bene Israel must have been living in the area before *all of* Cheul was renamed Revdanda.[43] We are told that Bene Israel fled from this area during the Maratha incursions and settled some distance away, in Kulaba and elsewhere. The *Gazetteer of Bombay Presidency, Kolaba*[44] *and Janjira* for 1883 says in its section on the Bene Israel (p. 421): "During the wars with the Marathas in the latter part of the 17th century, many Bene Israel families are said to have gone to Kolaba and Bombay."[45] At any rate, when the liberal Maratha rule was finally established, some of these Bene Israel families returned to Danda- Rajpuri.[46]

The Angreys (or Angrias) were a clan of Marathas who became the virtual rulers of the Konkan during the later years of the Maratha Empire. They came to be known as Kulabkar Angreys because the fortress of Kulaba became their headquarters. It is located on a promontory off the coastline at Alibag. This Kulaba of the Angreys is the place of origin for the Bene Israel surnames Khulabkar and Kolabkar. The original name of the place was Kulaba. Only much later did the area adjacent to the fortress come to be called Alibag. The fact that Alibagkar is *not* a Bene Israel surname points to a pre-Alibag date of residence in that area on the part of Bene Israel families.

Walter Fischel notes that Shivaji, in a letter to the Moghul Emperor Aurangzeb (who ruled from 1659-1707), specifically mentions Jews, contrasting Aurangzeb's intolerance with Emperor Akbar's 16th century adoption of "the admirable policy of perfect harmony in relation to all the various sects such as Christians, Jews,[47] Muslims, ... Brahmans and Jain priests. The aim of his liberal heart was to cherish and protect all people........."[48] One wonders whether Shivaji was aware of the community of Bene Israel in the Konkan, and whether any Bene Israel actually served in Shivaji's military forces.

That the Bene Israel were known to the Peshwas [49] (the dynasty which took over from Shivaji's line in 1713) is indicated by an interesting Bene Israel tale explaining the deed of land to the Bene Israel Talkar family : A wealthy Bene Israel oil-presser, Shelomo Abraham Talkar, owned considerable land and cattle in the village of Tala (Mangaon Taluka). He was much respected by his own community, by all the other villagers, and by the Muslim rulers of Janjira (who then ruled Tala), as well as by the rulers of the neighboring areas, i.e. by the Hindu Peshwas. But, after the Sidi Nawab of Janjira and the Peshwas began to war against each other (which would date the story somewhere in the first half of the 18th century), the false accusation was submitted to the Peshwa Court that Shelomo Abraham Talkar was conspiring with the Sidi Nawab against the Peshwas. Shelomo was called to the Peshwa Court (as he had been called many times before the two parties were at war with each other). His denial of charges availed him nothing and he was condemned to be trampled to death by an elephant (a form of execution in those days). Instead of killing him, however, the elephant gently picked up Shelomo and placed him on its back. The Peshwa ruler, taking this as miraculous proof of Shelomo's innocence, gave him a permanent seat at the Court as well as a *jagir* (assignment of hereditary land and right to the rents therefrom) of the village of Gangli. While the motif of this story is a common one, being often told also in respect of other Indian groups, it would still be worthwhile to try to trace the date and the actual sequence of events leading to the deeding of the Gangli *jagir* to the Talkar family.

The Konkan has had a very checkered history. The outline in this chapter of the main Konkan events and dynasties involving the Bene Israel heartland of settlement, has been sketched above as a guide and pointer to further research into the history of that Jewish community. A thorough search for reference to Bene Israel in Maratha and Peshwa archives (which do exist and are plentiful) is amply warranted.[50] Furthermore, research into Sultanate documents should reveal references to the Bene Israel antedating the arrival of the Portuguese, i.e. pre 16th century data, thus putting an end to the notion that Bene Israel origins go no further back than the 17th, or at best the 16th, century when "some foreign Jews must have introduced them to Judaism"

While it is deplorable that we have as yet found no early documentation about the Bene Israel, it should be pointed out that, with the exception of the diverse chronicles of Muslim rulers in India (most of them being little more than sporadic accounts), the writing of history with exact dating and precise historical detail (covering even important epochs on the subcontinent) is, more often than not, conspicuous by its absence. Therefore, the lack of more substantial historical documentation written by, or in respect of, the Bene Israel is not surprising. It is, however, not at all unlikely that a systematic search of all extant relevant archives and documents, village records, genealogies, and other family and synagogue [51] records might turn up numerous bits of information and produce evidence of the Bene Israel's existence as a community in the Konkan extending over many centuries previous to the 17th century. It cannot be urged too strongly that such a project of scholarly investigation should be undertaken *now*, before any such records—if they do exist—are further imperilled by the ravages of time, insects, weather, and human neglect.

NOTES

1. Replies to questions about Judaism from Diaspora Jews, originally addressed to the religio-legal heads (Geonim) of Jewish Academies of Babylonia, beginning about the 5th century A.D., and later to other learned rabbis.
2. Salo W. Baron, *A Social and Religious History of the Jews*, Columbia University Press, New York, 1937, Vol. I, pp. 221-2.
3. This Arabic treatise, edited by M.J. De Goeje, was published by Brill, Leiden, 1889.
4. English translation, as provided by Joseph Jacobs in his *Jewish Contributions to Civilization*, Jewish Publication Society, Philadelphia, 1919, pp. 194-6; also included by L. Rabinowitz in his *Jewish Merchant Adventurers, Study of the Radanites*, Edward Goldston, London, 1948, pp. 9-10.
   "Rādhānite" is the more accurate transliteration of the word used by Ibn Khurdadhbe.
5. D. Simonsen suggests derivation of the word "Radanites" from a term of reference used in those days, namely "Nautae Rhodanici" (meaning "sailors of the Rhone River"); in *Les Marchands juifs appelés Radanites, Revue des Etudes Juives*, Vol. 54, pp. 141-2, a la Librarie A. Durlacher, Paris, 1907.
6. Moshe Gil : "The Rādhānite Merchants and the land of Rādhān", in *The Journal of the Economic and Social History of the Orient*, Vol. 17, Part 3, pp. 299-328, Leiden, E.J. Brill, 1974.
7. Ibid.,p. 323.
8. Ibn Ezra; *Sefer Ha-Ehad* (Book of the One). Cf. Steinschneider, Moritz in *Zeitschrift der Deutschen Morgenlaendischen Gesellschaft*, Vol. 24, pp. 253-4; and *History of Hindu Mathematics, A Source Book* by Bibhutibhushan Datta and Avadhesh Narayan Singh, Asia Publishing House, Bombay, 1962, pp. 96-7.
9. Al-Idrisi wrote that Kandahar "is inhabited by Musulmans, and there is a quarter in which the infidel Jews live" (ibid, p. 127). Kandahar was located near the southern limits of Bactria.
10. The name "Kashmir", as used here, apparently refers to the wide plain of the Jhelum River Valley only.
11. This translation from the original Arabic is taken from Elliot and Dowson, op. cit. (n. 40 Ch. 1 above), pp. 87-8. (Other sources give the date of Al Biruni's birth as 973 A.D., and of his death as 1048.) His full name was Abu al Raihan Muhammed ibn Ahmed al-Biruni. He came into India from the north together with the invader, Muhammed of Ghazni, and saw the country at first hand. Al-Biruni is perhaps the greatest of the early Muslim writers on India. He was learned in many fields and wrote a comprehensive and perceptive book on India.
12. Rabinowitz, op. cit., p. 57.
13. An old Jewish custom forbids as sacrilegious the destruction of anything with Hebrew writing containing the name of God. Therefore such Hebrew writing (especially sacred books) and ritual articles which had to be discarded were either buried in a cemetery or assigned to a chamber especially set aside for the purpose within a synagogue. Such a storage place is called in Hebrew a *geniza*. Most letters of these Jewish international traders contained the name of God, invoking God's help or in giving thanks to Him, since travelling and being a merchant in those days were fraught with much danger. This accounts for the presence of such letters in the *geniza* of the Cairo synagogue.
14. Shelomo Goitein : *Letters of Medieval Jewish Traders*, Princeton University Press, 1973, p. 224.
15. Ibid., p. 64.
16. Professor Goitein's India book will be published posthumously and will contain English

translations of many of the "India Letters", which (as told to the present writer by Professor Goitein) will provide much information about India as such, and will describe what happened outside India in those days when selling Indian merchandise in other countries.

17. Professor Goitein suggested, as a possible explanation for this fact, that the indigenous Indian Jews might not at that time have engaged in *international* trade and therefore would not have had any reason for contact with foreign merchants. (This was also the case of the European Jews of that period, and in the Cairo *Geniza* letters there is no mention of European Jews being engaged in trade in India.) The India Letters already published by Goitein show that : "a spirit of friendly cooperation prevailed between Jew, Muslim and Hindu (also Christian, tho they are rarely mentioned), and between the free merchants and the bond-servants who served as their agents." (Goitein : *Letters of Medieval Jewish Traders*, p. 186). The writer of Letter No. 9 speaks of *Nakoda* (ship owner) Tinbu (a Hindu) who "has bonds with me of inseparable friendship and brotherhood" (ibid., p. 64). Some Jewish merchants remained many years in India. Very many items from the Cairo *Geniza* refer to a merchant, Abraham ben Yiju, a Tunisian Jew who lived in India at least from 1132-1149 A.D. In Valarapattnam (Dahbattan) on the Malabar Coast he ran a factory which made vessels of brass and of bronze. Old copper or bronze vessels were sent to India from the West, and new or repaired vessels were shipped from India to the West (ibid., pp. 186, 188, 192 & 195; and Goitein : *Jews and Arabs, Their Contacts. Through the Ages*, Schocken Books, New York, third edition 1974, p. 209). Elsewhere Goitein speculates that the "Abram" (definitely a Jewish name) who, together with slaves, assisted Ben Yiju at the brass factory, might have been "a local or a Yemenite Jew", but he produces no evidence whatever from the *geniza* documents to substantiate the "local Jewish" possibility; he tentatively is assuming that "As to the problem of 'local Jews' when a person with a Hebrew name and without an honorific epithet (such as 'sheikh'), engaged in a local industry is mentioned, I assume he is local." (From a personal communication to the present author.)

Goitein shows that Jewish merchants often had Indian women, usually slaves, as their concubines (Goitein: *Letters of Medieval Jewish Traders*, p. 335). Several female slaves of Jewish masters were given their freedom, plus considerable dowries, by their former Jewish masters, and with these dowries the women sometimes married Jews of a lower social status than their former master (ibid., p. 335). Abraham Yiju drew up

in his own handwriting a bill of manumission on October 17, 1132 to the slave girl Ashu in the city of Mangalore "given by her former proprietor"[who Goitein suspects later married her] "in the name of both the Exilarch of Baghdad and of the Palestinian Gaon" who at that time had his seat in Cairo. Jewish merchant colonies on the west coast of India originated partly in Iraq and Iran and partly in the Mediterranean Basin. Therefore the documents issued by their courts had to pay homage to the Jewish authorities predominant in each of these two areas (until a few years later). [Goitein : *A Mediterranean Society, the Jewish Communities of the Arab World as Portrayed in the Documents of the Cairo Geniza*, University of California Press, Berkeley and Los Angeles, Vol. II, 1971, p. 21.]

If more than mere verbal "paying homage" was involved, perhaps records of the Jewish Exilarchs of Baghdad and of the Palestinian Gaonim might, then, have included references to other relationships of foreign Jewish merchants while in India—not only in regard to manumission of slaves. If so, among such records there might be found some indication of the presence of *local* Indian Jews, not only in Kerala, but maybe even in the Konkan.

18. Goitein : *Letters of Medieval Jewish Traders*, p. 202.
19. From Dr Goitein's as yet unpublished translations of other "India Documents" from the Cairo *Geniza* it seems that Ben Yiju had a "brother-in-law Nair". This throws new light on the native community of Ben Yiju's wife. "Nair" is the name of a high and important matrilineal caste in Kerala. (Today, sometimes, a male member of this caste is called "Nair" rather than by his proper personal name.) Nairs were the warriors and administrators. It is not likely that even poor Nairs would have been slaves. Perhaps, then, Ben Yiju married a Nair woman and did not marry Ashu the manumitted slave. Nair women were free to have relations with men of the Nambudiri Brahmin caste, and often these were lifelong unions—the woman and her children

remaining with her own Nair joint-family. It might have been permitted to Nair women in those days also to have contracted similar unions with foreigners (in this case with foreign Jewish merchants), though this is very doubtful. Traditionally, Nair women were never allowed to unite with men of inferior status, not even with men of an inferior Nair clan. Most probably if a Nair, or any other non-Jewish Indian woman, actually married a Jew, she would have been excommunicated from her own caste or community and would have had to convert to Judaism. If they did not leave India altogether, were such converts and their children relegated to full, or to a lower status within the local Jewish community (if any)? Or, did they have nothing whatever to do with the local Jewish community? Similar questions would be as pertinent regarding Jews in the Konkan area as they are about this particular "Nair Case" in Kerala.

20. C.E.: an abbreviation for "Common Era", is often used by Jewish writers instead of A.D. (Anno Domini), and B.C.E. (Before the Common Era) instead of B.C.
21. Shelomo D. Goitein : *Yemenite Jewry and the India Trade*. This quotation is taken from the English summary on p. xiii of the Hebrew book entitled *Yahdut Teman-Pirkei Mehkar* (Papers of Research and Study of Yemenite Jewry), Ben Zvi Institute, Jerusalem, 1976.
22. Elliot and Dowson, op. cit., p. 124.
23. Ibid., p. 84.
24. Ibid., pp. 132-3.
25. J.W. McCrindle explains in his *Ancient India as Described by Ptolemy* :

    Simylla : Yule identifies this with Chaul and remarks : "Chaul was still a chief port of Western India when the Portuguese arrived. Its position seems to correspond precisely both with Simylla and with Saimur or Jaimur (i.e. Chaimur, the Arabs having no *ch*) of the Arabian geographers.........Istakhri [notes that] Ptolemy mentions that Simylla was called by the natives Timula (probably Tamula); and putting together all these forms, Timula, Simylla, Saimur, Chaimur, the real name must have been something like Chaimul or Chamul, which would modernize into Chaul." .... Chaul or Chenwal lies 23 miles south of Bombay. [J.W. McCrindle's *Ancient India as Described by Ptolemy*, a facsimile reprint, edited and with an introduction, notes and an additional map by Surendranath Majumdar Sastri, Chuckervertty, Chatterjee and Co., Inc., Calcutta 1927, pp. 42-3.]

    Cheul is a variant of Chaul. The Rev. J.H. Lord supplies additional links to the name when he points out that the present local pronunciation of the name of the village now known as Cheul (located on the outskirts of the ruins of Upper Cheul) is *Tsemvul* or *Tsemval*. This pronunciation is similar to the *Chemula* of the 130 A.D. Kanheri Buddhist cave inscriptions [located to the north of Bombay city, but still part of Greater Bombay]; to the already mentioned *Timulla* or *Simulla* of Ptolemy (150 A.D.); to the *Semulla* of the author of *Periplus Maris Erithraei* (247 A.D.); to the *Tchi-Mo-Lo* of Hwen Thsang (642 A.D.), the celebrated Chinese traveller; and to the *Chivil* of Athanasius Nikitin (1470 A.D.), the Russian. (Lord : *The Jews of India and the Far East*, p. 14.)

26. The English translation of this letter appears in *Letters of the Jews Through the Ages*, edited by Franz Kobler, published by the Ararat Publishing Society in conjunction with the East-West Library, London, 1952, Vol. 1, p. 217.
27. Goitein : *Letters of Medieval Jewish Traders*, p. 207.
28. J. Gerson Da Cunha : *Notes on the History and Antiquities of Chaul and Bassein*, Thacker, Vining and Company, Bombay, 1876, p. 74.
29. See below, Appendix 9, p. 369 of List of Bene Israel Surnames : and p. 156
30. Iravati Karve : *Maharashtra, Land and Its People*, Maharashtra State Gazetteers General Series, Bombay, 1968, p. 195.
31. See K.A. Nilakanta Sastri : *History of India, Part II, Mediaeval India*, S. Viswanathan, Madras, 1st edition, 1950, p.6.
32. Perhaps they were actually Somalis who were/are Muslim, while most Abyssinians (Ethiopians) were/are Christian. And, Somalia was part of Abyssinia for centuries.
33. The Bahmanis had also imported into western India many Abyssinians and other East Africans to serve as slaves.

Historical Data of Likely Relevance to Bene Israel

34. Lower Cheul, i.e. Portuguese Cheul, was also a port and trade emporium; while the port of Upper Cheul, sometimes referred to as "Moorish or Muslim Cheul", was located a mile and a half up-river and east of Lower Cheul.
35. Murud, Shrivardhan and Mhasla Mahals constituted the former Sidi State of Janjira before it was absorbed into Kolaba District in 1948. These mahals continue as subdivisions of Kolaba District.
36. For the only mention (found by the present author) of Portuguese attempts to convert Bene Israel, see below, the quotation on p. 101.
37. Jews who had converted to Catholicism in order to save their lives during the time of the Spanish and Portuguese Inquisitions, but who secretly continued to adhere to their Jewish faith and customs.
38. No record has yet been found of any knowledge about the Bene Israel even on the part of the world-famous Marrano medical-botanist, Garcia de Orta (died in 1568) who lived and did research on the then lush island called "Mombayin" (see Appendix 1). Marranos may have prudently considered it too dangerous, both for themselves, and ultimately for the Bene Israel, to show any interest in anything Jewish. Portuguese administrative and church sources name several Marrano refugees from both Spain and Portugal as settlers in Ahmednagar, Cheul, Cochin, Diu and Goa. The Portuguese in their Indian territories felt threatened by the Marranos because the Marranos were so numerous, had practically a monopoly on trade, and evinced a strong solidarity amongst themselves. It was discovered that some were actually reverting to Judaism, setting a very bad example for the indigenous population whom the Portuguese had forced to convert to Catholicism. In 1560, the Inquisition was formally established for Portuguese India where, with but a provisional suspension from 1774 until 1778, it continued to operate until 1812 in all areas remaining under Portuguese rule.

    The oldest *ketubah* (Jewish wedding contract) at the Israel Museum in Jerusalem happens to have been signed in *Bombay* in the Jewish year 5327 (corresponding to 1567 A.D.). The name of the groom was Avraham Haim ben Yehoshua Ezra, and the bride was Rahama bat Hacham Harav Yisrael ben Amozeg. The name Amozeg is a Judeo-Moroccan name. (One "Moshe ben Amozeg, Fez 1649", for instance, is cited in a list of names of Jews of Morocco.) Although the Portuguese Inquisition in India had already been established when this marriage contract was made in Bombay, and although the Portuguese had not yet ceded Bombay to England (see below pp 42-3), the Inquisition had jurisdiction only over Portuguese subjects (from Portuguese India as well as from Portugal). Hence, Jewish merchants from other lands, though in Bombay, were not questioned by the Inquisition. One can only conjecture that in 1567 a Moroccan Jewish merchant trading in Bombay married off his daughter to another foreign Jewish merchant there, namely to Avraham Haim ben Yehoshua Ezra. However, there is nothing in the groom's name which excludes the possibility of his having been a Bene Israel man from the Konkan. If so, the *ketubah* needed only to reconvert to Hebrew the Indianized forms of Bene Israel Biblical names—provided that the Bene Israel were actually using Biblical names in those days (we have as yet no proof one way or the other).
39. The Marathas, a high (non-Brahmin) Hindu caste of Maharashtra. In the 18th century they held sway over much of India.
40. In reaction against Muslim rule in the region, the Marathas (Hindu cultivators, landowners and soldiers), under Shivaji, by 1680 had taken possession of the entire area from Daman in the north to Poona and Kolhapur in the east, to Karwar in the south (except for Portuguese Goa, Cheul, Salsette and Bassein) and also excepting Sidi Janjira and British Bombay. Later, the Maratha power spread much further, and the Maratha Empire became the biggest adversary of the British in India.
41. The town of Rajpuri lies half a mile east of Janjira Fort (which guards the mouth of Rajpuri Creek). Two miles south of Rajpuri lies Danda, on the bank of that creek. The two places together are considered as one entity, Danda-Rajpuri. Danda-Rajpuri served the Sidis as headquarters for their possessions on land, including much of what is today Kulaba District. In the 16th century Rajpuri had been an important Konkan port, second only to Cheul. It continued to function as a trade emporium until the last quarter of the 17th century when the on-

going struggle between the Sidis and the Marathas ruined the normal life and business of Danda-Rajpuri.
42. *Bombay Presidency Gazetteer of 1883*, Volume XI, Janjira, p. 421.
43. However, according to Gerson Da Cunha, some believe that Revdanda had been the original name of the limited area on which the Portuguese built their section of Cheul. In 1907 the Rev. Lord, in his *The Jews of India and the Far East* (p. 14) mentions that Revdanda "now the site only of ruined churches and bastions" has "a village of the same name which happens to have a Bene Israel synagogue."
44. Following a recent official ruling, the word is to be spelled Kulaba instead of Kolaba.
45. One would like to know the source for this statement because, if the Bene Israel did settle in Bombay City in the latter part of the 17th century (the British themselves came there only in 1674), this would contradict the statement by Kehimkar that the first Bene Israel settled in Bombay in 1746. See below, p. 50.
46. Gerson Da Cunha writes that about 1871 the population of Cheul consisted mainly of Bhandaris, Prabhus, Bene Israel, Muslims and native Christians. The *Bombay Gazetteer* of 1883 states that Revdanda is the same as Lower Cheul and that the former Upper Cheul was then (in 1883) just a few scattered hamlets where, about one mile northeast of Revdanda, a thriving village named Cheul eventually developed. The 1961 *Census Handbook* records a population of 7,408 inhabitants for this new Cheul.
47. There were synagogues in the Moghul Empire under Emperor Akbar at the end of the 16th century. Dr Fischel in his *Jews and Judaism at the Court of the Moghul Emperors in Medieval India* states that

We read in one of those amazingly tolerant decrees of Akbar in 1594 : "If any of the infidels chose to build a church, or a synagogue, or an idol temple, or a Parsee tower of silence, no one is to hinder him". The reference to a synagogue, *kanisa*, as a terminological contrast to *bi's* (church) leaves no doubt that Akbar and his circle had a clear conception not only of the presence of individual Jews, but also of the existence of their house of worship. The existence of synagogues is also borne out by Sir Thomas Roe, who, in a letter of 1616 to the Archbishop, from the Moghul capital, refers to 'synagogue' in the Moghul Empire. [In *Proceedings of the American Academy for Jewish Research*, Volume 18, New York City, 1949, pp. 137-77. The above quote is from p. 147.]

Akbar's empire stretched from east to west over the entire north of the Indian Subcontinent—on the west coast as far south as Bassein, barely 30 miles north of Bombay. Were any of the above-mentioned synagogues located in the western part of Moghul India? No actual remains of any synagogues there have been found (nor for that matter have any been found in the vicinity of Agra, Delhi and Lahore either). We have as yet no evidence to indicate that the congregants of the synagogues in Moghul India were members of a permanently settled Jewish community rather than mere transient, or semi-transient, Jewish merchants, travellers or scholars. The Bene Israel themselves maintain that their own community never had a synagogue prior to 1796.

48. Ibid., p. 147
49. The Peshwas were Chitpavan Brahmins. They originally served as clerks and ministers for the Marathas, until they themselves took over as rulers, with their capital in Poona.
50. About the year 1920, a Bene Israel barrister, David Erulkar (see below, pp. 247, 252-53), then editor of the Bene Israel monthly periodical *The Israelite*, did propose that serious research should be undertaken into the Angria records, and to look for early mention of Bene Israel in the area of Navgaon and in Bombay. Nothing appears to have come of this proposal. What is known is that very soon after 1920, David Erulkar left India for work in Burma, and thereafter in London.
51. Although the first Bene Israel synagogue came into being only in 1796, the synagogue may have been the logical place to store for safe-keeping any precious old family documents, chronicles, etc.

Chapter 3
Earliest Known Documentation on the Bene Israel

As of today, documentary proof of Bene Israel settlement in the Konkan takes us back no farther than the beginning of the 17th century. However, Kehimkar tells us (pp. 81-2) of a *sanad* (a government document or warrant containing a title to land or to an office, or a privilege, or authorization for something specific to be done) in the hands of a Bene Israel Ashtamkar family (cf. Appendix 2a). There is a possibility that this document could prove that the Bene Israel were well established as oilmen in the Konkan at least during the 16th century. It concerns a dispute won, presumably by the Ashtamkars, because this *sanad* and the hereditary rights derived therefrom do belong to this family. The *sanad* specifies rights "enjoyed from time immemorial and from generation to generation" (Kehimkar, p. 82). Ambiguity arises because of the English translation of this *sanad* as presented by Kehimkar, and also because Kehimkar has not stated the date of this *sanad*. It deals with the contested rights of a village officer, a so-called Mheter (Kehimkar's spelling), and states that these rights were confirmed by referral to the records of the celebrated Malik Amber, Sidi Vizier of the Nizam Shahi Dynasty of the Ahmednagar Kingdom (cf. above, p. 26), for the oilman Dadawra, son of Nagawra,[1] and for his descendants in Ashtami (Roha) Taluka. The Bene Israel Ashtamkars, who presumably are the descendants of Dadawra, continued to own land in that area. The text of the *sanad*, which Kehimkar seems to quote in full (minus any date[2]), itself refers to the records of Malik Amber thus:

> It being therefore seen by a reference to the records of Mullik Amber, that the enjoyment of the said rights .... has been in the possession of your ancestors for five or seven generations .... (Kehimkar, p. 82)

The translation into English as presented by Kehimkar reads thus: "enjoyment of the said rights etc. *has* etc.", implying that the present *sanad* was issued five to seven generations *after* Malik Amber's record of the said privileges. On the other hand, if the word *has* actually should have been translated as *had*, the meaning would clearly be that *when Malik Amber's document was issued*, it was confirming privileges which had *already* been existing for five to seven generations. The *sanad* describes the parties concerned as being oilmen in the Konkan at least since the days of Malik Amber's rule there (i.e. from 1601 to his death in 1626)[3]. This provides the earliest evidence to date of the traditional Bene Israel occupation, oil-pressing. And, this *sanad* definitely establishes that these oil pressers were living in the Konkan during the first quarter of the 17th century. Furthermore, depending upon the actual wording of the original language of this *sanad*, it might, by inference, attest to their presence in the Konkan projected back well into the 16th century at least. If the *sanad* which Kehimkar quotes only in English translation could be found, scholars could then confirm or deny this latter point.

Kehimkar (p. 79) also tells of a Bene Israel named Aaron Churrikar who "was appointed Nayek or Commander of a fleet by Khanoji Angria about the beginning of the *seventeenth* century" (emphasis supplied). Aaron Churrikar also received hereditary privileges and land holdings, and the Churrikar family continued to hold the "most important and responsible post of Naik or Commander of the Angria's fleet until it was burnt by the Peshwa in about 1793" (pp. 79-80). Now, Kanhoji Angrey (or, in Kehimkar's spelling, Khanoji Angria) was born about 1669 and died in 1729. Aaron Churrikar could therefore hardly have been appointed Commander of a fleet by "Khanoji Angria about the *beginning* of the *seventeenth* century". Churrikar probably got his appointment early in the *eighteenth* century. Kanhoji Angrey was put in charge of the northern arm of the formidable Maratha fleet about the year 1690. He was later promoted to the position of Admiral of the entire Maratha fleet.[4]

Another Angrey edict, issued in 1761, cites yet another Bene Israel family on whom the title of *Naik* had been conferred much earlier. These appointments notwithstanding, Shellim Samuel believes that only a few Bene Israel had joined the Sidi or Angrey naval forces, because the risks were too great and the spoils for the lower ranks too insignificant. But he thinks that many of the Bene Israel who were living in the port towns were then most probably employed in the shipyards, while others prospered by selling the produce of their farms and oil-presses.[5] On this subject B.J. Israel, in a private communication, adds that, "In the biography of Kanhoji Angrey, written by Manohar Malgaonkar, there is no reference to any Bene Israel being employed by him. If any were, they must have been in very minor capacities." Yet, Aaron Churrikar's position as *Naik* was not a minor appointment.

The royal edict issued in 1761 (mentioned above) happens to be the first known written reference to Bene Israel *kajis*, stipulating that a Bene Israel *Naik* ranks just below a Bene Israel *kaji* in the Bene Israel hierarchy and in regard to the honors to which he is entitled.[6]

Another extant *sanad* dated 31 January 1808, Bombay, and signed by one S. Halliday, Superintendent of Police,[7] regarding the title of *Kaji* in the Rajpurkar family, names three generations of Rajpurkar *Kajis*, viz. Samuel, whose signature upon assuming the office of *Kaji* is dated 1799; his father, Nasemjee Musajee, who died in 1799; and Samuel's grandfather Musajee Aaronjee, who, depending upon the length of his life, may or may not have been a practising *kaji before* the date of 1761 (mentioned above as being "the first known written reference to Bene Israel *kajis*").

There are two more interesting *sanads* regarding hereditary *kaji* rights in the Rajpurkar family; one was issued by the Peshwa Government, the other by the Hubshi (Sidj) Government of Janjira. The former was issued in 1770 because (according to Kehimkar's translation, p. 46) "the old Sanad granted to them had been lost in a rebellion"[8]. If so, the old *sanad* which had been lost might well have antedated 1761. As for the Hubshi *sanad*, it was granted in 1840 confirming, for Hubshi territory, the hereditary *Kaji* rights for the same family which had received the *sanad* of 1770. This 1840 *sanad* explicitly says that copies of these edicts should be kept at the Royal Hubshi Palace. (For full text of this *sanad*, as well as of the *sanad* of 1770 according to Kehimkar's English translation, see Appendix 2b and 2c.) If a copy of the 1840 *sanad* was kept in the archives of the royal palace of the Hubshi rulers, how many other dated documents which also deal with Bene Israel might have been (or might still be) found in those archives, if thorough search had been (or still is) possible? This one *sanad* alone furnishes several clues as to where to start hunting.

Turning to another kind of documentation, we must include in this chapter a discussion of the inscriptions on the few Bene Israel tombstones which have as yet been found with "early" dates on them.

The ancestral burial mounds and the earliest markers in the Bene Israel cemetery at Navgaon have no writing at all on them. The oldest dated Bene Israel tombstones have been found, not at Navgaon, but in the vicinity of the Konkan town of Pen (southeast of Bombay), in an old burial ground which might have been either Muslim or Jewish, or both.[9] The earliest dates here are 1778-1780. One tombstone inscribed in Marathi only, marks the grave of "Mussaji Ballaji Tarantopkar [or Tarankhopkar?] of the Maratha[10] Regiment". The name "Mussaji" is a typical Bene Israel Marathi-ization of the name "Moses"; and "Tarankhopkar" is a traditional Bene Israel surname. In the old burial ground are several tombstones inscribed in English, Marathi and Hebrew, with later dates, all 19th century. But there are also several black rocks scattered as markers of graves which probably date to much earlier times. Because the place is located near a fortification of Shivaji (17th century) it suggests the possibility of Bene Israel having served under Shivaji and/or his successors in this area, and perhaps they lie buried here.

The date of 1715, attributed by Dr Strizower to a Bene Israel tombstone, is very questionable. In her earlier book *Exotic Jewish Communities*[11] (p. 65), and in her article, "Jews as an Indian Caste"[12] (p. 53), she mentions only one such tombstone : "For in an old Bene Israel cemetery in the Konkan I noticed a gravestone with a Hebrew inscription dated 1715—proof that Bene Israel were then not unfamiliar with at least the rudiments of that language"; whereas in her, *The Children of Israel : the Bene Israel of Bombay* (p. 43), she puts this in the plural, thus : "For in an old Bene Israel cemetery in the Konkan I noticed *gravestones* [emphasis supplied] with inscriptions dated 1715" etc. There is a tombstone in the Bene Israel cemetery at Navgaon which *almost* fits this 1715 date. It is inscribed both in Hebrew and in Marathi (Devanagri script). The Hebrew inscription on the stone contains a demonstrable mistake: its numerals—*hay, tav, ayin* and *het*— distinctly add up to the equivalent Christian year 1718; while its Marathi year (given according to the Shake Era 1740) is the equivalent of 1818 A.D., exactly 100 years later than the Hebrew date. Note that the Marathi inscription on the stone gives a date equivalent to *1818* rather than *1815*. It is quite understandable that here the final Hebrew letter *het* (which equals 8) might be mistaken for the letter *hay* (which equals 5, and which happens to be very similar to, although not identical in form with, the letter *het*). The old Bene Israel tombstone inscriptions require further study, especially as regards the use of specific styles of scripts, both Hebrew and Marathi, which might serve as a clue to the time at which a given inscription was actually incised. According to B.J. Israel,

> In the case of this particular gravestone, as far as its Marathi script is concerned, it looks more like the script developed for printing by moveable type in the early 19th century. I am convinced that the correct date for this gravestone is 1818 and *not* 1718. Furthermore, all the other gravestones near it also bear later dates in Marathi.[13]

We can safely say that any 18th century tombstone *with Hebrew inscription* which might be found in the Konkan is more likely to be that of a foreign Jew or of a Cochin Jewish merchant or teacher, or perhaps of a *Marrano* Jew rather than of a Bene Israel because, so far, we have no reason to believe that in the 18th century Hebrew was well enough known even to the Bene Israel *Kajis* to have been used on Bene Israel tombstones.[14]

When we get into the early decades of the 19th century, however, we do find Hebrew inscriptions on some Bene Israel tombstones, and not only at Navgaon. Some of these early Hebrew inscriptions marked Bene Israel graves in Bombay. Kehimkar tried, without success, to ascertain the dates of grant by the Government for the first two Jewish burial grounds in Bombay. B.J. Israel has pointed out that "In the account of the Bene Israel given in the *Gazetteer of Bombay City and Island, Volume I, 1900* it is stated that a gravestone excavated at an old Bene Israel cemetery on the Parel Road (the site of the present J.J. Hospital) proves that the community must have been resident in Bombay prior to 1776."[15]

Kehimkar mentions two additional inscriptions found here, each with name and date of Bene Israel who died in the last quarter of the 18th century. We do know that the *third* Bene Israel cemetery, located behind the Magen David (Baghdadi) Synagogue (founded in 1861) near the crossing of Bellasis Road and Clare Road, was granted in 1785. We have no evidence of any 18th century burials here, but we do have the name and date of death of several Bene Israel who died between 1817 and 1828, as evidenced by their tombstones inscribed in Hebrew, and, in other instances, in Marathi. David Sassoon, in his *Ohel Dawid*[16] (Volume I, p. 370, item 554) has listed the names of 45 deceased Bene Israel individuals whose remains are identified in this cemetery. Among the Bene Israel burials there were also some non-Bene Israel Jews who were buried here.[17]

In 1809 a non-Jew, Marcia Graham, mentioned a Jewish cemetery in Bombay and had located it quite precisely as being situated near

> Malabar Point on south-west of Island Road from Malabar Hill to Fort of Bombay [which] lies along beach of Back Bay, a dangerous bay formed by the point of Malabar and Old Woman's Island, or Coulaba, on which is the lighthouse. On the other shore is the general burial place of all classes of inhabitants......... Next to the British Cemetery is that of the Portuguese, after which follows those of Armenians, the Jews, and the Mahomedans, with a few Hindoos who bury their dead, in regular succession; they are all overshadowed by a thick coconut wood.[18]

In 1809 the Jewish cemetery was being shared by Bene Israel and Baghdadi Jews. However, the author's use of the term "Jew" need not imply that she was aware of the Bene Israel connotation of that term. On another page in her Journal and on another subject she again uses the word "Jew" and definitely means the Bene Israel.

A fourth Bene Israel burial ground—in Kamatipura—was granted in 1832. (The Baghdadis shared this burial ground too with the Bene Israel; but in 1836 they petitioned the Government that a wall be built in this cemetery to separate the two communities. See below, pp. 99-100.) In his *History of the Bene-Israel of India*, Kehimkar devotes pp. 160-165 to the location of each Bene Israel cemetery in Bombay and to the reasons why the 1st, 2nd and 4th Bene Israel burial grounds eventually were obliterated in the process of construction of various public works.[19]

There are numerous 19th century Bene Israel cemeteries scattered throughout the Konkan,[20] especially within Kulaba District. Besides, there are also Bene Israel burials in places other than the cemeteries which were associated with the various Bene Israel synagogues and prayer halls. Bene Israel cemeteries, most of which were in use during the 19th century, exist outside of the Konkan too. For many of these today, there are no longer any Bene Israel living in the vicinity who can maintain them. Those which are still being maintained and used for new burials are marked below with an asterisk (*).

BENE ISRAEL CEMETERIES OUTSIDE THE KONKAN :

In Maharashtra : Ahmednagar, Dissa, Kamti, Lonavla, Maow, Nagpur, Panchgani,

Earliest Known Documentation on the Bene Israel

Poona*, Satara and Sholapur.

In Gujarat : Ahmedabad* (Dudheshwar Road), Baroda, Rajkot, and Surat.
In Madhya Pradesh : Jabalpur.
In Karnataka (formerly Mysore State) : Dharwar and Hubli.
In Rajasthan : Ajmer.
In Delhi : New Delhi* (Humayun Road).

A third category of documentation of the Bene Israel relates to early contacts of the Cochin Jews with the Bene Israel. This will be dealt with in the following chapter.

NOTES

1. *Dadawra* and *Nagawra* are not names which are known to have been in use among the Bene Israel during the 18th or 19th centuries. In a government document, typical local names would have been preferred for citation to any name used strictly within the Bene Israel community, if indeed other communal (or Jewish) names had been in use then, or earlier among themselves.
2. Moses Ezekiel in his *History and Culture of the Bene Israel in India* (published by the author and J. and J. College of Science, Nadiad, 1948), on p. 96, about the document in question writes merely this :

   1612. Ashtamkers—Dadaora son of Nagaora—Mheters of the District of Ashtami had a SANAD. The "Sanad" refers to Malik Amber's Sanad given to him for seven generations.

   Moses Ezekiel does *not* state his source for the date "1612".
3. Cf. *History of the Rise of the Mahomedan Power in India till the year 1612*, translated into English from the original Persian of Mahomed Kasim Ferishta by John Briggs; (first edition, London 1829) reprinted 1966 by Editions Indian, Calcutta; published by S. Dey from Editions Indian. See Volume III, pp. 189-93, and also the "Comparative Chronology of the Deccan Kingdoms Principally during the Sixteenth Century"—at the very end of Volume III, for "Ahmudnuggur".
4. Kanhoji Angrey was the first of his family to adopt the surname Angrey, after the village of Angarwadi, near Poona. When the British took over (1818), the Angreys were allowed to continue (until about 1848) their rule in the southern part of Kolaba District which includes Alibag, Pen, and Roha Talukas (see Map 2), all of which were centers of Bene Israel habitation.
5. Shellim Samuel : *Treatise* etc., pp. 174-5.
6. To quote Kehimkar regarding the edict of 1761 : "His Royal Highness Raghoji Angria of Kolaba" affirms that "Tanaji bin Succoji Naik, the Israelite inhabitant residing in the province of Cheul......... by descent through a line of ancestors served His Royal Highness *from generation to generation* with great devotion and loyalty.........the office of Naik which the predecessors [presumably Kanhoji Angrey] of His Highness were graciously pleased to confer on his ancestors has also been held by the successive members of his family, and that on the occasion of weddings or festivities in the community certain honours and presents were accustomed to be rendered first to the *kaji*, then to the members of his family and lastly to the people of the community." [Kehimkar : *History*, p.80. Emphases supplied.]
7. This *sanad* of 1808 is mentioned by S.J. Kolabkar in his little pamphlet called *Kolaba Travels Investigations*, printed at the New Diamond Printing Press, Karachi, 1946, 9 pages; on p. 7.

   S.J. Kolabkar was very conscious of the need to document all extant information concerning the history of the Bene Israel. He travelled about in Kolaba District trying to collect such information, and requested members of the community to submit to him any relevant material. The present writer knows of nothing else published by Kolabkar. However, it is likely that he personally made a detailed survey of Bene Israel in certain Kolaba villages.
8. Kehimkar, *History*, pp. 45-6.

9. Dr. Shalva Weil visited this very inaccessible spot in 1978. She photographed some of the grave markers there.
10. A regiment of the Native Forces under the British, and *not* of the earlier Maratha rulers.
11. Strizower, Schifra : *Exotic Jewish Communities*, Thomas Yoseloff, London and New York, 1962, 157 pages.
12. Strizower : "Jews as an Indian Caste" in *The Jewish Journal of Sociology*, Volume I, no. 1, April 1959, pp. 43-57; published on behalf of the World Jewish Congress by William Heinemann Ltd. London.
13. From a personal communication to the present author. Here B.J. Israel refers to the four decipherable Navgaon tombstones (of which three bear both Marathi and Hebrew inscriptions). The equivalents of their *Shake* Era Marathi dates are as follows : 1740 = 1818 A.D., 1764 = 1842 A.D.; and 1786 = 1864 A.D. (which, in the latter case, is also inscribed as such). For further discussion on this matter see B.J. Israel : *The Bene Israel of India, Some Studies*, pp. 83-5.
14. However, relying upon Ezekiel Rahabi's Letter of 1768 (see below, p. 43-4) it is conceivable that an occasional (unknown) Cochin Jew *might* have been in the area in the 18th century and *might* have supervised the Hebrew lettering on a given tombstone.
15. From a personal communication to the author.
16. *Ohel Dawid. A Descriptive Catalogue of Hebrew and Samaritan Manuscripts in the Sassoon Library, London;* compiled by David Solomon Sassoon, in two volumes; Oxford University Press, London, Humphrey Milford, 1932.
17. Ohel Dawid specifically mentions Rev Meir Yehiel, who died in 1824, and Sharhanabai Haruna Silliman but not Silliman Jacob. (See below pp. 68-9) Was Sharhanabai Haruna Silliman the daughter of Silliman Jacob?
18. Marcia Graham : *Journal of a Residence in India*, Longmanns, London, 1812, p. 11.
    The entry quoted here was made on August 15, 1809.
19. Among H.G. Reissner's notes (now in Folios 654/1 — 3 at the Central Archives for the History of the Jewish People, located in the Sprinzak Building on the Givat Ram campus of Hebrew University in Jerusalem) there is a typewritten *Table of Jewish Cemeteries in Bombay*, and on separate notepaper are the following jottings : "Gazetteer of Bombay presidency, Volume 26, Part III, pp. 576-577 : Burial ground at Mendhane Point named and opened in 1675. Burial ground at Sonapur established in 1767." One wonders what, if any, connection there may have been between Jews in Bombay (if there were any there in 1675) and these burial grounds. Other jottings by Reissner about Jewish cemeteries : "Baghdad : Grant Road, opened 1830; Delisle Road, opened 1890; Jewish-Bene Israel, Bellasis Road and Clare Road, registered 1824; 6922 square yards; closed."
    (According to Kehimkar, p. 162, the land for the latter cemetery was granted in 1785 and it covered 6955 square yards instead of 6922 square yards. Perhaps it was first opened for use in 1785, but not officially registered until 1824.)
    The following table, typed as is, was also found among H. G. Reissner's notes (in Folio 654/1) :

JEWISH CEMETERIES IN BOMBAY

	Regd No.	Name & Address	Date of Registration	When first opened	Area in Sq. yds.	In use or closed *	Remarks
1.	5	Burial Ground, Grant Rd, North & South Sides	30-1-1874. re-registered in 1892	Jan. 1829.		Closed 16-10-1898	Bene Israel
2.	9	Grant Rd. Bene Israel Jewish Cemetery, 1, Grant Rd.			5927	Closed	Bene Israel

Earliest Known Documentation on the Bene Israel

Regd No.	Name & Address	Date of Registration	When first opened	Area in Sq. yds.	In use or closed	Remarks
3. 20	Burial Ground, Matunga, for Jewish prostitute** (Municipal managed)	1-6-1874	1869 when ground was granted by Gov't.	1573	In use	Taken over charge of this cemetery at Antop Hill from Mrs. A.K. Stewart by the municipality in 1936 ***
4. 48	Delisle Rd. East Side (Jewish)	19-5-1877 Re-registration 14-8-1891	30-4-1878* ****	11,621	In use	Jewish
5. 71	Mount Road	10-1-1899	16-10-1898	7000	Closed	Jewish-Bene Israel
6. 84	Haines Rd.	23-9-1926	10-1-1927	10,000	In use	Jewish-Bene Israel *****

(Additional plot of land reserved for Jewish Cemetery at Haines Road plot No. 3 & 4 and measuring about 2364 square yards and 2341 square yards respectively are not still in use. Granting of additional land for burial purposes adjoining the two plots is under consideration.)

* : Probably as of 1946 or 1947.
** : The words "for Jewish prostitute" were written in by hand. (See below, p. 109, n.11)
*** : Who was Mrs. A.K. Stewart? Had she offered her land for this cemetery? Was this cemetery only for prostitutes (of any religion)? In the Table, the word "prostitute" is in the singular.
**** : Reissner's handwritten note says this cemetery opened in 1890 and not in 1878.
***** : It is not clear whether "Jewish-Bene Israel" means only Bene Israel or Baghdadis and Bene Israel. For the first two cemeteries in this table, under *Remarks,* only "Bene Israel" and not "Jewish-Bene Israel" is given; yet we know that this was for the very period when Baghdadis were being buried in Bene Israel cemeteries.
The present writer did not have the opportunity to clarify the facts in this matter.

20. In folio 4558 at the Central Archives for the History of the Jewish People is a collection of postcard size, black and white photographs, taken at the following Bene Israel cemeteries in the Konkan : Alibag (new), Ashtami (old & new), Bandra, Borle, Chinchpokli, Jabulpada (big), J. J. Hospital graveyard, Korle, Kurla, Lonavla, Matheran, Mhasla (old and new), Nadgaon, Nagpada, Pali, Panvel, Pen, Perali, Pynad, Revdanda, Roha, Shrivardhan, Tala, Thana and Worli. (Unfortunately, the inscriptions on most of the tombstones as shown in these photographs are not clear enough to be read from the photographs)

Chapter 4
Earliest Contacts between the Cochin Jews and the Bene Israel

It is not entirely impossible that Cochin Jews did appear among the Bene Israel at a very early period. Indeed, given access to all Cochin Jewish Chronicles[1], documents and letters of merchants (both Cochini and foreign) who plied India's west coast even during the very early Middle Ages, one might conceivably find references to very early Cochin Jewish contacts with the Bene Israel. There does exist, in a chronicle called *Maggid Hadashoth*, a very garbled version of a possible contact of this sort.

Before proceeding it is necessary to note that the Cochin Jews were divided into three mutually endogamous groups: (1) the largest group, the *Malabari* Jews, who called themselves in Hebrew *ha-Meyuchasim* (those with a pedigree, i.e. descendants of the original Jewish community at Cranganore), and who are often referred to in English as the "Black Jews"; (2) the *Pardesi* (which literally means "foreigners") or "White Jews" (although among them some have rather dark skin)—probably never more than 200 in number, whose ancestors came from European or Levantine countries, except for three families from the ancient Jewish settlement in Cranganore; and (3) the *M'shuhrarim* (in Hebrew, meaning "manumitted") or "Brown Jews", who were descended from manumitted slaves or servants who had been converted to Judaism.[2]

Barbara Johnson (Hudson), in her significant M.A. thesis, *Shingli or Jewish Cranganore in the Traditions of the Cochin Jews of India*,[3] discusses the various Cochin Jewish Chronicles. In her category of "The Earliest Sources" she lists a chronicle called *Maggid Hadashoth*. She looks upon it as a *Malabari* (as distinct from a *Pardesi*) Cochin Jewish Chronicle because the Pardesis do not seem to claim it, and because parts of it appear in later *Malabari* Chronicles. To quote Barbara Johnson (p. 57), we learn from *Maggid Hadashoth* that:

In 866 B.C.E. Shalmanessar II sent 460 families of Jewish prisoners led by Simon Rabban of the tribe of Ephraim, to King Puruwa of Mokha in Teman (Yemen). In 344 B.C.E. King Prusus expelled thousands of Jews from Mokha, and Simcha Rabban led them to Puna and Guserate in the lands of the Great Mogul,[4] where they joined other Jews who were already there. In 340 C.E. 72 families of these Jews arrived in Malabar.

The original Hebrew text of *Maggid Hadashoth* has been lost. The complicated vicissitudes in the history of the text of this chronicle, and of the translations of it back and forth from the Hebrew are explained on pp. 174-177 of the thesis and are enough to warrant doubt about the authenticity of at least some of the statements attributed to *Maggid Hadashoth* in its present form. It is believed to have been either first translated into Dutch from the original Hebrew, or to have actually been authored by a Dutch

Jewish convert to Christianity, Leopold Emmanuel Jacob Van Dort, who found or produced *Maggid Hadashoth* during a visit to Cochin in the year 1757. Without concerning ourselves with the professed antiquity of the events, its reference to Jews who were already living in Poona and Gujarat, and to some Jews leaving these sites to settle in Malabar at an early date, is indeed intriguing. Poona is very close to the Bene Israel heartland, and most of Gujarat is closer to the Konkan than is Cochin. The text does not say, nor suggest, that "the other Jews who were already there" had preceded Simcha Rabban from Mokha. Therefore, the phrase could indeed refer to ancestors of the Bene Israel.

Naphtali Hertz Weisel (Weseley) discusses *Maggid Hadashoth* and reproduces parts of it (in Rashi script[5]). in a Hebrew journal called *Ha-Me'asef*.[6] The version which Weisel published and discusses is his own translation into Hebrew from a version of *Maggid Hadashoth* which had appeared in German. It says that Simcha Rabban and his group lived peacefully in Poona and Gujarat until a period of oppression occurred when most Jews there left Judaism and adopted idolatry. But only Joseph Rabban (a descendant of Simcha Rabban) and 72 Jewish families left Poona and Guzerati (transliterated according to *Ha-Me'asef's* Hebrew spelling) with him to settle in Malabar at the time of "Sheran Perumal". There follows this statement :

> The Jews who remained in the Moghul territory .... worshipped idols, did not know the name of Jews and if asked 'which people are you?', they say 'Bene Israel' .... Although they have forgotten the *Torah*, they keep *Shabbat*, *Yom Kippur* and *Brit Mila* [circumcision], and what is even more wonderful, they speak the Hebrew language in a pure and correct way.[7]

The dating and sequence of these events as *Maggid Hadashoth* tells the story is, to put it mildly, very odd. The oppression and reason for giving up their Judaism are blamed "on the Great Moghul" (i.e. Akbar in the 16th century, notoriously tolerant of all religions), while "Sheran Perumal" (i.e. Cheruman Perumal) of Malabar is erroneously catapulted forward by more than 500 years into Akbar's time.[8] Furthermore, the idea that the Bene Israel were speaking perfect Hebrew either in the 16th century or in the late 18th century (when this issue of *Ha-Me'asef* was published) is entirely unsupported by Bene Israel tradition. This source introduces yet another special twist : not only that the Bene Israel were possibly living in India as Jews *before* Simcha Rabban's band came to settle there (in Poona and Guzerati) with them, but that some of those original 72 Jewish families might themselves have been from the Poona-Guzerati Bene Israel stock! However, Weseley, in his discussion of *Maggid Hadashoth (Ha Me'asef*, p. 143) says that "Joseph Rabban and *his* [emphasis supplied] people, 72 families, went to live in Malabar".

Maggid Hadashoth was one of the *Malabari* Chronicles. The *Pardesi* Chronicles have different stories to tell or, perhaps more accurately, a different axe to grind.

During his stay in Cochin (1806-7, and in 1808), the Rev. Claudius Buchanan learned from the local Black Jews that "There are amongst us some of the children of Israel (Beni-Israel)[9] who came from the country of Ashkenaz, from Egypt, from Tsoba, and other places, besides those who formerly inhabited this country.[10] Because of the *Maggid Hadashoth* statement about Simcha Rabban and his band having joined other Jews who were already living in Poona and Guzarati, Buchanan's wording (above) might be construed to mean that "those who formerly inhabited the country" include (among others perhaps) the ancestors of the Konkan Bene Israel. Buchanan continues thus :

> The Black Jews communicated to me much interesting intelligence concerning their

brothers the ancient Israelites in the East .... They recounted the names of many other small colonies resident in northern India, Tartary and China and gave me a written list of *sixty-five* places. I conversed with those who had lately visited many of these stations, and were about to return again[11] .... They (the Black Jews) said that it was commonly believed among them, that the great body of the Israelites are to be found in Chaldea .... that some few families had migrated into regions more remote, as to Cochin and Rajapoor in India ....[12]

It is very interesting that the Black Jews here acknowledge that those Jews in Rajapoor also go back to the Biblical dispersal of the Israelites. Even though Rev. Buchanan's respondents make no mention of Jews in Poona and Guzerati, there *is* a connection linking Poona, the Bene Israel, and Rajapoor (Rajpuri) to the events mentioned in *Maggid Hadashot* : namely, that *all* of the Konkan (except Goa, Chaul, Salsette, Bassein and Janjira) was, until 1866, called "Rajpuri" and was ruled as such by the Maratha dynasty and then by the Peshwa dynasty out of Poona, their capital city. In 1866, after the British had taken over the Peshwa territory, what was formerly called Rajpuri became officially known as Roha[13] and Mangaon Talukas of Kolaba District. A look at Map. 2 will show how very many villages in these *talukas* were traditional places of Bene Israel habitation.

We skip now from the *"Maggid Hadashot* connection" and the Buchanan references, both of which take us far back in time, to the Portuguese period in India. The Portuguese began their occupation of the town of Cochin in the year 1500, ushering in a period of harrassment of the Jews in Cochin. In 1661 the Portuguese partially destroyed Cochin's Pardesi Synagogue. Shellim Samuel believes that the Jewish merchants of Cochin needed then to seek new trade prospects and that some of them might have tried to continue their trade by basing themselves on the port of Dande-Rajpuri, where they would have found their co-religionists, the Bene Israel. Shellim Samuel, however, ignores the fact that the persecutors of the Cochin Jews, namely the Portuguese, were then based also at Lower Cheul which lies uncomfortably close to Dande-Rajpuri. No record of Cochin Jewish merchants trading at the port of Dande-Rajpuri is known to the present author. However, even if one such merchant, in spite of the Portuguese presence in Lower Cheul and in spite of unsettling conditions of war, did carry on trade at Dande-Rajpuri, there might have been some contact with Bene Israel, and this might have led to the beginning of Cochin Jews giving religious instruction to some of the Bene Israel.

There may have been Bene Israel-Cochin Jewish contacts related to the port of Surat, 158 miles north of Bombay, near the mouth of the Tapti River on the southern coast of what is now the state of Gujarat. Surat had been conquered by the Moghul Emperor Akbar in 1572. It was in Surat (in 1608) that the British gained their first trade foothold in India. In 1610 the Moghuls also granted trading concessions to the Portuguese in Surat. At this time, and throughout the 17th century, there were several Jewish merchants (mainly in the jewel trade) who actually settled in Surat, established a Jewish congregation there, and influenced the city's economic life. Since this was then indeed "Guzarati in the land of the Great Moghul" (still under Moghul hegemony), one might well ask whether there were any Bene Israel also living in Surat or in its environs at that period; and whether they had any contacts with these Jewish merchants. So far these questions have remained unanswered.

Let us note the fact that the Portuguese in 1661 (the year in which they sacked the Jewish synagogue at Cochin) had ceded to England the port and islands of Bombay, as a wedding gift to England from the King of Portugal on the occasion of the latter's daughter, Catharine of Braganza, marrying the British King Charles II. Not until 1674, however, did the British transfer their East India Company headquarters from Surat to their recently acquired islands of Bombay. Here they established the city of Bombay.[14] It mushroomed rapidly under British rule and in 1818 became the capital of Bombay Presidency.[15] Thousands of villagers from the surrounding areas came to settle in Bombay. Among them were many Bene Israel.

Surat still remained an important trade emporium for several years after the British East India Company's headquarters had moved to Bombay. There are several extant documents which refer to a Jewish merchant in Surat, namely to Moses Tobias, the owner of many ships and the Director of the Portuguese factory[16] in Surat from 1728 until 1745. He served as official spokesman of Portugal in Surat (even after he had retired from his position as Director of the Portuguese factory there); and he also rendered services to the British East India Company branch office in Surat. He is buried there in an old Jewish cemetery and his tombstone reads as follows :

The revered Ha-Nasi[17] Moshe Tubi, from the holy community of Cochin, who died on Sunday the 20th of the month of Iyar, in the year 5529 (1769), at the age of 75 years.

This means that he himself was a Cochin Jew,[18] very likely of the Pardesi Cochin Jewish family of "Isaque Tobi from Berberia", as mentioned in the *List of Heads of Families* compiled by Mosseh Peyreyra De Paiva during his visit to Cochin in 1687. Professor Walter Fischel discovered Dutch records which document close personal and commercial relations between Moses Tobias in Surat and Ezekiel Rahabi II in Cochin. Also, Fischel found this bit of information in Volume IV, 1739/40 of *Tellicherry Consultations*, p. 11 : a letter from the Bombay President to Chief Wake of Tellicherry, dated November 23, 1739 : "We are advised from Surat that two carpenters would be sent you by a ship belonging to Moses Tobias which was to sail in a few days for the Malabar Coast." Many Bene Israel in 18th century Bombay were known to be skilled carpenters.

Tellicherry is on the coast of what is today the northern part of Kerala; in those days it came under the jurisdiction of the British. Even though Moses Tobias had dealings with the Bombay President, as evidenced by the letter, in 1739 the British East India Company had no foothold on the Konkan mainland and hardly any Bene Israel had yet settled on the islands of Bombay. One wonders whether or not Tobias received any reports about Bene Israel. If not, was he at least aware of the Bene Israel who were living in Surat in 1738, as recorded by the Danish missionary J.A. Sartorius in a letter to H.H. Francke in Halle? (See below, p. 49). Professor Fischel has found evidence in a British document dated April 1797 that the Jewish merchants (who were mainly Arabic-speaking Jews) of Surat at that time, had a synagogue with regular services.[19]) We do not know when this synagogue was first established, but those Bene Israel in Surat (mentioned by Sartorius), or their following generations, may have known about this synagogue. If so, this would mean that in the 18th century Bene Israel knowledge about synagogues stemmed from two sources : Cochin and Surat.

Next, let us consider a Hebrew letter to Tuvia Boaz of the Dutch East India Company in The Hague. It was written in 1768 by Ezekiel Rahabi II, a very important member of the *Pardesi* Jewish community in Cochin,[20] in reply to several questions mainly relating to the history and Jewish customs of the Cochin Jews. But of particular interest in the present context is Rahabi's mention in the letter of 1768 that

> There are Jews in India at Vijapur[21] and they are called Bene Israel. They are scattered in all Maratha towns and also under the Mogul. There are also tent-dwellers,[22] and some of them make oil, and some are soldiers and know nothing but the *Shema* and they keep the *Shabbat*; and a couple of times went to see wise men (*Hachamim*) to learn about Judaism, to be guided and taught. But they did not succeed. And one of them came to Cochin and stayed there for four years,[23] and learned *Torah* and a little of the laws and went away. And we heard that now he is their *Rav* and guides them according to the Jewish way. And, according to what we hear, there were about 10,000 souls there.[24]

Rahabi in his letter of 1768 makes no mention of the *Maggid Hadashoth* claim that Joseph Rabban and his followers originally sojourned in Poona and Guzerati, presumably with the Bene Israel. He does not mention Poona and Guzerati, but his specification of "Vijapur" and reference to being "under the Mogul" probably do relate to the same general area and, conceivably (although not necessarily), to the same context. This Letter of 1768 reveals clearly that there had been actual contact between Cochin Jews and the Bene Israel prior to 1768.

The time of the first Bene Israel religious revival, attributed to one David Rahabi who sojourned among them, is still an enigma. Indeed, David Rahabi I (1646-1726) was the name of the father of the famous Ezekiel Rahabi II (1694-1771) of Cochin. He had come from Aleppo to settle in Cochin in 1664. Was it he who had been among the Bene Israel and who had been responsible for persuading a Bene Israel to study *Torah* in Cochin "for four years"? Perhaps so, but Ezekiel Rahabi's Letter of 1768 does not say so. There was also Ezekiel Rahabi's own son (i.e. a grandson of David Rahabi I) whose full name was David Ezekiel Rahabi (1721-1791) and who is known to have been in touch with the Bene Israel. But, again his name is not mentioned in his father's Letter of 1768. About him Dr. Strizower has written:

> There is a Rahabi family in Cochin in whose unpublished family history, written in Hebrew, I have read that a member of the family, David Ezekiel Rahabi, went to western India in the middle of the eighteenth century, in the course of his work for the Dutch East India Company, there encountered the Bene Israel, and revived the Judaism he found existent among them.[25]

Also relevant is a 63-page document from the Pardesi Synagogue in Cochin, handwritten in Hebrew in the year 1939 by Naphtali Roby (Rahabi), entitled *History of the House of Rahabi in Cochin*. In a section specifically devoted to David Ezekiel Rahabi, it says (in English translation):

> In his days the people 'Bene Israel' saw the light of the Torah which they had never seen before because until then they did not know the Torah and the commandments except the tradition that they were descendants of the Jews. When David saw that their heart and eyes were for wanting God, he sent them men of God from Cochin to Bombay and to every other place where 'Bene Israel' live, to teach them Torah and commandments and to warn their wives of the 'idols' [or, of the 'bad things'][26] they had strayed after. Also, he sent (them) the books of the Torah of Moses. The teachers that went there succeeded in their task. (p. 21)

But, the 1939 Roby document nowhere mentions that David Ezekiel Rahabi personally encountered the Bene Israel in the Konkan. Instead, it only mentions his encounter in

Mysore with a Bene Israel prisoner-of-war (see Appendix 3a).

The Letter of 1768 makes no mention of David Ezekiel Rahabi's contact with Bene Israel as having had any relation to the one Bene Israel person who came and studied for "four years" in Cochin. The *sanad* issued in 1761 explicitly deals with *already customary* rights and privileges of Bene Israel *kajis*. Most probably, David Ezekiel Rahabi was not the David Rahabi who traditionally first discovered the Bene Israel and established the office of *Kaji* among them. If the 18th century David Rahabi of Cochin had instituted this Bene Israel office, why would *he* have given it a Muslim designation? David Ezekiel Rahabi, known for his scholarly interest in Hebrew and Judaism [27] would supposedly have preferred a Hebrew title for the persons who were to learn Hebrew and who were to be the religious guides among the Bene Israel.

Regarding the curious coincidence of David (Ezekiel) Rahabi's name with that of the David Rahabi of Bene Israel tradition, B.J. Israel comments that

> if the David Rahabi of Bene Israel tradition is the David Ezekiel Rahabi who visited them in the middle of the eighteenth century, it is inconceivable that, in the early years of the nineteenth century when several persons who had met him must have been still alive, his coming had been put back in the communal memory more than eight hundred years. The possibility is that the *name* was transferred to the legendary teacher who, if he ever existed, was an entirely different person.[28]

This need not, however, detract from Roby's statement, cited above, that David Ezekiel Rahabi sent Cochin Jewish teachers and Jewish books to the Bene Israel in the *18th* century.

If Naphtali Roby is correct, a group of Cochin Jewish teachers actually taught among the Bene Israel in the Konkan during the 18th century, i.e. earlier than detailed in Kehimkar's *History of the Bene Israel of India*. Kehimkar begins his Chapter III, entitled "Further Religious Revival Among the Bene Israel and the Adoption of the Name 'Bene-Israel'," by noting that

> a very noticeable religious revival among the Bene-Israel commenced about 1796, when the first synagogue in Bombay was built .... At or about this time the Jews from Cochin, Surat, Bagdad, and other places began to pour into Bombay, giving the Bene-Israel opportunities of learning more and more about their religion [p. 65] [and] a band of Cochin Jews arrived in Bombay in 1826, among whom the names of Michael and Abraham Sargon, David Baruch Rahabi, Hacham Samuel and Judah David Ashkenazi may be prominently mentioned. These exerted themselves not only in edifying the minds of the Bene Israel and of their children generally, but also particularly in turning the minds of those few Bene Israel, who through heathen influence had gone astray from the path of the holy religion of their forefathers to a right direction .... David Baruch Rahabi was engaged in effecting a religious revival at Revadanda .... (p. 66).

Roby too mentions a David Baruch Rahabi, born in 1790, a grandson of David Ezekiel Rahabi. He died in 1862. Although Roby does not mention his sojourn among the Bene Israel, he is most probably the person to whom Kehimkar here refers.[29] Enough, then, about the several different David Rahabis.

Eighteenth century contacts with Cochin Jews had sparked a religious revival among the

Bene Israel. We do not know all the dates, nor the frequency or extent of these eighteenth century interactions. But, we do know that in 1796 the first ever Bene Israel synagogue was built. (One hundred years later it was named Sha-ar Ha-Rachamim, i.e. Gate of Mercy Synagogue.) It is located at 254 Samuel Street, Mandvi, Bombay, and is still in use today. At the time of the founding of this synagogue practically all the Bene Israel of Bombay were living in Israel Mohalla (quarter) through which ran what came to be known as Samaji Hassaji Street (Samuel Street), named in honor of the founder of the first Bene Israel synagogue, Samaji Hassaji (i.e. Samuel Ezekiel) Divekar, one of a family of several brothers who were all army officers, and whose father, having come from Janjira State where he owned a lot of land, was the second member of the Bene Israel community known to have settled in Bombay.[30].

There is no doubt that Samaji Hassaji Divekar did build the first Bene Israel synagogue in 1796 after having fought in the British Native Army in the war against the Mysore Sultanate, following his release as a prisoner-of-war of the Sultan. However, different versions of the story give different dates and mention different persons as having been instrumental in securing his release. They also offer differing accounts of what transpired both in connection with his release from prison and with his subsequent activities. (See Appendix 3a.) Be all that as it may, it is at the very least certain that during the second half of the 18th century there definitely was contact between Cochin Jewry and the Bene Israel, and that before the end of that century, Cochin Jews had already begun to stimulate the revival of Judaism among the Bene Israel. A thorough search through Cochin Jewish documents of this period might disclose facts which would delineate the "who, when, where, and how" of these eighteenth century Bene Israel-Cochin Jewish contacts.

As soon as the synagogue was completed in Bombay, Samaji went to Cochin to obtain a Torah scroll for his synagogue. But he suddenly took ill in Cochin, died, and was buried there. The Hebrew inscription above his grave, which is located within the cemetery of the Cochin Jews, reads as follows:

This marks (the resting place) of Rav Samuel, son of Ezekiel Divekar, Commadan Israel, who died on Wednesday the 14th day of the month of Kislev in the year 1797.[31]

The death of Samaji coincided with the close of the eighteenth century. Before beginning the portrayal of the Bene Israel in the nineteenth century, let us see what Bene Israel life was like during the eighteenth century.

NOTES

1. The most important and the earliest chronicle, i.e. *Sefer Ha-Yashar*, is said to have been destroyed by the Portuguese when they burned the Cochin Pardesi Synagogue in 1661.
2. Barbara Johnson makes a point of distinguishing also between the *Pardesi M'shuḥrarim* and the *Malabari M'shuḥrarim* because each was endogamous and because the *Malabari M'Shuḥrarim* go much further back in history than do the *Pardesi M'shuḥrarim*. (Barbara Cottle Johnson: "The Social Context of Malayalam Songs among the Cochin Jews: Women's Folk Culture and Boundary Maintenance", a paper delivered at the Association for Jewish Studies Eleventh Annual Conference, Boston, December 1979, 12 pages; p.2.)
3. Barbara Johnson (Hudson), *Shingli or Jewish Cranganore in the Traditions of the Cochin Jews of India*, with an Appendix on "The Cochin Jewish Chronicles", a thesis presented to the Department of Religion, Smith College, in candidacy for the degree of Master of Arts, May 1975; 218 pages.

Earliest Contacts between Cochin Jews and Bene Israel

4. This obviously is meant only to identify the locale, meaning a specific area where *later* the Great Moghul ruled. It cannot mean that Simcha Rabban came there when that area was already under the sway of Emperor Akbar, the Great Moghul. Akbar was born in 1542; he reigned from 1556-1605.
5. Rashi script is the only rabbinical (non-modern) Hebrew script still being used today for commentaries on the Bible and Talmud. This script was used by Rashi (Solomon bar Isaac, b. 1040-d. 1105), a very important Jewish scholar and commentator who lived in France.
6. The Hebrew journal, *Ha-Me'asef,* was published "in der orientalischen Buch druckeri, Koenigsberg und Berlin, 1790". Weisel's article which discusses *Maggid-Hadashoth* appears in the *Ha-Me'*asef 1790 section for the Hebrew months of Tevet, Shvat and Adar called "2nd period", on pp. 129-160. The material also appeared in a separate 32 page booklet of *"Igeret Arachot Olam"* put out by Rav Avraham Fritzel, first printed in Prague in 1793, second printing in 1810.
7. Literal translation from the Hebrew on p. 143 of the *Ha-Me'asef* article.
8. Latest historical scholarship considers the year 1000 A.D. to be the date when the local ruler, Cheruman Perumal, presented to Joseph Rabban, in Cranganore, the Copper Plates Deed granting land and special privileges to the Jews of Cranganore in perpetuity.
9. This is Buchanan's own parenthesis.
10. Rev. Claudius Buchanan, D.D. : *Christian Researches in Asia, with Notices of the Translation of the Scriptures into the Oriental Languages;* published by Samuel T. Armstrong, Cornhill, Boston, 1811 (2nd edition). In 1812 a 5th edition of this book was published by T. Caldwell and W. Davis in the Strand, London. This quote is from p.173 of the 1811 edition (p. 222 of the 1812 edition).
11. This could mean that Malabari Jews themselves were among those widely travelled Jewish merchants; or that non-Cochin Jewish merchants happened to be around to talk when Buchanan was in Cochin.
12. Ibid., pp. 176-7 of the 1811 edition (pp. 225-6 of the 1812 edition).
13. Ashtami—the locale of the very early 17th century Ashtamkar *Sanad*, granted by Malik Amber (see above, p.33)—is within Roha Taluka; and Malik Amber was much involved with the Moghul governor of the adjacent territory.
14. Bombay originally consisted of seven separate islands (the Colaba, Fort, Byculla, Parel, Worli, Matunga and Mahim of today) which, through successive reclamations, have been transformed into a single peninsula attached to the mainland. The islands formed a fine harbor.
15. In 1818 the British East India Company divided all British territory in India into large administrative units, one of which was the Bombay Presidency.
16. A *Factory* in India of those days designated a foreign trading establishment. A list of the directors of the Portuguese Factory at Surat from the 16th into the 19th century shows that they were of many different nationalities and of many different religions, and that among them there were some Jews. For instance, it was to a Director Joseph Cohen that the Moghul Government in 1653 gave permission to hoist the Portuguese flag in Surat. At the head of the Portuguese Factory was the Representative to India of the King of Portugal. This Representative was stationed in Goa. The Directors of the Portuguese Factory were employed primarily to report to this Representative matters of interest about everybody in the area, i.e. matters relating to politics, economics, commerce, military affairs, etc. Such reports might reveal clues as to a Bene Israel presence in that area. If so, Dr. Fischel did not uncover any. He has, however, written at length about "Moshe Tuviah" in his Hebrew book *He-Yehudim B'Hodu (The Jews in India),* pp. 39-46. Moses Tobias is an Anglicization of Moshe Tuviah.
17. *Ha-Nasi* in Hebrew means *the President*. Moses Tobias must have been the President of the Surat Jewish community. Ten Hebrew-inscribed tombstones have been found in this cemetery; but only a few of them are decipherable. Of these, the marker on the grave of Moses Tobias bears the earliest date.
18. By the 18th century the Portuguese were no longer harrassing the Cochin Jews. The Dutch had taken Cochin away from the Portuguese in 1663. The Portuguese maintained their Inquisition in India until 1812, but it functioned only in those few territories still under Portuguese rule.

They seem to have had no reservations against placing their Surat Factory under the directorship of a Jew!

19. Walter J. Fischel : "The Immigration of Arabian Jews to India in the 18th Century", American Academy for Jewish Research, *Proceedings,* Volume XXXII, New York City, 1965, pp. 1-20; the reference cited is on pp. 15-6.

20. The paternal side of his family was relatively new to Cochin : his grandfather, Ezekiel Rahabi I, had come from Aleppo and settled in Cochin in 1646; his son David who was also born in Aleppo, married as his second wife a daughter of the old Pardesi Hallegua family; she was the mother of the famous Ezekiel Rahabi II.

21. Bijapur (Vijapur) was a 16th century independent kingdom, a large territory which included the Konkan coast from just south of Cheul to somewhat south of Goa, and extended far eastward beyond the Western Ghats (i.e. the north-south mountain range near and parallel to India's western coast line). Its capital city, also called Bijapur, is located in today's Karnataka State near its boundary with southern Maharashtra. The Bijapur Kingdom succumbed to the Moghuls.

22. The literal meaning of the Hebrew here is *tent-dwellers.* Were the Bene Israel of the Konkan ever tent-dwellers? *Tent-dwellers* presumably refers to nomads.

23. There is no known Bene Israel record of this four-year stay at Cochin on the part of a member of the Bene Israel community. He might have been a Bene Israel *Kaji.*

24. From "A Letter of 1768" written by Rav Ezekiel Rahabi in Cochin, addressed to Tuvia Boaz in the Hague. This letter was published and discussed in Hebrew in the 1790 Issue of *Ha-Me'asef,* section for the Hebrew months of Nissan, Iyar, Sivan-called "3rd period", on pp. 257-76; this quotation about the Bene Israel appears on p. 262.

25. Strizower : *The Children of Israel : The Bene Israel of Bombay,* p. 36. (Reprinted here by permission of Basil Blackwell Ltd.) The present writer has tried, unsuccessfully, to find out from Dr Strizower more details about this document to which she refers — minimally in order to verify whether it is the Naphtali Roby *History of the House of Rahabi in Cochin* (written in Cochin in 1939), or whether it is an entirely different document. In the latter case, the verbatim text of the information which it contains might help solve some questions.

26. The Hebrew word for "graven images" or for "idols" is *p'see-lim*; and from the same root comes the word *p'su-lim* the plural for "blemish, defect, disqualification". hence "a bad thing". Graven images are forbidden to the Jews in the Ten Commandments and elsewhere in the *Torah.* The distinguishing Hebrew vowels concerned (between *p'see-lim* and *p'su-lim* vary only in height one from the other. From examination of a photocopy of Roby's original hand-written text, it seems more likely to be *p'see-lim* rather than *p'su-lim* in this case. One cannot, however, be completely certain. On the other hand, Roby's account is largely copied from a much earlier account by Solomon Reinemann (See Appendix 6) where the word for "idols" is given very clearly (*p'see-lim*).

It is interesting that Bene Israel women are singled out as polluting the Bene Israel religion. While, according to the Bene Israel tradition, the "original" David Rahabi gives credit to Bene Israel women (for cooking only *kosher* fish), and while much credit is traditionally assigned to Bene Israel women in general for having been the guardians of the calendar of Jewish holidays and of whatever Jewish customs still survived among the Bene Israel before their Jewish revival. Could it have been only wives of non-Bene Israel origin who were holding on to their idols?

27. David Ezekiel Rahabi was the author of a study of the Hebrew calendar called *Ohel David.* It was published in Amsterdam in 1785.

28. Benjamin J. Israel : *The Bene Israel of India, Some Studies,* p. 56.

29. The name of one David Hyam Rahabi subsequently appears in the 1882-84 records of Bombay's Shaare Rason Synagogue, as that of the donor of a contribution of Rs. 6-12-0.

30. In mid-18th century, according to Kehimkar, *History,* p. 78.

31. Taken from David Sassoon : *Ohel Dawid,* Volume II, pp. 574-5. (Not to be confused with *Ohel David* written by David Ezekiel Rahabi, an entirely different book — see above, note 27.)

Chapter 5
The Bene Israel in the 18th Century

To gain some idea of the physical characteristics of the Bene Israel, picture a person with straight to wavy black hair, black or dark brown eyes, oval face, straight nose. Obesity was and remains rather rare among the Bene Israel. Skin color can vary from very light to very dark brown, and the average height used to be from five to five and a half feet (but by the 20th century they were on the average considerably taller). In their bodily appearance they were/are indistinguishable from many other Maharashtra groups, except perhaps to persons who are sensitive to the particular combination of distinguishing traits which does, in a vague unscientific way, to some extent differentiate each endogamous community.[1]

As to the name of the community which concerns us here, the early *sanads* which deal with Bene Israel never called them "Jews". Some referred to them as "Israel *Teli*" as well as "Shanwar Teli", or as "Israel *Lok* (people)", but never as "Yehudim" (Jews). The only actual reference to this community as "Yehudim" which the present author has ever found appears in an 1824 missionary report of Michael Sargon's description of some Bene Israel who were then living in Cannanore. (See below, p. 67).

We know that the designation "Bene Israel" was used in reference to what must have been members of this native Konkan Jewish community in a letter of 1738 by the Danish missionary J.A. Sartorius, referring to a group of them in Surat and Rajapoore who "do not call themselves Jews, nor understand the name, but Bene Israel, children or descendants of Israel."[2] And, as we have already seen above (p. 44), in his letter of the year 1768, Ezekiel Rahabi specifically wrote that "There are Jews in India at Vijapur and they are called Bene Israel, they are scattered in all Maratha Towns." The Dutch Governor of Cochin (1771-81), Adriaan Moens, in a memoir wrote: "some miles to the north of Bombay there dwell black men who call themselves Israelites and observe circumcision and also the Sabbath but no other customs or laws."[3] The important fact is that, according to documentation, the words "Bene Israel" *were* used to refer to this Konkan Jewish community at least as early as 1738; and in other early instances, if not "Bene Israel", then the word "Israel", not "Jew", formed part of the local name for them.[4]

Even though Sartorius based his information about the Bene Israel solely on hearsay, it is worth repeating here because he described the Bene Israel as they were reputed to be as of early in the 18th century. The following is Walter Fischel's quotation from Sartorius' letter of 1738 to Professor A.H. Francke of Halle :[5]

> They [the Bene Israel] have not the books of the Old Testament nor do they understand Hebrew but Hindustani (Mahratti), the language of the country where they reside. What they know of religion is not yet ascertained except that they make use of the word "Shema" as a formula of prayer of doctrine.........They are partly weavers, and partly boatmen, and supply the ships with necessaries. Others are

soldiers and workmen. They practise circumcision as a part of their religion. They wear turbans and a long dress reaching to their feet, and long trowsers, just as the Mohammedans do. They do not intermarry with other Indians, but keep to their own people.

This account I received from Indian and German Jews resident at Madras, who gained their information from other Jews who come from Cochin. One of these English Jews had seen and conversed with several of the Bene Israel in the country of Surat.

Some Bene Israel may have settled in Bombay during the latter years of the 17th century (see above, pp. 26 and 43). But, according to Strizower, "A document in the handwriting of one Samuel Nissim Kaji dated 1800 states that Bene Israel first settled in Bombay in 1746.[6]" Kehimkar (p. 78) too dates the first Bene Israel arrivals in Bombay in mid-18th century. B.J. Israel points out that Bene Israel from the mainland had actually begun enlisting as fighting forces for the British *before* the Bene Israel started to settle in Bombay, and that being in the service of the British military might well have been a contributing factor toward the Bene Israel move into Bombay. However, Professor Fischel writes that British "military records of August 1, 1759 and July 1760 which registered the various ethnic and religious groups of the population of Bombay who could be 'employed in the defence of the island in case of its being attacked by an enemy' .... make no mention of Jews."[7] In a private communication to the present author, B.J. Israel has explained that the military records of 1759 and 1760 (mentioned above) refer only to the population of Bombay and not to the neighbouring areas, and that

> it is a known fact that from the neighbouring areas outside of Bombay military personnel was enlisted by the British East India Company for some time before 1760. The Bene Israel enlisting in the East India Company forces were not necessarily already resident on the islands of Bombay......... I would put the Bene Israel enlistment in the East India Company, as preceding their formal embodiment as a regular force, in 1750 or so. Bene Israel also enlisted in the Bombay Marine.[8] Much of the first warfare engaged in from Bombay was at sea and on the coast with Angria and the Sidi. Employment in the marine preceded the organization of a regular Bombay Army and declined with the decline of the regular Maratha and Muslim naval power in the latter half of the 18th century.

According to Kehimkar (p. 78), sons of the first Bene Israel settler in Bombay enlisted in the British Army as early as 1760, but the first document to which Professor Fischel could attest

> which offered clear proof of the presence of Bene Israel Jews in Bombay is dated August 17, 1786 and is entitled "recruits to be chosen from particular castes"......... and listed along with Muslims, Shia and Sunni, native Christian converts, low caste Hindus, Marathis from the Deccan and Konkan (Perawarys or Fross, Rajpoot, Siedies) also members of the so-called 'Native Jew Caste' in Bombay.[9]

It probably took some decades before the Bene Israel came to the attention of the British as a group in its own right, and only then did the British designate them as "Native Jew Caste". Furthermore, it is clear that the British often incorrectly made use of the word "caste", as in this instance.[10] Further research may reveal earlier written recognition of the Bene Israel by the British and by others, and we must bear in mind

Professor Fischel's advice: "a systematic combing of all the material as far as humanly possible is imperative: only a part of this staggering abundance [of archival material] has been thus far subjected to a thorough analysis by me."[11] And, "A systematic collection of all the testimonies culled from the memoirs and biographies of British officials serving in India would be of great importance."[12]

In the 18th century, Bene Israel settlement extended southward as far as Bankot. Bankot was the recruiting center for the British Bombay Native Army, which the Bene Israel joined in large numbers. This prompts us to ask whether the Bene Israel already had a history of favoring enlistment in the fighting forces of their pre-British rulers as well. The mention of Bene Israel naval commanders in the Angria fleet (see above p.34) suggests that the answer may be in the affirmative. But as yet that is our only clue.

Most of the Bene Israel who enlisted in the Bombay Native Army attained the commissioned ranks of *Jemedar* or *Subedar*, while some acquired the additional title of *Sirdar Bahadur*.[13] Given the size of their community, relatively many Bene Israel fought in the 18th century in the 1st, 2nd and 3rd Anglo-Maratha Wars; and in the 1st and 2nd Anglo-Mysore wars.[14] In some cases a Bene Israel was put in charge of an entire fort. In the Native Army of the Bombay Presidency not only the total Bene Israel enlistment, but also the number of Bene Israel officers was quite out of proportion to the tiny size of the community.[15]

During the 18th century, although so many Bene Israel had joined the military services, and although so many others had been attracted from the rural areas to settle in Bombay, still, the majority of Bene Israel continued to live in obscurity as oil-pressers, dispersed throughout many (often contiguous) villages, with only a few of them living in each village.[16]

From the descriptions which follow, one finds some similarities and some differences which pertained to Bene Israel life and customs as compared to those of their Hindu counterparts.

As oil-pressers the Bene Israel were definitely on the lower (but not the lowest, let alone untouchable) rungs of the ladder in the social structure of the village. Technically speaking, Bene Israel (and also Muslim) oil-pressers did not really form part of the Hindu caste hierarchy *per se*. Their status in village or town was, therefore, almost by definition, higher than that of Hindu oil-pressers, and their contacts were less restricted because they were, so-to-speak, beyond the pale of the caste system. They were, however, inter-dependent in a caste-like way with all the other groups in the village, and they lived a thoroughly Indian village way of life except for their strict observance of the Jewish religion *as they knew it*. In the case of the Ashtamkar *sanad*, which takes us furthest back in time (see above, p. 33), we find early recognition of the Bene Israel as "oilmen". They are explicitly called *"Saturday* oilmen" in the *sanad* issued in 1770 (in replacement of an older document which had been lost; see above, p.34) in the district of Rajpuri to Abraham Kaji and Dawud Kaji. This *sanad* authorizes them "..........to come to the district without any hesitation and to exercise uninterruptedly your rights and privileges as kajis among the *Saturday Oilmen*."[17] [Emphasis supplied]

In their traditional vocation the Bene Israel worked their ancient type of oil-presses[18] to extract oil mainly from sesame seed and coconut. The oil-pressing was done right within the premises of one's own compound. The oil-mill was propelled by a blindfolded (in order to prevent dizziness) bullock walking round and round in its small orbit. After the oil had been extracted, the residue, in the form of sesame or of coconut oil cake, was used as feed for cattle, or as fertilizer. As his fee for pressing oil from seeds supplied by clients, the oil-presser was entitled to keep a certain portion of the produce of oil and of the oil cake, which he was then free to use for himself or to sell, or to barter in exchange for other necessities such as rice, salt, pulses, etc. The staple food was (and is) rice, with coconuts and mangoes also being plentiful and popular. From mid-June to the end of September there are heavy monsoon rains, with hot, humid weather. Average temperatures range from about 20° centigrade (January) to 30° centigrade (May). It was customary to dry and then to store in each household very large quantities of grains, spices and other foods at the time of their respective harvests in order to be able to feed the entire household during inclement weather and at all times when those items of food were otherwise not available.

While many Bene Israel, especially in the Sidi territory, spoke Konkani,[19] Marathi was, and is, the language most widely spoken.

It is doubtful that by mid-18th century there were more than one hundred Bene Israel living at any one place, even in towns, with the single exception of the city of Bombay. As early as the middle 1700s Bene Israel were not merely working as oilmen. As Kehimkar's own family history demonstrates, there were not only some Bene Israel men of wealth in those days, but there was also some mobility within the rural Konkan area, entirely separate from the lure of army service or of the city of Bombay:

> There lived in Kehim in times of remote antiquity [sic] a man by the name of Aaron, a Bene-Israel gentleman who had four sons by name Elloji, Abaji, Bhowji and Essaji. After the death of their father they went to Nadgam, a village in the Hubshi territory, being frequently molested by the Pindaries.[20] Of these four brothers Elloji had a son by name Joseph who came to reside at Ramraj, a village in the Angria's territory after the death of his father. He had a son named Jacob who was well-to-do in life and possessed a large herd of cattle which were let out to graze in the forest of Mahan where he had enclosed a large space for enclosing the cattle by night. He had also a great many rice fields and a park attached at Ramraj. He was besides a money lender,[21] but his house being several times plundered and burnt to ashes by gangs of free-booters such as the Pindaries, Dacoits,[22] etc., he was reduced to poverty. His grandson Shalom Samuel Kehimkar is still in possession of some of his lands which annually yield to him some income derived from the produce of rice. (Kehimkar, p. 83)

With the help of Kehimkar's Genealogical Chart (found at the beginning of his *History of the Bene Israel of India*), we can calculate with confidence that his ancestors Elloji and Elloji's son Isubji (or Joseph, who lived in Ramraj) lived in the first half of the 18th century, preceding H.S. Kehimkar, the author, by four and three generations respectively.

Then, about the Doodkar family, Kehimkar mentions that

> Bapuji Doodkar lived in the time of the Angrias, and was a wholesale merchant. He traded in oil from Jafrabad, in tobacco from the Ghauts and Surat, in betelnut from the Konkan, sandal from Malabar, cotton from Coomta as well as spices and many other commodities. It is said that he had his own ships wherewith he traded with other ports.[23] He did much business and held a considerable fortune for some time but he failed in consequence of almost all his warehouses being burnt in a great conflagration.[24]

Bene Israel religious observance centered on home ritual. Even group worship took place in someone's house rather than in a separate prayer hall. *Kajis* travelled from place to place to officiate at rites of passage and to arbitrate disputes within the community. So sparsely settled throughout numerous villages were the members of the Bene Israel community that sometimes they were buried in Muslim cemeteries, since separate Bene Israel burial grounds were not always within practicable distance. Most Bene Israel knew how to perform the Jewish ritual method of slaughtering animals for food. Out of deference for Hindu custom, beef was not included in the Bene Israel diet. Strict social sanctions from within, and equally strict caste barriers from without combined to assure the continuance of the small community from generation to generation.

From the information on the preceding pages, dealing with what is known about the Bene Israel in the 18th century, about their neighbours and the history of the area, there emerges the definite possibility that, even before the arrival in 1498 of the Portuguese in India, the Bene Israel were already living in what is now Maharashtra, as a distinct, separate small group of Jews, observing, however incompletely, basic elements of Biblical Judaism. Whether in this state they represent vestiges of immigrants from the Holy Land of Biblical times, or descendants of local converts to Judaism, or of a few foreign Jews who came to the area, or of a mixture of all three possibilities, and whether their own ancestral form of Judaism was vestigial or had never been more than fragmentary—the answer to these questions cannot reduce the likelihood that, as an entity, they antedated the arrival of the Portuguese in India; that, even then, they observed a religion different from that of their neighbours which probably contained more Jewish elements than are observed by some modern Jews whose status as Jews is not questioned by anyone.

Throughout the second half of the 18th century hundreds of Bene Israel left their villages for the attractive opportunities in employment and in education which the fast developing city of Bombay had to offer. By 1785 they were already numerous enough to have acquired their own *third* Bene Israel cemetery in Bombay.[25] Many Bene Israel became skilled laborers, especially in the field of carpentry. For the Bene Israel their several new occupations and city life represented quite a change from being rural oilpressers. And, in Bombay the Bene Israel for the first time developed into a substantial, vigorous community. Simultaneously their religious institutions also developed.

NOTES

1. One of India's leading anthropologists, Andre Beteille, takes congnizance of this factor in his book *Castes Old and New, Essays in Social Structure and Social Stratification,* Asia Publishing House, Bombay, 1969, p.43, where he states . "Perhaps there is room for a cultural theory of appearance which will go beyond the conventional anthropometric indices and probe into those subtle differences of carriage and expression which have such an important bearing on social interchange."
2. W.J. Fischel : "Bombay in Jewish History in the Light of New Documents from the Indian Archives", American Academy for Jewish Research, *Proceeding*, Volume 38-39, New York, 1972, pp. 119-44; p.128.
3. Ibid., pp. 128-30. Fischel mentions all these quotations from the *sanads,* Sartorius, Ezekiel Rahabi, and Moens. He does not, however, explain how he arrived at his conclusion that "the term 'Bene Israel' was not at all so generally applied by their neighbors until later in the 19th century." (Ibid., p.130)
4. Kehimkar, in *History,* pp. 74-5, suggests that, with the advent of Muslim power in the Konkan, his community had adopted the name "Bene Israel".
5. See Walter J. Fischel : "A Hitherto Unknown Jewish Traveler to India, The Travels of Rabbi

54 Beginnings

David D'Beth Hillel to India (1828-1832)", from *In the Time of Harvest, Essays in Honor of Abba Hillel Silver Jubilee,* New York, 1963, p.174. Fischel took this quotation from John Antony Sartorius : "Notices of Madras and Cuddalore in the Last Century," from *Journals and Letters of the Earlier Missionaries of the Society Promoting Christian Knowledge,* London, Longman and Co., 1858, pp. 162-64.

6. Strizower : *The Children of Israel : The Bene Israel of Bombay,* p. 39. (Reprinted with permission of Basil Blackwell, Ltd.)
7. Fischel : op. cit., p. 125.
8. A Marine Corps was established in 1769 and in the following year it became known as the Marine Battalion. In her *Journal of a Residence in India,* Mrs. Maria Graham records that in 1809 when she visited Bombay there were "three or four thousand Jews in Bombay......... many of whom were employed in the Marine........."
9. Fischel : op. cit., pp. 125-6.
10. Ibid. According to Fischel's footnote 10, p. 126, this quotation was extracted from the Fort Victoria Residence Diary of March 5, 1786, fols. 21-25, General Public Department, Bombay.
11. Ibid, Footnote 5, p.121.
12. Ibid., footnote 15, p. 127. The article in which these footnotes (5 and 15) occur was published in 1972, only a year before Professor Fischel's death.
13. Indian terms for various ranks and designations can be very confusing, largely because one and the same term often had different referents in different parts of the subcontinent or in different periods of time. To sort out the various ranks held by the Bene Israel, one must understand that under British rule, until 1919, Indians were not entitled to receive the King's Commission; instead, they were given Viceroy's Commissions of *Subedar Major, Subedar,* and *Jemedar.* These ranks still remain in the India Army, but are now referred to as Junior Commissions. In the days of the Moghul Empire a *Subedar* was a very high military-cum-civil official, the equivalent of a governor of a province. In general, under British rule, Indian officers received less pay than did their British counterparts. The equivalence of rank, although not of status, was as follows :

ARMY RANKS

INDIAN COMMISSIONED RANKS	CORRESPONDING BRITISH RANKS
Subedar Major (originally called Commandant)	Staff Captain
Subedar	Captain
Jemedar	Lieutenant
INDIAN NON-COMMISSIONED RANKS	**BRITISH RANKS**
Havaldar Major	Sergeant Major
Havaldar	Sergeant
Lance Naik	Lance Corporal
Naik	Corporal
Sepoy	Private

Indian officers were rewarded with the Order of British India for meritorious service, and the words *Sirdar Bahadur* were prefixed to their rank (if in First Class), or just the word *Sirdar.* (if Second Class).

Khan Bahadur was a distinction awarded to civilians, coming (in rank) between the title *Khan Saheb* and *Dewan Bahadur. Sardar Bahadur* was the civilian title given as an award to Sikhs, and was the equivalent of *Khan Bahadur.* The title when awarded to Muslims, Parsis and Jews was *Khan Bahadur.* For Hindus in western and in South India it was *Rao Bahadur;* in Bengal the "Rao" became "Rai".

14. Later, many Bene Israel fought in the 1st and 2nd Anglo-Afghan Wars, in the Abyssinian War, and in the 1st and 2nd Anglo-Burmese Wars. See Kehimkar's *History,* his chapter on *The Bene Israel as Gallant and Faithful Soldiers,* pp. 187-216.
15. We have no census figures for the Bene Israel in the 18th century, but Vol. 1 of the *Gazetteer of*

The Bene Israel in the 18th Century 55

Bombay City (1900) quotes from Mrs. Graham's *Journal of a Short Residence in India* that during her 1809 visit in Bombay the city contained

> upwards of 200,000 inhabitants, of whom the Parsis numbered from 6,000 to 8,000 and the remainder were Portuguese and Hindus, with the exception of *three or four thousand Jews* [emphasis supplied] who long passed in Bombay for a sect of Muhammadans, governed by a magistrate called "the Cazy [kaji] of Israel". Many of the latter were employed in the marine, but the bulk were petty traders.

The earliest official census was taken in 1814-15 for Bombay Island and counted 781 Jews. A census of all Bombay taken in 1833 recorded 2,246 Jews of whom about 2,000 must have been Bene Israel. (See B.J. Israel, *Religious Evolution Among the Bene Israel of India Since 1750*; Bombay, 1963, p. 21.) There is quite a discrepancy between Mrs. Graham's figure and those of the 1814-15 and 1833 Censuses. See below, p. 297 Table 17

16. In any Indian village (or in at least one of a cluster of villages) families of several of the services and supplies castes (washerman, barber, goldsmith, potter, oil-presser, etc.) are in residence, but often in small numbers as compared to the castes of the rest of the inhabitants of the village. It is important to appreciate the wider context of which the Bene Israel oil-presser formed a part. To quote the renowned Maharashtrian anthropologist, Dr. Irawati Karve (*Maharashtra, Land and Its People*, Maharashtra State Gazetteers, General Series, Bombay, published by the Director of Government Printing, 1968, p. 76):

> Somehow in medieval Europe [pottery oil] lamps were replaced by candlesticks which also made use of animal fat. The candle-stick-maker was one of the new types of artisan in Europe. In India, on the other hand, the easy availability of oil-seeds and the use of the oils for eating and for other purposes gave rise to a very important group of artisans, the oil-pressers.

Then on p. 37 Dr. Karve writes that the *Telis* (oil-pressers)

> are divided into numerous endogamous divisions according to the sub-regions, the particular oil-seeds which they use, and some other customs......... In Western Maharashtra they bear the same surname as the Kunbis [a peasant sub-caste] and have exogamous clans......... [The *Telis*] press oil from sesamum, hag plum (ambada), linseed, ground nuts [peanuts], niger seed, coconut, and castor seed. They allow cross-cousin marriage, marriage with one's mother's brother's daughter being the preferred form, though the other is tolerated. Divorce and widow re-marriage are allowed. The dead are cremated .... [The Hindu Telis] worship the usual gods of the Hindu pantheon, the planet Saturn being their special deity.

17. Kehimkar, op. cit., p. 46.
18. Shellim Samuel in his *Treatise* describes the Bene Israel archaic type of oil-press as follows:

> These primitive oil presses—even now in extensive use—are made from selected wood, usually the trunk of a large tamarind tree, 6 feet in height with a diameter of $3\frac{1}{2}$ to 4 feet. A bowl to a depth of 4 to $4\frac{1}{2}$ feet is hollowed out with a rim 3 to 4 inches wide on the topmost edge, the sides of the bowl gradually increasing to 6 inches, a foot to a foot and a half at the bottom of the hollowed trunk, a groove 3 to 4 inches wide is chipped out right round the trunk which is then sunk in the ground and well rammed, leaving the wooden pole from a straight branch or trunk of the Ain tree (Terminalia Tomentosa) with the outer bark and soft wood removed, exposing the hard inner core, about $6\frac{1}{2}$ to 7 feet long and 3 to 4 inches in thickness and rounded in shape, acts as the pressing agent for the contents of the oil press. The pole turns round and round when it works, a slightly slanted position being secured by two flat pieces of stout timber one being shaped in the form of a half arc at one end which weighted with heavy stones, slides along the groove in the waist, and the other projecting from the top of the pole, both planks being joined by a long light vertical piece of timber.

The contents of the bowl are thus able to be pressed when the contraption is worked round and round by a single bullock harnessed to the weighted projecting plank near the ground level. The person, usually a lad or a maiden in their teens, operating the press, sits on the rim and ducks his (her) head when the pole is near him; he not only adjusts the contents of the bowl and feeds the press, but arranges for the free flow of oil through four or five orifices provided at the sides, a foot or so above ground level, and fitted with hollow reeds let into them, the oil being collected in broad-mouthed jars or other metal vessels. (pp. 134-5)

19. Konkani is a distinct language popular from Goa northwards on the Konkan coast. It is spoken mainly in Goa and in Kanara (Mysore). The Konkani spoken by the lower classes in Kolaba District of Maharashtra was entirely different and was, in fact, a dialect of Marathi. Its use here has declined considerably with the increase in literacy. The speaking, reading and writing of Marathi had been popular in the Konkan long before the British made Marathi the official language of the Kolaba Collectorate.

20. *Pindaree* is a term used to refer to members of a community who, in the form of a shoddily mounted group of plunderers, would come in the wake of invading armies, pillaging and torturing indiscriminately. This "occupation" of theirs developed during the latter wars of the Muslim dynasties of the Deccan. Towards the end of the 17th century the Pindarees attached themselves to the Mahrattas. It was not until 1817 that the British began their concerted campaign to crush them and finally to put an end to the savage atrocities of the Pindarees.

21. Jews were not known as money-lenders in India. This is a very rare exception indeed; similar, perhaps, to the early 20th century instance of a rich Malabari Jewish family in Chennamangalam (Kerala) from whom Christians were wont to borrow as frequently as they also borrowed from local wealthy Brahmins.

22. A *Dacoit* is a robber belonging to an armed gang.

23. This is the only reference to this kind of Bene Israel enterprise known to the present author.

24. Kehimkar, op. cit., p. 83.

25. Kehimkar, ibid, p. 162

PART TWO

The Bene Israel in the Nineteenth Century : Development of Their Religious and Community Life

Chapter 6
The Influence of Cochin Jews

The builder of the first Bene Israel synagogue, Samaji Hassaji Divekar, had had two wives. Even so, he had only two children, both daugthers, and no sons. After Samaji's death his two wives adopted his brother Issaji's son, David, who later came to be known as "Dada Commadan".[1] The Divekar family endowed the new synagogue with an estate, the income from which went toward the upkeep of the synagogue. By virtue of the fact that Dada Commadan's father (by adoption) had built the synagogue, Dada became the headman or *Mukkadam*[2] of the Bene Israel community. He served as such, in spite of some ugly factionalism within the community, for 45 years, until his death in 1846. He tried to maintain a strict morality in the community, and especially tried to discourage the keeping of non-Jewish women by Bene Israel men. Under his aegis the synagogue became rich. Kehimkar depicts Dada Commadan in a favourable light.

Dada had inherited Samaji's title, "Commadan". The leadership of the community too became hereditary, the entire period 1796-1886 being known as "Commandan Rule", But Dada's descendants mismanaged (through a series of complicated and unsavory events[3]) the communal finances and administration which Dada had run so well. During the latter years of "Commandan Rule" there was a serious decline from the level which the Bene Israel had achieved during the first half of the 19th century, and the final quarter of the 19th century represented a difficult period of transition for the Bene Israel. It was during the first half of the 19th century that the Bene Israel had made great strides in their religious and communal life — adding up to a very interesting story, as we shall see in the following pages.

At the beginning of the 19th century the total number of Bene Israel appears to have been between 5,255 and 8,000 souls.[4] Most Bene Israel were still living in villages in the northern half of the Konkan. Gradually, large numbers of them moved to Bombay and Poona, while smaller Bene Israel congregations were also established in Ahmedabad, Indore and Ajmer. Furthermore, under British rule, considerable numbers of Bene Israel found either military or civil employment in Karachi, Quetta, Aden and Burma, and established their families in these places. But the center of development of Bene Israel religion, education and culture was in Bombay and in the towns of the Konkan.

Jews from Cochin, Surat and Baghdad had begun to settle in Bombay. Unlike the Bene Israel, many of them, such as David Sassoon, were already wealthy merchants upon arrival. In the 18th and early 19th centuries a few Bene Israel individuals had amassed considerable wealth as wholesale merchants and as successful contractors in the construction of public and private buildings. Because of one misfortune or another, however, their prosperity did not last long.

We learn from Ezekiel Rahabi's Letter of 1768 that prior to 1768 "a couple of times" Bene Israel had sought guidance in Judaism from "*hahamin*", who were, presumably, Cochin Jews; and also that one Bene Israel had studied Judaism in Cochin for four years. Beyond that we hear nothing more about such religious guidance until a group of dedicated Cochin "White" Jewish teachers arrived in the Konkan in the year 1826, followed by another group in 1833. These newly arrived teachers were able to effect a thorough-going religious revival not only in Bombay, but also in Revdanda, Alibag, Ashtami and Palli where they served among the Bene Israel as teachers, preachers, and interpreters of the Bible and of Jewish law. On week days they taught the Bene Israel children Jewish religion and how to read and write Hebrew. On Saturdays, in addition to the regular prayer service, many hours were devoted to the edification of the adults.

Among the Jewish teachers from Cochin, Shelomo Salem Shurrabi was outstanding. About the year 1838, coming from Cochin with his grandfather, the two were shipwrecked and cast onto the shore at Navgaon (as were the traditional Bene Israel forefathers of old). Shelomo's grandfather drowned. Shelomo was rescued and nursed back to health by a Bene Isreal man from Alibag. Thereafter Shelomo devoted himself to teaching the Bene Israel about Judaism most earnestly and persuasively. He served as *Hazan* (cantor) for the second Bene Israel synagogue in Bombay (called Shaare Rason, established by a faction which broke away from the first synagogue in 1841, and consecrated in 1844) from the time of its establishment until his death. His salary was a pittance, a meagre Rs. 100 per year. He himself was responsible for the establishment of other synagogues in Bombay, in Revdanda (1846), in Alibag (1848) and in Panvel (1849). He not only worked at his trade as a book-binder but also served the Bene Israel as *Mohel* (a person professionally qualified to perform Jewish ritual circumcision) and as *Shohet* (ritual slaughterer for *Kosher* meat). The Bene Israel deeply loved and respected him and followed his guidance. (For vivid details, see App.6. pp. 342-43) He died in 1856.

With the impact of the teachers from Cochin, Bene Israel Jewish observances and organization began more closely to resemble those of Jews elsewhere. Cochin Jewry had maintained contact with the Jewish mainstream at least since the late Middle Ages, and Cochin teachers were therefore able to give the Bene Israel access to the larger Jewish heritage, in this case the Sephardic, and parts of typically Cochini synagogue liturgy. Also, the Bene Israel imbibed a certain amount of specifically Yemenite Jewish influences, not only via Cochin, but also, and more especially, via those hundreds of Bene Israel who, from about 1839 onwards, were stationed in Aden,[5] employed in the British military or ancillary services, and who eventually returned to the Konkan after their retirement. At first, Bene Israel in Aden worshipped in Yemenite synagogues. Later they established their own Bene Israel prayer halls in Aden, hiring a Yemenite *Hazan* for themselves. Eventually Yemenite *Hazanim* came to officiate in some Bene Israel synagogues and prayer halls in the Konkan too. (These Yemenite *Hazanim* imported into the Konkan their own Yemenite brides.) The first *Torah* scrolls which the Bene Israel ever received came from Yemen, via Aden — rather than from Cochin after all!

For many years after Samaji's death in Cochin, the purpose of his mission to Cochin, namely to obtain a *Torah* scroll for his synagogue, remained unfulfilled. A Rev. Claudius Buchanan, commenting upon the Bene Israel as of the year 1808, wrote that he saw, just outside the walls of Bombay, a synagogue which had no *Torah*, and had only loose leaves of a few handwritten prayers; and that the congregation worshipping at this synagogue had little knowledge of Jewish scriptures or of Jewish history.[6] Similarly, Rabbi David D'Beth Hillel,[7] arriving in Bombay in 1828, writes about the Bene Israel that

> some years ago a fine synagogue was built by one of them named Samuel who was Captain in the Honorable Company's [i.e. the British East India Company] Army...... It is denominated in the native language Mesgad[8] Beney Israeyl, it is situated at Barcoot, not far from the Custom House. There is no manuscript [meaning, no *Torah* scroll]... no one Levite or Priest [Cohen] among them.[9]

The first Bene Israel *Torah* scroll was obtained by the second rather than the first Bene Israel synagogue, i.e. the Shaare Rason Synagogue. This newly formed separate congregation in 1844 acquired a proper parchment *Torah* scroll as a gift from Abraham Issaji Galsulkar, a Bene Israel surveyor in Aden. Samaji's synagogue did not obtain a scroll until the year 1847. When Israel Joseph Benjamin II visited Bombay in February 1849, he was able to observe the Bene Israel's

> pious veneration for the rolls of the Law which — although they are unable to read them — they preserve in their Synagogues. These manuscripts of the Law are very ancient; the writing is of a reddish colour, which is the result of the work of time; in all other respects they resemble ours.[10]

The evolution of the synagogue through the centuries as a diaspora institution had bypassed the Bene Israel. They had begun only some rudimentary congregational recital of prayers (especially preliminary to and during the High Holidays) when the synagogue was finally introduced to them as a fullblown institution. Partly because the Bene Israel had not participated in the historic evolution of that institution, the synagogue's scholarly and instructional functions, so characteristic of synagogues elsewhere,[11] did not become part of the Bene Israel institution. Typically, instruction in a Bene Israel synagogue was limited to teaching how to read (as distinct from understanding) Hebrew. Religious inspiration through discussion and study of Jewish matters was lacking. But the Bene Israel synagogue was secure in its firm foundation based on the simple faith of its congregants and on their traditionally strong sense of ethnicity and separateness of their religion.

Already in the 18th century many Bene Israel had begun to take advantage of the secular educational facilities made available under British rule. But, unlike the community as a whole, the Bene Israel *Kajis*, had not kept up with the times in general and had not improved their knowledge, religious or secular. Perhaps they had become too complacent with their high hereditary status. In the course of time they lost their functional importance, and subsequently no single Bene Israel official was ever again entrusted with all civil and religious duties. It became a matter of individual choice whether one would even invite a *Kaji* to be present at a given ceremony. Gradually, there was a waning of the former great respect for *Kajis*. Instead, wherever there were considerable numbers of Bene Israel, they organized themselves into a congregation under a *Mukkadam* (leader) assisted by four or five elderly councillors called *Choglas*. There was also a *Gabbai* (treasurer); a *Hazan* (cantor or reader of the liturgy at religious services) who was either a Cochini, Baghdadi or Yemenite Jew and who often also performed the duties of *Shohet*, *Mohel* and *Sopher* (scribe and teacher); and a *Shamash* (sexton) who also functioned as a herald and source of information about the members of the community, a veritable encyclopaedia. The *Jamat* or General Assembly of the congregation consisted of all of its adult male members.[12] There was no Rabbi, and sermons formed a part of the service only on rare occasions.

We learn from the *Gazetteer of Bombay Presidency of 1885*, Volume XVIII, (p. 536) that some *Kajis* were still functioning in their traditional fashion as late as 1885, but mainly in those villages which had no synagogues. Even where the old hereditary office of *Kaji* had ceased to function as such, synagogues often employed a *Kaji* to assist the *Hazan* in the conduct of synagogue services. He would also attend to funerals and ceremonies at the homes of members of the congregation (for which the latter paid him additional fees). Later on, with a decline in synagogue membership, the assistance of this kind of a *Kaji* was no longer needed. Or, in some instances a synagogue would carry on for years with a *Kaji*, but without a *Hazan*. Even today, men of traditional *Kaji* families still use that title, together with their *kar* (village-linked) surname, whenever they are honored by being called upon (or secured the privilege through auction) to recite the *Torah* blessings or to read from the *Torah* during a synagogue service.

In organizing administration for the new Bene Israel synagogues, the institution of the *Mukkadam* assisted by *Choglas* was practically a carry-over into the synagogue of a body known locally as *Mankaris* (i.e. "dignitaries") which had previously regulated Bene Israel life. As Solomon M. Vakrulkar explains it, "On the establishment of the synagogue, this body of Mankaris assumed their management without any protest on the part of the congregants, who had always been used to their rule."[13]

The judicial function of the *Kajis* was undertaken by the *Mukkadam* and the *Choglas*, who, if unable to arrive at an acceptable settlement, would convene a meeting of the *Jamat* for further deliberation. If the *Jamat's* advice also proved unacceptable to the complainant, and if the dispute was within the statutory jurisdiction of the civil courts (e.g. a matter of succession) as distinct from a strictly internal "caste" dispute, the case could then be referred to the government law courts. Synagogue verdicts imposed fines or excommunication, about which the *Bombay Gazetteer of 1885* tells us (p. 536) : "The faults generally punishable by excommunication are adultery with a Mahar, Mang [untouchable groups], or other degraded Hindu, or embracing Christianity or Islam."

The synagogue's imposition of fines, and of ostracism, sometimes disturbed the peace of the congregation and put a strain on the unity of the community. New and more complicated methods were now required to handle the large sums derived from income of synagogue properties, investments, etc. The office of *Gabbai* was new, and with it came a fundamental change from the previous custom of frequent, periodic distribution of any funds accumulated from marriage fees and the like which were beyond the *Kaji's* share.

The Bene Israel synagogue management had the responsibility for conducting synagogue ritual, and for providing guidance and/or direction for family ceremonies, and in virtually all social and religious matters.

The *Mukkadam* selected all the other officers who, except for the *Shamash*, then had to be confirmed by the *Jamat*. Only three officials — the *Hazan*, the *Kaji* and the *Shamash* — received wages for their services. All other synagogue officers served in an honorary capacity. The work of the *Gabbai* might have been conducted more efficiently had it been salaried rather than honorary. The office of *Mukkadam* remained hereditary from the time of Dada Commadan, but only as long as his descendants retained attributes of influence, leadership, and money. It was the duty of the *Mukkadam* to seek means of enlarging the synagogue's income; to direct the work of the *Hazan* and *Shamesh*; to sanction and fix the dates for all communal meetings, functions, rites of passage, vow-taking, etc. For all such events, except for burials, the synagogue received a fee. The *Choglas* assisted the *Mukkadam* in financial, as well as in judicial, decisions. The *Mukkadam, Choglas, Gabbai* and *Hazan* were invited to all functions and (in that order of priority) were honored, as were the *Kajis*, with double the portion allotted to other guests. In addition to salary and fixed fees, the *Hazan* and the *Shamash* received bonuses at the time of the Jewish New Year. The *Hazan's* duties were (and still are) to lead in Hebrew prayer[14] all the synagogue services and to perform all the religious ceremonies and rites. For this, he received a monthly salary paid by the synagogue as well as fees for each private ceremony (paid by the individual concerned and formerly paid to the *Kaji*). Moreover, a sum was paid to the *Hazan* for each sheep, goat or chicken which he slaughtered for food (for others) according to the *Kosher* ritual. The duties of the *Shamash* were (and still are) to sweep and light the synagogue; to prepare grape-juice for

Kiddush (the blessing special for Sabbath and festivals); to distribute invitations for all socio-religious functions, for which (except for funerals) he was entitled to receive additional fees; to announce community meetings; to attend all funerals; to collect all money-offerings to the synagogue and to hand them over to the *Gabbai*. One regular source of income for the synagogue was derived from its custom of selling to the highest bidder — at each synagogue service when the Torah was to be read — the privilege of reading the Torah portion, or of reciting the blessings that go with it, or of opening and closing the Ark, or of carrying the *Sefer Torah*, etc.[15]

Each Bene Israel synagogue was independent, with no central authority coordinating all Bene Israel places of worship. As was true of synagogues everywhere until very recently, the Bene Israel synagogue, too, was the focal point of all community life. Not so universal a phenomenon in Jewish life elsewhere, however, was the fact that Bene Israel synagogue leadership usually was strongly in the hands of the laity rather than from among the professional people of the congregation. They had no ordained clergy.

It was not long before the Bene Israel changed direction from the Cochin Jewish course to a somewhat less orthodox way of religious life, in circumstances shortly to be described.

NOTES

1. Both his real and his adopted father had been Commandants in the army.
2. The term *Mukkadam*, though of Muslim origin, was/is used by many non-Muslim groups in the area to designate the headman of a caste, of a community, or of an entire village.
3. Kehimkar.: *History*, pp. 256-72.
4. See below, p. 280 on census figures, and Rev. J. Wilson's estimate on p. 74
5. Aden became part of the British Bombay Presidency in 1838 or 1839. The Bene Israel who were stationed there were allowed to bring their wives and children to Aden also.
6. Rev. Claudius Buchanan : *Christian Researches in Asia*, 5th edition, London, 1812, p.234.
7. See below, pp. 72 – 74.
8. *Mesgad*, for *Masjid*, the Muslim word for house of prayer, a mosque.
9. Rabbi David D'Beth Hillel : *The Travels of Rabbi David D'Beth Hillel*. Madras, 1832, p. 134. This publication was printed in a private edition of 300 copies only.
10. J. J. Benjamin II : *Eight Years in Asia and Africa, from 1846-1855*, published by the author, Hanover, 1863, p.177.
    The scrolls from Yemen must already have been very old when they arrived in Bombay.
    There is another book, by an I. J. (i.e. Israel Joseph) Benjamin entitled *Un An de Sejour aux Indes Orientales 1859-1860*, written originally in Hebrew, translated into French by D.L., Imprimerie Typographique de Dubos Freres, Rues Bab Azoum et Sainte, Alger, 1854, 25 pages. The two books are by the same person : the *J* being interchangeable with *I* in the author's first name. In the French book the remarks about the Bene Israel are brief, unsystematic, and consist seemingly of hearsay in the form of disconnected tidbits of information. The salient points, which deserve mention mainly because of the date of Benjamin's visit and also because some statements are so curious, are as follows :
    (a) Benamin is convinced that the Bene Israel are real Jews.
    (b) Bene Israel told him that prior to the arrival of the Europeans, they had lived in isolation, governed by a chief whom they called "Sheikh", that they were forced to disperse and to look for refuge "beyond Calcutta" at a place 50 to 60 days' march from Calcutta, namely in "Gamek" where they still have a Sheikh at their head. (Does this have any relation to the Jews of Manipur? See above, p. xiii, n. 7.)
    (c) Not far from Bombay, 2 miles from Barkout, there is a colony of Bene Israel, about 2,000 souls, with a chief called "Babi". They are well-off. They possess several richly ornamented

Torot, but have forgotten how to read or write Hebrew. They do not know the *Shema*. They believe in the coming of the Messiah.
- (d) The Bene Israel make an effort to copy the Babylonian (i.e. the Baghdadi) Jews and would be happy to intermarry with them.
- (e) The Babylonian Jews of Bombay for some time now send their *shohatim* and rabbis to teach the Bene Israel, but they refuse to intermarry with them as co-religionists.
- (f) Benjamin has found Bene Israel in other places, especially in Cochin. (References to Bene Israel being in Cochin are very rare.)

11. Sometimes only relatively few members of any given congregation would participate regularly in Jewish studies. Synagogues have, however, always been foci for Jewish learning and scholarship.

12. *Mukkadam* and *Jamat* are Muslim terms; *Chogla* is a Marathi term for a village officer; the others are Hebrew terms. It is interesting that wherever Hebrew titles were not incorporated by the Bene Israel, their functionaries bore *local* Hindu or Muslim titles even though synagogue organization and administration as such had been introduced to them by their Cochin Jewish preceptors—who were using Hebrew terms for their own headman, elder councillors and general assembly of their own synagogues in Kerala.

13. *Our Synagogues and Their Functions*, an address to the Bene Israel by Solomon M. Vakrulkar; delivered in Bombay under the auspices of the Bene-Israel Club on December 8, 1907; published by Abraham Reuben Bhinjekar, Don Tad Street, Bombay, 1909.

14. Though the Ḥazan could read and chant the Hebrew fluently, he, more often than not, could not translate *all* the Hebrew words.

15. Shalva Weil's doctoral dissertation submitted to the University of Sussex's Division of Social Anthropology in 1977, entitled *Bene Israel Jews in Lod, Israel: A study of the Persistence of Ethnicity and Ethnic Identity*, deserves mention as an outstanding dissertation which includes much solid background material about the Bene Israel in general, assembled as a basis for her description and analysis of the specific Bene Israel group now living in Lod, Israel. On her pages 273-87 she discusses the auctions conducted in Bene Israel synagogues for the privilege of reading from the *Torah*, etc. She finds that, unlike the bidding for these privileges customary in some non-Bene Israel synagogues, "bid prices in the Bene Israel synagogue tend to be on average within easy reach of all synagogue members, and not just the monopoly of wealthier members"; that this kind of voluntary tax is re-invested in the synagogue as a symbol of the wealth of the community, uniting all Bene Israel through their synagogue and thus reinforcing their ethnic identity, in this case when living in Israel. The same practice, although competitive in form and motivated by the desire for prestige, had a strong cohesive effect among the Bene Israel in India also.

Chapter 7
The Influence of Christian Missionaries

The development of Judaism among the Bene Israel involves a context of situation entirely different from that of any other Jewish community within India or outside. The saga of how Christian missionaries actually fostered Judaism among the Bene Israel is unique.

It was noted above (p.25) that the Bene Israel were not living in those areas where the Portuguese forcibly converted the indigenous populations to Catholicism. And, the British did not allow certain categories of persons, including missionaries, inside British territories in India until 1813. Therefore, until that date, the center of Christian (Protestant) missionary activity in India was in Serampur,[1] in Bengal, then under Danish rule. Upon the urging of British free-traders and civil-servants in India, the relevant British ban was lifted.[2] After 1813, in Bombay and in Kulaba District, the American Congregational, the Scottish Presbyterian, and the Church of England Missions all quickly became very active; and the Bene Israel were heavily exposed to this activity. Surprisingly enough, the real result of this exposure was *not* proselytization. On the contrary, missionary activity strengthened Judaism among the Bene Israel. What is perhaps even more astonishing, the strengthening did not come as a reaction against pressure upon the Bene Israel to convert. Rather, the missionaries had, however inadvertently, enhanced Judaism in the eyes of the Bene Israel and had kindled their basic Jewish faith. The missionaries actually opened up the world of Judaism for the Bene Israel.

Even before the Cochin Jewish teachers and become very active in the Konkan, the American Mission at Bombay, founded in 1813, had established numerous primary schools throughout Bombay and the Konkan, teaching in the Marathi language. They employed several Bene Israel men as teachers in these schools, men who already had had some secular education under British auspices.[3] These schools were established for the education of the local children and included more than 100 Bene Israel children. The main activities of the American Mission, as of most Christian Missions, were:

> the translation, printing and circulation of the Scriptures; the publication and circulation of religious tracts; the establishment and direction of native free schools for the Christian instruction of the rising generation, and the preaching of the Gospel.[4]

They established schools not only for boys, but for girls as well. The following tables are extracted from the American Mission-at-Bombay's *Report for 1829*, as published in *The Oriental Christian Spectator*, Volume 1, No. 4, April 1830, Mission Press, Bombay, p.116:

TABLE 1 : SCHEDULE OF THE NATIVE FREE SCHOOLS, BOYS

Places	Teacher's Caste	Girls	Hindoos	Moohummudans	Jews	Christians	Total
T'hull	Jew	13	76	4	3	—	83
Allebag	Jew	10	65	10	14	—	89
Nagaum	Jew	15	70	—	17	—	87
Revadunda	Jew	6	79	3	27	1	110
Rohay	Jew	—	43	5	4	—	52
Parlee	Bramhun	—	45	15	—	—	60
Nagoatnay	Bramhun	2	86	2	2	—	90
Pane	Jew	3	56	—	12	—	68
Panwell	Jew	10	61	11	17	—	89
Joonnur	Weaver	2	59	3	—	—	62
Mahim	Maratha	—	30	9	—	—	39
BOMBAY No.1	Tailor	—	50	3	—	—	53
BOMBAY No.2	Weaver	2	24	1	2	2	29
BOMBAY No. 3	Bramhun	4	50	—	2	5	57
BOMBAY No.4	Bramhun	1	51	4	—	—	55
BOMBAY No.5	Bramhun	2	45	5	—	—	50
Mazagaum	Purbhoo	2	35	3	—	—	38
Allebag	Jew H.S.	6	—	—	30	—	30

"The numbers inserted in this table are those who actually belong to the Schools; but the average attendance in the schools on the continent [meaning, outside of Bombay Island] is, probably, nearly one fourth less."

NOTE : Even though this was a Table for *Boys* Schools, there were girls also in attendance. The only High School (H.S.) was at Allebag. All 30 of its pupils were Jews. (Undoubtedly these Jews were mostly, if not all, Bene Israel, because there were very few Arabic-speaking Jewish families even in Bombay at that time. The High School was in Allebag where many Bene Israel then lived.) Six of these high-school-level students were not only Jewish but female as well. There were Jewish girls in attendance at the all-girls schools too.

The Report on the Boys' Schools for 1829 mentions that some classes were

> under the instruction of Jewish teachers, who not only disallow the observance of heathenish customs in their schools, but also manifest considerable interest in giving religious instruction to their pupils. The good influence of these schools on the moral aspects of the villages in which they are situated, only goes to show the importance of having mission schools, *conducted strictly on Christian principles* [italics are in the original], established in every village in this land .... This influence is not limited to the children in the schools — nor to the families to which they belong, nor to any particular caste; but it is more or less felt by all castes, from the highest to the lowest.[5]

Of the more than 400 pupils at the Girls' Schools it was stated that

> 122 are readers, — all of these have committed the Ten Commandments, and the greater part have committed a catechism comprising a summary of Christian doctrines and precepts ....; all write a fair legible hand on sand boards, and a few have attended to the simple rules of Arithmetic...On Tuesday afternoons the teachers of all our schools in Bombay, and the larger girls in the female schools, assemble at the chapel for instruction in the Scriptures. The teachers and scholars, in classical order, read one

or more chapters, and are questioned respecting the same. Free discussion is encouraged on these occasions.....several natives are usually present on these occasions who are not connected with the schools.[6]

One of the teachers from Cochin who had come to the Konkan was Michael Sargon, the son of Isaac Sargon who had saved Samaji. But Michael was no longer Jewish. He had been converted to Christianity in Madras in 1818. He began his missionary career by conducting two schools for Jews in Cochin. *Annual Reports* of the London Society for Promoting Christianity Among Jews[7] describe Michael Sargon as "pious, prudent, steady and assiduous; and very well versed in languages". The section on India of the *16th Report,* in 1824, comments that Michael Sargon's Cochin "schools are well attended....the children have made considerable progress....The Jews entertain but few of these prejudices against him which they have against a clergyman, or other person, not so nearly connected with them as he is".[8] The *16th Report* goes on to say that the Madras Committee had directed Michael Sargon to pursue his investigations on the Bene Israel then living in Cannanore (on the northern coast of Kerala, just a few miles north of Tellicherry). A Mr. Jarrett, Secretary of the Madras Committee, wrote the following, as quoted verbatim in the *16th Report* :

> I come now to Mr. Sargon's visit to Cannanore, with whose information we have reason to be satisfied. The following important particulars, among others, are stated :— 1st, These people in dress and manners resemble the natives so as not to be distinguished from them, but by attentive observation and enquiry. 2nd, They have Hebrew names of the same kind, and with the same local terminations, as the Sepoys in the 9th Regiment Bombay Native Infantry. 3rd. Some of them read Hebrew and they have a faint tradition of the cause of their original exodus from Egypt. 4th. Their common language is the Hindoo.[9] 5th. They keep idols and worship them, and use idolatrous ceremonies intermixed with Hebrew. 6th. They circumcise *their own* children. 7th. They observe the Kippoor, or great Expiation-day of the Hebrews. 8th. They call themselves 'Gorah Jehudi', or White Jews, and they term the Black Jews 'Collah Jehudi'. 9th. They speak of the Arabian Jews as their brethren, but do not acknowledge the European Jews as such, because they are of a fairer complexion than themselves. 10th. They use the same prayer as those of whom we have heard, namely, 'Hear, O Israel, the Lord our God is one Lord'. Deut. vi.—1. 11th. They have no Cohen (priest), Levite, or Nasi amongst them, under those terms, though it appears they have elders and a chief in each community, who determine in their religious concerns. 12th. They expect the Messiah, and when he comes, that they will all go to Jerusalem : the time of his appearance, and their return, they think, will soon arrive; at which they would much rejoice, since at Jerusalem they would see their God, worship him only, and be dispersed no more!

This supplies us, for the first time (i.e. in 1824) with a few more details about Bene Israel beyond what we learned from Ezekiel Rahabi II's Letter of 1768; and these new details reappear in later accounts about the Bene Israel. However, it is very curious that Michael Sargon has referred to the Bene Israel sub-divisions as "Gorah and Collah *Jehudi*" instead of the usual "Gora and Kala Israel". Or was this a mistake made by Mr. Jarrett in his reporting about Michael Sargon?

Even though in some respects Sargon was an asset to the Missionary Society, year after year in the Annual Reports it was urged that a properly qualified missionary be appointed to superintend Sargon's Schools in Cochin, to meet the objections of the Cochin Jews against Christianity, to explain the prophecies (according to the Christian view), and to preach the Gospel to the Jews because Michael Sargon "is quite unable to meet their [the Jews'] objections and the consequence is that he seldom mentions the subject to them, as he says 'they only laugh at me and blaspheme' when he tries to do so."[10] Finally, in 1828, the *20th Report* (p.64) tells us that Sargon's services were no longer required in Cochin, so "it is the intention of the Madras Corresponding Committee to keep him in Bombay."

A few times prior to his actual transfer to Bombay Sargon had visited that city and the adjacent areas and had sent reports on his observations. From these we learn that only seven families of "White Jews"[11] then lived in the Bombay Fort area and that they did not mix with the Bene Israel; that the "White Jews" considered the Bene Israel to be "degraded" because they worked on the Sabbath, did not observe the Jewish feasts and fasts as they should, and kept idols in their houses.[12]

Once stationed in Bombay, Sargon usually held Sabbath meetings for the Bene Israel in order to explain to them each week's portion of the *Old Testament*. At first he served a missionary group called the Madras Jews Society (administered from Madras, it also had interests among the Cochin Jews). From the "Extracts from the Fifth Report of the Madras Jews Society" which appeared in *The Oriental Christian Spectator,* Volume 2, No. 1, January 1831 we learn that

> Mr. Sargon has been establishing several additional schools in the villages which he occasionally visits (out of Bombay), and many of them at the express request of the Jews themselves. (p.34)
> At present Mr. Sargon has schools at the following places, Bombay, Revadanda, Ashtumee, Paligaum and Panwel. They are attended by 165 children. The Old Testament and part of the New Testament in Hebrew are the only school books. The language is understood in a very slight degree by a very few of the people; and the necessity then of instructing children in Murathee, as Mr. S. endeavours to do, is very desirable. (p.35)

These Madras Jews Society schools, each of which also numbered a few girls among its students, were run exclusively for the Bene Israel; but they functioned only from 1825 until 1830. Sargon is quoted as having reported (in 1829) :

> At Bombay....No opposition is made now by the Bene Israels to our instructing their children the Hebrew meaning in Murathee; notwithstanding, I am concerned to state, that I cannot get them to come to a meeting in order to confer on religious subjects, but I occasionally have had some conversation with them. (p.35)
> Having been much urged by constant applications of the Hebrew Teachers of our different Schools for Bibles, and not having them in my possession, I inquired where I could obtain a few, at least to satisfy the Teachers. I was given to understand that the principal man of the Arabian Jews (Mr. Seleman Jacob) [Sargon's parentheses] had a few Bibles for disposal. I therefore called on him on the 2nd ultimo (Dec. 2, 1829) and requested him to let me have some. In the first instance Mr. S. Jacob refused to show me the Bibles, and replied that he could not dispose of them to any who are uncircumcised on account of their being consecrated by their Rabbins for their particular use. I affirmed to him that the books I wished to purchase from him were for the use of the Bene Israel's children in our schools. He repeated the same words as above, and said they consider the Bene Israels as such. (p.34)

We don't know whether or not Sargon actually obtained those Bibles. The wording is ambiguous. Does the "as such" mean that Seleman considered the Bene Israel to be proper Jews or not? If not, then this would contradict Kehimkar's assumption that "Seleman" had accepted the Bene Israel as Jews because "Silliman Jacob, the first rich man in Bombay, and his daughter" were buried in the Bene Israel cemetery (*History*, p.52). However, this fact need not necessarily have indicated any positive sentiment toward the Bene Israel; perhaps it was only a preference to be buried in a Bene Israel cemetery rather than in a Muslim cemetery, there being then no other alternative.

After the year 1830 Michael Sargon's work among the Bene Israel proceeded under the auspices of the Church of England Missionary Society of Bombay. He taught among the Bene Israel for thirty years. In Kehimkar's measured words : "He only spoke on Christianity when he was forced to do so."[13] And, according to Kehimkar, Sargon taught his Bene Israel pupils "the Hebrew Bible, ritual and songs with their proper tunes after the fashion of the Cochin Jews"![14] Kehimkar emphasizes Sargon's warm sympathy for, and sincere devotion to, the Bene Israel. Sargon died at the age of 80 in the year 1870.

Mention must also be made of quite another sort of missionary, namely the Rev. Joseph Wolff who passed through Bombay in the early 1830s and who wrote about the Bene Israel although he had spent practically no time with them. He was born in 1796, the son of a German Rabbi. In his teens Wolff left home and became a Catholic. Later he joined the Church of England and married an aristocratic Englishwoman. He travelled extensively, was an ardent proselytizer, and visited much of India in 1833. His book, *Researches and Missionary Labours among the Jews, Mahamedans and Other Sects*, was published in a second edition in 1835 in the form of a diary of his travels from 1831-34. Written in the first person, it is perhaps a more factual account than a later work of his, written in the third person, entitled *Travels and Adventures of the Rev. Joseph Wolff*. The latter book was published in 1861 and covers practically the same ground as his earlier *Researches and Missionary Labours*. He wrote on the Bene Israel, the Cochin Jews, and the Calcutta or Baghdadi Jews, but devoted only a few paragraphs to each. Indeed, he could not have had an opportunity to observe very much of them, having stayed not more than two weeks near any of these three Jewish groups, most of the time in the company of non-Jews at that. Thus, some of what little he wrote about the Bene Israel might have been based on hearsay and misinterpretation. It is of interest only because so very little had been written about these communities at the time of Wolff's visits :

Nov. 23, 1833 — I went with Mr. Stevenson among the Bene Israel, Children of Israel, who are resident at Poonah : they are totally distinct from the rest of the Jews in Europe and Hindoostaun. Soon after the destruction of the first temple, they came in seven ships (thus they relate their own story) from Arabia into Hindustaun, where they have since forgotten their law, but continue to repeat in Hebrew certain Hebrew prayers, which they have learnt from the other Jews; they also read the Pentateuch, but without understanding the language. They have synagogues; but they have not in them, like the rest of the Jews, the Sepher Torah, or the five books of Moses written upon parchment; for they say, "As we are soldiers, and do not keep the Law, the Sepher Torah may do us harm if it stands in the midst of us." They serve the English as volunteers in their armies and are esteemed the best native soldiers. They possess great simplicity and honesty of character, are faithful to their wives, and by far more moral than the Jews of Cochin. But they keep hidden in their houses some Hindoo idols, and beside this a great many charms, which they wear like the Kemias of the Jews. I conversed with several of them about Jesus Christ our Lord; they produced objections against his divinity, which they have evidently heard from other Jews. They know the

Ten Commandments of our Lord by heart in the English tongue; and they begin now to send their children to the schools of the Scotch Missionaries.[15]

NUMBER OF THE BENEE ISRAEL IN AND AROUND BOMBAY:

At Panwell, 800 families; Shwardhan, 5; Walwaticha, 10; Alibay Reodanda, 20; Karanja, 10; Rohe Ashtami, 20; Apta, 10; Rajpoore, 20; Poonah, 10; Bombay, 1000; in all 1905 families, or 9520 souls.[16]

....the whole body of the people at Bombay were dreadfully prejudiced against Wolff, for they had been informed that he made Christians by witchcraft; and one of them was especially adverse, whose name was Daood Captaan, i.e. "Captain David", a very fat man, and chief of the Benee Israel. He had actually issued an order that none of his people should even talk to Wolff, for fear of being overpowered by his black art when a breach would be made in Israel.... Wolff said, "Be not foolish, Captain David, but show me your synagogue, and bring me the people." Captain David replied, "I won't; you are a magician!" Wolff took no notice of his statements, but stared at him with all his eyes, muttered with his lips pointing sternly at him with his finger, said, "You are very fat." Captain David began to tremble, for he was afraid that he would get the evil eye... Captain David : "Let my fatness alone." Wolff again : "You are very fat." David : "What have you to do with my fatness?", holding his sides with his hands, "Let my fatness alone!"

Wolff then said, "Then show me your synagogue, and bring me your people."

He now said, "I will do so immediately." So the key was brought, the synagogue opened, and the Children of Israel were assembled.[17]

Wolff also discoursed at length to the "foreign Jews" in the house of "Sulliman Yacov".

Between 1831 and 1835 another Christian, also a European and also a former Jew, one Jacob Samuel, was trying his best to convince Jews in Calcutta, in Cochin and in Bombay to convert to Christianity. From *The Oriental Christian Spectator* we learn that he had come to India at his own expense and was not affiliated to any particular mission. As soon as various missions in India became convinced of his knowledge of Jewish tradition and of "the subterfuges of the Jews" (i.e. Jewish arguments against Christian theological reasoning), they did contribute to pay some of his expenses inside India. They noted, however, that :

> It seems greatly to be regretted that his [Jacob Samuel's] warmth of feeling, joined to imperfect acquaintance with our language and customs, should occasionally betray him into expressions, which through hasty judgment, are apt to be construed into serious errors; and thus hinder the Christian community from bestowing upon him that confidence which his other qualifications demand.[18]

He was well received by Arabic-speaking Jews in Calcutta, who gave him two letters of recommendation from the Jewish community in Calcutta to the Arabic-speaking Jews in Bombay. Mr. Samuel's Journal informs us that in January 1835 in Bombay he "Preached in the synagogue of the white Jews in the Fort, and in that of the Bene-Israel in the native town."[19] By 1835 the Baghdadi Jews were conducting their own prayer services and no longer worshipping in the Bene Israel synagogue (see below, p. 99). Also, they had their own *Nasi* who received Mr. Samuel graciously. Seven elders of that community engaged in discussion with him for four solid hours, mainly about the coming of the Messiah. Mr. Samuel was even permitted to preach about Moses and the

Prophets in their synagogue, on Saturday, January 10, 1835, when, he says,

> After they had finished the reading of the second lesson, which was the 37th Chapter of *Ezekiel*, I put on the veil with the fringes [i.e. the *talith*, the Jewish prayer shawl]. While the Law of Moses [i.e. the *Torah*] yet stood upon the altar, I addressed them, for about ten minutes, on the importance of studying the prophesies, and then I offered up three prayers; the first, for the King and Royal Family, under whom they enjoy the privilege of the exercise of their religion; the second, for all the house of Israel, the present congregation, and for a blessing on the Gospel amongst all nations. I concluded with the Lord's Prayer. They all seemed to reverence and join in the prayer, by repeating constantly Amen, every time when I said, O Lord bless us![20]

Thereafter, individuals, among them the Reader (*Hazan*) of the synagogue, came to Mr. Samuel to hear more about Jesus Christ. Samuel again preached in their synagogue on the following Saturday. On January 15th two Jews from Cochin called on him. On January 20th two Jews, one from Babylon and the other from Shiraz, requested baptism.

It was not until January 23 that Mr. Samuel was invited by the Bene Israel to preach in the Bene Israel synagogue.[21] Under January 29th, Samuel records:

> Three Jews were waiting for me, with whom I had a conversation about Christianity; and after a long argument, the conduct of the one was so rude, that I was obliged, for example's sake, to order him out by the *peon* [servant].[22]

And for January 31st:

> I intended to preach in the [Baghdadi] synagogue....; but, on account of being informed that the synagogue fell down, I was obliged to postpone the invitation. However, some Jews informed me that on account of my preaching there, and the elders not knowing how to prevent it, they broke in a wall in a part of the synagogue....I am inclined to think that the building gave way from age. In the afternoon, the reader of the black Jews' [i.e. the Bene Israel] synagogue called on me, informing me that he was discharged on account of having allowed me to preach so long in their synagogue about Jesus of Nazareth.[23]

The details are quoted here at some length in order to give the reader a better realization of the levels of interaction, and of the kinds of predicaments sometimes involved in these contacts with missionaries; and to show also that the Arabic-speaking Jews were as involved with the missionaries as were the Bene Israel. A thorough study of all such documents and other writings relating to missionary work among Indian Jews should be undertaken.[24] The present writer has made only a beginning, concentrating largely on *the* most important missionary in the Konkan, namely the Rev. Dr. John Wilson, to whom we now turn.

John Wilson, born in Scotland in 1804, came to Bombay in February 1829 as a missionary of the Church of Scotland, whose Scottish Presbyterian Mission in Bombay he headed. After the schism in the Church of Scotland, in 1843, Rev. Wilson chose to side with the newly established Free Church of Scotland, and his institutions became known as the Free Church of Scotland's Mission, School, and College respectively.

Wilson was an outstanding man with varied interests and great abilities, and he was a prolific writer. He has written at length on theology, philosophy, linguistics, and Indian archeology *inter alia*. His biographer, George Smith, describes him as a true "Orientalist who subordinated scholarly to missonary ends".[25] True, a certain disdain, arrogance and bigotry especially toward the "heathen religions", so typical in his day, do surface every now and then in Wilson's writings. But his actions and relations with people evidently earned him the love and affection of people of all religions and of all communities. In January 1830 Wilson founded the first Christian periodical in India, namely *The Oriental Christian Spectator*, a monthly magazine devoted to missionary projects (of which proselytization was only one) and progress in India and in other Southeast Asian countries. This periodical continued to be published for more than thirty years. Wilson was President of the Bombay Branch of the Royal Asiatic Society (1835-42; in 1842 he became its Honorary President). He served as Vice-Chancellor[26] of Bombay University from 1868 to 1870. It was he who was responsible for the inclusion of the study of Hebrew as a subject for matriculation and for higher examinations at Bombay University,[27] and for the encouragement of Hebrew scholarship among the Bene Israel. Except for a few journeys out of the sub-continent (one of them to "the lands of the Bible"), the Rev. Wilson lived and worked in Bombay for nearly half a century, from 1829 until his death in 1875.

A traveller, Rabbi David D'Beth Hillel, had been in Bombay for four months in 1828 and returned to Bombay only one month after Dr. Wilson's arrival in 1829. This Rabbi, who was born and educated in Vilna (Lithuania) and who later lived in the Holy Land, in Safed, had set out from Jerusalem in order to see the world and to visit Jewish groups, or vestiges of Jewish groups, settled in remote places. Before reaching India he had journeyed through Damascus, Aleppo, Kurdistan, parts of Persia, Baghdad, Basra and Muscat. He kept a diary, written in Hebrew, of all of his travels from 1824 until 1832. Parts of this Diary, translated into English, were published in Madras in 1832. The book's title page reads as follows : "*The Travels of Rabbi David D'Beth Hillel : from Jerusalem, through Arabia, Koordistan, Part of Persia, and India to Madras;* Madras, printed for the Author, 1832." From his own account we learn that D'Beth Hillel remained in Bombay

> for about two years, being engaged as a Hebrew teacher to some gentlemen. I stayed there very discontentedly owing to the Arabian Jews and the Arabs, for on exhibiting myself with a beard and English dress, they thought I was an Arab who had been proselytized to Christianity and I was in consequence many times badly treated by them in the streets and in my own dwelling.[28]

Although neither D'Beth Hillel nor Professor Walter Fischel (who has written at length about Rabbi D'Beth Hillel) mentions the names of D'Beth Hillel's pupils in Bombay, it is a fact that one of them was indeed the Rev. John Wilson. We know this from an amusing but rather affectionate account about D'Beth Hillel which appeared in a long *Review of the Travels of Rabbi D. D'Beth Hillel* published in *The Oriental Christian Spectator*, Volume 4, No. 5, May 1833, pp. 197-204, telling a lot about Rabbi D'Beth Hillel during his stay in Bombay from 1829 to 1831. (See Appendix 4)

Not only do we know that the Rev. John Wilson was being taught Hebrew by Rabbi D'Beth Hillel, but, according to George Smith, from April to November of 1829, he was also studying Marathi. Smith quotes Wilson as saying :

> For the last three months I have devoted the hour between seven and eight in the morning to the reading of Hebrew with the points.[29] I was very desirous, for the sake

of usefulness among the Jews here, and other important reasons, to attain to greater proficiency in this ancient language.

My teacher, who is a rabbi, is an excellent scholar. He is well acquainted with Mr. Wolff, whom he had frequently seen in Jerusalem; and he declared, even among his countrymen, that the Messiah has already appeared.[30]

If Rabbi D'Beth Hillel believed that the Messiah had already come — not necessarily in the form of Jesus Christ — such a belief alone would have discredited him in the eyes of the Arabian Jews, much more than his wearing English-style clothing. But there is no evidence of this belief on the part of D'Beth Hillel in the extant portions of his own diary. It is, however, also possible — and more plausible — to interpret Wilson's words in a different sense, viz. as meaning that his teacher — Rabbi D'Beth Hillel — had told Wilson that the Rev. Wolff (see above, pp. 69—70) had declared "even among his countrymen", i.e. the Jews of Jerusalem, "that the Messiah had already appeared."

The original Hebrew diary of Rabbi D'Beth Hillel's travels amounted to 600 to 700 pages. Even the short Madras version of the diary contains useful information about all places he visited, data relating to transport, lodgings, prices, currencies, weights and measures, climate, food, places of worship of various religions, some local customs, and estimates of numbers of Jewish families resident in a given place, together with the number of synagogues. The Rabbi also compiled a vocabulary of words useful to any traveller, expressed in Arabic, English, Hebrew, Hindustani and Persian — all in Latin characters.

After eight months of travel from Bombay, the Rabbi reached Madras in January 1832. While waiting for a return passage home, he spent his few months in Madras earning money as a Hebrew teacher to some English clergymen there. The Anglican Archdeacon of Madras, T. Robinson, encouraged the Rabbi to publish the diary of his travels. But the Rabbi prepared, or perhaps the British clergy and/or officials in Madras, perferred, for their own reasons and purposes, to use only a very condensed version, in English, printed in Madras in 1832 in a private edition of only 300 copies for British Colonial civil, military and religious officials in the areas of the Madras and Bombay Presidencies. Today, only six copies are known to be extant: one in the Carey Library at Serampore near Calcutta; three copies in the United States; and two in England. Unfortunately, the original Hebrew version has been lost.

Professor Walter J. Fischel was responsible for bringing Rabbi D'Beth Hillel to the attention of modern scholars[31] and in 1973 Ktav Publishing House Inc. of New York published, *Unknown Jews in Unknown Lands, the Travels of Rabbi David D'Beth Hillel (1824-1832)*, a book of 130 pages, edited and with an Introduction and Notes by Walter J. Fischel. This book is based on the 1832 Madras publication, but it does *not* include the entire 1832 English text.

According to Fischel, the Rabbi made two more trips to India and died in Calcutta in 1846. His burial place is unknown.[32]

It is to be greatly regretted that the original 600 to 700 page Hebrew diary of Rabbi D'Beth Hillel's travels has never been found. Speaking only on those of his jottings on India which appear in English in the 1832 Madras publication, with a few rare exceptions, one gets the overall impression that the Rabbi was a rather superficial sort of observer; or else that he was very unwise in what he (or his missionary-minded patrons) selected from his original Hebrew travel notes for inclusion in his English version, which, furthermore, includes too many of this own untenable "theories".[33] To give him the benefit of the doubt, let us say that a truly fair assessment of D'Beth Hillel's observations and thinking could have been made only from the original diary *in toto*. From the printed 1832 condensation of the diary, however, it is difficult to understand how Professor Fischel arrived at the conclusion that, "For an understanding of the Jews in India, the Bene Israel in Bombay, the Cochin Jews on the Malabar Coast, and the Arabian Jews, Rabbi David's account has to be reckoned with as a major source of information."[34]

For a Jew who lived in Bombay for two years, the printed version of the Rabbi's diary included disappointingly few lines about the Bene Israel (or about the Arabic-speaking Jews there). This is all the more inexplicable since the Rabbi was particularly interested in forgotten remnants of Israel : he devoted fewer than two pages to the Bene Israel, and fewer than five pages to the Jews of Cochin out of a total of 71 pages on India in his 1832 English publication. One must deplore the fact that he has not provided a detailed account of Bene Israel life in Bombay on the eve of their second religious revival. What's more, in the very little which he has published about the Bene Israel, there are two demonstrable errors.[35]

The earliest source of *substantial information* about the Bene Israel is an article about them written by the Rev. John Wilson. Although Rabbi D'Beth Hillel's account was published a few years before Wilson's, the latter provides us with much more information. Wilson seems to have had a more intimate relationship with the Bene Israel, and to have collected his information more systematically than did Rabbi D'Beth Hillel. Although some of Wilson's observations may not have been typical of the whole community, his own words on the subject do invite careful attention. In an address read before the monthly meeting of the Bombay Branch of the Royal Asiatic Society on January 27, 1836, the Rev. John Wilson noted that : "The Beni-Israel of Bombay and the adjoining territories amount to about eight thousand. It is to be regretted that no considerable account of them has yet appeared, particularly as they have been long settled in the country, refuse the appellation of Jew, and are probably a portion of the Ten Tribes...." In 1838 he himself undertook the task of writing "a considerable account of the Beni-Israel".

In this own book, *The Lands of the Bible*,[36] Wilson begins his section on the Bene Israel by saying : "I submitted an account of the Beni-Israel to the Bombay Branch of the Royal Asiatic Society, on its anniversary meetings in 1838 and 1839. An abridgment of that document I here present to my readers" (p.667). Years later, in *The Indian Antiquary* of November 1874 (pp.321-3), he published a very much briefer account of "The Bene Israel," using the same material. Obviously, the original account, with no abridgment whatever, would be most significant for our purposes. However, neither the libraries and archives of Bombay University, of the Church of Scotland (at the National Library of Scotland), of the Royal Asiatic Society,[37] of Harvard University, of Princeton University and others — to whom the present author addressed inquiries — have been able to locate that original account. Therefore, we must make do with the next best thing, viz. an "Abstract of an Account of the Beni-Israel of Bombay, read before the Bombay Branch of the Royal Asiatic Society, at the Anniversary Meetings in November 1838 and 1839, by John Wilson D.D. President of the Society" as published in *The Oriental Christian Spectator,* Volume 11, No. 1, January 1840, pp. 27-36.[38] All we know about the *original unabridged* account is learned from George Smith (*Life of John Wilson,* p. 124) i.e. that it was in the form of "two careful and learned papers written for the Bombay Branch of the Royal Asiatic Society."

Because of its fundamental significance to any serious study of the Bene Israel, *The Oriental Christian Spectator's* abstract[39] of Wilson's account is reproduced in full as Appendix 5. (See below).

From Wilson's account the reader cannot help but gain insight into his feelings and the reasons for his particular devotion to the Bene Israel. Thus he explains:

> In the view which we have been led to take of the Beni-Israel, they must be considered as possessed of peculiar interest, even among the seed of Abraham....Amongst us who are Christians, they must be "beloved for the father's sakes"; and it must be our desire and endeavour, that "through our mercy, they may obtain mercy." Their situation, if properly explained to the Hindus among whom they dwell, might facilitate the illustration of the Prophetical testimony to the truth of the Scriptures. (p.35)

It is interesting that nowhere in his abridged account does Wilson make any mention of the Bene Israel tradition about having been "discovered" by a David Rahabi; nor does he mention anything of their pre-first-Jewish-revival observances as such, which Bene Israel claim to have been their pristine traditions.[40] Ezekiel Rahabi's Letter of 1768 specifies at least that the Bene Israel "knew nothing but the Shema and they keep the Sabbath". Similar statements by earlier writers, presumably about this vestigial group, had *not* specified the Bene Israel by name. Kehimkar, at the end of the 19th century, wrote at length on the Bene Israel tradition about their vestigial Jewish observances. Not on this matter (because Wilson is silent on this point), yet concerning many other details, it is clear that Kehimkar borrowed heavily from Wilson's account. And it is important to notice those points where Kehimkar's account differs from Wilson's in substance or in points of detail.

The better to pursue his intended program vis-a-vis the Bene Israel, Wilson, as soon as his proficiency in Hebrew enabled him to do so, set about compiling his *Rudiments of Hebrew Grammar in Marathi* which was published in Bombay in 1831. A pre-publication announcement of this *Grammar* appeared in *The Oriental Christian Spectator*, Volume 2, No. 7, July 1831, p.9, thus:

> *A Grammar of the Hebrew Language, with points, in Murathee,* by the Rev. John Wilson, Bombay:
>
> This Grammar is intended for the benefit of the Native Israelites in the Bombay Presidency, whose number is estimated at 8000. In addition to an explanation, and an exemplification of the different parts of speech, it will contain an account of the Creation, the Fall, and the Flood, the Ten Commandments, Selected Moral Sentences, and passages relating to the Messiah contained in the Old Testament, and contrasted with the corresponding ones in the New, both in the Hebrew and Murathee languages, so as to form a set of useful and constructive exercises.

Inasmuch as Rabbi David D'Beth Hillel was actually the person who helped perfect Rev. Wilson's Hebrew proficiency preparatory to Wilson's composition of *The Rudiments of Hebrew Grammar in Marathi,* Rabbi D'Beth Hillel thus unwittingly played a definite, albeit very indirect, role in shaping the future history of the Bene Israel. Therefore it is fitting to include herewith (below, as Appendix 4) a copy of a rare vignette which describes an aspect of the Rabbi's life in Bombay, i.e. his relationship with Christians in Bombay. Since D'Beth Hillel did not leave Bombay until 1831, the year of publication of the Hebrew-Marathi Grammar, he *may* even have assisted in the preparation of the Hebrew parts of its text. But the present author has found no indication, let alone proof, that D'Beth Hillel had anything directly to do with the preparation of that book.

In the January 1834 issue of *The Oriental Christian Spectator* (Volume 5, No. 1, p.32) Wilson wrote :

> The native Israelites, who were at one time shy in their intercourse with me, now pay me frequent visits at my own house. They have purchased within a few months, 70 copies of my Hebrew and Marathi Rudiments, and some Old Testaments [which had already been translated into Marathi].

By the time Volume 13, No. 4, of April 1842 appeared, we read (p.182) that Wilson had, among his older male pupils, more than 20 Israelites who

> regularly attend me once a week to study the elements of the Hebrew language. The more advanced of them have nearly finished an outline of the Grammar, and are able, with little help from a Lexicon,[41] to read any prose portion of the Hebrew Scriptures. I am aware of more than one of my pupils giving instruction in Hebrew — so far as they themselves know it — to their countrymen... The lessons I give my young Israelite pupils frequently lead us to the discussion of the claims of Jesus to the Messiahship.
> Like their countrymen, they are full of prejudice; but perhaps one of the most effectual means which man can employ to remove these prejudices is to lead them to a correct and critical acquaintance with the original Scripture....
> One very interesting and important occupation during the last year has been intercourse with Jews in Bombay. (I speak of Jews as distinct from the Beni-Israael.) In particular I have sought the acquaintance of those Jews who have passed through Bombay on their way to or from Arabia and Persia. I have to regret my ignorance of the Arabic language,[42] with which nearly all the Eastern Jews are acquainted — Hebrew not being so well fitted as Arabic for a medium of intercourse. Several Rabbis of high acquirements have passed through Bombay during the past year, and I have several documents in my possession written by them in answer to the arguments in support of Christianity to which I had directed their attention.

One wonders how many, if any, of these Rabbis[43] spent time with the Bene Israel to give them Jewish religious inspiration and instruction. We read only of Bene Israel responding (with donations of money) to itinerant Jews' pleas to help the needy Jews in the Holy Land.[44]

As for the Missionary Bibles :

> By a recent regulation of the depository, the Old Testament is sold for half the cost price to Jews and to persons who purchase them for distribution among the Jews. And to every Jew [here this included the Bene Israel] who purchases the Old Testament a copy of the New Testament is to be offered gratis.[45]

In 1835 Rev. Wilson had 215 youths as students in his Church of Scotland's English College.[46] Here Hindus, Parsis, Jains, Muslims, Jews (most, if not all of whom were Bene Israel), and native Christians associated together and, as G. Smith puts it (p.87), quoting Wilson, "helped remove caste prejudices which so much impede missionary operations in India". But — as Wilson surely realized — encouraging a spirit of enquiry, whether in secular or in religious education, and the broadening influences of secular education *per se* created a two-edged sword as far as the chances for conversion to Christianity were concerned. In March of 1842, of the 155 students then in the College, 78 were Hindus, 38

Jews, 33 Christians (of all sects), and 6 Muslims. In G. Smith's *Life of John Wilson*, we read among many quotations from Wilson's letters that he wrote to his home missionary committee on May 10, 1850 : "The students of Elphinstone College (of Bombay University) have been setting up some schools of their own from which all Christianity is excluded and they have sought to fill them from our schools by prejudicing the minds of their parents". (p.449) It took the Bene Israel another quarter of a century before such an independent school was set up by them : the Israelite School was not founded until 1875 (see below, pp. 169-71). However, by mid-19th century because the missionaries had not had sufficient success in proselytization — not only among the Bene Israel but among other Indians in general — all Christian missions began to phase out their free schools for non-Christians.

Many missionaries were women who would begin by trying to persuade Bene Israel girls, whom they chanced to pass on the street, to join their particular Christian school; or they would go from house to house to teach women. But the Rev. Wilson's first wife, Margaret, nee Bayne, was an extraordinary person, a true educationist, and it was she who was responsible for the rapid progress of female education in Bombay. She set up six girls' schools in Bombay, all under her own supervision. After her death in 1835 her two sisters took over the supervision of female education on the part of the Scottish Mission in Bombay. They enlarged the number of its Girls' Schools from 6 to 19. In 1841 these schools had a total of 568 students of whom 65 were "Israelites". Unlike the schools for boys (but which always had a small proportion of girl students too) the Girls' Schools of the Scottish Mission (as also the Girls' Schools of the American Mission) had no Jewish teachers. They taught the Marathi language and did not teach Hebrew. Christian religious instruction was given to the girls (originally by Mrs. Wilson) on the premises of the Scottish Mission on Saturday mornings. Wilson's second wife, Isabella, nee Dennistoun, whom he married in Scotland in 1846 and who died in Bombay in 1867, also took a very active part, among her many other missionary programs, especially in her mission's Girls' Schools and in its one school which was only for Bene Israel students. According to G. Smith (pp.599-600), she "had proved so potent a force that it was difficult to realize how these organizations could prosper without her. Her social intercourse for the highest ends, with Hindu, Parsi, Jewish, and Muhammadan families had been closer than that of any other English lady in all India."

In 1841 the Rev. Wilson wrote in a letter that in preparation for his forthcoming trip to the Holy Land, he had

> called a meeting of the principal Arabian Jews which was held at the house of David Sassoon, the most opulent merchant of their body. R.T. Webb, Esq., Major Jervis, Mr. Mitchell, Mr. Glasgow, and Mr. Kerr were present with me.... We were very politely received, and obtained much of the information which we asked, as well as the promise of every assistance being granted to a Jew whom I have employed to commit to writing whatever he can learn of the circumstance of his brethren in Yemen, Busora, Bombay and other places. Toward the close of our interview we entered on the infinitely important question of the Messiahship of Christ....They ordered all their children to leave the room when we first mentioned the name of the Saviour; and we could not help observing how much more reserved they appeared in this matter than the Beni-Israel. They otherwise evinced, however, no improper feelings; and they freely discussed with us the different points to which we averted. I told them of the deputation to Palestine, the objects of the General Assembly's Committee, and its readiness to aid in the instruction of their countrymen; and they seemed pleased with the interest which our Church takes in their welfare.[47]

Wilson's visits with Jews in Jerusalem, Safed, Hebron and Tiberias were greatly facilitated by a letter of introduction given to him by the Arabic-speaking Jews of Bombay.[48]

After his return to Bombay, Rev. Wilson was ever solicitous of the welfare of the Jews in the Holy Land. On the inner face of the back cover of the November 1854 issue of *The Oriental Christian Spectator* we even find a notice about the

RELIEF OF THE JEWS AT JERUSALEM :
The Rev. Dr. Wilson begs to acknowledge the receipt of the following additional contributions for the Relief of the Jews at Jerusalem, through the industrial plantation.
Received since 1st September....

The total donation amounted to Rs. 315/—. The names of all seven donors are listed; all are non-Jewish, European names.

There is one more item in connection with Wilson's travels in the Holy Land : namely, discussion which directly involved the Bene Israel of Bombay. When Wilson was in Nablus in May 1843, he was shown Jacob's Well by the local Samaritans who told him that they were just then preparing a letter to the Bene Israel of Bombay. In his *Lands of the Bible* (Volume II, p.47-8) Wilson records that Salamah Ibn Tobiah, the priest of the Samaritans, upon learning that Wilson had come from Bombay, asked :

"Have you brought a letter from the Samaritans there?" "I have brought" I said in reply " a communication from the Beni-Israel of Bombay, whom you suppose to be Samaritans." "This" he cried "is what we have long wanted...." Our host was much disappointed to find that we had strong doubts about the propriety of ranking the Beni-Israel of Bombay among Samaritans.

Later (p.64) Wilson brings up the subject again :

The Beni-Israel of Bombay were among the first topics of a conversation which we maintained till near midnight. The Samaritans were pleased with a good deal of what we said about the object of their inquiry; but they were awfully shocked when we told them that when the Beni-Israel were discovered by the English, they were found reverencing the serpent as well as Jehovah and serving other gods which neither they nor their fathers had known, even wood and stone. They expressed the utmost horror at this idolatry, and exclaimed, "They cannot be Samaritans; they do not make Gerizim their Kiblah."[49]

To Rev. Wilson, however, the Bene Israel remained an important Jewish remnant most worthy of his attention. They were "very near Mr. Wilson's heart....Long after he ceased to receive support for them [i.e. Wilson's projects relating to the Bene Israel] from the home churches, he made it his special care to raise funds on the spot."[50] Then, from an announcement in *The Bombay Times and Standard* of July 20, 1860 (p.2) we see that more than 31 years after Rev. Wilson came to settle in Bombay, he was still soliciting funds on behalf of "Bene Israel elevation, both social and religious".

The Rev. Wilson was certainly *the* one man most responsible for significant advances among the Bene Israel both in secular and in Jewish education. But, if one measures Wilson's success only in terms of proselytizing the Bene Israel to Christianity, he was a dismal failure; and so were all other efforts to proselytize among the Bene Israel. This can be seen even from incomplete research into missionary records. For instance, let us examine *The Oriental Christian Spectator*[51] (which first appeared in Bombay in January 1830). Each issue carried information covering a wide variety of categories: "Sermons"; "Religious Controversies"; "Intelligence" – about the life, work, death, etc. of missionaries; "Literary Reviews" of books, articles, journals, etc. which were in any way helpful to or related to missionary work;[52] "Poetry"; "Notes to Correspondents"; "World-wide Communication"; and "Religious Intelligence" – specifying the name, community, occupation, date of baptism, etc. of new converts. From this well-informed source, from the Rev. Wilson's own published writings, and from George Smith's biography of John Wilson, the present writer has been unable to find the name of (or any reference to) even a single convert won over specifically from the Bene Israel community.[53] This is particularly surprising in view of the fact that especially in Wilson's case, he had worked so very closely with Bene Israel in educating them to become teachers in his own institutions. He so often cites the names of, and the circumstances relating to converts from among the Hindus, Jains, Parsis, Muslims and Arabic-speaking Jews, always especially mentioning many details about the first convert from each community; but nothing ever about a Bene Israel convert. Actually, as of 1877, the total number of all converts made by the Free Church of Scotland in Bombay and in the stations of the Free Church founded by Wilson during the 46 years of Wilson's missionary service in India amounted only to 1,071 souls. It would, however, be quite wrong to measure Wilson's very great impact upon the vast numbers of people whom he knew purely in terms of this rather modest record of conversions.[54]

The History of the London Society for Promoting Christianity Among the Jews, from 1809 to 1908, by Rev. W.T. Gidney,[55] mentions not a single Bene Israel convert to Christianity, although it acknowledges (p.112) that "there are now some 18,228 Bene Israel in the neighbourhood of Bombay"; also that Michael Sargon's brother, Abraham, came to teach in Bombay in 1826, followed later by yet another brother, J. Sargon; and that one Jew and two Jewesses were baptized in Cochin in 1828 (p.114). On p.115 the book names all the places where the Rev. Dr. Wolff preached in India, without, however, referring to even a single resulting convert. On pp.384-5 the book tells of Rev. J.M. Eppstein (himself probably of Jewish birth, judging from the name) who arrived in Bombay in 1860. He was ineffectual due to ill health; but, in general "with regard to the Jews of India, amongst the Arab and German[56] Jews [note, there is no mention of Bene Israel] the preaching of the Gospel has not been entirely without effect. Two from amongst the latter, both very intelligent young men, have lately been baptized in Bombay."

Tables of statistics on conversions, which the present writer has seen among reports of the Annual Meetings of the Bombay Missionary Union (including the American, London, and Scottish Missionary Societies) specify whether the convert (to Protestantism) was originally "Heathen" or "Romanist" (i.e. Catholic). But we cannot assume that they included Jews, Muslims or Parsis in this category of "Heathen". Somewhere there must be reports by the various member groups of the Bombay Missionary Union which document the actual numbers of Parsi, Muslim, "German", Arabic-speaking Jewish, and Bene Israel converts specifically.

Other statistical tables of the above-mentioned missions in India were compiled in 1852 and again in 1862.[57] Because the findings proved to be so helpful, in the November 1862 issue of *The Oriental Christian Spectator* (Volume III, fourth series, No. 11, pp.540-8) the taking of a census of Indian Missions regularly every ten years was strongly recommended. However, under its proposed census category of "Converts" it did not, unfortunately, require or specify the "original religion of the convert".

In appraising the work of missionaries among the Bene Israel no one can deny that the missionary translation of the Bible into Marathi, whatever its faults from a Jewish point of view, was *the* cornerstone for Bene Israel understanding of the Bible. In the words of Rebecca Reuben, a well known Bene Israel educationist : "The translation of the Bible into Marathi by the missionaries, in spite of the faulty language and the poor literary value of the publication, in spite of many textual misinterpretations and the general Christian tone of the interpellations, was a great boon to the Bene Israel."[58] In the words of B.J. Israel, the missionaries

> profoundly influenced the Bene Israel attitude to the Bible, which, for better or worse, differed materially from that of the Orthodox Oriental Jew. They taught them to regard the plain text of the Bible as a self-sufficient guide in matters of religion and to rely on their own individual reading of the Bible to learn God's law. And, ever since, although the Bene Israel have professed to accept rabbinical teaching and law like their fellow Jews elsewhere, they have never given rabbinical teaching the attention it received elsewhere.[59]

Also stressed by B.J. Israel is the fact that at a time when illiteracy, especially among women, was "appallingly high" an extraordinary proportion of Bene Israel children — both boys and girls — received a secular education in missionary schools.

The Bene Israel appreciated the benefits which accrued from their contacts with missionaries. The Rev. Wilson, in particular, they held in very high esteem. But, as far as anything about Rev. Wilson written (at least in English) by members of the Bene Israel community goes, one usually finds remarkably little more than an acknowledgment of Wilson's *Hebrew-Marathi Grammar* and some passing references that such-and-such a Bene Israel, or so many Bene Israel children, had been educated in Dr. Wilson's schools. Even Kehimkar gives no real praise or thanks to Wilson for the latter's role in the enlightenment of the Bene Israel. He does mention Wilson's schools, and Wilson's theories as to Bene Israel origins, and that "there was no regular class for teaching English before the time of Dr. Wilson".[60] But we find no warmth of feeling. And yet, it was the missionaries who had made accessible the Hebrew Scriptures in Marathi translations so that the entire community of the Bene Israel could — for the first time — easily and thoroughly grasp their contents; they had published a Hebrew-Marathi Grammar; they employed Bene Israel teachers in missionary schools throughout the Konkan area; they provided hundreds of Bene Israel pupils with a good secular education and a thorough grounding in Hebrew and in English.

The entire story of Bene Israel relations with Christian missionaries presents a fascinating and exceptional experience in history, an unparalleled example of a Jewish remnant, unfettered by the minutiae of *halachic* rules, not only obtaining secular education, but simultaneously strengthening its *Jewish* religious life *under Christian auspices*! What made such a state of affairs possible may have been the fact that the Bene Israel were unsophisticated, staunch in their loyalty to what little they knew of Judaism and its practice, yet without bigotry, exhibiting the peculiarly Indian facility to absorb much from other cultures without losing one's own identity and ethnicity.

This chapter has introduced us to the Christian missionary point of view, often through the words of missionaries, regarding the 19th century development of the Bene Israel. An altogether different kind of source about the Bene Israel of this period, and

The Influence of Christian Missionaries 81

which, among other things, deals with one Bene Israel who converted to Christianity, is a Hebrew book published in 1884 called *Masa'ot Shelomo* (*The Travels of Solomon*) by Solomon Reinemann. (See Appendix 3a, pp. 314-315 and Appendix 6.) Reinemann devotes thirteen pages to the Bene Israel.[61]

Scholars usually refer to Solomon Reinemann only as the first writer (except for the one sentence in Ezekiel Rahabi's *Letter of 1768*) to have mentioned and described pre-19th century contact between the Bene Israel and Cochin Jewry. Actually, the Rev. John Wilson, in the abstract of his 1838-39 *Account of the Beni-Israel,* had already stated that "The Jews of Cochin have all along considered themselves distinct from the Beni-Israel of Bombay, of whose circumstances they have from time immemorial been well aware." (See Appendix 5, p. 335) But, in any case, what *The Travels of Solomon* tells us about the Bene Israel in other respects should also have received some attention because it brings to life certain additional aspects and nuances based on first-hand contact with Bene Israel in 19th century Bombay. Reinemann was visiting among the Bene Israel at least as early as 1846.

As explained by its publisher at the beginning of the book, Reinemann was born in Galicia (Europe), travelled extensively through Asia as a merchant, married a daughter of the Cochin Jewish Rahabi family, and ended up in Vienna where the publisher encouraged him to write the memoirs of his travels, and where he died in 1872. But Reinemann did not write well and his material was very disorganised. When the publisher learned that a well-known traveller, Wolff Schur, was then in Vienna, he commissioned Schur to complete the task, begun by the publisher himself, of preparing Reinemann's memoirs for publication. Not only did the original manuscript have to be reorganized and rewritten, but Schur added to it details which he had seen with his own eyes, as well as some which other travellers had documented. Although this is sometimes acknowledged in a footnote, the fact remains that one cannot always be sure what part of the information comes from Reinemann, what part from Schur, or perhaps from some other unacknowledged source. It is the present writer's impression, however, that Schur added less to Reinemann's original manuscript whenever the text deals with *Jews* of India than he did in the (more numerous) sections dealing with non-Jewish details from Reinemann's travels.

Be that as it may, the background of the writing and publication of *The Travels of Solomon* must be borne in mind for any evaluation of the reliability of each point of information which it contains. This caution applied as much to each detail in Reinemann's story of Samaji's release from prison and of his first visit to Cochin, as it does to any of the other anecdotes which he relates, but which he did not witness at first hand. All these caveats notwithstanding, *The Travels of Solomon* contains certain *first-hand* observations of the Bene Israel and expresses a certain empathy toward them which is not to be found anywhere else. This warrants its reproduction here as Appendix 6 — a literal translation into English from the original Hebrew of Reinemann's pages on the Bene Israel. His section on the Bene Israel happens to end with a lengthy account of how a certain Bene Israel doctor converted to Christianity, realized the mistake he had made, and asked to be reinstated as a Jew and to rejoin the Bene Israel community. Reinemann beautifully describes the reinstatement ceremony. (See Appendix 6, pp. 347-48). We finally find here a Bene Israel who did convert to Christianity — but he quickly changed his mind.

The fact is that there were remarkably few conversions on the part of the Bene Israel in spite of persistent missionary efforts (among young and old, male and female) and of intensive exposure to Christianity during impressionable school years.

It seems that even Dr. Wilson converted very few, if any, Bene Israel; but he certainly wanted to do so and also helped other missionaries who were actively trying to convert the Bene Israel. He wrote a booklet called *The Bene Israel of Bombay : An Appeal for Their Christian Education,* to which various missionary writings sometimes refer. One reference asserts that it was first published in Edinburgh in 1852; another says that the first edition appeared in Bombay in 1854, and that a second edition was published in Edinburgh in 1865. Most 20th century serious writers on the Bene Israel have included this tract in their respective bibliographies, but all searches on the part of the present writer, even in Edinburgh and in Bombay, have failed to turn up the full text of this booklet by Wilson. Fortunately, for our present purpose, *The Jewish Chronicle* (London) of December 7, 1866 (p.2), quotes from what must have been this very document:

> We [i.e. *The Jewish Chronicle*] make the following extract from a pamphlet by Rev. Dr. John Wilson which was published in 1854 and reprinted in July 1865. Our object in so doing is to show the dangers to which the branch of the Jewish Stock is exposed....

> "In 1853 the Jews' Committee of the Free Church of Scotland withdrew from the Bene Israel the annual grant of £ 200 on which our schools and a few scholarships were dependent....2) This interesting people, we think are more willing to receive instruction in the doctrines of Christianity than perhaps any other community of their brethren throughout the world. We have seldom experienced any difficulty in collecting, in any place where they reside, a considerable congregation of them whenever we have sought to prove to them that Jesus whom their fathers crucified is indeed the Annointed. In our schools they regularly use the New Testament as well as the Old; and even commit our Christian Catechisms to memory....3) Though the labours among the Bene Israel of the Bombay Missions have not yet [sic!] been blessed to the conversion of any of their number, they are most evidently preparing for them the way of the Lord...."*

> * Since this was written, an Asiatic Jewish pupil of the institution (our principal institution in Bombay), who has received an excellent education, has embraced Christianity. Another is at present (1865) a candidate for Baptism.

When this appeal was published in 1854, Wilson had been working in Bombay for 25 years and he admits that he had not yet been able to convert a single Bene Israel. Furthermore, the missionary footnote to the above quotation, dated 1865, does not specify a Bene Israel, but only a rather vague "Asiatic Jewish pupil" (who was very likely a Jew of Asiatic, but not of Indian, origin) as being the only Jewish convert.

More than half a century after Wilson began his work in Bombay, the Anglican Rev. J. Henry Lord was very diligent in trying to learn as much as possible about the background of the Bene Israel in order to find more effective methods for proselytizing among them. With this in mind, he published a 94-page tract called the *The Jewish Mission Field in the Bombay Diocese* wherein he made some very pertinent observations, such as :

> We shall feel sure at the outset that, owing to the centuries of isolation from their fellow religionists, and to the total loss for centuries of whatever religious books they may have once possessed, this community [the Bene Israel] will present features of a very different description to the generality of Jews. Moreover, we see them just now (1893) in a sort of transition period — when the disadvantages of centuries of past

The Influence of Christian Missionaries 83

ignorance and depression are fast giving way to the enjoyment of fresh educational and religious experiences.[62]

They seem possessed by the belief that a great deal more can be said in defence of Judaism than they themselves know how to put into words, and evince not uncommonly a disposition to fall back on their own ignorance and incapability, and to say "We cannot answer these questions; our more learned rabbis elsewhere can; ask them."[63]

In the Rev. Lord's *The Jewish Mission Field in the Bombay Diocese* occurs the rare phenomenon of citing the name of an actual Bene Israel convert to Christianity, in a context which does credit to Bene Israel resistance to proselytization.

> About 21 years ago [i.e. 1872] something like a religious crisis took place amongst them [the Bene Israel]. They were much aroused by a Marathi treatise called *The Watchman's Voice*, which had been published and addressed to them, and an active correspondence for some time was carried on in the columns of the native Christian paper called the *Dnyanodaya*.[64]

There were especially two members of the Bene Israel community who took part in this correspondence, one of them

> Mr. Banduji Bhonkar became a Christian; the other, who was a most cultivated man, remained a Jew. The end, for the time being, of the crisis was that controversial books on the Jewish side were procured from England and translated into Marathi, and the movement in the direction of Christianity was, at any rate temporarily, delayed.[65]

The only other name of a Bene Israel convert to come to the present author's attention in the course of extensive reading of missionary and other writings, is found in Volume VII, Nos. 1-2, January-February, 1923, of *The Israelite*, Bombay (p.46), in a notice about a "Karachi Jewish Marriage Case" which says that

> Abraham Benjamin Talkar was converted to Christianity in his early youth. He married one Laxmi, an Indian Christian, according to the Christian rites. Two years ago the appellant relapsed to Judaism on account of religious convictions. As the respondent continued to be a Christian and as the Jewish Law does not recognize a Christian wife and the Christian form of marriage, the appellant decided to take a wife from the Jewish community and marry her according to the Jewish rites....It was urged for the appellant that the rights of Christian wife, after the appellant had relapsed to Judaism, extended merely to an appellation for dissolution of Marriage.

Rev. Lord makes several quite candid comments about his experiences in trying to convert Bene Israel :

> ....Nothing could be more pleasant than the courtesy and friendliness with which the Christian missionary is generally received by them [Bene Israel]— *would that there were but commensurate earnestness in weighing his message*. To one familiar with the bitterness and open hostility apt to be vented on a missionary by orthodox Jews in

other lands, no greater contrast than the courtesy and kindness usually accorded here could be imagined.⁶⁶ [Emphasis supplied]

Later in the same article, discussing missionary work among Bene Israel villagers, Rev. Lord mentions the head of one of two sole Bene Israel families in a village who almost looked upon the Rev. Lord as a Rabbi and who did not know what the *Old Testament* was. He records that in another village some Bene Israel village children were wearing Hindu charms. The Rev. Lord used picture books of the Scriptures, showed magic lantern slides of sacred views, and read portions from the translation of the Old Testament in Marathi. He writes that the Bene Israel would attend his first and second meetings *en masse,* and then stay away from the third, also *en masse*; that the Bene Israel did not discuss Christianity on merits, but rejected it because "with a large number [of Bene Israel], Christianity does not seem to be wrong for any other reason than because it is not Judaism."⁶⁷

A further picture of the Rev. Lord's relations with the Bene Israel is to be found in a missionary book called *On the Bombay Coast and Deccan* :

> In 1882 there had come to the Diocese of Bombay a young priest, the Rev. J.H. Lord, who had been working among the Jews in the East End of London. It was his intention to devote himself to the study and service of the Bene Israel community in the Bombay littoral....From Umerkhadi he would cross the Harbour to the mainland and visit the Bene Israel in the scattered villages of the Konkan. As early as 1888 he had established outposts in Pen and Panvel. (He died at Panvel in 1924 in his 70th year.) Father Lord, though not a member of the Society, was associated with the S.S.J.E.⁶⁸ during all his Indian service. They became the executors of his work among the Bene Israel....He was Examiner in Hebrew for the Bombay University and wrote the article on the Bene Israel in *Hastings' Encyclopaedia of Religion and Ethics*. He had considerable medical knowledge. In 1905 his dispensary at Sai, a village between Panvel and Pen, was built and equipped by the S.S.J.E. .... Year after year Fr. Lord travelled about the Konkan in his tonga,⁶⁹ going from village to village winning the hearts of the simple people, in parts little known to white men. "So he went on in faith *without a single convert* [emphasis supplied]. But in those years there must have been many a life touched by the power of Jesus as in Palestine long years ago. There was a ploughing and a sowing of seed which will surely germinate in time."* (* From Bombay Diocesan Magazine, September 1928.)⁷⁰

This was the way the missionaries rationalized the lack of Bene Israel converts.

Of the Arabic-speaking Jews in Bombay the Rev. Lord mentions that they spoke some Hindustani, but not Marathi; that they were well versed in Hebrew and spoke it for religious purposes; but that he himself had very little to do with them because they were too few in number; and that his missionary endeavors were almost wholly concerned with the Bene Israel. Yet, with all the goodwill and effort directed toward proselytization of the Bene Israel by such remarkable personages as the Rev. Wilson and Father Lord, so very very few Bene Israel converted to Christianity. Indeed, after more than 132 years of Bene Israel exposure to missionaries

> Rev. C.J. Buffam, late of the Baptist Church in Bombay, estimated that *in all of India in 1945* [emphasis supplied] there were 20-25 families of the Bene Israel origin and 5 Baghdadi families that had been converted to various Protestant denominations.... He was not aware of the number of Jewish converts to the Roman Catholic Church.⁷¹

The Influence of Christian Missionaries 85

The Bene Israel experience was not the only instance of missionaries concentrating on remote Jewish communities and wanting to teach them Hebrew and the Bible. A superficially comparable example was the missionary effort among the Kaifeng Jews of Honan, China during the late 19th and early 20th centuries. But, neither here nor elsewhere have missionary efforts resulted in so directly nurturing, and so thoroughly vitalizing, the Jewishness of a community as was the case among the Bene Israel of the Konkan.[72]

NOTES

1. Missionaries at Serampur (in West Bengal, slightly northeast of Calcutta) were the first to publish, between 1812 and 1821, a Marathi translation (by Casey) of the Old Testament. Old Testament translations into Marathi were also published in Bombay where the Marathi translation of Genesis was completed about 1819; about 1833 the Book of Exodus appeared in Marathi, followed in 1837 by a Marathi translation of the Book of Psalms. It was not until 1855 that translation of the entire Old Testament into Marathi was completed in Bombay. See below, p. 241, n.6.
2. In 1600 A.D. British merchant adventurers received from Queen Elizabeth I their charter to form The British East India Company. They had to renew this charter every twenty years. Before 1813 The British East India Company would not allow anyone, except their own company officials and chaplains — i.e. no one not under the Company's control — to enter their territories in India. In 1813 an Act of Parliament, Section 33, granted entry to British territory in India to non-British East India Company personnel, inclusive of missionaries. In 1833 the British East India Company lost its trading monopoly. See Raymond Renford : *The Non-Official British in India to 1920*, Oxford University Press, Delhi, 1987.
3. Some had been educated under army auspices, as soldiers themselves or as children or family of soldiers, in so-called "regimental schools".
4. *The Oriental Christian Spectator*, Volume I, No. 4, April 1830; printed for the Proprietors by James Garrett at the American Mission Press, Bombay, 1830, p.113.
5. Ibid., p.113.
6. Ibid., pp.114-5.
7. These reports are located at the Mocatta Library, London University. The present writer is grateful to Dr. Barbara Johnson for the use of her notes taken from these Reports.
8. The *16th Report* was written by Rev. Henry Baker. This quotation is to be found on p.59 in the volume of *Jews Society Reports* 1-20, from 1809 to 1828.
9. That these Bene Israel living at Cannanore spoke "the Hindoo" language, would indicate that they were in some way connected with the army, because Hindu(stani) was developed as the language of the army. However, Michael Sargon (through the writer Mr. Jarrett) seems to distinguish between Bene Israel Sepoys of the 9th Regiment and these Bene Israel whom he found in Cannanore. What had brought these Bene Israel so far south? Could this in any way have been connected with Maratha settlement in South India, either with the Maratha political domination established in mid-17th century, or with the Maratha colonies along the southwest coast of India whose establishment probably antedates the 17th century? This particular aspect should be investigated, looking (for our purposes) for the presence of any Bene Israel among Marathas in South India. An early presence of Bene Israel as far south as Cannanore would have facilitated equally early Bene Israel contact with Cochin Jews. In her article, "The Bene Israel", which appeared in the *Journal of the Anthropological Society of Bombay*, 1956, p.53, Schifra Strizower also suggests that the Maratha settlement in Malabar "might have been conducive to further contact between the Malabar Jews and the Bene Israel of the Konkan."
   To quote M.G.Ranade, in *Rise of the Maratha Power and Other Essays,* published by the University of Bombay, March 1961, Chapter XII on the Marathas in Southern India, p.128 :

South Kanara and Malabar, Cochin and Travancore with a Maratha population of one and half lakhs [the 1881 Census shows exactly 153,497 souls] were of course colonized from the coast, and these settlements had no connection with the political domination established in the middle of the 17th century by the army of Shahaji (Shivaji's father) and his son Venkoji, the step-brother of Shivaji.... The military settlers included both Brahmans and Marathas, and by reason of their isolation from their distant home, the subdivisions which separated these castes in their mother country were forgotten, and they were all welded together under the common name of Deshastas. [a *lakh* = 100,000]

Furthermore, Tanjore, in southeast India, was dominated for some centuries by Maratha rulers. One wonders if their archives might have contained an occasional reference to the Bene Israel.

10. From the *18th Report*, 1826, p.85.
11. It is not clear here whether Sargon is referring to Arabic-speaking Jews or to White Cochin Jews.
12. From the *19th Report*, 1827; Appendix (I) : Third Report of the Madras Corresponding Committee, p.173.
13. Kehimkar : *History*, p.67.
14. Ibid., p.237.
15. Rev. Joseph Wolff : *Researches and Missionary Labours Among the Jews, Mahomedans and Other Sects,* second edition, James Nisbet and Company, London, 1853, p.502.
16. Ibid., p.503.
17. Rev. Joseph Wolff : *Travels and Adventures of the Rev. Joseph Wolff, D.D. LL.D.*, Saunders, Otley and Company, 66 Brook Street, Hanover Square, W. London, 1861, pp.471-2.
18. *The Oriental Christian Spectator*, Volume 6, No. 2, February 1835; printed at the American Mission Press, Bombay, p.70 (under the heading "Religious Intelligence").
19. Mr. Samuel always uses the term "Jews" to refer to the Arabic-speaking Jews; and he specifies "Bene Israel" or "black Jews" whenever writing about the Bene Israel.
20. Ibid., Volume 6, No. 10, October 1835, p.382; from the *Journal of Mr. Samuel,* for the month of January 1835.
21. Ibid., p.383.
22. Ibid., p.384
23. Ibid., pp.384-5. Samuel explains that this "reader of the black Jews" was "a man of family, and a white Jew" (p.385). By "white Jew" he probably meant a White (Pardesi) Cochin Jew.
24. The records of the Bombay Union of Christian Missions are said to have been transferred to Ahmednagar College (about 100 miles from Bombay). Microfilm collections of historical church-related documents and other records are kept in the Indian Church History archives at the United Theological College, Bangalore 6, Karnataka (Mysore) State, and at the Carey Library of Serampore College, Serampore, Hooghly District 712-201, West Bengal. There are also records at the Cambridge Brotherhood Library in Old Delhi. Various missionary headquarters and missionary libraries abroad, especially those in London, Edinburgh, Glasgow, Boston (Massachusetts), and New York City very likely also contain records of missionary activities among the Jews in India. Dr. Raymond K. Renford, in his 9-page article, "Missionary Records in Indian Ocean Studies" (published by the International Conference on Indian Ocean Studies, Perth, Western Australia, 1979; in Section VI, "Archives and Resources for Study" notes that the Library of the Church Missionary Society in London is a very important source for missionary journals; and that the "foreign" (mission) records of the Church Missionary Society are in process of transfer to the Birmingham University Library. He recommends as useful : *A Guide to Archives and Records of Protestant Christian Missions from the British Isles to China, 1796-1914*, by Leslie R. Marchant, published by the University of Western Australia Press in 1966; Rosemary Keen's *A Survey of Archives of Selected Missionary Societies*, published by the Church Missionary Society, London, 1968; the *Catalogue of Indian Church History Archives,* Bangalore, 1968; and the *Christian Handbook of India 1959*, published by the National Christian Council of India, Nagpur.
25. George Smith, LL.D : *The Life of John Wilson, D.D. F.R.S.* – *for 50 Years Philanthropist and Scholar in the East,* John Murray, Albermarle Street, London, 1878; 652 pages, unabridged first

edition. See Preface, page x.
26. The title of "Chancellor of the University" was always reserved for the Governor of Bombay Presidency and, since Indian Independence, for the Governor of the State of Maharashtra.
27. Hebrew was first taught at Wilson College and later also at St.Xavier's College, both colleges being affiliates of Bombay University (founded in 1856). Today, although Hebrew, like Greek, is listed as an optional subject at the University, there are no longer even part-time professors of Hebrew. However, it is still a subject for the State Government School-Leaving Examination, although the University has discontinued the matriculation exam in Hebrew.
28. David D'Beth Hillel, op. cit., (Madras, 1832), pp.129-30.
29. Wilson had begun his study of Hebrew in Scotland during his student days. With greater proficiency in Hebrew, one learns how to read without "points", i.e. the vowels. Hebrew is frequently written without vowels.
30. Smith, op.cit., p.59.
31. In 1957 a short article by Walter Fischel entitled "David D'Beth Hillel : An Unknown Jewish Traveller in the Middle East and India in the 19th Century", was published in *Oriens*, Journal of the International Society for Oriental Research, Volume X, No. 2, 1957, Leiden, pp. 240-7.
32. One admires the Rabbi's bravery, curiosity, and persistence in executing his extensive travels to remote places. He is intrigued by many customs or happenings in the course of his travels, often sees parallels to Jewish customs, but usually does not follow up with enquiries so as to learn more about whatever happens to have crossed his path, not even when the inhabitants were friendly, willing and able to communicate either directly or through an interpreter. Amidst the trivia, misinterpretations and lacunae, there are also some remarkable observations, such as the following quotation taken from p. 184 of the 1832 publication :

> As far as I understand I am of opinion that all classes of Hindoos believe in the one everlasting Being, as the chief of the whole universe, and he is likewise distinguished by a separate appellation which they never make use of for any idols, as for instance in Tamil Chooyambee means self-existence or self-existing being, in Teloogoo Sweehamboo which has the same meaning, and they have many poems regarding this point for instance in Teruvalluven's Cural, Mr. Ellis' translation.

That the Rabbi noticed *The Tirukkural* of Tiruvalluvar and gave the correct meaning for "Chooyambee" and "Sweehamboo" ("Swayambhu" in Sanskrit) are definite points in his favour : too few people, including too few modern Indians, have ever heard of this superb Tamil classic, *The Tirukkural*, of the first century B.C.

Fischel, in basing his *Unknown Jews in Unknown Lands* on D'Beth Hillel's 1832 book, has reproduced, though in abridged form, the bulk of what appeared in D'Beth Hillel's 1832 publication. However, on this point, for instance, Fischel has omitted all of pages 182, 183, 184 and the top of page 185 from D'Beth Hillel's 1832 publication. (Had Fischel included these pages in his own presentation of D'Beth Hillel's text, the omitted pages would appear on page 129 of Fischel's sequential quotation from D'Beth Hillel's book.)

33. Rabbi D'Beth Hillel asserts that very likely the Bene Israel are descendants of the converts to Judaism in the Kuzari Kingdom (mentioned as the "Kingdom of the Khazars" by Ben Zvi in his, *The Exiled and the Redeemed,* see above, p.xiii n. 5) since, he argues, some Bene Israel live in the "Coojoorati [Gujarati] country". (D'Beth Hillel, op.cit., p.135) This "theory" is based on the rather slight similarity in sound between "Kuzari" and "Coojoorati"!
34. Fischel : *Unknown Jews in Unknown Lands,* p.42, n. 81.
35. Both of which Professor Fischel in his book points out as being errors on the part of D'Beth Hillel who wrote :

   1. "They [the Bene Israel] are circumcised and sanctify the day of atonement, but no other customs belonging to the Mosaical law." (D'Beth Hillel, 1832, p.133)
   2. "In the Mahratta countries around Bombay are about eight thousand families of them [Bene Israel]...." (Ibid., p.134)

The Rabbi's estimate of about 600 families in Bombay itself as of 1831 was probably close to the actual figure at that time. However, in his estimate of the numbers of Bene Israel then living outside Bombay he probably meant eight thousand *individuals* rather than "eight thousand families".

36. Rev. John Wilson : *Lands of the Bible,* William Whyte and Company, Edinburgh, 1847, in 2 volumes. The section on the "Beni-Israel of Bombay" is in Volume II, pp.667-78. The section on the "Jews at Cochin" is in Volume II, pp. 678-82.
37. The difficulty in locating a copy of the original account of 1838-39 is, no doubt, related to the fact that the Bombay Branch of the Royal Asiatic Society (established in 1830) did not begin publishing its *Transactions* (in the form of a quarterly issue) until 1841.
38. Wilson's account of the Bene Israel as it appears in his *The Lands of the Bible* is practically identical with this account from *The Oriental Christian Spectator*.
39. Wilson must have written this Abstract himself, although it is not credited to him (nor, indeed, to anyone else). Much of what appeared in most issues of *The Oriental Christian Spectator* was written by its editor, Wilson.
40. We cannot be sure whether or not the Rev. Wilson may have mentioned the Bene Israel "pristine" Jewish observances in his earlier, unabridged account on the Bene Israel.
41. The Rev. Wilson surely had Hebrew-English, English-Hebrew dictionaries at his disposal. He must have composed some Hebrew-Marathi word lists for his pupils, although no mention of a Hebrew-Marathi Dictionary has been found by the present author. It seems strange that no such dictionary was produced in the 19th century. Hebrew type was then available for printing in Bombay. Even the Government Press in Bombay had Hebrew type at one time, mainly for printing University examination papers for those studying Hebrew (but nowadays this is no longer the case). Equally strange is the fact that no Marathi-Hebrew, Hebrew-Marathi Dictionary has yet been published in Israel where there was, and continues to be, a real need for it among new Bene Israel immigrants, and also for the benefit of elderly Bene Israel who have not become proficient in Hebrew. Mr. Shimshon Menasseh, one of the very few Bene Israel members of a kibbutz (Kibbutz Afikim), has written and completed such a dictionary which, it is hoped, will soon be published.
42. Wilson had already mastered Hebrew, Marathi, Gujarati, Hindustani and Persian.
43. Wilson and others often use the word "Rabbi" not necessarily to signify an ordained rabbi, but as a term of respect for any Jew who was learned in Jewish religious literature.
44. Several other writers have mentioned such Bene Israel contacts with many different messengers (sh'liḥim) from the Holy Land who came through Bombay, especially in the 19th century.
45. *The Oriental Christian Spectator,* Volume 13, No. 1, January 1842, p.48.
46. In 1836 a College Division was added to the Native English High School, the latter having been founded by the Rev. Wilson in 1832. In 1835 both the High School and the College were called "The General Assembly Institution". After the Church of Scotland split in 1843, the name changed to "The Free General Assembly's Institution". The College was affiliated to Bombay University when the University was first established in 1857. The subjects taught, and the textbooks used at the College were the same as in Scottish universities, not excluding Greek and Hebrew. Only in 1889, when it moved into its own building, did the College of the Free General Assembly's Institution acquire the name "Wilson College", while the school became known as "Wilson High School".
47. From a letter by Rev. John Wilson to Robert Wodrow, Esq. in Glasgow, written on July 10, 1841.
48. For the full text, in an English translation, of this letter see Wilson, *Lands of the Bible,* Volume I, pp.369-71; for much, but not all of the Hebrew text, see Volume II, p.630. The names of the signatories nowhere appear.
49. Unlike the Five Books of Moses (the *Torah*) as venerated by the Jews, the version of the *Pentateuch* accepted by the Samaritans contains a verse with the express commandment that an altar should be built on Mt.Gerizim (near the town of Nablus, i.e. the ancient city of Shechem, capital of the Biblical Northern Kingdom of Israel). For the Samaritans, Mt. Gerizim has the sanctity which the Temple Mount of Jerusalem holds for the Jews. Samaritans believe that it was on Mt. Gerizim that Abraham was commanded to sacrifice his son Isaac.

Because of the Jewish Prophet Ezra's stringent reforms against mixed marriages, and with the subsequent rejection of the Samaritans' offer to help rebuild the Jewish Temple at Jerusalem, the Samaritans had become a sect distinct from the Jews, although their ancestors were Jews who never left their homeland even when most Jews were taken captive into Babylonian exile. In 332 B.C., by permission of Alexander the Great, the Samaritans built their own temple on top of Mt.Gerizim, which had always been their holiest place of worship. Hence, their *Kiblah* (the direction to be faced in worship and in ritual) is that facing toward Mt. Gerizim. The Samaritans observe the laws of the *Pentateuch* very literally, but they do not accept the other books of the *Old Testament*, and they have none of the Jewish traditions, writings or customs which developed among Jews after the era of the *Pentateuch*.

In the 19th century the Samaritan community in the Holy Land had dwindled to such an extent that their leaders conducted correspondence with the outside world, seeking "lost" groups of Samaritans. Their hopes were falsely raised by unscrupulous Europeans trying to get hold of priceless old Samaritan manuscripts from the community in the Holy Land.

50. G. Smith, p.124.
51. In searching for information relating to the Jews of India the present author has examined the following issues of *The Oriental Christian Spectator* :

Of Series I (1830-39)
   Volume 1, 1830 : complete.
   Volume 2, 1831 : complete.
   Volume 3, 1832 : complete
   Volume 4, 1833 : complete
   Volume 5, 1834 : all issues except May, June, July.

Of Series II (1840-49)
   Volume 11, 1840 : January only.
   Volume 13, 1842 : all issues except November and December.
   Volume 16, 1846 : October only.

Of Series III (1850-59)
   1854 : November only.

Of Series IV (1860-63)
   Volume 2, 1861 : all issues except January, February, May, July, August, October and December.
   Volume 3, 1862 : all issues except April, July and August.
   Volume 4, 1863 : all issues except May-June, September-October and November-December.

The publication ceased in 1863. According to information received from the National Library in Edinburgh, in the U.S.A. Yale University (New Haven, Connecticut) owns the most complete collection of *The Oriental Christian Spectator*, i.e. volumes 2-17 (1831 through 1847).

52. An announcement in *The Oriental Christian Spectator*, Volume 17, No. 10, October 1846, p.396 (under the heading of "Books in Press") mentioned that the Mirzapore Mission (located in North India, in the southeastern part of the present State of Uttar Pradesh) reported a book entitled *"A History of the Jews*, prepared in Hindustani by Mr. Buyers of Benares", adding that it "is now being lithographed in the Persian character, and is half finished".

53. On page 565 of Smith's *Life of John Wilson*, two converts to Christianity, obviously of Jewish origin, are mentioned by name, one Mattathias Cohen, the other a Mikhail Joseph. "Joseph" might be part of a Bene Israel name; but, although "Mikhail" or "Michael" today is sometimes used as a Bene Israel name, it is not included in Rev. Wilson's own list of common Bene Israel male names of his day. (See Appendix 5) It is rather unlikely that the convert Mikhail Joseph was of the Bene Israel community. As for Mattathias Cohen, there were and are no *Cohanim* among the Bene Israel community.

54. From Smith : *The Life of Wilson*, p.617 :
   Statistics are no adequate test of such work as Dr. Wilson's. But the latest figures for 1877 show that in Bombay and the stations of the Free Church founded by him, 1071 converts

have been admitted, on the intelligent profession of their faith, since the beginning of his mission; while there were 2877 pupils and students in 56 schools.
55. Rev. W.T.Gidney : *History of the London Society for Promoting Christianity Among the Jews, from 1809 to 1908,* London Society for Promoting Christianity Among the Jews, London, 1908.
56. "German Jews" here refers, presumably, to *all* Ashkenazi (i.e. non-Sephardi) Jews and is not necessarily limited to Jews from the area of Germany.
57. These tables are based on information found in *A Brief Review of Ten Years' Missionary Labour in India between 1852 and 1861* published by Messrs. Nisbet and Company, London, 1862. Two such tables were reproduced in the November 1862 issue of *The Oriental Christian Spectator,* on pp. 547 and 548 respectively; these deal with the missions in Bengal only.
58. Rebecca Reuben : "Religious Reorganization", an article in the *Bene Israel Annual and Year Book, Volume III, 1919-1920,* edited by Rebecca Reuben, p.xviii.
59. Benjamin J. Israel : *The Bene Israel of India, Some Studies,* p.68.
60. Kehimkar : *History,* p.238.
61. Although *The Travels of Solomon* (edited by Wolff Schur at the Georg Breg Press under P. Smolenskin, Vienna) was not published until 1884, Reinemann's observations among the Bene Israel go back to mid-19th century. Somewhat later than Reinemann, another Jewish traveller, Yaakov Sapir Halevi, visited the Bene Israel, in 1860. The book about his travels is called *Even Sapir,* two volumes in one, published in Hebrew by M'kitze Nardin, L. Silverman, Lyok, 1866. It contains eight pages on the Bene Israel.
62. Rev. J. Henry Lord : *The Jewish Mission Field in the Bombay Diocese,* being a paper read before the Bombay Diocesan Conference held in March 1893, Bombay; printed at the Education Society's Steam Press, Byculla, 1894, pp.11-12.
63. Ibid., p.14.
64. Ibid., p.13.
65. Ibid., p.13.
66. Ibid., p.15.
67. Ibid., pp.25-8.
68. S.S.J.E. : The Society of St. John the Evangelist, founded in 1866, for men only, clergy and lay, of the Anglican Church. (Present headquarters are at 16 Marston St., Oxford OX41JX, England.)
69. A two-wheeled, horse-drawn carriage.
70. *On the Bombay Coast and Deccan, the Origin and the History of the Bombay Diocese, A Record of 300 Years Work for Christ in Western India,* by W. Ashley-Brown, Archdeacon of Bombay, senior Chaplain, Indian Ecclesiastical Establishment, Chaplain of Poona : published by the Society for Promoting Christian Knowledge, Northumberland Avenue, W.C.2, London, 1937, pp. 222-3. This book does not mention any Bene Israel converts.
71. H.G.Reissner : "Indian Jewish Statistics 1837-1941", in *Jewish Social Studies,* Volume XII, 1950; edited for the Conference on Jewish Relations, 1950, New York City, p.351. In 1945, it must be emphasized, the Bene Israel community was more numerous than ever before in its history, comprising about 23,000 souls.
72. For a comparison of missionary contacts with, and influences upon, the Bene Israel and the Kaifeng Jews respectively, see Isenberg : the final pages of "Paradoxical Outcome of Meeting of Bene Israel and Christian Missionaries in the Nineteenth Century", in *Jews in India,* edited by Thomas Timberg, Vikas Publishing House, Delhi, 1985; pp. 356-8.

Chapter 8
Arts and Letters

It seems that in the 19th century, although Bene Israel were skillful artisans, very few Bene Israel excelled in the fine arts or in creative writing. But Kehimkar tells us that "there arose a poet about a century and a half or two centuries ago (1690-1740) among the Bene-Israel, by name Elloji Nagawkar, surnamed Elloji Shahir i.e. Elloji the Ballad Singer." (p.228) He enjoyed the patronage of the Angria rulers and participated in singing contests at the Peshwa's court. Some of his Marathi and Hindustani songs on religious and moral themes were remembered in Kehimkar's day although they were not handed down in printed form. If Kehimkar's dating and the 20th century translation (inserted as an Appendix to Kehimkar's book on pp.283-90) are correct, the Biblical allusions and Hebrew words contained in the songs make one wonder how a Bene Israel (i.e. Elloji Shahir) was conversant with these at such an early date. Indeed, Olsvanger has inserted a footnote (p.290) saying that the style of the songs indicates a 19th century date of composition. Another famous Bene Israel singer, Robenji Isaji Nawgaonkar,[1] was born in the 1830s. He was a prolific composer of *lavnis* (extemporaneous folk poetry). Still very popular in India today, *lavnis* are performed by two contesting groups. They are an unsophisticated equivalent of the more literary, classical Indian *mushaira* or *kavi sammelan*. In *lavnis* the singer made use of puns (sometimes the Bene Israel singers used Hebrew words), riddles, acrostics, arbitrary limitations as to which letters of the alphabet were allowed to be used, etc.

It was not until the 19th century that the Bene Israel adopted the typically Hindu form of the *kirtan* as a very appealing means for religious education of the masses. *Kirtan* literally means "song", but the term also designates a form of story-telling and preaching, largely through songs, to an audience. Even today attendance at *kirtans* is a very popular pastime for both men and women in India. The Bene Israel *kirtans* were Bible stories presented in Marathi verse and sung to Hindu tunes by the *kirtankar* (singer) either solo or with choral and/or instrumental accompaniment. The songs were interspersed with simple sermons evoked by the Bible story. Because of popular demand sometimes the texts of the songs were made available in print.[2]

A Bene Israel musical group, called Subodh Prakashak, was formed for putting on *kirtan* performances. We read that "a narration, punctuated by music, about Queen Esther" was premiered by the most prolific author of Bene Israel *kirtans*, Benjamin Samson Ashtamkar, on January 6, 1895. Another *kirtan,* this one about the Maccabees, was performed by the Subodh Prakashak group on January 12, 1895. On February 2, 1895 they performed in the new synagogue (i.e. the Share Rason Synagogue). Each time their performances were followed by talks given by two different lecturers.

The missionary translation of the Bible into Marathi had been the original inspiration for the Bene Israel *kirtans*. Then, in the 1840s, teachers from Cochin, in collaboration with some Bene Israel, published translations of certain Jewish prayers from Hebrew into Marathi, as well as a book of songs and a book of rules for fixing the dates of Jewish holidays. As a result of the strange combination of influences—i.e. Hebrew language training and vernacular translation of the Bible under Christian auspices, together with an introduction to Jewish liturgy and to Jewish literature through Cochin Jewish orthodoxy—the Bene Israel Jewish spirit suddenly began to flower in the 1850s and produced an impressive array of Hebrew-Marathi books of Jewish liturgy and on other Jewish topics. This was made possible by the establishment of Jewish-owned Hebrew printing presses in Bombay.

The first Jewish printer of Hebrew in Bombay was a Cochini of Yemenite origin, Shelomo Salem Shurrabi (see above, p. 60 and Appendix 6) whose first Hebrew book was printed (lithographed) in Bombay in 1843, a book of penitential prayers.[3]

In 1874[4] a book of Hebrew *Songs of Prayer* (or Songs of Praise or Exultations) for all ritual occasions—entitled *Shirei R'nanot* in Hebrew—was prepared by a Bene Israel *hazan*,[5] Shalom Joseph Penkar. The book's contents closely follow the Cochin Jewish customary liturgy for Jewish holidays, Sabbaths, weddings, and circumcisions. On the reverse side of the book's Hebrew frontispiece is a Marathi frontispiece written in Devanagri script.[6] This lithographed edition was as much used by the Jews of Cochin as by the Bene Israel. Today it is a valuable and rare book. The present author noticed a book from this edition—frayed, brown with age, and greatly treasured as a family heirloom—on a bookshelf in the home of a Cochin Jewess in Israel. Mishael M. Caspi discusses this book, together with four other collections of Cochin Jewish prayers, in his article entitled "Wedding Customs of the Jews of Cochin according to the Book of Poems and the Songs of Praise".[7] Caspi, however, has made a mistake due partly to his lack of familiarity with Bene Israel surnames: he attributes the compilation of this book to some (western?) source whom he calls (in English) "Salom Fincher" rather than correctly transliterating the Hebrew letters *pay, yud, nun, caf, resh* as Penkar.

Other Bene Israel Penkars also published some Hebrew prayer books. In 1889 Ezekiel Benjamin Penkar brought out *The Daily Prayers* "translated from Hebrew into Marathi by Joseph Ezekiel Rajpurkar (see below, pp. 93-94), printed for the use of the Bene Israel community by Aaron Jacob Divekar at the Anglo-Jewish and Vernacular Press, Bombay". A second edition of this book was published by Hyam Ezekiel Penkar, printed by Simeon Jacob Kharilkar at the Bombay Hebrew Publishing and Printing Press, Bombay, 1934. The content of this prayer book varies considerably from Shalom Joseph Penkar's *Shirei R'nanot*.

Eighty-eight titles of Hebrew books authored by Baghdadis, and fifty-eight Hebrew books written by Bene Israel were published in Bombay. Hebrew printing started at a later date in Poona where the first Hebrew press was owned by one Ezekiel Samuel Talkar, a Bene Israel who published six Hebrew titles between 1870 and 1871. The second Hebrew press in Poona was established in 1888 by a Baghdadi printer, Abraham Solomon David Hai Yehezkiel; it also lasted only a short time during which nine Hebrew titles were published. Another Poona printer, called Vithal Sakharam Agnihotri, printed a *Hebrew-Marathi Haggadah* in 1874.[8]

But the first *Hebrew-Marathi Haggadah* (the text for the service to be conducted at home on the eve of Passover) was published in Bombay in 1846. Individuals from different groups of oriental Jewry (a Cochin Jew, two Bene Israel, and a Baghdadi Jew) who were then in Bombay collaborated in the publication of this work. Walter Fischel contributed a short but valuable introduction to a facsimile reproduction (in reduced size) of this *Haggadah of 1846*.[9] Fischel cites seven details in which this *haggadah* varies from customary *Haggadoth*, adding that:

Despite these and other discrepancies, due mainly to a borrowing from other versions of the *Haggadah*, from Cochin, Yemen, Baghdad and Livorno, the text does not constitute an original rite in itself or a special independent liturgy.

    This *Marathi Haggadah* is the first Hebrew book printed (lithographed) in India with illustrations....It is noteworthy that for instance, each of the three Mazzoth, the Cohen, Levi and Israel, are differentiated in the drawings....by three different conspicuous signs[10] [i.e. by, respectively, one, two and three protrusions from the circumference of each round matzah].

This *Haggadah* was very much in demand. It was re-published in Poona in 1874, in Bombay in 1890, and again in 1935 (with a new title, *The Institution of Passover*). B.J.Israel has supplied (privately) some additional comments and translations of the Marathi preface and title page of each of these various editions. His notes are reproduced below as Appendix 7 because they disclose additional facts which do not appear in Fischel's Introduction to the *1846 Hebrew-Marathi Haggadah* and because they give the reader certain insights into the Bene Israel community at that time.

    In 1911 another Bene Israel *Haggadah* was published. This one was unique because its full Hebrew text was presented in transliteration into the Indian Devanagri script instead of being printed in Hebrew script.

    Throughout the second half of the 19th century several Bene Israel, most of whom had themselves been recipients of missionary-school education, published a variety of books in Marathi, on Jewish subjects, translations from the Hebrew liturgy for the daily prayers and for each of the Jewish holidays, and translations of other important Hebrew writings. Benjamin Samson Ashtamkar (Bombay and Poona), Elijah Shalom Walwutkar (Poona), and Joseph Ezekiel Rajpurkar (Bombay) — all were prolific in this field. All were scholars of the Hebrew language without, however, being "Hebrew scholars" as that term has come to be understood in the Jewish world : a person referred to as a Hebrew scholar or as a learned Jew is usually a person steeped in knowledge not only of the Old Testament, but also of most, or even all, the Jewish commentaries on the Old Testament, or the Talmud, or the entire body of customary Jewish law, and of Jewish literature through the ages. The relatively few Bene Israel real scholars of Hebrew of the 19th century were not specialists of that sort, but they were proficient in Hebrew; and, in the course of translating into Marathi all the Jewish liturgy and many other Jewish writings, they did absorb a great deal of Jewish knowledge.

    The life of Joseph Ezekiel Rajpurkar (1834-1905) illustrates the constellation of forces and relationships (Bene Israel, Baghdadi and Christian) that prevailed in Bombay and in the Konkan as a whole during this period. His family was one of the few Bene Israel families devoted to the field of education in a period during which military service was still regarded as the most desirable career for Bene Israel. His father, Ezekiel Joseph Rajpurkar, was Superintendent of Schools of the Free Church Mission in Bombay and Kolaba District. Joseph's school and college education proceeded under the tutelage of such Christian missionaries as the Rev. John Wilson, Dr. J.M.Mitchell, and the Rev. R. Nesbit. He began his career in 1860 as an assistant teacher in the David Sassoon Benevolent Institution of the Arabic-speaking Jews. After five years he became Headmaster of this school, a post he held for forty years during which several members (who later became famous) of the Sassoon family attended the same school. The difference between Christian and Jewish interpretation of certain passages of the Bible stimulated Joseph Ezekiel Rajpurkar to master the Hebrew language so as to be able to study the Hebrew sources directly in the original. In 1871 he was appointed Examiner in Hebrew at Bombay University and in 1876 also became Examiner in Arts. He was made a Fellow of Bombay University in 1879. In 1890 he was appointed as Justice of the Peace. During his lifetime he delivered many lectures on the Hebrew language and writings, as well as on Jewish religion as such. On these subjects he has a total of twenty volumes to his credit, being either original writings or translations from the Hebrew into Marathi. His first book, *The Confession of Sins on the Day of Atonement,* a translation from Hebrew into Marathi, was published in 1858.

One avenue for Bene Israel publication of tracts on Jewish subjects in the Marathi language was the Subodh Prakash Samaj (Society for the Diffusion of Knowledge), especially established for this purpose. (The publication and distribution of Christian religious tracts had long been standard procedures of Christian missionaries.) A note appended to the Subodh Prakash Samaj booklet entitled *Peace,* published in 1891, had this to say about the organization :

INTIMATION TO ALL BENE ISRAEL BRETHREN :

Dear Brethren, It is now five years since the establishment of the Subodh Prakash Samaj in this city of Bombay. The aim of the Society is to print very short, instructive books, and place them on sale at prices within the reach of all....It is the intention of this Society to print and publish books which will increase the religious knowledge of our younger generation and will increase the fear and love of God in them... In some Israelite homes "Malidada re Malidada" or "Yashodachè Palna" ["Mr.Gardener, oh Mr. Gardener" or "The Cradle of Yashoda"—Yashoda being the mother of the Hindu god Krishna], or other songs composed by Christians or Hindus used to be sung. Now songs composed by an Israelite are available... The Society meets every fortnight and discusses worthwhile subjects....The Society is making every effort to insure that the work it has undertaken is efficiently carried out. In this connection we appeal to you to give the Society the maximum support. Thereby you will earn its gratitude.

Bombay dated 15th August, 1891. Signed, David Solomon Pezarkar.

The annual subscription to the Society was only four *annas,* a very small sum.[11]

There exist rather substantial listings of Bene Israel publications in India. These lists appeared in *The Bene Israel Annual and Year Book,* edited by Rebecca Reuben, in Volumes I, II and III, 1917-1920.[12] For the Volume III list of Bene Israel publications, see Appendix 8. The earliest date of publication mentioned in Miss Reuben's lists is 1842, the year in which *Hebrew Penitential Prayers,* a book written by Solomon David Divekar and Haeem Isaac Galsoorkar, was published. All but a few publications by Bene Israel authors and translators appeared in Bombay, the earlier ones among them having been lithographed rather than printed. Despite a few omissions, Miss Reuben's lists of publications are impressively comprehensive. They show that most of the writing by Bene Israel authors was in the Marathi language, only a very few titles appearing in English.

The first published piece of Bene Israel creative writing in Marathi was Bahais Joseph Talkar's *Gul and Sanobar,* published in 1867.[13] Soon thereafter appeared *Bago Bahar*, a novel by one M.D.Talkar.[14]

Several Bene Israel periodicals in Marathi appeared during the last quarter of the 19th century : weeklies, fortnightlies, monthlies, and annuals. Very occasionally they included articles in their original English, taken from American or British Jewish papers.

Arts and Letters   95

Many articles which were published in these periodicals served to educate the Bene Israel in things Jewish. These publications also provided a forum for airing community controversies. A thorough combing of all of these periodicals, particulary those articles written in Marathi, should be undertaken in order to bring to light old Bene Israel customs, attitudes and other types of information which have been forgotten or remain unclear. The 19th century Bene Israel periodicals were, in order of their appearance :

Satya Prakash (subtitled *Or Emeth* in Hebrew), *Light of Truth;* 1877-84.
T'ruah (a Hebrew word meaning *Trumpet Call*); 1878-79.
Israeli Dharmadeep, Lamp of Judaism; 1881-85 and 1893-96.
Stri Soundharyalatika; 1886. *The Tendril of Female Beauty* (articles on female education, cooking, needlework, dressmaking, health, etc.)
Israeli Gyan Sangraha, Compilation (or treasury) *of Jewish Knowledge;* 1886.
Bene Israel : 1893-1900.
Israel Mitra, Friend of Israel; 1898-99; and 1916-21.
Israel Ashram, House (or retreat or refuge) *of Israel.*

(The Bene Israel periodicals of the 20th century will be discussed below on pp. 238-40.)
B.J.Israel points out that in their 19th century periodicals the Bene Israel show that they

> had begun to regard the missionaries as enemies rather than as friends (as they had done earlier) and had begun to answer them back when mission activity began to be overtly conversionist — the Scottish and the American missionaries were much subtler than the English, who had no hesitation in attacking Judaism and the Talmud. Another thing the Bene Israel Journals bring out is the amount of material which was being fed to our people from Jewish sources in the U.S.A. and England, and which was received indiscriminately whether it was orthodox or reform, whether fundamentalist or critical — all was grist to the mill. This confirms my view that the opening to the West was one of the reasons why the Bene Israel ceased to look to Cochin and to the Baghdadis.[15]

There was a very talented Bene Israel artist who also bore the surname Talkar. It was he who painted the portrait of Haeem S. Kehimkar (which Olsvangar included as one of the photographs in Kehimkar's book *The History of the Bene Israel of India,* a reproduction of which is presented elsewhere as photograph no. 1).[16] This artist married a Janjira princess, was converted to Islam, and changed his name, to Fayizee Rahmin (thus retaining his father's name, Rahamim.)

NOTES

1. Kehimkar, *History,* pp.229, 230, 278-90 (a few songs of Elloji and Robenji).
2. The *kirtan* form of group religious edification never developed among the Cochin Jews, mainly because all along they had had synagogues as the center of their religious life, and also beause of other factors in Kerala which did not pertain to the Bene Israel in the Konkan. However even without any thorough analysis, there are evident similarities between the traditional folksongs of the Bene Israel women and those of the Cochin Jewish women — in regard to Biblical content and to the occasions for singing specific songs. But the content and the language of many of the traditional Malayalam folksongs of the Cochin Jewish women — replete as they are with archaic

Malayalam words, Biblical stories, Jewish customs, and the history of the community — indicate that they originated in the Middle Ages, while the Bene Israel women's folksongs with Biblical content can date back only to late 18th century at the very earliest. On the other hand, those Bene Israel women's Marathi folksongs which have other than Biblical content (such as lullabies, wedding songs, etc.) must go back to pre-Jewish revival days (see below p. 229). The occasional Biblical reference now within the texts of these songs probably represent later insertions into the older Bene Israel folksongs. It would be worthwhile to study those now traditional Marathi folksongs of the Bene Israel women which tell Bible stories, in order to see what, if any relation they may have to the texts of well-known Bene Israel *kirtan* songs, and also to compare them with the Biblical folksongs of the Cochin Jewish women.

3. The first Hebrew book printed in Calcutta was printed by the Baghdadi Jew, Elazar ben Mari Aharon Saadiya Araki Hacohen. The book was also lithographed and it too appeared in 1843.
4. This volume was published in 1874 but it was first registered in 1847.
5. Abraham Yaari: "Hebrew Printing in the East" (in Hebrew), Part II India and Baghdad, Special Supplement to *Kiryat Sepher*, Volume XVII, Jerusalem, at the University Press, 1940, p.74.
6. The only part of the book appearing in Marathi is this second frontispiece, the book's title in Marathi being *Ivri Gitasangraha*.
7. Mishael Maswari Caspi: "Wedding Customs of the Jews of Cochin According to the Book of Poems and the Songs of Praise," in *Jewish Tradition in the Diaspora, Studies in Memory of Professor Walter J. Fischel*, edited by Mishael M. Caspi, Judah L. Magnes Memorial Museum, Berkeley, California, 1981, p.231.
8. Yaari: *Hebrew Printing in the East*, pp. 52-71, pp.83-7.
9. This was issued from New York in 1968, entitled *The Haggadah of the Bene Israel of India*, as Volume VIII in a series of interesting old *Haggadoth*, published annually by The Orphan Hospital Ward of Israel, 673 Broadway, New York, 48 pages.
10. These quotations are from Prof. Fischel's Introduction to the facsimile reproduction. The pages of the Introduction are not numbered.
11. The "Intimation to All Bene Israel Brethren" and the following list of Marathi titles published by the Subodh Prakash Samaj have been translated from Marathi into English by B.J. Israel and appear here with his permission.

Serial Number	Year of Publication	Title	Author
1.	1887	Songs of Praise of God	Benjamin Samson Ashtamkar
2.	1888	Songs of Praise of God	David Solomon Pezarkar
3.	1889	Prayer	David Solomon Pezarkar
4.	1891	Peace	Abraham Solomon Pezarkar
5.	1891	Hebrew is the Language of Prayer	Benjamin Samson Ashtamkar
6.	1891	*The Talmud and the School System of the Talmud	Isaac Abraham Talegaonkar
7.	(not listed in the Bene Israel Annual & Year Book; see below, note 12)		
8.	1894	Account of Queen Esther	Aaron Samson Ashtamkar
9.	1894	Greatness of Patience, or An Account of a Great Soul, Job	David Solomon Pezarkar
10.	1895	The Greatness of Faith in God or The Heroism of the Glorious Maccabees	David Solomon Pezarkar
11.	[not listed in the Annual and Year Book, but must have been *The Torah of Moshe*]		
12.	1895	Why Should I Remain a Jew?	Samuel Haeem Pezarkar

* This book (No. 6.) consists of Talegaonkar's long essay in Marathi on the Talmud, and his Marathi translation of an English essay by Rabbi B. Spiers on "The School System of the Talmud".

Some other Bene Israel titles in Marathi were
> *Tefilat Hodesh* (Prayer of the Month)
> *Shashtraniyam* (Religious Ceremonies)
> *Travel to Jerusalem*
> *How to Abide by the Jewish Religion*
> *Biography of Sir Moses Montefiore*
> *The Book of Esther and Purim Songs*
> *What Is Unique About the Jewish Religion?*
> *Stories and Proverbs from The Talmud*
> *Questions and Answers About the Jewish Religion for Children to Memorize*
> *The Messiah — What, When and How?*

12. In each of its three years of publication *The Bene Israel Annual and Year Book* included a list of Bene Israel publications, that of the first year being the least comprehensive. In Vol. I (Bombay 1917-1918) on pp.98-106 is a list of "Bene Israel Authors and Publications", exclusive of periodicals, and listed according to the alphabetical order of the authors' names. In Vol. II (Bombay 1918-1919) on pp. 101-13, again according to the alphabetical order of authors' names, there is a more extensive list, and this is followed on p. 114 by a "List of Periodicals", with the dates during which these periodicals existed and the names of their respective editors. Vol. III (Junagadh 1919-1920) on pp. 56-78 also includes a "List of Bene Israel Authors and Publications", but this time the titles are arranged chronologically, beginning with the year 1842; the "List of Bene Israel Periodicals" is on pp. 79-80. In all three volumes the date of publication is given for each title; and, whenever the publication was in Marathi, it appears in these lists in Devanagri script, sometimes with translation of the Marathi title into English also. The vast majority of titles are in Marathi; the names of all authors and editors are printed in Latin type. The lists from Vol. III are the ones reproduced below as Appendix 8.

13. B.J.Talkar is not mentioned by Rebecca Reuben in any of her lists of Bene Israel publications, but is mentioned by Moses Ezekiel in his *History and Culture of the Bene-Israel of India*, (pp. 78 and 80) and by Walter Fischel in his *Literary Activities of the Bene Israel* (p.9). Also, Moses Ezekiel says that Bahais Joseph Talkar in 1874 published a *History of the Bene Israel since their Advent in India* (p. 80); but Rebecca Reuben's list mentions Haeem Joseph Talkar and David Haeem Divekar as co-authors of this title. Whoever the author(s) was/were, the present writer located no copy of this book, but would have liked to have been able to compare it with Kehimkar's *History of the Bene Israel*.

14. According both to Moses Ezekiel and Walter Fischel. Rebecca Reuben mentions a Moses Daniel Talkar as the author of *Bago Bahar* and adds this information : "Translated from the English — 1869-73"

15. From a private communication from B.J.Israel to the present author.

16. Mr. H. D. Haeems, Kehimkar's grandson (i.e. son of Kehimkar's youngest son David) remembers a portrait of his maternal grandmother which this artist also painted

Chapter 9
Caste-Like Patterns

As the various Jewish teachers from Cochin died, no one came to take their place among the Bene Israel and the hold of the synagogue was loosened. A further complication was the lack of goodwill between the Bene Israel and the local community of the so-called Baghdadi Jews.

In the present context, the terms "Baghdadi" and "Iraqi", strictly speaking, refer to Jews whose native place, or that of their immediate ancestors, was in the general vicinity of the Tigris and Euphrates Rivers, for centuries a center of Jewish learning and culture. The term "Arabian Jews" is also used and includes not only Baghdadis or Iraqis, but also Jews from many parts of the Ottoman Empire, Aleppo, the Holy Land, Damascus, Aden, Yemen, etc.; all of them were Arabic-speaking and steeped in orthodoxy and Jewish tradition. The Bene Israel also included in this latter category Jews in India who had come from Persia (of whom there were several in Bombay), although these Jews spoke Persian rather than Arabic. In the Bombay area in particular the term "Baghdadi" in its overall meaning seems to have been preferred (although it is/was often used interchangeably with "Arabian") to include all of these peoples. We shall therefore use the term "Baghdadi" in its cover-all meaning hereafter in discussing their relations with the Bene Israel.

Jewish merchants from Baghdad and Aleppo are known to have flourished in Surat at least since 1770[1] for a few decades, until the commercial importance of Surat declined while that of Bombay rose at the very end of the 18th century, when some of these merchants transferred to Bombay. Rabbi David D'Beth Hillel (p.116 of his Madras publication) has written that

> I arrived in Bombay in October 1828 and remained there forty days in great inconvenience. I found there few Jews from Arabia and they are domineered over by Solomon Yakob a rich man and the first Arabian Jew who established himself in Bombay. He is a man of bad disposition and notorious character....and is conciliated by flatterers of the grossest kind. I had not been accustomed to such dishonorable subterfuges and I am a man who worships only my Creator. For this cause and on account of my refusing to conform to their unlawful usages which they have learnt from the Arabs and the Hindoos, and concerning which there is a prohibition in Leviticus 18·3 verse, "In their statutes", etc. I was the object of his persecution.

This statement about "their unlawful usages" would indicate that the Arabic-speaking Jews in Bombay at that time were themselves following customs forbidden in *Leviticus*. Later, during Rabbi David D'Beth Hillel's second stay in Bombay (1829-31), he observed that

> there are about twenty families of Jews collected from Arabia who have hired a small house from a Parsee for divine service (p.132); [and that]

Caste-Like Patterns

since the Arabian Jews came to Bombay they [the Bene Israel] commenced to learn some of the Hebrew language and purchased some of the Hebrew books. (p.134)

This introduces a fourth source of Hebrew instruction for the Bene Israel : the Cochin Jews, Yemenite Jews, Christian missionaries, and the Baghdadi Jews (whom Rabbi D'Beth Hillel here refers to as Jews from Arabia).

Solomon Yakob (Seleman or Silliman Jacob) is also mentioned by Michael Sargon (see above, pp. 68-9). According to the Rev. Lord, however, (in his *The Jews in India and the Far East*, p.90) the first Baghdadi Jew to settle in Bombay was not Solomon Jacob, but Jacob Semah who arrived in 1777, having come from Surat. Be that as it may, after the founding of the first Bene Israel Synagogue in 1796, the early Baghdadis coming into Bombay were made welcome in the one and only Bene Israel synagogue of that time, and when Baghdadis died they were buried in the Bene Israel cemetery. Kehimkar names Silliman Jacob and his daughter specifically as having been buried there.[2] (See above, p.38, n. 17).

David S. Sassoon (1792-1864), originally of Baghdad, arrived in Bombay in 1832 when, according to Cecil Roth, there were some Baghdadi families in Bombay who were already worshipping on their own "in a small house, hired from a Parsee and approximately adapted for synagogue use. At their head was Solomon Jacob."[3]

On the other hand, the Rev. Lord (p.90) clearly states that

It is on record that when the Sassoon family first came to Bombay from Baghdad in the very early days of the White Jewish community in this city, the members of that family at first frequented the synagogue of the Bene-Israel community, and were indebted to them for the ministrations of their religion.

Yet we know from Michael Sargon that as early as 1827 the "White Jews" did not mix with the Bene Israel. (See above p. 68) Fischel seems to support Rev. Lord's contention by documenting cooperative relations between the Baghdadis and the Bene Israel at least until 1833 :

The prevailing unity and harmony expressed itself in the fact that the leaders of both groups submitted jointly petitions to the President and Governor-in-Council of Bombay in November, 1831, and September, 1833, in which the leaders of the Jewish merchants of Arabia, inhabitants and residents of Bombay, as well as those of the "Native Jew Caste", voiced their grievances in regards to matters connected with the Jewish cemetery (General Public Department, Bombay 1833, No. 284,fols. 163ff). These petitions were signed in Hebrew and English by the "Arabian" and in Marathi by the "native" Jews.

Then Fischel goes on to cite the incident which led to the definite rupture between the two communities :

This harmony did, however, not last very long. In October 1836 a petition was sent to the Bombay authorities signed by Haskel Abdul Nubee, David S. Sassoon and eight other leading "Arabian" Jews requesting that a partition-wall be erected to divide the burial-grounds of the two groups....[stating] "Two components and distinct tribes of Jews inhabit this country, one having adopted the customs of the natives of India, and the other faithful to their Arabian fathers, which is that of the petitioners." They are, as the petition continues, "For a long while in a state of painful excitement against each other, occasioned by the place of their sepulchre where they...bury their departed friends and relatives....unproperly and indiscriminately preserved."

The petition went on to explain : "To obviate for the future any disturbances or objections whatever on this important matter between the tribe above alluded to and that of the petitioners, they readily propose and agree that a wall should be built as soon as possible in the middle part of the burying place...."[4]

Kehimkar adds (p.163) that "Government by their letter dated 17 February 1837 declined to comply with the request." Much later, one of David Sassoon's sons purchased land for the Baghdadi Chinchpokli Cemetery.

The first Baghdadi families who settled in Bombay were very wealthy, and several Bombay Baghdadis continued to be people of means, while the Bene Israel, even when urbanized and when many of them were educated and somewhat westernized, were in moderate to meagre financial circumstances. Besides, the life-style of the Baghdadis was very different from that of the Bene Israel. The Baghdadis had absorbed practically nothing that was Indian and did not speak the Marathi language although many knew some basic Hindustani. They kept the orthodox Jewish customs and lived according to the minutiae of *halacha*. To the Bene Israel many of the rules of *halacha* were a new addition to Judaism as they had known it, and many Bene Israel were pragmatic and/or eclectic in the degree to which they accommodated themselves to this complicated body of Jewish tradition so recently brought to their attention — particularly if they were poor and if it impinged upon the (by then) prevailing western system of education and of office employment. The poor could not afford two complete sets of all eating and cooking utensils in order to observe strictly *kosher* food regulations; such utensils as they did own were mostly made of clay. When they could afford to eat meat, they would eat only *kosher* meat, i.e. no meat at all if *kosher* fare were not available. If they had only one pot to use, when changing from cooking in it anything involving milk products to something containing meat, they did first make that utensil *kosher* by causing water in it to boil by immersing in it a heated stone. Yet many *hazanim* from Cochin and Baghdadi *Cohanim* who officiated in Bene Israel synagogues would not eat in Bene Israel homes because they feared that these households did not measure up to every prerequisite of *kashrut*.

Some Bene Israel rode to and attended work on the Sabbath. But they did what little they could to lessen the sin. Large numbers of Bene Israel were employed as clerks in offices and had to report for work usually between 10 and 10 : 30 a.m. So, first the synagogue of the Israelite School (see below, p.170), and subsequently the Tiferet Israel Prayer Hall[5] obliged by arranging to have Saturday morning services between 7 and 9 a.m. instead of continuing the services into later hours of the morning. They considerably shortened the Sabbath morning service by having only one *Amidah* (the long section of silent prayers read by the entire congregation while standing, is normally repeated at three different times on Saturday morning).

In 1876, in a request for financial assistance to the newly established Bene Israel Israelite School, as "Answers to Questions Put by the Anglo-Jewish Association to the Directors of the Bene-Israel Benevolent Society and Mr. Haeem Samuel (Kehimkar) of Poona", the Bene Israel painted the following picture of their Jewish inter-relationships, making no mention of any Baghdadi discrimination against them :

The Baghdad and Cochin Jews attend our synagogues, and we theirs, and we eat together. We had the same burying ground until recently. We converse with each other in Hindoostan dialect [Urdu] which is composed of Arabic, Persian and Sanskrit and is the lingua franca of India. There exists a distance between us, chiefly owing to difference in costume and language. We have among us a class of Beni Israel whom we designate "Kala Israel"or "Black Israel" (see above p. 67 and below pp. 104-7). Between them and ourselves no inter-marriages ever take place. They are descendants of Beni-Israel with heathen wives. Some of these are also proselytes [to Judaism]. They have separate burying grounds. There are no congregations of the Beni Israel whose customs differ from those of the Beni Israel in Bombay....Most of our people having providentially settled in the Hindoo territories were looked upon as outcaste. This afforded a protection which otherwise we should not have obtained. The Portuguese at Goa made some attempts at conversion, but they did not find many of our people within their reach.

The place of the Prophet Elijah among the Bene Israel is of unusual importance, and this was an additional feature which differentiated them from the Baghdadis, even though all Jewish groups have a closer and warmer feeling for the Prophet Elijah than for any other prophet (see below pp. 112 and 113). Some of the ways in which the Bene Israel gave prominence to the Prophet Elijah were completely foreign to the Baghdadis.

Toward the end of the 19th century the Baghdadis numbered about 1,000 in Bombay. Having a fairer skin color than the majority of Bene Israel, and being relative newcomers to India, the Baghdadis made every effort to identify themselves with the European inhabitants of the city. Before the advent of Indian Independence their success in doing so, and their wealth, placed them on a socially higher plane than the Bene Israel. They built their own synagogue in 1861, and usually shunned all contact with the Bene Israel community. Paradoxically, the Baghdadis, who were so un-Indian and such very orthodox Jews, in preventing the Bene Israel from being called upon to read the Torah in Baghdadi synagogues, acted in way which is untenable in relations between Jew and Jew. The Baghdadi argument, however, was that they not only saw that the Bene Israel were not practicing every bit of *halachic* ritual, but they believed some Bene Israel were not *halachically* pure Jews from birth — displaying an attitude akin to Hindu discriminatory caste behaviour. It is rather strange that it took the Baghdadis so many years — years during which they used Bene Israel religious facilities and maintained religious relations with them — before they "discovered" them to be *halachically* impure. If, during the period of sharing, the Baghdadis had, in a friendly manner, undertaken to give the Bene Israel a thorough grounding in Judaism (supplementing the work of the Cochini Jewish teachers among the Bene Israel), and if this effort had been successful, at that time making every thing about the Bene Israel *halachically* acceptable, the subsequent history of Baghdadi-Bene Israel relations would have been somewhat different from what it actually turned out to be. Even so, the very many points of difference in aspirations and in background of the two communities would inevitably have created caste-like barriers between them, given the Indian context and coupled with the Baghdadi preference to disassociate themselves from native Indians (inclusive of the Bene Israel). Hence, no Baghdadi-Bene Israel intermarriages, etc.

The Baghdadi attitude toward the relatively few Bene Israel who lived in Calcutta was more liberal than in Bombay and Poona. Even in the 1870s and 1880s in Calcutta Bene Israel were allowed to sit anywhere in Baghdadi synagogues and to be called up for honors during the reading from the Torah. Also there were some Baghdadi-Bene Israel intermarriages in Calcutta. Perhaps relations between Baghdadis and Bene Israel in Calcutta were generally far less prejudiced just because in Calcutta there were so few Bene Israel.[6]

The focal argument upon which the Arabic-speaking Jews in Bombay based their allegation of Bene Israel impurity centered on the facts that, in cases of Bene Israel divorce, there was no *kosher* certificate of divorce; and that the Bene Israel had never observed the orthodox rules of *Yibum* and *Halitzah*. *Yibum* is the Hebrew word for "levirate marriage", i.e. a man's marriage to his brother's widow. *Halitzah* (which literally means "untying") has been defined as

> The ceremony of taking off a brother-in-law's shoe by the widow of a brother who had died childless, through which ceremony he is released from the obligation of marrying her, and she becomes free to marry whomever she desires (Deuteronomy XXV, 5-10). It may be noted that only one brother-in-law need perform the ceremony. The old custom of the levirate marriage (Genesis XXXVIII, 8) is thus modified in the Deuteronomic code by permitting the surviving brother to refuse to marry his brother's widow, provided he submits to the ceremony of *halitzah*.[7]

What worried the orthodox Jews was the technicality that if a Bene Israel divorcee or widow remarried without, respectively, a Jewish divorce certificate, or without having gone through the ritual of *halitzah*, any children of the remarriage and the children's descendents would be illegitimate children according to Jewish law and could not be considered to be *halachically* pure Jews. The incidence of divorce (see below, p.138) and of widow remarriage (see below, p.138-9) among the Bene Israel was anyway probably less than the average among any other Jewish community because of the prevailing Hindu ambience against both practices. Nevertheless, the entire Bene Israel community was suspect in the eyes of the Arabic-speaking Jews because of those few Bene Israel women who—in the past when Jewish divorce certificates and the *halitzah* ritual were not common practices among the Bene Israel—either had been divorced or whose husbands had died childless.

So the Baghdadis considered themselves superior to the Bene Israel. They believed that the Bene Israel were not entitled to "pure" Jewish status. Eventually, in Bombay and Poona, they refused to accept Bene Israel for the purpose of a *minyan* even though at the beginning Baghdadis in Bombay had had no compunctions against worshipping in the Bene Israel synagogue and had been counted as part of the Bene Israel *minyan*. Nor would the Baghdadis intermarry with the Bene Israel. Moreover, the ample Baghdadi charitable funds and institutions were not made available to needy Bene Israel, whereas needy Baghdadis could always rely upon these funds and also upon Baghdadi enterprises for employment and other forms of assistance. Stanley Jackson in his book, *The Sassoons*, tells that in the early 1880s the Sassoons' fellow Baghdadi Jews had "earned rapid promotion as overseers and managers [in the Sassoon mills], and shiploads of eager recruits soon began to arrive from Baghdad. They were promised full employment and the now standard Sassoon guarantees of Hebrew schools, trade apprenticeship for their children, synagogues, medical care and holy burial grounds."[8]

The first instance of Sassoon-family financial aid given directly to the Bene Israel, however, was the donation in 1882 to help the Israelite School (see below, 171-2, n.4 & 5) which was a Bene Israel institution.[9] Furthermore, this Sassoon aid was given only after the Anglo-Jewish Association of London had taken the school under its wing. Sassoons also aided the Israelite School Building Fund. A David Sassoon Hebrew Scholarship had been endowed at Bombay University and most of the recipients of this scholarship happened to be Bene Israel because it was mainly Bene Israel, rather than Baghdadis, who were studying Hebrew as a second language at the university.

The Anglo-Jewish Association at one time had high opes of bringing about a rapprochement between the Bene Israel and the Baghdadis. *The Jewish Chronicle* (London) of February 9, 1883 (p.3), recorded that :

> Notwithstanding that they practise all Jewish observances, the Beni-Israel in Bombay are looked down upon by the Arab Jews....owing to a custom having prevailed among them of marrying Hindoo women. They thereby lost caste in the sight of the pure Jews, who....regarded them in the same light as in England the Portuguese Jews did their German brethren [sic !]....About five or six years ago the Anglo-Jewish Association established a branch in Bombay, the members of which belonged exclusively to the Bene Israel. Last year, on the occasion of the distribution of prizes to the pupils of the new school, founded by this branch with the aid of the London Council,[10] an *entente* was established between the two communities through the circumstance that the ceremony of the day was presided over by the Hon. Solomon David Sassoon, the most prominent member of the 'Baghdad' community. This *entente* has now been further strengthened through the judicious action of Mr. David Schloss, who has succeeded in re-organizing the existing Branch, which now included members of both the Arab and the Beni Israel communities. In fact, with the exception of Mr. Haeem Samuel (Kehimkar), the honorary officers consist entirely of 'pure' Jews. The difference in the vernacular, the one speaking Arabic and the other the Marathi dialect, will for some years prevent the intimacy between the two bodies from becoming of the closest character, but with a more thorough diffusion in their schools of a knowledge of the English language, this difficulty will eventually be removed and there is no reason why the Beni Israel and the Arab Jews should not be merged into one important and extensive community.

The prognosis proved to be very unrealistic.

On their part, the Bombay Bene Israel actually preferred to keep apart from the Baghdadis, and not merely as a reaction to the Baghdadi superiority complex. To the Bene Israel the typically Indian tradition of strict endogamy was a powerful factor; also, the Bene Israel found the Baghdadi way of life distasteful. In the eyes of the Bene Israel, the Baghdadi children were less disciplined and more boisterous than other children in India; the average Baghdadis did not encourage education for their daughters; and, in general, they did not place as much emphasis as did the Bene Israel on higher education (even though Baghdadi scholarships were available especially for Baghdadis) because they knew that a job was waiting for them in the Sassoon Mills whether they studied or not, and that *they* could rise to the position of head clerk or of weaving master, and receive good salaries. Negative feelings on the part of the Bene Israel toward Baghdadis were also engendered by the fact that Baghdadis followed many superstitious practices. Another aspect very distasteful to the Bene Israel was the sight of Baghdadi women sitting on the roadside, or working in the Baghdadi-owned eating stalls by the wayside.[11] Both sides no doubt magnified their respective objections to each other, and not until very recently did a rapprochement of sorts take place. But, certain manifestations of separateness were attributable neither to bigotry nor to ideas of "caste impurity" — they were simply practical arrangements in consideration for difference in custom as practised by Jewish communities of varying backgrounds. Thus, in Calcutta's Baghdadi Jewish cemetery, separate sections were marked off not only for the Bene Israel but also for Cochin Jews and for western Jews (because each community practised somewhat different burial customs).

A situation very analogous to sub-caste behavior existed *within* the Bene Israel community itself. Strizower has written at length on the caste-like aspects of the Bene

Israel from within the group and also in respect of relations with their Hindu neighbors.[12] Accounting for the fact that Judaism elsewhere did not evolve along these lines, Strizower observes that "certain aspects of Bene Israel assimilation can readily be duplicated in other Jewish communities" but that "The peculiarity of Indian Jewry's situation lies in the fact that *it is assimilated to a system not usually associated with Judaism* — unlike Islam and Christianity which have confronted Judaism for many centuries."[13] [Emphasis supplied]

Even though strictly speaking Hindu castes and sub-castes consist only of members of the four *varnas* (see above, p. 16 n.48), the word "caste" is often (mis)used (see above p. 50) when designating specific Indian non-caste communities because a caste-like mentality and structure pervaded most non-Hindu-caste communities living in India, and much of this is still retained to this day. The British Government, in documents and letters, referred to the Bene Israel as a caste. Kehimkar too repeatedly refers to the Bene Israel as a caste as, for instance, when he describes the officers of a Bene Israel synagogue and states that the appointment of Reader and Sexton is made by the Leader of the synagogue "and is confirmed by the *caste* [emphasis supplied] in a meeting [of the general assembly of the synagogue congregants] held for that purpose"; or that the synagogue Leader takes advice from the Councillors "in all matters of *caste* questions [i.e. of the Bene Israel community]."[14] Caste-conditioned Bene Israel behavior shows up where Hindu ideas of untouchability have reinforced Jewish dietary rules, as illustrated by Kehimkar's statement that "The Bene Israel never employ as servants the Mahar and the Mang castes, who use as articles of food dead beasts and fowls, a touch of which alone defiles a Bene Israel."[15] Not only did the Bene Israel keep their distance from untouchable carrion-eaters, but out of respect for and in imitation of their caste-Hindu neighbors, Bene Israel in general abstained from beef-eating altogether even though Bene Israel could have eaten beef if slaughtered according to regulations of *kashrut*.

The Bene Israel community itself was divided into so-called *Gora* (white) and *Kala* (black) sub-groups. This dichotomy does not correlate with a person's actual skin color. But the terminology reflects the widespread Indian concern about skin color. It is expressed in the Indian term for "caste", *varna*, which literally means "color" and which is the generic term applicable to all Hindu caste society. The term does not, however, apply to non-caste communities. Actual skin color has today[16] no correlation with the *varna* hierarchy. Community labels descriptive of dark skin color (and in India such labels are not only peculiar to the Bene Israel and Cochin Jews) are *not* literal in meaning. Members of such groups are not all of uniform skin color. Light-color group designations do, however, always signify higher status, and imply an emphasis on the preservation of this status. The late Prof. Dr. Umar Rolf von Ehrenfels, former Head of the Department of Anthropology at Madras University, shows in his writings[17] that color consciousness, if not actual prejudice, often interwoven with concomitant differences in social organization became a vital factor in India's social history ever since the immigrant Aryans first established casteism and Brahmin supremacy in India. Ehrenfels goes on to point out that subsequent immigrant groups and imported religions in India have adopted the Hindu *jati*[18] system together with the whole complex of colour prejudice — or where there has not been deliberate and schematic segregation into sub-sections, the group will discriminate on a color basis against individuals. Together with this color complex is a desire to trace back the ancestry of one's group to extra-Indian origins. All these characteristic features fully apply to India's Muslim groups, to its various Christian sects, as well as to its Jewish communities.

Among the Bene Israel the *Gora* are the upper class, the full-blooded Bene Israel.

There has never been an actual census of the two groups as separate entities, but the *Kala* were always much fewer in number than the *Gora*. The Bene Israel pride themselves on the chastity of their women and they excommunicated the rare Bene Israel woman who had sexual relations or a solemnized marriage with a non-Jew; so that at least until well into the 20th century, most unions with non-Jews, more likely than not, were due to Bene Israel male indiscretions or concubinage with non-Jewish women. This *Kala-Gora* dichotomy seems to have been the Bene Israel way of accepting responsibility for the progeny of their irregular unions dating back to the time when there was among the Bene Israel no practice of conversion to Judaism. The offspring of such unions and their descendants were forever set apart as *Kala* Bene Israel. They could not intermarry with Gora Bene Israel, nor could they interdine with them;[19] nor were the *Kala* allowed to handle the cooking utensils of the *Gora*. *Kala* were buried apart from the *Gora*, in a separate corner of Bene Israel cemeteries. As a matter of fact, Kehimkar (pp.162-3) mentions that the fourth Bene Israel cemetery in Bombay, which was located in Kamateepura and allocated to the Bene Israel as early as 1832, was divided into a northern and southern section by a public road. The southern section was used for *Kala* Bene Israel burials, while the northern section was for *Gora* Bene Israel.

Kala Bene Israel worshipped in *Gora* synagogues and did not maintain synagogues of their own. Their seats were located in a far corner of the synagogue. Originally, *Kala* had to wait for their portion of sanctified grape juice until all the *Gora* had been served at the conclusion of the Sabbath and Holy Day services in the synagogue. In the year 1840, however, the *Kala* as a group strongly and successfully objected to this practice and it was abolished.[20] Strizower mentions that *Kala* were not permitted to wear the *talith* (ritual prayer shawl).[21] If this had ever been the case, this particular manifestation of discrimination has long since been discontinued. One elderly Bene Israel repondent remembers that, as of 1910, *Kala* men, wearing the *talith*, were being called up to read from the *Torah* in the Bene Israel Prayer Hall in Poona; and, that even in 1910, there were sometimes instances of *Kala* and *Gora* dining together. In any event, *Kala* and *Gora* children did play together. There was no difference between *Kala* and *Gora* in terms of occupations and the *Kala* stigma of descent proved to be of no impediment to *Kala* in obtaining higher eudcation or in improving their economic status. The traditional modes of discrimination were apt to be far more strictly observed in small villages where the fact of indiscretions by Bene Israel men with non-Bene Israel women (more often than not from the lowly toddy-palm-tapping community) were more difficult to hide than in the city, and the resultant unfortunate offspring were set aside and well known as *Kala*. Even today, members of the older generation still know to which section a Bene Israel individual belongs; and to some it still makes a difference when arranging for marriage partners.

A certain letter from a *Gora* Bene Israel written to a White Jew of Cochin shows how obsessive this *Gora-Kala* idea was in the minds of Bene Israel especially in the 19th century. The holographic letter is in possession of the Judah Magnes Museum in Berkeley, California. It reads as follows:

To : Hayeem Isaac Hallegua, Esq.,
     Jewish Town
     Malabar Coast, Cochin,

Bombay, 14th November, 1899.

Dear Sır :
    We, the undersigned, Wardens of the Synagogue at Rewdunda [Revdanda], Kolaba

District, beg to solicit the favour of your kindly supplying us with the following information.

In the town of Alibag, Kolaba District, one Moses Elia Madai has been engaged as Hazan and Shohet of the synagogue of that place on his giving them to understand that he was a White Jew from Cochin and is now doing all the requisite duties in connection with that synagogue. But we are justly suspicious about his descent from White race to which we have the honour to belong.

Our notions about the Black Jews have been strengthened by our late venerable Hazan Abraham Yehuda Gemal, who served the Rewdunda synagogue over about 25 years and who made us acquainted with the difference between the Black and White Jews—differentiating the former from religious duties. The said Hazan Moses Elia Madai of Alibag, if a Black Jew, makes all the ceremonies performed by him irreligious.—according to our notions.

Under the circumstances, we beg of you, in the cause of our holy religion, to kindly favour us with the following explanation on the following heads, viz :—

1. To what distinctive class, i.e. White or Black, the said Hazan Moses Elia Madai belongs?
2. If in the case of his being born from Black descent are we justified in having all the religious ceremonies performed by him?
3. What distinction you as White Jews in general keep between Black Jews in respect to religious affairs, i.e.
    a. Do you call upon them to read the Torah in your own synagogue?
    b. Do you appoint them to be your Hazan, Shohet, etc.? If ever a case of the kind has happened, be good enough to cite.
4. Whether any marriage connection has ever been formed between the two distinctive classes?

The reason of our troubling you with the above is that we, as White Jews, observe the custom from a very long time of not bestowing upon them, i.e. to Cochin Black Jews, the permanent office of Hazan and Shohet as that of a White one, which rule is observed intact *for centuries* [emphasis supplied] amongst us to the present time.

We, with a view to perpetuate amongst us and not to assimilate ourselves with the Black ones, and if this view of ours is just and right,—are led to make this reference to your goodself in the cause of our holy religion, to which you will vouchsafe us a reply to the following address, for which act of kindness our whole community of Rewdunda will be highly obliged.

We beg to remain   Dear Sir,
Yours faithfully,
Shallom Elizah Shapoorkar, Gabbai
Shallom Aaron Dhokehkar
Issac Solomon Ashtaumkar
Jacob Benjamin Shapoorkar

Mr. Shallom Elizah Shapoorkar Gubbai
    Kolaba District
    Taluka Alibag
    at Rewdunda.

The above letter plainly reveals two points :
(1) These *Gora* Bene Israel writers were equating (although quite mistakenly) the Bene Israel Black (*Kala*) sub-group with the so-called Black Jews (Malabari Jews) of

Cochin. The subdivision of Cochin Jewry into Black and White groups had had an entirely different history and rationale than did the *Kala-Gora* sub-division of the Bene Israel; and

(2) The concerned *Gora* Bene Israel were being more papal than the pope, a well-known phenomenon among neo-converts. Although not themselves neo-converts, their religious revival and introduction to minutiae of *halachic* Judaism were then matters of barely 100 years' standing.[22] Their *Kala-Gora* restrictions, however, seem more deeply rooted.[23] Their first Cochini Jewish preceptors had been White Cochin Jews who probably had not explicitly informed the Bene Israel that the Black (Malabari) Jews of Cochin were *halachically* pure even if the White Cochin Jews kept them out of their Pardesi synagogue, lorded it over them, and did not intermarry with them. The Cochin Black Jews not only were *halachically* pure Jews, they were, if anything, more learned and more orthodox than the Cochin White Jews. But the *Gora* Bene Israel who wrote the above letter did not want to be tainted with anything Black.

Basically, the Bene Israel *Kala-Gora* distinction was one of purity of descent, essential from the Jewish point of view and, at the same time, fitting the general Indian pattern of contempt for the half-caste. On this subject Kehimkar argues that the *Kala* were offspring of illicit unions, either temporary or permanent, but *never* by marriage; and that this very separation of *Kala* from *Gora* is what strictly maintains purity of origin on the part of the *Gora*.[24] Solomon M. Vakrulkar has put it another way:

> people who would pose as our judges....have caught at the words "White" and "Black" Israel used by us as at a catchword, without understanding the significance we attach to them, and think that they have condemned us out of our own mouth. Now it is sheer common sense that the people who classify themselves as "White" and "Black" could not be all "Black"....But the logic of these remarks has not appealed to our self-styled judges and they have been assiduous in publishing to the world that the Bene Israel are all "Black" Jews. They should have known that the term "Black Israel" is applied by the Bene-Israel to the offspring of mixed marriages, or of connection with alien women, and a community capable of instituting and preserving this distinction from generation to generation could not be of tainted origin.[25]

The strict *Kala-Gora* cleavage within the Bene Israel community seems not to have had any positive influence upon the Baghdadi attitude at least toward the *Gora* Bene Israel majority.[26]

As for inter-community relations, as in the case of other Indians, so also in that of the Bene Israel (vis-à-vis the non-Jewish communities) the change to urban conditions in the 19th century afforded an opportunity for upgrading their social status in general. Especially in the milieu of Bombay, social status no longer derived so much from caste as from class, and many Bene Israel in Bombay were generally identified with the white collar middle class (which mainly consisted of the higher Hindu castes). Besides, despite the disdain of the Baghdadi Jews towards them in Bombay, the Bene Israel had greatly strengthened their own knowledge of Judaism and had absorbed a large body of Jewish customs, in the process opening up meaningful contacts with non-Indian Jewry. It was not until the 20th century, however, that the social gap between the Bene Israel and the Baghdadis narrowed, due largely to the leavening influence of Indian Independence and to the fact that all three Jewish communities in India were drastically shrinking in size as a result of emigration.

The Bene Israel in the Nineteenth Century

NOTES

1. Dutch merchants of Portuguese descent had established themselves in Surat in 1686, and were soon followed by English and other west European Jewish merchants, as well as by Jewish merchants from Cochin.
2. Kehimkar : *History*, p.52.
3. Cecil Roth : *The Sassoon Dynasty*, Robert Hale Ltd., London, 1941, p.57.
4. Fischel : *Bombay in Jewish History*, etc., pp.138-9.
5. The Tiferet Israel Prayer Hall eventually gave up this innovation.
6. The problem of Baghdadi Jews looking down upon Bene Israel was recognised by a Baghdadi Jewish journal in Calcutta, viz. *The Hebrew and the Voice of Sinai*. The journal tried to change Baghdadi Jewish attitudes by publishing the text of a letter written about 1887 which also addressed itself to this problem. The following are the journal's own words in introducing the letter and its full text as reproduced in *The Hebrew and the Voice of Sinai*, Volume III, No. 9, January 11, 1907 :

THE LATE RABBI* JOSEPH EZEKIEL, J.P. AND THE ISRAELITES
Some light on their origins and customs.
Questions solved by the late Rabbi Joseph Ezekiel,
J.P., Fellow of the Bombay University and Headmaster of the Sassoon Jewish School [see above, pp. 93-94.]
The following letter was sent to the Calcutta congregation about twenty years ago :

(1) Several Jewish and Christian travellers have proved that the Bene-Israelites are of pure Jewish blood. They have kept very strict distinction between themselves and those of mixed blood of several generations, also they do not intermarry and eat with them in the same plate.

(2) There are some among the Bene-Israelites as also among the Arab Jews who do not observe the Sabbath, but the Bene-Israelites do not count such persons in the number required for *Kaddish* and *Kedusha*, while the Arab Jews do, and they never touch or kindle fire on the Sabbath.

(3) *Hakhamim* from Jerusalem and other holy places pray with the Bene-Israelites, say *Kadish* and *Kedusha*, and allow their *Hazan* to read *Sepher* for them when they are called.

(4) There are two cisterns attached to the two Bene-Israel synagogues for the purification of their women.

(5) In Poona not only are they called to the *Sepher*, but are also allowed to read *Zemiroth*, *Haftara* and *Selihot*.

(6) The pilgrims that went to Jerusalem were called to the *Sepher* and one of them was asked to read *Haftara* and *Musaf*.

(7) Before the formation of the Arab Jewish Community, the Arab Jews attended the Bene-Israel synagogues and buried their departed relations in the Bene-Israel burial grounds. The late Silliman Yacob and his servant Asher (both of whom died on the same day), Elyahoo Haeem, Ezekiel Abdal Nabee and several respectable gentlemen and ladies were interred there and some of their monuments still exist.

(8) They do not eat meat without *Nekawa* and with milk and ghee, and for great feasts they have vessels belonging to the synagogues.

(9) There are instances of divorce according to the Jewish customs. Those women that are left by their husbands without any good reason remain without remarrying. Some obtain their divorce according to the Civil Law, and this is allowed by the Rabbins of Europe and America. Divorce according to the Jewish Custom is so easy that if the practise be followed it would, they fear, increase adultery among them. An adultress is generally punished by being obliged to remain like a widow all the remainder of her life.

* Joseph Ezekiel (Rajpurkar) was a Bene Israel scholar of Hebrew, and not an ordained Rabbi. The use of the title "Rabbi" at the beginning of the quotation is honorific.

(10) It is only because the Bene-Israelites are real Jews that the Sassoons pay Rs. 1,000 and the Anglo-Jewish Association of London more than Rs. 3,000 every year for the Israelite School (of the Bene-Israel).

(11) In their religious practises they are orthodox.

(12) Their marriages and circumcisions are allowed to be performed in both the Arab Jewish synagogues of Bombay and also Poona [see below, pp. 149-50] and these are registered in the books kept in these synagogues.

(13) As the Bene-Israelites have two Synagogues and two Prayer Halls of their own, and pray according to Cochin *minhaj*, they do not go to the Arab Jewish synagogues.

(14) There are some instances of intermarriages between Bene-Israelites and the Arab Jews.

(15) When Bene-Israel marriages take place in the Arab Jewish Synagogues, the Bene-Israel *Hazan* is allowed to pray *Minha* and *Arbith* and the Arab Jews pray with him.

(We give publication of the above letter for the enlightenment of the uncultured Jews, as there exists some ignorance and prejudice among them regarding this noble race, their origin, customs, rituals and ceremonies, etc. We are in possession of their full history and would be glad to meet any enquiry on the subject. Ed.H)"

In its next issue-Volume II, No. 10 of February 1, 1907, *The Hebrew and the Voice of Sinai* reprinted from the newspaper, *The Statesman* (Calcutta) an article on the history and present position of the Bene Israel, asserting as a fact their arrival 2,000 years ago, and dwelling upon their military record with the British, the professional and other well-educated members of the community, their institutions, etc. The article was very complimentary toward the Bene Israel. Publication of this article notwithstanding, the Baghdadi-Bene Israel relationship was usually characterized by deliberate mutual separation.

7. *The Jewish Encyclopaedia*, Funk and Wagnalls, New York and London, 1912, Volume VI, pp.170-1.
8. Stanley Jackson : *The Sassoons*, Heinemann, London, 1968, p.63.
9. Kehimkar, op . cit., p.243.
10. The school was founded in 1875 by Bene Israel individuals and not by the Anglo-Jewish Association of London, nor by its Bombay Branch (See below, p. 169). It had been in existence for six years before the Anglo-Jewish Association began to subsidize its finances.
11. Far more shocking than the ways of Baghdadi Jewish women was the ugly fact that in the latter decades of the 19th century white slavers were bringing into Bombay East European Jewish women as prostitutes.* Rev. Lord (*The Jewish Mission Field in the Bombay Diocese*, pp. 20-21) discusses this subject under the heading "The European Jewish Community in Bombay" :

of course it has its virtuous members, but I know not by what sad reversal of the general rule it is that the usual high standard of Jewish morality to which one can almost invariably point with such confidence in Europe generally, has here seemed to belie itself....a very considerable portion of the small European Jewish community of Bombay are the victims or votaries of vice....the Government has deported some of them....there are at least some 200 European Jews and Jewesses engaged in the nefarious traffic or the open vice....Amongst the Bene Israel, preeminently the standard of Jewish virtue is exceedingly high; and therefore by these [Bene Israel] the usual character for morality in the matters alluded to receives its vindication.

12. Schifra Strizower : "Jews as an Indian Caste", pp. 43-57 and *The Children of Israel : The Bene Israel of Bombay*, pp. 21-34.
13. Strizower : *The Children of Israel, etc.*, p.31 (Reprinted with the permission of Basil Blackwell Ltd.)
14. Kehimkar, op.cit., p.254.
15. Kehimkar, ibid., p.93. In Hindu Society the Mahar and the Mang were outcaste,untouchable groups. While this is a typically Indian sort of proscription, for Hindu reasons of pollution, it is

---

* The problem of burial for deceased (Jewish) prostitutes must have been solved by the allocation of Bombay Burial Ground No. 20. (See above, p. 39, n. 19).

also quite common for orthodox Jews to refuse to allow non-Jews to do their cooking or to handle their utensils out of fear lest the non-Jews may not observe all the rules of *Kashrut*.

16. The usage very likely originated when the fair-skinned Aryans invaded the land of the dark-skinned indigenous Dravidians. As pointed out to the present author by the Indian historian, Professor Romila Thapar : Vedic texts speak of dark (black) DASAS and of the lighter (white conquering), Aryans "White" and "Black" came to be symbolic, respectively, of high and low status. Similarly in Central Asian culture the upper strata of society are called "The white bones" and the lowest are "The black bones".

17. And also in personal communications to the present author.

18. The word "caste" is of Portuguese origin. *Jati* is the proper Indian term, sometimes loosely used for "caste" or "Varna", but more often it refers to the numerous sub-divisions of a *varna*. There are in India thousands of different *jatis*. The *jati*, i.e. sub-caste, is the most meaningful unit, and *it* determines one's caste-behavior and relationships. Based as it is on common descent, the term *jati* is sometimes used to refer to non-Hindu racial, linguistic or religious groups. Even in its strictest Hindu usage, however, there are different categories of *jati* segmentation relevant for different purposes (such as marriage, doctrine, sect, occupation or territory); but a *jati* cannot be defined on the basis of any single set of attributes.

19. Moses Ezekiel, in his *History and Culture of the Bene-Israel of India*, says that even the cups served to the *Kala* Bene Israel in synagogues were separate cups for them only and that they were "served after the 'white' Israel had been served" (p. 69).

20. Kehimkar, op cit., p.33.

21. Strizower : *The Children of Israel* etc., p.28.

22. But *not* "for centuries". A few Cochin Jews had had sporadic contact with Bene Israel before the first Bene Israel synagogue was built in 1797, but there were then no *hazanim* regularly among them. However, recitation of a few simple prayers at rituals, and also the Jewish ritual slaughter of animals for food could go back much earlier, to the time of the first Bene Israel religious revival and to the functions of the Bene Israel *Kajis*, but not of Cochini *hazanim* and *shohetim* among the Bene Israel "for centuries" past.

23. Mention of this *Kala-Gora* Bene Israel division was made in 1824, in the 16th Annual Report of the London Society for Promotion of Christianity Among Jews, (see above, p. 67). It is strange that the Abstract of Rev. Wilson's account of the Bene Israel, written in 1838-39, makes no mention of the Kala-Gora cleavage within the Bene Israel community; neither does S.Reinemann, who was among the Bene Israel in the 1840s.

24. Kehimkar, op.cit., p.51.

25. Solomon M. Vakrulkar : *Our Synagogues*, etc., pp.11-12.

26. The Baghdadi attitude toward all Bene Israel in the Bombay area was undoubtedly a significant underlying factor prompting rabbinical questioning, in certain cases, of Bene Israel Jewish purity. This came to a head at the beginning of the 1960s in Israel, with the rabbinical concern being focused not on the *Kala-Gora* distinctions, but rather on *halachic* technicalities of observance in relation to the Biblical law of the levirate and to past cases of divorce in the family — in the event of a Bene Israel intending to marry a member of any other Jewish community *in Israel*. Had there been fuller knowledge about the Bene Israel community and more empathy, the whole distasteful affair need never have assumed such proportions, nor lasted as long as it did. The fact that rulings of the Israeli Chief Rabbinate specifically singled out the Bene Israel community and were not stated as general dicta concerning all Jews, finally aroused the Bene Israel in Israel to protest and strike. Eventually, in 1964, the Israeli Parliament passed a resolution orering the Chief Rabbinate to remove the words " Bene Israel" from those Rabbinical directives; and the then Prime Minister of Israel announced that "the Government of Israel reiterated that it regards the community of the Bene Israel from India as Jews in every respect, without any restriction or distinction, equal in their rights to all other Jews in every matter, including matters of matrimony."

For a short but clear account of this affair, see Shalva Weil's doctoral dissertation, op.cit., pp.71-9.

Chapter 10
Typical Features of Bene Israel Jewish Life

This chapter describes those 19th century aspects of Bene Israel Jewish life which were typical of the Bene Israel but *not* of other Jewish groups. Not only do Jewish customs vary according to the two major divisions of Judaism, the Sephardic and the Ashkenazic, but even within each of these two divisions, Jews of different countries, and of different localities within a single country, have always had the freedom to develop their own variations in liturgy, ritual, and socio-religious customs. It goes beyond the scope of the present book to describe and compare the variety of local Jewish customs around the world. While mentioning some Bene Israel customs which they do share with certain other Jewish communities, the main purpose here is especially to describe those Jewish customs which are unique to the Bene Israel. For whatever custom or ritual is not specifically mentioned in the present section on the Judaism of the Bene Israel, it should be assumed that the Bene Israel of the 19th century followed the general Sephardic rather than Askenazic tradition.

The following information is based largely, even if not entirely, on Kehimkar's book *The History of the Bene Israel of India*, written in 1897. It will be noted that many of the Bene Israel customs of the 19th century are still being observed by the Bene Israel today.

First, let us go a long way back for a moment. After the split into two parts of the Solomonic Kingdom (c. 930 B.C.), the Northern Kingdom was deprived of the services and ceremonies revolving around the Holy Temple in Jerusalem, and therefore had to eliminate much of the Jerusalem Temple ritual or to improvise substitutions, for instance, for the various offerings prescribed in the Book of Leviticus. Whether or not the Bene Israel ancestors actually did hail from that Northern Kingdom and had made ritual adaptations in those days, the fact remains that many of the very offerings which are prescribed in Leviticus took the form of home rituals among the Bene Israel and were prepared by the housewife.[1] The main feature in the Bene Israel giving of offerings is the so called *Malida* and this particular observance is unique in Judaism. The *Malida* is an auspicious ceremonial offering which the Bene Israel describe as "a dish offered in the name of God" (Kehimkar, p.25), accompanied with an invocation for the presence and blessings of the Prophet Elijah.At the end of the Sabbath it has been customary for Jews to invoke Elijah requesting him to bless the affairs of the new week. Certain Jewish communities have a special *Eliahu ha-Navi* ceremony for the Prophet Elijah at the close of Sabbath; in some Jewish communities important rituals accompany the taking and the fulfillment of a vow *(neder)* (see below, p. 116) and even include a food "offering" which is later distributed among the congregants. But the affiliation always of Eliahu ha-Navi, the actual components of the *Malida* offering, and the many specified occasions at which the *Malida* ceremony is performed — all together make it a uniquely Bene Israel custom. It is interesting that Kehimkar uses the word *Malida* to mean *only* the food component, i.e. the actual offering, and not the ceremony as a whole; whereas Bene Israel today often use the word *Malida* to refer to the entire ceremony (the offering, the prayers, and the distribution of the offering) even though the more common Bene Israel term for the ritual as a whole is "an Eliahu ha-Navi". They are accustomed to say that they will "make" or "have an Eliahu ha-Navi" on such and such an occasion.

The historian, Abram L. Sachar, describes Elijah's position in Judaism as follows:

> He [Elijah] is the most popular personality in Hebrew history, the patron saint of Jewish life....Curiously enough, in the Biblical narratives he shows few of the gentle qualities calculated to endear him to a peaceloving people. He is harsh, severe, relentless, of the typical dervish type, intolerant of all the effeminate corruptions of civilized life. Yet through centuries of folklore the austere figure who never knew the meaning of peace, whose every word was a challenge, is mellowed and softened into the gentle comforter, the solicitous friend, the chivalrous companion of the weak and the oppressed. In the memory of his people it is Elijah who opens secret doors through which the martyred escape, who provides dowries for the unfortunate daughters of the poor, who saves the defenceless victims of powerful swindlers. There is a chair for him at every circumcision, and a cup of wine on every Passover table. He is stationed at the crossroads of paradise to welcome every worthy person; he weaves garlands for God from the prayers of the truly pious. He will be the precurser of the Messiah, ushering in the new world in which the sufferings of Israel and of all peoples will be no more.[2]

Without belittling the folkloristic significance of Elijah to most Jewish communities, there is no doubt that, even today, in the lives of the Bene Israel, Elijah is a figure of more central importance to them than to any other Jewish community. This is reflected in the fact that the Bene Israel have established a formal ritual which intimately connects Elijah with the individual Bene Israel throughout all the most important aspects of life — not only for rites of passage but also in times of any crisis or danger; and on all happy occasions; as well as in undertaking and fulfilling vows. In all such circumstances the Bene Israel turn to Eliahu ha-Navi.

When, where and why did the Bene Israel adopt the Prophet Elijah as their particular patron? Although the Bene Israel tradition of having been discovered by David Rahabi does not include any mention of Elijah or of a *Malida* offering — neither as having been an aspect of Bene Israel religion at the time of the "discovery", nor as having been introduced to them by David Rahabi — it might be that, as Rebecca Reuben has suggested,[3] when David Rahabi revived Judaism among the Bene Israel he deliberately substituted the Prophet Elijah for the numerous local Indian saints invoked for help against the evils in this life. However, there *is* a Bene Israel legend that Elijah, immediately after the shipwreck of the Bene Israel ancestors (i.e. much earlier in time than the discovery of the Bene Israel by David Rahabi) appeared at Navgaon and revived the unconscious survivors; and that Elijah's footprints are visible on a rock at that place.[4] Elijah is believed to have again appeared to the Bene Israel much later at a place called Khandala (a Konkan village near Navgaon, *not* the hill-station by the same name) where he promised that the Bene Israel would be redeemed. At Khandala the impression of the footprints of Elijah's horse is supposed to have remained. After Elijah's appearance on the spot, Khandala became the traditional site for an annual Bene Israel fair called "Elijah Hanabicha Oorus".[5] There is food for thought in Rev. Lord's theory that "The observance of such a festival as this seems indicative of a very prolonged sojourn of the Bene-Israel in India, for such a mixture of knowledge and ignorance in regard to the prophet Elijah, and its incrustation into such a practice as that mentioned, can hardly have sprung up and taken fixed form in a short time."[6]

The Elijah Hanabicha Oorus used to take place on the fifteenth day of the Hebrew month of *Sh'vat* (about the beginning of February), the day on which Elijah is believed to have appeared to the Bene Israel at Khandala before re-ascending to heaven. Among Jews elsewhere the same day is called *Tu b'Shvat*, a kind of Jewish Arbor day,[7] sometimes referred to as the "New Year's Day for Trees". It is a minor Jewish holiday celebrated by reading a special liturgy for the day, by planting tree saplings, and by eating many different fruits (especially carob fruit imported from the Holy Land). On this day the Bene Israel serve their traditional *Malida* offering (see below, p. 114) with many kinds of fruit, an aromatic twig and burning incense. Elijah is invoked and prayers are said in thanksgiving to God for causing everything to grow in its proper season. Kehimkar thinks that this Jewish Arbor day was introduced to the Bene Israel by David Rahabi and was lately transformed into the uniquely Bene Israel holiday together with the fair. The venue for the fair was eventually shifted from Khandala to the grounds opposite the first Bene Israel synagogue in Bombay. A few decades later the custom of holding this fair was abolished

at the instance of one Judah Kindil, who, it is said, was a Cochin Jew,[8] and a Reader in the Bene Israel synagogue. He told the Bene Israel that though Elijah the Prophet might have appeared to them as they believed, yet to celebrate the day in the manner in which they did, with such an exaggerated degree of festivities, was almost the same as worshipping him, an act which is opposed to the very spirit of their faith.[9]

There is, however, a sentence in universal Jewish liturgy which says "Make us to rejoice, O Lord our God, in Elijah the Prophet, Thy servant, and in the kingdom of the house of David, Thine anointed."[10] Actually there is no evidence of Bene Israel overt adoration of Elijah, not even in the invoking of Elijah for the *Malida* ceremony.

We are told that the ancient Bene Israel custom during the Malida ceremony was to repeat the words of the *Shema* (perhaps only the first few lines — see above, p. 3 and p. 14, n. 6). But, early in the 19th century the words of the *Shema* (for recitation during the *Malida* ceremony) were replaced by a different recitation, in unison, of specific Hebrew passages in the following order:

1. The entire *pizmon* (a hymn with a refrain) which begins with "Eliahu ha-Navi, Eliahu ha-Tishbi".
2. Several different blessings quoted from the Bible, the first of which begins with the Hebrew words *"Va-yi-ten-l'ha"* (May He [God] give to you). These Biblical passages are recited in the following order:
   Genesis : Chapter 27, verses 28 & 29.
   Chapter 28, verses 3 & 4.
   Chapter 49, verses 25 & 26.
   Deuteronomy : Chapter 7, verses 13, 14 & 15.
   Chapter 28, verses 3, 6, 5, 4, 8 & 12.
   Chapter 15, verse 6.
   Chapter 33, verse 29.
3. All the above verses are recited only once, after which *Genesis*, Chapter 48, verse 16 is repeated thrice.
4. The *Malida* recitation concludes with Psalm 121 in its entirety.

While the particular Eliahu ha-Navi *pizmon* which opens the *Malida* ceremony is only an optional feature in *Motzei Shabbat* (end of Sabbath) observances, the Bene Israel have chosen also to include in their *Malida* ceremony several passages which are taken directly from the regular liturgy for *Motzei Shabbat* (i.e. the above-mentioned Biblical verses) and they recite this combination of selections on whatever day of the week they may choose to perform the *Malida*. A *minyan* is not required for this ceremony, and a *hazan* may or may not be present to lead the recitation.

In speculating upon possible Cochin Jewish influence regarding the passages chosen for this ceremony, it should be noted that the Cochin Jews, in their various services, pick from several different *pizmonim* which invoke Eliahu ha-Navi, and they do not especially favour the particular *pizmon* which is used in the *Malida* ceremony of the Bene Israel. The Cochin Jews do observe a special ceremony connected with making a vow in the name of Eliahu ha-Navi, and with the fulfillment of vows. But the Cochin ceremony differs from the corresponding Bene Israel custom in the following respects:

1. The Cochin *neder* (vow) ceremony takes place only during the *Motzei Shabbat* service; or on the eve of Channukah, which happens to coincide with the death anniversary of their revered saint Nehemiah Mota (on this latter occasion no offering is given, but a feast is prepared for all persons present).
2. On those occasions when it is customary among the Cochin Jews to give a food offering, the offering consists only of *appams* (rice cakes) and bananas. The ingredients of the Bene Israel *Malida* are always more in number and they vary specifically according to the occasion.
3. There are many other reasons besides vows for performing the Bene Israel *Malida* ceremony. (See below pp. 116 – 117)

The Bene Israel offering usually consists of a mixture of so-called beaten rice,[11] grated fresh coconut, raisins, nuts, ground cardamom, rose water, and sugar, thick discs of rice or wheat cakes; and five different kinds of fresh fruits. All this is nicely arranged together on a large platter. About the fresh fruits, some say "there must be dates plus one fresh fruit from a real tree (i.e. the wood of which can burn) and also another fresh fruit from a soft tree like a banana"; or, "from a tree which bears fruit annually and fruit from a plant which bears only once"; others specify five kinds of fruit including one for the *pri ha-adamah* (fruit of the earth) blessing, one for the *pri ha-aitz* (fruit of the tree) blessing, and one new seasonal fruit". Other specific items are added according to the particular purpose of the offering. For an auspicious occasion, for instance, a sprig of *subja*[12] or flower blossoms is added for fragrance.

For the Bene Israel *meal*-offerings, rice is more often used than wheat as an ingredient.

In their *meat*-offerings the Bene Israel seem simply to have substituted goat or lamb (usually only the cooked liver of these animals) for the bullock prescribed in the Bible in many different verses of *Leviticus*,[13] and they have substituted domestic fowl (usually only its cooked liver and/or gizzard[14]) in place of the prescribed turtle-dove and pigeon. One finds no Hindu or Muslim meat-offering analogous to this use of cooked liver and gizzard, although lower-caste Hindus, especially in rural areas, do sacrifice fowl and goats with prayers to their local deities at the times of sowing and reaping, or in order to be protected against danger of disease, etc. Their offering is of the whole bird or animal, not of just the liver or gizzard. In the case of vegetarians (higher castes usually), there are no animal or meat offerings. Upon the conclusion of the Hindu ritual, portions of the offerings (called *prasadam*)[15] are distributed among the supplicants. After the Bene Israel ceremony, the *Malida* is distributed among those present – *Kajis*, if present, partaking of it first.

The *Malida* ceremony of the Bene Israel has its obvious analogue in the Hindu *Puja* (which means : honor, respect, homage, or ritual worship). "Of all the Hindu rites," wrote Abbe Dubois, "*puja* is the one that occurs most frequently in all their ceremonies, both public and private, in their temples and elsewhere. Every Brahmin is obliged to offer it at least once a day to his household gods."[16] Every *puja* minimally includes the following elements : sandalwood powder; grains of rice colored with saffron; flowers; incense; a lighted oil-lamp; an offering composed of cooked rice, fruit, ghee (butter clarified through boiling) and sugar; and areca nut.

The word *Malida*, according to the Rev. Lord,[17] derives from the Persian language and describes a confection offering as part of local[18] Muslim custom : viz. the *Dargah* at the tomb of a saint, where prayers are recited over a platter of food offerings which are later distributed to those present. However, nowadays the Bene Israel never bring the *Malida* platter to a grave site, although Kehimkar mentions that "There was in former times a practice among the Bene Israel of offering food at the grave." (p.158) Today at the grave only the *Hashkaba* memorial prayer is recited, accompanied by a vow to give to charity (customary at the cemetery among many Jews). Yet, the ritual use of the *Malida* platter seems to be a common element among both Muslims and Bene Israel, even though their respective contexts and purposes differ.

The word *Malida* as such is in common use among Marathi-speaking people and is not limited to the Muslims and Bene Israel. It is defined in one Marathi-English dictionary as "a cake made up with milk, sugar, butter, etc. especially as offered at the shrine of a Muhammedan Pir. 2. Figurative : anything much crushed or squeezed, and any mash or mess."[19] There is an old expression (now out of fashion) : "to make *malida* out of one's opponent", meaning to crush him; it conveys contempt. The book *Folklore of the Konkan*,[20] in its glossary of terms occurring within the text, lists *malinda* as "a sweet preparation of wheat flour fried in ghi". No doubt the word *malinda* is etymologically related to *malida*. In *Folklore of the Konkan* the *malinda* is mentioned as a feature in Hindu worship of a Muslim saint :

> The Hindus of Bhuvan in the Murbad taluka of the Kolaba district worship the Pir [Muslim saint] of the locality. It is said that the cultivators of the village once lost their cattle, and that a *Fakir* [Muslim mendicant] attributed the loss to the rage of the Pir. Since that time they are careful to worship the saint, and the result is that there has been no disease among their cattle. They offer *Malinda* i.e. bread and *jagri* [unrefined sugar], to the Pir every Thursday. (p.46)

This is by no means the only example in the Konkan of adoption or adaptation of rituals from one faith into another. In a milieu such as this, it is remarkable that the Bene Israel have incorporated only some forms, but usually not the substance of neighboring faiths. Kehimkar mentions one deviation : i.e. Bene Israel invocation of the Hindu deity against smallpox (see below, pp. 131–32). There were other similar instances (as mentioned by Rev. John Wilson, see App. 5, pp. 329 & 330) certainly before the Bene Israel Jewish revival, and even in Kehimkar's day. But the overall Bene Israel pattern always differed markedly from Hindu, Muslim or Christian custom. Thus, the Hebrew Prophet Elijah served as Bene Israel patron, but *not* as a deity, for all Bene Israel folk ritual. The Bene Israel flouted the "general belief among all classes of Hindus in the Bombay Presidency that Saturday is an unlucky day." (*Folklore of the Konkan*, p.65) To the Bene Israel, even as of the time when they were first "discovered", Saturday has alway been the most holy and auspicious of days.

While the ceremonial giving of offerings is a universal phenomenon, the Bene Israel offerings conform largely to the ancient Hebrew custom as described in *Leviticus*. Kehimkar lists (pp.25-9) the following offerings which the Bene Israel combine with their *Malida* ceremony :

Sebah Todah — Thanks offering (*Leviticus* 7)
 The word *zebah* in Hebrew literally means an "animal sacrifice". Instead of actually sacrificing an animal, the Bene Israel add the liver or gizzard to the usual items on the *Malida* platter. Sometimes a goat was released as a token of thanks by a person recovering from an illness, or for some other reason; more frequently donations were made to the synagogue on such occasions.

Sebah Shelamim — Peace Offering (*Leviticus* 7)

Korban Nedaba — Voluntary or Free-Will Offering (*Leviticus* 7)

Korban Neder — Vow Offering (*Leviticus* 7)
 In various books of the Old Testament instances occur of persons making vows. But the *Mishnah* and the *Talmud* generally discourage this practice which, however, must have been prevalent enough in those days to have warranted the enumeration (in the *Mishnah* and *Talmud*) of different kinds of vows and of the various contingencies involved. To absolve a person from a vow, the Bene Israel *Kaji* (or other officiating person) with appropriate prayers, gives the *Malida* to the person concerned who, if a woman, receives it in the front fold of her *sari* in her lap, or, if a man, in his handkerchief or other clean cloth.
 Note that the taking of vows is a very important feature also to Hindus and to Muslims in the Konkan. The Hindus make vows in honor of different deities, or at different phases of the moon, or to request a great variety of different favors (e.g. health, children, wealth, education, etc.). Among the Hindus each kind of vow has its own name and specifications for its proper performance (such as fasting, silence, hair-shaving, circumambulation of temples or of sacred trees, etc.). Hindus make vows at the tombs of Hindu saints also. Native Indian Christians make their vows to Christian saints. Offerings are usually a feature in fulfilment of a vow.

Korban Neser — Offering of the Nazirite
 A woman with no male offspring, in hope that a male child will be born, may vow that if a boy is born to her, that child's hair will not be cut. This was quite common among the Bene Israel before the 20th century. After the period specified in the vow for not cutting the child's hair[21] was completed, the shaven hair was weighed against gold or silver which was then given in charity or presented to the synagogue: the hair was then thrown by the Bene Israel into the sea, there being no Temple altar on which to burn it as provided in the *Book of Numbers*, (6 : 18).

Korban Tehara — Offering of purification of a woman after childbirth (see below, p.131).

Other occasions on which the *Malida* ceremony is always performed are :

1. Before the start of the preparations for a wedding : first the *Hashkaba* memorial service is performed at the family grave site, or at home; on the next day the *Malida* ceremony is performed with the liver and gizzard of fowl added to the regular *Malida* platter, except that sweets are omitted from this particular ceremony which memorializes one's ancestors in the hope that they will be present in spirit at the coming wedding.
2. The evening following a circumcision.
3. On the holiday of *Tu B'Sh'vat*, to celebrate the first fruits, and also to pay respect to the Prophet Elijah at Khandala.

Typical Features of Bene Israel Jewish Life

4. Usually on all auspicious occasions; and in times of illness or of other difficulties or crises; or, whenever else divine help is sought (even at such moments as previous to taking a school examination); or, whenever there is reason to express deep gratitude.

In spite of its similarity in some respects to the *Neder* ceremony of the Cochin Jews (which suggests its introduction to the Bene Israel by Cochin Jews), the actual origins of the Bene Israel *Malida* ceremony remain a mystery. Kehimkar has presented a case based on parallels between the Bene Israel *Malida* and the prescribed Biblical offerings. It would be more convincing, however, if we had some clue, at least, that some aspects of this custom were prevalent among the Bene Israel *before* their religious revival — even if only it had been mentioned in Ezekiel Rahabi's Letter of 1768. Yet, the fact that the *Malida* ceremony seems to be so ingrained and basic to Bene Israel thinking and to their way of life, forces us to speculate :

1. that the core, at least, of the Bene Israel *Malida* ceremony must go back *many* centuries; and
2. if its Biblical components — including the importance of Elijah — do constitute additions or adaptations to an already deeply rooted Bene Israel indigenous custom, then
3. the addition of Biblical elements is more likely attributable to *the* David Rahabi or to the early Bene Israel *kajis* than to any of the late 18th or early 19th century Cochin Jewish teachers.

However, the question still remains : Why don't the earliest (or, for that matter, any) accounts of and/or by the Bene Israel mention the *Malida* either as one of the Bene Israel "pristine" traditions, or as something traceable to the time when they were "discovered" by David Rahabi?

Although in the *Malida* ceremony the original Bene Israel custom of repetition of the *Shema* had been replaced by the recital of other Biblical quotations, Kehimkar stresses that the words of the *Shema*, namely "Hear, O Israel, the Lord our God is one Lord", were and are "the watchwords of the Bene Israel who repeat them with heart and soul thrice a day." (p.166) Twice daily, i.e. morning and evening, is the regular rule for the rest of Jewry. In the 19th century and to this day, whenever a Bene Israel would say the *Shema*, he/she would touch the right eye with the right thumb, the left eye with the right little finger, and the forehead with the three middle fingers, as is the custom for most Shephardi Jewish communities. The positioning of the fingers in this way simulates the two Hebrew letters *Shin* and *Daleth*, which are the first two letters of the word *Shaddai* (an early word for the Almighty, but it is not *the* Holy Name of God). It is an Ashkenazi custom to cover the eyes otherwise while saying the *Shema*, they say, in order better to concentrate upon the unity of God.

Kehimkar has divided the Bene Israel Jewish holidays into two main groups : those already observed by the Bene Israel in the days before their religious revival (see above, pp. 4–6); and those to which David Rahabi introduced them; all the former being known by Marathi names, and all the latter being commonly known by Hindustani names as follows (according to Kehimkar, *History*, p.23), in order of their occurrence during the year :

Hindustani name	*Hebrew name*	*Significance*
(a) Ramzan	Month (Ellul) of S'lichot	Month of semi-fasting and propitiatory prayers prior to the New Year and Day of Atonement.

Hindustani name	Hebrew name	Significance
(b) Naviacha Roja	Tzom Gedaliah	3rd day of the month of Tishri; the Fast of Gedaliah in commemoration of Gedaliah's assassination.
(c) Sababi Roja (in month of Tevet)	Tzom Tevet	10th day of the month of Tevet; a fast day to mark the beginning of the siege of Jerusalem by Nebuchadnezzar.
(d) Elijah Hanabicha Oorus.	Tu B'Shvat	15th day of the month of Sh'vat; New Year for Trees, planting of saplings.
(e) Sababi Roja (in month of Tamuz)	Tzom Tamuz	Fast on 17th day of month of Tamuz commemorating both Nebuchadnezzar's capture of Jerusalem and the day when Titus broke into the walls of Jerusalem.
(f) Birdiacha Roja	Tisha B'Av	Fast on 9th day of month of Av, commemorating the destruction of both the First and the Second Temples.

Conspicuous by its absence from both lists, *San* (see above, p. 4) and Roja, is *Hanukkah*, the Feast of Dedication commemorating the cleansing and rededication of the Second Temple by Judas the Maccabee in 164 B.C., after it had been desecrated by Antiochus Epiphanes. This leads to the theory that the Bene Israel ancestors must have left their homeland at least *before* 164 B.C. Furthermore, note that four (i.e. numbers (b), (c), (e) and (f) out of six of the *Roja* holidays are days of fasting relating to the Babylonian conquest of Jerusalem and destruction of the First Temple (586 B.C.). All four of these fasts had been officially discontinued after the rebuilding of the Temple in 520-515 B.C. They were reinstated only after the Second Temple was also destroyed (70 A.D.). The absence of these four fasts from the list of Bene Israel holidays bearing Marathi names (i.e. those which, according to Kehimkar, they traditionally celebrated before their first religious revival) is one of the arguments in favour of the thesis that the ancestors of the Bene Israel arrived in India *before* 70 A.D. In addition to the Hindustani-named holidays, Kehimkar says that the Bene Israel of his day observed *Shavuot* (the Pentecost, or the Feast of Weeks) seven complete weeks after Passover, but that "it is of quite late introduction among them" (p.169). Also, see above, p. 5, paragraph (4).

As for the observance of *S'lichot* (the period for propitiatory prayers, beginning in the month of Ellul), the number of days observed and the actual prayers and their arrangement differ in Sephardic and Ashkenazic practices. Within these two major sections of Jewry there are also various local differences in *S'lichot* observances. It seems that the Bene Israel are the only group whose custom (since their 19th century religious revival) it was to observe *S'lichot* for the *entire* month of Ellul[22] while conscientiously *observing semi-fasting during this whole period*. According to Kehimkar (p.23), the Bene Israel referred to this period as *Ramzan* (*Ramadan*) using the same name as do the Indian Muslims for their month of semi-fasting. During the entire month of Ellul (which always occurs about August-September, unlike Muslim *Ramzan* which wanders, from year to year, in all the seasons,[23] the Bene Israel ate and drank only at the evening meal (the Muslims fast during *Ramzan* from sunrise to sunset also), except on the Sabbath when they (the Bene Israel) ate as usual. This could be a simple example of superficial influence upon the Bene Israel by their neighbors. Other Sephardi Jewish communities, who also lived among Muslims, adapted other features from their neighbors. It is interesting to note that, when asked about a Bene Israel month of semi-fasting named *Ramzan*, most modern Bene Israel respondents denied knowing that such a name was ever used for the month of *S'lichot* observance. In the 20th century very few Bene Israel still observe this fast by eating only an evening meal; some, however, still do so (especially women who do not go out to work); or, some men and women consume nothing but tea during the day and eat nothing solid until the evening meal. Naphtali Roby, in his chronicle *History of the House of Rahabi in Cochin* (see above, p. 44), wrote that David Rahabi (whom he does *not* here call "David *Ezekiel* Rahabi") "changed the fasts of Ramadan that they [Bene Israel] observed to the fasts of the 29 days of Ellul." (p.22) This statement implies that the Bene Israel had previously been observing Muslim *Ramadan* as such. However, as explained above, what Naphtali Roby has written about the Bene Israel is too imprecise for us to be certain as to which David Rahabi he has in mind, or to learn whether the Bene Israel *Ramadan* used to take place always about August-September, or according to the Muslim calendar, etc.

The Bene Israel *S'lichot* prayers began every day before dawn. According to Kehimkar :

> At the time of the propitiatory prayers the *shofar* (ram's horn) is blown in the synagogue thrice... On the last day of this month [Ellul] the *shofar* is not blown, but when the morning service is over, the congregation divides into two parties facing each other. One party stands while the other sits. Those standing read the *Hattara*, or the prayer of forgiveness. Those sitting say "As we forgive you, so may you be forgiven from on High." Then those that are standing sit down and those that are sitting stand up and in their turn ask and receive forgiveness. This having been done, they kiss one another's hands and return home, where children kiss the hands of the mothers and sisters. During this month new clothes are made and houses are whitewashed. (p. 17).

Wearing new clothes was almost obligatory on Rosh Hashonah. After their religious revival the Bene Israel celebrated two days at New Year instead of their traditional one day. They also performed *taschlich* (casting sins upon the waters)[24] on the afternoon of either the first or second day. Kehimkar singles out the *kapporoth* ritual (the atoning sacrifice of a white fowl on the day before Yom Kippur) as being something that "some of the Bene Israel performed in imitation of the Jews" (p.173) (meaning the Baghdadis). Although "casting one's sins upon the waters" and the sacrificing of fowls are almost universal in the history of religion, the introduction of the *Taschlich* and of the *Kapporoth* rituals to the Bene Israel came about at the time of their religious revival through the agency of other Jews. However, the Bene Israel were no doubt already familiar with similar practices on the part of their neighbors, and therefore the expectation would have been for them to have readily incorporated *both* Jewish customs into their growing body of Jewish ritual. But *Taschlich* has been much more popular than *Kapporoth* among the Bene Israel.[25]

As of old, the Bene Israel before Yom Kippur bathe first with hot and then with cold water; they dress in white clothes; and, in Bombay, for instance, even if they do ride to the synagogue, they'll go preferably in a private rather than in a public vehicle so as to avoid the touch of non-Jews on Yom Kippur (see below, p. 221).

Kehimkar comments that on Yom Kippur "the Bene Israel synagogues are more than crowded, as those who are so careless as not even to pay their visit to the synagogue at any other time in the year, are careful to be present on that day." (p.174). The same is true in many congregations of western Jewry too. Yet, for all that, Yom Kippur is verily a day of awe and of deep meaning. Every Bene Israel in the synagogue, even today, at specific points during the Yom Kippur service, spreads his/her handkerchief on the floor, exclaiming : "Blessed be the name of the glory of His kingdom for ever and ever", and then fully prostrates on the floor (with face on the handkerchief).

The celebration by the Bene Israel of *Shila San* (see above, p. 5 is difficult to account for. Kehimkar (pp.18-19) thinks it goes back to the day of rejoicing for the High Priest (*Simhat Ha-Cohen*), from the days of the Second Temple when it used to be observed. It may be connected with the Bene Israel belief that the souls of the dead visit their relatives on the day before *Yom Kippur* and remain until the night of *Shila San*, during which time one invokes intercession by the dead for the granting of a good new year. Just as on the afternoon before *Yom Kippur* they had held a *Hashkaba* (memorial prayers) and *Malida* service calling on three generations of ancestors to come and be with them for *Yom Kippur* so, on the morning of *Shila San*, after *Hashkaba*, the ancestors were requested to go away. The word *shila* means "stale", referring to the fact that all the sweets and refreshments for consumption on this holiday had to be prepared before *Yom Kippur*, because there was no possibility of preparing fresh food for *Shila San* which was observed on the day immediately following *Yom Kippur*. Perhaps *Shila San* was celebrated out of sheer relief that *Yom Kippur* had passed and, one hoped, with good portents. Other Jews have a celebration on *Yom Kippur* night immediately after the fast, rather than on the following day.

Kehimkar wrote (p.19) that the Feast of Tabernacles (Succoth) "was totally forgotten by the Bene Israel" before their religious revival. According to Rev. John Wilson, as of 1840 the Bene Israel did construct *succoth* and celebrated the holiday for nine days (see Appendix 5, p.333). As of the end of the 19th century Kehimkar explained that the community celebrated eight days of *Succoth*. Their temporary booths they constructed out of fronds of the coconut palm (very readily available in the Konkan). They ate all their meals in these *succoth* and, as prescribed, they carried the bundle of palm, myrtle and willow together with a citron in the synagogues. They also observed the day after *Succoth* as *Simchat Torah* (Rejoicing in the Law), making seven circuits while carrying scrolls of the *Torah* around the reading desk in the synagogue. Kehimkar offers the very patronizing comment that on "Simchat Torah some illiterate and ignorant males dance on this occasion, but they are laughed at by the educated." (p.177) Either he is referring to inappropriate forms of dancing, or he was just being snobbish, and also unaware of the fact that it was (and is) customary, even for sophisticated Jewish intellectuals all over the Jewish world to participate in joyous song and dance in the synagogues on the holiday of *Simchat Torah*.

Devout Bene Israel even observed three fasts during the month of *Heshvan* or *Marheshvan* to atone for any shortcomings of which they may have been guilty in their observances during the High Holiday season.

In the 19th century all Bene Israel began celebrating the eight days of *Hanukkah*, the Feast of Dedication, with special prayers for the lighting of the *Hanukkah* lamp, called the *Hanukkiah*, each night in each household, and also in the synagogue. The *Hanukkiah* in use by the Bene Israel was usually hung against a wall and was in the form of a brass frame holding eight glasses in a row, with a ninth glass pendant above the row of eight. When in use, the glasses are partly filled with oil. There is a cotton wick in each glass.

The holiday of *Purim* too came to be celebrated by the Bene Israel according to usual Jewish custom, as was also the preceding day, namely the Fast of Esther. In the synagogue, during the reading of the *Book of Esther*, at every mention of the villain Haman, the congregation loudly knocked against the wooden benches upon which they sat, to show their contempt for Haman.

Typical Features of Bene Israel Jewish Life 121

According to Kehimkar (p.167), Bene Israel local custom was not only to abstain from all forms of leaven during the eight days of Passover, but also from the use of tea, sugar, jaggery and clarified butter. (All Jewish communities abstain from eating leaven, but different areas have their own local customs in regard to abstention from specific other foods.) On the day before Passover, all the first-born of the Bene Israel, both male and female over the age of thirteen, or the parents of first-born under the age of thirteen fasted in gratitude that the first born of Israel were spared when, as the *Book of Exodus* tells us, all the first-born among the Egyptians died (the Tenth Plague) prior to the exodus of the Hebrews from Egypt. At the Passover *Seder* (ritual meal) the *harosheth* (one of the symbolic foods) of the Bene Israel was made from a thick syrup of dates; and the bitter herbs were served in a cup of lime juice. Grape juice, not wine, was used. Not until 1846, when the first *Marathi-Hebrew Haggadah* was published, could the Bene Israel fully understand the prayers for the *Seder* service. Kehimkar indicates (p. 168) that those Bene Israel who were illiterate could not read the story of the exodus in any *Haggadah* and presumably did not perform the *Seder* ritual, but only refrained from using any kind of leaven during the eight days of Passover. But all Bene Israel prepared for Passover by thoroughly cleaning and whitewashing their houses, retinning the insides of their metal pots, and replacing old earthenware utensils by new ones. New clothes were worn as part of the celebration. On the fourteenth day of Iyar (the month following Passover), Kehimkar says, "a second Passover is observed by those persons who for some reason were prevented from keeping the first, but no instances of the observance of the second Passover in olden times can be found among the Bene Israel." (p.169)

Kehimkar mentions that in his day only some of the Bene Israel prayed regularly each morning wearing *Talith* and *Tefillin* (phylacteries); but that all Bene Israel males wore the *tzitzit* (an undergarment with fringes at four corners, worn by orthodox Jews).

Kehimkar (p.180) writes that women were busy preparing food for the Sabbath from about 2-5 p.m. on Friday. Two particular dishes were traditional among the Bene Israel for the Sabbath : *Chavlya* and *Kadhi*.[26] For the rich, the Friday evening meal consisted of fowl, curry, rice, bread, vegetables, fruit and wine; for the middle class, mutton, curry, rice, bread, liquor; for the poor, fish, rice and bread. The leftovers were eaten on Saturday. Women did not usually attend the Sabbath services in the synagogue, although when and if they did attend, they sat separately from the men, usually in a gallery; and women did customarily go to the synagogue on *Rosh Hashonah* and *Yom Kippur*. In the synagogue, at the close of the Friday evening and of the Saturday morning services, the reader blessed the grape-juice in a large silver chalice, tasted it and then distributed the rest among all the congregation present (to sip from the chalice, or else an additional supply is served to all in tiny glasses). At the close of the Sabbath the *Shamash* lit the synagogue lamps; the Prophet Elijah was invoked, using two cups of grape juice (one of which was for Elijah), and reciting the *Va-yiten l'cha* (see above, p. 113) and *Ha-mavdil* (the prayer recited at the end of Sabbath — separating the Sabbath from the mundane week ahead).

At the end of all synagogue services, the entire Bene Israel congregation participated in a very pleasing custom referred to by the Bene Israel as *Hath Boshi* (Kissing the Hand) : a senior person, thumbs uppermost, approached a junior, took the junior's hand in both of his/her own hands, while the junior placed his/her remaining hand on the outside of the hand of the senior; then both released hands and immediately, putting the tips of their fingers to their respective mouths, kissed their own fingertips; they then proceeded to repeat the process with another person until the entire congregation (if possible) had thus greeted each other. Rev. Lord calls this custom "The Kiss of Peace",[27] although the Kiss of Peace of the early Christians was really a kiss on the cheek. A practise similar to

122 The Bene Israel in the Nineteenth Century

that of the Bene Israel is observed not only by the Jews of Cochin but also by the Syrian Christians of St. Thomas in Malabar, by Nestorian Christians of Kurdistan, by Assyrian Christians, and by Indian Muslims.[28] The Parsis of India also observe a very similar custom, but instead of kissing the fingertips, they touch them to the head while slightly nodding the head. There is an article on this subject, written by a Parsi, J.J.Modi, pointing to a connection between the Jews of India and Persia : that, especially if the forefathers of the Bene Israel, coming from the Persian Gulf, landed near Cheul (al-Kazwini mentioned Jews and Parsis at Cheul in the 13th century), the Bene Israel might have learned this custom either in Persia itself or from Parsis in Cheul; and that the custom itself "probably came to the Jews and Christians of Malabar from [their historic contacts with] the Jews and Christians of Persia who must have taken it from the custom of *Hamazor* of the Zoroastrians of Persia."[29] However, it is more likely that the custom was introduced to the Bene Israel by the Cochin Jews who served as *Hazanim* in Bene Israel synagogues, rather than in medieval times from Parsis in Cheul.

Last but not least, the Bene Israel, unlike other Jews, had no tradition of "returning" or of making a pilgrimage to Jerusalem. It was not until as late as February 1880 (according to Kehimkar, p.77) that any member of the Bene Israel community ever visited the Holy Land : Issac Solomon Ghosalkar and Joel Samuel Shirkolkar were the first Bene Israel to go there on pilgrimage. Yet, cemented into the wall of the building (near Bethlehem) which according to tradition houses the Matriarch Rachel's Tomb, together with an adjacent small well, there is a large plaque with a Hebrew inscription. The English translation of its text runs as follows :

> The construction of this well was made possible through a donation from the esteemed, our brothers the Bene Israel, who are living in the city of Bombay, may the Lord protect it well! In honour of the whole assembly of the community of Israel, [through those] who came to bow over the gravestone at the burial place of our Mother Rachel. May her memory protect us. Amen.
> Given in the year 5625 — according to the Jewish calendar.

The Jewish year 5625 corresponds to c. September 1864 — September 1865 A.D.. Thus Kehimkar either erred in dating the first Bene Israel pilgrimage to the Holy Land to the year 1880; or, Bene Israel funds were sent in 1864-65 through an emissary from the Holy Land who had solicited donations among the Bene Israel in Bombay, to be used in the Holy Land. It would be interesting to know whether the Bene Israel had been given any say in the matter of the actual use of their donation. It so happens that among Hindus the construction of wells and water-tanks, as well as their proper maintenance, are considered to be meritorious acts of the highest order, and such a value might well have been shared by the Bene Israel. The amenity of having a well at the site of Rachel's Tomb (then a very arid place) was a comfort to pilgrims, whom it enabled thereafter to observe the Jewish custom of washing the hands immediately after visiting a grave; and they could also enjoy the advantage of a readily available supply of drinking water. At this writing (1980) the custodian at Rachel's Tomb happens to be a member of the Bene Israel community, one Solomon Benjamin, who immigrated to Israel from India in 1971.

NOTES

1. To the Bene Israel housewife is attributed not only the strictness of the observance of each ritual detail (i.e. according to Bene Israel custom) but also the conscientiousness in remembering from

Typical Features of Bene Israel Jewish Life   123

generation to generation (before they were "discovered" by David Rahabi) the dates of all the Jewish holidays known to them.
2. Abram Leon Sachar : *A History of the Jews*, Alfred A. Knopf, Inc., New York, 1965, 5th edition, revised and enlarged, pp.50-51. © 1964 by Alfred A. Knopf., Inc. Reprinted with permission of the publisher.
3. Rebecca Reuben : *The Bene Israel of Bombay*, Cambridge Jewish Publications-4, Cambridge University Press, Cambridge, 1913, p.12.
4. The first element is reminiscent of the Chitpavan Brahmin legend (see above. p. 13, n.2). Secondly, it is not uncommon in the Konkan that the *padukas* (footprints) of Hindu saints and ascetics are worshipped after their death. The "footprint" features in Islamic lore also, such as the footprint of the Prophet Mohammed at the Dome of the Rock in Jerusalem where he is believed by Muslims to have ascended to heaven; or the "footprints" in a rock in Kashmir, thought by the Ahmadiya Muslims to have been those of Christ, whom they believe died in Kashmir.
5. *Oorus* is Kehimkar's spelling of the *urs* (see Kehimkar : *History*, p.20) which refers to the Muslim commemoration of a death anniversary. The *urs* of a Muslim saint or mystic is sometimes regularly celebrated with a big fair. Large annual fairs (*melas*) are also celebrated by Hindus to honour *sanyasis* (very holy Hindu ascetics) at their respective tombs. (According to Hindu custom a *sanyasi* is buried rather than cremated.)
6. Rev. J.Henry Lord : *Bene Israel*, in Hastings' *Encyclopaedia of Religion and Ethics*, Edinburgh, 1901, Volume II, p.472.
7. There is now an official Indian holiday for tree-planting, called *Vanamahotsava*.
8. In *Solomon's Travels* (on p.98 of the Hebrew text, just previous to the section on the Bene Israel) Reinemann mentions a Meir Kindil who was a Cochin Jew and who served as *Hazan* in Bombay. He was also a scribe for writing out marriage and divorce contracts.
9. Kehimkar, op.cit., p.65.
10. This is always recited in synagogue on Shabbat after the reading of the Torah.
11. Soaked and pounded rice.
12. In his book, *The Jews in India and the Far East*, the Rev. J.H.Lord discusses *subja*. Its Latin name is *Ocymum pilosum vel basilicum*, being of the same genus as the *tulasi* plant (*Ocymum sanctum*). Lord suggests that the unidentified hyssop (*aizoy* in Hebrew) of the Bible might also have been of this genus of fragrant herb. (*Aizov* has since been identified by a Biblical botanist, Nogah Hareuveni, as *marjorama Syriaca labiate* or *Oreganum Syriacum*). For *havdala* (the prayer at the close of each Sabbath) the Bene Israel made use of the *subja* plant (instead of the usual Jewish *havdala* spice box containing pleasant smelling spices and herbs); and they used *subja* on several other ritual occasions as well. It was also used a great deal by their Muslim neighbors. Among Hindus, the *tulasi* plant is believed to be an incarnation of the wife of the Hindu god Vishnu and, as such, is especially sacred to Vaishnavite Brahmin families who use the tulasi leaf for ritual purposes. But many other Hindus also keep a *tulasi* plant in their home compound. The daily circumambulation of the plant is an act of worship, and there is a Hindu belief that *tulasi* leaves purify the soul and body. A few tulasi leaves are eaten after each meal as an aid to digestion, and also before and after washing in cold water, in order to prevent catching cold. To give a sprig of *tulasi* to anyone is believed capable of averting danger, of alleviating problems, etc. A distinction is made between the *sham tulasi* variety Ocymum basilicum L. (know as subja) which is used by the Bene Israel and the *Ram tulasi* variety Ocymum cannùm Sims (hoary basil) which is used by Hindus (and never by the Bene Israel). Rev. Lord did not mention the curious similarity in form of the Jewish four-horned altar, as described in the Bible (*Exodus* 27:2) to the typical form of container-cum-pedestal in which the sacred *tulasi* plant grows in Hindu courtyards, especially in west and south India. The pedestal is about three feet in height, broadened at its top and placed in such a way that its four sides face the four points of the compass. Each corner of the top (container portion) ends in a pointed protrusion. Such square shapes with a protrusion at each corner (these protrusions are called "horns" in the Bible), on top of a wide square pedestal (usually of stone, but sometimes of clay) have been found at Megiddo, Beer Sheva, and several other excavations in Israel, dating back to the 8th

century B.C. and onwards, Most of these were found in association with domestic artifacts and formed part of household worship as home altars. The Bene Israel do not use this kind of object at all, although *tulasi* (*subja*) is an important ingredient in many Bene Israel rituals.

13. Because of Jewish dietary restrictions (which sanction the eating only of animals which have cloven hooves and chew the cud), and out of respect for the Hindu revulsion against the eating of beef, the flesh of no other animals except goat and, less commonly, sheep, was ever eaten by the Bene Israel.

14. There is an intriguing reference to the existence of a similar custom among tribes on India's Northwest Frontier. The Rev. Lord in his *Jews in India and in the Far East,*(pp.44-5) calls attention to an article by M.E.Solomon which appeared in *The Jewish Chronicle* (London) of 29 August, 1902. It tells (p.20) of a recently published work by

> Sheikh Sadikali, entitled *A Short Sketch of the Musalman Races found in Sind, Baluchistan, and Afghanistan* [who] notices that three of the dominant tribes, the Ansari, the Afghans or Pathans, and the Birahoi, all described by Sadikali as originally Jews or Bene- Israel....The following practices and customs which Mr. Solomon describes amongst these people certainly bear remarkable likeness to some of those of the Bene-Israel. He relates : "I was once told here by a friend that an Israelite going to Jacobabad was invited by a Mahomadan family to their house. He found that a dish containing cakes, goat liver, and incense was prepared. He was shown a very old book, and asked if he knew how to read the portion pointed out. He found that it was a Hebrew book, which was the same used by Israelites in vow ceremonies. viz. *Eliahu HaNabi* and *Vayitten I'cha*. This Israelite entreated him much to give him the prayer book, but the Mahomadan Sheikh would not part with it. On enquiry he found that there were only two families of this sort living in Jacobabad who yearly performed this ceremony. If they found none to read their prayers, as they called it, they simply prepared the dish, kept it on a clean white piece of cloth, burned the incense, and kissed the prayer book, the only scripture book they had with them. When I myself went to Jacobabad, I found that these two families were lost to us. Although they followed, my friend told me, the Mahomadan faith, yet they did not intermarry with other Mahomadans, and hence when they found they were few in number, they always went to places where other families of their sect still settled. I tried my best to find out who these people were. Jacobabad once belonged to Baluchistan territory. They followed the oil-pressing profession like the Bene-Israel of old, but I am sure they were not descendants of Bene-Israel. They buried their dead east and west, in contradistinction to other Mahomadans, and followed the Mishnaic customs of sacrifices, which the Bene-Israel exactly did."

15. *Prasadam* : Consecrated small object (often a bit of food) usually from an offering to a Hindu deity or to a holy person, afterward presented to an individual, or divided among a group of congregants as an auspicious gift. Gussin, on p.141 of his doctoral dissertation, *The Bene Israel of India : Politics, Religion and Systematic Change,* points out that after an Hassidic Rabbi at the Sabbath meal has eaten his portion, he will distribute the rest among his followers; that this food is considered to have been made holy and potent by the Rabbi. While seeing in this a similarity to the function of *prasadam*, he concludes that "the distribution of *Malida* food more likely is a syncretic element from the dominant religion in the environment, rather than a doctrinal diffusion from an esoteric Jewish sect; or convergence."

16. Abbe J.A.Dubois : *Hindu Manners, Customs and Ceremonies,* translated from the author's later French manuscript and edited with notes, corrections, and biography by Henry K.Beuchamp, third edition, Oxford at the Clarendon Press, Great Britain, 1906, reprinted in 1953, p.147.

17. Rev. J.H.Lord, op. cit., p.27.

18. The Rev. Lord in this case refers to the Konkan. But the term *malida* was and is in use in North India too. *Bharghava's Standard Illustrated Dictionary of the Hindi Language*, compiled and edited by R.C.Pathak, Hindi-English revised and enlarged edition, published by P.N.Bharghava, Benares, N.D.(Preface 1946), on p.857 defines *malida* as "a kind of sweetmeat", with a second meaning, "a kind of soft woolen cloth".

Abdul Halim Sharar's book *Lucknow : The Last Phase of an Oriental Culture,* translated and edited by E.S. Harcourt and Fakir Hussain, from the original Urdu; published by Paul Elek, London, 1975, as part of the Indian Series of the Translations Collection of UNESCO, mentions (p.162) that "Pieces of bread mixed with ghee and sugar are an everyday sweet dish generally partaken of on occasion of the ceremonies *Fatiha* and *Niyaz*. From this developed the preparation of *malida*, a sweet dish with semolina." On p.273 of Sharar's book, notes 495 and 496 explain that

> "*Fatiha* is the opening *sura* of the *Quran*. It is also the name of the ceremony in which this *surah* is read with a prayer, usually over food, for the souls of religious saints but occasionally for relatives as well. The food is intended for distribution to the poor but can be eaten by members of the household.
>
> The (Niyaz) prayers are for the souls of relatives and friends. The food over which the prayers are said is usually not eaten in the house but given to the poor."

From this passage one can easily see those Muslim elements which the Bene Israel have incorporated into the Bene Israel *Malida* context. But, distribution of the *Malida* food among the participants at the end of a Bene Israel *Malida* ceremony resembles more the Hindu element of distribution of *prasadam*.

19. *Dictionary of Marathi and English*, compiled by J.T. Molesworth assisted by George and Thomas Candy; Government Publication, Bombay, second edition, 1857, p.635.
20. *Folklore of the Konkan*, compiled from materials collected by the late A.M.T. Jackson, Indian Civil Service; R.E. Enthoven (compiler), C.I.E., I.C.S.: Cosmo Publications, Delhi, first published in 1915, reprinted in 1976; 92 pages of text and 37 pages of appendix-glossary.
21. The Bene Israel did not associate with the Nazirite Vow, the usual abstention from intoxicating drink; only the abstention from hair-cutting during childhood, usually continuing only until the child was six or seven years of age, rather than into manhood (in such circumstances abstention from alcoholic drink was of course irrelevant).
22. Cochin Jews observe *S'lichot* during all of *Ellul* plus the ten days between *Rosh Hashonah* and *Yom Kippur*, but with no regular fasting.
23. The Jewish and Islamic calendars are both lunar, but the Islamic calendar does not adjust the lunar year to the solar year, while the Jewish calendar does do so.
24. Gussin (pp.120-121 of his thesis) mentions that in the 1960s more than 60 percent of Bombay's Jews still participated in the *Taschlich* ritual. He saw it largely as a kind of picnic for them to enjoy, but also pointed out a parallel Hindu ritual, the *Avabhṛta Snana* (expiatory bath), through which personal sins are believed to be washed away at a large body of water.
25. The *Kapporoth* ceremony is a much older custom among Jews than is the *Taschlich* ceremony. Orthodox Jews still observe both customs. The *kapporoth* ritual involves the swinging of a white cock (by a male), or of a hen (by a female), about one's head for nine times. First, some Psalms are recited. Then the person says: "This is instead of me, this is an offering on my account, this is in expiation for me; this rooster (or hen) shall go to his (or her) death, and may I enter a long and healthy life." At the end, the fowl is ritually killed as an atoning sacrifice. The bird is either eaten by the family or given to a poor person.

Not only in the Konkan, but in many parts of India (and elsewhere) as well, fowl are still presented as offerings, especially to local deities in villages, for a variety of reasons, such as: in order to avert the evil eye; to ward off danger or disease; to propitiate local deities or ghosts; to ensure good harvests at the beginning of sowing and of reaping in the fields; and to express respect at the time of setting up a new statue of a deity. Even the custom of waving a fowl around a person is a common ritual practised in the Konkan, for example: "When a man is very ill or frequently becomes unconscious, coconuts, *fowls* [emphasis supplied] and boiled rice are waved around him and thrown away." From *Folklore of the Konkan*, p.61; also see pp.25 & 26.

26. These are Kehimkar's spellings. For *chavlya* (a kind of *cholent* – which is a traditional European Jewish dish for Sabbath meals, a stew basically of dried beans and potatoes, kept hot overnight over a slow fire), white beans are soaked overnight to be cooked on Friday with fried

onions, spices, saffron, and water. Kadhi (from which is derived the English word "curry") is basically a sauce of coconut liquid, garlic, hot chillies, saffron, cummin and other spices, curry leaves and a tamarind-like fruit called *cocum* — all boiled together until thickened.

27. Rev. J.H.Lord, op. cit., pp. 30-1.
28. The touching of each other's hands is noticeably different from the Hindu way of greeting — never touching the other person but placing the palms of one's hands together and raising them in that position, higher or lower, according to the status of the person being greeted.
29. Shams ul-ulma Jivanji Jamshedi Modi : "Kiss of Peace among the Bene Israels of Bombay and the Hamazor among the Parsees," in the *Journal of the Anthropological Society of Bombay*, 1907-08, Volume VIII, No. 2, pp.84-95; the passage quoted here is from p.92.

Modi adds that participation in the Hamazor is no longer so common among the Parsee congregants in Bombay, but that it continues to be practised between officiating priests, among congregants in Parsee towns of Gujarat and also as part of certain religious ceremonies.

See Appendix 6 (p. 339) for Solomon Reinemann's version of the Bene Israel ancestors, *together with the ancestors of the Parsis,* fleeing from Islamic persecution in Persia in the 7th century A.D. and *together* being shipwrecked off the shore not far from Bombay.

Chapter 11
Life–Cycle Rituals

Much of this chapter consists of a digest of Kehimkar's descriptions of Bene Israel Rites of Passage (Kehimkar : History, pp.111-160) which are intended here not only to supply a picture of 19th century Bene Israel customs, but also to serve as background closely related to additional material and comment within this chapter which supplement Kehimkar's information. Not only have the verbatim quotes from Kehimkar been identified here, but also each précis (by the present author) of Kehimkar's descriptions is acknowledged as such at the end of each paragraph concerned — in fairness to Kehimkar and to the reader; thus : "according to Kehimkar, p. —". However, this latter form of citation does not imply that the entire paragraph is based solely on Kehimkar's words because within the "précis" of Kehimkar's description, or as footnotes, the present author has often taken the liberty to interject information additional to that of Kehimkar, even though most of any given paragraph in this chapter which has been followed by a page citation from Kehimkar does follow Kehimkar's detail and sequence. It should also be mentioned that many (but not all) of the details as described by Kehimkar have appeared in other published sources, or have been reported by respondents; and many have actually been observed by the present author as rituals still being performed by Bene Israel in the 1960s and 1970s.

Rites of passage typically involve both religion and folkways. As elsewhere in this book, when dealing with the customs of the Bene Israel, it is always to be assumed that, unless otherwise indicated, in all cases in which a specific ritual is prescribed by the Jewish religion, such a ritual has been — ever since the second quarter of the 19th century — observed by the majority of the Bene Israel to the best of their ability and according to the Sephardic rite; and that those Bene Israel customs which are unfamiliar to other Jews are usually performed *in addition to* the customary Jewish practices. Some of them are old customs antedating the Bene Israel religious revival; others are later accretions, adaptations, etc. In describing Bene Israel rites of pasage, mention will be made primarily of customs not common to other Jewish communities. Many such usages had already been discontinued at the time when Kehimkar wrote his book. Previously prevalent, they had been assimilated from the local folk customs and their incorporation did not imply Bene Israel participation in Hindu or Muslim worship. There was, rather, an unsophisticated lack of discrimination on the part of the Bene Israel; and, more than that, a felt need to rely on amulets, exorcism, and local superstitious customs and terminology to help overcome fears of evil spirits, etc. Similar phenomena have characterized the practices of Jews in other places the world over, both in the past and in the present. For that matter, some Bene Israel in the 19th century adopted certain superstitions, amulets, etc. which had been introduced to them by the Baghdadi Jews.

Pregnancy and Birth

Since during four or five months after delivery a woman was not supposed to eat sweets or fancy foods, nor wear beautiful clothes nor flowers in her hair, during pregnancy she was actually encouraged to indulge herself in all of these things. In the case of a first pregnancy only, a special ceremony was performed in the middle of the seventh or during the ninth month of pregnancy, but nowadays it is by no means as widely practised as it was fifty and more years ago. At home, the pregnant woman was presented with five fresh fruits which were placed in her lap. Then she, her husband, and a few others together had to cross a body of water in a boat. For Bombay and surroundings, the Mahim creek, in north Bombay, was the popular place for the boatride part of the ceremony. From the boat, the pregnant woman dropped a coconut into the water.[1] Upon returning home, she donned a new sari and new green glass bangles, and participated in a *Malida* ceremony during which Elijah the Prophet was invoked and asked to grant the woman a safe childbirth. Then a small dinner party was held. This custom is certainly related to the Bene Israel's proximity to the sea and to the many creeks and tidal inlets along the Konkan Coast. The Bene Israel look upon the whole ceremony as a means of protecting their progeny from the dangers and fear of the sea. However, no respondent has ever mentioned what seems to be a logical inference, namely that there may be in this ceremony some connection with the legend of their ancestors' shipwreck.

A woman's first confinement used to take place always at the home of her own parents, where she would suffer less embarrassment and receive more intimate care during delivery. The delivery took place in a sparsely ventilated room and with the assistance of a midwife familiar to the family. She received as a set fee for her services one pound of rice and a coconut. As soon as labour pains began, the mother-to-be was fed gruel with a certain leaf (*lepidum sativum*) added to it, and, if in labour too long, she was given hot milk with pepper to drink. Immediately following the delivery, she ate a few pieces of nutmeg, "for warmth". A brass or copper plate was beaten to announce the birth to others in the house. (According to Kehimkar, p.112)

Drops of cold water are then sprinkled on the body of the babe to encourage it to respire, and at the same time to ascertain that it is alive. The child is then laid in a winnowing fan and has its navel cord cut. It is also made to lick castor oil mixed with honey. Its body is rubbed over with the white of an egg that it may have no eruptions on the skin. It is then bathed in lukewarm water, and water is being poured on its head....some families do bore the nostril of the first child born alive (the right nostril if a male and the left one if a female) if the mother has been unfortunate enough to lose the first four or five of her children. This custom has probably been borrowed from the Hindus.[2]

The new mother then bathed and lay down to the left side of the baby near whom had been placed the knife which was used to cut the umbilical cord. Later, upon awakening, the baby was given a honey mixture and then, at intervals, a piece of cotton soaked in cow or goat milk was given to the child to suck. Only a dim lamp was kept in the otherwise dark room. For three days the mother was given dry coconut, dates, chicken soup, spices mixed with jaggery, and a paste made of wheat flour, jaggery and ghee. She did not leave the delivery room for one week. She kept head, ears and body well wrapped and wore sandals on her feet. She and the baby bathed with warm water twice a day for twelve days, and thereafter once a day. After each bath the baby's body was rubbed with turmeric and the white of an egg. The mother drank a thick solution of dill seed, jaggery and coconut milk in order to ensure sufficient flow of her breast milk. On the third day female relatives and friends visited the new mother, bringing her cloves and nutmeg. They were served *pan supari* (basically : arecanut and sugar rolled in a betel leaf). On the fourth day the mother could add warm water or tea to her diet. (According to Kehimkar, p.112—116.) On the fifth day a party was given for female friends who gathered

> between seven or eight in the evening, each provided with a coconut which is a symbol of fruitfulness. A low wooden stool is placed in the middle of the room in which the confinement actually took place : a white handkerchief is spread over it and a copy of the Scriptures is nowadays placed on it; but formerly only a lamp with five lighted wicks was suspended from the roof in the centre of the room. Sitting at some distance both from the stool and the lamp, the woman who has been lately confined stretches forth her hand in the direction of the copy of the Scriptures and the lamp and kisses it in token of her gratitude to the Almighty for having removed the cloud of darkness which had overhung her and for having shown her the light of a lamp again. Her lap is then filled with five dry dates as a symbol of fruitfulness. Presents are given to the child by its relatives in the shape of a silk frock, a *jari* [gold or silver embroidered] cap, and of gold or silver bangles. The guests partake of a feast provided by the child's father or the mother's father, when they sing a song or two and spend an hour or so in merrymaking.[3]
>
> Bene Israel ladies, it is true, wave copper coins around the puerperal woman and her child, but they do not consider that any evil is transferred thereby to the person who takes these pieces, for if that were the case, they would not give them to their own children as they usually do. In short, women gather on the fifth day not in honour of Panchvi, whom they never consider to be a deity, but simply because it is usual among the Bene Israel to give a feast whenever there is the slightest occasion for showing joy.[4]

On the sixth day a party was given for male friends and relatives.

> ...on the seventh day a mother comes out of her room and receives her female relatives. As soon as they come in, the mother takes the child in her arms, and moves in and out of the door of her confinement room several times. Water mixed with turmeric powder is sprinkled over her. A cot having been placed in another room.... covered with a white clean sheet. This was undoubtedly a local usage borrowed from Gentile neighbours. The mother then laid her child in the middle of the cot....and handfuls of boiled gram and pieces of coconut were placed round the child on the cot. When this had been done, each little boy and girl who had been invited to this party went in turn near the child, and said "Come away, child! let us go to play and eat a dish of rice cakes on the sixth day".[5]

Kehimkar occasionally acknowledges the fact, or his assumption, that a given Bene Israel custom "was borrowed from Gentile neighbours". Actually, beyond what Kehimkar acknowledges, the instances of borrowing are so numerous that it is impossible to point out here each and every detail of ritual which the Bene Israel have adopted and/or adapted. An example of the sort of borrowing that has taken place can be appreciated by comparing the above mentioned post-delivery rituals of the Bene Israel with the following information taken from *Folklore in the Konkan* (p.3), discussing the days immediately after childbirth among the Hindus :

> There are no cases recorded in which women after childbirth are exposed to the Sun. But on the 12th day after her delivery, the mother puts on new bangles and new

clothes; coconuts, betelnuts and leaves, grains of rice, plantains and grains of wheat are placed in her lap. She then comes out and bows to the Sun. Wealthy persons on this occasion perform a *homa* sacrifice in their houses by kindling the holy fire and feeding Brahmans.

Compare : (1) not exposing the mother to the sun, with the Bene Israel feature of dim lamp-light only; (2) the mother bowing to the sun, with the Bene Israel mother stretching forth her hand toward the lamp and the scriptures; (3) Hindu mother and child not going out of doors until the 12th day, with the 7th day for Bene Israel; (4) new bangles and new clothes for the Hindu mother on the 12th day, but for the Bene Israel babe on the evening of the 5th day; (5) placing foods symbolic of fertility in the Hindu mother's lap on the 12th day, and for the Bene Israel mother on the evening of the 5th day; (6) a ritual (bowing to the sun) when the Hindu mother first goes outdoors, with the Bene Israel ritual on the 7th day when the Bene Israel mother first goes out; the holy fire and feeding of Brahmins, with the Bene Israel 5-wick lamp and hosting a feast on the 5th day. In addition to the above details, practically every other element of 19th century Bene Israel post-natal ritual (except for circumcision) was also a part of Hindu custom or a variant thereof.

Naming

No *Malida* ceremony accompanied the naming of a female child. However, if the mother, for a long time previous had not been able to conceive and had made a vow in connection with her desire to do so, after the birth of the child, she would perform a special *Malida* thanksgiving. There is no fixed time for the naming of female babies. According to Kehimkar (p.117), the naming ceremony for girls took place with a minimum of ten Jewish men (a *minyan*) in attendance, either at home or in the synagogue on either the 6th, 12th, 30th, or 80th day after birth. A cup of milk and honey was placed on a white cloth-covered stool in the middle of the room, and the *Hazan* or *Kaji* recited certain verses from *The Song of Songs*. The child was given the milk and honey to lick, was blessed, and the guests then sang Psalms of David in Hebrew and in Marathi. The naming of a male child invariably takes place on the eighth day after birth, at the time of his circumcision.

Circumcision

The Bene Israel mother was not present at her own son's circumcision. The mother's brother had the privilege of carrying the baby into the synagogue. Among the Bene Israel the operation was performed according to the Jewish ritual either by the child's father (if qualified), by the *Hazan*, or by a *Mohel*. Whether the circumcision was performed at home or in the synagogue, a chair with a copy of the *Bible* on it was set aside near the west wall (to the left of the Ark, if in a synagogue) for the Prophet Elijah, who was believed to be present at every circumcision; there was another chair for the circumciser, and a third chair for the *Sandek* (godfather); there was also a table on which was placed a citron which, together with one or two coconuts, was opened after the ceremony, and distributed to the guests while invoking the Prophet Elijah. Afterwards, a cock was killed outside, cooked and distributed among the circumciser and members of the family, excluding, however, the parents of the baby boy. A fee was paid to the synagogue and another fee to the circumciser. A *Malida* ceremony was optional. If performed, it was done in the evening, at home. (According to Kehimkar, pp.118-20)

On the twelfth day the child was bathed and laid in a cradle for the first time, to the words of "B'Shem Adonai" ("In the name of God"), followed by a lullaby in Marathi. A coconut[6] was broken, the coconut milk was sprinkled on all sides of the cradle, then the kernel was sugared and given to any children present. (According to Kehimkar, p.120)

Purification after Childbirth

The mother had to be purified on the fortieth day after having delivered a male child, and on the eightieth day in the case of a daughter.[7] On the day of the mother's purification, the barber shaved the baby's head. The hair was collected in a handkerchief and given to the barber, who was then dismissed with a gift of rice, a coconut and a small fee. Then a twig of *subja* was twisted inside a pot of cold water, while verses from *I Chronicles* (29 : 11-13) and from *Nehemiah* (9 : 5) were being chanted. These Biblical verses have replaced the chanting of the *Shema* of the Bene Israel's pre-religious-revival days. (According to Kehimkar, pp.122-3)

First the mother bathed herself, and then the child, with warm water; and herself again, this time with cold water. A plate of rice-flour balls was later held over the baby's head and the balls were caught by children of the household as they were dropped off the plate. After that a *Malida* platter was prepared (cf. the purification offerings in *Leviticus* 12 : 6-8) with rice, bread, jaggery, coconut kernel, *subja* or myrtle, and the legs, gizzard and wings of a cock. After the proper blessings and invocation of Elijah, the *Malida* was served to members of the household, who alone were present, unless perhaps also the *Hazan* may have been invited. After her purification, the woman's hair was adorned with flowers and her parents gave her a new sari, blouse, and glass bangles; and for the child they gave gold or silver bangles. If the baby was a girl, her ears were pierced and she was given earrings, a dress, a cap and a cradle. Then a feast was provided, and gifts were given, by the husband's family in honor of his wife's parents, if they had borne all the expenses of the childbirth and of the attendant rituals. Even if the child had not been born at the home of its maternal grandparents, the mother and child went there on the twelfth day, remaining there until the day of the mother's purification (according to Kehimkar, p.124).[8]

Childhood

At the age of one or two, the ears of a female child were pierced in four places along the rim of each ear (for four different kinds of earrings), and the left nostril was pierced for a nose-ring. Kehimkar (p.26) reminds us that even the wearing of nose-rings was a Biblical practice mentioned, for instance, in *Isaiah* 3 : 2 and in *Ezekiel* 16 : 12). In India there are very many different kinds of nose- and ear-rings.

At least for the State of Janjira we know that smallpox vaccination was made compulsory in the year 1873. But, before the introduction of vaccination against smallpox, the Bene Israel sought help from Shitla Devi, a local Hindu smallpox goddess[9] (see Kehimkar, p. 126). It should be noted that during epidemics of this dread disease, Muslims of the area did likewise.[10] In its section dealing specifically with the Bene Israel, the *Gazetteer* of 1885 mentions that :

The ceremonies connected with vaccination and small-pox are generally performed with much secrecy except in places without a synagogue where, till lately, they were done openly in the same manner as among cultivating Marathas and other low class Hindus. The small-pox goddess Shitaladevi, seven married women or *savasins*, a boy or *govla* are worshipped. When the lymph has taken, songs are sung in praise of the sores and of the goddess; the child is considered sacred and bowed down to, and neither fish nor flesh is eaten.[11]

Vestiges of this custom persisted among some of the Bene Israel even into the 20th century. Sometimes they called the smallpox goddess "Mata" (meaning "mother"). One elderly Bene Israel respondent explained that

> The only Hindu custom that my mother followed, and which I remember, is the worship of Mata on the occasion of bathing a child who had suffered an attack of smallpox, of chicken pox, or even of measles. This was done at the time of announcing the end of the segregation of the family due to illness. There was great fear of smallpox as a fatal disease. The difference between the Hindu worship of Mata and that of the Bene Israel being that the Hindus visit the goddess' temple on this occasion, while the Bene Israel honor the child who has recovered from the disease. On this occasion some foods are distributed to other children as well.

When a child began to take its first few steps. a coconut was broken in front of the child's feet, and the coconut kernel together with sweets were then given to the children of the household (according to Kehimkar, p.126).

Kehimkar (p.126) mentions a skirt ceremony which used to be common "when a married girl became twelve years old.... in imitation of local custom...." But he mentions no ceremonies or customs in connection with menstruation or puberty as such.

The *Bar Mitzvah* ceremony, celebrated by most Jews at age 13, marking a boy's passage into adulthood, was not usually observed by the Bene Israel in India, although in the 20th century it has been occasionally performed in some Bene Israel synagogues in India.

Marriage

Kehimkar (pp.128-9) begins his discussion of Bene Israel marriage customs, of his own day and of earlier times, by enumerating

> some of the customs introduced amongst our people in imitation of local usages. Fixing an auspicious day for marriage:[12] calling out five unwidowed or unmarried women, as is done on every auspicious occasion; putting on bangles on the wrist of the bride a day previous to her marriage; waving copper or silver coin round the bride and bride-groom (not to avert evil, like the Hindus, for the latter throw the same afterwards to people of the lower castes in order that evil may be averted from the pair....whilst among the Bene-Israel, the pieces are presented to the very sisters of the bride and bride-groom;[13] throwing rice on their bodies as a sign of fertility; rubbing their hands and feet with Mendi (Henna); fastening together the hems of their handkerchiefs as a symbol of union; the tying of a necklace (*Lacha*) [see below, note 25] of glass and golden beads around the neck of the bride at the conclusion of the marriage ceremony; making the newly married pair tear out rolls of leaves, held between the teeth, from the mouth of each other; making them play the games of odd and even; the bride-groom's going away from the bride in pretended ill humour; the hiding by the bride-groom of a betel-nut or some ornament which is to be searched for and found by the bride; the breaking of the bangles and of the *Lacha*, worn by a woman, after the death of her husband; and the discontinuing of the use of the nose

ring by a widow....most of the local customs named have been gradually given up by our people during the last fifty or sixty years....Early marriages were common amongst the Bene Israel in former times, and children of eight or ten years old were married[14]....everything in connection with their espousals was naturally managed by their parents or guardians....No marriage as a rule now-a-days takes place unless the bridegroom is a young man of twenty or twenty-one years old, and the bride be 14 or 15.[15]

Cross-cousin marriage,[16] a favoured form in most of south India, was sometimes practised also among the Bene Israel. Double weddings were, and are, even today, not uncommon, with a brother and sister marrying, respectively, a sister and brother from another family.

Parents of a boy, in trying to arrange for his marriage, first made sure that the girl's family was, in Kehimkar's words, "of pure Hebrew blood"[17] and had no hereditary diseases. If the boy approved of the parents' choice, two relatives were sent as matchmakers to the girl's family. A male matchmaker would speak to the girl's father; a female, to the mother. Then the girl's family would begin its inquiries. If the verdict was favourable, the next step was for the matchmakers to negotiate about presents for the girl from the boy's family, who in turn negotiated about the number and kind of household items, clothing and jewelry that the bride would receive from her own parents. When agreement was reached, the boy's parents brought sugar to the girl's house and a few days later an espousal ceremony took place in the presence of relatives from both families. Five women brought sugar also to the girl's home where the girl, facing eastward, and her mother both sat on stools. The women put sugar into the mouths of mother and daughter while saying "*B'Shem Adonai*" ("In the name of the Lord"). Guests were served sweetened rice with coconut milk, and *pan*. That evening the community elders and the boy's father visited the girl's house and the matchmaker announced the betrothal. The girl again sat on one stool, and this time her father on the other, and the *Hazan* or *Kaji* put sugar into the mouths of the girl and of the two fathers. All were treated to snacks, wine and *pan*. (According to Kehimkar, pp.131-2)

If the marriage itself were not going to take place for another six months or more, after one or more weeks there was another ceremony, beginning with five women bringing sugar to the bride's house in the morning. That evening the groom (if rich) rode either on horseback, or in a palanquin; or (if poor) he walked, to the bride's house, attended by guests, torchbearers and music (in true Indian-wedding fashion), all preceded by the *Hazan* singing "*Yigdal Elohim Hai*" (a Hebrew hymn). Once again, at the bride's house, the bride and her mother sat on two stools now covered with white sheets. The groom sat down in front of the bride, a plate of sugar and a ring placed between them. The *Hazan* or *Kaji* gave the ring to the groom, who put it on the bride's left forefinger and said three times in Hebrew : "Behold, thou art betrothed unto me by this ring according to the law of Moses and of Israel." (This—said once and not three times—is part of every Jewish wedding ceremony. Kehimkar claims that the ring-giving was a pre-religious-revival custom among the Bene Israel.) Now sugar was put into the mouths of the bridegroom and of the two fathers. The bride's father gave the groom a ring. Then food was served, after which the prospective bride had to escort her groom to the threshold when he was ready to leave her home. (According to Kehimkar, pp.132-37)

Traditionally, among the Bene Israel, the actual wedding ceremony for first marriages (but not for re-marriages) took place toward the beginning of the week. Especially in villages, and before the introduction of synagogues among the Bene Israel, large marriage tents were erected in open places (as was and is still customary among Hindus and others in India). These tents were very colorful and richly decorated with foliage. (According to Kehimkar, p.134)

Before any wedding preparations were begun, a special memorial *Hashkaba* service was held for the deceased members of the family; and their spiritual presence at the forthcoming wedding was invoked. This ceremony is referred to as the "Wedding *Ud*" because, as for all Bene Israel *Hashkaba* ceremonies, it was customary to burn a particular tree resin called *ud*. A pellet of this *ud*, about the size of a raisin, when placed on a fire, burns with a characteristic odour which the Bene Israel associate only with a memorial for the dead. *Ud* is burned at Muslim tomb-shrines, and it seems that the Bene Israel adopted this custom from their Muslim neighbors, except that the Bene Israel never burned the *Ud* at the cemetery, only in the home during a *Hashkaba* service (and *never* in a synagogue). After completion of the Wedding *Ud*, the family performed a *Malida* ceremony. The custom of burning the *ud* resin is no longer practised today.

Five married women were asked to assist in preparing the wedding feast. As a sign of a marriage, copying practices considered auspicious among the Hindus, they first applied turmeric to the handmill for rice-grinding, and they also tied mango leaves on to it. While grinding the grain, the women sang songs in Marathi about the bride and groom. (According to Kehimkar, p.135)

It was customary for both the bride and groom to take separate ritual baths at their respective houses[18] on the day previous to the marriage. This was accompanied by the playing of music in the house. After the bride's bath, a female bangleseller was called in to put glass bangles on the bride's wrists and also on the wrists of the five (virgin) bridesmaids; dark green (symbolizing fertility) bangles for the bride, five on her right wrist and four on her left.[19] *Haldi* (turmeric) used to be applied to the entire body, but in Kehimkar's day it was applied only to the head and forearms of both bride and groom. After their baths, the bride and groom were fed milk with rice and sugar, and then went to sit together on a cot, the groom wearing a white turban; the bride in a green sari, and a shawl on her head, was bedecked with garlands of flowers. *Mehndi* (henna) was then applied to their hands and feet, with a special bit of henna (brought from the groom's house) being applied to the forefinger of the bride's left hand. (According to Kehimkar, pp.136-8)[20]

Around noon on the day of the marriage a festive meal was served to their respective guests at the bride's as well as at the groom's house. In the midst of the guests there was placed a tinned copper platter containing rice cakes, liver, fried eggs, and *subja*—i.e. the *Malida* platter; and also a glass of wine and some burning incense.[21] The invocation of Elijah was followed in earlier times only by the shaving of the groom's hair, and the subsequent shaving of the hair of his companions. All of them then took baths and dressed the groom in new clothes. In the evening the male guests of the groom were seated in the marriage tent, and female guests were seated apart from the men or in the house proper; and similar arrangements were made at the bride's house. Two men, to the accompaniment of music, carried two large platters bearing gifts : mainly auspicious foods (rice, wheat, unrefined sugar), saris, blouses and gold and silver jewelry. These gifts were for the bride from the groom's parents. When the men bearing the gifts arrived, the bride and her father, seated on stools placed midway between the male and female seating sections were fed sugar by the *Hazan* or *Kaji*. The gifts were then examined and the bride adorned in her new jewelry. (According to Kehimkar, pp.138-9)

During some of the wedding rituals the bride and groom wore a sort of crown of sweet-smelling jasmine or tuberoses. This crown, called a *sherra*, had several strings of blossoms pendant from it, each string ending with a rose flower and hanging over the face of the wearer. For the actual wedding ceremony the groom wore a highly decorated turban. In earlier days he also wore a dagger at his side, as in Muslim custom, and held a tinsel-covered coconut as a symbol of fertility. According to custom (typical of most of India, but not of south India), the groom rode to the bride's house on a caparisoned horse. He was preceded by musicians, while two attendants fanned him, and another held a large ceremonial umbrella over his head as if he were king — the umbrella being an ancient Indian symbol of royalty. (According to Kehimkar, p.142)

Already in Kehimkar's time, especially in cities where space was at a premium, the synagogue, with the women guests seated in the gallery, was replacing the marriage tent on the premises of the bride's family as venue for the marriage ceremony and for the reception thereafter. Previous to the ceremony, the bride's father sat behind the chair of the bride, and the groom's father behind the groom's chair. The hair of a virgin bride was worn hanging loosely and a small sheer shawl covered her head and face during the ceremony. The groom wore his *talith*.

An especially appealing feature of the Bene Israel marriage ceremony is the singing of a love poem written by Israel ben Moses Najara (c.1555-1625 A.D.). The song begins thus in Hebrew :

Yonati ziv yifatayh domah lehseel v'heemot,
V' ahnee l'ahavatayh asheer alamot.

In rough translation :

My dove, your splendour resembles Orion and the Pleiades,
And I, for love of you, shall sing a song.[22]

One wonders whether this song was introduced to the Bene Israel by a Yemenite or by a Cochini *hazan*.

On page 143 of his *History* Kehimkar says, "When the bridegroom enters the synagogue a song is recited and he is seated on a chair until the arrival of the bride." He does not, however, mention the name of the song; nor does he mention a unique Bene Israel tradition which is still sometimes part of the Bene Israel wedding ceremony of today : when the ceremony is about to begin and the groom is already standing under the wedding canopy (*hupah*), the groom sings Najara's medieval Hebrew poem, singing the entire poem *solo* as the bride enters the synagogue and very slowly approaches the *hupah*. A few weeks in advance of the wedding ceremony the Bene Israel groom would begin to prepare for this solo performance. Only if he was for some reason incapable of singing the song alone, would the song be sung in unison by those present at the ceremony. This song is part of Cochin Jewish liturgy too. It is sung in unison by the Cochin Jews especially on *Shavuot*, also in the *Succah*, during the *Simhat Torah* procession, at all sorts of festive dinner parties, and on *Shabbat Hatunah* (the Wedding Sabbath). But, it was and is *not sung solo* by the groom as part of the Cochin Jewish wedding ceremony. Shalom Joseph Penkar's *Shirei R'nanot* (see above, p. 92) contains this poem together with instruction that it is to be sung on the eve of the Wedding Sabbath.

With the bride, groom and their respective fathers all standing under the *hupah*, the groom held a glass of wine or of grape juice in which lay a special gold or silver elongated ring (like a small pointer) called *akda* or *akkara*.[23] Once the prayers and blessings had been recited, the groom drank half of the contents of his goblet. Thereafter the *Hazan* or

Kaji read aloud the marriage contract, which the Bene Israel call *akhtana* (*ketubàh* in Hebrew). Then it was signed by the *Ḥazan* or *Kaji* and by two witnesses. The groom handed the document to the bride who, in turn, gave it to her father for safe keeping. The guests sang a special wedding song. Another full goblet was given to the groom and to the *Ḥazan* or *Kaji*, and *Kiddush* was recited over it. Again the groom drank only half, giving the other half to his bride. (It was not a Bene Israel custom for the groom to break a glass under foot.[24]) Next, the bride's father tied a *laccha*[25] around the bride's neck. The *Ḥazan* or *Kaji* drank a sip from his glass and the remainder was poured into a large full punch bowl, the contents of which were distributed to all those present. The bride now sat to the right of the groom while the hems of their garments or of their handkerchiefs were tied together. Likewise, the two fathers, now seated behind the newlyweds, had their own handkerchiefs or garment hems tied together as a sign of union of the two families. The *Ḥazan* or *Kaji* then pronounced a blessing upon the bride and groom. And the gift-giving began. The bride's parents fed a bit of sugar to the groom and presented him with a gold ring. Then came a description by the *Ḥazan* or *Kaji* of each gift received[26] and announcement of the name of its donor. (According to Kehimkar, pp.144-6)

Before the bride and groom left the synagogue they went up to the Holy Ark together and kissed the *Torah* scroll.[27] They left the building with their little fingers interlocking. A pompous parade of guests on foot, the bride in a carriage or palanquin, and the groom on horseback then proceeded, accompanied by music and fireworks, to the bride's house. There her parents had arranged for a feast for all the guests of both families, after which the newlyweds spent their first night together in a separate room in the bride's home. Even the middle and poor classes tried to keep up with the wedding pageantry and feasting. Frequently they went deeply into debt because of this (a common occurrence all over India). (According to Kehimkar, pp.146-7)

The entire day after the wedding was devoted to several games and little rituals prescribed by custom ending in yet another procession, taking the bride and groom to the groom's house. Although Kehimkar does not mention this, it was customary at the entrance to the house for the sister or the brother of the groom to exact a promise from the newlyweds that the newlyweds would give their children in marriage to the children of the brother or sister concerned. This custom had almost completely died out among the Bene Israel by the beginning of the 20th century, largely because parents could no longer enforce such an arrangement once child-marriages had gone out of fashion.[28]

Having arrived at the groom's house, the groom sat on his father's lap and the bride on the lap of her mother-in-law.[29] The feet of the newlyweds were washed by the groom's sister and husband, or by the groom's brother and wife. Now the groom's parents gave a feast, also for the relatives of both bride and groom. On the following night the floral marriage "crowns" were removed and either thrown into the sea or tied to the roof of the house. (According to Kehimkar, pp.149-50)[30]

While the Bene Israel by no means incorporated the unique Cochin Jewish wedding procedure, they did observe several elements of it, such as: recitation of many passages from the special Cochin Jewish marriage liturgy, and placing the wedding ring in a goblet of wine (although the Cochini ring was not at all shaped like the Bene Israel *akda*). The Bene Israel of the 19th century also shared with the Cochin Jews numerous features of marriage ritual which are clear derivatives of Hindu custom, such as: the marriage ceremonies being protracted over several days; tying a marriage locket around the bride's neck; women singing songs in the local language at specific stages in the celebration; marriage processions; simulation of the bride and groom as "king" and "queen" (among Hindus, as Krishna and Radha) during certain aspects of the celebration (the Bene Israel to a lesser extent than among the Cochin Jews); "games" to be played by the bride and groom; some feasts or parties hosted by the groom's family, others by the bride's family; and the fact that fixed responsibilities for and active participation in specific aspects of the marriage celebrations involved many members, both male and female, of one's particular Jewish community (for Hindus, one's *jati*) beyond the immediate families of bride and groom.

At the beginning of this section on *Marriage* (p. 132) a quotation from Kehimkar pointed out many Hindu marriage customs which the Bene Israel had incorporated or adapted as features of traditional Bene Israel marriage custom. Of course, the most significant difference is the Hebrew ceremony as such. But, even in the carry-overs from Bene Israel pre-religious-revival days, there *are* differences; to mention only a few : for the *mehndi* ceremony the Bene Israel bride always wears a green sari (the Hindu wedding sari is red); the Bene Israel *laccha* is unlike any for other local communities; and the number of glass bangles for a Bene Israel bride also differs from the number worn by brides of other local communities.

The following apt remarks about Indian marriages in general would have been equally applicable to the Bene Israel in the days before their religious revival, i.e. before the introduction to the Bene Israel of the *ketubah*, the formal Jewish marriage contract :

...the family and friends as witnesses [of the wedding ceremonies] accept the legality of the marriage, which has traditionally been sufficient proof of marriage. Even today [1974] few marriages are registered as a statistical entry and no marriage certificate is issued nor is any marriage license required. In many cases the wedding invitation is the sole documentary proof of the marriage and this is admissible as legal evidence.[31]

In Maharashtra, however, for more than 20 years, there has been a State Law requiring that all marriages be registered.

A certain petition was signed by "23 Bene Israel Ladies" of Poona. It shows us not only how enlightened these Bene Israel women already were in the year 1891, but that they were even then acting in truly progressive feminist fashion — i.e. lobbying on behalf of women of *all* communities, since their own community, the Bene Israel, least of all Indian communities needed a raise to age 12 for legal Age of Consent. By 1891 only a very small percentage of Bene Israel were marrying below the age of 15. The petition, as printed by the Government Press and as it appears in *India Bills, Objects and Reasons, Part 1, 1891, for Act 19 of 1891*, reads as follows :

Petition from Aryan Ladies Association, Poona
To the Government of India :
We, the undersigned members of the Poona Arya Mahila Samaj [Aryan Ladies Association] and other Hindu Ladies of Poona humbly submit our petition :
We hope that the Bill, which has been introduced before you by the Hon'ble Sir Andrew Noble for the purpose of raising the age of consent will be finally passed by you in law, whereby you will protect your poor female subjects in this country from being outraged by men during their immature state.
We now submit our petition that the age of consent may be raised to at least 12 years. [The age of consent was at that time 10 years.]... If the aforementioned Bill be passed by Government into Law, we shall ever pray as their well-wishers.
Signed by 65 Hindu Ladies and 23 Bene Israel Ladies.

(The closing line is, as printed by the Government Press, exactly as quoted above; no names were mentioned.)

B.J. Israel has made a useful analytical study of the actual marriage statistics of the Bene Israel of the Kolaba and of Poona Districts, based on the Government Census of 1881.[32] It includes a comparison of the Bene Israel with the Hindus, Muslims and Parsis in respect of marriage-related statistics. The 1881 statistics for Bene Israel show that a very small proportion of Bene Israel males and females were still being married below the age of 15 years. After the age of 24 the number of unmarried individuals becomes negligible. The extremely small number of widowers below the age of 30 years indicates that Bene Israel men who were widowed early, usually remarried. That the men were generally substantially older than their wives is seen from the fact that in the age-group of 30 years and over, as many as 44·9 percent of all the Bene Israel women in Kolaba District and 36·8 percent in Poona District were widows. B.J. Israel points out that this shows that, except for very young and childless widows, the remarriage of widows was rare. The 1881 Census Tables give no indication of the extent of polygyny, but a childless first marriage usually led to taking a second wife rather than to divorcing the barren first wife.

The Bene Israel followed the general Indian practice of extended families living in patrilocal[33] joint-households. Most households consisted of a father, mother, unmarried daughters and sons, and married sons with their respective wives and children. A house may have had enough sleeping quarters to allow for some privacy, but a daughter-in-law was otherwise under the thumb of her mother-in-law. Sons who could not get along in a joint-family found a ready way out by joining a Native Indian Regiment (though this was by no means the sole Bene Israel motive for joining the army). In a joint-family, when the pater-familias died, all family financial matters and settlement of affairs, big and small, devolved upon the eldest son. The original joint-family might, or might not then break up and each married son might or might not set up his own household which, in turn, would eventually become a joint-family household of its own.

In the 19th century, polygyny was frequent among the Bene Israel, the husband, two wives, and their offspring all living together. If, however, the co-wives were not on friendly terms, the husband had to maintain them in separate households. Ashkenazic Jewry, since the 11th century, has been bound by a ruling against bigamy established by Rabbi Gershon ben Juda of Metz and Mayence. But bigamy was never forbidden among the Bene Israel in spite of the frequent outcries against polygyny appearing in Bene Israel journals and other forums. However, in the early decades of the 20th century polygyny became much less common among the Bene Israel and was usually resorted to only in cases in which there was no chance of issue from the first wife. In Bombay, both Shaare Ha-Rachamim and Shaare Rason synagogues decided not to perform bigamous marriages under their auspices (but Judaism does not stipulate that marriages have to take place in a synagogue).

Folklore of the Konkan describes how "remarriage of a [Hindu] widow among the lower classes is generally performed at night, and under an old mango tree. It is never performed in the house. A widow who has remarried cannot take part in any auspicious ceremony such as a marriage, etc." (p.73). Among the Bene Israel a widow was also allowed to remarry, but a widow could only marry a widower. A Bene Israel widower, however, was allowed to marry any Jewish unmarried woman. A man had to marry a virgin for his first marriage; a widower too could marry a virgin, but was under no obligation to do so. Remarriages could not be performed in a synagogue. In the case of a remarriage, the ceremonies lasted for only one day, and no music was allowed. Although Bene Israel widows were not excluded from attendance at weddings of others, they were barred from serving as functionaries in the actual ceremonies. (According to Kehimkar, p.143)

The custom of _Halitzah_ (see above, p. 102) was not practised by the Bene Israel; and Levirate marriage was impossible if the Bene Israel widow's brother-in-law had not yet been married and widowed since only Bene Israel widowers were allowed to marry widows. However, when a widower did marry a widow, he did have to obtain the consent of the brother of her deceased husband.

Adoption sometimes took place. It was not obligatory for childless couples, nor did the adopted child have to be a relative, nor was the consent of the families of the adopting couple necessary, nor were the Bene Israel bound by any outside laws in this matter (according to Kehimkar, p.108).

Adultery was the only cause for divorce, which was rare among the Bene Israel. A letter of divorce was a prerequisite, and in former days was written in Marathi. (According to _halacha_, it must be written in Hebrew.) Only the husband, not the wife, could request a divorce; and a divorced Bene Israel woman could not remarry. The Hindu revulsion against divorce, and also against widow remarriage, was reflected among the Bene Israel in a distaste for both of these options, and they relatively rarely resorted to either of them, considering that both divorce and widow remarriage are sanctioned according to the Jewish religion.[34] The statistics show, however, that there was more widow remarriage among the Bene Israel than among their Hindu and Muslim neighbours.

According to Kěhimkar (p.109), in practice, although not according to legal stricture, upon a Bene Israel man's death, his estate was divided among his widow(s) and sons, with a portion also being set aside to cover the marriage expenses and dowry of any then unmarried daughters. In the event of no sons, daughters could and did share in the inheritance. In the case of a childless marriage, the widow was supposed to inherit all the property. In 1853 Haeem Samuel Kehimkar founded the _Bene Israel Benevolent Society_ in order to afford relief to poor and helpless widows, destitute orphans, and infirm men and women of the community.

Death

Until about 1917 there existed no Bene Israel _Hevrah Kedushah_ Society to minister to their dying and dead. Finally, when this kind of traditionally Jewish burial society was established, it functioned only in Bombay City. However, even though there was no Bene Israel _Hevrah Kedushah_ in the 19th century, there was a charitable society founded in 1887 called _Beni-Israel Kullianechhu Sabha_ (Bene Israel Association for Communal Welfare). The objectives of this association were :

> to guarantee upon a member's death, to the heirs and nominees of the deceased, a sum equal to one rupee and eight annas for every member on the roll, according to the class to which the deceased belonged at the time of his demise; to bury the homeless; and to defray the expenses of burial in the case of those whose relatives are too poor to do so, according to Jewish rites; and also to help other charitable schemes. This Association has, from the first July 1894, introduced a marriage fund. [From _The Indian Directory_, Thacker, Spink & Co., Calcutta, 1905, p.1321.]

When anyone of their community died, the traditional Bene Israel custom was to call upon relatives and friends to do the needful.[35] Partly because of universal Jewish custom, but also because of quick decomposition of the dead body in India's hot climate, burial had to take place as soon as possible after the death occurred (preferably within 24 hours), but never on the Sabbath.

Psalms of David were read in Marathi to a dying person, and sugar water or grape juice was poured into his/her mouth. Immediately after the moment of death, the eyes and mouth were closed, and the *Shema* was recited. Then the water was poured out of every water container in the entire household; a tear was made in the garment of each mourner; the dead body was covered with a white sheet; and the bed upon which it lay was turned with its head toward the east and feet toward the west (i.e. facing Jerusalem). Women beat their breasts, and there was wailing and weeping. Where there was a synagogue, the *Shamash* was informed of the death; he, in turn, informed the rest of the community; and he arranged for the grave-digging, shrouds for the body, etc. (According to Kehimkar, pp.152-3) To quote from Kehimkar (p.154) :

> The dead body is then rubbed with coconut milk and soap and is washed in warm water on the cot[36] under which a large tub is placed to catch the water used, and while this is done the *lunghi* [ankle length waistcloth] is tied around the waist. The Kaji or the Reader or any one else of the Bene Israel who can repeat Hebrew texts, recites the prescribed text. The body of the deceased is then bathed in cold water in the following manner : cold water brought in an open-mouthed copper vessel called a *Handa* is placed near the dead. It contains *Subja* and rose flowers. The minister takes water from the vessel in a new earthen pot, and pours it over the dead, from the head to the feet, and the earthen pot is then dashed to pieces on the ground near the feet. After seven pots have been thus poured over the body and in turn dashed to the ground, the eighth one is kept filled with cold water together with a towel used for wiping the dead body, and a lamp is kept constantly burning near it, day and night, for seven days, as the spirit of the deceased is supposed to visit this apartment during the whole 7 days of mourning.

A male body is washed and dressed by men, that of a female by women. The deceased was dressed in a full outfit of clothing and was then brought out into the gathering of men. The *hazan* or *kaji* chanted a dirge while the *talith* and *tzitzith* of the deceased (if a male) were put on him. Prior to putting on the *tzitzith* one of its fringes was bitten off. The big toes of the body were tied together with a thread, A twig of *subja* was tied by means of a handkerchief to the right hand, and the palms of the hands were placed one over the other. Already in Kehimkar's day it was customary to place a bit of earth from Jerusalem on the eyes and mouth of the deceased, then to cover the entire face with a handkerchief. A winding sheet was next wrapped around the body in special way, and tied at the top of the head, at the waist, and at the bottom of the feet. Rose water was sprinkled over the shroud, while the officiating person asked the community to forgive all faults of the deceased. The body, wrapped in its shroud, was placed on a portable bier (the property of the synagogue), made of woven cane, and was strewn with rose petals, *subja*, and sometimes with camphor. Usually the Bene Israel did not use coffins[37] but, if a coffin was/is used, it was/is made of plain wood covered inside and out with black or white cotton cloth. The lid is removed before the actual burial. (According to Kehimkar, pp.154-5)[38]

Kehimkar (p.153) seems somewhat on the defensive when he mentions that Bene Israel widows perform the same custom as do Hindu widows, even if not immediately upon the expiration of the husband :

> The [Bene Israel] widow of the deceased does not "dash her bangles" and "break them

against the cot", nor does she break her black bead necklace called "Lacha" immediately after life is extinct, as stated by the Gazetteer (Bombay Gazetteer vol.XVIII part 1 page 532). Breaking the bangles and the necklace of black beads and taking off the nose-ring takes place after the corps [sic!] 'has been washed (Tahara), and when it is lifted to be taken either to the coffin or to the bier to be buried. The ornaments above-named are never worn by a [Bene Israel] woman as long as she remains a widow, and she only wears them [again] after remarriage.

The *Gazetteer* to which Kehimkar refers was published in 1884-85. Whereas a Hindu widow was (except in some of the lowest castes) forbidden to remarry, some **Bene Israel** widows did remarry.

First, male members of the family, and after them all other men of the gathering, in groups, took turns at carrying the body to the cemetery (either on a bier or in a coffin). In rural areas there usually was a Bene Israel cemetery[39] close enough to most villages. After the establishment of synagogues, a cemetery was affiliated to each synagogue.

After the *Shema* was recited, prayers were intoned during the funeral procession, either by the *Kaji*, *Hazan*, or other officiating person. The corpse was placed in the grave with its head toward the east and its feet toward the west. A bag, containing a handful of earth presented by each person present, was placed under the corpse's head. If a coffin was used, its lid (or else a simple wooden marker) was firmly stuck, end down, at the foot of the grave, to serve as a marker until later when a tombstone would replace it. The mourners, and after them all men present threw handfuls of earth into the grave. Volunteers from among the gathering completed the burial, covering the entire grave with earth. Prayers were recited. On leaving the cemetery, each person plucked some grass and threw it behind his/her back, symbolic of resurrection of the dead. Upon return to the house of mourning, relatives and friends washed their hands and feet before entering. (According to Kehimkar, pp.156-7)

The following description of Hindu mourning customs (quoted from *Folklore of the Konkan*, p.69) is inserted here in order to bring out the obvious parallels, almost point by point. Although certain terms and rites in Bene Israel death ceremonies are due to Muslim influence, it is especially interesting to note the Hindu parallels particularly because Hindu disposal of the dead is characteristically by cremation and not by burial. (Some low class Hindus do bury their dead and do not cremate; but the customs described below pertain to Hindus who cremate their dead.)

The earthen pots that are required for the funeral rites are all broken....All the members of the family of the dead have to observe mourning for ten days. They are purified on the eleventh day after taking a bath....A man in mourning does not touch those who are not in mourning....The son of the deceased or, in the absence of a son, any male member belonging to the family....performs the funeral rites....during the first twelve days....and he has to take his meals only once a day....During the period of mourning, every morning a Brahmin comes to the mourner's house and recites some passages from the *Garud Purana*....On the eleventh day the house is besmeared with cow dung....All the clothes are washed.

One will see in this a remarkable similarity to many standard Jewish mourning procedures : a certain number of days of mourning at home : *Kaddish* said by the son of the deceased; prayers said daily at the home of the deceased by a *minyan*; etc. as well as to several specifically Bene Israel mourning customs, some of which are described in the following paragraphs.

Father, mother, brother, sister, son, daughter, husband and wife of the Bene Israel deceased went into mourning for seven days, doing no work and never leaving the house during this period. Meals were supplied by friends and relatives. The mourners covered the lower part of their faces, and sometimes their heads; observed silence; were allowed to sit or lie only on mats directly on the floor. They were not allowed to wear shoes or jewelry, nor to cut their hair, shave, wash or change their clothes—not even on the Sabbath. Daily, morning and evening prayers were recited at the home of the mourners, always with at least a *minyan* present; and each time the chief mourners would recite the Mourners' *Kaddish* (a glorification of God and a prayer for peace). Many friends and relatives paid condolence calls all during the week of mourning. On the third day, they purified the house by spreading cow-dung[40] or water over the floors; and they washed all the household clothes. On the seventh morning, the eighth clay pot (which had been filled with water on the first day) was taken to the burial ground by at least a *minyan*. They compacted the earth over the grave and then the water from the eighth pot was poured over the grave, after which the pot was thrown away. The *Huzan* or *Kaji* again recited prayers, and the chief mourners recited the *Kaddish*. Upon returning home, the mourners bathed and donned fresh clothes. A piece of the shroud that had been set aside was placed in a room together with a *Malida* tray containing pieces of cakes fried in oil, goat's liver, *subja*, a bit of boiled rice, and some wine. The *Shema* and some Psalms were chanted. *Kaddish* was recited once more. And the week of mourning concluded with a small feast at which the chief mourner was given a new turban. That evening, in the synagogue, memorial blessings for the deceased were recited, and a donation was usually given to the synagogue for reciting special blessings for the deceased every morning and evening throughout the next eleven months. (According to Kehimkar, p.158)

One month after a death, family and friends would gather at the grave for prayer, and each person present was given a sprig of *subja*.[41] Memorial services and a feast were provided by those who could afford to do so on the 15th and 30th days after a death, and at the end of the 6th and 11th months. The male mourners themselves attended synagogue and recited the Mourners' *Kaddish* every Sabbath for eleven months. Either on the seventh day, or at some time during the sixth or eleventh month after a death, some Bene Israel families placed a stone marker at the head of the grave, engraved (in Hebrew or in Marathi, or in both) with the deceased's name, age and date of death.

In the 19th century, and still continuing today, memorial anniversaries were reckoned according to the Jewish calendar. In observing the annual death anniversary of one's immediate kin, the Bene Israel recited *Kaddish*, either at the synagogue or at home, with a *minyan* present. A speical memorial oil-lamp, consisting of a white bowl with a thick wick, was lit at home on the eve of the anniversary and kept burning for 24 hours. When in use, it was set on a table rather than being suspended in a hanging position. On the death anniversary, the grave of the deceased was visited and *Hashkaba* prayers were recited there. Donations were made to charity. On the Sabbath nearest the death anniversary, the head of the family was honored by being called upon to read from the *Torah* during the synagogue services. On the death anniversary of their parents, some Bene Israel would fast for the entire day. Another custom was to read aloud from *Psalm 119*, but only those verses beginning with the (Hebrew) letters which spelled out the deceased's name : the Psalm has verses beginning with every letter of the Hebrew alphabet. Those who could afford it, hosted a small dinner for close relatives. (According to Kehimkar, pp.159-60)

If the Bene Israel life-cycle rituals seem strange, this merely reveals ignorance of India and her customs. Anywhere in the world it is precisely the details of folk customs absorbed from non-Jewish neighbours which, more than any other factor, differentiate one Jewish community from another. This chapter has shown the degree and flavor of Indian influence upon much of the ritual, sociology and material culture of the Bene Israel. It is really not possible to weigh Hindu influence against Muslim influence upon the Bene Israel. B. J. Israel suggests that it was easier, and therefore more likely, for the Bene Israel to have absorbed more from the Muslims than from the Hindus simply because the Hindu caste system created barriers between Bene Israel and Hindus which did not exist between Bene Israel and Muslims. But we must bear in mind that the local Muslims had also been considerably influenced by Hindu customs and superstitions.[42]

Many old Bene Israel habits — too numerous for all of them to have been described in this chapter — became less and less popular among the Bene Israel toward the end of the 19th century. Yet, in all those instances of Bene Israel customs and rituals traceable to non-Jewish influences which persisted after the Bene Israel's religious revival, we find that the prayers and blessings which the Bene Israel attached to them were wholly Jewish in their referents, content, and religious core.

NOTES

1. In the Konkan area, Hindus offer coconuts to the sea on several different occasions. Green glass bangles are often worn by pregnant women in North India, especially in Rajasthan.
2. Kehimkar : *History*, p.112.
3. Ibid., p.116.
4. Ibid., p.117. Here Kehimkar has in mind the coincidence with a local custom in connection with *Panchvi*. *Panch* is the word for the number "five", and by *Panchvi* Kehimkar is probably referring to the term *Panch Deva* or *Panchayatan*, both of which, as used in the Konkan, refer to five Hindu deities together, namely : Shiva, Vishnu, Surya, Ganapati and Devi. (*Folkore of the Konkan*, p.xxiv). Kehimkar stresses that, in spite of the similarity, the Bene Israel custom does not imply that they believed in the local idea of transference of evil through coins which are meant to avert the evil eye. Nor did the Bene Israel think of the custom in terms of the presence of a Hindu deity.

   To Hindus "five" is a very auspicious number, and the Bene Israel have absorbed this belief. The reader will note in the present text frequent specification of the number "five" in the following descriptions of Bene Israel customs : for instance, on p. 114 & p. 128 "five different kinds of fresh fruits", on p. 132 "five unwidowed women", p. 133 "five women bringing sugar", p. 134 "five married women assist in preparing the wedding feast" and "five bridesmaids". However, in Jewish numerological lore the number "five" is not particularly significant. But the customary Jewish way of writing numbers involves the use of the letters of the Hebrew alphabet according to their accepted fixed order. Of some significance may be the fact that it is the fifth letter, called "*hay*", which the Jews use in writing to mean "God". The fact that there are five books of Moses (the *Torah*) might also be relevant. In this context one Bene Israel respondent invited attention to a Hindu proverb : "Wherever five people collect together, there is God." She also mentioned, as of possible relevance, the fact that there are five fingers on a hand, five senses, and five elements (air, earth, ether, fire and water).

   The presence of five married women whose husbands are alive is required in several Hindu rituals; also, mixtures of five holy foods : milk, curds, ghee, honey and sugar; and vessels made of five metals. Amulets and anklets made of an alloy of five different metals are worn to ward off the evil eye. The number five is also auspicious in Islam.
5. Ibid., p.118.
6. The coconut is almost always an important element in auspicious Hindu rituals.

7. *Leviticus* 12 : 4 & 5 prescribes, in the event of a male child, seven days of separation and thirty-three days of uncleanliness, with fourteen days of separation and sixty-six days until purification if a female baby is born. Among some Brahmins the mother's pollution lasts for thirty days in the case of a son, and forty days in that of a daughter.
8. The *Pidyan Ha-Ben* ceremony for the redemption of the first-born has only relatively recently been adopted by the Bene Israel, performing this ceremony on the fortieth day after birth, but only when and if a Cohen happened to be available. After the ceremony the father would give a feast marked by *hookah* (water-pipe) smoking and the distribution of *pan supari* (according to Kehimkar, p.125).
9. Kehimkar, p.126 : "It is said that some of the Bene Israel worshipped in former times....the small-pox goddess Shitla Devi in imitation of Hindus; but several years have already elapsed since the abolition of this superstition from their midst."
10. *Folklore of the Konkan*, p.30 : "There is a famous temple of the goddess Shitala at Chaul where the deity is worshipped by Brahmans, who recite Vedic hyms, whenever smallpox prevails in the village....The women walk around the temple every day as long as the signs of the disease are visible on their children.......It is worth noting that even Musulmans ask for a Kaul [a favour from the deity] from this goddess."

We learn from the *Bombay Gazetteer* of 1882, discussing Thana District, p.273, that "tho they know it is contrary to their religion, village Parsis have adopted many of the practices of their Hindu, Musulman and Christian neighbours....They offer vows and sacrifices of goats and fowls to the goddess of small-pox. Some reverence the shrines of Musulman saints, offer vows and make presents to them, and a few offer vows and presents to the Virgin Mary and to Christian saints in the Catholic village churches....The Parsis believe in ghosts and in magic. They attribute many diseases to possession by evil spirits and employ Musulman, Hindu and Parsi magicians to drive out the spirit and to cure the effects of the evil eye."
11. *Gazetteer of Bombay Presidency, Part III, Deccan-Poona*, printed at the Government Central Press, Bombay, 1885, p.531.
12. Certain days of the week are preferred; according to Kehimkar (p.134) these were Sunday, Monday and Tuesday. The Bene Israel do not rely on horoscopes. On the other hand, horoscopes feature very importantly in choosing marriage partners and in setting an auspicious date for a Hindu marriage.

This is quite different from the Jewish custom of forbidding marriages on certain dates (or periods) which commemorate historical Jewish national tragedies.
13. Kehimkar stresses that the Bene Israel intention when waving coins around a person was not to avert the evil eye, but to bring good luck and prosperity. *Folklore of the Konkan* cites many instances of Hindu custom where copper coins, fowls, limes, coconuts, etc. are waved around a person in order to avert the evil eye. Surrounded as the Bene Israel were by the prevalence of such customs, the amazing thing is that they did not incorporate many more superstitions of their neighbours.
14. The Bene Israel followed Hindu custom in this respect. On p.134 of *Rabbi D'Beth Hillel's Travels*, Madras 1832, we are told that "They [the Bene Israel] are accustomed to marry their children when very young from three years and upwards" and "they are accustomed to marry two or three children at once." Such child marriages as occurred among the Bene Israel were in reality binding betrothals and were not consummated until puberty. The practise of more than one couple being married at one and the same ceremony is also a not uncommon practice among Hindus.
15. Kehimkar, pp.128-9. For a discussion of age at time of marriage and of other marital statistics, see above, p. 138.
16. Cross-cousin marriage : marriage between two cousins, the parent of one cousin being a sibling of the parent of the other cousin, but of the opposite sex.
17. Kehimkar, p.130. This is a reference to the separation of *Kala* and *Gora* Bene Israel.
18. Ibid., p.136. The custom was to bathe at home and not in the *mikve*. Ritual baths are also important in the Hindu religion.
19. It is customary to put on new green glass bangles for other auspicious occasions (such as when

making a vow, purification after childbirth, or for the 7th-month-of-pregnancy ceremony), but never as many as at the time of marriage. On other occasions they don the same number of bangles on each wrist. Putting new glass bangles on girls is also a prevalent Hindu custom on several occasions, such as at the time of first menstruation or during pregnancy ceremonies.

20. For a full description of the *Mehndi* Ceremony as practised today, see Shalva Weil's doctoral dissertation, pp.215-9.
21. Kehimkar (p.138) says that the Bene Israel gave up the practice of burning incense "fifty or sixty years ago" when they "received information from the Jews [i.e. the Baghdadis or Cochin Jews] that it was improper to do so. However, incense is prescribed for this particular offering in *Leviticus* 2 : 1. Since the destruction of the Second Temple, the only incense forbidden to Jews is the specific mixture of aromatic ingredients previously used in Temple offerings.
22. This poem is in the form of an acrostic, in that the first letter of the first three verses in succession, followed by the first two letters of the fourth (the last) verse spell out the word Israel and the poem expresses a love for Israel. Looking at the poem metaphorically, a mystic, spiritual interpretation is often attributed to it, as to other love poems. Its author, Najara, was born in Damascus and wrote secular poems and love songs, as well as sacred compositions. *Z'mirot Yisrael* (Hymns of Israel, a collection of Najara's poems was first published in Safed in 1587, followed by other books of his poetry. This particular song appears in the *Tsafir* (the Yemenite prayer book for the Sabbath) as well as in the *Shirot Cochin* (Songs of Cochin), the first edition of which came out in Bombay in 1846. It also appears in collections from Saloniki, from Aden, and in some rare manuscripts from Persia. See Israel Davidson's *Thesaurus of Medieval Hebrew Poetry*, Ktav Publishing House Inc., Jerusalem, 1970, Vol.II, p.357, no.2118.
23. This ring was put on the forefinger of the bride's left hand, and formerly the Bene Israel woman always continued to wear it. The custom began to go out of fashion at the turn of the century, the *akkara* being replaced for daily wear by a simple wedding band. Also, nowadays sometimes the *laccha*, (see below, note 25) instead of the *akkara*, is placed in the glass of wine.
24. The common Jewish custom is for the groom to crush the wine glass under foot. Some say this is to remind us of the destruction of the Temple; others see in it the symbolic defloration of the bride. The Bene Israel modern custom is to wrap the glass in a handkerchief and knock it against something solid, or on the ground until it breaks; but some of them stamp it under foot.
25. A Hindu token of marriage is called a *tali* or *laccha*, a symbolic gold bead or pendant. The Bene Israel married woman also wears a *laccha*, which might be faceted or smooth, and in the 20th century often is in the shape of a six-pointed "Jewish" star set within a circle. The traditional Bene Israel *laccha* necklace was of intertwined strands of tiny black glass beads. If and when the couple could afford to do so later on they might change the plain black necklace to a chain of slightly larger black glass beads interspersed with small gold beads. But the pendant always remains the original *laccha* pendant.

Tying the *tali (laccha)* around the bride's neck is an essential feature of Hindu marriages in south the western India. The pendant cum necklace is not removed from the woman's neck during the lifetime of her husband. The *tali* of the Hindu woman usually bears, or is actually in the shape of, the symbol of the *jati* (sub-caste) of the newlyweds concerned. At the time of the Hindu wedding ritual, the tradition is to tie the *tali* around the bride's neck on saffron-dyed yellow cord.
26. According to Kehimkar, p.146 :

When cash was presented to the bride or bridegroom or to anybody else, an *anna* [16 *annas* equalled one rupee] for each gift was given by the presenter to the Kaji or Reader in former times....The practice of filling up the lap of the bride with five pieces of almonds, dry dates and betelnut, as well as of giving these articles to the headman and the Kaji has also gone out of use.

27. This custom is maintained by the Bene Israel today, even in Israel. See Shalva Weil's doctoral dissertation, pp.215-21, for a detailed description of Bene Israel marriage customs as practised today.
28. The promise made at the entrance to the groom's house was a way of perpetuating cross-cousin

marriage (still common in western and southern India, inclusive of the local Muslim population). Cross-cousin marriage kept property within the same extended family. Often it was only within this family circle that young people had any opportunity to get to know members of the opposite sex; so, at least in a cross-cousin marriage the bride and groom were not marrying total strangers.

29. This was symbolic of her new relationship. Throughout patrilineal India, in extended-family households, the son's wife was under the thumb of her mother-in-law, often until she herself became a mother-in-law.
30. Immersing ritual items in the sea after a religious ceremony, and also tying things to the housetop to ward off the evil eye, are customs common to both Hindus and Indian Muslims.
31. Margaret Ann Sood : *The Urban Middle Class Family in India*, Experimental Study Unit Series, Educational Resources Centre, New Delhi, 1974, p.27.
32. B.J. Israel: "Age of Marriage Among the Bene Israel : Some Statistics of 1881", in *The Bene Israel of India : Some Studies*, Orient Longman Ltd., 1984, pp.167-84.
33. However, several communities in the areas of Kerala and Assam were both matrilocal and matrilineal.
34. The same is true of Islam. To use the terminology of anthropologist M.N. Srinivas, a kind of "Sanskritization" has taken place in both communities in this respect. The Indian Muslims are surprisingly reticent, particularly in regard to divorce. Even after civil divorce initiated by the wife became possible in India, the present author has known educated Indian Muslim women who had more than sufficient grounds for divorce but who considered it unthinkable, not because of Muslim mores, but "because in this orthodox Hindu milieu of South India it is just not proper". To quote from a recent study of the subject, namely *Marriage Customs Among Muslims in India. A Sociological Study of the Shia Marriage Customs* by Sheikh Abrar Husain, Sterling Publishers Pvt., Ltd., Delhi. 1976 :(In rural Maharashtra Sunni Muslims predominate while many Bohras and Khojas — Muslim converts from Gujarat — who are Shias live in Bombay.) Sunni and Shia Muslim ideas on marriage are quite similar but

> a great point of difference between Sunnis and Shias on the subject of marriage is that whilst the former insist on the presence of witnesses at the contractual ceremony, they do not require any testimony for the dissolution of the contract by the husband. The Shias, on the contrary, do not require any evidence of marriage so long as the parties agree that it has been performed regularly, but they insist upon the presence of witnesses for the dissolution of the contract by the husband. (p.41)
> Hindus on the whole abhor it [divorce] and their views have influenced Indian Muslim Society as well. (p.157)
> Shia Society is also extremely averse to divorce and considers it a family dishonour. Generally a Shia may prefer his daughter or ward to die of family torture than be separated from her husband. This is no doubt due to a great extent to the long impact of Hindu culture. But now with the broadening of liberal views....we find occasional cases of divorces as well as remarriages, though rarely in Shia society. (p.158)
> Widow remarriage was not prohibited but, on the contrary, encouraged by Islam. But in the atmosphere that prevailed in Indian society, widow remarriage among Muslims had also begun to recede and was looked down upon. (p.165)
> Though the prejudice against remarriage had begun to disappear rapidly in towns and cities, it still lingers among orthodox families and in rural areas. (p.169)

On the other hand, both divorce and widow remarriage were traditionally allowed among the Hindu oil-pressers of the Konkan—which is another indicator of their low status within the Hindu caste hierarchy, and probably preferring not to be comparable to people of low status is another reason why the Bene Israel and the Muslims did not often have divorces or widow remarriages in their respective communities.

35. To this day it is being carried out in this fashion by the Bene Israel even in modern New Delhi.

36. The typical Indian cot, called a *charpoy*, has four wooden legs and a frame through which is laced a webbing of rope or woven cane.
37. The Bene Israel looked upon the use of coffins as a Christian practice.
38. A few ultra-modern Bene Israel burials have the coffin sealed with its lid on, but not before sprinkling a handful of earth upon the body inside.
39. The Bene Israel use the Muslim words *kabrastan* and *kaffan* respectively for "cemetery" and "shroud"
40. Hindus regularly use cow dung as the base of a mixture with which they cleanse, as well as ritually purify, the floors of their home.
41. In place of the twig of sweet-smelling myrtle which is used by other Jews in order to dispel evil. After the destruction of the Temple, myrtle instead of incense came into use for this purpose.
42. Personal communication to the present author.

Chapter 12
Bene Israel Synagogues

During the last quarter of the 19th century the religious life of the Bene Israel was substantially different from what it had been during the first half of that century. After considerable numbers of Bene Israel had mastered the English language (in Rev. Wilson's day), they not only moved away from the missionaries, but, because they were now able to obtain and understand the wealth of material about Judaism written in English, they were no longer so dependent upon Cochinis and Baghdadis in matters of religion. Even so, Cochin *Hazanim* still officiated in many Bene Israel synagogues. The Baghdadis were still acting on their belief that Bene Israel did not qualify as part of a *minyan*, and they were angered by the fact that the Cochini *Hazan*, Isaac Elias Sargon,[1] not only prayed at Bene Israel synagogues but considered the Bene Israel to be better Jews than the Baghdadis, expressing great admiration for the former for having so faithfully clung to Judaism throughout their centuries-long isolation.

The second half of the 19th century had witnessed the construction of several Bene Israel synagogues throughout the Konkan area. They were funded through the efforts of their respective local congregants as a whole, as well as through contributions from individual benefactors. The more affluent Bene Israel would donate elaborate cloth coverings for the table on which the *Torah* was placed when being read, or curtains for the *heykhal* (i.e. cabinet where the Torah scrolls are kept), or benches for worshippers. The *Torah* scrolls were fitted by their winding poles into well-made hinged boxes of wood, often overlaid with ornately decorated silver. The scroll remained in its casing while being read at services. Two large arm chairs were placed beside the Ark, one for the Prophet Elijah and the other for the godfather who held the child during the ritual of circumcision (which customarily took place in the synagogue). On the wall facing Jerusalem, on either or on both sides of the *heykhal,* there always were hung, in frames, one or more auspicious representations of a Menorah, the shape of the entire candelabrum being composed of calligraphic holy writings in Hebrew.[2] There was a women's balcony overlooking the main hall of the synagogue, positioned aloft on one, two, and even sometimes three sides of the hall.[3] Located next to the synagogue was a small building housing a regulation-size pool for the ritual bath, the *mikveh*. In rural areas where there were usually very few Jews in any one village, several near-by villages would share a central synagogue. (Some of the villages concerned were separated by backwaters which could be crossed on foot only during low tide.) The congregation as a whole owned the synagogue building and the land on which it stood. Often there was enough synagogue land to be rented out to tenant farmers, the income going into the synagogue treasury. Urban synagogues also owned their building(s) and land, and some had considerable sums in the treasury out of which they paid the salaries of *Hazan* and *Shamash,* supported communal welfare cases, maintained synagogue premises, and purchased utensils, mats, etc. for ready use at communal as well as at private Bene Israel functions.

There were *IN BOMBAY CITY* at the close of the 19th century a total of two Bene Israel synagogues and two Bene Israel Prayer Halls, namely :

Shaarei Harachamim Synagogue, popularly known as The Old Synagogue, at 254 Samuel Street, Mandvi; founded in 1796.
Shaarei Rason Synagogue, popularly known as The New Synagogue, at Don Tad Cross Lane, Khadak; founded in 1840.
Tifereth Israel Prayer Hall, at 92 K.K. Marg, Clerk Road, Jacob Circle; founded in 1886.
Aitz Hayyim Prayer Hall, at 19 2nd Cross Lane, Umerkhadi; founded by H.S. Kehimkar for the Israelite School in 1888.
(The *Magen David Synagogue* of the Baghdadi community was established in 1861, built in Byculla by the Sassoons. *The Knesset Eliyahu Synagogue* in Fort, Bombay, was built by the Baghdadis in 1888.)

IN THANA DISTRICT (north of Bombay)

In Panvel (Panvel Taluka), *Beth El Synagogue*, on Mahatma Gandhi Road; built in 1849.
In the town of Thana, *Shaar Hashamayim Synagogue*, at Temil Naka, Tembi; opened in 1879.

IN KOLABA DISTRICT[4]

In Revdanda (Alibag Taluka), *Beth El Synagogue;* built originally in 1842, and rebuilt in 1876.
In Alibag (Alibag Taluka), *Magen Avoth Synagogue;* built originally in 1848, rebuilt in 1910.
* In Tala-Ghosale (Mangaon Taluka), *Knesset Israel Synagogue*; built in 1849, rebuilt in 1876.
In Pen (Pen Taluka), *Beth Ha-Elohim Synagogue*; built in 1863, rebuilt in 1893.
* In Poynad (Alibag Taluka), *Hesed El Synagogue*, built in 1866, rebuilt in 1933.
In Borlai (then Janjira State, now Alibag Taluka), *Shaarei Shalom Synagogue;* built in 1869.
** In Ambepur (Alibag Taluka), *Ambepur Synagogue;* built in 1874, rebuilt in 1884.
* In Ashtami (Roha Taluka), *Beth El Synagogue;* built in 1882.
In Mhasla (Mhasla Mahal), *Shaar Ha-Tefila Synagogue;* built in 1886, rebuilt in 1921.
* In Post Chordei, Talekhar (Murud Mahal), *Talekhar Synagogue*; built either in 1892 or around 1870.[5]
In Nandgaon (then Janjira State, now Alibag Taluka), *Or L'Israel Synagogue;* begun in 1896, rebuilt in 1945.

IN AHMEDABAD, Gujarat State, a Bene Israel congregation had been meeting for prayers since mid-19th century, but it was not until 1934 that their *Magen Abraham Synagogue* was built in the Bukhara Mohalla of Ahmedabad.[6]

IN POONA (now spelled *Pune*), the Bene Israel started two prayer halls in 1877. Later, the two united but eventually disbanded when the Bene Israel *Succcath Shelomo*

Synagogue, at 93 Rasta Peth, was built in 1921. (The Baghdadi *Ohel David Synagogue*, in Poona Camp, was built in 1867.)[7]

IN KARACHI, now in Pakistan, a Bene Israel synagogue, *Magen Shalom*, was established in 1892. A bigger synagogue with the same name was built in 1912, financed wholly by the sons of the founder, Solomon David Oomerdekar.

Those synagogues marked above with an asterisk (*) had to stop functioning during the third quarter of the 20th century because there were no more Bene Israel residents in their respective areas. (**) The Ambepur Synagogue became defunct as early as 1916 — much before the Bene Israel emigration to Israel had begun — because no more Bene Israel continued to live in Ambepur. Here a Muslim resident was entrusted with the duty of keeping the everlasting light aflame even though the synagogue was no longer in use.

The 19th century had witnessed a real flowering of Bene Israel Judaism. Already by mid-19th century almost all Bene Israel were observant Jews, even if not following the ultra-*halachic* stream. In this respect they resembled considerable numbers of other Jews, especially in western Europe and in America, who, about fifty years later and for different reasons, began to attach less and less importance to much of *halacha*.

Unfortunately, Bene Israel congregations would all too often split into two factions: Kehimkar singles out the synagogues at Revdanda and at Tale-Ghosale as being rare and notable exceptions (p.182). He himself analysed the problem and devoted his life to efforts aimed at improving the condition of the Bene Israel. Due to his untiring work, the Israelite School was founded, and closely associated with it he established the *Aitz Hayeem Prayer Hall* with the following aims:[8]

1. To teach the new generation to pray in intelligible Hebrew and to provide religious education.
2. To introduce into the synagogue service sermons in the local language.
3. To establish harmony in the congregation, and to maintain order and solemnity during the synagogue service.
4. To publish religious books and other related materials.
5. To use the income from and the donations to the synagogue for providing Bene Israel children with secular, vocational and religious education so that they need not attend other schools attendance at which involved violation of the Sabbath. And, if possible, to establish workshops for the community.

Some of Kehimkar's other proposed synagogue reforms were: recitation of the prayers by the congregation in unison; shortened services, in order to enable worshippers to attend office on Sabbath; no more celebrations with dancing and eating to be allowed to take place within the synagogue; and no more bidding for the privilege of being called up to the *bimah* for blessing or reading from the *Torah*. For his contemporary fellow-Bene Israel, however, Kehimkar was too much ahead of his time. He was practically ostracised by the congregations of other synagogues. After Kehimkar's death the Aitz Hayeem Prayer Hall became an independent institution. However, for some time thereafter it continued to pay about Rs. 300/— annually to the Israelite School's funds.

Kehimkar felt that "During the past century and a half, those who came later than we did to Bombay [i.e. the Baghdadis] have risen to power and affluence, and it is advisable that we should inquire into the causes of our own backwardness." (p.185) He believed that before their religious revival, the Bene Israel, in their ignorance, probably followed their relatively few religious precepts with less internal discord than after they had developed into congregations; and that it now was imperative for them not only to increase their religious knowledge, but also to employ a spiritual guide, a Rabbi of high character, to teach and preach and restore harmony amongst them. He also advocated a temporal guide to represent the community in civil and political matters.

Many of Kehimkar's far-sighted ideas never saw the light of day, and the opposition to him made his latter years very difficult. He had put his finger exactly on what had kept the Bene Israel from prospering : disunity, individual self-interest, jealousy, apathy, indifference. In the administration of Bene Israel communal affairs there was total absence of rules. Kehimkar's advice was to frame a code of laws for the control and guidance of the officers of the community; to choose as leaders only men of high morals and liberal education; annually to examine, print and circulate all accounts for the information of the congregation as a whole; to record the minutes of all meetings of the managing committee and of the general assembly; to invest synagogue money in Government Loans or in buildings; and never to mortgage any synagogue estate.[9]

For the light which they throw on some actual synagogue affairs it is worth noting here a few passages from a 35-page booklet brought out in 1975 in Bombay entitled, *Shaare Rason Synagogue* (90 Tantanpura Street, Khadak, Bombay 400 009, India) *1840-1968, a Brief Retrospect*. It is largely based on the accumulation of the synagogues's financial accounts, but it also names all its executives, trustees, *Hazanim*, etc. in succession since the founding of the synagogue, and it reveals many interesting facts, such as :

> In 1882-83, a special service of intercession was held and a fast observed on account of the fierce persecution of Jews in Russia and a sum of Rs. 100 was collected from the members for their relief. (p.35)
> In the same year Dy. Rabbi Hacham Morenu of Jerusalem attended a Sabbath service and gave an address. A sum of Rs. 40 was collected from the members and given to him. (p.35)
> In 1888-89 [the synagogue received] (i) Rs. 1-4-0 from fee for conversion to Judaism; (ii) payments amounting to Rs.19-14--0 in 1888-89, Rs. 28-8-0 in 1889-90 and Rs.27-8-0 in 1890-91 by persons making vows; and (iii) Rs.2-8-0 in 1889-90 for widow remarriage. (p.15)
> [In 1911] a new item of regular expenditure was the payment of Rs. 10 a year for blowing the *Shofar*.[10] (p.16)
> For the first time in 1925 there is evidence of the use of a bank for keeping the balances of the Synagogue. (p.18)

The booklet contains narration and explanations as well as financial accounts, for instance :

> ....surprise is often expressed by foreign observers at the miniscule membership fees levied by Bene Israel synagogues....Bene Israel synagogues have never relied on such fees for their maintenance. The fees have always been regarded as merely token payments acknowledging identification with the community. (p.25)
> Right from its establishment the Synagogue had the good fortune to be served as *Hazan* by a very remarkable *Hacham* from Cochin, Shelomo Salem Shurrabi, who bravely persevered in his post despite pressure and even physical violence from leaders of the Old Synagogue. (p.27)

So far as available records show, only once was a serious attempt made to adopt a proper constitution for the Synagogue before that in 1968. (p.30)
[Between 1888 and 1891] there was a serious rift between the management of the Synagogue and the authorities of the Israelite School. One of the results of this rift was an attempt by the Synagogue to run a rival school....for the teaching of Hebrew and Marathi....It could not afford to divert sufficient funds for the maintenance of the school for boys without detriment to its religious functions, and the school was closed in 1891. (pp.31-2)
In the year 1917 a British Jewish soldier paid Rs.3 in the form of a bid for Synagogue honours and in the year 1918 two British Jewish soldiers paid smaller amounts as bids. The fact deserves mention only because it was very unusual for British Jews in India to profess their religion so openly (many highly placed officials successfully concealed their religious affiliation) and even more unusual for any of them to attend a service in a synagogue of the Bene Israel when those maintained by Baghdadi Jews were more easily accessible. (p.35).

If only the records of each synagogue in India would be studied, and if booklets similar to the one about Shaare Rason Synagogue could be written, we'd get a closer look at and a more inclusive picture of the Jewish communities of India of days gone by.[11] A development in this direction is the fact that the Central Archives for the History of the Jewish People, located in the Sprinzak Building on the Givat Ram Campus of Hebrew University in Jerusalem, is gradually acquiring a collection of original synagogue documents obtained from various synagogues of the Konkan. Almost all of this material is written in Marathi, and most of it is in the form of accounts of expenditures and income. Some of these records, such as those from the Beth El Synagogue at Revdanda, go back as far as 1873. But most of the records thus far collected relate to the first half of the 20th century.

A study of these accounts alone indicates the whole gamut of synagogue activity. Besides expense accounts, there is the occasional list, for instance, of each and every cooking utensil owned by the synagogue for use at functions; or such information as the fact that Bombay's Shaar Harachamim Synagogue, before the days of *aliyah* to Israel, usually had about 600 members, and that it has trustees and/or representatives on the boards of all of the following institutions in Bombay : the Bene Israel Home for Destitutes, Jewish Cemeteries, Sir Elly Kadoorie School, the *Hevrah Kedushah*, and the Central Jewish Board. All but the *Hevrah Kedushah* and the Central Jewish Board were affiliated concerns of the synagogue during the second half of the 19th century as well as at the present time.

NOTES

1. Isaac Elias Sargon was of the same family as Isaac Sargon (reputed to have saved Samaji Hassaji, see App. 3a, pp.317-18 and Micheal Sargon (see above, pp. 67-9). Originally, the Sargon ancestor had fled from the Inquisition in Spain. The family lived in Turkey, and later in the Holy Land. From there they came to settle in Cochin. Isaac Elias Sargon himself had married a Baghdadi Jewess. Their son is Joseph I. Sargon (now living in Brookline, Massachusetts, U.S.A.), the founder and editor of *The Jewish Tribune* (subtitled *The Organ of Indian Jewry*), a fine English language monthly journal on matters of Indian and worldwide Jewish interest, published in Bombay from 1930 until 1941.
2. This kind of picture is called a *Shivti* or a *Mizrah* (the Hebrew word for the "East") because. for most of Jewry, Jerusalem lies to the East. This ornament is a typical feature especially in

Sephardi synagogues. It has Kabbalistic associations, and is also meant to concentrate the mind of the worshipper on the unity of God.

3. At the entrance to the Magen Avoth Synagogue in Alibag, as a mural on the wall of its entry verandah, is painted a sign with a floral border, painted by a Bene Israel who signed it simply "Ghosalker". The text of the panel on the left is in Marathi; the panel on the right is in English, as follows :

Manners to be observed in the Synagogue :
1. Please before entering the synagogue boots, chappals, sleepers, footwears, etc. should be taken off and left them outside.
2. No noise except the praying should be made while the prayer is going on.
3. Any enquiry to be made should be asked from PANCHAS [i.e. the five councillors or *choglas*] on any day but enquiry should not be made at the time of prayer.
4. Those against whom the balance of previous years' bid is outstanding are prohibited to give further bids.
5. Outsiders are allowed to give bids offering oil but they will have to pay the price of bids in cash.
6. Everyone should behave in the synagogue in good manner so as not to insult others.
7. On every Shabbat or bid festival at least one member of each family from the local residents of Alibag should attend the prayer.
Magen Avot. Alibag.

4. The location of all these synagogues may be found on Map 2 which shows all the Bene Israel surname-linked villages.
5. S.J.Kolabkar in his *Kolaba Investigations Travels* (p. 3) gives the date as "about 1870", while on p.78 of the *Indian Jewish Year Book of 1969* (published by Emanuel Joseph for Abi-Emu Publishers, Bombay) in its list of Synagogues in India the date of the founding is given as 1892.
6. For other Bene Israel houses of prayer which were established in the 20th century, see below, p.232
7. Actually, the Ohel David Synagogue in Poona, built by the Baghdadi Jewish financial tycoon and great philanthropist, David Sassoon, in 1867, was much more capacious than warranted by Poona's relatively small Baghdadi Jewish population. However, this synagogue was not only distant from the Bene Israel neighborhood in Poona, but segregation between Bene Israel and Baghdadis was maintained in Poona as it was in Bombay.
8. In many respects, Kehimkar's ideas anticipated and/or paralleled those of the Jewish Conservative Movement in the West.
9. Kehimkar : *History*, pp. 272, 274, 275, 276.
10. *Shofar* is the Hebrew word for the ram's horn. It is blown in a certain way, especially at specific points during the Rosh Hashonah synagogue services, and at the end of Yom Kippur.
11. A great deal of this sort of "inside" information is recorded about the Shaar Harachamim Synagogue on pages 1-10 of E.M. Jocob's *The Religious and Cultural Heritage of the Bene Israels of India*, Book II, in an article by E.M. Jacob entitled "History of Shaar Harachamim — Gate of Mercy-Synagogue". The present writer is grateful to E.M. Jacob particularly for additional information which he gave me concerning the *heykhal* of Shaar Harachamim Synagogue.

Chapter 13
Bene Israel Names

We do not know when the community first began calling itself "Bene Israel". The name might reflect the possibility that they were indeed of the "Children of Israel", i.e. of the Biblical Northern Kingdom of the Ten Tribes of Israel as distinguished from the Kingdom of Judah. Even if the "Bene Israel" designation was not adopted until the days of Islam—perhaps mindful of the favourable connotation assigned by Muslims to the term "Bene Israel" (see above p. 25)—the presence of Muslims in the Konkan goes back long enough to support the claim of Bene Israel settlement in that part of India in the remote past. Currently available Bene Israel family genealogies, however, go back to a time no earlier than late 17th century.

Formerly many male and female Bene Israel bore local Hindu names exclusive, however, of names of specific Hindu deities (the latter type of name being very common among Hindus). The local vernacular names of the Bene Israel were based on words signifying attributes, or epithets, or relationships (ending usually in the suffix "ji" or "bai"—the former an honorific, the latter signifying affectionate respect). For men there were such names as Babuji, Balaji, Banduji, Bhuooji, Dadaji, Ittuji, Nathuji, Sakuji, Tanaji; for women: Akabai, Baiabai, Balkubai, Ladubai, Nanubai, Sonabai, Thakubai, Zaitubai. A non-Biblical first name, especially if combined with a village-linked surname which is known to be in use also among non-Bene Israel-groups, can make it difficult, if not impossible, to identify some persons as being definite members of the Bene Israel community, unless other accompanying facts are available and supportive. At least since the Bene Israel religious revival, a Bene Israel had, in addition to a vernacular name, also a Biblical name, always used together with the family surname ending in *kar*, in rites of passage and other religious matters. It is not clear how far back beyond the 18th century the Bene Israel use of Biblical names goes. On the one hand, the 18th century contacts with Cochin Jews might have introduced Biblical names to the Bene Israel. On the other hand, there is the fact that Biblical names crop up as names of known Bene Israel soldiers who fought in the Mysore Wars, and also in Bene Israel genealogies as names of *early* 18th century progenitors (some of whose lives might have extended into the last quarter of the 17th century) where one sibling would have a Biblical name, another a local Indian name—and we can't be sure that Cochin Jews had contacted these families at such an early date.[1] Nowadays most Bene Israel have only Biblical rather than Indian names. But Biblical names were often given a local touch, for instance by changing Abraham to Abaji, Benjamin to Bunnaji, David to Dawoodji, Elijah to Elloji, Ezekiel to Hassaji, Isaac to Essaji, Jacob to Akhoobji, Joseph to Essobji, Moses to Mussaji, Rachamim to Ramaji; or simply by adding the suffix to the actual Biblical name as follows: Dinahbai, Hannahbai, Miriambai, Ruthbai, Segullahbai, Simhabai, Shebabai, Sipporahbai, Yochebedbai. Similarly, Jews all over the world have usually altered their Hebrew names to conform more closely to local non-Jewish names.

Generally speaking, family surnames as such came into vogue in India only in the 20th century, prompted by the world-wide needs of modern business, banking practice, registration of all sorts, etc. Previously it had been the Indian custom to identify a person by a triad consisting of the name of one's native place, father's given name, and one's own given name. Even where *kar* (or its equivalent) had been added to the name of one's native place, it still did not function as a surname in the modern usage of the term. This does not imply that one's "place-name" had no significance; but it was not what it is today, namely the main identifying criterion of an individual (except in cases of intimate personal relationship), with one's surname, and not one's given name, always the determining factor in alphabetical listings of individuals. With the exception of common practice in a few Indian communities, although names of sub-caste or of kinship groups were known to each individual, he/she did not use such a name as part of his/her own name *per se*. In establishing surnames for modern nuclear families, some Indians nowadays chose their sub-caste names, others prefer place-names, or the given name of their father or grandfather. For several generations the Bene Israel, however, have not only preserved the name of their particular ancestral village (although the family may have left it one or two centuries earlier) but used such village names (with the suffix *kar*, meaning "belonging to" or "from") as regular surnames.[2] Since Hindu Maharashtrians of various castes often have the same custom, it cannot be assumed that every name ending in *kar* belongs to a Bene Israel; indeed, in some instances non-Bene Israel and Bene Israel sometimes bear the very same *kar* name, meaning that their respective ancestors came from the same village.[3]

In her article *The Bene Israel of Bombay* (p.9), Miss Rebecca Reuben claimed that "not found in any other Indian community, but peculiar to the Bene Israel alone" is the use of the suffix *kara* instead of *kar* to designate the village-name or surname of a married Bene Israel woman. Miss Reuben, however, was wrong on this point because occasionally Hindu female names also use the *kara* form.[4] The practice was prevalent among the Bene Israel until about 1925, after which it began to die out. The addition of the final "a" to the suffix reminds one of the regular use of the suffix "ah" (*kometz-hay*) in the Hebrew language to denote feminine gender. But this is perhaps not the origin of the custom (which seems to have been widespread at the beginning of the 19th century), because, on the Hebrew inscriptions of early 19th century Bene Israel tombstones this suffix, added to surnames of women, was spelled with the Hebrew letter *aleph* at the end much more often than with *kometz-hay*. Yet, the surname of most females then was given the *kara* ending.[5]

Pingle seems to be the only *traditional* surname without the suffix *kar* (it derives from the village Pingalsai); with Doodkar or Dootkar being the only surname which does not refer to a place. Kehimkar (p.83) explains the name Doodkar as follows : "There was a certain Bapuji Doodkar who belonged to the family of Kamarlekars and said family had received the name of Doodkar from the fact that his [Bapuji's] ancestors supplied the Government of Angria with *Dood* or milk."

Some Bene Israel families have changed their traditional surnames in various ways :

(1) by dropping the suffix *kar* : Jhirad instead of Jhiradkar, or Kolet instead of Koletkar; or
(2) by adding the letter "s" to a given name, as in the non-traditional surname Hyams or Reubens; or
(3) By anglicizing a traditional surname[6]: Rogers, from Rajpurkar; Cherry, from Charrikar; Ashton, from Ashtamkar.

In modern times such names seemed preferable to some Bene Israel who chose to give up the village-derived surname either in an effort to westernize,[7] or simply to get rid of this vestige of former rustic background. B.J.Israel explains the choice of his own surname in yet another way :

> It belonged to the third generation of a family which adopted "Israel" as its surname, following the practice of the East India Company's Bombay Army of enlisting Bene Israel recruits under their first names, the first names of their fathers, and the common surname "Israel" as a caste name....But despite this, the traditional village-derived surname of "Wargharkar" is still remembered and applied to the family....almost every member of the community knows his or her traditional village-derived surname and is identified by this name within the community rather than by the more recently adopted surname.[8]

In his study entitled *Bene Israel Surnames and Their Village Links* B.J.Israel defines a genuine traditional village-linked surname as one which has come down from generation to generation and which does *not* change with change of residence to another village, town or city. It should be noted that place-linked traditional surnames did not invariably refer only to villages. The name Cheulkar, for instance, is based on the place-name Cheul, which place (with variations in the spelling of its name — see above, p. 30, n. 25) traces back to antiquity, not as a village, but as a port city of historical importance. Bene Israel also lived in relatively large numbers in the towns of Danda and Rajpuri. That they were living in these towns before the 16th century is a distinct possibility, although it has not been proven.[9]

An impediment to correct identification of location is the confusion of place names in a given locality, a phenomenon discussed by Dr. Burnell in Volume III, pp.333-334 of *The Indian Antiquary* of December 1874, as follows :

> Every town in South India which is known to foreigners by one name....in reality consists of a larger or smaller number of hamlets, each with its distinct name; and, as one or the other of these rises in importance, by being made a royal residence, or the harbour being altered, or for similar reasons, the whole town changes its name with strangers. Hence the difficulty of identifying some towns in South India, which were formerly well known.

The same observation applies with equal force to place names in the Konkan.

B.J.Israel's chapter *Bene Israel Surnames and Their Village Links*, in his book *The Bene Israel of India, Some Studies*, contains a wealth of information and is a fine example of the kind of meticulous research and reasoning which are necessary to further our knowledge about this community previous to the 18th century.

A major source for B.J.Israel's research into Bene Israel surnames was a study made by Abraham Samuel Tarankhopkar, a reputed Marathi scholar. His article on Bene Israel surnames was published in the journal, *The Friend of Israel*, Volume V, Nos. 7, 8 and 9 of July, August and September 1920; written in Marathi, it supplied a list of 133 Bene Israel surnames, the villages which Tarankhopkar thought were connected to these surnames, and the area where each village was located.

Another source is a list of 91 village-derived Bene Israel surnames included by the Rev. J.H.Lord in his book *The Jews in India and the Far East* (as Appendix II, p.11 of Lord's Appendix section). A third source is a list (anonymous) of 103 surnames published in Marathi in *The Israelite* magazine, Volume II, Nos. 9 and 10, September—October 1919. A fourth list of 107 surnames occurs as Appendix V (p.102) of Moses Ezekiel's booklet *History and Culture of the Bene Israel in India* (Nadiad, 1948). Various written records found in old Bene Israel synagogues also proved helpful to B.J.Israel, especially in establishing and in dating names of places no longer extant today.

However, seven Bene Israel surnames which do not occur in B.J.Israel's compilation are to be found in the *Ohel Dawid* of David Sassoon, Volume I, p.370, item No.554. Here we find names copied from Hebrew inscriptions on tombstones in Bombay for burials which occurred from 1817 to 1828. The Bene Israel surnames mentioned in item no.554 are as follows :

```
NOTE :     + = surnames not appearing in B.J.Israel's list.
           * = surnames with feminine ending -kara (either ending with the Hebrew
               letter aleph or hay).
          ** = surnames ending in -karani.
              AVASKAR
            + BADREKAR
          * + BARAZKAR
          * + BILAKAR
              BONKAR (BONKIR)
            * BORUPKAR
            * DIVEKAR
              GALSUKAR, GARTZURKAR
            + GAMARLEKAR
            * GARKAR
         ** + HAZRASHOLKAR
            + HORAMKAR
              KARLEKAR
              MAZGAMKAR
            * NAUGOKAR
            * PANSAPURKAR
              PEZARKAR
              PENKAR
            * PUGAOKAR
         ** RAJPURKAR
              SANKAR
          * + SASOOLKAR
              TALKAR, TALEKAR
            + ZARHAPURKAR
```

Maybe some of the transliterations into Hebrew were incorrectly rendered on these particular tombstones. Bilakar might be a variant of Belkar, Gamarlekar of Kamerlekar, Mazgamkar of Mazgaonkar. Were Badrekar, Barazkar, Bilakar, Gamarlekar, Horamkar, Sassolkar and Zarhapurkar *traditional* Bene Israel surnames still in use at the beginning of the 19th century, but since then came into disuse? Or did those names relate to then new Bene Israel residence locations and, as Bene Israel surnames, have since died out?

Another list, of 127 Bene Israel surnames, which the present author found among the notes of H.G.Reissner, mentions seven other names which are also not included in B.J.Israel's list, namely : **GORDEKAR** (in Janijra State), **KANENKAR** (Rohe), **KHAJAWKAR** (Pen), **NOWSHERKAR** (Pen), **THUGKAR** (Alibag), **WARSHERKAR** (Janjira), and **WARUKAR** (Janjira). The respective locations given here in parentheses are also taken from Reissner's notes. Kanenkar might be a variant of Kankekar, Warsherkar of Varsulkar, and Warukar of Warulkar.

B.J.Israel's own list of *Bene Israel Village-Linked Surnames* (see below, Appendix 9) enumerates 142 different Bene Israel surnames, eighteen of which have variant spellings,[10] and seven of which are not attributable to specific place-nemes.[11] All in all, about 200 different villages (all located within Kolaba District of Maharashtra) are mentioned as possible places of origin for Bene Israel surnames. *These are the villages in which research into all extant records* (of village, family, religious institutions, etc.) *should be carried out*[12] in the hope of finding relevant references to persons of the Bene Israel community.

Rebecca Reuben stresses the need to correlate Bene Israel surnames with historical facts of Kolaba District. She offers the following suggestion :

On the Konkan Coast there are two somewhat important towns — Revdanda and Alibag. Curiously enough there are no Bene Israel surnames derived from these two towns. And yet two other insignificant little villages, Rohe and Ashtami, quite close to the first-mentioned, give us the [Bene Israel] Rohekars and the Ashtamkars. This might tell us that the Bene Israel arrived in India long before the towns of Alibag and Revdanda grew up. And the history of these towns would help to fix the date of the arrival of the Bene Israel in one direction at least.[13]

It seems strange, especially in India, where reference to one's "native village" or "ancestral place" is so frequently alluded to (the former even by veteran city-dwellers, the latter even by second and third generation urbanites) that many (though by no means all) contemporary urban Bene Israel not only have never visited the village from which their family surname has been derived, but do not seem to have any idea as to where it is/was located.

NOTES

1. A word of caution for future researchers : if in future we should be fortunate enough to find pre-18th century official documents definitely referring to Bene Israel individuals, and if no Biblical names should appear among them, it would not necessarily mean that such Bene Israel did not then also have Biblical names. It might mean simply that for official (governmental) purposes the Bene Israel cited their non-Biblical names of local flavor. Often Jewish parents in English-speaking countries, for instance, will give a child a Hebrew name, which is used only for religious ceremonies; but in the municipal register of births the parents will assign a non-Jewish name (usually one which begins with the same letter-sound as has the Hebrew name), for example : Moshe (Moses) becomes Mark, Sarah becomes Sylvia, etc. It is the non-Jewish name which is used throughout life, even at home.
2. Similarly, many Jews from all over Europe took as surnames the names of the towns or cities where they lived, some with and some without adding a locative suffix to the place-name : "Berlin", Berliner", etc.
3. Such Bene Israel surnames as Dandekar, Penkar, Pingle, Rajpurkar, Rohekar and Shirgaonkar, for instance, also belong to Brahmins and other high castes among the Hindus.
4. For instance : Maharani Ahilyabai Hol*kara*.
5. See the list (in Hebrew) of names on old Bene Israel tombstones in Bombay, from David Sassoon's *Ohel Dawid*, item No. 554 in Volume I on page 370 — as transliterated below, p. 157. Nine of the twenty-four surnames listed in item No.554 have a *kara* suffix, usually (but not always) together with the plain *kar* suffix to the same place-name. Interestingly, two other

names end in *karani*, i.e. Harsholkarani and Rajpurkarani. Some of the *kara* names are spelled with the Hebrew letter *aleph* at the end while others end with the letter *hay*.

6. In Israel, a Bene Israel will sometimes Hebraize his/her traditional village-based surname for instance, by changing Shapurkar to Sopher (which in Hebrew means a "writer", "author", or "scribe") the literal meaning of the word having no relevance to the person who adopts it as his/her new surname.
7. Some eastern European Jews in England and America have adopted Anglo-Saxon surnames in place of what have come to be known as "typically Jewish" names, retaining only the same initial letter not only in an effort to westernize, but sometimes also in order to hide their Jewishness.
8. From an earlier (1974) draft (never published as such) of an article by B.J.Israel on Bene Israel Surnames. Changed slightly, this article now appears in B.J.Israel's book *The Bene Israel of India, Some Studies* as the chapter called *Bene Israel Surnames and Their Village Links*, pp.120-66. The surname *Israel* is discussed on pp.124-5.
9. See above, p. 33 about the *sanad* in the hands of the Ashtamkar family.
10. These sixteen variants appear in the list with tally numbers 6, 10, 15, 23, 32, 36, 39, 41, 58, 59, 62, 76, 83, 104, 118, 122, 128, 137.
11. For this, see Appendix 9, p.373
12. In any village, especially the temples and the Brahmin households would be the most likely to have in their possession old records since, before modern times, the Brahmins were often the only functional Hindu literates. Not only Hindu records, but also local Muslim, Christian and Parsi records of all sorts might reveal occasional mention of Bene Israel or "shanwar telis". And, in the towns and ports, certainly the Sidi and the Maratha records should be combed also. Obviously, to carry out this type of research, persons must be found who have the ability to read the various scripts (both the archaic and the more recent forms) and to understand the different languages involved.

    To begin with, any researcher intending to visit many of these Bene Israel-Surname-Linked villages will find useful *The Directory of Villages and Towns of Kolaba District*. This lists a total of 1,976 places and give for each place-name its "Direction", "Travelling Distance", "Area in Square Miles", "Population", "Number of Households", "Number of Agriculturalists", "The Nearest Post Office and Its Distance Away" "Weekly Bazaar" with the distance away and the Bazaar Day, "The Nearest Motor Stand" (how far away), "Sources of Water Supply", "Institutions", and "Other Information". This *Directory* is to be found on pp.981-1129 of the 1964 revised edition of the *Kolaba District Gazetteer*.
13. Rebecca Reuben, op. cit., p.10.

Chapter 14
19th Century Bene Israel Occupations

Although not ranked anywhere near the top of the social hierarchy, the Bene Israel were always looked upon as a respectable community. Even as *telis* (oil-pressers) they actually enjoyed a different and higher status than that of the lowly Hindu oil-presser because the Bene Israel did not form part of the Hindu caste system. Being a small and unique entity on their own, the Bene Israel, under Muslim, and later under British rule enjoyed a distinct status advantage. Their status was raised still further by their move to cities and large towns where their *Shanwar Teli* label receded in importance as they came to be associated more and more with the white collar middle-class which included (and still does) people of many different castes (especially the high castes) and religions.

During the 19th century the Bene Israel still lived mainly in villages of Kolaba District. Sometimes there were as few as only two or three Bene Israel families per village; more often there were between 15 to 30 families in a single locality; in no village did they ever constitute a majority. They were not, however, isolated from other Bene Israel. Occasional social and shopping visits to Bombay and to the larger towns were customary, facilitated since 1874 by the introduction of steamships calling at Bombay and Janjira every other day, and since 1882, every day. The 1885 *Bombay Gazetteer* (p.430) tells us about customary weekly markets and annual fairs; also that "Shopkeepers are found only in large villages. They are Gujaratis and Marwaris, Vanis, Sonars, Kasars, Shimpis, Bhandaris, Musalmans and Beni Israels.... Their trade has grown considerably of late years."

In the more out-of-the-way villages, the Bene Israel lived amid very primitive conditions, without access to religious or secular learning. Some owned their own land and used hired agricultural labor. But almost all rural Bene Israel themselves also worked in the fields. Typically they were not affluent. Many lived on and tilled leased land; but they usually did own their own house, oil-press and a few sheds, as well as the site on which these stood. Their main cash crop was rice. Only the wives of oil-pressers and farmers (but not of craftsmen and others) helped their husbands in their work. Some of the richer Bene Israel farmers owned their own cattle for ploughing. But the average Bene Israel lived on a small plot of land, usually much less than an acre in size, with a well for irrigation and drinking water. He owned only a few chickens and a few cows (for their milk). In the 19th century the Bene Israel were the *main* oil-pressers in all of Kolaba and Janjira.[1]

In the larger villages Bene Israel of the 19th century not only worked as oil-pressers and small farmers, but also found employment (in the towns and cities as well as in their own villages) as day laborers, skilled furniture-makers,[2] carpenters, masons, building contractors and construction laborers. Only few of them were cart-drivers; timber, grain or hay merchants; or *small* grocery-shop owners. As farmers or laborers they worked on a bare subsistence level, from dawn until dusk. Many Bene Israel became skilled workers only after they left their village homes and went to live and work in Bombay or other towns. It was mostly the younger people who migrated to the towns and cities (for jobs

and for education), while their elders usually remained in the villages. Even though we definitely know of Bene Israel carpenters, artisans and building contractors working in Bombay during the first half of the 19th century, the Konkan *Gazetteers* do not mention these as Bene Israel occupations.

As secular education spread among the Bene Israel, the most readily available lines of employment for them were in government civil service jobs in the towns and cities as clerks, draftsmen, telegraph signallers, hospital assistants; others became teachers or printing compositors; and a few of them entered the fields of medicine, law and engineering. Those who had jobs in government or in business offices usually worked from 10 a.m. to 5 p.m. on an average wage of Rs. 50 to Rs. 60 per month; an apprentice learning to become a hospital assistant earned only Rs. 8 per month, but when he achieved the grade of First Class Hospital Assistant his monthly earning went up to Rs. 60. As for doctors, some Bene Israel rose to be put in charge of entire hospitals. Toward the end of the 19th century a Bene Israel, Abraham Samuel Nagawkar, served as Executive Engineer in the then princely state of Mysore.

While not particularly enterprising, the Bene Israel, nevertheless, enjoyed the reputation of being very hard-working, loyal, honest and diligent. Among the less praiseworthy characteristics that seem to have been too often evident among them in civilian life one reads that they tended to quarrel among themselves (although not with others) and were not of a forgiving nature. There was among them too much pettiness, back-biting, jealousy, self-righteousness without real self-confidence, and a general lack of sophistication. Also, they were perhaps overly fond of drink; but, to their credit, the Bene Israel were not at all prone to other vices.

There are frequent references in Bene Israel periodicals and elsewhere calling for temperance among the Bene Israel. On the other hand, we find so many favourable references made by non-Bene Israel sources describing Bene Israel civilians (the carpenter class included) and soldiers, that it is very unlikely that there was any degree of clinical alcoholism among the Bene Israel before the days of prohibition in Bombay. A rare instance of strong condemnation comes from *The Bombay Times* of March 3, 1846 (p.31) which, while describing the Bene Israel community, says : "It is stated in a printed journal of one of the earlier Missionaries, that the Magistrate described them at that time [30 years previous, i.e. 1816] as being the most drunken and troublesome people on the island [i.e. Bombay]." In *The Jewish Chronicle* (London) of February 6, 1852, we find a much less drastic statement attributed to a source labeled "Jewish intelligence" :

> I always found the Jews [i.e. the Bene Israel] amongst the most cleanly, well-behaved, and I must say, by far the most intelligent of our native soldiers. And, with the exception of being addicted to drink, and when this was carried to excess, to quarrel among themselves, it was very seldom that a Jew was ever brought up for any offence to the orderly room. They never intermarry with the Hindoos or Mahometans, and live by themselves.

Volume XI of the *Bombay Gazetteer on the Konkan* (1883), discussing the Bene Israel in Janjira (p. 422), makes the point that, "Though fond of liquor and extravagant on ceremonial occasions the Bene Israel are a steady, hardworking and successful people." The Deccan-Poona section of the *Bombay Presidency Gazetteer*, 1885, Volume XVIII, Part III (p.509), says that "They [the Bene Israel] may be called temperate drinkers of both country and European liquor – but only in the evening before supper, and they will not stir from the house after they have taken it."

Attention should be called particularly to the fact that in Bombay the period covering the 1860s was (for several complicated reasons) one of uncontrollable inflation, speculation, scandals, army changes, and influx of a different type of Englishman and of other Europeans. Gambling, prostitution and drinking were much in evidence. There is no doubt that there were enough instances of heavy drinking on the part of certain Bene Israel in urban areas (one finds no references to excessive toddy drinking among Bene Israel in rural areas) to have caused serious problems, and this is what the Bene Israel periodicals, etc. were deploring. There had been for a long time a strong emphasis on the need for temperance in many sectors of Bombay's population, coming from the Bombay Union of Missionaries which encouraged the establishment of temperance societies.[3]

We find the call for temperance among the Bene Israel continuing into the 20th century, again, symptomatic of a general problem among the local population (see below, p. 163, n.3 and p.244), with the poor squandering their money in the local toddy shops, the middle classes drinking *arak*, and the rich getting drunk on imported brandy. As for the Bene Israel, drinking alcoholic beverages was and continues to be an integral part of every celebration, cutting across all Bene Israel social, economic, and educational lines. In addition, especially on pay day among the poorer Bene Israel in towns and cities, instances of wife-beating during drunkenness did sometimes occur. This was not a problem among their Muslim friends and neighbours, forbidden to drink alcoholic beverages by the *Koran*. Unfortunately, in this respect the Bene Israel modelled their own conduct on a non-Muslim local pattern.

Many Bene Israel built careers based upon enlistment in the army.[4] H.G. Reissner has shown that, "In 1837, 19% of the Bene Israel (1,000 including family members, out of a total sample of 5,255 souls) depended for their livelihood on professional military service in the territorial units of the East India Company's Army."[5] Relatively large numbers of Bene Israel military officers were active in breaking up Thuggery, in putting down the lawlessness and vandalism of the so-called Criminal Tribes, and in actions on the Northwest and Northeast Frontiers. *Sirdar Bahadur* (see above, p. 54, n. 13), the highest military honor which was then possible for a Bene Israel to achieve, was awarded to considerable numbers of Bene Israel. For example, one Sirdar Behadur Silliman Abajee Waskar in 1809 had enlisted in the lowest rank, rose to the highest rank, and was decorated with the Star of the Order of British India, 1st Class. Sirdar Bahadur Solomon Daniel Ghosalkar of the Bombay Native Light Infantry also obtained this honor. He had served in very many campaigns and was so well liked and appreciated by the European officers of his regiment that when he died of cholera in 1869, the latter, at their own expense, erected a monument at Dhulia in his honor.

There is more than enough material to fill a separate book with facts about Bene Israel service in the armed forces of the subcontinent, and their contribution of excellent service in the various branches of independent India's armed forces continues to the present day. However, the unusually large percentage of Bene Israel enlistments decreased when, after the 1857 Mutiny against the British (in which no Bene Israel took part),[6] a new ruling made army[7] promotions contingent upon criteria other than merit alone. Under the new British rules for the Native Army there could be only one officer from a given caste or community per every one hundred enlisted men from that same caste or community.[8] When the new rules came into force there were already many more Bene Israel officers than the 100 : 1 ratio would have warranted even if all Bene Israel in India had enlisted. (The entire Bene Israel Community was not numerous enough to furnish a sufficient number of eligible males to form a separate Bene Israel regiment.) The reorganization of the Indian Army was completed in 1863. With their chances for rising in rank practically eliminated, the fighting ranks of the army became much less popular among educated

Bene Israel, and many then turned to ancillary services (public as well as military), especially in the accounts department and in medical services. Bene Israel army enlistment almost ceased by 1870, due as much to the growing attraction of civilian careers as to the restructuring of the Native Army Regiments according to caste. So many Bene Israel school graduates became clerks in public and private offices that the Bombay Bene Israel often refer to themselves as a "clerk caste".[9] Be that as it may, a very large number of Bene Israel were carpenters, building contractors and artisans; and later, into the 20th century, many Bene Israel became mechanics of all sorts.

NOTES

1. The 1883 *Gazetteer of Bombay Presidency*, Volume XI, on Kolaba and Janjira (p.67) specifically states that HINDU *telis* in these areas were then living only in Alibag, Mangaon and Mahad.
2. The *Kolaba District Gazetteer* of 1883 specifically mentions that there were cabinet makers in Upper Cheul. Some of them might have been Bene Israel.
3. The Bene Israel must have started a Temperance Society of their own because in 1917 the President of the First Bene Israel Conference mentioned it in his Presidential address, thus :

    Temperance requires the most prominent place in the programme of social reform in our community....I am however glad to note that now drink is not to be seen so much in our community as before....[but] a Temperance Association is ....needed.... I know there formerly existed a Temperance Society in our community. [From the Report of the First Bene Israel Conference, 1917; compiled and published by Solomon Moses, in English and Marathi; pp. v, 160; Bombay 1918; pp.56-7].

4. Sir Patrick Cadell, in his *History of the Bombay Army*, Longmans, Green & Co., Bombay, 1938 (p.13), has written :

    In addition to those already mentioned as belonging to Sivaji's army, the Bombay Army drew on the Bene-Israel, that interesting little community of Jews who have been for much more than a thousand years on the coast near Bombay, and who supplied so many good native officers to the Bombay regiments.

5. H.G. Reissner : *Jews of India*, quoted in *India and Israel*, August 1948, p.14.

    The *Jewish Chronicle* (London) of February 6, 1852, in an article about "Jews in the Indian Army" (p.142) says that : "Almost every Jew in the ranks of the Bombay Army has been either born or brought up from infancy in their respective regiments."
6. Cadell : *History of the Bombay Army* (p.201) :

    Why then, did the Bombay Army stand firm against the incitements of mutiny to which their brethren in Bengal succumbed? The principal reason for the mutiny was the sad decay of discipline in the Bengal regiments. The morale of those regiments had been shaken by a pandering to caste which affected alike the ranks and the Indian officers. The men were practically all of the same high castes, and promotion was almost entirely by seniority, so that the Indian officers were too old and inefficient to exercise control. In the Bombay regiment, on the other hand, men of all castes, some high, others extremely low, stood and worked together. Promotion was by merit and selection, and men of low extraction were constantly promoted to the commissioned ranks; while those of exceptionally intelligent, though numerically small classes, such as *the Bene Israel*, supplied a large number of officers who had no caste ties....But the main reason was the superior discipline of the Bombay sepoys." [Emphasis supplied]

7. With the passing of the Government of India Act (August 2, 1858) the British East India Company, as such, ceased to exist. Henceforth the British-led army in India was no longer

known as "The Honourable Company's Forces", but instead was called "The Indian Army" (with its Native as well as British units).

8. Ibid., p.15 :

> ....caste feeling caused the elimination of the lower castes from the Maratha armies of the Peshwa and his feudatories. It is sad to think that it was the increasing caste consciousness of the Maratha soldier himself, fostered doubtless by the introduction of the system of class companies, that led to the exclusion from the Bombay Army of the valuable elements found among the lesser castes and communities of the Western Presidency. Not the outcaste Parwari only, but the Bhandari, the Koli, *the Bene Israel*, the Native Christian, and even castes such as the Dhangar and Mali closely connected with himself [i.e. with the Maratha], were not considered good enough by the true Maratha for association in the ranks. [Emphasis supplied]

And, ibid., p.249 :

> The system of class companies had been introduced into the regiments of the Northern Army largely as a measure of greater safety. No such precaution was needed in the Bombay Army, but other administrative advantages led to the introduction of this measure, thereby sounding the knell of the old mixed system and closing valuable sources of recruitment.

Changing circumstances, especially the industrial development of Bombay, had already seriously affected the old patterns of recruitment.

9. There is a curious little booklet with the deceptive title *Colonel Wahab's Notes on the Jews Serving in the Bombay Army* (printed at the Education Society's Press, Byculla, Bombay, 1879). Colonel C.W.Wahab was the officer commanding the 8th Regiment of the Bombay Native Infantry. Benjamin Samson Ashtamkar translated into Marathi the 12 pages of Wahab's English text which very briefly dealt with the traditions, character, occupation and customs of the Bene Israel. His text does not devote itself at all to the Bene Israel in military service! However, Benjamin Samson Ashtamkar was "late assistant Master in the Robert Money Institution and now *clerk* to E.D.Sassoon Esq." and in his preface to the booklet he includes his own appreciation of the Sassoons (he was employed by them) as of the 1870s :

> The wealthy and eminent members of the Sassoon family, especially E.D.Sassoon Esq., always try their best to better our [the Bene Israel's] condition by engaging the services of our people in their firms, offices, mills etc., etc., etc. and paying them according to their ability.

In the interest of objectivity it would be useful to learn from Sassoon files just how many Bene Israel in the 19th century were in their employ, and in what positions. We do have a few statistics of this sort for the 20th century. (See below, p. 205, Table 4)

Chapter 15
Home Life

Bene Israel homes were distinguished from all others only by the presence of a *Mezuzah* (typically 4 to 5 inches long and one inch wide) on the front doorpost. According to the *Revised Bombay State Gazetteer* of 1954, for Poona District (p.148):

> They [Bene Israel] live in houses of the better sort. Fixed to the upper part of the right doorpost is a box with a small square glass let into the front of it, and inside in a wooden or metal case is a piece of parchment with carefully written verses from Deuteronomy vi, 4-9 and xi, 13-20 [should be 21], so placed that from the outside through the holes in the case and box, the word *Shadaya* (Almighty) can be read. Both in going out and in coming in, the members of the household touch this box with reverence.

Village houses consisted of

> a ground floor only and are built with bricks or with wattle and daub walls, and have thatched or tiled roofs. They have a verandah of about 8 or 10 feet in front, sitting and sleeping rooms in the middle, and a kitchen at the back. In the compound at the back of the house there are a few coconut or other trees, and a shed which is used either as an oil-press or as a shelter for cattle.[1]

Bene Israel originally owned 200 to 300 houses in Bombay alone (also many in Poona), but because of financial difficulties during the 19th century most of them lost the ownership of their houses, after which time most Bene Israel in cities lived in rented houses. The city houses consisted of two or three stories, built of brick with tiled roofs and lime plastering. The Bene Israel usually whitewashed the interior walls of their houses, or flats, twice a year, before Passover and once again just before the Jewish New Year.

Shining copper utensils, if they could afford them, were used for cooking; they were tinned on the inside in order to avoid unhealthy chemical reactions during cooking. Other kitchen utensils were clay jugs for water; a grindstone for making flour; a stone slab and roller for grinding curry condiments; a wooden mortar and pestle for pounding rice; a cast-iron disc for preparing unleavened bread. Some brass vessels were also used. Sometimes the very poor had only clay pots to cook with. As was/is the custom all over India, food was usually cooked on small portable stoves (called *segris* or *chulas*) made either of iron, tinplate, or of clay, using wood or cow-dung cakes for fuel. Later, charcoal was introduced as cooking fuel even in the villages. If the pots had any handles at all, they took the form of small loops. Lids of pots were flat, and sometimes two or three different recipes were cooked simultaneously by stacking two or three pots (with lids) on top of each other, making maximal use of the single grid of the *chula*.

Furniture in a middle class home consisted of low wooden stools, boxes (often of tin) for storing clothes, etc., a few chairs, and *charpoys*. Only the richer families had such items as tables, cupboards, wardrobes, framed pictures and modern lamps.

Bene Israel in city and village, unless very poor, employed one or two male or female servants who came either from their own, or from Maratha or Muslim communities, but never from communities engaged in occupations which Hindus considered to be defiling (such as scavenging).

Bene Israel husbands generally treated their wives with respect and wives had considerable say in family affairs. Copying Hindu custom, a Bene Israel husband and wife would not address each other by their personal name. The women of the Bene Israel household, with or without the help of servants, performed the duties of grinding wheat and corn, pounding and husking rice, and cooking. Women also shopped for rice and for fuel; men usually did the other kinds of shopping. Women brought the water from the well or from city taps; and they did much of the family sewing, house-cleaning, and washing of their own and of their children's clothes. (Washerman, of the outcaste *dhobi* community, did the rest of the laundry.)

Bene Israel women wore their long thick black hair in a knot at the nape of the neck, and wore mainly Hindu style clothing. For ordinary wear they dressed in cotton sari and bodice. During the 19th and early 20th centuries the sleeves of the bodice came down to the wrist or at least to the elbow — a feature which might be attributable either to missionary influence or to Muslim custom. For special occasions Bene Israel women, like their Hindu neighbours, always wore a silk sari and bodice, several of which had been given to them at the time of their marriage. They carried the *pallu* (i.e. the most heavily decorated portion, at the end of the sari) over the left shoulder, and then usually draped it over the top of the head. They wore the sari at ankle length (as did the local caste-Hindus and the Muslim women, while low-caste Hindu women in the area wore the *sari* almost at knee length), according to Kehimkar (p.103). But the 1885 *Gazetteer* in its section on Deccan-Poona (p.511) states that: "Bene Israel women dress like Kunbis (peasant cultivators) in a full robe and loose bodice passing the skirt of the robe between the feet and tucking it into the waistband behind." This probably was the most common style originally for the Bene Israel women in villages. The 1964 Revised Edition of an old *Maharashtra State Gazetteer* says (p.197):

> Till recently the [Bene Israel] women dressed like Kunbis....In recent years there has been a considerable change, the young women taking to the *golnesana*, round mode of wearing the sari [winding it round the hips and not between the legs], and a few copying the Parsi or the Western style. Their ornaments are generally the same as those worn by the middle and low class Hindus of the same rank.

Among educated women, nose-rings and silver anklets were becoming less popular, but not so with earrings or bangles (of gold, silver or glass). Bene Israel women, however, did *not* adopt the Hindu custom of wearing a red dot or round spot of vermilion (*kumkum*) powder on the forehead just above the nose.[2]

Bene Israel men copied elements from both Hindu and Muslim styles of dress, but usually preferred the Muslim wide trouser to the Hindu loin cloth. They also wore the Muslim style of long jacket; a collarless shirt; and for headwear, a Muslim type of turban or the velvet Turkish-style or Persian cap; and a skull cap for indoors. They wore country shoes or sandals. Some Bene Israel already were wearing English-cut jackets, pants, boots and shoes. Often they mixed items from all three styles (Muslim, Hindu, English) in their mode of dressing. The practice of men wearing ornaments (such as earrings) was

Home Life 167

dying out. Many of the non-westernized Bene Israel men wore Jewish-style earlocks. Some shaved their heads, others did not. Most wore a short beard and a moustache. Bene Israel did not tatoo their bodies.

Kehimkar describes how the first daily meal consisted of tea and bread or porridge, eaten very early in the morning; it was followed by a large full meal between 9 and 10 a.m.; and another meal between 7 and 9 p.m. To eat a meal between 1 and 2 p.m. was less usual. Both at home and at group functions, the men always ate first, the women afterwards, while the children could eat with either. In April and May, before the monsoon set in, poor and rich alike put aside enough stores of grains, pulses, onions, firewood and oil to provide food during the following three or four difficult months.

The local kind of unleavened wheat bread, called *chappati* or *bhakri*, as well as rice, pulses, potatoes, millet, local fruits and vegetables, sesame-seed oil, butter and salt were the staples. *Puris* of deep-fried dough were delicacies for Friday evenings or for special occasions. Fish was eaten far more frequently than meat and never beef. The Bene Israel had so thoroughly assimilated the Hindu ban on beef-eating that some uninformed Bene Israel actually believed that beef-eating was prohibited by the Jewish religion. Whenever they did eat meat and fowl it was only the kinds allowed by Jewish dietary laws, provided these had been slaughtered according to Jewish ritual. However, they sometimes did use butter with fowl, a practice forbidden by *halacha*.[3] In reference to this custom, Immanuel Olsvanger offered the following footnote-comment in Kehimkar's book *The History of the Bene Israel of India*:

> According to the *Babylonian Talmud, Yebomoth* 14a, there is mention of the fact that "In the place of Rabbi Yossi the Galilean, meat of fowls was served with milk." This passage might form an additional argument in support of the author's [i.e. Kehimkar's] theory of the Galilean origin of the Bene Israel.[4]

Kehimkar does not make clear exactly which details of *Kashruth* were observed before the Bene Israel's religious revival, except that the "forbidden" animals and fish were not eaten; that pork was especially abhorrent to them;[5] that when slaughtering an animal only the words of the *Kiryat Shema* or *B'Shem Adonai*, instead of the appropriate prayer, used to be recited; that the prerequisite examination as to the health of the animal's internal organs was not then carried out; and that the sciatic nerve, but not the tendons, used to be removed.

Feasts were given upon reaching various stages of one's life cycle, or on the occasion of making or fulfillment of a vow, and took place either between 9 a.m. and noon or from 7 to 10 p.m. The list of invitees was given to the *Shamash* (sexton) who, in turn, delivered the actual invitations (written or verbal). The community-owned (purchased out of synagogue funds) massive cooking utensils were put at the host's disposal, and either his female relatives and friends, or some hired Bene Israel cooks, prepared the food. The synagogue could provide ample quantities of separate sets of utensils and dishes for meat, milk or Passover meals, respectively. The invited guests left their shoes on the verandah, and all the male guests were seated on the mat or carpet-covered floor, with the *Hazan* or *Kaji* and the community leaders in the places of honor. The appropriate blessings and grace were first recited, the *Hazan* or *Kazi* partaking of bread and salt, then distributing some among all those present. Next, the various kinds of food were served in large china platters. The practice of two or three guests eating from the same platter was already giving way to that of each guest having his own plate. In July 1865, the Bene Israel community agreed that neither local nor European liquor was to be served at their public parties. Such liquor was allowed at private parties, but was served only before the meal. Both before and after the feast, a copper pitcher of water and a widelipped copper bowl were passed around, in Muslim fashion, for each guest to wash his hands. The _Hazan_ or _Kaji_ said grace after the meal and tasted salt, a bit of which was then passed to each guest. After the distribution of *pan*, the dishes were removed to be washed and thereafter to be used to feed all the women guests.

Countless little details of Bene Israel (and of Muslim) life in the Konkan, like the chewing of *pan* after a meal, were the same as that of their Hindu neighbors. The custom of removing one's shoes before entering a house, particularly a house of worship, was practised alike by Bene Israel, Hindus and Muslims. But in spite of so many examples of assimilation, the Bene Israel tenaciously clung to the uniqueness of their Jewish faith during centuries of isolation from other Jews and even in instances where only a handful of them were living in a given locality. There are anecdotes telling of Bene Israel who themselves had been enlightened by the 19th century religious revival, and who happened to come across fellow Bene Israel living in "untouched" rural areas, and who were surprised and enormously impressed by the fact that those isolated individuals still continued to observe the old traditional Bene Israel ways of honoring the Sabbath day.

NOTES

1. Kehimkar : *History*, p.92. Many details throughout this chapter can be found in Kehimkar, pp.92-104.
2. Among Hindu women, the *teepa* (also known as *bindi* or *puttu*) is worn as an auspicious cosmetic sign, and is *not* a caste symbol. Hindu widows are forbidden to wear the *teepa* because a woman whose husband had died was regarded as unlucky (i.e. inauspicious).
3. There are a few other scattered Jewish communities which also do not observe the prohibition against eating any dairy products together with flesh of fowl.
4. Olswanger prepared Kehimkar's *History* for publication. This footnote occurs on p.95.
5. The Jewish abhorrence of pork was reinforced by the fact that the Bene Israel's Muslim neighbors did not touch pork (because eating pork is forbidden in Islam); and also by the fact that only outcaste groups in India ate pork.

Chapter 16
Haeem Samuel Kehimkar and the Israelite School

Assuming that any writings which the ancestors of the Bene Israel may have brought with them were lost in the shipwreck, and realizing that in Konkan villages the only literates were traditionally the Brahmins, one can understand the lack of any but the most rudimentary kind of education among the Bene Israel before the arrival of the British and of the Cochin Jewish teachers.

After the Bene Israel religious revival, they learned to read Hebrew but without being able to translate word by word. Bene Israel who enlisted in the army in the early days must have received some elementary schooling connected with the regiments. But their first real enlightenment (in Hebrew, Marathi and English) had come through their attendance at Christian missionary schools. Eventually, several qualified Bene Israel teachers were trained and put on the staffs of these schools throughout the Konkan. Actually, both the first (Samuel Jacob Kehimkar) and the second (Ezekiel Joseph Rajpurkar)[1] Inspectors of these schools were members of the Bene Israel community, the missionaries themselves only occasionally visiting their schools. With the deaths of Rev. Wilson and Michael Sargon, the teaching of Hebrew was discontinued at the mission schools (except at one mission high school).

Even though in 1842 there had been 38 Bene Israel students at Wilson's College, there was no Bene Israel graduate in Arts from Bombay University until 1884. Evidently the need to earn one's living took precedence over higher education among the Bene Israel of this period. In order to attract large numbers of Bene Israel once more to attendance at school, there was a definite need for the Bene Israel to have a good school of their own. In 1875, through the devoted efforts of Haeem Samuel Kehimkar, his brother Joseph Samuel Kehimkar, and A.D. Pezarkar, the Bene Israel themselves were able to open a school which taught both Hebrew and Marathi among other subjects. Soon, however, in spite of promised contributions, the school could not manage with its meagre finances. In 1881, after A.D. Pezarkar, and later H.S. Kehimkar brought the problem to the attention of the Anglo-Jewish Association of London which responded generously, the school came under its continuing patronage, and it became known as the Israelite School.

Indifference and a lack of a sense of responsibility marked the attitude of too many members of the Bene Israel community. Still, with great difficulty, and without the participation of some of its leading members, the community did manage to raise the required amount of matching funds, and the Government agreed to allocate to the new school an annual grant of Rs. 1,560/—, which they soon increased to Rs. 2,000/—. The grant was justified on the grounds that, although many Bene Israel youngsters had begun primary education, only very few had continued beyond that stage[2] because of poverty and inability to pay school fees; attendance at other schools was undesirable for them because it involved the necessity of attending classes held on Saturdays and on Jewish holidays, conflicting with observation of Jewish respect for the Sabbath, etc.; and also because no instruction in Hebrew[3] or in the Jewish religion was by then available in other schools.

Haeem Samuel Kehimkar was completely devoted to the cause of the Israelite School. Three generations earlier his family had come from Ramraj to Alibag where he himself was born in 1830. He was educated by his father, then Inspector of the Mission Schools. His first employment was at the Military Board Office; and thereafter, for twenty-two years, in the Office of the Inspector General of Ordinance in Bombay, and later in Poona. He reached the rank of Second Assistant to the Inspector General of Ordinance. In 1853 be founded the Bene Israel Benevolent Society to give help to needy Bene Israel. Under the auspices of this society the Hebrew-Marathi School (as the Israelite School was first called) was founded in 1875. Following his retirement from Government service in 1878, H.S.Kehimkar dedicated the rest of his life to the school and to the general improvement of his community.

In 1881 H.S.Kehimkar was appointed President of the Israelite School.[4] In 1890 its first matriculation class began. The school's premises changed three or four times during these years, as rental fees became prohibitive. Older boys were allowed to study at school at night, and night sessions were also held to teach Hebrew to working people.

In 1892 Kehimkar published his *Sketch of the History of the Beni-Israel and an Appeal for Their Education* which he later (1897) developed into his significant book *The History of the Bene Israel of India* (although the latter was not published until 1937). In his *Sketch... and Appeal ....* his plea was not only for funds for a spacious building with playground and gymnasium, but also for a permanent endowment sufficient to maintain a teaching staff of the highest quality; for a "good library furnished with English and Hebrew classical and religious works"; and for a large workshop (closed on Sabbaths) able to train up to 300 needy Bene Israel children at a time in learning trades to prepare them for earning their own livelihood. Of all these desiderata, only the spacious building and grounds materialized. It was Kehimkar who spearheaded the campaign for collection of money for the Israelite School Building Fund.[5]

Finally, in the year 1896, a commodious building (inside a large compound wherein there were three heart-shaped gardens), located in the Mazgaon section of Bombay, was purchased for the Israelite School at a cost of Rs. 80,000/—.

Against great opposition, and to the dissatisfaction of the Israelite School Committee, Kehimkar fought for the establishment of a synagogue for the Israelite School. He ultimately prevailed, and a prayer hall for the use of students and the community at large was opened on the school premises, then in Umerkhadi, in September 1888. It was called the Aitz Hayyim (Tree of Life) Prayer Hall, and Kehimkar had very specific ideas of the important purposes which he intended it to serve (see above; p. 150).

He had to fight for everything, and was by no means always successful. He pleaded with his people to spend less on family ceremonies and on feasts, and to spend more on education. He saw the need for a permanent endowment fund sufficient to maintain the Israelite School out of income. He persuaded his sister-in-law to bequeath her Rs. 22,000/— estate toward such a fund. He wanted, but never attained, a school dormitory which would have enabled Bene Israel children from outside Bombay to attend the school.

Kehimkar wrote several articles on Jewish subjects and often lectured on the Jewish religion. Also, he translated into Marathi some sermons of English-speaking Jews and many English articles on a variety of useful subjects. In 1881 he, together with his eldest son Samuel, started a magazine called *Israel*. But, due to the sudden death of Samuel who had been the editor, publication of this magazine ceased.

The widespread opposition to Kehimkar centered on his reluctance to delegate authority to others. He was Chairman, Secretary and Treasurer (according to E.S. Divekar's *Life Story of the Late Haeem Samuel Kehimkar*) of the School Committee and served as Head of the School's synagogue. Committee Members felt that they themselves were little more than puppets. Some say that Bene Israel with university degrees, something which Kehimkar did not have, felt that they were more qualified than he was to direct the school. It did not matter to them that Kehimkar's motives were not selfish, nor that he lived a life of self-sacrifice for the benefit of the Bene Israel community. It is a sad fact that just before the onset of his final illness (1909), because of the Israelite School Committee's dissatisfaction with his services, Kehimkar felt forced to submit his resignation as President of the Israelite School.

After his death, H.S. Kehimkar's deeds, ideas and writings gained more and more appreciation. The 1927 Marathi translation of Paul Goodman's *A History of the Jews* has been dedicated by its Bene Israel sponsors to Kehimkar, with these words :

This book has been dedicated with great love by the managing committee of the Aitz Hayyim Prayer Hall to the late Haeem Samuel Kehimkar, who devoted the last twenty-seven years of his life to spread education among the Bene Israel community.

NOTES

1. While Ezekiel Joseph Rajpurkar was a teacher at a missionary school, he simultaneously served as *Hazan* in the Shaare Harachamim Synagogue in Bombay as well. Samuel Jacob Kehimkar, the first Inspector of Mission Schools in the area, was the father of Haeem Samuel Kehimkar, the author of *The History of the Bene Israel of India*. He had some 40 schools under his authority, according to a 24-page booklet called *The Life Story of the Late Haeem Samuel Kehimkar*, written by Ezekiel (Ujial) Solomon Divekar; printed by Moses Abraham Gadkar, Bombay, 1923. This booklet was written in Marathi and has been kindly translated into English for the present author by Mrs. Mary (Shapurkar) Sopher of Beer Sheva.
2. During a three-year period, in Bombay Presidency which then had a Bene Israel population of 10 to 12,000, only one Bene Israel boy had passed the matriculation examination.
3. Government was at that time sponsoring the teaching of Sanskrit, Persian or Latin in other schools.
4. According to Kehimkar (*History*, p.246), the annual income for the Israelite School during its early years was as follows :

The Anglo-Jewish Association of London	Rs. 3,000
The Bombay Government	Rs. 2,000
The Sassoon Family	Rs. 800
The Joint Schools Committee of Bombay Municipality	Rs. 600
The Bene Israel in fees and subscriptions	Rs. 1,000
Surplus from School Synagogue income	Rs. 300
TOTAL	Rs. 7,700

Kehimkar does not supply any actual date for this accounting. We do know from him, however, that the school synagogue was not opened until September 1888. He explained (pp.242-3) that the Rs.800/– from the Sassoon Family was originally made up of Rs. 400/– from Messrs. David Sassoon and Company, and an equal amount from Messrs. E.D. Sassoon and Company; and that Messrs. David Sassoon and Company, from the first of April 1888, had increased its subscription from Rs.400/– to Rs. 600/–; but that beginning on April 1, 1895, after the death of S.D.Sassoon, they reverted to the former sum of Rs. 400/–. Before this withdrawal of the additional Rs.200/–, Kehimkar expressed his appreciation thus : "....the Anglo-Jewish

Association and the Sassoon family have placed the Beni-Israel community under an obligation which they will ever remember with a sense of deep gratitude." (Kehimkar's *Sketch*, p.35)

5. The list of donors for the Israelite School Building Fund reads as follows :

" FROM LONDON	Rs.	FROM INDIA	Rs.
Anglo-Jewish Association	29,485	Messrs. David Sassoon & Co.	5,000
Bombay Government	20,000	Mr. S.E.Sassoon	1,000
Messrs. Rothschild & Sons	8,343	Mr. Shalom Issac Sagavkar	1,000
Mrs. N. Montefiore	7,500	Bai Motlabai	700
Mr. C.G.Montefiore	3,750	Mr. J.N.Khatav	300
Baroness De Hirsch, Paris	3,700	H.E.Lord Harris	250
Mr. F.D.Mocatta	2,345	Mr. Jacob E.Sassoon	1,500
Mr. E.A.Franklin	750	Mr. D.M.Petit	1,000
Mr. O.A.Goldsmid	750	Bai Dinbai N. Petit	800
Other Donors	400	Mr. Joseph Samuel Kehimkar	500
		Mr. Ezekiel J.Pugavkar	300
		Mrs. Leahbai Kehimkar	250
		Other Donors	1,150
		Mr. Shalom Samuel Kehimkar	1,000
		Dr. V.S. Divan, in memory of Dr. Abraham Hyams	500
		Mr. Hanabai Ezekiel Jacob Bhorupkar, a house and	7,000
		Mr. Mordecai Aaron Mazgavkar	2,000"

(Kehimkar : *History*, p.249).

6. See above, Preface, p. xiv, note 10.

Chapter 17
Bene Israel in Konkan Towns

Some remarks are in order concerning the Konkan towns and larger villages in which Bene Israel had concentrated. For the sake of better coherence and continuity, these paragraphs will include information going beyond the 19th century.

No single village was ever inhabited exclusively by Bene Israel. As a rule, Hindus, Muslims and Bene Israel lived side by side in friendship and harmony. Some villages had very few Bene Israel families; in others, like Kehim, lived 20 to 25 Bene Israel families; above average in numbers of Bene Israel were the 50 to 60 families living in Pen. Some villages, such as Tala (155 miles from Bombay) once had a relatively large Bene Israel population, enough at any rate to have supplied at one time "125 sturdy young Bene Israel *jawans* (soldiers)". Tala was not a military cantonment town; it is one of the traditional Bene Israel surname-linked villages. In Tala the Bene Israel established their own synagogue in 1846. It also served the Bene Israel who lived in the surrounding area. However, in 1960, when Tala's total population stood at 4,000, there were only 20 Bene Israel residents (from four different families) in Tala. The same year, also worshipping together in Tala's synagogue, having come from surrounding villages, were: five Bene Israel from Salshet, six from Nigudshet, three from Walis, three from Hardi, fifty from Ghosale, and ten from Satambe.

Some villages, such as Alibag and Pen had developed into small towns by the 20th century. Alibag had a considerable Bene Israel population even in 1848 (about 300 Bene Israel families) when its Magen Aboth Synagogue was first built.[1] Alibag became a favorite place where many Bene Israel military men chose to settle with their families upon their retirement. But, according to the 1971 Government of India Census, only thirty-two Jews remained in Alibag.

The synagogue at Pen owns about fifty acres of land. About five miles outside of Pen are located Bene Israel tombstones with the oldest dates yet found anywhere for Bene Israel burials (see above, p. 35). According to the *Gazetteer of the Bombay Presidency*, 1882, Volume XIII, Part I, Thana (p.273-4): "Bene Israels [in Thana District] returned as numbering 775 souls, are found in Panvel, Salsette, Bassein, Karjat, Bhiwandi, and Kalyan. They are also known as Yahudis[2] and Telis or oilmen. They are believed to have come into the district from Alibag in Kolaba about a hundred years ago."

Each Bene Israel urban congregation seems to have developed its own special character. Panvel is a trade center and, formerly, before its inlet to the sea became silted up, was a port town of Kolaba District (transferred from Thana District after 1882). It lies 16 miles east of Bombay on the Bombay-Poona Highway. Rabbi D'Beth Hillel found 30 Bene Israel families living in Panvel (which he called "Panoovellee") in 1831. The Bene Israel settled here in even greater numbers in the early 1840s when the British formed the Special Ghat Police Force (by taking servicemen from the regular Indian Infantry units) in order to put a stop to the plundering and violence being carried on by hill tribesmen in the area. Many Bene Israel formed a part of this Special Ghat Police Force which had its base in Panvel. Bene Israel prayer services were held in the house of a

Bene Israel settler in Panvel. Later, the Cochin Jewish teacher, Shelomo Salem Shurrabi, encouraged the establishment of a synagogue in Panvel. One Joseph David donated his house and grounds on which Panvel's Beth-El Synagogue was built in 1849. The Panvel Oomerdekar family, being related to the hereditary President of the Karachi Synagogue, a *Torah* scroll from Karachi was gifted to the Panvel congregation. As of 1980 the synagogue's properties were being well managed, Hebrew classes for children provided, and the cemetery maintained.

Several Bene Israel families, each on its own, had purchased houses in Panvel's "Israel Alley".[3] Many Bene Israel of Panvel earned their livelihood from the products of their groves of jackfruit, mango, and coconut and areca ("betel nut") palms. Atypically for Bene Israel in general, those of Panvel also engage in other forms of trade, as well as in small-scale and cottage industries. Some Bene Israel in Panvel own horse *tongas* and motor buses as public conveyance services catering to Panvel and adjacent areas. Several Bene Israel, both past and present, have been elected as Chairmen or members of the Panvel Municipal Committee or Local Board. The Bene Israel population in Panvel Taluka declined from 503 souls in 1872 to 147 in 1971 (108 of them were living in Panvel town in 1971).[4]

Also in Thana District is Thana town, 21 miles northeast of Bombay, another place in which the Portuguese had built a large fort. After 1817 British forces were brought to the area. Many Bene Israel enlisted both in the Indian Infantry and in the Special Armed Police here. There even were Bene Israel who belonged to the Police Band. One of the oldest graves in the Thana Bene Israel cemetery is of one "Subedar Major Bahadur and Native Commandant Thana Ghat Police, Moosaji Balaji Oomedkar" who died in 1868. The town's first permanent Bene Israel settlers were oil-pressers (see above, p. 173) who in Bombay had found keen competition from the more numerous and wealthier Hindu and Muslim oil-pressers, and so they came to Thana in search of better prospects and became successful oil-sellers here. The town really began to develop quickly once the railway line, India's first, was built (1853) connecting Thana with Bombay. During the four years while this was being constructed, Bene Israel carpenters, masons, supervisors, and contractors were employed on the project, and there were further employment opportunities thereafter in building the railway extension to Kalyan, and in the spanning of Thana Creek. Many Deccani Muslims were similarly employed, and both communities settled with their families in the Tembi area, on the outskirts of Thana town.

Some Bene Israel who were connected with the railway operation also moved into Thana proper, where good schools had been established both by the government and by the missionaries. Some Bene Israel residents of Thana commuted via the new railway to Bombay where they worked. Hindu, Muslim and Jewish retired military personnel began to settle in Thana. Jewish religious services had been sporadic until the Bene Israel community built the Shaar Hashamayim Synagogue in 1879 on land donated by a Bene Israel, situated on the edge of Tembi locality, within 200 yards of a Muslim mosque, symbolizing the friendship between the two neighboring communities which had now lasted for more than one hundred years and which is not limited only to the descendants of those retired military men.

In 1928 the railway was converted from steam to electric power, making the ride to Bombay much quicker and available at more frequent intervals. More and more families moved into Thana, many Bene Israel among them. This was reflected in the greater prosperity of the Thana Shaar Hashamayim synagogue. In 1959 ORT [5]—India built a hall adjacent to the synagogue, to be used for educational purposes, later adding a second storey. Elementary manual-training courses, for both boys and girls, are held there, as well as classes in home-science, home-nursing, and Hebrew.

Thana *District* had a Bene Israel population of 629 in 1851, 662 souls in 1861, 775 in 1871 and 892 in 1881. In 1881, 165 Bene Israel were living in Thana *town*[6]; in 1941 their number had grown to 306; and as of late 1970 there were still about eighty Bene Israel families there.[7]

The Thana Bene Israel community is outstanding for its vitality, its good synagogue attendance on Sabbath eve and on the Sabbath itself, its Hebrew classes, and its programs of lectures (in Marathi), discussions and entertainment, all on Jewish subjects. As of 1945, all Bene Israel children attended school, and 70 percent of Thana's Bene Israel males and 20 percent of Bene Israel females were able to speak, read and write English.

NOTES

1. The present Magen Aboth Synagogue has on its entrance doorpost an impressive, nine inch long *Mezuzah* of marble.
2. The author of this *Gazetteer* article may here have confused the Bene Israel with the Baghdadis; they were lumped together for census purposes and the preceding sentence gives a census figure. However, the rest of the article definitely describes only the Bene Israel.
3. This name does not carry any derogatory connotation.
4. Information on Panvel has been based largely on an article, *The Bene Israel of Panvel*, written by Daphne Samuel Pinglay, Advocate, High Court, Bombay; in *Shalom* 1969-1970, Bombay, pp.9-11.
5. ORT is the abbreviation for the international Jewish Organization for Rehabilitation through Training.
6. The following are the 1891 and 1901 Census figures for the Jewish (i.e. Bene Israel) population of the Konkan towns described in this chapter :

	JEWISH POPULATION	
	1891	1901
Alibag	90	104
Pen	182	156
Panvel	301	185
Thana	209	180

7. Most of the above information on Thana (now called Thane) is largely according to Shellim Samuel's article, *The Jews of Thana*, in *Shalom*, 1969-1970, Bombay, pp.1-5.

Chapter 18
Bene Israel Beyond the Konkan

This account of the spread of the Bene Israel into areas of India beyond the Konkan will also cover the 19th and 20th centuries.

Relatively large communities grew up in the places listed here in the order of the pre-1948 density of population of their Bene Israel inhabitants: Poona, Ahmedabad (Gujarat), Iqatpuri, Bhor and Satara. Poona, Bhor, Iqatpuri and Satara are located somewhat inland in western Maharashtra, i.e. not along the Konkan coast. Small groups of the community were scattered far and wide throughout India in various other places in which individual Bene Israel had come to settle with their immediate families, on assignment in army service, or as employees in government civil service, more especially in the departments of railways, customs, posts and telegraphs. These services employed many Bene Israel as mechanics, electricians, artisans, etc.; while some Bene Israel held responsible administrative positions. That was how small groups of Bene Israel came to settle in Ajmer (Rajasthan), Indore and Jabalpur (Madhya Pradesh), Belgaum (Karnataka, near Goa), Nagpur (eastern Maharashtra), and in Delhi. In some of these places they and their children remained for life. In other instances, both as military and as civil servants, some were shifted from one station to another every two or three years. In such cases a family often remained permanently in an "adopted" town in which there were at least a few other Bene Israel families as well as facilities for the children's schooling, while the husband was stationed elsewhere. The pattern of being stationed far from one's native place was also common among many non-Jewish Indians in government or in military service. Traditional extended-family households were more suited to coping with this kind of situation than was a single nuclear family unit. But Bene Israel families seemed more ready to establish themselves in an adopted town relatively close to the husband's work rather than in their native place. In such towns, the Bene Israel and their children adopted the language of the region. Thus, Bene Israel living in Ahmedabad spoke Gujarati; in Delhi, Hindi; etc. But they did not forget their Marathi and the children understood that language as well.

The dispersion did, however, separate those Bene Israel who lived outside the Konkan from the mainstream of community life as it had developed in the 19th century. Except for the greater distances involved, it was in a sense, a kind of reversion to the old traditional Bene Israel pattern of living not within a large Bene Israel group but rather with just a few families of their community per village. Indeed, this reversion to type may have been a considerable factor in the impressive record of progress and enlightenment generally so characteristic of the Bene Israel from such outlying regions. Not being a large enough group to have had communal institutions, etc., they at least were not torn and handicapped by factionalism. Their isolation, while depriving them of Jewish community life and services, did not alienate them from their Jewish faith and there was emphasis again upon the maintenance of Jewish customs in the home. Their neglect of certain details of *halacha* cannot be wholly blamed on their isolation, since other Jewish communities, including very large ones, have accepted similar reforms and non-*halachic* adaptations to modern life. In India there never was any need to hide their Jewishness. But, many times it happened that a Bene Israel child found him/herself to be the only Jewish pupil in an outlying convent or mission school, and this occasionally, but by no means always, placed the child in an awkward and sometimes difficult situation.

In the event of a birth of a son, a Bene Israel family would have to "import", often at great expense, the services of a *mohel*. On the other hand, these dispersed Bene Israel themselves knew and performed the Jewish ritual method for slaughter of fowl; and they ate lamb or goat only on the rare occasions when a *shochet* happened to be travelling in the vicinity, or had been "imported" in celebration of a holiday or other special feast. Especially in places where there were only one or two Bene Israel families, each scattered family maintained ties with the Jewish congregation and synagogue nearest to where they were living. The entire family would visit such a place during the Jewish High Holidays, and sometimes during other holidays as well; or they would visit with their own extended families who were living in Bombay or elsewhere in the Konkan, especially during holidays, marriages, etc. Larger groups, even of ten or more Bene Israel families, who regularly conducted their own prayer services in their adopted town, still maintained contact, as a group, with synagogues and with Bene Israel families where there were larger communities. And, always they staunchly maintained their Jewish identity in the places in which they had settled.

Karachi

The 1941 Government Census recorded 1,199 Jews living in what is now Pakistan; almost all of them, i.e. 1,051 (513 men and 538 women) lived in Karachi. At the time of partition of the subcontinent (August 15, 1947), some estimate that there were about 1,500 Jews living in the entire area which became (West) Pakistan and 36 Jews in East Bengal (which later became Bangladesh). About 85 percent of these Jews were then residents of Karachi and almost all of them were Marathi-speaking Bene Israel who had settled in Karachi only two generations earlier, while serving in the British civil or military cadres. There were also enough Bene Israel living in Quetta to have established their own prayer hall.

According to the 1891 Census, there were 128 Jews in Karachi City where in 1892 they founded a substantial synagogue – called Magen Shalom (see above, p. 150). Most Bene Israel in Karachi worked for the government as petty clerks, either in railway offices or at Karachi Port. Few were tradesmen. It was not a wealthy community, but it was on the average better off than the Bene Israel community in Bombay or Poona.

The first anti-Jewish riots in Pakistan (demonstrating solidarity with Palestinian Arabs) occurred in December 1947 in Peshawar. The Jews involved were almost all of Persian or Middle Eastern origin. All of them, as well as five Jewish families from Multan, fled first to Karachi and thereafter joined the first group of Karachi Bene Israel in their flight to Bombay. When, on May 21, 1948, the so-called Palestine Day demonstrators attacked the Karachi synagogue, the local police intervened and saved the synagogue from extensive damage. However, when the Bene Israel saw that Mohammed Ali Jinnah's assurances of no discrimination against minorities in the new country of Pakistan had not saved the exposed large Hindu and Sikh minorities of Pakistan, the Karachi Bene Israel community considered it wiser to leave Pakistan. The great majority went to live in Bombay. As for the handful of Jews who chose to remain in Karachi, they became renewed targets of demonstrations in 1956 and 1967, both occasions coinciding with warfare involving Israel and its Arab neighbors.

By April 1948 some 130 Jewish refugee families from Pakistan (about 650 souls) had arrived in Bombay, to be joined soon thereafter by another 350 Bene Israel refugees. According to the periodical *India and Israel*, Bombay, December 1948, the Relief and Rehabilitation Department of the Government of Bombay announced that "Jews who were Indian nationals immediately before August 15, 1947 and who have come to India as refugees are to be treated like any other non-Muslim refugees and given the usual facilities". Most of the Karachi refugees had relatives or friends in Bombay, still spoke Marathi, and were relatively easily rehabilitated. Only about thirty families of the Jewish refugees from Pakistan were completely destitute, knew no one, and had to be housed in Bombay synagogues and Jewish schools, remaining for a considerable period of time under the care of the Central Jewish Board of Bombay (see below, p. 266.)

Poona[1]

Poona (110 miles east and slightly south of Bombay, located in the plateau beyond the Western Ghats) was the capital of the Peshwa rulers of Maharashtra (1750-1817). Later, under the British, it became the administrative capital of the Bombay Presidency during Bombay's humid and unpleasant monsoon months (June through September); and it also served, and still serves, as Headquarters of India's Southern Command. After 1818 a large contingent of troops was always stationed in Poona. Bene Israel came to the city not only with the military and the ancillary services, but also settled there as army pensioners. On the other hand, relatively few Baghdadis ever settled in Poona, and they too only after the Sassoons chose Poona as their place of residence during the monsoon season.

Rabbi David D'Beth Hillel visited Poona in 1831 but makes no mention of any Jews there. The Rev. Joseph Wolff, however, specifically mentioned ten Bene Israel families living in Poona at the time of his visit in 1833. The *Revised Bombay State Gazetteer*, 1954, Volume XX in its section on Poona District (p.147) notes that the Bene Israel did not settle as civilians in Poona until 1856. We know that Bene Israel, in large numbers, came to settle there with their families after one of their number, Subedar Abraham David Churrikar, had been appointed Assistant Superintendent of Police in Poona in 1863. A few years later the railway link between Bombay and Poona was completed and Poona's favorable climate, lower prices, and growing opportunities attracted additional Bene Israel families. Abraham David Churrikar had become Chairman of the Poona Municipality and in that capacity he was in a good position to render help and advice to the newcomers in finding homes and work. Similar to their residence patterns in villages and in Bombay, the Bene Israel in Poona too settled originally in a cluster, mostly in one particular street which, in the case of Poona is still called — officially — "Israel Alley". Subsequent Bene Israel newcomers to Poona did not spread far afield. Almost all Bene Israel living in Poona reside within the Rastha Peth and Nana Peth sections of the city. The period of their settling was marked by extensive construction work: building of military and public edifices as well as of private villas for wealthy Maharashtrians coming to live (permanently or for part of the year) in Poona. Many incoming Bene Israel carpenters, masons and artisans found ample employment, enabling them comfortably to establish their families. Other Bene Israel found local work in civil or military service, in ordinance or other factories, in educational institutions, or in private businesses. In general the Bene Israel enjoyed a more open life, bustling with social and cultural activity, and free of Bombay's congested living conditions. Yet there were some Bene Israel families in Poona who needed extra help, especially those with large families, and in 1880 the Poona Jewish Benevolent Association was founded. It not only helped members of the community to find housing and jobs, but it also enabled poor children to obtain a proper education.

A few interesting observations of Jews in Poona were made by a Britisher, W.F. Sinclair, in an article entitled "Notes of Castes in the Puna and Solapur Districts" in the *Indian Antiquary*, No. 3 of 1874 (p.338) :

> The Bene Israel now number about two hundred souls....These Indian Jews seem to have no aptitude for trade, although many were formerly in business in the Kulaba District especially as dyers[2]....The Jewish Carpenters, too, rank high in their trade....The Bene Israel do not eat nor marry with the Kala Israel, but permit community of worship. The latter seem to prefer military service to any other profession....The writers [i.e. clerks] among the Bene Israel being "Progresistas", and the carpenters and military men strong Conservatives....There are two or three families of Mesopotamian Jews, connected in one way or another with the Sassoon family.... Except for small internal differences [among the Bene Israel]....there is probably no race in India whose members so seldom come in the way of penal justice."

Poona's Ohel David Synagogue was built by Bombay's wealthy Jewish (Baghdadi) trade magnate, David Sassoon, although only a handful of Baghdadi Jews had settled in Poona. It is located in the Cantonment area of Poona and was opened in 1867. Although Albert Sassoon, Solomon Sassoon and Sir Jacob Sassoon had built palatial homes for themselves in Poona, large numbers of Baghdadi Jews were not inclined to settle there. Despite its size and imposing steeple, the Ohel David Synagogue mainly served as a Sassoon family chapel. It was crowded only during the Jewish High Holidays when Baghdadi Jews from Bombay who could afford to do so, flocked to Poona so as to avoid the crowds in Bombay synagogues, and perhaps also to be seen worshipping in the company of the Sassoons.

The Ohel David Synagogue was not only socially distant for the Bene Israel of Poona, but, actually, it was not conveniently close enough to the Bene Israel neighborhood. In 1877 the first of four Bene Israel prayer halls was opened in the Rashta Peth house of Joseph Solomon Jhiradkar, who personally conducted the services. This first Bene Israel prayer hall in Poona possessed one *Sepher Torah*. Classes in Jewish religion and teaching Hebrew were held on the verandah. Poona's three other prayer halls, also located in Rastha Peth, were known respectively as the Bene Israel Prayer Hall, which had three *Torah* scrolls and a regular *hazan* (Baghdadi); the Hebrath Beth Yakob Prayer Hall, with four *Torah* scrolls; and the Ghosalkar Prayer Hall. In 1916 these congregations decided to cooperate; they purchased the property and house of the first, i.e. the Jhiradkar Prayer hall, and collected funds for erecting on this property a large Bene Israel synagogue inaugurated in 1921. Hindu, Muslim, Christian and Parsi places of worship are to be found in the same locality. The new synagogue was named the Succath Shelomo (Booth of Solomon) Synagogue in honor of Solomon Aaron Bhonkar and his wife who had made the largest donation toward the synagogue building fund. (S.A. Bhonkar had been a Karachi wine merchant who had come to Poona to retire.)

The Succath Shelomo Synagogue has a seating capacity of about 500 persons, with a women's gallery on three sides; it also has office space and a classroom with its own small library of Judaica. The Holy Ark contains twelve *Torah* Scrolls. This synagogue was a very lively centre of Bene Israel life in Poona until the mid-1960s, i.e. until the bulk of the congregation emigrated to Israel. As of 1970 Friday evening services barely managed to muster a *minyan* of men, some 10 to 12 teenagers and, seated in the upstairs balcony, 10 to 12 women with a few babies and youngsters. In spite of advertising and other efforts, the congregation could not find a permanent *ḥazan*-cum-*shohet* (as well as a *mohel*). For a while, in an effort to maintain some Jewish content for the younger generation, a teacher used to come from Bombay every Sunday to give Hebrew lessons.

In May 1971 Succath Shelomo Synagogue celebrated its Golden Jubilee. Bene Israel from all over contributed to the cost of the celebrations. The Mayor of Poona was guest of honor, and Bene Israel from many parts of India attended. The Jubilee evoked its own nostalgia and it led to a realization that all the scattered Jewish communities in India should join in a central organization and devise a scheme to maintain, as landmarks of the history of the Jews in India, those synagogue buildings, cemeteries and institutions which can no longer be sustained by the congregation which had originally established them; and that those Jews who remain in India should assist in enriching the Jewish content of their lives.[3] The concluding paragraph of an article written by Shellim Samuel, entitled "The Succath Shelomo Synagogue, Poona", which appeared in the *Succath Shelomo Synagogue Golden Jubilee Souvenir*, offered these reflections:

> Whether or not there will remain a community at the time of the Centenary of the Synagogue is a moot question; but one thing is certain, that the Bene Israel Community of Poona will leave its mark on the sands of time, and the Synagogue which is an embodiment of the will and the spirit of the Bene Israel of Poona will remain a memento to that enlightened and progressive Bene Israel Community of Poona.

In an effort to produce sufficient supplementary income for current maintenance of the Succath Shelomo Synagogue, the congregation was able, as late as 1971, to construct a hall on nearby premises, gifted to the synagogue by one Ratanbai Joseph Kamerlekar. In addition, a donation was received toward this construction from Bombay's Noar Memorial Trust (set up by the Navgaonkar family), leading to the structure being named the Noar Memorial Hall. Its facilities are rented out, for a fee, to members of all communities as a venue for various private functions, etc., thus providing income for the Synagogue.

An unusually large proportion of the Poona Bene Israel community had availed itself of the city's educational facilities. Especially noteworthy was the good education in Poona of large numbers of Bene Israel girls (some of whom came from as far as Bombay) who attended the Huzoor Paga Girls High School (also known as the High School for Indian Girls), today known as His Highness Chintamanrao Patwardhan Girls School. In former days, a special Bene Israel hostel, with a Bene Israel matron, was maintained at this school; and some of its Bene Israel girl students achieved first or second place in the Bombay University Matriculation Examinations. Many of these young women subsequently had careers in education and social service. It was a young Bene Israel woman, Sarah Sampson (Mrs. Sarah Ezekiel), who, in 1917, became the first female student at Poona's Shiksan Prasarak Mandali College, now called Sir Parshuram Bhau College. About the same time, she, together with Abigail Hyams, founded the Poona Bene Israel Stree Mandal for the benefit of the women and girls of Poona's Bene Israel community. It continued to function until 1935. Sarah devoted the greater part of her life to teaching and social welfare work in Bombay. Abigail first taught at the High School for Indian Girls at Poona; then, after her marriage to Dr. E. Moses (who later became Mayor of Bombay), she continued her teaching career at the Government High School for Girls in Thana, commuting daily from Bombay.

In 1916, the Young Men's Hebrew Association (YMHA) of Poona was founded for social, intellectual, and sports activities. A praiseworthy and exceptional Bene Israel venture was the establishment, as early as 1887, of the Poona Jewish Reading Room and Library. This library prospered thanks to the dedicated efforts of David Eliezer Koletkar, Khan Bahadur Dr. Judah Hyam Mhasilkar, Solomon Samson Penkar, and a few others. Located near the Succath Shelomo Synagogue, it is open to Jews and non-Jews alike, holds more than 2,000 books in English and 3,000 in Marathi, and subscribes to some periodicals. Its holdings include a modest collection of books on Judaism. For a while it received a grant-in-aid from the Poona Municipality, but now is financed exclusively through membership fees and donations.

Another feature of Poona's Bene Israel community was its relatively large membership in Freemason Lodges, with some Bene Israel reaching advanced Masonic degrees.

A member of the community, Daniel Elijah Benjamin Gadkar, has for several years been collecting what is now a disorganized mass of photographs of Indian Jewish synagogues (interior and exterior) and other institutional buildings, cemeteries, monuments (with details of inscriptions, etc.), personalities and events. He has also collected much written material bearing on Jews in India : books, pamphlets, brochures, news clippings, articles, etc., in English as well as in Indian languages. Daniel E. Benjamin's father, Elijah Benjamin Gadkar, born in 1898, was for several years active in Ahmedabad's Bene Israel community. Since moving to Poona, almost until his death in 1985, he was the mainstay of Poona's Jewish religious life. Were it not for him and a very few others, the lives of the Jews remaining in the city would long ago have been deprived of Jewish content. He formerly served as President, and later as a Trustee of the Succath Shelomo Synagogue; also, and in spite of his advanced years, he served as regular *hazan* in the Baghdadi Ohel David Synagogue.[4] He taught Hebrew to classes of children and of adults; he served as *shohet*; and officiated at Jewish funerals, memorial services, marriages, and Bar Mitzvah ceremonies. On his 75th birth anniversary, in memory of his departed wife, Rachel, he donated to Poona's Raja Kelkar Museum some Jewish ceremonial items and a small library of Jewish publications and books on Jewish history, philosophy and culture.

Dr. Judah Hyam Mhasilkar F. Z. S. (Fellow Zoological Society) (1862-1935), also of Poona, was awarded the title of Khan Bahadur for his outstanding service as a veterinary surgeon. He was an avid reader, a past President of the Poona Jewish Reading Room and Library, a founder-member of the Succath Shelomo Synagogue, as well as a founding member of the Bene Israel Conference. New Delhi's Judah Hyam Prayer Hall is named in his memory.

There were many notable individuals of the Poona Bene Israel community, sometimes several in the same family. After the death of his father, namely Subedar Major Bahadur Daniel Rahamin Talkar, who had founded the Poona Bene Israel Prayer Hall, Aaron Daniel Talkar became the head of this congregation. Among his other activities he was a staunch supporter of the Indian freedom-fighter Lokamanya Bal Gangadhar Tilak. Talkar became the first Bene Israel ever to serve as an elected member of Poona's Municipal Council (from Rastha Peth constituency, 1902-7) and was appointed by the Judge of the Small Causes Court to settle intra-communal disputes of the Bene Israel in Poona.

Dr. Jerusha Jhirad, the first Jewish Padma Shri Award winner (see below, p. 209), is the granddaughter of Joseph Solomon Jhiradkar in whose house the first prayer hall conducted its services. Poona's Killekar family has family members with a variety of successful careers : civil and mechanical engineering, law, medicine, chemistry and aviation.

Poona was home to Shalom Bapuji Israel Wargharkar (see below, p. 208) and his wife and children. His son, Abraham Shalom Wargharkar, established Poona's Israelite Press which catered to the general public and at one time was one of the largest presses in Poona. He also started an English daily newspaper, with an Englishman as editor; but it was unsuccessful financially and failed. Eventually he sold his Israelite Press to a Parsi who, interestingly enough, retained the name for the establishment. Abraham Wargharkar later started a new business venture, first in Kolhapur and then in Ahmednagar. This rare example of Bene Israel business endeavor flourished during World War II. There were only a few other Bene Israel business ventures in all of India. Perhaps the one with the longest history of success is a shipping agency in Bombay, called D. Abraham and Sons, which, however, today is mainly controlled by a Gujarati financier, although members of the Bene Israel family which started the firm still have a share in it.

The Bene Israel's only member of the elite Indian Civil Service, namely David Ezra Reuben (see below, p. 209) of the Navgaonkar family, studied in Poona at Deccan College. Rebecca Reuben, the educationist, was his sister, who studied and then taught for some time at Huzoor Paga Girls High School in Poona.

Poona had a two-way relationship with Bene Israel who lived elsewhere. The careers of several of its sons and daughters took them away from Poona. On the other hand, Poona continued to hold an attraction for Bene Israel living within a wide radius of the city. Such towns as Ahmednager (where many retired Bene Israel once made their homes), Lonavala (a hill resort), Sholapur (where Bene Israel were employed in mills and in railway offices and enterprises), Satara and Panchgani — all of these places formerly had small Bene Israel communities and these families would regularly come to Poona for holidays and Jewish festivals. The small Bene Israel cemeteries in each of these towns are mute evidence of earlier days of Bene Israel residence there.

The older of Poona's two Jewish cemeteries is the Babulbund cemetery in Wanowarie in the Cantonment area, which had been allotted to the Bene Israel of the Old Indian Sepoy regiments and is now closed but maintained by the Succath Shelomo Synagogue. The "new" Jewish cemetery is situated in Chorpuri on the edge of Koregaon Park. In 1885 the *Bombay Presidency Gazetteer*[5] reporting on the "Jews' Graveyard" noted that "A wall divides it inside into two unequal parts, the western half belonging to the Konkan Jews or Bene-Israels, and the eastern half to other Jews."[6]

Already in 1893 the Rev. J.H. Lord, in his, *The Jewish Mission Field in the Bombay Diocese* (pp. 7-8), observed that in Poona the Bene Israel were the main worshippers in the Sassoon Synagogue, and that there were at that time 930 Jews in the city of whom only a trifling few were Arabic-speaking Jews. Yet social separation of the two communities, i.e. the Baghdadis and the Bene Israel, was strictly maintained until large-scale emigration of both communities made it practically untenable. However, even after large-scale emigration had taken place, the two communities still did not really pool their remaining manpower and resources to cooperate in Jewish affairs.

According to H. G. Reissner, in 1945 there were in Poona 621 Bene Israel and only 184 Baghdadis, a 3.4 : 1 ratio.[7] The peak total population of all Jews in Poona was reached about 1949 when it is estimated that the number stood at approximately 1,200. Estimates of the breakdown into numbers of Bene Israel and of Baghdadis are offered by various sources for various years, but vary far too widely to be taken seriously. At most there never seem to have been more than 300 to 400 Baghdadi Jewish residents in Poona, and these peak figures were apparently reduced early in the 20th century.

Jewish relations with non-Jewish neighbors in Poona had always been so cordial that it is difficult for many non-Jews to understand why so many Jews have emigrated. In the words of a Bene Israel remaining in Poona : "It is hard to give them a satisfactory answer, because we have *never* had any trouble from non-Jews in Poona."

Bene Israel in Gujarat

Bene Israel settlement throughout what is now the State of Gujarat began with soldiers who were stationed in various early British garrisons and cantonments in this region. Later, when communications and peaceful conditions were established, the Bene Israel soldiers were joined by their families. (There is no Bene Israel tradition of having lived in Gujarat in pre-British times.) A second wave of Bene Israel settlement in Gujarat followed the construction of the Bombay—Baroda railway line and its extensions when large numbers of the community obtained employment in the newly created railway complex. The Bene Israel families who moved to Gujarat became bi-lingual in Gujarati and Marathi.

There are small Bene Israel cemeteries in Surat and in Baroda, with early 19th century dates on the tombstones. The number of Bene Israel in Baroda was never very large. Abraham Aaron Kehimkar, a nephew of the Bene Israel historian, lived in Baroda, serving as High Court Judge (*Sur Nayadish*) of Baroda State. After the State of Baroda merged with that of Bombay in 1948, a Bene Israel, Solomon Benjamin Dandekar, became Collector of Baroda District. In Surat, the Bene Israel were numerous enough to maintain a prayer hall of their own, separate from that of the local Baghdadi Jews. In northern Gujarat, at Deesa, it is known that there were 72 Bene Israel men and 38 women living in the cantonment in 1872. Here, too, as well as in Rajkot and Wadhwan, there were Bene Israel cemeteries. Kehimkar mentions (pp.75-6) that a few Bene Israel were also living in Daskroi, Dhanduka, Prantej, Kapadvanj, Broach, Kutch, Palanpur, Mahi Kanta, Kathiawar, and Rewa Kanta. For all these outlying groups, Ahmedabad served as their social and religious center.

Ahmedabad (Gujarat)

Ahmedabad, the site of many important milestones in Mahatma Gandhi's life, is located some 300 miles north of Bombay. Bene Israel began to settle there about 1840. It is recorded that, as of 1846, 40 Bene Israel persons were living in Ahmedabad, most of them being clerks or hospital assistants. When Dr. Abraham Benjamin Erulkar (1822-87) came to Ahmedabad in 1848, in his capacity as House Surgeon in charge of Ahmedabad's Civil Hospital, he (being well-versed in Hebrew) organized the Bene Israel residents into a congregation which met regularly for religious services in a special room of his own house. He encouraged and helped other Bene Israel to settle in Ahmedabad where he and others had already purchased some land. In 1866, Dr. Joseph Solomon Dandekar was posted in Ahmedabad, in charge of Ahmedabad's Lunatic Asylum; he too became quite active in community affairs.

Dr. Abraham Benjamin Erulkar had sent his own son (later Dr.) Solomon Abraham Erulkar, to study medicine at Durham University in England. After his father's death Dr. Solomon A. Erulkar became the head of the Ahmedabad Bene Israel community. He, in turn, sent his own sons (later Dr.) Abraham Solomon Erulkar and David Solomon Erulkar (see below, p. 209) for professional studies in England.

In his will, Dr. A.B. Erulkar had set aside a large sum of money for the erection of a synagogue in Ahmedabad at a time when the size of the growing community would warrant it to be built. Another substantial sum for the same synagogue was donated by Aaron Solomon Charrikar, Station Master at Baroda. The Ahmedabad congregation was foremost among all Bene Israel congregations in systematically keeping a register of all its births, circumcisions, marriages and deaths.[8]

In 1920, when their religious services were being held in a rented hall, the congregation began concentrating on raising more funds for building a proper synagogue, and a 750 square yard plot of land was purchased in the so-called Bokhara section of the city. At the laying of the foundation stone in 1933, it is said that 800 Bene Israel were present, there being at that time about 300 Bene Israel *families* living in Ahmedabad. The new synagogue was inaugurated on September 2, 1934, and was named Magen Abraham, in fitting memory of Dr. Abraham Erulkar. It is a handsome structure and was built largely by Bene Israel artisans. On the premises there is a separate store-room as well as residential quarters for the *Hazan* and *Shamash*. The storey above these quarters is rented out, and one-third of the rental fee is allocated to an education fund. The synagogue also maintains a cemetery, on Dudheshwar Road.

The first *Hazan* in Ahmedabad was Hyam Samuel Jhiradkar, of a Bene Israel *Kaji* family. He was succeeded by a Cochin Jew, Moshe Madai, and his son Yakob. For many years, the present *Hazan*, also from Cochin, Eliahu Hai Isaac, has served the Ahmedabad congregation faithfully. Like his predecessor, whenever he has received a telegram announcing the birth of a baby boy, he has never failed dutifully to appear exactly on the eighth day in order to perform a ritual circumcision, even in places 200 or more miles distant from Ahmedabad, such as at Indore or Ajmer. He also travelled extensively to conduct Jewish burials for bereaved Bene Israel families who lived very far away from Ahmedabad.

In the 1960's a Bene Israel boy from Ahmedabad went to Israel to study. He returned to Ahmedabad where he taught Hebrew in the congregation for four years, but ultimately he settled in Israel.

The Ahmedabad community has few close ties with Bene Israel in Maharashtra. It has always had a special character of its own. Among its congregation there were several nurses, teachers and doctors; many others were government employees; or workers and a few engineers in the local textile mills, none at the very top nor at the lowest levels in the industry; most recently a few Bene Israel in Ahmedabad have started working in banks.[9]

Among the notable Bene Israel of Ahmedabad are: Dr. Joseph Benjamin (Bamnolkar) who took an active part in the Indian National Congress until about 1910, was an intimate friend of Mahatma Gandhi, was a strict prohibitionist, served as President of the first and the thirteenth sessions of the Bene Israel Conference, from the beginning of the 20th century for about 35 years he very effectively served as Secretary and Treasurer of the Magen Abraham Synagogue, and it was his idea to start keeping a synagogue register; Dr. Jacob E. Solomon (Warsulkar), a Theosophist and a physician in government service who, after his retirement, ran a very popular free dispensary for the poor, received the Kaiser-i-Hind Silver Medal for his social service, and served as Secretary of the Ahmedabad Branch of the Indian Home Rule League (among several other important offices which he held); Dr. Rachailbai David who was Superintendent of the Municipal Maternity Home; the well-known Dr. Abraham Solomon Erulkar and David Solomon Erulkar (already mentioned above); Khan Bahadur Reuben Benjamin, Deputy Political Agent, Western India State; Khan Bahadur Solomon Benjamin, Collector and District Magistrate in Baroda; Reuben Hyam Dighorkar, Superintendent of Police in Saurashtra; Isaac Ellis Erulkar, Inspector of Police in Surat and later in Petlad; Reuben David (Dandekar), the imaginative Superintendent of Ahmedabad's Zoo and founder of Ahmedabad's Children's Park; Dr. Esther Solomon, Head of the Sanskrit Department, School of Languages of Gujarat University in Ahmedabad; J.M. Penkar, a prominent Gujarat architect; Dr. Eliezer

Moses Best who in 1962 became Dean of the B.J: Medical College and Superintendent of the Civil Hospital in Ahmedabad, and thereafter held similar posts in Surat; Ralph Best and his wife, co-founders of one of Ahmedabad's outstanding high schools, appropriately called Best High School, of which they are, respectively, Managing Trustee and Principal.[10] All in all, three schools were established in Ahmedabad by Bene Israel, largely because there were very few mission schools in the city, so that there was a need for English-medium schools, and qualified Bene Israel were able to meet the need.

Among the above-mentioned Bene Israel achievements in so many different fields of endeavor, such occupations as Superintendent or Inspector of Police, or Zoo Superintendent, or artisans physically building their community's own synagogue are particularly noteworthy, for such careers are not exactly common among Jews, past or present (except of course in the State of Israel).

Unlike the Bene Israel in the Konkan, Bene Israel in Ahmedabad spoke Gujarati, dressed in Gujarati fashion, and were, on the whole, more successful financially than their Konkan brethren. However, the life of the Bene Israel community in Ahmedabad (especially in the early 1920s), as was equally true of Bene Israel in Bombay and Poona, was ridden with internal strife, law suits, and even excommunications, all of which sapped the vitality of the community as such.

According to Reissner (p.356), as of 1941, places in Madhya Pradesh such as Nagpur had 142 Jews, Jubbulpore had 105 Jews; Patapatnam of (the then) Madras province had 107 Jews. Many, but not all, of these Jews must have been Bene Israel.

Ajmer in Rajasthan, is an example (as is also Indore in Madhya Pradesh) of a much smaller congregation of Bene Israel, never numbering more than 15 to 20 families, reaching the latter peak in the 1920s. Most Bene Israel men in Ajmer were employed in the Railway services.[11] Such jobs frequently took the husband of the family away from Ajmer for weeks, even months, at a time, while the wife and children remained in Ajmer. At that time, the Bene Israel met for prayers, including High Holiday services, in a special room at the home of Dr. Samuel Korlekar. The older men knew how to conduct services and the youngsters learned purely by ear and rote. The *Brit Mila* ceremony, the prayer services (especially on the High Holidays), and the maintenance of household Jewish traditions were their main, but very meaningful, bonds with Judaism. Ajmer's Jewish cemetery is larger than that of Delhi and contains many tombstones. By the 1960s, however, the remaining handful of Ajmer Jews had to come to Delhi to worship on the High Holidays because of the lack of a *minyan* in Ajmer. Today there are no Jews at all in Ajmer.[12] When the Ajmer Prayer Hall stopped functioning, its *bimah* found a proper home at the Judah Hyam Prayer Hall in New Delhi.

Other small Bene Israel settlements, such as at Belgaum, Karwar and Yellapur (all now in Karnataka) were begun not because of local railway employment, but because Bene Israel in army service were stationed there. *Gazetteers* tell us that in the early 1880s there were about 90 Bene Israel at Belgaum and "Beni-Israels, numbering 25 of whom 14 were males and 11 females, are found in the towns of Karwar and Yellapur."[13]

Delhi

In 1911 the capital of British India was transferred from Calcutta to Delhi. Through the ages Delhi had been the Capital of several important kingdoms and empires, beginning in ancient Hindu times and continuing (with interruptions) through the Moghul Period. From the 10th century onwards, Hebrew literature and synagogue records in the diaspora make mention of individual Jews from Europe, Egypt, West Asia and Persia who had gone to northern India as seekers of greater religious freedom, or for purposes of trade, or a combination of both reasons. Most of them were active in India as merchants, agents or jewellers; some remained only temporarily in India, others merged with the Indian population. Unlike their role in other lands, these Jews did not serve as bankers or as money-lenders, an occupation which in most of India was practically a monopoly of specific Indian communities. Persian was the *lingua franca* of the Moghul Empire, making the subcontinent particularly attractive to Jewish merchants from Persia, Khorasan and Afghanistan, even more so after the Emperor Akbar abolished (in 1564) the poll tax which Muslim rulers had previously levied on "non-believers". It is a fact that during Akbar's reign Jewish merchants were living in the important Moghul cities of Agra, Delhi and Lahore, as well as in Kashmir. These Jews traded in expensive cloth, shoes, bracelets, iron, junk, locks and bolts, and all sorts of utility items.[14]

One of the Persian Jews who came to India as a merchant, called Sarmad, converted to Islam and is known in the literature variously as Mohammed Said Sarmad or as "Sarmad the Jew", "the Hebrew pantheist", "the Jewish mystic", "the Hebrew atheist". He became a Sufic mystic, went about as a naked *fakir*, and expounded in poetry his Sufic philosophy, but, as Fischel says, "Sarmad's views show no leanings towards either Christianity or Islam".[15] His *rubaiyats* are still being sung in Delhi and elsewhere even today. Emperor Akbar's great-grandson, Dara Shikoh (himself an important writer and thinker), was a close friend and disciple of Sarmad. Dara Shikoh (eldest son of Shah Jehan, the builder of the Taj Mahal) was beheaded in 1659 by his ruthless brother Aurangzeb who wanted no rival to the Moghul throne; and in 1661 Aurangzeb had Sarmad beheaded as well. Professor Fischel cites from the decree pertaining to Dara Shikoh's execution as follows : "It became manifest that if Dara Shikoh obtained the throne and established his power, the foundations of the faith would be in danger and the precepts of Islam would be changed for the rant of infidelity and Judaism."[16] Sarmad is revered to this very day. His tomb is a sort of shrine, located northeast and very near the broad main stairway to Delhi's Jama Masjid, the largest mosque in India (also built by Shah Jehan).[17]

Several other Jewish merchants, of a much more prosaic bent than Sarmad — especially from Afghanistan — were also attracted to Delhi even when it was the Capital city of India under the British. These Jews dealt in hides and skins, brought their wares first to Delhi, thence to be shipped by rail to Bombay, and abroad by sea. In the 1920s and 30s a few French and Russian Jews[18] in Delhi also engaged in the skin export business which they conducted in the Sardar Bazaar section of the city. The few Bene Israel then living in Delhi, working in government jobs, would join all these other Jews for prayers in Sardar Bazaar. The group called themselves the Jewish Association of Delhi. In the course of a decade they had rented three or four different rooms in which they held their High Holiday services. About 1930, the government allotted them land on Reading Road on which to build a synagogue. (In the same neighborhood were located a church, two Hindu temples and a mosque.) But the Jewish Association objected to their allocation because it would have necessitated building a place of worship over an old grave-site, in contravention of Jewish law.

Actually, the most pressing need for the Jews in Delhi was to have a Jewish cemetery. At that time a Bene Israel by the name of Moses Jacob Solomon was serving as Railway Station-Master at Delhi Junction. It was through his efforts that the Jewish Association of Delhi in 1932 acquired from the government a plot of land (97' × 100') for a cemetery on Humayun Road, then on the outskirts of *New* Delhi.

Among the Allied forces stationed in Delhi during World War II were several Jewish soldiers, one of whom is buried in the Delhi Jewish cemetery. In those days, places (near the Masonic Lodge) in Delhi were reserved for worship by troops of various faiths. It was one of these places that served all the various Jews in Delhi (servicemen included) as a Jewish Prayer Hall from 1939-45. At the time of partition of the subcontinent there lived in Delhi about eight Bene Israel families and a few bachelors, three Afghan Jewish families, and about half a dozen individual Jews from western countries. Due to the partition of the subcontinent, the usual access route from Afghanistan was no longer open, putting a stop to their trade, and so the Afghan families left Delhi. As part of the massive population exchange at the time of partition, government employees in both Pakistan and India were given the option of either remaining where they were, or migrating to the other country. Many Muslims left India for Pakistan and multitudes of Sikhs and Hindus left Pakistan for India. In this catastrophic upheaval most Bene Israel, who had been working especially in the government Railway and Post and Telegraph services in the Pakistan area, chose to come with their families to India. Refugees who had held government jobs in India were often transferred to government employment in Pakistan, and vice versa. But, when the Bene Israel fled from Karachi, after the sack of their synagogue, it all happened so quickly that in many cases there was no time for them to collect or obtain important documents, etc. This subsequently caused problems for the Bene Israel concerned when they wanted to benefit from their Provident Fund assets, etc. accrued in Pakistan. Fortunately for them, their fellow Bene Israel in Delhi enlisted the help of Muslim friends, formerly serving in the Ministry of Finance in Delhi, who, resettled in Pakistan, were able to intervene successfully in such personal matters — a particularly striking example of the close ties of friendship between Indian Muslims and the Bene Israel.

About the same time, the "Jewish Association of Delhi" changed its name to the "Delhi Jewish Welfare Association", taking the word "welfare" in its broadest sense, i.e. for the mutual benefit of all Jews in Delhi: religiously, socially, culturally, educationally, charitably.

The Association's first *Torah* scroll had been borrowed from a Bombay synagogue. The group met every Friday evening for Sabbath eve services at the residence of one of the members. They inserted notices in newspapers to announce their High Holiday services for the information of any Jews who happened to be in Delhi at that time as tourists, students, employees in the various diplomatic corps or United Nations agencies, or as consultants in various fields. A few of these foreign Jews and their families became "regulars" of the congregation for as long as they remained in Delhi, sometimes for a number of years, as did also a few Baghdadi Jews and an occasional Cochin Jew. All have always worshipped and socialized together in Delhi in complete amity and equality; and there are no dividing walls in the cemetery to separate one group from another. But the core and spirit of all Jewish life in the city since the days of partition has been, and continues to be vested in the few Bene Israel families permanently resident in Delhi and numbering never more than twenty families at any one time, reaching a peak in the 1950s and 1960s. On the High Holidays at least one hundred persons would attend services. About 1954, one of the members began conducting children's classes on Sunday mornings, teaching them Jewish history, customs, songs, and Hebrew.

The community needed premises of its own. The original contract for land for the cemetery had sanctioned the construction of a room to be used for religious purposes. Government approval for construction of a synagogue on part of the land was sought and obtained through the efforts of Ezra Kolet, then Honorary Secretary of the Delhi Jewish Welfare Association. Only one quarter of the Association's land had been used as a cemetery, situated along one side of the plot. The cemetery is separated from the rest by a high substantial wall and has its own separate entrance from the street. The Association applied to the *Bet Din* (Jewish religious court) in London for *halachic* advice on the Jewish rules governing the construction of a synagogue in proximity to a burial ground. For consideration by the *Bet Din* the property was inspected by a British Jew (who happened to be a Member of Parliament then on a visit to Delhi). The *Bet Din* ruled that the distance away from the graves and the separating wall made construction of a synagogue there acceptable according to orthodox Jewish rules.

Joshua M. Benjamin, who came to live and work in Delhi in 1947 and who is Vice-President and Secretary of the Jewish Welfare Association and Retired Chief Architect, Design Group, Government of India Ministry of Works and Housing,[19] created the design and the blueprint for the proposed small synagogue. An appeal for building funds was sent out to friends in India and abroad. A Bene Israel woman, Dr. Rachel Judah (then in charge of the Women's Section of the Jodhpur Government Hospital) gave the largest single donation (Rs.4,000/−) towards the building fund and the new building was named in memory of her late father, Khan Bahadur Dr. Judah Hyam of Poona. It is called the Judah Hyam Hall and was inaugurated in 1956. Baruch B. Benjamin, a Bene Israel and at one time Under-Secretary in the Ministry of Irrigation and Power was the first President of the Delhi Jewish Welfare Association and its President when the new building was inaugurated.

Judah Hyam Hall's single large room serves principally as a synagogue. Its Ark (the *heykhal*) of light and dark wood, is situated in the further right corner. In front of the Ark, from the ceiling, hangs a brass oil-lamp (a gift from Cochin) for the everlasting light. The Ark contains three *Torah* scrolls : one was donated to the congregation by Jewish communities in Philadelphia, Pennsylvania; another by the Knesset Israel Synagogue of Minneapolis, Minnesota; and a third (smaller) scroll by S. David Rohekar of Bombay. The scrolls donated from Philadelphia and Minneapolis have ornamented velvet covers, in Ashkenazic fashion. The scroll from Bombay is in its traditional wooden encasement. The *bimah*, originally from the now defunct Prayer Hall in Ajmer, a fenced-in wooden pulpit-platform, is moveable, but usually remains in the center of the room, in the fashion of Sephardic synagogues. Judah Hyam Hall serves the Delhi congregation also for social gatherings on occasions other than for prayers, and which sometimes take place immediately after prayers : for wedding ceremonies, Sunday-school classes. Purim plays, lectures, meetings with visiting foreign Jews, committee meetings of the Delhi Jewish Welfare Association, *Bar* (and *Bat*) *Mitzvahs*, etc. There are no fixed benches or chairs. The seating arrangement is flexible. With additional folding chairs, the hall can seat a maximum of one hundred persons.

Nowadays, except on the High Holidays, on special occasions, or for special memorial prayers, a *minyan* in attendance is a rare event. There are only six Indian Jewish families (all of whom are Bene Israel) and one bachelor now living in Delhi (1984), a total of twenty-five persons. The few men who do come, conduct the service themselves, with Sabbath eve services being conducted regularly; Sabbath morning services occur only irregularly. Almost every week there is some sort of Sunday-school program for the children. For the High Holidays a *Hazan* from Bombay or from Cochin is engaged to conduct the services. Basically, the Sephardic De Sola Pool Prayer Book is followed, but the chants and melodies are those used in Cochin and/or in customary Bene Israel worship; and many of their own traditional prayers are interspersed as frequent additions to the De Sola Pool service.

Judah Hyam Hall is a center for Jews of all sects and backgrounds in the Indian capital. In spite of all the differences in the backgrounds of all its congregants, it has somehow managed to accommodate them all without frictions or fissions. The driving force behind this achievement has been its present President, Ezra Kolet, who has for decades successfully guided and assisted the congregation. He participated as one of the representatives of Indian Jewry at a meeting of the World Jewish Congress held in Jerusalem in February 1975. In May 1982 he very effectively represented (together with one other Jew from the U.S.A.) the World Jewish Congress at the United Nations Seminar on Regional, National and Local Arrangements for the Protection and Promotion of Human Rights in the Asian Region. Currently Ezra Kolet is developing, on the premises of Judah Hyam Hall, a Centre for Jewish and Inter-Faith Studies, including a Judaica Library, open to interested Jews and non-Jews alike. With this in mind, a modest building has already been constructed behind the Judah Hyam Hall. It is planned to transport to Delhi from the Konkan a full oil-press apparatus which belonged to a Bene Israel *Shanwar Teli* villager—this to be installed in the compound of Judah Hyam Hall as a fitting reminder of the traditional name and occupation of the Bene Israel. The Center publishes Bulletins about Indian Jewry and also on Jewish topics in general.

Ezra Kolet, grandson of Dr. Judah Hyam of Poona, was born in Calcutta in 1914, but grew up in Ajmer. He moved to Delhi in 1938 and, until his recent retirement, saw government service in the Secretariat of the Finance Ministry, and later in the Ministry of Shipping and Transport as Chief Comptroller of Chartered Shipping, and as Additional Secretary to the Ministry. In quite a different sphere, it was through his efforts that the Delhi Symphony Orchestra was founded, enhancing the cultural life of Delhi as a whole. Until very recently, he served as Secretary of the orchestra; he continues as one of its violinists.

At Indian Government functions, such as memorial services on Indian Independence Day, at the death of a national figure, or in times of war or calamity, when representatives of various religions are gathered together, Ezra Kolet is usually invited to participate and to recite a Jewish prayer as part of the official ceremony. The Government of India also shows its consideration for Jews by issuing to its offices each year a circular of the dates of the Jewish holidays. This is sent to each of the State Governments as well, and all Jewish government employees are assured of casual leave with pay on those days.[20] In such ways India shows respect for her Jewish citizens, although the Jews have never been more than an extremely tiny minority in the nation's population—currently constituting a microscopic 0.001 percent or so.

To conclude this chapter on Bene Israel Beyond the Konkan, the following condensed genealogy of the Erulkar family of Ahmedabad is presented as a very graphic example of Bene Israel mobility:

1782 : SAMUELJI ERULKAR, died at the siege of *Mangalore*. His son SATKELJI worked as a carpenter in *Bombay*, and acquired some property there.
BENJAMINJI (Satkelji's son) squandered his late father's money and joined the army.
1817 : He won a medal at the Battle of Kirki (near Poona).
1857 : He died.
1819 : ABRAHAMJI (son of Benjaminji) born at *Deesa* (Gujarat); instead of enlisting in the regiments, he served as a doctor in the ancillary (military) services; died in 1887.

1851 : ISAAC (first son of Abrahamji) born at *Poona*.
1856 : SOLOMON (another son of Abrahamji) born in *Ahmedabad*, where he died in 1907.
1887 : ABRAHAM (Solomon's first son) born in *Ahmedabad*; died in *Bombay* in 1960.
1891 : DAVID (Solomon's second son) born in *Ahmedabad*; died in *London* in 1970.
1924 : SOL (David's son) born in *Calcutta* : now lives in *Pennsylvania*, U.S.A.

Another example of relatively common Bene Israel family mobility comes from the life history of Mrs. Sarah S. Ezekiel (see above, p. 180). Her mother's family was from the village of *Kehim*; her father's family was from *Waluk* (very near Pen). Sarah was born in 1897 in *Bombay*, but her father's work took the family to *Poona* where Sarah grew up and received her education. After her marriage, she lived several years in *Bombay*. When her husband died, she went to stay with one of her sons in *Delhi*. When he and his family emigrated to *Israel*, she went to live with another son, an air-pilot, first in *Agra*, next in *Wellington*, New Zealand; thence in *Perth*, Australia; and finally in *Israel*, from 1970 until her death in 1985.

In an age when mobility was not yet widespread, it had nevertheless long been quite characteristic for many Bene Israel. In this respect they were "Wandering Jews", never, however, for reasons of anti-Semitism.

NOTES

1. Quite recently the spelling of Poona has been officially changed to "Pune".
2. The assertion that in those days Bene Israel worked as dyers has not been found elsewhere by the present writer.
3. Regrettably, the systematic, all-inclusive, dynamic tackling of these problems has not yet been achieved, or even adequately begun. However, in 1972 the Bene Israel in Poona did establish their own Jewish Welfare Association for the urgent purpose of collecting and disbursing funds and comfort to aged persons of the community who are left with no means of adequate support for themselves. This Welfare Association of Poona is entirely separate from any other fund-raising group.
4. It is interesting that the Baghdadis were relying upon Bene Israel : another Bene Israel, John Joseph Borgavkar, was for several years the administrator of the Sassoon family estates in Poona as well as of the estates of other Baghdadi families in Poona. The David Sassoon Management in Bombay had appointed Elijah Benjamin Gadkar to serve as Torah Reader in the Ohel David Synagogue.
5. Vol. VIII, Part II, "Poona"; Government Central Press, Bombay, 1885, p. 374.
6. B.J.Israel comments that the wall, if it ever existed, is not there now; perhaps the *Gazetteer* refers to an older cemetery; but in the present cemetery there is a corner reserved for non-Bene Israel.
7. H.G.Reissner in 1945 obtained figures for the Bene Israel and for the Baghdadis then resident in Poona, as follows :

"POONA'S	BENE ISRAEL		AND	BAGHDADI JEWS		
	Male	Female	Total	Male	Female	Total
Children	119	70	189	35	30	65
Married	107	108	215	30	31	61
Unmarried	96	71	167	22	21	43
Widow(er)s	9	41	50	5	10	15
Total	331	290	621	92	92	184

Among the Bene Israel in 1945 in Poona there were 518 literate persons and 103 illiterate.

Among Poona's Baghdadi Jews in 1945 the following numbers were :
    Literate in *Arabic* : 155 could read, 18 could also write
    Literate in *Hebrew* : 68 could read, 2 could also write
    Literate in *English* : 140 could speak and read, 125 could write

Reissner listed occupations only for Poona's Bene Israel (males) at that time (1945). The numbers of male Bene Israel of Poona with the following types of livelihood were :

    2 Professionals
    1 Merchant
    68 Salaried Clerks
    16 Government Officials
    29 Government Pensioners
    70 Craftsmen
    1 Supported by Charity
    ―――――――――――――
    187 TOTAL"

("Indian Jewish Statistics, 1837-1941", *Jewish Social Studies*, Vol. XII, p.357.)

8. If this register had been consulted by the present writer, no doubt some accurate figures for the Bene Israel population of Ahmedabad would have emerged. As it is, the figures supplied for Ahmedabad by Rev.Lord, H.G.Reissner and Shellim Samuel are contradictory; also, they are impossible to collate because some refer just to Bene Israel, some to "all Jews", some to Ahmedabad city, some to Ahmedabad cantonment, and some to Ahmedabad District. We know from the Presidential Address to the First Bene Israel Conference (December 1917, see below, p. 243) that this register was already functioning then. In his address, Dr. J. B. Bamnolkar strongly recommended that all other Bene Israel congregations should adopt the same system of registration.

9. In 1947 H.G. Reissner found that 389 Bene Israel in Ahmedabad were earning a livelihood in the following categories of work : independently, 155; government service, 75; clerks, 70; arts and professions, 55; miscellaneous, 21; religion-related work, 10; business, 3. However, about 50% of *all* Bene Israel earners in Ahmedabad were employed in the City's textile mills.

10. Much of the above information about the Bene Israel of Gujarat has been based on an article entitled "The Jews of Gujarat", written by Shellim Samuel in *Shalom*, Bombay, 1971, pp.1-11.

11. Jaipur, also in Rajasthan, had no Bene Israel "congregation". Its Railway Station-Master as of 1960 was Moses Jacob Solomon, a Bene Israel.

12. Nor are there any Jews any more at Indore, where there once was a small Bene Israel community with a prayer hall.

13. *Gazetteer of Bombay Presidency* of 1884, Volume XXI, p.229; and of 1883, Vol. XV, Part I, "Kanara", p.411.

14. Walter J. Fischel : *Ha-Yehudim B'Hodu*, p.77.

15. Walter J. Fischel : "The Bible in Persian Translation", in *The Harvard Theological Review*, Vol. XLV, No. 1, January 1952. Cambridge, p.23.

16. Walter J. Fischel, "Jews and Judaism at the Court of the Moghul Emperors in Medieval India", *Proceedings of the American Academy for Jewish Research*, Vol. XVIII, 1948-49; Bloch Publishing Company, New York, 1949, p.171.

17. For further information on Sarmad, see :
    (1) Maulavi Abdul Wali Khan Sahib : "A Sketch of the Life of Sarmad", in the *Journal and Proceedings of the Asiatic Society of Bengal*, printed at the Baptist Mission Press, published by the Asiatic Society of Bengal, Calcutta, 1925, article No. 11, pp.111-22.
    (2) Isaac A. Ezekiel : *Sarmad, Jewish Saint of India*, Radha Soami Satsang Beas, Punjab, 1966; printed by N.K. Gossain & Co., Pvt. Ltd., Calcutta; contains translation into English of 321 Rubaiyats of Sarmad on pp.296-382.

18. They left India during World War II.

19. Joshua M. Benjamin drew up the design for the Indian Parliament Annexe and for the Defence Headquarters Building, both in New Delhi; also for India House in Paris.

20. Government servants are allowed up to fifteen days of casual leave with pay, but not automatically on the days they would prefer. However, Jews can be sure, if they want it so, that they *will be able* to get off on the Jewish holidays.

Chapter 19
At the Turn of the Century

At the close of the 19th century it was still too early to expect the Israelite School to have been able to effect any appreciable change for the better in the generally poor condition of the Bene Israel community. Most Bene Israel children had to leave school at a very early age and, because of the poverty of their parents, begin to earn a pittance as apprentices in some workshop. Slackening of the former widespread Bene Israel attendance at schools was certainly one factor responsible for the deterioration of the general level of Bene Israel circumstances. But there were other reasons too why they did not continue to prosper and progress as a significant urban community following the initial spurt in education and improvement of their financial condition during the first half of the 19th century.

A comparison is sometimes made in the light of the outstanding and continuing success of another very small minority group centered in Bombay, the Parsi community. The Parsis, a community larger than the Bene Israel, although still a tiny minority,[1] had come to India (sometime between the 7th and 10th centuries A.D.) as a cohesive group, refugees from religious persecution in their native Persia. They brought with them a continuing zeal to preserve their religion in all its features. From the very start they formed an articulated, highly self-conscious, well-organised *community*. Their economic importance in India is far out of proportion to their small numbers. Even in pre-British days, Parsi businessmen were prominent in places such as Surat, Broach, Navsari and Baroda, not to mention the friendly relations which Parsis enjoyed at the Moghul Court. With their businesses, they began settling in Bombay before the Bene Israel did so. In addition to large private enterprises, the Parsis developed almost a monopoly as purveyors of consumer goods in the British military cantonments. Wealthy Parsis established good schools and scientific and charitable foundations. As a result, the Parsis have long been one of the best educated groups in all of India.

As for the Bene Israel, however, the initial gains which they had made during the early development of Bombay city petered out, probably because by tradition they were not merchants or businessmen (apart from selling of oil and some petty trading). While a few Bene Israel have been rather well-to-do, there have never been any persons of very great wealth among them. They simply did not have the necessary spirit of enterprise or of co-operation. They soon lost out to Hindu and Muslim businessmen with their greater financial resources. Also, perhaps in the 19th century (as in the 20th century) many Bene Israel lacked the necessary social confidence for getting ahead.

But from the beginning in Bombay the most serious obstacles to the progress of the Bene Israel community stemmed from the bitter intra-communal schisms, scandals and immorality involving some of those aspiring to communal leadership – beginning in 1839 with a most unfortunate story of self-seeking, unscrupulous contenders for power while Mukkadam Dada Commodan was still alive. The total lack of inspiring progressive leadership at that time was aggravated, if not actually caused, by the fact that, scattered as the Bene Israel had been for generations, with only a few Bene Israel in each village, they had never learned to function as a single cohesive community, sufficiently unified and organised for self-help and advancement. The condition was especially detrimental to them in the face of the pressure of the new, challenging, and harsh urban conditions which confronted them.

Compared to the Parsis, the Bene Israel had only a vague tradition of their own origin, beginning in India, so the story goes, with only seven men and seven women. Even so, however, before the period of their large-scale urbanization, the Bene Israel had developed in the course of time (for several centuries at least) a stable way of life with fixed and familiar patterns of leadership, hierarchy, relationships and functions, within as well as outside their community. The city uprooted these patterns. The constant flow of newcomers, the pressures of finding and keeping a job, the unfamiliar or not yet stabilized patterns of leadership, responsibilities and privileges—all made for insecurity, intrigue and divisiveness. The Bene Israel response showed itself in an overwhelming preference for the security, even at the price of relative mediocrity, offered by government employment as contrasted with seeking financial successes based on individual initiative. This "playing-it-safe" mentality kept them, as a whole, out of city or national politics, channeling such political instincts as they possessed into internal Bene Israel affairs, often in very negative ways. To make matters worse, the questioning of their status as pure Jews came at just about the same time as the major rupture with their traditional life-style. All these factors hindered the progress of the Bene Israel and to some extent still continue to haunt them today.

However, as we have seen in preceding chapters, certain important achievements do stand to their credit, even if the community was always riddled with fissions; even if it was very difficult to remove entrenched leaders of institutions and to introduce new ideas; and even if only a minority of the community ever went on to secure a university education.

By the end of the 19th century the seeds of education and of westernization, earlier sown among the Bene Israel, had caused a full-blown split of a new sort in the community: one side consisted of the old establishment of conservative, non-westernized Bene Israel, whose leadership and supporters came from the class of master craftsmen and petty contractors; the other side was the new class of English-speaking, educated white-collar workers and persons in the professions. The latter class was responsible for many changes and innovations, which also affected the old guard, sometimes in rather subtle ways, sometimes more directly.

Just before the close of the 19th century, in 1896, following on the heels of a serious famine, Bombay was struck by a terrible epidemic of bubonic plague. Volume III of *The Lamp of Judaism 1896/97* tells us that at the height of the plague in Bombay alone there were 1,500 deaths per week, and that "The combined effect of famine and plague was disastrous to some Bene Israel families who were leading happy and peaceful lives before August last, and who have now sunk into poverty, misery and woe."

Many people left Bombay for their native villages. Some Baghdadis fled also, but no Bene Israel (we are told). The plague spread to Bandra, Thana and Poona. The Bene Israel received some help from Jews outside India. Only a few Jews were among those who had died, but the government, in establishing burial grounds outside the heart of the city, allotted one also to the Bene Israel. In May 1897 a hospital for Jews was opened in Bombay with Sassoon funds. An article in the *Bene Israelite* noted with relief and pride that "It is a matter of great comfort to hear that Dr. Haffkine, who is an Israelite, has found out 'prophylactic lymph' with which persons are being inoculated."[2]

Although Jewish and living in Bombay, Dr. Waldemar Haffkine does not seem to have had any contacts with the Bene Israel.³ It is very likely, however, that some Bene Israel in the medical profession may have known him.

NOTES-

1. According to Government of India Censuses, the peak for the Parsi community was reached in 1941 when their total number in all of India was 115,000. The peak for the Bene Israel in all of India was reached in 1951 when the total Jewish population was listed as 26,512, of which about 20,000 must have been Bene Israel. However, taking into consideration the likelihood of underestimation in official censuses, the actual number of Bene Israel was probably higher than 23,000.
2. This article (date unspecified) was reproduced in *India and Israel*, February 1950, Volume II, No. 8, p.23.
3. Dr. Waldemar Mordecai Wolff Haffkine was born in Odessa in 1860. As a bacteriologist who had developed the first effective vaccine against cholera (at the Pasteur Institute in Paris in 1892), he came to Calcutta in 1893, at the invitation of the Government of India, to help combat a cholera epidemic. In 1896 he was asked to try to subdue the bubonic plague epidemic then afflicting Bombay. Haffkine discovered an effective anti-plague inoculation. In 1899 he became the founder and first Director of Bombay's Plague Research Laboratory, later renamed the Haffkine Institute in his honor. He remained in India until 1915.

PART THREE

The Bene Israel in the Twentieth Century

Chapter 20
20th Century Bene Israel Occupations

Socially and culturally, many old customs were discontinued or altered in the 20th century. Modern times brought new ways of life, new institutions, new relationships and new occupations for the Bene Israel.

Among the urban Bene Israel of India the degree of assimilation to British, western or other modern ways varies, as it indeed does among Hindu and other city dwellers. The Bene Israel observe the Jewish religion but are otherwise thoroughly Indian. Their distinctiveness as a community, however, remains. Just how did the Bene Israel fare in the 20th century?

Educated Bene Israel entered new occupations or (as in the late 19th century), worked as clerks or administrators for the government railway, customs, or post and telegraph departments. To such places of employment all over the map of India many a Bene Israel man brought along his wife and children. The family often took root in its new location, and sometimes the father's job eventually passed on to his son. Members of the community frequently enlisted for officer-training, especially during World War II, but it was no longer popular among them to enlist in the rank-and-file fighting forces as they had done in the 18th and first half of the 19th centuries. In independent India commissioned officers can come from any community and no regiment is composed of but one caste or community; if the regiment's name still indicates something of that kind, it is no more than an anachronism. The highest army rank ever reached by a Bene Israel officer is that of Major General (see below, pp. 210 – 11 Major General Jonathan Reuben Samson). Several members of the community also serve in India's Navy and Merchant Marine, and there are Bene Israel pilots and officers in India's civil as well as in its military aviation services. There are also Bene Israel civil, electrical and mechanical engineers, contractors, architects, textile engineers and labor officers. Some Bene Israel are engaged in various aspects of the film industry and a few are in journalism. (See below, p. 201, "Occupations or Means of Livelihood of Jews of Bombay City, in 1872 and 1931".)

About ten percent—among them many women—of the community are active in the professions of medicine, nursing,[1] midwifery, social work, law, and teaching (both as school principals and as teachers). Unless an urban Bene Israel woman in India has had professional or secretarial training, or is in poor financial circumstances, she usually does not seek work outside the home. In 1961, fourteen percent of all adult Bene Israel females in Bombay were wage earners. Bene Israel women teachers especially were highly qualified, competent and much in demand, not only teaching regular subjects, but also gym, music and handicrafts. They were not timid and even accepted positions in out-of-the-way schools. One reason for the relatively large number of Bene Israel spinsters (out of proportion to the total size of the community) is that many Bene Israel women were professionally more highly qualified and more successful than most Bene Israel men. Therefore it was difficult for them to find Bene Israel marriage partners. Many of these women remained spinsters, and some of them married men of other religions.

It is interesting to note that, especially in the cities, in keeping with a general Indian trend, Bene Israel men have adopted western style clothing. On the other hand, most Bene Israel women in India—whether working in the professions or not—continue to wear *saris*.

The majority of Bene Israel working men chose employment in offices as clerks, with employment in factories and workshops running a close second. As early as the 1920s Bene Israel with vision had deplored the then widespread "clerk mentality" among the community, and the denigration of carpentry as a source of livelihood. In Bene Israel periodicals, articles written by independent thinkers contain such statements as :

> A working man should be made to realize that he "may do better for his son by fitting him to become a responsible foreman, than if he makes him a second-rate clerk or school-master : for the foreman will probably do the higher work and rightly get the higher wages." It must be shown to him that a skilled artisan, provided he uses his leisure well, can lead as intellectual a life as a member of any other profession....that a higher intelligence is required in this [skilled manual work] than in a profession requiring a knowledge of reading and writing only.[2]

Actually, those Bene Israel who were carpenters usually were above average in their craft and were therefore much appreciated and sought after for the good and durable furniture which they made.

The beginning of the 20th century was marked by immigration into Bombay on the part of large numbers of Bene Israel from the villages. By mid-century only 10 percent of the community remained as agriculturalists. Typically in the 20th century the Bene Israel villager would first sell his home and property.[3] He would then come to Bombay and begin work there, often in carpentry, earning no more than a rupee a day, paying more than he could afford on rent for one undesirable room for himself and his family, and getting deeply into debt whenever births, marriages or deaths occurred in the family. Even eventual pay raises of up to two rupees per day did not really improve matters and, more often than not, he took to drinking to forget his troubles. He would withdraw his son from school at the age of twelve; the boy would begin working, for nothing at first, as an apprentice under his father, before he too would begin earning a pittance. Ten percent of the Bene Israel community were carpenters, but only in the rarest instances did they establish themselves as owners of their own carpentry shops.

H.G. Reissner's list of "Occupations or Means of Livelihood of Jews of Bombay City in 1872 and 1931" enumerates a great variety of specific occupations (see below, pp. 201 – 3). Reissner also provides us with tabulations of categories of "Sources of Income" for Indian Jews all over India, indicating clearly those places where the date could refer only, or mainly, to Bene Israel. It is unfortunate that in this table carpentry, mechanical work and factory work are not listed as separate categories. Instead, they are all subsumed under the heading "Transport, Crafts and Industry" (see below, p. 204).

Among H.G. Reissner's notes at the Central Archives for the History of the Jewish People, in their Folio 654/1 is a long list of different occupations in which Jews of Bombay City were engaged as of 1872 and 1931. Local official censuses for these two years included tabulations on occupations of Jews specifically. We have no way of identifying whether any given occupation was a livelihood mainly or only for Bene Israel or for Baghdadi Jews. However, in certain occupations we can be sure that mainly if not only Bene Israel and NOT Baghdadis were engaged. These have been marked by the present writer with an asterisk (*) in the table prepared by Reissner which follows.

Table 2 : OCCUPATIONS OR MEANS OF LIVELIHOOD OF JEWS OF BOMBAY CITY IN 1872 AND 1931

	1931 Male	1931 Female	1872 Male	1872 Female
Class A : *Production of Raw Materials*				
1. * Cultivation Proprietors	4	1		
2. * Market Gardeners	1			
TOTAL	5	1		
Class B : *Preparation & Supply of Material Substances*				
1. Cloth ginning & pressing		1	2	
2. Cloth spinning, weaving, etc.	149	12		
3. Jute pressing, spinning, etc.	2			
4. * Carpenters, turners, joiners, etc.	370	2	214	
5. * Smelting, forging, etc.	4			
6. * Makers of guns, etc.	1			
7. * Blacksmiths	4			
8. * Brassworkers	2			
9. Chemical products	1			
10. Butchers	8			
11. Miscellaneous food makers	1	2		
12. * Technicians & craftsmen			69	2
13. Tailors, milliners, dressmakers	14			8
14. Hatmakers, embroiderers	4			
15. Washing & cleaning	2			
16. * Cabinet makers	1			
17. * Upholsterers	1			
18. * Lime burners, builders, etc.	4	1		
19. * Power production & distillation	14			
20. Printers, engravers, book-binders	35			
21. Clocks & scientific instruments	7			
22. Scavenging	1			
23. Boat Owners	3	1	6 shipping agents	
24. * Docks & canals	1			
25. * Maintenance of roads & bridges	6			
26. Harbour workers	12			
27. Taxi-drivers, owners, etc.	71			
28. Porters etc.	6			
29. * Railway employees	140			
30. * Labour employees	5			
31. * Telephone linesmen	16	1		
32. Bank managers, money-lenders, etc.	8	1	2	
33. Brokers, commission agents, etc.	35	2	3	

(continued)

Table 2 (continued)

		1931		1872	
		Male	Female	Male	Female
34.	Trade in goods, etc.	5	1		
35.	Trade in chemical products	1			
36. *	Dealers in animal food, etc.	3	1		
37.	Hotel owners, managers, etc.	7	1		
38.	Trade in ready-made clothes	10			
39. *	Dealers & hirers in cars & cycles	3			
40.	General stores & shopkeepers	151	6	45	
41.	Peddlars & hawkers (other than food)	44	2		
42.	Dealers in bangles, beads, etc.	1			
	TOTAL	1,150	35	341	10

Class C: *Public Administration & Liberal Arts*					
1. *	Army	5	1	23	
2. *	Navy	1			
3. *	Police	6		13	
4. *	Service of State	31			
5. *	Municipal & other local service	60	5		
6.	Priests, ministers, etc.	6		8	
7.	Rabbi	1			
8.	Religious workers	11			
9. *	Lawyers	16			
10 *	Law clerks, etc.	6			
11. *	Burial ground supervisors (Baghdadis too)	2			
12. *	Registered medical workers	11	1	5	
13. *	Unregistered medical workers	16	1		
14. *	Midwives, nurses, compounders	4	26	14	
15. *	Veterinary surgeons	2			
16. *	Professors & teachers	37	41		
17. *	Clerks connected with teaching	2			
18. *	Stenographers	4	8	90	(Clerks)
19. *	Architects, surveyors, etc.	21	1	3	(Engs.)
20. *	Authors, editors, journalists (Baghdadis too)	14	1		
21.	Artists, sculptors, etc.	3			
22.	Managers of public entertainments, homes, clubs	61			
23.	Musicians	4			
	TOTAL	324	85	156	

(continued)

Table 2 (continued)

		1931		1872	
		Male	Female	Male	Female
Class D : *Miscellaneous*					
1.	Proprietors, etc.	29	3	2	(agri. prop.)
				79	(contractor builders)
				31	11 (rentiers)
2.	Private motor drivers & cleaners	3			
3.	Other domestic servants	25	36	82	28
4.	Manufacturers, businesses (not specified)	45	2		
5.	Cashiers, clerks, accountants	522	35		
6.	Mechanics, etc.	129	2		
7.	Labourers, not specified	22	2	1	(agri.)
				22	4
8.	Unproductive	1		209	858
9.	Vagrant	1			
10.	Prostitutes		10		12
	TOTAL	777	90	426	902

For 1872 : Children :   457   362
Class A :   —   —
Class B :   341   —
Class C :   156   —
Class D :   426   902
Grand Total 2,644 = 1,380 + 1,264

NOTE :
In this Table, the coverage of Jews for 1931 was far less inclusive than for 1872. The total Jewish population of Greater Bombay in 1931 was 8,946 but this Table accounts only for 2,264 Jewish males and 211 Jewish females as of 1931.
According to the *1872 Census,* the Total Number of *Jews in Bombay City* was :
.... 2,666

The following table combines gainfully employed and dependents according to the sources from which their livelihood is derived.

Table 3 : SOURCES OF INCOME FOR INDIAN JEWS IN THE 1940s

Location	Cochin	Kolaba	Thana	Ahmedabad	Karachi	Poona	Bombay	Calcutta	Scattered outside communities	Total	
Subdivision	Cochin Jews	Bene Israel	Bene Israel	Bene Israel	Bene Israel	Bene Israel & Baghdadis	Bene Israel & Baghdadis	Baghdadis	Mostly Bene Israel & Some Baghdadis & Cochin Jews	No.	Percent
Agriculture	248	1,220	—	—	—	—	—	—	—	1,468	6·5
Domestic Service	4	79	—	—	3	—	268	—	50	404	1·8
Transport, Crafts and Industry	230	720	117	155	220	241	4,934	150	200	6,967	31·
Commerce	1,238	167	—	3	70	62	1,667	400	300	3,907	17·4
Clerical	77	18	137	70	358	274	2,496	1,400	280	5,110	22·7
Government Service	15	184	4	75	150	65	474	100	870	1,937	8·6
Religious Service	26	44	8	10	10	—	89	150	—	337	1·5
Arts and Professions	85	—	4	55	80	34	921	150	300	1,629	7·3
Pensioners, Retired and Living on Income	12	132	36	21	160	99	—	261	—	721	3·2
Total	1,935	2,564	306	389	1,051	775	10,849	2,611	2,000	22,480	100·—

(From "*Indian Jewish Statistics 1837-1941*" by H.G. Reissner in *Jewish Social Studies*, Volume XII, New York, 1950; p. 362)

There are still very few Bene Israel businessmen,[4] probably because of lack of initiative and of capital, combined with a fear of bankruptcy. Those few Bene Israel businessmen who do exist, do not tend in their hiring policies to favor members of their own community. Nor do Bene Israel necessarily seek the services of those Bene Israel who are in the professions. Intra-communal work affords income to some Bene Israel, such as the salaried officers and employees of the synagogues and cemeteries, Hebrew teachers, teachers and clerks in Bene Israel schools, superintendent and cook in the Bene Israel Home for Orphans and Destitutes, agents for the sale of Hebrew books and religious articles, or clerks in the Bene Israel Cooperative Banking Society.[5] This Society, which started as a Cooperative Credit Society in 1918, prided itself upon being very particular about persons to whom they granted loans. Consequently, for loans of ready cash most Bene Israel prefer to belong to and borrow from savings clubs (so-called "chit-funds") composed of fellow workers (of many different communities) at their respective places of work.[6]

During World War II the Sassoons sold ten out of their thirteen textile mills. Before the sale, they had in their employ about 16·5 percent of all Jewish employees in India. The Manchester Mill in Bombay, a relatively small enterprise which belonged to E.D. Sassoon and Company, gave preference to Baghdadis and to Bene Israel in hiring employees. A table of statistics from the offices of E.D. Sassoon and Company Mills[7] shows the number of Baghdadis and Bene Israel in its employ in 1943 :

Table 4 : JEWISH EMPLOYEES AT THE MANCHESTER MILL, BOMBAY IN 1943

182 male Jews (Baghdadis) and 26 female Jews working as operatives
208 male Bene Israel and 20 female Bene Israel as operatives
159 male Jews and 4 female Jews working as clerks
172 male Bene Israel and 1 female Bene Israel as clerks

Thus the total number of Baghdadis employed here in 1943 came to 371 as against a total of 401 Bene Israel. While in absolute numbers there were 30 more Bene Israel than Baghdadi employees, the respective totals represented approximately 54 percent of the Baghdadi population of Bombay at the time, as compared to about 37 percent of the city's Bene Israel population at the time. While several Europeans and Parsis held managerial jobs in the larger Sassoon Mills, only one Bene Israel ever held the position of Manager of a Sassoon Mill, and that was at the Manchester Mill. In Gujarat, in mills which were not owned by Jews, there were some Bene Israel managers and other Bene Israel who had risen to important positions, or who had come in as engineers.

Most of the Bene Israel who had studied at technical schools preferred technical jobs offered in Government services. In general the Bene Israel were conservative and cautious. But there were significant exceptions, namely : their leaving the villages and their traditional occupation as *telis* for military and civil service and for urban life; the importance they gave to secular and religious education for both boys *and* girls; and later their mass emigration to Israel.

Within the Bene Israel community there is no such thing as rigid stratification based on occupation. It is not at all uncommon to find living together, within a single joint-family, persons in a variety of occupations covering a wide range of the status spectrum. To paraphrase Strizower (pp.117-118) : formerly the leadership of the community was entrusted to the more highly educated Bene Israel; but gradually those who are/were employed as clerks typically have become the leaders of organized Bene Israel community life. Those working in carpentry, masonry, or in factory or transport work, or as mechanics, fitters, turners, moulders—they are the ones who support the "domination" of the community by the clerk element, and who are responsible for orthodoxy in synagogue ritual and organization, as well as for the retention of the Marathi language[8] for communal transactions and records.

To a certain extent the Bene Israel social stratification is built up on the basis of language : i.e. determined by those who speak only Marathi; those who speak Marathi at home and English at work; and those who know some Marathi, but usually speak English both at home and at work. The cleavage between the well-educated Bene Israel and the others is based not only on language, but also on a wide difference in ways of thinking, as is true of any society. On the other hand those well-educated, English-speaking Bene Israel who do not have a good command of spoken and written Marathi are missing, especially today, much of the most attractive cultural life in Maharashtra. But there *are* educated Bene Isreal who also are fluent in Marathi and they usually speak a better style of Marathi than do their non-educated fellows. It is said that the Bene Israel of Poona in general speak a better form of Marathi than do other Bene Israel.

The kind of intellectual with a broad knowledge of the humanities and the arts, which evolved out of western Jewry's original emphasis on the (Talmudic) scholar and out of the period of Jewish emancipation (*Haskalah*), was a rarity in the Bene Israel community, although many Bene Isreal had received a university education and were outstanding in their own professions. Those with higher education could move freely in higher circles, but often were reticent to do so, through a lack of self-confidence and not because of outside discrimination against them. This characteristic was mentioned in the Presidential Address to the First Bene Israel Conference, in 1917 :

> ...it is a matter for deep regret that our community as a rule remains aloof from the other communities, who are in advance of us in Education and in Social Life. The result is that we lose the golden opportunity of finding out what is best in them, and if so of adopting it. It is therefore necessary that if our community seriously wants to rise, its educated members must not fail to join all movements that would help to uplift the community directly or indirectly.[9]

The average Bene Israel lived like other Indian lower-middle-class people. It was often difficult for Bene Israel, particularly in government service or in other offices, to make ends meet. In these jobs they had the added burden of having to wear more expensive clothes and of having "to keep appearances to suit the exigencies of their service",[10] while their actual salaries were quite meagre. But, the jobs were secure and pensions would eventually be forthcoming.

NOTES

1. Bene Israel nurses were much in demand. Christian girls, especially from what is now Kerala, also went into the nursing profession in large numbers; however, the Jews of Kerala did not do so. Only very recently have some emancipated and educated Muslim girls also entered nursing. Caste Hindus did not do so because they looked upon nursing (as distinct from a career as a medical doctor) as being defiling work (an attitude which is slowly changing). Because Bene Israel and Kerala Christian girls were educated girls and were not part of the Hindu caste structure, they were much better qualified to become nursing candidates than were illiterate low-caste and outcaste girls.

2. From "A Communal Problem", by Joseph Israel; *The Israelite*, Volume IX, Nos. 7-8, July-August 1925, p.101.
3. Rural Bene Israel tended less to follow the example of many other Indian villagers in the 20th century who, rather than leave the village forever, left only their traditional occupation; found more remunerative work (as casual laborers, milk sellers, drivers, clerks, servants, messengers, etc.); but they, or some members of the family would continue to live in the village. Those who took work and lived in far off cities often eventually returned to live in their native village.
4. Daniel Abraham Satamkar was an exception. He was a self-made man who began his career by working on the docks for several years, and eventually founded his own shipping agency which became a very prosperous business during World War I. Daniel Abraham donated much of his wealth to Bene Israel charitable institutions.
5. Strizower, op.cit., p.75.
6. Strizower, op.cit., p.144.
7. Found among the papers of H.G.Reissner, now kept in Folio 364/1 at the Central Archives for the History of the Jewish People, Jerusalem.
8. In describing the mother-tongue of the Bene Israel in Kolaba District, the 1964 edition of the 1883 *Kolaba District Gazetteer* says : "The home-tongue of the Bene Israel is Marathi often mixed with words of Arabic or Hebrew origin." (p.198)
9. *Report of the First Bene Israel Conference, 1917*; compiled and published by Solomon Moses in English and Marathi, pp.v and 160; Bombay 1918, on p.80.
10. Ibid, p.58.

Chapter 21
Bene Israel Individuals of Distinction

(in approximate order of year of birth)

In spite of the relatively small size of the Bene Israel community and its unremarkable economic achievement, there is a very long list of 20th century Bene Israel individuals, both men and women, in Bombay and in places scattered all over India, who have served, or continue to serve, in very important and varied positions in Indian life and have set standards of excellence in doing so. Included among them are:

SHALOM BAPUJI ISRAEL (1853-1942) : Started his career as police constable. Was first Bene Israel to be appointed as a magistrate. Rose to become Dewan (roughly equivalent to prime minister) of Janjira State. The road from Shrivardhan to Mhasla (in what used to be Janjira State) is even today named after him in appreciation for his services to the people. Became Deputy Collector in Khandesh (c.1890-1910). Was the first Bene Israel ever to hold the post of Deputy Collector. (His brother, Jacob Bapuji Israel, was the second Bene Israel to do so.)

KHAN BAHADUR JACOB BAPUJI ISRAEL (1863-1933) : Joined the Revenue Department in 1885. From 1902-1913 was Chief Karbhari[1] of Aundh State (in southern Maharashtra of today). From 1906-1910 was in sole charge during the suspension of powers of the Ruler of Aundh. Pioneered with his ideas and measures in matters of medicine, education, ecology, communications and agriculture toward improving life in rural communities; was far ahead of his day in all this.[2] Was awarded the title of Khan Bahadur in recognition of his work, in 1911. In 1913 became a Freemason. Deputy Collector in Ahmednagar and Thana Districts (1913-1916). Active in the creation of the All India Israelite League and presided over its first session in Karachi in 1918. Was the last editor of *The Israelite*; wrote many articles for this and other journals covering a wide variety of subjects.

JUDGE EZRA REUBEN (1864-1950) : Chief Justice in Junagad State (in peninsular Gujarat). He presided over the Second Bene Israel Conference in 1919.

JOSEPH DAVID PENKAR (1872-1949) : Pioneer of the Indian film industry of the early 1920s. Wrote the final script and songs for the first "talkie' feature film produced in India in 1931 (an adaptation of the stage play *Alam Ara*). Writer of film scripts in Marathi, Hindi, Urdu, and Gujarati. Author of more than a hundred stage plays (tragedies as well as comedies; some with religious or mythological themes). Author of Biblical *kirtans* in Marathi. Theatre Manager.

DR. ELIJAH MOSES (RAJPURKAR) (1873-1957) : M.D., J.P.. Mayor of Bombay 1937-38. Member of Bombay Muncipal Council. Examiner in materia medica, Bombay University.

Bene Israel Individuals of Distinction 209

DR. ABRAHAM SOLOMON ERULKAR (1887-1960) : M.D. London University. Began medical practice in Bombay 1917. Honorary Physician and Professor of Medicine at K.E.M. Hospital of Bombay Municipality and the attached G.S.Medical College, Fellow of Bombay University and Dean of its Faculty of Medicine. For several years President of the Medical Council of India. He was an ardent nationalist. It was in his capacity as the President of the Medical Council of India, and not as personal physician, that he atttended on Mahatma Gandhi on the occasion of several of the Mahatma's fasts. Was influential, against a great deal of local opposition, in allowing Jewish doctors, who had fled from the Nazis before and during World War II, to practise medicine in India. During 1939-45 he was attached, in an honorary capacity, as Consulting Physician to the Military Hospital in Bombay, with the honorary rank of Lieutenant Colonel.

REBECCA REUBEN (1889-1957) : Matriculated in 1906 with first rank in Bombay University, being the first female to do so. Teaching Diploma from London University (Maria Grey College). Principal of the Israelite School (later called the Sir Elly Kadoorie School), 1922-50. Edited the *Bene Israel Annual and Year Books* of 1917 through 1920, Issued *Nofeth*, a monthly journal in Marathi, for Bene Israel children. Author of a series of readers in English for secondary schools, a grammar, and guides for teachers. Honorary magistrate in juvenile courts.

DR. JERUSHA JHIRAD (1890-1984) : M.D. London University, and Fellow of the Royal College of Obstetricians and Gynaecologists. Superintendent of Bombay's Cama and Albless Hospitals for Women and Children, 1928-49. Under the auspices of the Association of Medical Women in India, the Dr. Jhirad Postgraduate Research Library was set up at Cama and Albless Hospitals in 1971 in appreciation of her services and in honor of her 80th birthday. Was President of the Gynaecological and Obstetrics Society, and edited its journal. In 1913 in Bombay she founded the Bene Israel Stree Mandal, and in 1925 she founded the Jewish Religious Union. Just before India became an independent country, Dr. Jhirad was awarded the M.B.E. (Civil).[3] She was recipient of the Padma Shri Award in 1966.

DAVID SOLOMON ERULKAR (1891-1970) : B.A. Cambridge University. Bar-at-law, Lincoln's Inn, London. In 1917 started the monthly Bene Israel journal *The Israelite*. Frequent delegate from India to the International Labour Organisation at Geneva; member of its Governing Body and of its Maritime Committee. Held high executive positions in the Scindia Shipping Company, in Calcutta, Rangoon and London. Director General of Shipping, Government of India.

DAVID EZRA REUBEN (1893-1980) : Graduated from Bombay University and from Cambridge University (Wrangler). Secured first place in examination for admission to the Indian Civil Service in 1917; was the first and only Bene Israel ever to serve in the Indian Civil Service (I.C.S.). In Bihar and in Orissa he served as District Magistrate and as District Judge; 1951-52 as Chief Justice of Patna High Court. Member of Labour Appellate Tribunal in Bombay, after his retirement.

JUDGE ABRAHAM AARON KEHIMKAR : District Judge in Baroda State, later its High Court Judge.

DR. SARAH JACOB : M.D., Principal of the Jaipur Government Medical College.

DR. E. BENJAMIN : Assistant Director of Public Health, Sind. Later, Director of Public Health, Bombay State. Was awarded the M.B.E. (Civil), just before India became independent. .

SHALOM BENJAMIN NAGAVKAR : Postmaster General of Bombay. Retired in 1948.

DAVID ABRAHAM (CHEULKAR) (1906-82) : Character actor in Indian films. Also a popular compère. International Wrestling Umpire. He was awarded the Padma Shri in 1969.

BENJAMIN J. ISRAEL (1906 – 1987) : M. A. First Class in Philosophy, Elphinstone College, Bombay University. Served in Secretariat of Government of Bombay 1929- 59, in various departments, including ten years as Secretary, Bombay Public Service Commission. President of the Bombay Philosophical Society 1962-64. Researcher and writer about the Bene Israel community.

DR. ELIEZER MOSES BEST : Dean of the B.J.Medical College and Superintendent of the Civil Hospital in Ahmedabad, 1962.

DR. SEGULLA APTEKAR : Superintendent of Cama and Albless Hospitals, Bombay, 1966-68.

REUBEN DAVID (DANDEKAR) (1912-   ) : Veterinarian and Naturalist. Superintendent (now retired) of Ahmedabad's Zoo and founder of Ahmedabad's extraordinary Children's Park. He was awarded the Padma Shri in 1975.

EZRA KOLET (1914-   ) : Government service in the Secretariat of the Finance Ministry. Later served as Chief Comptroller of Chartered Shipping and as Additional Secretary to the Ministry of Shipping and Transport. Violinist in Delhi Symphony Orchestra.

VICE-ADMIRAL BENJAMIN A. SAMSON (1916-   ) : Began his career in the Merchant Marine. Was awarded the Viceroy's Gold Medal. Saw service in the Royal Indian Navy in several theatres of war during World War II. After India's independence, served as Naval Attache at the Indian High Commission in the United Kingdom. Was given title of Commodore when he was posted as Commandant of India's National Defence Academy at Khadakvasla.[4] Commanded Indian Western Fleet during hostilities with Pakistan in 1965. Retired with rank of Rear Admiral. Subsequently was appointed as Managing Director of Mazgaon Dock, Ltd., a government-owned shipbuilding and ship-repair yard in Bombay. On the occasion of the launching of the second frigate built under his supervision, he was awarded the rank of Vice-Admiral. Later became Director of Phillips Ltd., in Delhi.

SAMUEL ISRAEL (1920-   ) Editor. Director of India's National Book Trust 1974-77. Author of *The Wonderful World of Books* and *A Career in Book Publishing*, both addressed to young people. Editor : *Grand Tour, India*.

MAJOR GENERAL JONATHAN REUBEN SAMSON (19 -   ) : of the Indian Engineers Corps of the army. After retirement from the army he became Director of the

Defence Research Establishment. Later was General Manager of the Armoured Vehicles Factory at Avadi, Madras in Tamilnadu.

JOSHUA M. BENJAMIN (1920-   ) : Chief Architect, Ministry of Works and Housing, Government of India 1972-1978. Secretary, Delhi Urban Art Commission, 1978-1980.

NISSIM EZEKIEL (1924-   ) : Outstanding poet (in English). There are several published anthologies of his poems. His *Latter Day Psalms* (Oxford University Press) won the Sahitya Akademy Award in 1983. Also writes plays and essays in English. Member of the Board of Trustees of The National Book Trust. Ex-editor of *Quest* magazine. Professor (Retd.) of American and English Literature, Bombay University.

JUDAH REUBEN : India's only Jewish cricket umpire. Was admitted by examination as member of the All India Panel of Umpires, 1960.

A.S.ABRAHAM : Journalist. Assistant Editor of *The Times of India*

JESSICA JACOB : Journalist. Feature writer for *The Times of India.*

MRS. MEERA JACOB (MENDREKAR) MAHADEVAN (1930-1977) : Conceived of and implemented a unique, very practicable scheme for a network of Mobile Creches, schools and health services for the impoverished, neglected infants and children of itinerant road-and-building-construction laborers; these facilities were later extended to city slum-dwellers as well and in many places, especially Delhi and Bombay.[5] She was also an author of fiction in Hindi. See below, pp. 240 – 1.

Before Indian independence Bene Israel had received such titles and decorations as *Khan Sahib*,[6] *Khan Bahadur*, O.B.E. (Order of the British Empire), and M.B.E. When India became independent it started its own tradition of recognizing, through the granting of awards, its citizens of outstanding merit. The highest national awards are given out annually on India's Republic Day. There have been four Jewish recipients of the Padma Shri Award,[7] granted for distinguished service in any civilian field. Of the four Jewish recipients of this award, three belong to the Bene Israel community, namely :

1. Dr. Jerusha Jhirad (see above), in 1966;
2. David Abraham Cheulkar (see above), in 1969; and
3. Dr. Reuben David Dandekar (see above), in 1975.

The fourth Jew to have received the Padma Shri Award was a Baghdadi Jew from Calcutta, Mr. Ezra Mir, for his work on documentary films in the Government of India Films Division, in 1970. In 1974, a Bene Israel police officer, Sub-Inspector Samson Joseph Talkar, was awarded the Government of India President's Gold Medal for Gallantry and Exceptional Courage (during a case of rioting in Bombay).

The above-mentioned names do not by any means complete the roster of all the Bene Israel who have distinguished themselves to date in the 20th century. Some additional individuals are mentioned *en passant* in other parts of this book. Even so, these notices are illustrative only, not exhaustive, to convey to the reader an appreciation of the wide spectrum of Bene Israel careers and achievements.

NOTES

1. The dictionary meaning of *karbhari* is "manager". It was the designation of the Chief Minister in the smaller Indian States especially of the Deccan, corresponding to the title *Dewan* in the larger States. Before India became independent, there were several quasi-autonomous "Princely States", such as Aundh.
2. *Khan Bahadur Jacob Bapuji Israel, A Personal Sketch*, by Benjamin J. Israel, Bombay, 1960; published for private circulation by B.J.Israel, printed at Popular Press Private Ltd.; see p.16. (Republished in B. J. Israel's *The Bene Israel of India : Some Studies*, Orient Longman Ltd., Bombay, 1984, pp.187-242.) This booklet gives a vivid picture of Khan Bahadur Jacob Bapuji Israel and of his ideas and achievements. It also affords insight into a kind of Bene Israel family life and upbringing of children specific to a family where the father held important civil service positions outside the Konkan.
3. M.B.E : Member of the British Empire, being the lowest rank in the Order of the British Empire. This order has a civilian as well as a military wing. Solomon Jacob Israel, a Bene Israel Captain in the Indian Engineers in World War II, received the M.B.E. (military) Award. Another Bene Israel, E.O.Samson of the Indian Forest Service, was awarded the higher rank of O.B.E. (Order of the British Empire). Bene Israel who received the M.B.E.(Civil) Award were Hyam S. Israel (son of Shalom B. Israel), M.R.Reuben and Dr. E. Benjamin.
4. This place is near Poona, where army, navy and airforce officers, in turn, are appointed to train cadets gathered here from all branches of the armed forces together, before the cadets go off to their respective specialized academies.
5. The first Mobile Creche was begun in 1969, the year of the Gandhi Centenary, as a fitting living memorial to Mahatma Gandhi. Meera Mahadevan died in the prime of her life.
6. The first time the title "Khansahib" was awarded to a Jew was in April 1887, awarded to Sub-Engineer Hyem Shelomo Chincholkar, a Bene Israel.
7. The highest Civil Award in India is the *Bharat Ratna*, followed (in that order of approbation) by the *Padma Vibhushan*, the *Padma Bhushan*, and the *Padma Shri*.

Chapter 22

Bene Israel Village Life in the Twentieth Century

It is to be greatly regretted that, to date, no one has made a thorough study of Bene Israel villagers, either of the few still remaining in India or of the many who have emigrated to Israel; nor has any one properly examined the villages themselves in which groups of Bene Israel were still living at mid-20th century. This means that the most likely keys to unraveling the real roots and traditions of the Bene Israel community have been ignored.

While no thorough study (historical, ethnographic or sociological) has been made of Bene Israel villagers, there was one attempt at a demographic survey of Bene Israel families living in villages of Kolaba District. In file No. 654/3 at the The Central Archives for the History of the Jewish People containing some of H.G. Reissner's notes and correspondence, the present writer found nine long sheets of paper with lists of heads-of-families from the congregations of nine, out of a total of fourteen, Bene Israel synagogues in Kolaba District : 39 families from the Revdanda Synagogue; 21 families (of which 13 bore the surname Ashtamkar) from the Beth El Synagogue at Ashtami; 14 families from the Tala Synagogue; 48 families (of which 36 bore the surname Satamkar from the Virjole (Satambe) congregation; 34 families from the Murud congregation; 37 families from the Talekhar Synagogue; 46 families from the Nandgaon Synagogue; 51 families (of which one bore the surname Mhasilkar) from Mhasla's Shaar Ha-Tefila Synagogue; and 14 families from the Shriwardhan Congregation : a total of 304 Bene Israel families living in Kolaba District, but *not including* all the Bene Israel families affiliated with Bene Israel places of worship in Alibag; Ambepur, Borlai, Pen or Poynad (all of which are also located within Kolaba District). Neither the date when the survey was made, nor the name of the surveyor is indicated anywhere on these lists, but, from the handwriting and other clues, it would seem that this survey was made by S. Joseph Kolabkar (the author of *Kolaba Travels Investigations*) in 1946-47. (See above, p 37, footnote 7). For each synagogue, the information is divided according to the village of residence of its congregants; for example : members of the Talekhar Synagogue resided in one or another of the neighboring villages of Chorde, Chandgaon, Chanera, Kokban, Mhawa, Parankhar, Sarsoli, Shigaon, or Tadgaon. The survey gives the number of families; the occupation of the head of each family; the sex, age-group, marital status, literacy (or illiteracy), and "remarks" regarding the head-of-family and all his/her dependents.[1] The occupations mentioned in these lists are as follows : cartman, oil-presser, landlord, landlady, clerk, carpenter, cultivator, coachman, laborer, housewife, housework, shopkeeper, motor driver, tailor, jobber, mechanic, milkman, rice-miller, egg merchant, electrician, soda factory worker, railway driver, shepherd, *kaji*, *hazan*, *shamash*, field-owner, *mheter*, Postal Department worker, military, R.A.F. (Royal Air Force), State Service, student, turner (in Bombay), weaver (in Bombay), and "retired".

Within Kolaba District in the 1940s rural Bene Israel in certain places needed additional prayer halls; they also required Hebrew teachers for their children. Pleas were therefore circulated among "Jewish Brethren and Sisters in and outside India", appealing for the necessary funds. This and other projects were undertaken by S.J.Kolabkar, a Bene Israel living in Karachi, who published his ideas and a few findings in a small pamphlet called *Kolaba Travels Investigations* (Karachi 1946). Kolabkar hoped that just as the missionaries had once set up schooling for Bene Israel in rural areas, so the authorities of the Sir Elly Kadoorie School (formerly called the Israelite School) and of the Sir Jacob Sassoon High School (see below, p.261, using money from the Bene Israel Education Fund, might send their own Hebrew teachers during school vacations to inspect and improve the teaching of Hebrew in the villages. But no such plan was ever implemented. Kolabkar also suggested the "composition of a list of Bene Israel surnames by Talukas of Kolaba District and a map showing position of those villages from which the surnames were adopted" (p.2). B.J.Israel's research into "Bene Israel Surnames and Their Village Links" (see above, pp. 156 & 158) came practically three decades after Kolabkar's suggestion was published.

Tourists and others have peeked into "Bene Israel villages", but no one except Gerry Zalizar seems to have taken the trouble to write about the Bene Israel living there. Because of its rarity value, and also because it shows us a realistic slice of Bene Israel village life, it is worth choosing certain cogent details from Zalizar's Hebrew article and re-telling them here:

A Bene Israel by the name of Judah took Zalizar by car to Wakrul Village in Pen Taluka about ninety miles from Bombay. Judah owned land with nut trees, mango trees and rice fields nearby. To get there, they had to drive through hilly jungle land and Judah carried with him a revolver against panthers and robbers. They actually saw a black panther en route.

Three Bene Israel families (25 persons in number) lived then in Wakrul in three thatch-roofed houses situated side by side. Judah introduced Zalizar as "Ray" (although this honorific title was not warranted), whereupon the villagers began respectfully to kiss his feet. The visitor, through his interpreter, explained that other Jews did not have this custom. On the verandah of his house the leader of this group of Bene Israel (he was dressed in white trousers, white shirt, and white Nehru-Congress cap) touched Zalizar's fingertips with his two hands and then put his hands to his own lips. He was the employer of everyone in the village who cut down tress, which were then taken to Pen and Panvel and sold for firewood. He sat on his verandah with his brothers and male cousins (all wearing caps embroidered by their womenfolk) by his side. The women and small children were listening from inside the two-room house (which had no windows, no sanitary fixtures, no running water, no electricity — and there was but a single kerosene lamp in the entire village). Each of the three families had had eight or nine children, and in each family two or three children had died of malaria or typhus.[2] The nearest doctor now was a Jewish [no doubt Bene Israel] woman doctor living in Pen — impossible to reach during the monsoon. Above the entrance to the house, near the *mezuzah*, hung a piece of paper on which, in brown color, there was an impression of a hand. It was made by a child who, having put his hand in the blood of the lamb slaughtered on Passover in memory of the paschal sacrifice, put it upon the paper.[3]

The men sat and talked with Zalizar for three hours. Only the three household heads did the talking. Only the eldest among them had ever travelled south to Bombay and had seen the sea-coast. The grandfather of this old man had left Wakrul forty years ago to live in Bombay where he set up a firewood business. Since then the family had enjoyed relations of mutual respect and admiration with Wakrul's non-Jewish residents. The relatives in Bombay never came to visit their relatives who still remain in Wakrul.

On Jewish holidays the three Bene Israel families go to the town of Panvel more than 10 miles away. There a synagogue was built about fifty years ago serving as central house of prayer for all the Bene Israel who were scattered in 20 to 25 surrounding villages. A Bene Israel congregation in Bombay customarily sent Panvel a *hazan* for the holidays. His knowledge of Hebrew gave the villagers some opportunity to familiarize themselves with the prayers. They explained that the *hazan* pronounces each word loudly so that most of those present, who do not understand the meaning of the verses, can at least listen and say "Amen" at the proper places. Kosher meat is brought in cars to Wakrul and to the other outlying villages where Bene Israel are living. During the monsoon, however, it is impossible to travel on the roads and during this period the Bene Israel eat only vegetarian food like their Indian neighbors. *Brit Milah*, *Pidyan ha-Ben*, and kosher meat slaughtering are all performed for the villagers by qualified Bene Israel from Bombay.

According to Judah, the villagers in Wakrul had never heard anything about Jews of Europe until shortly before Zalizar's visit when Judah had told them something about other Jews. But they did ask Zalizar if it was true that Americans erect buildings of fifty stories and can get way up to the fiftieth floor in "a machine driven by hand".[4]

The striking thing is that these observations were made in *1962* or *1963* and not several decades earlier. Many details from Zalizar's article about Wakrul are/were true of Bene Israel in other villages too, varying according to the degree of isolation of the village concerned. The *Kolaba District Census Handbook* for 1961 states that, as of that year, Wakrul had one functioning oil-press (which undoubtedly belonged to a Bene Israel family — although Zalizar made no mention of an oil-press there).

From a much broader sample, based on several interviews by the present author with Bene Israel from other villages, certain common themes have emerged. The unselfconsciously-told life-histories of elderly Bene Israel villagers convincingly reveal a long-ago firmly established Bene Israel *modus vivendi*; a specific pattern of relationships with their non-Jewish neighbors; and a very strict adherence to the Bene Israel's own old way of Jewishness, a kind of Bene Israel *'halacha*, which evolved during their isolation from other Jewish communities. Rural Bene Israel, wherever possible, still cling to the nearest synagogue as *the* focal point of their religious life. It is not uncommon for a Bene Israel villager to pedal one and a half hours (one way) on his bicycle until he reaches the nearest synagogue — the synagogue service being far more important to him than the stricture against riding on Sabbath. Until the time of their emigration to Israel, the villagers have remained more faithful to their own Jewish traditions than is true of many Bene Israel in the cities. A few true vignettes of actual Bene Israel villagers can best illustrate these points:

1. ABAJI

Abaji (Abraham) was born at the turn of the century, about 1901, in the village of Parali in Sudhagad *Tehsil*[5] where, he says, his family had lived for seven generations. But, his family name, i.e. his surname ending in *-kar* relates to a totally different village, in Roha

Taluk. [The evidence from his study of village-based surnames indicates to B.J. Israel that it is very likely that most Bene Israel settlement in Sudhagad (*Taluka*, *Tehsil* or *Mahal*) must have taken place *after* the Bene Israel had already assumed their village-based surnames.[6] What's more, there is no Bene Israel surname such as Paralikar.]

Abaji is tall and erect. He speaks unhesitatingly and knowledgeably, in his mother-tongue Marathi. He lived in Parali from the time of his birth until 1968 when he emigrated to Israel. Before the Bene Israel began emigrating to Israel, the total population of Parali consisted of 150 families, 25 of them Bene Israel, 10 Muslim, and all the rest were Hindu.

Abaji lived in the family-owned homestead together with the members of his joint-family, usually about 13 persons altogether : Abaji, his wife, and their only child; Abaji's two brothers and their respective wives and children; plus Abaji's three unmarried sisters. The family owned not only the house, but also ten acres of land. Abaji said that in Parali twenty of the Bene Israel families, owned their own land. The remaining five families rented land, retaining the entire profit from their agricultural produce. [Usually, the landlord was given a major portion of the produce in kind, although rent was sometimes paid in cash. After land-reform laws were established in independent India, tenants of absentee landlords became owners of land, the absentee landlords being given some compensation by the government. Many Bene Israel, living in Bombay, thus lost much land to their tenants. On the other hand, many cases of ancestral tenancies continued as such, with the actual tiller being considered as a hired laborer for the purposes of the official records only.]

Before continuing with Abaji's life-history and his own descriptions of life in Parali, inclusion of some actual data about Parali may not only bolster the reader's confidence in Abaji's descriptions, but will provide a more comprehensive and vivid picture of that village. Luckily, Parali was one of thirteen villages in Sudhagad Tehsil singled out for a detailed survey as part of the 1961 Census. From this survey and from the 1971 *Census Report* one learns that :

Parali Village is situated in the northeastern part of Sudhagad Tehsil, not far from the border of Poona District. Before 1948 it belonged to the Indian Princely State of Bhor. Sudhagad Tehsil is that portion of Bhor which was incorporated into Kulaba District. In 1961 Sudhagad Tehsil had the largest Jewish population among all the Tehsils of Kulaba District; and in 1971 (by which year the Jewish population of Sudhagad Tehsil had fallen from 493 to 195) it was second to Alibag Tehsil (which in 1971 had a Jewish population of 261).

In 1961 the village of Parali had a total population of 730; in 1971 it had fallen to 710. [How many of these were Jews in either year is not recorded.]

Parali is situated very close to the Amba River, which rises on the Poona border. It is situated on a State Highway running from north to south, with no direct road connecting to the nearest town which is Pen (in Pen Tehsil), 55 kilometres to the west. As late as 1971 there was still no bus stop at Parali, the nearest one being a kilometre away, to the east, at Karchund. The nearest telegraph office was at the Sudhagad Tehsil headquarters in Pali, 20 kilometres away. In 1961 Parali had no Post Office, the nearest one being about two kilometres away; but by 1971 a Post Office had been opened at Parali, although Pali was still the only telegraph office in the Tehsil, and it also had a telephone. In 1961 Parali had a Primary School, but the nearest Secondary

School was at Pali. In 1971, 289 persons were literate in Parali. By 1971 a Secondary School had been opened at Varhad Jambulpada, two kilometres from Parali. The nearest (modern) medical dispensary was also at Varhad Jambulpada. Electricity had not reached Parali in 1961, but had done so by 1971. Drinking water was drawn from the river, wells and tanks.

In 1961 a weekly market was held at Parali on Saturdays, but by 1971 it had been discontinued. In 1971, of the total area of 153 acres, 85 were put under cultivation. No irrigation was available. Rice was the staple food and the rice crop was dependent upon heavy monsoon rains (June to September).

As of 1961 there were in Parali 11 rice mills employing 24 persons; one small oil-pressing *ghani* [this must have been Abaji's oil-press] employing one person; 3 garment-making places employing 6 persons; one place making unspecified chemical products; and 5 metal-working places [no doubt, mainly for manufacturing, and repairing agricultural implements], employing 12 persons.[7]

Long before Abaji's time, the family house had started out as one big room plus a kitchen. Each generation kept repairing and adding to it especially in order to be able to provide each married couple with a separate room. A storeroom was also added to the house, to keep produce used by the family, to be available for use from one harvest to the next; and also a small room in which about ten chickens (for family use only) were kept safe from possible depredations by fox or mongoose. There was, in addition, an entirely separate structure, a shed, for the family's fifteen water buffaloes, a couple of oxen and a few cows. The family oil-mill was attached to this shed. Until the advent of competition from large modern oil-mills (which made the traditional processing of oil no longer profitable), Abaji worked his own mill, the only one in Parali. Some of the seeds which he processed, he grew on his own land; but outsiders, too, brought seeds to him and paid him to have them ground. Abaji prepared edible and inedible (for lamp lighting) oils as well.

Without looking into personal and village records of those Konkan villages inhabited by Bene Israel for generations, it is impossible to ascertain the correct figure; but, according to certain information from Bene Israel respondents, it seems to be a conservative estimate that more than 50 percent of all Bene Israel joint-families living in Konkan villages owned their own land. However, the size of each holding varied greatly. A Bene Israel Chandgaonkar family in Roha Taluka owned 1,000 acres. Not necessarily for such huge land-holdings, but for Abaji's family with its ten acres of land, as well as for families who owned relatively large amounts of land, the usual Bene Israel practice was for at least some male members of the joint-family to work the land in person (and to hire additional labour when, as, and if necessary); or else to sell the land; but not to give it on rent and thus to become an absentee landlord (i.e. with no one from the owner's joint-family living and working there).

A large proportion of Abaji's family land was devoted to rice cultivation, which involved a cycle of very strenuous tasks. Even with everyone in the family working in the fields for certain seasonal operations, the family had to hire 25 additional helpers. Usually such hired laborers were Muslims, but Hindu Thakurs[8] were also employed. At such times Abaji's wife prepared food not only for the entire joint-family (for whom food was regularly prepared together anyway), but also for all 25 hired laborers, who received their daily food in addition to wages for their services. After the rice seeds had been removed from the harvest, the leftover hay was used to feed the cows and buffaloes.

Ample supplies of rice were kept for family use, enough to last until the next harvest; the surplus was offered for sale. Abaji himself seasonally took his bullock-cart and piled on to it his own surplus produce of rice and of oils, as well as products from others (such as charcoal and fishnets). All this he peddled and sold throughout the surrounding villages.

The family never had much cash as such, but then their cash needs were very few; they produced their own food except for salt, sugar, tea and a certain kind of already powdered chili.

Abaji married when he was 25 years of age. His bride was 15 years old and hailed from another village. Neither Abaji nor his wife had ever attended any school nor could they read or write. There was a Primary School but no Secondary School at Parali and they sent their only child, a daughter, to this school where she completed the 7th standard. After the girl's marriage, she and her husband went to live in Bombay where her husband let her continue her schooling through the 10th standard. This illustrates a new priority among Bene Israel villagers : a desire for education, not only for boys, but for girls as well. Abaji's daughter got as far as filling out an application form to attend a teacher-training course in Bombay, but instead had to devote herself to three small children who came in rapid succession. Later, she and the family emigrated to Israel, followed a year later by her parents.

It used to take Abaji about four hours in "the good old days" to travel from Parali to Bombay. With his wife and daughter, he would make the journey usually once a year, staying at the home of relatives in Bombay. On these occasions he took the opportunity to attend holiday or Sabbath services in a real synagogue. However, he never learned to read Hebrew, and since he had not learned the liturgy by heart, he concentrated on just listening to the chanting of the *hazan*, and he would stand up with the rest of the congregation whenever they did so in unison. At Parali there was neither synagogue nor prayer-hall. Pen, situated about 55 kilometres to the west, was the nearest town with a synagogue. But there was no access road between Pen and Parali. During the three-week period of Jewish holidays (Rosh Hashonah, Yom Kippur, Succoth, Shemini Atzereth, Simchat Torah) prayer services were held in Parali, in one Jewish house or another, sometimes with a hired *hazan*, sometimes with one of the villagers to lead all the prayers. (A few villagers did know how to do so.) During the rest of the year, except for rites of passage, each Bene Israel family, while in Parali, did not attend religious services, limiting themselves to a Sabbath *Kiddush* at home. Abaji performed this ritual in his home every Sabbath. Other Sabbath customs which Abaji and all Bene Israel in Parali observed were as follows : Punctually at 4 p.m. every Friday, all work outside and inside the home ceased; no chore was performed by any member of the family until 7 p.m. on Saturday; and the oxen too on the Sabbath had a full day's rest from turning the oil-mill. No fire, be it for cooking or any other purpose, was lit during this period. The mistress of the household would light the special Sabbath lamp on Friday at 4 p.m., using home-made coconut oil which filled a single container suspended from a wall of the "front room", and she recited the appropriate blessing. The previously-prepared food for the Sabbath was kept hot over a typically Indian simple type of stove, using dung patties as fuel, which burned with an odorless, slow, constant flame, generating a very low heat.

Their way of observing Passover was very strict : a total ban on eating any item of food which they themselves had not harvested and processed. Thus they did not even drink tea; instead, they made a brew of certain green leaves which grew on their own land. They used no sugar at all during Passover, because that too had not been prepared by Jews. They used no dried condiments because they had been prepared long before Passover. Their *matzoh* was *bhakri*, the same type of unleavened bread (made from rice flour) which they were accustomed to make and to eat during the rest of the year, except that for Passover the dough was rolled and baked immediately, whereas during the rest of the year the dough was allowed to stand for a while so that a bit of natural leavening could take place.

No one can attribute these customs to Hindu or to Muslim influences. They are, rather, manifestations of the Bene Israel villager's firm desire to preserve and to observe the Jewish Sabbath and the Passover, even if only so far as their circumstances permitted. And, the universally Jewish referent for each of these observances is easy to recognize. What we do not know is how far back in time these Jewish practices of the Bene Israel villagers took root.

More than three-quarters of the population of Parali were Hindus, and Abaji was not immune to the lure of some of the Hindu celebrations. For instance, on Pola, a certain Hindu festival, it is customary to paint the horns of all oxen in bright colors and to adorn the horns with flower garlands and small bells, then to parade the animals around. This was, among other things, a way of honoring one's beasts of burden for their faithful services. Abaji, too, was a farmer and he too decorated the horns of his oxen on that day each year; and he would make a modest cash donation to his Hindu neighbors, to be added to their collection to defray expenses for the culminating function of the day, a feast, which, however, Abaji did not choose to attend. "After all," he said, "they are my neighbors and my good friends, and I like to help them. But their religion is not my religion."

Mutual respect for another's religion was a way of life not only in "backward", isolated villages but also in the larger villages whose populations had been exposed to more secular education and to more modern ways of life. In Ashtami, for instance, every three years, coinciding with the eve of Yom Kippur, as part of a certain Hindu festival a noisy crowd, with rather rowdy singing, dancing and drunkenness, carried an image to immerse in the nearby Rohe Creek. At the same time, the *hazan* of the local Bene Israel congregation would be taking his flock for their ritual bath (*tebila*)[9] prior to the Yom Kippur fast. Always without any fuss the Hindu celebrants would respectfully quiet down and the crowd parted, making way for the Bene Israel group to proceed to a peaceful spot on the bank of the creek. This kind of behaviour reflects the prevailing basic decency and consideration for customs of others.

2. RIVKA

Unlike Abaji, many Bene Israel who lived in the Konkan villages during the first half of the 20th century were literate in their mother-tongue, Marathi, some of them having completed several grades at their respective local schools. Thale, although it could boast of having a real, one-storey synagogue, was still a village, not a town. At mid-century there were only the Bene Israel residents in Thale. Especially for the Jewish holidays, all the Bene Israel residents from the nearby villages of Ghosale, Satambe, Halde, Walis, Nigushet and Salshet would walk the three or four miles to the Thale Synagogue, usually arriving before sundown on the eve of the holiday and spending the night(s) at one or the other local Bene Israel home so as to be able to attend synagogue for the entire holiday service. The house of Rivka, for instance, whose family name was indeed Thalkar (indicating that Thale had been the native place of her family for generations), was a huge house, large enough to accommodate as many as fifty persons overnight, with each guest bringing his/her own bedroll, or just sleeping on a mat, all of them on the floor. Like most Indian joint-families, such a household was well equipped and geared for cooking for large numbers of simultaneous overnight guests belonging to one's extended family.

Rivka's father worked his own land (they grew a wide variety of green vegetables) and he also worked as a carpenter. Thale had its own high school, conducted in Marathi, as well as several other separate schools run by Muslims, Gujaratis, etc., but it had none specifically earmarked for the Bene Israel. Rivka and her siblings were sent to Bombay to attend high school and/or to obtain jobs. In Thale, the Brahmins, as well as the Muslim community (most of the latter being shopkeepers and farmers) lived in their own separate sections of the village. Not so, however, with the Bene Israel : the houses of three Bene Israel families were located among Sonars (the Hindu goldsmith *jati*); another four Bene Israel families lived among tailors; and each of the remaining three families lived in different parts of Thale.

3. RACHEL

The situation in another Konkan village[10] presented quite another pattern. Here there were thirty Hindu families, no Muslims, and only three Bene Israel families. Rachel's family owned its own lands and a large one-storey house in this village. To them their Hindu neighbors were almost as close as their own kith and kin. Rachel's father and his three sons worked the land and hired additional help when necessary. But her father, and his father before him, were also carpenters by trade. Her father learned his carpentry skills from his own father. Later, Rachel's father learned new techniques as well : as time went on he began using modern implements which his father had never seen. From carpentry, he entered the house-building trade. He had finished the fourth standard at school and even his wife knew how to read and write.

Under their thatch roof, condiments and vegetables were left to dry for use in the rainy season. The family grew their own sesame and made their own oil, but only for their own use. There was another Bene Israel family in the village whose main business was the making and selling of oil. Rachel's family owned a bullock and cart, four or five cows, and a few chickens. The chickens were kept only for the family : they would be eaten on holidays, a treat in which the family indulged on Jewish as well as on Hindu festival days. They did share several superstitious folk customs[11] with their Hindu neighbors, but they never confused their own Bene Israel *religion* with that of the Hindus. The Bene Israel always kept their own religion distinct and were respected for that. To orthodox Jewry, on the other hand, nothing but adherence to every detail of traditional *halacha* is acceptable. The typically Bene Israel Jewish customs, the eclecticism and new ways of Reform Judaism, and even the much more traditional ways of Conservative Judaism, all are unacceptable to Jewish orthodoxy.

Rachel's father once obtained a building job with a major foreign company in Bombay and thereupon took his wife and children with him to Bombay. They rented and lived in a flat in Byculla; all the other members of the joint-family remained back in the village. Her father learned to read and write Hebrew while in Bombay. He, his wife and children invariably returned to their village during all vacations. The foreign company closed down after Rachel's father had worked for them for four years and the little family promptly returned, once again, taking up residence in their ancestral village home.

While they lived in the village, Rachel's family sometimes attended synagogue services in another not-too-distant village which, unlike their own, did have a synagogue. But Rachel's family preferred the sanctity of their own home especially on Yom Kippur. She refers to the atmosphere of her home on that day as being "very like that of a synagogue. Everything was covered with white cloth for the occasion and all members of the joint-family (there were no guests on Yom Kippur) were dressed in white." Before Yom Kippur eve, everyone had bathed by first anointing his/her entire body with home-made coconut oil, thereafter removing the oil with a certain kind of flour, and finally bathing with fresh water. Not only did they fast from sundown of Yom Kippur eve until nightfall of the following day, but they spoke very little during this entire period, and no one was supposed to utter or hear anything bad. Anyone in the family who knew Hebrew would recite prayers. "None of us did any chores on that day. We did not even milk our cows. Our Hindu neighbors quietly took care of that for us. The Hindus of the village knew and respected our custom and would say "Today the Bene Israel will not talk". At the close of Yom Kippur, with the benediction (outdoors) for the new moon,[12] our neighbors would very unobtrusively come into our courtyard, leave the milk, which they, in our stead, had collected from our cows, and then they would silently go away."

Rachel remembered how, in preparation for Passover, all the brass cooking pots of the household were freshly re-tinned so that the Passover foods would not be "contaminated" by contact with pre-Passover cooking traces. The walls of the entire house were whitewashed, inside and out, just before Passover (and also before Rosh Hashonah). Everything inside the house was cleaned from top to bottom. Before Passover, the red imprint of a full hand (dipped in the blood of a goat) was pressed on to the outside wall at the entry to the house, and they took care not to cover over the imprint during the pre-Rosh Hashonah whitewashing.

Rachel married a man from the village of Ghosale where, as of 1967, eleven Bene Israel families were still living in their ancestral family houses. Soon after their marriage, Rachel and her husband emigrated to Israel. Within less than a deade, all of Ghosale's Bene Israel inhabitants followed their example and also emigrated to Israel, so that today not a single Bene Israel remains there. However, Rachel's own parents remained in her father's native village for several years after the departure of its other two Bene Israel families. Eventually, however, they also came to Israel.

4. DANIEL

It must be pointed out that if a Bene Israel lived in a village or small town *outside the Konkan area*, even though he/she may have been born there, the reasons for living there, as well as his/her education, occupation, and Jewish life — all differ distinctly from those aspects (as described above) relating to Bene Israel native villagers of the Konkan. The relatively small number of Bene Israel fathers, whose civil or military jobs had brought them and their families to live in small towns or in larger villages scattered throughout India, is sufficiently large to warrant recognition that Bene Israel experience in such a village or small town has practically nothing in common with that of the Bene Israel who lived in Konkan villages. Furthermore, the Bene Israel in such non-Konkan villages or small towns did not usually establish permanent homes there from generation to generation.

The following Bene Israel mini-biography shows that life for a Bene Israel in a rural area outside of the Konkan was not rustic, and differed markedly indeed from the life of Bene Israel residing in Konkan villages.

Daniel was born in 1905 in a Gujarat village where his father was serving as a medical doctor. There were no other Bene Israel living in this village. The town nearest to the village was Viramgam, a railway junction. The only indication of Jewishness at home which Daniel remembers were the Jewish Holidays. The family annually received the current calendar of Jewish holidays from Bombay. The holidays were celebrated merely by a festive family meal, with parents and children all together. Hebrew prayers were not recited. Daniel received no religious instruction whatever. When he was old enough, he was sent to Rajkot (some 150 or more kilometres away) for his secular (English medium) education, returning only during vacations to be with his parents. He studied law in Bombay. A suitable wife was chosen for him from among the Bene Israel community of Ahmedabad, and he and his bride then settled in Bombay. Eventually, they too emigrated to Israel, in 1970. Other Bene Israel families in equally isolated spots outside the Konkan often retained a more Jewish atmosphere at home than that which obtained in Daniel's family. But, observant or not, those Bene Israel whose jobs or professions scattered them and their families in villages elsewhere in India, were not living the lives of agriculturalists or of oil-pressers.

NOTES

1. The villages of residence of Bene Israel who were affiliated to a rural Bene Israel house of worship were listed, respectively, as follows :

Revdanda	:	Revdanda.
Ashtami	:	Ashtami, Pui, Dew Kaneh, Dolwal, Damkhadi, Rohe.
Tala (Rohe Taluka)	:	Hardi, Wali, Salset.
Virjoli-Satambe (Rohe Taluka)	:	Virjoli, Satambe, Ghosale, Gowalwadi.
Murud (Janjira State)	:	Murud, Dande, Korlai.
Talekhar (Janjira State)	:	Talekhar, Chorde, Chandgaon, Chanera, Kokban, Mhawa, Parankhar, Sarsoli, Shigaon, Tadgaon.
Nandgaon (Janjira State)	:	Nandgaon, Oosrolly.
Mhasle (Janjira State)	:	Mhasle, Agerwada, Gowala, Kharsai, Majrona, Rewli.
Shriwardhan (Janjira State)	:	Shriwardhan, Galsure, Walwati, Ningdi, Borlai-Panchatan.

   These demographic lists were found in folio 654/1 at the Central Archives for the History of the Jewish People, under the letter "K". (Were they filed under "K" for "Kolaba", or for "Konkan", or for "Kolabkar, S.J."?)
   Kolabkar must have been the one who compiled these lists, and must have done so either at the request of, or in conjunction with, H.G. Reissner. On p.8 of *Kolaba Travels Investigations* Kolabkar thanks "Dr. H.G.Reissner....for taking great interest for Bene-Israel community."

2. The malaria victims must have died some years earlier because, by the mid-1960s, after a concerted and very thorough war against malaria, this disease was almost completely wiped out all over India. However, a new DDT-resistant strain of malaria-bearing mosquito developed in the 1970s.

3. In mid-20th century Rabbi Louis Rabinowitz observed something in the Panvel Synagogue which, to him, was unique : posted above the door there was a square of paper on which appeared the figure of a hand. He explains that :

   On the eve of Passover they slay a goat and, dipping their hand in the blood, they press the gory hand on piece of paper which is affixed to the upper lintel of the door. The reference is obviously to the 12th chapter of *Exodus*, and the goat chosen instead of a sheep in order to avoid the transgression of sacrificing the Paschal Lamb in non-Temple times. Although Scripture specifically permits goat, the custom was to sacrifice only a lamb. (Rabbi Louis Isaac Rabinowitz : *Far East Mission*, printed by Eagle Press, Johannesburg, 1952, p.79.)

   Moroccan and other oriental Jewish communites also have this custom, even though Rabbi Rabinowitz had never heard of it, at least not on a synagogue wall.

4. Gerry Zalizar : "The Road to Wakrul", a Hebrew article in the quarterly journal, *Gesher*, June 1963, 9th year, (35)2; published by the Israel Branch of the World Jewish Congress pp.118-21. Mr. Zalizar seems to have confused the town of Panvel with Pen. It is Pen that is "more than 10 miles away from Wakrul". Panvel is much further away. Also Pen's synagogue was *re*-built in 1893 (closer to "about 50 years ago") than the building of Panvel's synagogue in 1849.
5. *Tehsil* is now the official name for the old *Talukas* and *Mahals* (i.e. districts).
6. This surmise is based on the fact that, for all of Sudhagad *Taluka*, Bhurgekar and Bhorupkar are the only definitely Sudhagad-based Bene Israel surnames, with the possible exception of two others, viz. Mangaonkar and Palkar (although the latter two may have stemmed from villages of the same name in Mangaon Taluka or in Khalapur Taluka, respectively).
7. Taken from *Census Reports* of 1961 and 1971, on *Village Surveys in Maharashtra*, including the *Kolaba District Census Handbook for 1961*, p.230.
8. In Bengal, Thakur is the name of a Brahmin family (Tagore), but in Maharashtra the Thakurs are of very low rank. They used to be largely cultivators, genealogists, some ballad singers, occasional puppeteers, or beggars. Today most of them are landless laborers and are officially classed as a Scheduled (backward or deprived) Tribe.
9. The women-folk bathed at home, but the men and children did so at the "river" bank.
10. This village is deliberately unnamed. Otherwise the identity of the respondents would be easy to detect. Personal names of all respondents mentioned in this chapter are not their real names. Names of villages, however, wherever stated, are the actual places under discussion.
11. Superstitions of the following ilk : "making a stain on a part of the body of an old woman and giving her name to a babe who happened later to be born with a similar mark on its body". This has nothing to do with religion; nor does feasting on chicken on a Hindu holiday.
12. Any date from the first to the sixteenth of the Hebrew lunar month had been fixed by Maimonides as being appropriate for blessing the new or waxing moon, preferably with at least a *minyan* being present, just outside the synagogue at the close of the appropriate Sabbath. Orthodox congregations regularly do this also at the close of Yom Kippur, after the evening prayers have been recited inside the synagogue.

Chapter 23
Bene Israel Life - Styles in Bombay

More so in Bombay than in other centers where large numbers of Bene Israel live, the successful Bene Israel maintain less and less contact with the community as such, except on the Jewish High Holidays and for the performance of rites of passage; even then, after the ritual portion has been completed, receptions are often held privately rather than in the synagogue where all the members of the congregation could socialize together (as they used to do). Only a very few of the wealthier Bene Israel have retained residence in the original Bene Israel neighborhood of Bombay. Those whose work has taken them outside Bombay and removed them far from Bene Israel centers, do travel with their families to be back "home" for the Jewish High Holidays and for the celebration of rites of passage; or at least they try to be in the nearest (often still quite distant) place in which they can find a prayer hall and a *minyan*. The Bene Israel synagogues in Bombay aid[1] these small outlying communities in such matters as supplying *Torah* scrolls, and in sending a *hazan* for the High Holidays, etc.; while modest sums are donated by the outlying groups to the Bene Israel Orphanage and to charity and education funds administered by the Bene Israel in Bombay.

A certain percentage of educated and successful Bene Israel are active in public life and in non-sectarian organizations, but not as many as might be expected, given the cosmopolitan atmosphere of Bombay. On the whole, most Bene Israel of Bombay have followed the traditional Indian pattern, conservatively keeping themselves *socially* separate from other communities even though Bombay offers innumerable cultural and social opportunities for mixing.

Long gone by, however, are the days when there was a communal neighborhood in Bombay. The original neighborhood was located where the Byculla, Nagpada, Mazgaon and Umerkhadi sections of Bombay meet. At that early time all the residents had been within walking distance of each other. Today there are several areas of Bene Israel concentration in Bombay, with no one sector being inhabited exclusively by them. The new Bene Israel clusters of residence are at least two or three miles away from the old center. Many had moved away from the original communal neighborhood because of a growing lack of adequate accommodations. By the late 1950s there were about 500 Bene Israel living in very small groups even at the very outskirts of Bombay. Here as well as elsewhere, however, the Bene Israel population has since been greatly diminished because of large-scale emigration to Israel.

The following sections of Bombay are today still favorite areas of Bene Israel residence. (They did not settle in the most exclusive residential areas, namely Malabar Hill and Colaba.) The Bene Israel neighborhoods are listed here in the chronological order in which they became favored by members of the community.

1. *Israel Mohalla*, in the Mandvi area : this is adjacent to the Memon Muslim and to the Khoja Muslim settlement.[2] The Khojas rented their houses to Bene Israel in what then came to be known as Israel Mohalla, which today still has a large

Muslim population. At one time Bene Israel owned several houses in Israel Mohalla. As they move out to other neighborhoods, the place is gradually once again becoming mostly Muslim.
2. *Dongakherry* (Dongri) and *Umarkhadi*.
3. *Noorbagh* and *Mazgaon* : many Parsis and the Baghdadi Sassoon family also lived in Mazgaon.
4. *Byculla* and *Nagpada*, also inhabited by some Baghdadis.
5. *Jacob Circle*, about four miles north of Israel Mohalla, between Byculla and Parel.
6. *Parel*.
7. *Dadar, Matunga,* and *Mahim*.
8. *Bandra* and *Khar* : not settled by the Bene Israel until the late 1920s , it is part of Greater Bombay, about ten miles north of Israel Mohalla.
9. *Kurla*.
10. *Santa Cruz, Kalina, Vile Parle,* and *Andheri* : even further north into Greater Bombay, and with relatively fewer Bene Israel.

Not only is there an Israel Mohalla in Bombay, but some of the city's streets have been officially named after Bene Israel individuals. Thus we find Dr. E. Moses Road (formerly Haines Road), after Dr. E. Moses who was Mayor of Bombay; Samuel Street (or Samaji Street) where the first Bene Israel synagogue, built by Samual Ezekiel Divekar, still stands; and Issaji Street, named after Samuel E. Divekar's brother.

Strizower[3] gives the following table of Jewish residence in Bombay as of the mid-1960s :

	Bene Israel	Baghdadis	European Jews
Communal Neighborhoods	7,000	800	—
Areas similar to the Communal Neighborhoods	1,500	—	—
Middle-class Suburbs	900	—	—
Best Residential Area	100	100	100
Total	9,500	900	100

Although the majority of Bene Israel and Baghdadis lived near each other, and although once again, in mid-20th century, the Headmaster of the Baghdadi School was a Bene Israel, the two communities still did not freely fraternize. However, the barriers are no longer as strict as they had been in the 19th century. In the President's Address to the First Bene Israel Conference (1917) we nevertheless still find this statement : "There have been a few instances of mixed marriages in our community, so also marriages with Baghdadi girls. We may hope that such marriages will be few in number." (pp.55 – 6) We wonder whether it is just a matter of unclear phrasing or whether marriage with a Baghdadi was frowned upon as much as intermarriage with a non-Jew! During the first half of the 20th century, at any rate, some conservative Bene Israel mothers preferred to have their children (daughters especially) play with Hindu children rather than with those of the Baghdadis because the Baghdadi youngsters were already living according to freer, more modern, western life-styles. At a time when there were already one or two famous Baghdadi Jewish cinema actresses, some Bene Israel parents even objected to their sons going to see motion pictures. If Bene Israel girls did go to see films, they were always accompanied by father, uncle or elder brother. Some Bene Israel also discouraged[29] association with Christian children, in this case because they had reason to fear attempts at proselytization.

Only one of the new Bene Israel neighborhoods, at that time the most distant, i.e. Parel, had its own prayer hall (until recently when it had to close due to emigration); but even its congregants would return to perform their rites of passage in the synagogue of their old neighborhood. Bandra has no prayer hall, but local services are held in Bandra, on the High Holidays only.

A very special accommodation for Jewish street-car passengers in Bombay was arranged through official issuance by the Tramway Company (later, the Bombay Electric Supply and Transport Undertaking) of tram tickets which could be purchased on weekdays, in advance, for use on the Sabbath and Jewish holidays. When, in the 1930s, buses were introduced for public transport, these special coupons were valid for buses also. The gesture enabled Jewish passengers to respect at least the *halachic* rule against carrying money on those days. The special ticket bore these words :

> The Bombay Electric Supply and Tramways Co., Ltd.
> One anna ticket coupon
> For Jews only
> No. ....
> (Good only for Sabbath and Holidays)
> To be handed over to the Conductor who will issue a ticket in lieu thereof.
> C. Lucas
> Asst. Manager.
>
> Initials :

There often was no other way for Bombay's Jews to meet the requirements of their jobs or to attend synagogues located too far from their homes to make walking either practicable or, indeed, *halachically* acceptable.[4] In such ways many Jews in Bombay, like many of their fellow Jews in Europe and in America after the industrial revolution, altered or relaxed their former Sabbath observances.[5] Sir Sassoon J. David, as chairman of the Bombay Electric Supply and Tramways Company,[6] was the originator of this special arrangement for the pre-Sabbath and pre-Jewish holiday purchase of tram tickets. It seems that such tickets were obtainable only from officials of Baghdadi synagogues and not many Bene Israel took advantage of this facility. Such tickets are no longer being issued, having been discontinued some years ago when buses and trams were taken over from the private company by the municipality of Bombay.

By 1920 the average Bene Israel housing in Bombay had become crowded and unsanitary. There is a pamphlet of that year, written by Judge Ezra Reuben, entitled *The Housing Problem and Bene Israels*. Judge Reuben made this subject the main topic of his Presidential Address to the Second Bene Israel Conference (1918). He recommended that the Bene Israel undertake to develop a cooperative housing project for themselves, as some other communities had already done in Bombay Presidency. He cites the Hindu Cooperative Housing Society, the Catholic Cooperative Housing Society at Santa Cruz, and the Gaud Saraswat Housing Society. Although such a scheme was discussed and urged at the Bene Israel Conference, it does not seem ever to have been implemented, another example of Bene Israel lack of enterprise in cooperating as a unit for the benefit of all concerned. (When asked about this scheme, only one out of many Bene Israel spondents did remember one attempt at Bene Israel Cooperative Housing, but he could remember no details.)

The average resident in the Bombay Bene Israel communal neighborhood lives in very crowded tenement conditions; but crowded or not, each home has its *mezuzah* at the entrance; a hanging oil-lamp[7] to be lit on the eve of Sabbath and of Jewish festivals; prayer books and a copy of the Hebrew Bible with Marathi or English translation; and on the wall some framed photographs of family members and pictures (usually colorful) of Biblical scenes. Similarly, Indians of other religions also display in their homes scenes from their respective religious epics, even the most humble hut having on its interior walls unframed posters depicting in color religious (and nowadays other) subjects. When and if figurines of Hindu deities are occasionally found in Bene Israel homes, they are there as purely decorative folkart objects, not as objects of worship.

For non-Indian readers it may be helpful to mention some general features of Indian joint-family life which the Bene Israel, as Indians, shared in every respect. As with most Indians, certain attitudes engendered by living in joint-families still persist, even when large extended joint-families no longer live under one roof or within one compound. The individuals continue to have strong emotional ties to and real involvement in extended family affairs. The sense of privacy confines itself to bathing, dressing and sexual relations, but there is no "room-of-one's own" mentality. As many as ten additional relatives (invited or unexpected) are made welcome as house guests for weeks at a time, even in already crowded quarters. Servants and all the women present cooperate in the cooking and care of children. Disruption of order and lack of quiet do not seem to disturb the genuine pleasure of family togetherness. Margaret Ann Sood has very aptly distilled some of the essence of Indian family life:

Indian parents rarely insist on a prescribed routine once the child is out of infancy. When he visits any of his relatives, the child slips into their food habits, daily routine and rules of the house—neither his mother nor any one else worries about his nap time, in which room he plays, where he sleeps or whose clothes he borrows. Nevertheless, the traditions which the family as a whole or a particular set of parents hold dear are taught to the child; for example, a brief prayer upon awakening in the morning or a reverent nod when passing a religious shrine and the more significant cultural and religious traditions such as fasting or not eating certain meat. In addition, respect for elders, restraint of emotions in public, hospitality to guests and a patience and calm in the face of difficulty are inculcated in a child from his earliest years. The middle and upper classes place great emphasis upon instilling in children politeness, refinement and the habit of doing kindnesses gracefully for others....An Indian child is rarely excluded from even the most solemn ceremony and often accompanies his parent in public or winesses a family argument—with no apparent ill effects....As he will absorb familiarity with people, with moods, with ways of behaving, American children absorb the inventiveness, self-reliance and individuality that a narrower circle encourages....his [the Indian child's] consciousness of his place in the social gradations encourages confidence.... Boys in particular must be self-reliant and competent for they have to look after their sisters and their mother....Girls learn the art of dealing gently with family members and while they are not expected to be real leaders, they must be able to oversee, protect and unite the family. Girls use quiet persuasion and persistent cajoling to influence their brothers and even elders and the family expects them to be a guiding moral and personal force in the home—and in their husband's house after marriage....In spite of the collective nature of children's experience within the family, Indian children do not develop much ability in group thinking or cooperative problem solving. This may stem from the fact that decisions are deferred to elders or follow a traditional pattern.⁸

While arranged marriages are still very prevalent among the Bene Israel (they are still prevalent among most other Indian groups too), the number of love marriages, however *with* the parents' consent, is steadily growing. Strizower makes the point that, on the positive side, a love-match can serve as an excuse for more modest wedding celebrations, since there is less need for the parents to impress each other, and less of a tendency for them to quarrel between the time of the engagement and the marriage.⁹ Still, many parents sense — correctly — that unless they themselves choose their children's marriage partners, the stability of the whole traditional pattern of family life will be threatened. Actually, love-marriages often do alter many lifelong responsibilities and relationships traditionally assigned to specific family members of the married couple. With the trend toward love-marriages, there is also a greater possibility of inter-marriage, either between *Kala* and *Gora* Bene Israel, or of marriage outside the Bene Israel community altogether. To date, however, the strong preference for marriage within the community still remains.

Instances of a man keeping more than one wife are rare nowadays, although Jews in India are not governed by the 1955 Hindu Marriage Act which forbids polygamy to Hindus, Buddhists, Jains and Sikhs. As regards marriage, the Jews of India are bound by their own religious laws. Bene Israel marriage customs (as distinct from religious marriage laws) have been changing rather rapidly and even drastically, sometimes leaving only vestiges of former usages. On the other hand, many Bene Israel still observe at home — no matter how modernized the actual wedding ceremony may be — the sequence of traditional Bene Israel marriage rituals, using the traditional accoutrements, even such things as a winnowing fan (a feature of the so-called *mehndi* ceremony).

Kinship terms, used as appellations, continue to be much in use, in common Indian fashion, on a generational basis, being applied also to those who are not one's real kin. Thus, non-relatives sufficiently older than oneself are addressed, in whatever language they speak, as "uncle" or "aunt", or (more rarely) as "father" or "mother"; persons more or less of one's own age-group as "brother" or "sister". A person younger than oneself is addressed simply by his/her given name, and this is acceptable too for persons of one's own age-group. Respect is expressed for persons of rank and for people in the professions by prefacing the given name with the person's proper title, for example: "Dr. Sarah" or "Mrs. Ruth".

By mid-20th century the average Bene Israel lived in a nuclear family household typically with one or both surviving paternal grandparents and/or perhaps one or two unmarried or widowed aunts or uncles, but in conditions which were much more crowded than those prevalent in the homes of the larger joint-family households of the 19th century. It is today considered quite proper for a couple to set up a separate household of their own, largely because this is the example set by modern, well-educated people, but also because it relieves the over-crowding. Whether the senior male in a family of today is the real "ruler" of the house depends on whether he himself happens to be a domineering and successful person. Families in the cities may accommodate relatives from rural areas who are attracted to the city by prospects of work, education or marriage. But the binding obligation, in the traditional sense, of being responsible to help one's kin-in-need is a value of the past. Today everyone is more on one's own, particularly among the Bene Israel in Bombay, who find it very difficult to make a living even just for themselves. Kinship ties are meaningful today primarily in respect of the various rites of passage and are otherwise no longer so important.

Until mid-20th century the Bene Israel, especially the women (and through them their children) maintained and strengthened their Judaism through the medium of their familiar, dearly-loved folk-songs : songs regularly sung by the entire family at home at the close of the Sabbath; songs sung by the women at the time of marriages and at other important times in the life-cycle. There were the songs sung by the women during the *mehndi* ceremony; and songs traditionally sung by the bride's friends while she is sitting on a swing[10] (the Indian melody – used also for non-Jewish marriages – imitated and evoked the rhythm of swinging; but in the Marathi text of the Bene Israel the blessings of Abraham, Isaac, Jacob, Moses and Elijah were invoked). Four days before the wedding (and four days before the rice was ground for the wedding feast) the women sang a song which described an offering presented on a tray of gold covered with a gold-embroidered cloth, and being sent to the bridegroom "to the palace of the Patriarch Abraham". Other songs were sad, being sung at the moment when the bride left her mother's house. The content and melodies of these Bene Israel folksongs were similar to those wedding songs of their non-Jewish Indian neighbors, but the characters mentioned in the Bene Israel songs belonged exclusively to the Old Testament.[11]

The songs were in simple Marathi or Hindustani. Some had been set to music for the Bene Israel by British or American missionaries or by Bene Israel themselves, some of whom were known by name, others unknown. For some songs there were several different melodies. As for contents, they related stories from the Old Testament, or included Old Testament characters (especially the patriarchs and the Prophet Elijah) conceptualized as actual participants at a given Bene Israel ceremony, or simply invoked for their blessings. Some songs were purely devotional; others were lullabies. The blend of music and words very effectively evoked the desired moods and emotions. Although the custom of women singing together to celebrate the various rites of passage is very Indian, the texts sung on such occasions by the Bene Israel were unique to their community. An individual, today in his forties, recalls that as a small child he always used to cry at the sad parts of the song about Joseph and his brothers. Older respondents, who had attended Christian mission or convent schools, have remarked that even if there was only one Jewish pupil at a given school at any given time, the Marathi songs their own mothers used to sing about the Bible and various Jewish precepts "stuck in their minds" and kept them staunch Jews. The refrain of one song is : "We are the children of Jacob. We must not worship graven images."

But today only the older Bene Israel women remember these songs well enough to enable those interested to record at least some of them before they are lost forever. Too many ultra-modern Bene Israel mothers today in India know very little of Judaism which they might pass on to their children, an ignorance true of too many Jews elsewhere as well.

Especially in the first half of the 20th century, a noticeable dichotomy among urban Bene Israel resulted from two different patterns of raising children. On the one hand there were the self-segregated Jewish orthodox Bene Israel families who sent their children to Hindu schools and whose friends were Hindu and Muslim, but – deliberately – not Christian. Other Bene Israel families sent their children to Christian schools; such families may or may not have lived according to orthodox Jewish tradition, but they did tend to be more westernized, modern, fashionable; and a few members of such families actually converted to Christianity. There was another kind of loss to the community; one due to bigotry on the part of its non-liberal element, who were the actual leaders of the community. The case of Rebeka and Simeon Walkar is a good example. Both were very cosmopolitan and modern in their outlook, and completely dissociated themselves from Judaism and from the Bene Israel community, without adopting any other religion instead. Rebeka studied midwifery and ayurvedic medicine, and earned a diploma from Grant Medical College. From a lecture hall in her "Temple of Hygiene" she explained to public gatherings about sanitation and medicine for the layman. She and her husband were reformers, educators and philanthropists. When Rebeka died, her husband wrote her biography in Marathi. It was rendered into English by I.A.Isaac.[12] Reviewing it in 1926, Khan Bahadur Jacob Bapuji Israel wrote in *The Israelite* :

> A quarter of a century ago the Walkar family was well known not only among the Bene Israel, but among all the communities of Bombay. Mr. Isaac does not mention however, in the Life [i.e. the biography of his wife] the fact that Rebekah and her husband left the Jewish fold....The reasons were social, about 30 years ago the community was very intolerant and could not brook any departure from certain fixed modes of worship and thought. If only the community had allowed the Walkars to follow their own ideas and ideals so long as they were good, the family would have remained Bene Israel, but as it is, the family is lost to the community.[13]

In 1875 the Bene Israel community had excommunicated Simeon Benjamin Walkar calling him a Brahmo, an atheist and a Christian.[14]

By the beginning of the second quarter of the 20th century there were liberal Bene Israel voices speaking out in their journals and conferences and forming progressive institutions, such as the Jewish Religious Union (see below, pp.235 –7); although most Bene Israel remained basically conservative. Yet, during the 20th century so many traditional Bene Israel folk-customs have been given up completely by all Bene Israel. However, certain distinctively Bene Israel customs related to rites of passage, as well as to the all-encompassing feature of the *Malida* ritual, are still being observed; and faith in the prophet Elijah remains potent.[15] Most 20th century Bene Israel continue to perform the household *Malida* ceremony as a votive offering, or as a thanks offering. There are also modern reasons for its performance, such as, for instance, on the occasion of emigrating to Israel.

NOTES

1. The older synagogues were relatively well off. In 1917, for instance, Shaare Ha-Rachamim, the first Bene Israel synagogue, had an estate which yielded Rs. 982/- per month, a considerable sum in those days.
2. The Khojas are followers of the Aga Khan and belong to the Shia sect of Islam. They are mainly traders, originally from Gujarat.
3. Strizower : *The Children of Israel, The Bene Israel of Bombay*, p.59.
4. There is a *halachic* limit to the permissible area within which one is allowed to walk during Sabbath. *The American Jewish Year Book*, (prepared by the American Jewish Committee and published by the Jewish Publication Society of America, Philadelphia, 1953) Volume 54, p.420, lines 19 – 27, discusses *halachic* considerations relating to transportation on the Sabbath, as follows :

> An interesting innovation in Bombay is the use of special bus and tram tickets for Jews on the Sabbath and holidays to enable them to travel without handling money, a practice that has been followed for more than thirty years. Its authority is based on the passage in the Talmud Tractate *Sabbath* (Ch. 16) mentioning that what is used by the non-Jew (in this case public vehicles) may be made use of by the Jew, and on the decision given by Haham Abdulla Somekh of Baghdad in the second volume of *Zivhe Tzedek*, permitting travelling by train within city limits. This is being subjected to various interpretations and further inquiry.

5. Both Reform and Conservative Judaism developed in mid-19th century as religious alternatives to rigid orthodoxy in response to the social, educational and cultural emancipation of Jews from their former Ghetto restrictions. Actually, the Conservative Movement (i.e. the less radical break with tradition) developed not in rebellion against Jewish Orthodoxy, but rather because of dissatisfaction with the extremes of the Reform Movement.
6. Israel Cohen : *The Journal of a Jewish Traveler*, The Bodley Head, J. Lane, London, 1925, pp.254 & 255.
7. The suspended glass for this lamp is filled with three parts of water on top of which floats one part of oil (coconut or sesame oil). A slice of raw potato floats on the oil and has a sliver of bamboo protruding from it. The entire length of the sliver is wrapped in cotton and serves as a wick. These lamps keep lit for 24 hours without any need of pouring in additional oil. Such lamps were often set in a frame of two concentric circles, the inner with six glasses (used for the Sabbath) and the outer with seven-used in the days when oil was not so expensive.
8. Margaret Anne Sood : *The Urban Middle Class Family in India*, pp.30, 31, 33.
9. Strizower, op. cit., p.89.
10. In many places it is traditional for Hindu bridal couples to hold court (as it were) while seated on a swing, just as the Hindu deities Krishna and Radha are sometimes depicted together. A large smooth plank of fine wood, suspended from the ceiling by metal chains, is a truly indigenous kind of furnishing found inside many South Indian homes; and beautifully ornamented swings (seating two persons), suspended from frames based firmly on the ground are as numerous in variety of design as are the many different folk-art styles in North and Central India.
11. It would be interesting to make a comparative study of the traditional Marathi (and Hindustani) folksongs of the Bene Israel women and of the Cochin Jewish women's traditional Malayalam folksongs. The present author, under a research grant from the Yad Hanadiv (Rothschild Foundation) collected extant notebooks of Cochin Jewish women's folksongs in Malayalam, and is working on this project, together with Professor P.M.Jussay (recently retired Head of the Department of Humanities at Calicut Regional Engineering College, Calicut, Kerala) who is making translations of these songs into English; and with Dr. Barbara Johnson (Hudson), an anthropologist who has studied Cochin Jewish Chronicles and whose doctoral dissertation *"Our Community" in Two Worlds : The Cochin Paradesi Jews in India and in Israel* discusses the maintenance of tradition by Cochin Jewish women, past and present. Many of the words of their folksongs are of medieval usage. The songs will be analyzed from the points of view of history, linguistics, musicology and folklore; and will be compared with similar Malayalam folksongs of non-Jewish communities in Kerala. The entire collection of recordings and texts has been deposited in the Israel National Phonoteque Archives of the Jewish National and Hebrew University Library in Jerusalem, as documentation and for further study.
12. Simeon Benjamin Walkar : *Rebeka Simeon Benjamin Walkar* (in Marathi); translated into English by I.A. Isaac, Calcutta, 1925.
13. *The Israelite*, Vol. X, Nos. 3 & 4, March-April 1926, pp.39-40.
14. *The Bene Israel Review*, Vol. 1, No.11 12, 1926, p.8.
15. In Israel, young Bene Israel couples sometimes vow a pilgrimage to, coupled with performance of the *brit milah* (circumcision) at, Prophet Elijah's cave (in Haifa), if a son should be born to them.

Chapter 24
Bene Israel Places of Worship in the Twentieth Century

During the first half of the 20th century there had been a large increase in Bene Israel population and several new places of worship were added to those established in the 19th century : some were entirely new congregations; others were formed when already established congregations split into two separate groups.

In Bombay

In 1904 the congregation of the Tiferet Israel Prayer Hall (founded in 1886 at Jacob Circle) split up : the old one remained at 92 K.K.Marg, Clerk Road, and a new one was also formed. In 1931 the latter built the *Magen Hassidim* Synagogue at 8 Moreland Road, Jacob Circle. Both houses of prayer are still functioning today.

The Jewish Religious Union (see below, pp.235 – 7 was established in 1925, but not until 1959 did they occupy premises of their own, at 23 Sussex Road, Byculla. The synagogue of this congregation is called *Rodef Shalom*.

Kurla Bene Israel Prayer Hall, at 275 S.C.Barve Road, Kurla West.

Parel Bene Israel Prayer Hall, at 28b Elphinstone Road, Parel; started in 1930, it closed in 1978.

A Prayer Room in Bandra, originally intended for, and is still used only on the High Holidays.

In Kulaba District :

In addition to those 19th century synagogues referred to above on p. 149, S.J. Kolabkar (p. 3) mentions the following congregations without, however, giving the date for the year of founding :

    Congregation in *Ghosale-Virjoli* (Satambe), Roha Taluka.

    Murud, Murud Mahal.

    Shriwardhan, Shriwardhan Mahal.

In New Delhi :

On Bene Israel initiative, the Judah Hyam Hall, at 2 Humayun Road, was dedicated in 1956 to be used as a Prayer Hall and Jewish Community Center by all Jews who happen to be in the nation's capital.

Dedicated Jewish teachers from Cochin had worked among the Bene Israel during the first half of the 19th century. Later, a constant, though small stream of Cochin Jews kept coming to settle in and near Bombay until well into the 20th century. Most of these later immigrants from Cochin were Malabari ("Black") Jews from the Kadavambakkam Synagogue in Cochin. They gained employment in Bombay mills and as *hazanim* in the growing number of Bene Israel places of worship.

At mid-20th century there were in Bombay eight fully active places of worship functioning the year round. But this does not mean that they attracted enough persons in daily attendance to warrant holding regular daily prayer services. However, most of them conducted services every Sabbath and on all Jewish holidays. What usually distinguishes a synagogue from a prayer hall is the fact that the former consists of a special separate building (sometimes with a few buildings in a separate compound) owned by the congregation and it has its own *mikveh* (ritual bath place); while a prayer hall usually consists of just one or two rented rooms[1] of a building, the other rooms of which may be used for non-Jewish purposes; and there is no *mikveh*. But a prayer hall has the same sort of membership fees, officers and administration as does a synagogue. As in many modern Jewish communities elsewhere, the advent of plumbing facilities within one's own home reduced the importance and use of the community *mikveh* to the point where it has all but disappeared except among the orthodox. A *mikveh* is used for the ritual of conversion to Judaism; also it is available to any Jew for other ritual purposes.

Bene Israel places of worship are struggling to remain the focal points of community life, even though they lack their former dynamic vitality. In Bombay these places of worship are located in the poorer neighbourhoods except for Rodef Shalom which is in a better class section of Byculla. Early in the modern period most urban Bene Israel had adjusted to new conditions by riding and even going to work on the Sabbath. Those living at a distance commute to places of worship on the Jewish holidays, to recite the *Mourner's Kaddish* prayer, to attend rites of passage, and occasionally for Friday evening or Saturday morning services. On the other hand, there are some orthodox Bene Israel individuals, not only in Bombay, but also in Poona, Delhi and elsewhere, who either walk long distances to the nearest house of prayer on each Sabbath, or else they say the Sabbath prayers and perform the Sabbath *kiddush* and *havdala* ceremonies at home.

To fill the *kiddush* cup, in synagogue or at home, a juice made of raisins is, more often than not, used instead of wine. In the synagogue a large full silver goblet is held by the *hazan* (or by the father of the family, if at home) as he recites the *kiddush*, after which he takes a sip from the goblet, then pours the rest into a larger container from which is decanted into small wine glasses one portion for each person present. Or, as Rev. Lord described it in 1907 (*The Jews in India and the Far East*, p. 27) : two little silver cups were filled alternately until each person present has had a sip.

At least during the first half of the 20th century the Sabbath for most Bene Israel retained a distinctly Jewish atmosphere : hymns were sung by all the family together; the food, prepared on Friday, was kept continuously warm; and even for those who may have gone to work, once at home, it was the Sabbath for them.

Modern education did divert Bene Israel from many traditional Jewish paths just as it did for Jews elsewhere. Early in the century (1913) Rebecca Reuben perceptively wrote about the Bene Israel that :

English education so far has proved a centrifugal force, which tends to cut off all English-educated members from the community (in language, dress and social customs). While believing that Anglicisation is both inevitable and desirable....[the Anglo-Jewish Association and the Israelite School] should fight against the growing indifference to and the alienation from Jewish ideals and moral, religious and institutional influences. We must make the Bene Israel understand and appreciate Judaism in harmony with Anglicisation and modernization.[2]

And such alienation was indeed avoided in some cases by intelligent flexibility. Similar to the modern development of synagogue sisterhoods in the west, a Ladies Association was established in the Poona Bene Israel congregation. There was serious opposition to the Poona ladies' request to hold meetings of their association in the synagogue (on the grounds that some women might attend meetings during their menses and thus pollute the synagogue). But one of the influential male members of the community was able to persuade the men of the congregation to allow the women to hold meetings in the synagogue, arguing that : "We know that our women on their own never come to the synagogue during menses; so why not trust them that they will also be honorable about the matter in regard to attendance at their Ladies' Association meetings in the synagogue?" Thus the women gained permission to hold their meetings in the synagogue, and another dimension was added to the synagogue's functions. In Bombay the women of congregation Rodef Shalom also began to express themselves through a sisterhood group. And, in the 1960s the first female was installed as a synagogue official : a woman held the office of synagogue treasurer for two terms at the Magen Hassidim Synagogue in Bombay.

The premises of Bene Israel synagogues and prayer halls were never used solely for the purpose of worship. They served, and still do, as venues for most social events; meeting places for the congregation; or as a place just for idle chats; as overnight shelters for out-of-towners (in an adjoining room or small building on the synagogue premises); the site of the community's administrative offices and bulletin boards; a place where the children are taught how to read and how to chant the prayers. In order really to understand Hebrew as a spoken language, however, some Bene Israel children are given private lessons; and also they used to have lessons in Hebrew and in Jewish studies as part of the curriculum either at the Bene Israel or at the Baghdadi school.

In Bombay, where there are several Bene Israel places of worship, there is no longer one overall leader of the entire Bene Israel community as the Commodan had been in former times. Each congregation is autonomous, and its leadership is usually in the hands, not of the more highly educated and wealthier Bene Israel, but of the less well educated and poorer clerk elements, who are more truly representative of the majority of the Bene Israel. Synagogue or prayer hall members pay very modest annual dues,[3] and in return are entitled to pay low fees for private use of synagogue halls and facilities (inclusive of cooking and serving utensils, seating arrangements, etc.) for various kinds of functions and rites of passage. The synagogue's main source of income is by no means from membership fees, but rather from rental of its premises and from gifts well invested over the years. The synagogue, on its part, annually makes donations to the Israelite (Kadoorie) School, the Orphans Home, funds for destitutes, and cemetery maintenance —while the synagogue has representatives on the committees of each of these institutions.

The Shaar Ha-Rachamim Synagogue, the oldest in Bombay, in 1906 was entrusted with an estate of seven warehouses. The income received from this property is used by the synagogue for charitable and administrative purposes. Synagogue property is held by the Synagogue Trustees, and each synagogue trust is registered under the Bombay Public Trusts Act of 1950.

The salaried synagogue officers are kept busy with their essential duties, but are not accorded any special marks of respect therefor.[4] Among the Bene Israel there were, and are, no *cohanin*. Sometimes, however, a non-Bene Israel *cohen* may be present at services and he will then at least give the special priestly blessing and be invited to read from the *Torah*.

Early in the 20th century many educated Bene Israel had lost patience with the (to them) meaningless rattling of Hebrew prayers, and with the un-inspiring concerns and quarrels of synagogue management and congregants. Some urged Bene Israel synagogues to adopt the instructional discussions and adult *Torah*-study groups which had always played an important role in houses of worship (orthodox, conservative and reform) elsewhere. A report of the Bombay Shaar Ha-Rachamim Synagogue conveys the feeling of the situation then prevailing, in such remarks as :

> Hitherto we have had *Hazans* or prayer-readers either Bene Israel, Cochin Jews or Bagdhdad Jews whose function has been nothing more than to read prayers during the service and to conduct ceremonies. Almost all of these persons have been ignorant of the Hebrew language, i.e. they did not understand it....The *Hazan* should be not only a prayer-reader but also a minister, and should lead a life of the highest morality....We leave it to our brethren to decide for themselves whether our past *Hazans* have fulfilled this condition....Our *Hazan* should be competent to teach our brethren especially the younger generation, the tenets of our religion and to explain to them the ethics and the morals of our religion....For this we require a man who understands and who has studied the principles of the Jewish religion....a person who is to administer to the spiritual needs of the community must be a Bene Israel because firstly he must understand their language....and secondly, only a Bene Israel can best appreciate the feelings and sentiments of the people, as he would know their peculiar habits and customs....and will be able to understand everybody and be able to converse freely even with the most backward person....we shall have to select a suitable young man from among our community and send him for training to the Jews College in England....such a trained minister should conduct synagogue services and on Saturdays and holidays deliver suitable sermons to the congregation....his services should be placed at the services of the School Committee for employment as Principal of the Israelite School. The teaching of Hebrew and religion in the school should be entrusted to his care....He may be sent on tours of religious lectures to stations where Bene Israel reside in numbers....agreement will have to be entered into by them [the trained ministers] to serve the Synagogue for a certain number of years, say ten....and there should be a life insurance and an endowment policy for the minister at the end of twenty or twenty-five years of approved service.... if no funds can be spared immediately for this purpose .... the latest by which the first man should be sent out to England should be in the year 1928 and the second one in the following year....[5]

But, as in the case of Kehimkar's insights, the congregation did not concert its efforts towards implementing those suggestions. To combat "the spirit of doubtfulness running through the discussions on communal and religious questions", another wise suggestion was made (by Benjamin David Shahapurkar) : to utilize some of the synagogue's Rs.980/- per month income to purchase and maintain a library of books of Jewish interest. This too prompted no effective action. A couple of Bene Israel synagogues, however, did start Sabbath classes for ladies to read and explain to them in Marathi the weekly portion of the Torah (from the Pentateuch) and the *Haftarah* (the concluding portion, from other books of the Old Testament).

Some Bene Israel congregations have affiliated themselves to the World Council of Synagogues[6] (Conservative Judaism), others to the Union of Orthodox Jewish congregations of America, without, indeed, much actual change in their beliefs, practices or prayer-services. However, a Bene Israel woman physician was responsible for a true innovation : the setting up in 1925 of the Jewish Religious Union by a small group of highly educated and financially better-off Bene Israel who chose to adopt the liberal Judaism of England to which Dr. Jerusha Jhirad (back from her medical training in England) had introduced them. This new group, the Jewish Religious Union of Bombay, was one of the founding members (1926) in London of the World Union of Progressive

Judaism. It continues to follow the Union's reforms and type of religious service, at which men and women sit together (unlike the customary separate balcony or area set aside for women only). The new group received some assistance (in the form of literature and prayer books) from the world body. The Jewish community of Hamburg (Germany) donated a beautiful *Sefer Torah* with silver crowns, pointer and shield. It was only in the 1950s that the Bombay congregation of the Jewish Religious Union began to receive financial aid from circles of Progressive Judaism outside India, and this enabled them to become the only Bene Israel congregation ever to have a resident, qualified Rabbi. For a few months in 1951-2 Rabbi Bernard Heller (from the U.S.A.) conducted classes for adults and youths of the Bombay Jewish Religious Union; he also started the Young Men and Women's Hebrew Association (YMWHA) of Bombay. In 1954-5 a student rabbi, Richard Israel (also from the U.S.A.), ministered to the congregation. Then, in August 1957, Rabbi Hugo Gryn, born in Europe and ordained by the Reform Rabbinate in the U.S.A., came to the Bombay Jewish Religious Union and was formally inducted as Rabbi of that congregation by Rabbi Ezekiel Musleah of the Baghdadi Jewish community of Calcutta and a graduate of the Jewish Theological Seminary of America. During Rabbi Gryn's tenure of more than two full years, the congregation grew from about 60 to more than 300 members, his influence, however, extending far beyond the members of his own synagogue, now called Rodef Shalom. All services at Rodef Shalom were well attended, as were also its Hebrew language and Jewish religion classes for children and for adults, Hebrew-school teacher-training classes, Youth Group[7] (which once a month was given the honor of conducting the Friday night service), the Sisterhood, and several committees. Not only were special Bar Mitzvah services held for boys, but Confirmation Services were also instituted for girls. Even some orthodox parents joined this Reform synagogue hoping that its modern approach might better appeal to their own children and thus succeed in keeping them within the fold of Judaism. Baghdadi Jews often came to listen to lectures by Rabbi Gryn, and Rodef Shalom had three or four Baghdadi regular members. Some Europeans and Yemenites also joined the congregation.

Rabbi Gryn was succeeded by Rabbi Elisha Nativ (born in Israel), another Reform Rabbi, who remained with the congregation about three years. The salaries for these rabbis were paid partly by the Rodef Shalom congregation, and partly by the World Union for Progressive Judaism and by the U.S. National Federation of Temple Sisterhoods. In 1959 the Rodef Shalom congregation bought premises of their own, occupying a large hall in an upper storey of a building located at 23 Sussex Road, Byculla. To help them pay for this purchase, they borrowed Rs.50,000/- from the Victor Sassoon Trust (which later wrote off the debt), and from the Union of American Hebrew Congregations. A young Bene Israel man had been sent to the U.S.A. on a scholarship given by the National Federation of Temple Sisterhoods, to be trained for the Reform Rabbinate at Hebrew Union College in Cincinnati, Ohio in the hope that he would subsequently take up the pulpit at Rodef Shalom. Unfortunately this did not materialize; in fact, instead, the American Rabbinate now has a Bene Israel rabbi.

Following Rabbi Nativ's departure, the congregation continued to function on its own as best it could, guided by the teachings and inspiration of their former rabbis and of the wives of those rabbis. Even in the 1970s, when membership in all Bene Israel synagogues had been steadily declining, the rate of decline was smallest at Rodef Shalom, which even now still continues to attract the younger generation.

Not many of the better-educated clerk-class belong to the Rodef Shalom group. Most Bene Israel still look upon members of Rodef Shalom as being of a higher social status than they themselves. The fact that Rodef Shalom practises a liberal, reform Judaism is to them, a matter of only secondary concern. It is interesting that some members of Rodef Shalom have retained their membership in their original orthodox synagogue as well, where their "higher status" does not qualify them for general community leadership or representation. As a matter of fact, the opposite is true.

Whether orthodox or reform, Bene Israel have real respect for and appreciation of the several other religions of their neighbours, with whom many Bene Israel have an intimate friendship without it ever impinging upon their own community affiliation and religion. Yet, typically, they do not encourage non-Jews to attend their synagogues or prayer halls during services (this is not true of the prayer hall in New Delhi), although they frequently invite non-Jews to the synagogue as guests for social functions; and they, in turn, are invited as guests to non-Jewish functions and ceremonies. In many respects the relation of the Bene Israel community as a whole to its non-Jewish neighbours parallels that of the free atmosphere of American Jewish life.

Before closing this chapter on Bene Israel places of worship, what about the Bene Israel synagogues and prayer halls in small towns and villages? Because of the mass emigration to Israel on the part of Bene Israel coming directly from the Konkan *villages* (which occurred later than the mass exodus to Israel from the cities) in the late 1960s and first half of the 1970s, the rural Bene Israel congregations are today too small to maintain their local synagogues. Even though there is still some income from the synagogue land holdings rented out to tenant farmers, there are so very few worshippers at each synagogue that they are unable to pay the taxes due on the synagogue land and property. In several cases, however, the few Bene Israel villagers who do remain do not agree as a group to sell the synagogue and its property, since doing so would deprive them of the synagogue which is dear to them even if they are too few to constitute a *minyan*.

NOTES

1. Except for the Aitz Hayim Prayer Hall which owns the building in which it is located; but it occupies only a large hall in this building, the rest is rented out. Congregation Rodef Shalom at the beginning owned only its own hall, which is located in a large building the rest of which was only later acquired by the congregation.
2. Rebecca Reuben : *The Bene Israel of Bombay*, Cambridge Jewish Publications 4, Cambridge University Press, 1913, p.19.
3. This is in stark contrast to the prevailing custom in synagogues in the United States, for instance, which charge very steep membership fees needed to pay for the luxurious facilities which they offer, for the rabbi's salary, etc.
4. This is similar to the Hindu attitude toward a *pujari* priest (but not toward holy men and *gurus*) whose position is purely that of religious technicians adept at performing the necessary rituals and does not necessarily imply any particular honor or status other than that to which the *pujari* is entitled by virtue of his Brahmin caste as such (if he is a Brahmin). However, *pujaris* are not always Brahmins, especially not in connection with ritual for worship of minor local deities. *Pujaris* of deities which are believed to prevent contagious disease are always of the lower castes. The *pujaris* of the guardian goddesses of Chaul in Kolaba District belong to a low caste (*Folklore of the Konkan* : pp. 1-2, 21, 23, 24).
5. *The Israelite*, Volume VIII, Nos. 3-4, March-April 1924, pp. 35-9.
6. The first meeting of the United Synagogues of India, an affiliate of the World Council of Synagogues, took place on Jaunary 16, 1960. Through their membership in this organization Bene Israel synagogues have received (from the U.S.A.) Torah scrolls, prayer books, *talesim*, *tefilin*, *mezuzot*, Hebrew language texts, and also a scholarship for study in Israel.
   As of 1981 this Youth Group was still very popular and had 78 members in regular attendance!

Chapter 25
Bene Israel Publications of the Twentieth Century

As a logical outgrowth of 19th century patterns, at the turn of the century there came a spurt of Bene Israel writings in Marathi on a variety of Jewish subjects, many being based on Biblical stories (the *kirtan* technique) with such titles as *The Life of Esther in Verse* (1890), *Daniel's Moral Courage* (1894), *The Song of Daniel, a six-act musical* (1899), or *The Song of Joseph, a musical in three acts* (1906), all by Solomon Shalom Aptekar who, after 1919, also published a number of plays.[1] But Bene Israel publication in the 20th century was mainly in the field of periodicals. Before going into this matter, however, deserving of mention are two very different, little-known publications, each important in its own way : in the publication of one a Bene Israel was very instrumental; and the other was authored by a Bene Israel.

The former is a rare series of five volumes, beautifully bound and printed, called *Wonderful Testimonies*, with the Hebrew title *P'La-ot Aydot*.[2] The series was published by Pandita Ramabai,[3] Mukti Mission Press, Kedgaon, 1910-11. A Bene Israel, Aaron Jacob Divekar, not only ran the Mukti Mission Press but he was of great assistance to Pandita Ramabai in translating from Hebrew into Marathi.[4] *Wonderful Testimonies* is remarkable not so much because it contains all the books of the Old Testament in Hebrew, but because beneath the Hebrew text on each page, verse for verse, there appear *four* well-known translations of the Bible into English which differ from one another in certain details;[5] and there are copious footnotes which give additional meaning(s) or variant etymologies for certain Hebrew words or roots occurring within the text. This work is not mentioned in any of *The Bene Israel Annual and Year Book* lists of publications; nor is it mentioned by Fischel or Yaari; nor is it listed in any of the several world catalogues on the Bible. *Wonderful Testimonies* seems to have been compiled as a preliminary to Pandita Ramabai's Marathi translation of both the Old and the New Testaments of the Bible. It was probably not listed by Miss Reuben in the list of Bene Israel Publications because it was not essentially a Bene Israel production. 50,000 copies of Pandita Ramabai's *Marathi* translation of the Bible were printed.[6] It would be interesting to learn how many, if any, of these 50,000 copies wound up in the homes of Bene Israel families.

I.A. Ezekiel does not appear in any list of Bene Israel authors, but he was born of a Bene Israel family and did write an uncommon book. He is a journalist and a free-lance writer and for some years was Principal of a college of journalism in Bombay. Although active on behalf of the short-lived Jewish Nationalist party in his youth, he soon dissociated himself from the Bene Israel community and things Jewish, and this makes it more rather than less interesting that he should have written *Sarmad, Jewish Saint of India*[7] (See above, p. 186), a Judaica curiosity. Although the text of the book contains very little original writing and tells very little about Sarmad's life, it is replete with parallel ideas to Sarmad's, quoting from other mystics of various other times, places and religions. It is important because it includes 321 quatrains (*rubaiyats*) attributed to

Sarmad, in English translation.[8] There is no other translation into English of so many quatrains attributed to Sarmad.[9]

Of all the new Bene Israel periodicals which appeared in the 20th century, the most significant were those published between 1916 and 1930 (See Appendix 8, p.367). The period between 1916 and 1922 witnessed a very lively dialogue between two new English-Marathi monthlies : i.e. *The Friend of Israel* (1916-21) and *The Israelite* (1917-27). The former was succeeded, if only briefly, by *The Bene Israel Review* (1925-26) which also had both English and Marathi sections. A separate publication called *Prasangik Vichar* (Occasional Thoughts) used to appear irregularly as the vehicle for S.S. Mazgaonkar's trenchant comments on current affairs and personages, in Marathi. Sometimes the Bene Israel Marathi periodicals would carry an occasional article in English. Many pamphlets on controversial issues were privately published, either in Marathi or in English.

Rebecca Reuben issued a monthly Marathi paper for Bene Israel children, called *Nofeth* (a Hebrew word meaning flowing honey or honeycomb). Although this publication continued for only about three and a half years, it was extremely popular, and copies are still in demand among Bene Israel for teaching children about their Jewish religion and heritage.

The most enduring Bene Israel periodical has been *Maccabi* : from 1946 through 1971 it appeared regularly as a Marathi monthly; even now it still is being published two or three times a year. From 1959 to 1961 Baruch B. Benjamin edited, out of Delhi, a bulletin in English called *And Ye Shall Teach Them* which aimed at being "published occasionally for the educational, social, cultural and religious uplift of the Bene Israel community of India". B.B. Benjamin and his bulletin favoured Conservative Judaism and its World Council of Synagogues. Its rival, the Union of Orthodox Congregations in India, issued a journal called *Mebasser* (Messenger).

To go into further detail about one of these publications : *The Israelite* was founded in January 1917 by David S. Erulkar. At first it appeared monthly, but after two to three years it began coming out six times a year. It was about equally divided between a section in English and a section in Marathi. The two sections differed in their contents, the Marathi one being more lively and presenting a fuller picture of the Bene Israel community of those days. Each issue contained "Domestic Announcements" (of births, deaths, marriages and other notices and advertisements of interest to the Bene Israel wherever they were living in India); it also featured "think pieces", mostly by the editor, on all sorts of Jewish as well as non-Jewish matters; reports on proceedings of the Bene Israel Conference, the All India Israelite League, Bene Israel synagogues and other institutions; articles on Jewish subjects, including Zionism, reprinted verbatim from Jewish and non-Jewish publications throughout the rest of the world; current accounts of the British Viceroyalty year by year (usually, but not always, refraining from expressing or discussing opinions about these matters); and articles relating to India's Independence Movement. The Marathi section regularly published a whole series of translations of stories from the *Talmud*, as well as dissertations on liberal Judaism (also translated into Marathi). *The Israelite* sometimes published articles which had no perceptible link whatever to the general sphere of interest of the periodical or to the community which it served. Thus it would reprint entire articles taken from publications outside India, too often with insufficient data as to their source. But, on the whole, *The Israelite* was a most worthwhile and significant vehicle of information for the Bene Israel community. Its founder, David Erulkar, served as editor until December 1922 when he was succeeded by I.J. Samson, then a practising lawyer, later a Judge of the Small Causes Court in Bombay. In February 1926 Samson was succeeded by Khan Bahadur Jacob Bapuji Israel who continued as editor through publication of the last issue of *The Israelite*, i.e. Volume XI, Nos. 5-6, May-June 1927.

A few Bene Israel authors, in fields other than journalism and translation, appeared on the scene in the 20th century. In the field of history, Hayeem S. Kehimkar had already completed his masterwork in 1897, although this was not actually published in book form until 1937. In 1948 Moses Ezekiel published a small booklet called *History and Culture of the Bene-Israel in India* (see below, Bibliography) which supplements Kehimkar with a few additional details and goes on with some facts about the Bene Israel of the 20th century. Shellim Samuel, in his *A Treatise on the Origin and Early History of the Beni-Israel of Maharashtra State*, published in 1963 (see below, Bibliography), explores his chosen subject in great depth. Most scholarly of all is Benjamin J. Israel whose writings (see below, Bibliography) reflect meticulous research.

As for purely creative writing on the part of 20th century Bene Israel, Joseph David Penkar (see above, p.208 was prolific in writing filmscripts, stage plays and biblical *kirtans*. The single Bene Israel writer of world-wide acclaim is the poet, Nissim Ezekiel. Born in 1924, he is (and so regards himself as) essentially an Indian poet writing in English. Among his published writings are : *A Time to Change*, Fortune Press, London, 1952; *Sixty Poems*, Strand Book Shop, Bombay, 1953; *The Third*, Street Book Shop, Bombay, 1959; *The Unfinished Man*, Writers' Workshop, Calcutta, 1960; *Indian Writers in Conference*, P.E.N. All India Centre, Bombay, 1964; *The Exact Name*, Writers' Workshop, Calcutta, 1965; *Writing in India Today*, P.E.N. All India Centre, Bombay, 1965; *An Emerson Reader*, Popular Prakashan, Bombay, 1965; *Three Plays*, Writers' Workshop, Calcutta, 1969; *A Martin Luther King Reader*, Popular Prakashan, Bombay, 1969; *Snakeskin and Other Poems*, Poems by Indira Sant, translated from the Marathi in collaboration with Vrinda Nabar, Popular Prakashan, Bombay, 1974; *Hymns in Darkness*, Oxford University Press, Delhi, 1976. His Sahitya Akademy Award-winning volume of poems entitled *Latter-Day Psalms* (also Oxford University Press) annotates biblical psalms in verse.

A set of two books, each with the title *Gate of Mercy, "Shaar Haraḥamim" Synagogue* on its cover and the title *The Religious and Cultural Heritage of the Bene Israels of India* inside, were published in 1984 by E.M. Jacob Gadkar for the Gate of Mercy Synagogue, Bombay. The first, a book of 54 pages, is a collection of 136 black and white photographs mostly of Bene Israel personalities (some are reproductions of photos taken in the late 19th century) — individual portraits as well as group photos; also a few sites relevant to the Bene Israel; and interior and/or exterior views of most of the synagogues in India, be they Bene Israel, Cochini, or Baghdadi. The second volume (182 pages) contains 118 more photographs, mostly portraits, but is mainly devoted to anecdotes from or resumés of the lives of outstanding Bene Israel personages, interspersed with a potpourri of bits of information about various synagogues, about the Jewish religion, or Bene Israel history, folklore, institutions, etc; plus, at the bottom of every page, sayings of wisdom, most of them anonymous, with several attributed to specific non-Jews. The publication of a collection of so many photographs relating in one way or another to the Bene Israel (even if many of the photos are poorly reproduced) is a first-time, very valuable achievement. And, even though parts of the text are irrelevant, there is a wealth of detail contained within Volume II.

Meera Jacob Mendrekar Mahadevan, a Bene Israel woman, wrote several short stories and novellas in Hindi. A full-length novel of hers, entitled *Apna Ghar* (A Home of One's Own) was published in Hindi in 1961 by Rajkamal Prakashan Private Ltd., Delhi. In 1973 another edition of this book was published by Akshar Prakashan Private Ltd.,

Delhi. A translation into English of this novel was published in 1975 by Arnold Heinemann, Delhi, with a new title, *Shulamit*. It is an absorbing story of the various members of a Bene Israel family part of which emigrated to Israel and part of which remained in India, telling of the life-stories, motivations and ambivalencies of each of the characters. The present writer is unaware of any other novel ever written about the Bene Israel as such.

NOTES

1. This particular Bene Israel author was the first President of the Bombay Jewish Religious Union, the first and only Reform Jewish congregation of the Bene Israel.
2. The Israel National and Hebrew University Library in Jerusalem has Volumes I, III, IV and V of *Wonderful Testimonies*, kept among its rare books.
3. The appellation *Pandit* designates a Hindu Sanskrit scholar of the male sex; *Pandita* is applied to a female Sanskrit scholar. Pandita Ramabai (1858-1922) was indeed a learned Sanskrit scholar. She was widowed early in life. Though born a Brahmin, she converted to Christianity and established a home in Poona for the care, uplift and liberation of widows. She later established the Mukti·Mission in Kedgaon, a small town in Poona District, where she started her own press for printing Christian tracts. She taught the girls of her Widows' Home how to set type in Marathi, Hindi, English, and later in Greek and Hebrew. Padmini Sengupta, writing about *Pandita Ramabai Saraswati* (Asia Publishing House, Bombay & London, 1970), tells us that

   > Ramabai in the last two decades of her life, studied two new languages, Greek and Hebrew, in order to translate the Bible straight from the original. [p.291]....Miss Victoria Brazier and *a Jewish printer Mr. Aaron Jacob Divekar of the Bene Israel community played an important part in the publishing house*. [p.292] In 1904 she [Ramabai] started her translation of the Bible into Marathi....Ramabai began to feel more and more strongly that the Marathi in which the Bible had already been translated was not pure, but *Padri* or Missionary Marathi. With this was also combined the wish to eliminate Sanskritized allusions. [p.294]...When Ramabai did translate the Bible she made it simple enough for the lower class literate people to understand [p.293]....Pandita Ramabai is the only woman in the world who has translated the whole Bible single-handed, and from the· original Greek and Hebrew. She further achieved the superhuman task of having it published by her own girls in her own press. [p.296] [Emphasis supplied]

4. For titles of his own publications, see Appendix 8, pp. 359, 361, 362, 363.
5. The first translation is the King James Authorized Version. The other three have not been identified by the present author.
6. *The Bible in India* by J.S.M. Hooper, Oxford University Press, Humphrey Milford, London, 1938, explains that :

   > In 1807 the Serampore Press (Bengal) issued 1,000 copies of the Marathi *New Testament*, followed in 1819 by the *Old Testament*. The work was in the first instance done by a pandit (employed by William Carey)....But the pandit spoke a dialect (of Marathi) peculiar to a district near Nagpur, and the language thus proved useless for the general circulation in the Marathi country....It was hardly even a foundation on which others could build. [p.75]....the saintly Pandita Ramabai [wished] to produce a translation of her own of the whole *Bible* which she hoped would be more in harmony with the Marathi mind. *She was helped by a man of the Bene Israel community who knew Hebrew* [emphasis supplied] and by her own daughter Manoramabai who learnt *New Testament* Greek when she was in America. It is said that the excessive literalness of this version has in a number of places proved fatal to the Marathi idiom, and for this and other reasons her work remains as a monument to her love of the *Bible* rather than as a permanently valuable contribution to Marathi *Bible* translation. [p.82]

In passing, it is interesting to note that, toward the end of the 19th century, Pandita Ramabai helped David J. Solomon (Kurulkar), a member of the Bene Israel community, by paying for his room and board while he studied at Hebrew Union College (of the Reform Jewish Movement) in Cincinnati, Ohio, where he had received a scholarship covering his tuition. Upon graduation from this college he received the BHL Degree (Bachelor of Hebrew Literature). His hopes of obtaining a position at the Israelite School never materialized, and he therefore took no part in Bene Israel community activity thereafter. Here we have another example of Christian help in promoting Bene Israel knowledge of Judaism. But the outcome of this particular story also exemplifies Bene Israel ineptitude, in the failure to employ David J. Solomon at the Israelite School, not taking advantage of his academic Jewish education.

7. Issac A. Ezekiel *Sarmad Jewish Saint of India*, published by Radha Soami Satsang (a Hindu sect), Beas, Punjab, 1966; printed by N.K. Gossain & Co., Pt. Ltd., Calcutta; 384 pages.
8. Translated by Kashiram Aggarwal (Munshi Fazal) in cooperation with I.A. Ezekiel. This English translation was based on an Urdu translation of Sarmad's original Persian.
9. The only other translation *into English*, namely by B.A. Hashmi in his "Sarmad, His Life and Quatrains" (*Islamic Culture*, Vol. 7, 1933, pp.663-72 and Vol. 8, pp.92-104) contains only 55 quatrains. Hashmi maintains that various collections of Sarmad's Persian quatrains contain from 310 to 321 quatrains. Since some of these quatrains have also been attributed to other Persian poets, Hashmi has chosen to translate only those which have *not* also been attributed to other poets. Hashmi sticks strictly to quatrain format in his translations, but Ezekiel and Aggarwal do not usually do so. The resulting translations are so different from Hashmi's that it is difficult to identify each of the 55 quatrains translated into English by Hashmi among Ezekiel and Aggarwal's 321 translations.

Chapter 26
The Bene Israel Conference and the All India Israelite League

Not only had David S. Erulkar founded *The Israelite*; he was also one of the few persons who originally pressed for the establishment of a Bene Israel Conference for the community's general benefit. (The Parsi, Muslim, Christian and Jain minority communities, as well as Kayasth, Kunbi and other caste groups had already established Conferences for their respective communities.) The Bene Israel Conference was visualized as a central policy-making and coordinating body for the community as a whole; thus, it was hoped, it might counteract the tendency toward quarrelsome factionalism. But at the very first preparatory meeting for the Conference there was a split over the definition of the scope of the new body. At that meeting Khan Bahadur Jacob Bapuji Israel pointed out that every community was striving to protect its interests in the then emerging Independence Movement, and that the Bene Israel should see that, even if they got no new privileges, they did not lose their existing rights.[1] Following this statement there was considerable opposition against bringing political questions into the Conference, Jacob Bapuji Israel and David S. Erulkar withdrew, and the Conference decided that its objective would be "to deliberate upon social, religious, educational and economic questions *not of a political nature* affecting the Bene Israel community." The first general meeting of the Bene Israel Conference was held in Bombay from December 25 to 27, 1917, presided over by Dr. Joseph Benjamin Bamnolkar (of Ahmedabad). In his Presidential Address, following expressions of loyalty to the Throne and wishes for the success of Allied Arms and for lasting peace, he added:

> In this connection it may not perhaps be out of place to say that our holy city of Jerusalem has, we are rejoiced to learn, surrendered to British Arms, and His Majesty's Government has already declared itself in favour of the setting up in Palestine of a National Home for our people. Thus the desire of many of our coreligionists in the West to colonize there is within sight of fulfillment, and their dreams are likely to be realized.[2]

Little did any Bene Israel (or anyone else at that time) dream that the majority of the Bene Israel would some decades hence emigrate to Israel!

This First Bene Israel Conference passed 31 resolutions[3] on a variety of subjects including: recommendations to put an end to polygamy (resolution No. 6); to establish a free dispensary (No.11), a *Hevra Kedusha* burial society (No.12), a hostel for the Israelite School (No.13), an orphanage and widows' home (No.14), housing units for poor Bene Israel (No.15), a *Bet Din* court of arbitration of communal and religious matters (No.19), a provident fund (No.21), and a cooperative credit society (No.22); to form a federation of all Bene Israel houses of prayer (No.18) and that every congregation should keep a register of births, marriages and deaths (No.21); to do research and publish an authentic history of the Bene Israel community (No.23); to appoint committees to administer an education fund of the Bene Israel Conference (No.8); to carry out a Bene Israel census (No.9); and to draft a Conference constitution (No.28). Other resolutions bore on such matters as the following:

That this Conference respectfully appeals to Government to give some of the new higher commissions to some of our deserving educated youths in consideration of the services rendered by their forefathers in the Military Line and as an incentive to the young men to render similar services. [No.16]

That this Conference recommends the advisability of publishing a Directory of all successful students at the various University and other examinations from year to year as well as of all title-holders and of others who have received other honours. [No.24]

Having withdrawn from the Bene Israel conference, Jacob Bapuji Israel and David S. Erulkar proceeded to form a second Bene Israel organization called The All India Israelite League, the first meeting of which was held in Karachi in 1918. Subsequent Israelite League sessions were held in Bombay. Some of the items discussed, for instance, at the Fifth Annual Session of the All India Israelite League, held in Poona on December 31, 1922, were:

1. Regrets that the long-needed unity between the League and the Conference had not been achieved.
2. Lack of proper encouragement for present and potential community workers.
3. Lack of housing for the poor and middle-class Bene Israel, both in Poona and in Bombay.
4. Appeal for funds to build a compound wall around the historic burial ground of the original Bene Israel ancestors at Navgaon.
5. Condemnation of resort to synagogue excommunication as practised by some Bene Israel in cases of internal quarrels about administrative matters not at all involving religious precepts.
6. Expression of "horror and indignation at the atrocities committed on the Jewish people in Eastern Europe",[4] and an appeal for funds for ameliorating the suffering of the victims.
7. The necessity for physical culture activities for the young Bene Israel men and women.

Items discussed at the Sixth Annual Session of the Bene Israel Conference included:

1. Dissatisfaction with Bene Israel divine services described as being "as unattractive as ever", with no attempts to improve matters.
2. Boycott of all those in the community who "participated in bigamies and polygamies".
3. Regret that nothing had been done to further the temperance movement in the community.
4. The importance and urgency of executing the Bene Israel Cooperative Housing Scheme.[5]

It should be noted that often, although not always, the very same points were discussed both by the League and the Conference, just as both the Conference and the League would issue, year after year, many resolutions and desirable recommendations which somehow, however, they never implemented—such as the taking of a thorough communal census, publishing Kehimkar's manuscript on the *History of the Bene Israel*, or the establishment by each Bene Israel congregation of a *Hevra Kedusha*. While both the Conference and the League were fully cognizant of the many pressing needs of the community, and lists of resolutions were always long and well-meaning, the actual achievements of these two bodies were disappointingly few.

To the credit of the Conference was its establishment of the Bene Israel Education Fund, meagre though it was (Dr. Judah Hyam of Poona was the driving spirit behind the establishment of this fund); and of the Bene Israel Home for Orphans and Destitutes. The Bene Israel Benevolent Society, started by Kehimkar, had already started raising funds for the latter and subsequently the Home was assisted by the Shaar Ha-Rachamim Synagogue (which much later became its main support); the Home itself did not begin to function until 1934. The one long-lasting achievement of the All India Israelite League was the establishment of a Jewish Cooperative Credit Society (see above, p. 243), the idea having been suggested by Jacob Bapuji Israel. A copy of each successive Balance Sheet of this Jewish Cooperative Credit Society, Ltd., used to appear (both in English and in Marathi) in concurrent issues of *The Israelite*. The Society later changed its name to the Bene Israel Cooperative Banking Society and functioned until 1971.

A valuable glimpse into the Bene Israel past as well as into their sentiments and problems as of the early 1920s may be had from the following excerpts taken from the President's (i.e. I.J.Samson's) speech on the occasion of the Sixth Annual Session of the All India Israelite League, on December 30, 1923, held in Bombay at the Israelite School :

> How many of us envy the local Yahudi [Baghdadi] community for their institutions which almost all have been provided by the munificence of one individual? Has the community any voice in the management of their institutions? About a century ago our position was similar and our institutions then were mostly in the hands of a single family [i.e. the Commadans]. Was our position any better then than it is now? The whole community then was under the autocratic rule of that family and a good deal of our poverty and want of mutual confidence can be traced back to that dictatorial rule[6]....The present advance of the community may be said to have commenced about 40 years ago. This synchronized with the establishment of the Israelite School....our people easily got posts as clerks in Government offices on fairly decent salaries...It only produced in them a sort of mentality by which they became content only with their clerical work in the hope that in due time they would rise to one of the higher posts that the service allows. They had no thinking to do for themselves. It would have been better if our people instead of taking Government service had more taken to service in commercial firms where they would in time have learned business....More of our young men should take training under the many and competent *maistrys* [i.e. master craftsmen, most Bene Israel *maistrys* being carpenters or masons] we have in the community as building contractors. It is a great pity that that profession is fast disappearing from the community....
>
> I am glad to see that polygamous marriages which a few years ago were pretty common have been rapidly disappearing....the question arises about divorces. In Bombay it is very difficult for our people to resort to the law courts as they must go to the High Court and there the cost of litigation is prohibitive....I would suggest the formation of a communal tribunal for trying matrimonial cases....to be constituted of men of known integrity and fairness in the community or appointed under an Act of the Legislature as in the case of the Parsis....
>
> It is alleged by our detractors that we have not really emigrated from Palestine but

have been originally residents of India and have been converted to the Jewish faith. It is therefore extremely important to preserve this piece of land [i.e. the Navgaon Bene Israel cemetery] which is connected so intimately with our first arrival in India and about which we Bene Israels have no manner of doubt....regarding the removal of the cart track which runs through the cemetery and is desecrating the graves of our ancestors....the League would be prepared to pay for the land but in that event the cemetery should be transferred to the name of the Community....I have appealed to the whole community simply because this work is being done not for and in the name of the League but for and in the name of the whole Community.[7]

The several aspects of Bene Israel concern as revealed in the above passages speak for themselves and are significant to students of the social history of the Bene Israel.

As regards the League itself, David S. Erulkar and Jacob Bapuji Israel, each for personal reasons of his own, were all too soon no longer available to give it the kind of leadership which it needed; and no others came forward to take their places. In Karachi and in Poona the League proved to be more popular than the Conference. However, the League became defunct about 1925. Its rival, the Bene Israel Conference lasted for some twenty years (until 1937), led by the more educated and successful members of the community who, unfortunately, did not live up to the challenge of moulding the community into a cohesive unit capable of achieving improvements in many spheres. During the second quarter of the 20th century, many well-educated Bene Israel either moved away from or kept aloof from involvement in Bene Israel community affairs. Community leadership, now completely in the hands of the so-called "clerk class" of the Bene Israel, concentrated on relatively trivial issues and generally failed to tackle major community problems.[8]

However, as Prof. Joan Roland once phrased it : "The period from 1917 to 1927 was certainly the most vital in the history of the Bene Israel communal organization and development. Its interest cannot be measured only by its lasting accomplishments; rather it lies in the serious, self-conscious communal awareness that prevailed."

NOTES

1. The only time Jacob Bapuji Israel, and other Bene Israel, went further than this and advocated constitutional safeguards for minorities in India was when they presented their November 22, 1917 Memorandum to Montagu, Secretary of State for India (see below, pp.248 – 9). This Memorandum supported the joint proposal of reforms put forward by the Indian National Congress and the All India Muslim League.
2. *Report of the First Bene Israel Conference*, Bombay, 1917; p.36.
3. Ibid., pp.2-20.
4. The worst wave of *pogroms* (a Russian word meaning "destruction, loot, murder and rape perpetrated by one section of the population against another") against Jews in Eastern Europe occurred between 1917 and 1921, especially in the Ukraine, perpetrated mainly by groups of soldiers from the disintegrating czarist army, killing 60,000 Jews and wounding many more.
5. *The Israelite*, Volume VII, Nos.1-2, January-February 1923; p.8.
6. Cf. Kehimkar : *History*, pp.256-72. Also, see above, p.59, re Commadan Rule.
7. *The Israelite*, Volume VIII, Nos.1-2, January-February 1924, pp.4-10.
8. For additional details about the Bene Israel Conference and the All India Israelite League, see Joan Roland's article, "A Decade of Vitality : Bene Israel Communal Development, 1917-1927" in *Jews in India*, edited by Thomas Timberg, Vikas Publishing House Private Ltd., Delhi, and Advent Books Inc., New York, 1986; pp. 285-347. This article presents a great deal of information about an important phase of Bene Israel history which other scholars have hitherto ignored.

Chapter 27
Bene Israel in India's Independence Struggle

To the best of our knowledge, the Bene Israel were never—not before, during or after the British Raj—"in the political arena" as such,[1] partly because they were too pre-occupied trying to eke out a living and so could not afford the time and money needed to be active in local politics. For a Bene Israel to run for a public office was very rare, and such a person had to be well known outside his community because the backing and votes of such an infinitesimally small community as the Bene Israel would carry only negligible weight. It was therefore quite a compliment to the community that they (in this case, all of Bombay's Jews together) were systematically given a turn (as were the Hindu, Muslim, Christian and Parsi communities, each of which heavily outnumbered the Jews of Bombay) at having a Jew nominated for the position of Mayor of Bombay (a ceremonial rather than an executive office). Mayors of Bombay are elected by the Councilors of the Municipal Corporation of Bombay from among themselves. Most of these Councilors had reached that office through public election (though a few of them were nominated by the Government). Dr. Elijah Moses was one of the rare Bene Israel ever to have stood in a public election: he was elected to the office of Councilor and later became Mayor of Bombay.[2] Actually, before this, however, Aaron Daniel Talkar had served as an elected member of Poona's Municipal Council (1902-07).

India's independence struggle was no ordinary political fight. As far as the Bene Israel were concerned, we have already seen that consensus, followed by concerted action, simply was never characteristic of this community. There was, however, some noteworthy participation by Bene Israel in their individual capacities actively supporting the independence movement, as for instance, Dr. Joseph Benjamin's early role in the Indian National Congress; Dr. Jacob E. Solomon serving as Secretary of the Ahmedabad Branch of the India Home Rule League; and Aaron Daniel Talkar's strong support of Lokamanya Tilak.

India's fight for freedom was, at the beginning, a wholly secular movement. When in 1916 the great Hindu freedom-fighter, Lokamanya Bal Gangadhar Tilak (a Chitpavan Brahmin from Maharashtra and a staunch Hindu revivalist) appealed in the Bombay High Court against an order of the District Magistrate of Poona demanding security for "good behaviour" in an amount of Rs.40,000 (on charges that Tilak had been making seditious speeches), Tilak's Senior Counsel was none other than Mohammed Ali Jinnah (a brilliant advocate, President of India's Muslim League, who later—at the partition of the sub-continent—became Governor General of Pakistan), with a Bene Israel Jew, David Solomon Erulkar, as his Junior Counsel. (At that time David S. Erulkar, after his return from studying law in England, had already started a law practice in Bombay.) In these proceedings David Erulkar assisted in securing a most far-reaching re-definition of the law which secured greater scope for nationalist agitation.[3] Soon thereafter, David

Erulkar turned his efforts for a few years toward Bene Israel community affairs through his editorship of *The Israelite* journal.

In regard to India's independence struggle there were written expressions of opinion on the part of the most articulate thinkers among the Bene Israel, but hardly a political act, except for the addressing of the following joint-letter to the Secretary of State for India :

Bombay, 22nd November, 1917.

To
> THE RIGHT HONOURABLE
> EDWIN SAMUEL MONTAGU, P.C.M.P.
> Secretary of State for India.

Sir,

We, the undersigned members of the Bene Israel Community beg to submit, in the interests of our community, the following representation in connection with the constitutional changes in the administration of the country at present under consideration of the Government of India and the British Cabinet.

2. The scheme of reforms adopted by the Indian National Congress and the All India Muslim League has been before the country for some time past. This scheme has our entire approval and hearty support.

3. We would urge the granting of these reforms at an early date. We also pray that the same be granted liberally and generously, not as a reward for services rendered by our country, but as a recognition of our countrymen's fitness for a responsible share in the Government of this country after over a century of British rule, and also as a faithful fulfilment of promises made by British Sovereigns and Statesmen.

4. In connection with the questions of communal representation, though we belong to a microscopically small community, the past history of our community in India, extending over the long period of two thousand years, has convinced us of the spirit of tolerance and fairness practised by those Indian communities who command the majority towards their numerically insignificant sister communities; and hence we are of the opinion that the interests of small communities will not suffer in any way by a general representation as distinct from communal representations.

5. For a large community such as the Mahomedans, a separate representation may be necessary for a time, but we feel that smaller communities stand to lose by communal representation, inasmuch as they are marked out, and whatever special representation they may get, can never be very effective. The Jews in England are a minority, and yet they have never suffered for the want of communal representation. We are, therefore, of the opinion that the principle of communal representation, if applied at all, should be limited to Mahomedans only.

6. On the other hand, if the principle of communal representation be extended to smaller communities, we beg to submit, that there should not be separate communal electorates. In place of communal electorates or Government nominations, we would recommend that communal representatives be co-opted by the representatives of the general electorate, which must then necessarily include all the persons with franchise irrespective of caste or community.

7. By giving a separate electorate to a community, the racial feeling is accentuated and the interest of the community is narrowed down to its own activities. Such communal elections do not foster the development of the Indian nation; they rather retard it. In our opinion these disadvantages of communal electorates can be overcome and communal representation be secured, if considered necessary, by some such plan as we have submitted to you.

8. We feel sure, that a nation which has sacrificed so much for the liberty and freedom of small nations cannot but uphold the same principle in the case of a large nation.

9. We also feel that you, sir, whose co-religionists have suffered for centuries in many Western countries, disabilities based on race and creed, cannot but sympathize with the just and legitimate aspirations of three hundred millions of your fellow subjects, whose disabilities are mainly based on creed, colour and race.
We beg to remain,
    Sir,
Your most obedient servants, [signed]

Shalom B. Israel	Abraham S. Erulkar, M.D. (London)
B.J.Samson	Samuel S. Mazgamkar
M.S.[4]Ezekiel	Jacob B.Israel, B.A.
Rahamim J.Ezekiel	I.J.Samson, B.A.L.L.B.
	Jacob E. Solomon, L.M. & S.

On December 5, 1917, a Bombay newspaper, commenting on the above-reproduced letter, states :

The members of the Bene Israel community have submitted to Mr. Montagu a very sensible representation on the subject of constitutional reforms....an oasis in the desert of bewildering, silly and stupid clamour for representation on the basis of class, creed and caste which self-seeking elements in some of the most advanced communities like the Parsis and Anglo-Indians have chosen to claim.

However, many Bene Israel disagreed with the ideas expressed in the petition and insisted that the petitioners did *not* represent the community.

Mahatma Gandhi (addressing his co-workers in November 1921) kept emphasizing that

There must be a heart union between Hindus, Mussalmans, Parsis, Christians and Jews. The three latter communities may and will distrust the other two. The recent occurrences must strengthen that distrust. We must not molest them if they do not become full non-cooperators, or do not adopt Swadeshi [i.e. Indian-made products] or the white Khadi [hand-spun and hand-woven cloth] cap which has become its symbol. We must not be irritated against them even if they side with the Government on every occasion. We have to make them ours by right of loving service.[5]

Again, on the eve of Gandhi's arrest in March 1922, he stressed that "If I am arrested....the four pillars of Swaraj [i.e. self-rule] [must remain, namely] non-violence, Hindu-Muslim-Sikh-Parsi-Christian-Jewish unity, total removal of untouchability, and manufacture of hand-spun and hand-woven *Khaddar* completely displacing foreign cloth."[6]

In 1921, during Gandhi's fast at the time of riots in Bombay (with nationalists attacking, in spite of Gandhi's call for non-violence, those Indians who had welcomed the visit of the Prince of Wales) and at a time when Gandhi's efforts had already been focused on developing Hindu-Muslim unity, Dr. A.S. Erulkar asked Gandhi what the role of Indian Jews should be in the struggle for freedom. Gandhi scribbled in ink on the back of an envelope his answer to the question : "If you could influence the Jews, or put me on to some, I would like it. They must feel also absolutely secure from molestation by Hindus and Musalmans." And, on a scrap of paper : "If the Bene Israelites have not been injured or affected, one need not worry. The English Jews I class among Englishmen, who don't need any special assurance."[7] By the latter remark presumably Gandhi meant to point to the example of British Jews who needed no special minority rights or assurances; similarly, the Bene Israel in India, were like any other Indians.

Quite apart from the fact that Dr. A.S.Erulkar was among the physicians attendant upon Mahatma Gandhi then and in subsequent years during several of the Mahatma's fasts,[8] it was he who, together with I.J.Samson, tried to establish a Jewish (Indian) Nationalist Party. On the other hand, however, even though there was no united Bene Israel front for or against India's Independence Movement, both the All India Israelite League and the Bene Israel Conference did pass similar resolutions of loyalty to the British.[9] Among some of the Bene Israel there were feelings of understandable ambivalence in view of the fact that under British rule the Bene Israel, together with the Anglo-Indian community, were enjoying a privileged status in government employ, in the form of preference in employment and with higher rates of pay. This element and the fact that so very few Bene Israel were really active in the Independence Movement, should not, however, becloud the reality that all Bene Israel were proud of being Indian, even while acknowledging that they benefited from the British rule.

In 1922 there appeared in *The Bombay Chronicle* an article written by "a Bene Israel", entitled *Passover and India : the Great Festival of Freedom*. The article concluded with this paragraph :

> The Almighty....will surely hear the cries of millions of his creatures and send a deliverer. Perhaps one has already come in the presence of Mahatma Gandhi and it is only a question of time. Perhaps the Almighty is trying the heart of the British as He did that of Pharaoh and freedom will come at an unexpected moment. Let us wait in hope and expectation, doing to the best of our abilities all that our great leader requires of us.[10]

And, in the January-February 1923 issue of *The Israelite* (p.35), in a long article by M.D.Borgawkar (a Bene Israel) covering the second year of Lord Reading's Viceroyalty, the Viceroy was strongly criticized for his adamancy in having doubled the Salt Tax against the majority vote of the assembly. Here the fact that Lord Reading was himself Jewish[11] did not color Borgawkar's objective reporting of the Viceroy's tenure.

There is an interesting memorandum of the early 1920s called *The Problem of the Minor Communities*, written by a member of the Bene Israel community in Ahmedabad, Dr. Jacob E. Solomon who was Secretary of the Ahmedabad Branch of the Indian Home Rule League. The memorandum was forwarded through Dr. Annie Besant, then General Secretary of the National Convention, to the committee concerned. Some of the points made by Dr. Jacob E. Solomon in the Memorandum bear reproducing. With the idea of Home Rule in mind, but even under British rule, these proposals for obtaining reasonable democratic representation were quite basic, taking into account India's very heterogeneous population.

> I am of the opinion that reserving seats in the Provincial Councils or the Assembly for the Minor Communities, or even for the Mahomedans alone, is detrimental to the interests of India even though the reserved seats be filled by mixed election. Unless the ideal is straightaway introduced, there is likely to be percolation of the communal

principle through all the lower strata of state life, and introduce an element of separativeness instead of promoting unity of Indian ideal for all communities in India....We are Indians first and Muslims or Jews or Parsees afterwards."

To handle certain problems requiring more light on them from the religious point of view [he suggested for each Province] a Religious Board of five representatives of each religion because of the religious equality that ought to be maintained....Comparing the percentage it will be seen how utterly impossible it would be to fix the number of seats to be reserved for each community in a just manner without giving extra consideration for some, than the ratio of population demands.

In his Memorandum, Dr. Solomon presented the figures from the 1921 Government Census for the *British Districts of the Bombay Presidency*.

Religion	Population	Percentage to the Total Population
Hindus	148,12,545[12]	76.78%
Sikhs	8,027	00.04%
Jains	2,14,401	01.11%
Buddhists	1,734	00.01%
Muslims	37,75,098	19.57%
Christians	2,62,620	01.36%
Zoroastrians [Parsis]	82,696	00.43%
Jews	11,571	00.06%[13]
Animists	1,22,937	00.64%
Others	90	
Total	19,291,719 [which is the same as 19,291,719.]	

The ideal was "to promote the solidarity of all religionists in India in civil matters."[14]

It was in 1930 that certain Bene Israel made an attempt to form a Jewish (Indian) Nationalist Party. *The Bombay Chronicle* of July 21, 1930, in a long news item with the caption "Jews Can't Stand Aside", tells us that:

A Jewish Nationalist Party was formed on Sunday afternoon at a meeting of Jews sympathizing with the present national struggle, held at Mr. I. J. Solomon's office at Kalbadevi. About 75 members mostly of Bene Israel community had responded to the call. Dr. [A.S.] Erulkar presided. Mr. Solomon explaining....It was the duty of the Jews to sympathize with the present national movement...they should take up the Swadeshi and boycott programme of the Congress and devote special attention to the temperance movement. Mr. Samson Nagaonkar and Mr. Shalom Abraham suggested to persuade other members of their community to join....they [the Bene Israel] were treated like brothers in India by the Hindus and Muslims and they would be ungrateful to them if they did not stand by their side. Dr. Jacob Ezekiel who was in charge of the St. John Ambulance said that they have now been allowed to be present whenever their services were needed. Dr. Erulkar welcomes the move to form a Nationalist Party of Jews. He felt proud of the Jew Mr. Eli Abraham Nagaonkar who was sentenced for picketing in Bombay. He did not like to join any institution conducted on communal lines; but as the proposed party was meant for the political education of the Jewish community and its object was national service, he felt glad to offer his services. He condemned the repressive measures of the Government and described the harrowing effects of police lathi [cudgel] charges on unarmed people. He had himself to treat some patients at the Congress Hospital and he could say that the charges were brutal. He made a strong appeal for the boycott of British goods....In his opinion a microscopic community like the Jews was not at all in need of special representation at the conference....a provisional committee with Dr. Erulkar as President and Mr. I.J.Samson and Mr. S.M.Benjamin as Joint Secretaries and a half a dozen members was formed to carry on the work and to convene a public meeting of the Jewish sympathizers of the National Movement. Many of those present signed the boycott pledges of the B.P.C.C.[16]

It seems that nothing much happened beyond the establishment of this provisional committee, although several Bene Israel as individuals, rather than as a group, did fully identify themselves with the struggle for Indian independence. Dr. A.S.Erulkar and David S. Erulkar, for instance, completely agreed with Gandhi's aims and, while they were not sure that Gandhi's method was the most effective one, they certainly were activists in India's cause.

In his own way, David Erulkar, throughout his entire career, continued to fight effectively for the cause of Indianization, and this in the face of strong British opposition. He did so in each successive position held by him. In 1919 he joined the Scindia Steam Navigation company; in 1922 opened the Calcutta office of the firm, and later managed its Rangoon office; in 1928 he went to England as chairman and Managing Director of Scindia Steamship (London) Ltd. Also, the Government of India appointed him as Technical Adviser to the Empire Chartering Committee, and he twice served as President of the International Organization of Industrial Employers (at Brussels). Since 1930 for practically two decades he was on the Governing Board of the International Labour Organization (started by the League of Nations). From 1948 to 1951 he served as Joint Comptroller of Shipping at Bombay Port, under the Indian Ministry of Commerce. From 1951 to 1955 he held the position of London Representative of the British Steamship Company.

In 1928, while David Erulkar was with the Calcutta Office of the Scindia Steamship Company, he was prominent among those who agitated for Indianization of the service under the Port Trust, insisting upon the appointment of only Indians to future vacancies in certain departments, but this was vehemently opposed by the then 19 European members of the Calcutta Port Trust (which had only five Indian members). He was more successful in persuading the British to allow native Indians to serve as pilots on ships sailing into and out of Calcutta's Hooghly River port. Actually, the first Indian pilot allowed by the British to guide ships on the Hooghly was a Bene Israel pilot, one Arthur Judah Daniel (Korlekar), a nephew of David Erulkar. He had served in the merchant marine and was the first Indian accepted by the British to be trained as a Hooghly River Pilot.[17] Because he was an Indian, encroaching for the first time on a hitherto British preserve, he suffered humiliating discrimination and sadistic physical hardships at the hands of his non-Indian peers and superior officers all during his training (which began in March of 1931). (That he was also a Jew was never a factor in this matter.) Finally he won respect.[18]

David Erulkar persisted in his "crusade" in every avenue open to him. To Chambers of Commerce he pointed out that Britain had debased Indian industries, that Indo-British trade had reached a precarious position and that Britain was now threatened with the loss of her best customer, India. He urged the appointment of Indians (with business experience) as additional trade commissioners. Based on Indian public opinion, Erulkar opposed any scheme savoring of Imperial preference in trade with India. On September 28, 1937, David Erulkar wrote a long Letter to the Editor of the British *Journal of Commerce and Shipping Telegraph* which published it on October 4, 1937. Some of the salient points made in the letter were as follows :

> ...before the sea-borne trade between India and England was opened up, £ 600,000 per annum was sent from Europe through Mocha to India for calicoes, drugs, sugar, rice, tobacco and other articles....Had not such prohibitory duties and decrees (for protection and profit of British-made goods) existed, the mills of Paisley and Manchester would have stopped in their outset, and could scarcely have been again set in motion, even by the power of steam. They were created by the sacrifice of the Indian manufacture. Had India been independent, she would have retaliated, would have imposed prohibitive duties upon British goods, and would thus have preserved her own productive industry from annihilation....Facilities for better transport, as also the increasing demand for raw materials, gave the Indian trade an impetus, but to assert that the British shipowners fostered and built up India's trade, and but for them India's wealth would have lain dormant, is not consistent with historical facts. Indian shipping enterprise has not been lacking. It has from time to time tried to establish itself in the country's carrying trade, but has met with relentless hostility from the powerful British shipping interests.

At the International Labour Organization (1945) Erulkar did not hesitate to state his contention that if Indian problems would continue to be handled by an Imperialist staff at the I.L.O., no justice could be expected for India. And no one was more active than Erulkar in campaigning at the I.L.O. for Bengal Famine Relief (1943-44). In 1955 he finally resigned from the Scindia Steamship Company as a protest against interference against Indian shipping interests, in this case on the part of non-Indians in the Company.

It is said that although David Erulkar fought tenaciously for his principles, he did so always in an affable and sportsmanlike fashion. In his various capacities and career positions he consistently fought for Indian rights.[19]

NOTES

1. Some Bene Israel, during and after the British Raj, held responsible administrative posts in government; and many Bene Israel, as clerks, obtained employment and were scattered throughout almost all the different govenment ministries and departments. The genesis of giving these jobs to Bene Israel to an extent way out of proportion to the size of the community is traceable to *British, not* Bene Israel, political motives. The Bene Israel characteristically were, if anything, a-political (although many Bene Israel have held very high civil administrative posts) in all but intra-Bene Israel affairs and (after mid-20th century) in all-India Jewish affairs. The long roster of famous Bene Israel persons shows only three individuals ever to be involved in external politics. On the other hand, Cochin Jews (of the Rahabi and a few other families) had for centuries actually wielded much political influence and were active in political dealings with their Hindu, Dutch and (to a lesser extent) their British rulers.
2. The practice of rotating the office of Bombay's mayor among its several different religious communities has since been discontinued.
    One of Bombay's Jewish Mayors, Meyer Nissim (a Baghdadi Jew) wrote about Bombay's Jewish Councillors and Mayors in an article called "When I was Mayor of Bombay", published in *India and Israel,* No.3, September 1948, Bombay, p.14 :

I had the privilege of being Councillor (of the Municipal Corporation of Bombay) for 25 years. When Government had the right to nominate a certain number of Councillors, it was customary for Government to include a certain number of representatives of minority communities also. It was therefore possible for several years for a Jew to be a member of the Corporation apart from other Jews who as the result of their own efforts were returned as Councillors by contesting the Municipal elections. Of the *five Jews* who *have been members of the Corporation during the past 40 years*, Dr. Elijah Moses and myself have been the only Councillors who have succeeded regularly at general elections. The late Sir Sassoon J. David was nominated by Government. Commencing from the General Ward Election of 1923 till my retirement in 1940, I was privileged to represent the Fort area.

Of the two other Jewish Councillors, the late Mr. D. S. Shellim was a Government nominee, whilst Sir Alwyn Ezra, apart from nomination, represented the British Chamber of Commerce.

The late Sir Sassoon J. David, Dr. E. Moses and myself have had the honour of being elected President of the Corporation or the Mayor, as the Presidents have been designated in recent years. Sir Sassoon David presided over the Municipal Corporation in 1921-22 I in 1929-30, and Dr. Moses in 1937-38.

Although Jews are a microscopic minority, with the result that if they had to count merely on the backing of their own community, it would have been absolutely impossible for any Jew to obtain a sufficiency of votes to be returned to the Corporation, yet in practice Jews have received good support from the other communities. Be it said to its credit, no sectarianism prevails in the Bombay Municipal Corporation. All religions and religious observances are respected.

3. About this court case, D.V.Tamhankar in his *Lokmanya Tilak* (John Murray, London, 1956, p.238) remarked that:

The speeches the Government had taken objection to were those delivered in Belgaum and Ahmednagar. The gravamen of the Government's charge was that Tilak had incited the people to be disloyal to the Government established by law. But, Tilak's counsel Mr. Jinnah and Mr. Erulkar were able to show that Tilak had made a distinction between the Government established by law, which is a permanent institution, and the administration which was subject to change. As the personnel of the administration changed from time to time, the nature of their work also changed. This was a very important distinction and the High Court Judges, Mr. Batchelor and Mr. Shah, accepted it and declared the speeches did not contain sedition.

The judgement which Tilak secured in this security trial was of paramount importance, not only to him but also to the Home Rule movement. It established the principle that the seditious character of any speech ought to be assessed not by quotations taken at random, but by passages taken in relation to their context and by the general effect of the whole. The judgment also quashed the definition of sedition which had hounded Tilak's work since 1897—his first sedition trial—when Mr. Justice Strachey had defined sedition as "absence of affection". In the 1916 trial the Judges of the High Court by setting aside this definition made the path of Home Rule agitation smoother and less perilous and gave it the character of a legitimate agitation.

4. This signatory was probably M.S.Ezekiel, a solicitor. But, the indecipherable hand-written initials of the signature look more like M.M. or W.W.
5. *Gandhi's Letters on Indian Affairs*, published by V. Narayanan and Company, Madras, 1923, p.113.
6. Ibid., p.164.
7. Dr. Sol Erulkar, son of David S. Erulkar and nephew of Dr. A.S.Erulkar, has a large collection of newspaper clippings and other mementos relating to his famous father and uncle. The two jottings by Mahatma Gandhi which are cited here are part of that collection. The present author is grateful to Dr. Sol Erulkar for giving her access to his collection and for sharing with her his recollections of his father and uncle.
8. Dr. A.S.Erulkar was called in almost every time when Gandhi undertook a fast, Dr. Erulkar

representing the Indian Medical Council, in his capacity as President of that Council, David S. Erulkar was also in close touch with Gandhi. There is a photograph of David Erulkar together with Gandhi, taken in England when Gandhi attended the Round Table Conference.

9. For example, Volume VII of *The Israelite*, Nos. 1—2, January-February 1923, records the following from the President's Address at the Fifth Annual Session of the All India Israelite League on December 31, 1922:

Point No. 10 : As regards politics I may mention, keep aloof from the same. If it does effect our community in any way, do by all means approach the Government through constitutional means, keeping on the right side of the Government and bearing in mind that we Jews are peaceful and loyal subjects of the community and Government which gives us shelter and protection. [p.7]

The same issue of *The Israelite*, in reporting on the Sixth Session of the Bene Israel Conference, quotes one of their resolutions as follows : "This Conference of the Beni-Israel Community expresses its sense of deep loyalty and devotion to the person and throne of His Gracious Majesty, the King-Emperor."[p.9]

10. This article from *The Bombay Chronicle* was reprinted in *The Israelite*, Vol.VI, Nos. 7-8, July-August 1922, pp. 109-110.
11. Born of a Jewish family, Rufus Daniel Issacs—who later became Lord Reading—(1860-1935), left his home in England as a boy and ran away to sea. He first made a career for himself on the stock exchange. This was followed by a highly successful practice in common law, culminating in his appointment as Lord Chief Justice of England (1913-21). He was Viceroy of India from 1921 to 1926, and became British Foreign Secretary in 1931.
12. Positioning the commas in this Indian fashion, the figure 148,12,545 must be read as *one crore, 48 lakhs, twelve thousand five hundred and forty-five*. One hundred thousand equals one *lakh;* one hundred *lakhs* equals one *crore,* or, in other words, ten million. In general notation :14,812,545 (fourteen million, eight hundred and twelve thousand, five hundred and forty-five). Sometimes this same figure in India is written with another comma, thus :1,48,12,545.
13. Bear in mind that the statistics in this Table relate to the British part of Bombay Presidency *only* (the area of highest concentration of Indian Jews), and not to all of India.
14. *The Israelite*, Volume VIII, Nos. 9-10, September-October 1924, pp.124-7.
15. This must have been a misprint. Read "I.J.Samson" for "I.J.Solomon". I.J.Samson did have an office at Kalbadevi, and fits all the other circumstances too. Note that I.J.Samson's signature appears on the November 22, 1917, letter to Montagu also.
16. B.P.C.C. stands for Bombay Provincial Congress Committee. Until the year 1936 the Indian National Congress divided Bombay Presidency into five Provinces, namely : Sind, Gujarat, Maharashtra, Bombay City and Karnataka.
17. The Hooghly River (on the shore of which is situated the port of Calcutta), is treacherous and unusually difficult to navigate, even in the best weather. Being qualified as a Hooghly River Pilot required great skill, intelligence, quick thinking and good judgment.
18. Daniel not only kept a detailed personal diary but also committed to writing (in the mid-1950s) a very interesting (unpublished) document consisting of 171 typed pages which describe his entire training experience and contain copious details of background information on the Bengal Pilot Service as such. The manuscript contains an additional 29 pages taken from Daniel's diary, covering the period from 28-3-31 through 31-5-31, i.e. his first two months of pilot apprenticeship. This is followed by yet another 41 pages of copy of 16 different articles which had appeared in print (since 1840 to 1954) relating to the Bengal Pilot Service. The manuscript also contains some 14 illustrative drawings done by C.H.Blaney.

Arthur Judah Daniel died in England on September 15, 1970. His widow, Mrs. Alma V. Daniel, and his son, Captain Lawrence J. Daniel, kindly allowed the present writer to read this entire document. It is of significance here because he, Arthur Judah Daniel, the first Indian accepted by the British into the Bengal Pilot Service, happened to belong to the Bene Israel community.

19. During his lifetime David Erulkar assembled an extensive collection of writings dealing with the Indian Merchant Marine. After his death, this unique library was offered for sale to several appropriate Indian institutions, but without success; regrettably this important unit of documentation was dispersed. During his long stay in London David Erulkar used to hold community dinners in celebration of the Hindu festival of Diwali, the Muslim festival of Id, and the Parsi festival of Jamshed Nawroz, at which functions all Indians, whatever their religious beliefs, could meet together as citizens of one country. The fact that Erulkar had memorized a long repertoire of Bene Israel Jewish folksongs in Marathi and Jewish hymns in Hebrew reveals yet another side of his personality. He obviously was a man of varied interests and significant achievements.

Chapter 28
Education

At the beginning of the 20th century it took courage for Indian girls to continue their education beyond the primary level. At Hindu schools non-Hindus (both boys and girls) were made to sit separately, to one side. One Bene Israel female respondent from Poona recalled that even if the teacher at such a school were a European, menstruating girl pupils had to sit in a separate row. Girl students on their way to school were often teased, pelted with stones, or shot at with pea-shooters, by youths along their path. Kehimkar, who lived in Poona for a time and who was convinced that girls too must receive a good education, used to accompany his cart driver daily in a large wagon pulled by two bullocks and would go from house to house in order to pick up his female pupils and bring them to school, protecting them against those who ridiculed. The harassment was not because the girls were Jewish : all over India (except perhaps in the state of what is now Kerala, a largely matrilineal area) education for girls was a pioneering struggle in those days.

Jacob Bapuji Israel was among the few with liberal ideas on this and on other subjects. Writing for *The Israelite* in 1923 (in connection with new Bombay Government laws against prostitution), he had the courage to quote the following paragraph from a doctor's article which had been published in the American magazine called *Physical Culture* :

....sex ignorance was responsible for ninety-nine out of a hundred girls' going wrong, and for three quarters of the cases of venereal disease in the world today....if sex lectures were to be delivered to an audience of males and females, I can see how the situation might prove very indelicate at times....The only proper way to teach such a course is to take the boys and girls separately.[1]

In other articles written for *The Israelite* he championed a combination of the most modern type of liberal arts and of practical education for girls, holding that it is "as important as the blending of practical education with literary studies in the case of boys".[2]

Those girls with special desire and aptitude could then undertake learned professions, enter politics and wield sway for the benefit of the country.[3]
We have a large number of graduates and passes, men who are neither fit to prosper in the learned professions nor can they now take to other professions, to which they should have been directed at a much earlier stage in life.[4]

Unfortunately, J.B. Israel was not in a position to implement his ideas on education among the Bene Israel.

Writing in 1913 Rebecca Reuben observed that most Bene Israel girls were attending Indian schools; but that many Bene Israel parents preferred to send their sons to schools for Europeans and Eurasians, after which the boys were admitted into Government service which, although not overly lucrative, was at any rate secure.

With the development of the Israelite School, Bene Israel girls as well as boys gained a great advantage. Still, in 1917, Resolution No.3 of the First Bene Israel Conference proposed having a separate school for Bene Israel girls as being "needed from [an] educational, moral and physical point of view."[5] Although proportionately large numbers of Bene Israel girls had received secondary education in the 19th century, in regard to higher education, there was no Bene Israel "lady graudate" until 1907, while the first Bene Israel male to graduate from a college did so in 1871.

In 1884 the first two Bene Israel graduated in the Arts, from Bombay University. The first Master of Arts degree received by a Bene Israel was awarded in 1902; the second only in 1913. The first Bene Israel Barrister at Law also graduated in 1913; the first Bene Israel Bachelor of Science in 1915. According to the Presidential Address to the First Bene Israel Conference, the Bene Israel

had by the end of 1914 about 64 graduates of whom 32 were B.A.'s, 13 L.M.&S's, 9 LL.B's, 2 M.B.B.S's, 2 M.A.'s, and 1 M.D. of the Bombay University, in addition to the three graduates from British Universities, one in Arts, one in Law, and one in Medicine. If our community had kept pace with the Prabhu community we should have had more than 500 graduates from our community according to our population by this time.[6]

No doubt our community has made some progress in education, but it cannot be denied that we are still lagging in this matter far behind other advanced communities.[7]

At this same Conference a Mr. Solomon R. Songaokar, in proposing Resolution No.8 for the establishment of a fund for higher education, said:

If the boys discontinue their studies at the secondary stage of education....that is a great loss to the community. In such cases the community must come forward to help and lead them to the right path....The fresh matriculate boy is, except in rare cases, hardly able to think rightly for himself. Besides, our young men are not, as a rule, like young men in other communities grown up in the atmosphere that is suitable to education which creates an ambition for acquiring knowledge and information....the student in question should be taken in hand....create a taste for higher education in our community and once the desire is created they will win the goal anyhow and under any adverse circumstances....Now I come to the point of post-graduate education....they should be given all the help we can.... [and we should] help even a deserving man to go abroad to further his studies.[8]

The community had, in a period of about 75 years since its introduction to secular education, made considerable strides. Its own well-educated members realized that much more could and should be done to make higher education available to the rest, i.e. to the majority of the Bene Israel. The Israelite School did, to some extent, further this goal, although the desire for and acquisition of higher education never did become as widespread among the Bene Israel as it did among European and American Jews, even in families who were very poor.

In the early years of the 20th century the Israelite School offered education to boys and girls from the primary grades up through matriculation for Bombay University. The school had its main building in Mazgaon, a branch in the Israel Mohalla in the heart of the original Bene Israel community neighbourhood, and a second branch in Jacob

Circle. The school was run by a supervisory committee composed of educated members of the Bene Israel community. It did (and still does) obtain funds from the Anglo-Jewish Association of London, from the Indian Government, and from the Bombay Municipality. From 1922 to 1953 it had the good fortune to have as its Principal Miss Rebecca Reuben, a very capable and highly qualified Bene Israel woman. While in England, besides getting her Teaching Diploma from London University, she also took some courses at Cambridge University and, while there, perfected her knowledge of Hebrew by studying under Dr. Israel Abrahams. On her return to India she taught for a few years in teachers'- training colleges, but, being anxious to serve the Bene Israel community in particular, she settled in Bombay, at first doing social work among women there. Following her appointment as Headmistress of the Israelite School (where she served on a nominal salary), she introduced many changes in the school, including improved methods of teaching Hebrew.

During Rebecca Reuben's years as Headmistress, the Israelite School was *the* school attended by Bene Israel children, rich and poor alike, and Bene Israel students constituted some 95 percent of its student body. The following table[9] indicates its evergrowing popularity during the 1920s, when its student body was almost wholly Bene Israel:

NUMBER OF STUDENTS ATTENDING THE ISRAELITE SCHOOL IN													
	1921		1922		1923		1924		1925		1926		1927
(B = boys, G = girls)	B	G	B	G	B	G	B	G	B	G	B	G	B	G
High School	18	23	21	24	36	17	48	18	65	16	59	12	59	12
Middle School	59	19	70	28	72	17	83	28	84	25	86	24	105	38
Marathi School Mazagaon	98	69	101	69	152	88	183	113	160	113	149	126	151	113
Marathi School Jacob's Circle	85	61	91	61	96	52	103	56	103	58	90	69	86	64
TOTAL: Boys sep. Girls sep.	260	172	283	182	356	174	417	215	412	212	384	231	401	227
TOTAL: Boys and Girls together	432		465		530		632		624		615		628	

The table shows that during the 1920s an average of 560 Bene Israel students were in attendance at the Israelite School, a rate out of proportion to the size of the community, as well as, in terms of girls' attendance at schools in the India of that decade. Besides, according to Rebecca Reuben (*The Bene Israel of Bombay*, p.18), as of 1913:

In an English High School for Indian girls, where only one quarter were Bene Israel, out of 27 scholarships awarded for merit, the Bene Israel girls held 19. The Bene Israel appreciate the advantages of education and eagerly send their children to school, and usually contrive to contribute something towards schooling expenses even though they be very poor.

Whether they sent their children to the Israelite School or elsewhere, it seems that education, even of daughters, was a priority for many Bene Israel parents; but that did not alter the fact that the *majority* of Bene Israel did not complete their secondary education, even in the 1940s. However, according to the 1941 Census of Bombay Province, there were 4,712 Jewish children in school, i.e. 28.83 percent of the total Jewish population of the Province, a percentage much higher than that of all other communities.

While in London, Miss Reuben had met Sir Elly Kadoorie, a wealthy Baghdadi Jew whose business was based in Hong Kong. Later, in 1931, when visiting Bombay, he agreed to donate Rs.200,000 for purposes of repairing and enlarging the school building, on condition that the Israelite School be named after him. In spite of strong objections, the name was changed to that of Sir Elly Kadoorie School.[10]

Notwithstanding Rebecca Reuben's proven ability and the school's remarkable record during her tenure as Principal, there was a sizeable group of Bene Israel who were constantly seeking to thwart her. When she retired, however, she was made Honorary Principal and served in this capacity until her death in 1957. None of her successors bore the title of Principal. After Miss Reuben's retirement, Mr. B.G. Kher, a Brahmin, became Headmaster of the entire school, with the Headmaster of the Primary School, S.S. Karsulkar (a Bene Israel), under him. Mrs. Flora Samuel, B.A. (Honors in Sanskrit), B.T, and M.Ed. — a member of the Bene Israel community — replaced Mr. B.G. Kher in June 1955 and continued as Headmistress of the entire school until December 1964, when she and her family emigrated to Israel. Although Rebecca Reuben was too ill to come to the school in her capacity as Honorary Principal, Mrs. Samuel used to go to her for consultations from time to time. In the management of the school strong factional conflicts continued between the original supporters of Rebecca Reuben and those opposed to her. While this factor seemed to remain a constant, many other factors relating to the school changed quite drastically.

For one thing, the Bene Israel community no longer lived mainly in the Mazgaon neighbourhood, but had dispersed into several other suburbs (some of them quite distant from Mazgaon). For this reason alone the Elly Kadoorie School lost many pupils to schools (private or municipal) in other neighbourhoods nearer to the pupils' homes. Another factor was related to the growing popularity of English in Bombay. At the Sir Elly Kadoorie School, before Indian Independence, English was taught only in the higher grades; and this was eliminated after Independence when the Indian Government favoured only regional languages as the medium of instruction, resulting in withdrawals of many pupils from the Elly Kadoorie School in favour of schools teaching in English. Nowadays classes of the population (including many of the lower classes) who never before learned English want to know English as a key to a more remunerative livelihood. Many new private schools, teaching in the English medium, sprang up and the English medium is now available even in Bombay municipal schools. Although English is more widespread in Bombay than ever before, the general standard of teaching it and of speaking it has gone down perceptibly.

It has always been the policy of the Israelite – Elly Kadoorie School to accept every Jewish child who applies for admission and to keep every child in school well into his/her teens even though the child may not be achieving passing grades. There have always been freeships available for pupils too poor to afford tuition fees, as well as scholarships awarded on merit. Inevitably the average standard of pupil achievement at the school is affected by these factors. Furthermore, practically every week during Mrs. Samuel's tenure as Headmistress, fifteen to twenty Bene Israel pupils were discharged from school because they and their families were leaving for Israel. The vacancies were filled by non-Jewish pupils and the municipality's subsidizing of the school grew proportionately. For the first time in its history, its teachers received decent salaries. Previously the school never had adequate funds to pay proper wages to its teachers. Because of this, Sir Elly Kadoorie School had lost several teachers who opted for better-paying positions elsewhere, some at the wealthy Baghdadi school, namely the Jacob Sassoon School. Originally the Sassoon School accepted very few Bene Israel students and only if and when they were ready for the upper grades of the school. The first choice of the few most westernized of the Bene Israel elite was to send their children to St. Xavier's or St. Mary's or St. Joseph's schools; or, if they could not easily afford the fee, then to try to gain admission for their children at the tuition-free Sassoon School (which offered the study of French, as one attraction). The school was founded for Baghdadi children; it teaches in English medium, offers classes in Hebrew and Jewish subjects, and nowadays will willingly admit Bene Israel pupils. In Bombay today the Jacob Sassoon School is the only school where Hebrew is being taught.

By no means all the old-time Elly Kadoorie School teachers "defected" to jobs in other schools. Many of them remained at the Bene Israel school and served it with great dedication and self-sacrifice. New teachers practising modern teaching methods were added to the faculty, and the old teachers were given in-service training in up-to-date pedagogy, etc. Their services were retained until they reached retirement age.

In an effort to keep the school attractive to Bene Israel families, Flora Samuel kept her teachers on their toes, introduced one class in English medium, added a kindergarten (which the school previously never had), and involved the pupils in inter-school activities (such as singing, drama and folk-dancing). Rather than deteriorating, one year the Elly Kadoorie School results in the matriculation examination rose considerably. But it was no longer the pride of the Bene Israel community that it once had been. Fewer and fewer Bene Israel parents were sending their children there even though, in some cases, this meant sacrificing the Jewish and Hebrew components of their education. For reasons enumerated above, most of the pupils at the Sir Elly Kadoorie School nowadays come from the lower-middle and poorer classes of Bombay. The medium of instruction continues to be Marathi.

Flora Samuel was succeeded as Headmistress by Sybil Benjamin, B.Sc. and M.Ed., a well-qualified Bene Israel woman who remained at the Kadoorie School only two years. A Hindu teacher, Mrs. Purao, succeeded her for one year, followed by another Hindu Headmistress, Mrs Joshi. Both Mrs. Purao and Mrs Joshi had previously served as teachers at the Elly Kadoorie School.

In 1975, its Centenary Year, there were about 1,250 pupils in attendance, but only 5 percent of them were Bene Israel. The standard of the school has declined and of late has had a very poor record. On the other hand, the Jacob Sassoon School has in the last decade become a very good school, obtaining excellent results in the preparation of its pupils. The Bene Israel prefer it to the Sir Elly Kadoorie School. Today's student body at the Sassoon School is one-third Jewish (mostly Bene Israel) and two-thirds Muslim.

In 1962, however, the Sir Elly Kadoorie School was still Jewish enough for the American Joint Distribution Committee[11] to contribute toward the feeding, clothing and medical aid of its needy pupils. The A.J.D.C. set up on the school premises a dispensary for pupils of all denominations, and it supplemented an already existing Sir Victor Sassoon donation for provision of free meals, at that time for about 300 needy students. Also, the A.J.D.C. contributed largely toward the construction (in 1965) of two new wings which were added to the school building. Another Jewish Organization, Organization for Rehabilitation and Training (O.R.T.), which also functions on an international level, was permitted to construct (in 1962), within the Sir Elly Kadoorie School Compound, a most modern technical school for giving mechanical and technical training of high standards. In the second half of the 1970s this O.R.T. School was training 70 to 80 students per year, only a very few of whom were Jewish. A separate O.R.T. School for Girls is located at Worli (another section of Bombay) and offers courses in domestic science, languages, typing, shorthand, hair-dressing, cooking, etc.

Since the early 1970s easy access for young and old alike to study Jewish religion, world Jewish history and culture, and the Hebrew language has been, and continues to be, the most pressing Bene Israel need in the educational sphere. To help compensate for the present scarcity of qualified teachers, the Jews of India would welcome and benefit enormously from a well designed program of correspondence courses in English on a wide variety of subjects of Jewish interest.

NOTES

1. *The Israelite*, Volume VII, Nos 11-12, November-December 1923, p.161.
2. Ibid., Nos. 3-4, March-April, 1923, p.38.
3. Ibid., p.39.
4. *The Israelite*, Volume VII, Nos.5-6, May-June, 1923, p.74.
5. *Report of the First Bene Israel Conference, 1917*, Bombay, p.92.
6. Ibid., pp.47-8.
7. Ibid., p.46.
8. Ibid., pp.120-22.
9. *The Israelite School Bulletin,* No.4, July 1927, p.2.
10. Sir Elly never again returned to Bombay; but his sons came once and donated money for needy pupils at the school who required uniforms, eyeglasses and raincoats; and umbrellas were bought for the school servants.
11. The American Joint Distribution Committee is a relief and rehabilitation agency, which brings together a number of separate Jewish charities, and is ready to help Jews anywhere in the world.

Chapter 29
Some Community Activities and Inter-relationships

In 1913 a Bene Israel physician, Dr. (Miss) Jerusha Jhirad, with the help of her sister and of Rebecca Reuben, founded a women's association called Stree Mandal (similar to already-established Hindu and Muslim women's organizations) through which, in its early years, qualified women volunteers offered free medical advice and other help to poor Bene Israel women and children. They also arranged for discussions on social, religious and moral subjects; taught needlework; and conducted classes for the study of English, Marathi and Hebrew. All of the Stree Mandal's activities took place in a rented hall located in Nagpada. Their free dispensary was also set up here; and it was in this same hall that the growing congregation of the Jewish Religious Union held its services and meetings, usually on Saturday afternoons, renting the premises from the Stree Mandal. By the 1960s only the Stree Mandal's sewing classes had survived, attended by teenage girls and conducted by a government-supplied sewing teacher, the pupils earning a certificate at the completion of the course. Today the Stree Mandal has ceased to function, for all practical purposes, but in its day it was a well-run, much appreciated service.

Among early 20th century social and cultural efforts of the Bene Israel mention must be made of a Young Men's Jewish Debating Club, started in 1905, later becoming the Israelite Brotherhood and more than just a debating society. It held weekly meetings and offered lectures. It also started a Reading Room cum Circulating Library, with a good collection of modern Jewish books and newspapers, and a nucleus of Jewish reference and scholarly works. In 1918 the Shaare Ha-Rachamim Synagogue began to contribute an annual amount to the library. In November 1922, Boy Scout and Girl Guide troops were introduced among the Bene Israel under the auspices of the Israelite High School. A Bene Israel Youth Convention was inaugurated in 1936, meeting annually until 1943. While outlets such as these filled some needs of Bombay's Bene Israel teenagers and young adults, often they also formed groups of about five or six persons of the same sex who shared a common background, such as same school and same neighbourhood, as well as common interests, and who spent much of their free time together. Sometimes non-Bene Israel friends were included. Such groups frequently developed into real clubs of about twenty members, with officers and a stated purpose. Their activities included fund-raising for community charities or for the school; sports; entertaining neighbourhood children; specifically Jewish or Zionist-oriented discussions and programs, classes in English and in Hebrew; organizing *kirtans,* or picnics and outings. Although the clubs usually broke up after a few years, they were enjoyable and worthwhile while they lasted.[1] Similar to those in Bombay, Bene Israel clubs and charities were established wherever large centers of Bene Israel existed.

The longest-lasting association (aside from the synagogues) is a club of school alumni started in 1917 under the name "Israelite School Old Students' Union" to sponsor social get-togethers; to purchase and study books especially on Jewish subjects; to arrange debates, public lectures, fund-raising and other types of aid for the Israelite School. In 1928 this club, which had been practically dormant, was revived under its new name "The Israelite School Maccabean Fellowship". Its main event was an annual festival of lectures, sports, competitions and other forms of entertainment held during the week of Chanukah, the holiday commemorating the successful revolt of the Maccabees. (However, according to Bene Israel tradition, Chanukah was unknown to their ancestors. It is the Jewish holiday of lights, symbolic of rededication.) While persons in their twenties always constituted the Fellowship's most active age-group, the entire community participated in its functions. On the Sunday following the last day of Passover, they always held a community outing.[2] An enterprising venture on the part of the Fellowship was the acquisition of about two and a half acres of land from the government, in the hill-station of Matheran. There they own a cottage and a pavilion, both of which are open to all, at a modest rental fee, regardless of whether they are members of the Bene Israel community or of the Fellowship. This gave poorer people a chance for a holiday in the hills, something which they could not otherwise afford. The wealthier Bene Israel participated in Fellowship committees, made donations and attended functions, but they did not really mix socially with the poorer members of the community. A lot of hard work was involved in arranging Fellowship activities, and though there may have been bickerings among individuals, this one Bene Israel organization somehow succeeded, in striking contrast to other communal efforts. It endured and gave pleasure to the entire Bene Israel community for about half a century.[3]

Not many Bene Israel joined non-Bene Israel associations. As for Free Masonry, it was originally confined in India to the few large cities, drawing its members from the British and from the Indian upper classes only. However, by the second decade of the 20th century, middle-class, English-speaking Bene Israel began to be admitted more and more to membership, especially in the Masonic Lodges of Bombay and Poona.[4]

During the 20th century, not only did the Bene Israel develop new types of relationships; they also were confronted with changes in some of their old, well-established social patterns. For instance, in mid 20th century a *Kala* Bene Israel man was elected as President of one of the Bene Israel synagogues with *Kala* and *Gora* worshipping together without distinction. But, as in India generally, a marked hesitancy to intermarry remains the last stronghold of restricted relationships between originally endogamous groups. And, it can still be a factor within the Bene Israel community vis-a-vis the *Kala* and *Gora* sub-sections.

In general it can be said that, as in the 19th century, so also in the 20th century, although the Bene Israel were too often quarrelsome and fissiparous among themselves, they lived amicably with their non-Bene Israel neighbours. Even in respect of their co-religionists, the Baghdadis, there was usually no strife : separatioin, rather than overt antagonism was the preferred rule. There were, however, exceptions. Mention has already been made of the fact that more and more Bene Israel children were being admitted to the Sassoon School. The school was gradually becoming more attractive to Bene Israel than the Sir Elly Kadoorie School. By the late 1950s the student body at the Sassoon School was 90 percent Bene Israel, even though it had no policy to accept every Bene Israel who applied for admission. By the mid-1970s, however, the pendulum had swung the other way : the school had no more than twenty-five Jewish students altogether (not because of bad Bene Israel-Baghdadi relations, but because of the volume of emigration on the part of those Jewish elements for whom the school had been attractive).

As for Bene Israel-Baghdadi relations, the Baghdadis had always allowed the Bene

Some Community Activities and Inter-relationships 265

Israel to pray in their synagogues, but they would not accept Bene Israel as part of their *minyan* or as eligible for being called up to the *bimah* for chanting the *Torah* blessings or for reading from the *Torah* scroll. This discrimination involving different *levels of purity* (in this case, of Jewishness) was similar to the Hindu concept, but by no stretch of the imagination could it be attributed to Hinduizing influences in the case in point. Understandably, most Bene Israel continued to resent the Baghdadi attitude toward their community, minimizing the Baghdadi's *halachic* excuses for discrimination against the Bene Israel, while occasionally accusing the Baghdadis of not admitting the Bene Israel as brothers lest doing so should spoil the Baghdadis' success at passing themselves off as Europeans. The irony of it all is that, ultimately, the Baghdadi synagogues began hiring (for a pittance) Bene Israel men to attend their synagogue services since only thus could a *minyan* be secured!

Long before Baghdadis had agreed to consider Bene Israel as eligible for their *minyan*, their Sassoon School had been, practically from its inception, dependent upon Bene Israel not only for its teachers of Hebrew, but even for its Headmasters. Joseph Ezekiel Rajpurkar served as Headmaster of the David Sassoon School, from 1865 until 1905. Another of its Bene Israel Headmasters was E.M. Ezekiel (who was also Prof. of Hebrew at St. Xavier's College of Bombay University). From 1922 until 1960 Shalom Abraham taught Hebrew and English History at the Jacob Sassoon School, and served as its Headmaster from 1953 to 1960. It was about five years after he came to teach at the school (about 1927) that he persuaded the Sassoon School Trustees to accept Bene Israel pupils at the school, as a matter of principle. Until then only a handful of Bene Israel pupils had ever been admitted. Around that time he also persuaded the two Baghdadi synagogues in Bombay to accept Bene Israel for their *minyan*. It was not, however, until the 1960s that they accepted Bene Israel for the honor of coming up to the *bimah* in their synagogues to recite the blessings or chant from the Torah.

Even after the removal of the Baghdadi restrictions against Bene Israel, today in Bombay very few Bene Israel ever worship in the Baghdadi synagogues, although one is located right within a Bene Israel neighbourhood.

From time to time tension mounted between the Bene Israel and the Baghdadis. The former needed larger quarters in which to hold their marriage celebrations. Baghdadis had begun allowing well-to-do Bene Israel to hold the marriage ceremony, as well as the reception, at the Baghdadi Magen David Synagogue in Byculla, until it was discovered after one such wedding that the bride concerned was a widow by a previous marriage. Since there was a rule against the marriage of a widow taking place inside a synagogue (which has nothing to do with Hindu prejudice against widows), the Baghdadis were incensed by this Bene Israel infraction.[5] Thereafter they refused to make their synagogue premises available for Bene Israel weddings. Hence, we read in *The Israelite*, Volume VII, Nos.7-8, July-August 1923, p.97 : "The Baghdad Jews have within the last few years thought it fit to preclude our people from using their commodious Byculla Synagogue and this makes it insistent upon us to arrange to have a commodious synagogue of our own at an early date." Seven years later, in 1930, Sir Victor Sassoon allowed the Bene Israel wedding of Captain J.S. Samson to take place at the Magen David Synagogue. After that, certain other Bene Israel weddings also were allowed to take place from time to time at that synagogue.

A particularly ugly incident of discrimination occurred in 1935 when an unsuccessful attempt was made by Baghdadis in Bombay to have the Bene Israel barred from the use of ten hospital beds which an endowment by Sir Sassoon J. David had reserved for Jewish patients at the Government J.J. Hospital in Bombay. The Government ruled that the Bene Israel were fully entitled to use of these beds since Bene Israel had always been considered part of the Jewish population.

A visiting American Rabbi, Bernard Heller, founded the Young Men and Women's Hebrew Association in Bombay in 1957, in order to try to bring Baghdadi and Bene Israel youths together. It also brought young men and women together, which most other Jewish clubs in Bombay had not done. The group met on the premises of The Jewish Club on 137 Mahatma Gandhi Road (which is not located within any Bene Israel communal neighbourhood) which the Baghdadi community had rented for social purposes. However, the Baghdadi members of the Y.M.W.H.A. were outnumbered by its Bene Israel members. Most of the Baghdadi members came from poor families while the Y.M.W.H.A. attracted only the more sophisticated Bene Israel youths. This Y.M.W.H.A. is now defunct, but the Jewish Club as such is still there and serves as a venue for its now predominantly adult Bene Israel clientele.

During World War II, in 1943, all Jewish synagogues, organizations and institutions in Bombay — with Bene Israel, Baghdadis and other Jews all joining together — affiliated under a cover organization called the Central Jewish Board of Bombay. During and immediately following World War II it rendered important service. Its founder and first President was Sir Victor Sassoon, followed in office by Dr. Elijah Moses of the Bene Israel community. Later, Meyer Nissim, a Baghdadi Jew (who had also served once as Mayor of Bombay), became President of the organization. Its membership, 90 percent Bene Israel, consists of sixteen different Bombay Jewish organizations. Formation of the Central Jewish Board *of India* followed in 1967, comprising the Central Jewish Board of Bombay, the Jewish Association of Calcutta, and the South Indian Jews Association of Cochin. The Central Jewish Board of India is supposed to represent the Jews of India as a whole in their relations vis-a-vis India and in their concern for Jews in India and abroad. Today, however, when there is a greater need than ever for such a body, no all-India Jewish organization is really devoting itself to the urgent requirements of the small remnant of Jews (of all denominations), wherever they may be in India, coordinating their religious, social, financial and material resources for the benefit of them all. A Council of Indian Jewry was recently (1979) established, with Ezra Kolet (of Delhi) as President, Shellim Samuel (of Bombay) as Organizing Chairman and Satu Koder (of Cochin) and Nissim Ezekiel (Bombay) as Vice-Presidents. It remains to be seen how effective the new organization will prove to be. It plans to promote and coordinate the interests of Indian Jews, especially in the dwindling congregations of Bombay, Poona, Ahmedabad, Delhi, Cochin and Calcutta and to act on their behalf; also to preserve synagogues and Jewish cemeteries; and to represent Indian Jewry at international conferences.

As a breath of fresh air, early in 1985 the Federation of Indian Jewish Youth (F.I.J.Y.) was formed in Bombay in order to serve as a non-partisan coordinating body for Jewish young people (ages 13-35) of India. It especially represents the approximately one thousand young Jews (Baghdadis, Bene Israel and Cochinis together) who live in Greater Bombay. Member bodies of the Federation are: the Bombay Zionist Association; the Jewish Cultural Association; the Jewish Religious Union, Youth Wing; and the Maccabean Sports Club. The founders, among whom are college students and young professionals, are enthusiastic, creative and capable individuals. The goals of the federation are to "reactivate Jewish awareness from one focal point, and to serve as a community resource that receives and disseminates information within and without the community." They propose to achieve these goals through organizing seminars and Jewish religious camps, publishing a newsletter, and coordinating inter-group activities.

The leadership is receptive to ideas for useful and meaningful programs and special projects. They even are intrigued with the prospect of seriously undertaking specific assignments of research and documentation about the Jews of India!

NOTES

1. Cf. Strizower : *The Children of Israel : The Bene Israel of Bombay*, pp.148-52.
2. On the day after the last day of Passover the Moroccan Jews have similar picnic festivities for the entire community (and for the public at large). It is called *"Maimouna"*. The time of year for this outdoor Bene Israel event might perhaps have been chosen with this custom of Arabic-speaking Jews in mind.
3. Cf. Strizower : Ibid., pp.152-60.
4. A great uncle of B.J. Israel was made a Free Mason in the late 19th century.
5. One wonders whether this Bene Israel bride and groom were actually aware that they were breaking a rule. In his *History of the Bene-Israel* Kehimkar says (p.143) that "....a spinster may marry a widower but a widow marries a widower only. A remarriage is not performed in a synagogue." The bridal couple in the case concerned must have been rather affluent and westernized, since otherwise they would not have been considered eligible for renting the Baghdadi synagogue premises in the first place; and very likely they were not very observant Jews. They probably forgot, or wanted to forget, Bene Israel old customs. For the Bene Israel the custom of not solemnizing a widow-remarriage in a synagogue could not have antedated 1796 (when the first Bene Israel synagogue was built), and it is possible that if the Bene Israel had been aware of the restriction at all, they might have attributed it to an old-fashioned Hindu-like custom which, in their judgment, the Baghdadis would therefore have ridiculed.

Chapter 30
Emigration to Israel

The Indian anthropologist, Irawati Karve, says that

As long as historical records go these people [the Bene Israel] have lived on the West Coast, i.e. the Konkan.... This community, for all practical purposes, was a native Maharashtra community, but this sentiment has been shaken by the creation of Israel as an independent state, and many young, educated and enterprising Jews have left Maharashtra to settle into what they consider to be their ancient home-land.[1]

The story of the Bene Israel emigration to Israel should also be prefaced by Kehimkar's own words written at the close of the 19th century in his *History of the Bene-Israel of India*. Significantly, these words are from the concluding paragraphs of his 9th chapter which he has entitled "The Bene-Israel as Gallant and Faithful Soldiers" (pp.224-225) :

The Bene-Israel and the Jews in general have no ambition to gain even an inch of ground anywhere except in Palestine....it is ever before the eye of every individual of that race by day and night, and ever does he remember "If I forget thee O Jerusalem, let my right hand forget her cunning. Let my tongue cleave to the roof of my mouth if I remember thee not, if I prefer not Jerusalem above my chief joy." Psalms CXXXVII, 5-6 ....This sentiment however does not lessen their patriotism for the country where they live at present, for they have been distinctly commanded by God through the Prophet Jeremiah to look to the country of their residence and naturalization with feelings of great love and true patriotism. (Jeremiah XXIX, 4-7).

It is on this very account that in the prayer of the Bene-Israel on the night of the Day of Atonement for the Empress of India, the Prince of Wales, the Royal Family, the Governor General of India and the Governor of the Presidency the following words are inserted : "In their days and in ours, may Judah be saved, Israel dwell in safety and the Redeemer come to Zion. May such be the Divine will and let us say Amen."

In 1897 the First World Zionist Congress was convened. But the Bene Israel declined an invitation to participate in this Congress on the grounds that Jewish settlement of the Holy Land could occur only with the coming of the Messiah. In 1919 a Zionist leader, Paul Tolkovsky, came to Bombay and tried to ascertain the attitude of the Bene Israel community toward Zionism. Most members of the Bene Israel Conference were in favor of Zionism, while strong opposition to it came from the All India Israelite League. This encounter was featured in *The Israelite*, Volume II, Nos.5-6, 1919, pp.73-7. Its editor at the time, David Erulkar, as well as his brother Dr. A.S. Erulkar, held a rather negative opinion of Zionism, largely because they felt that most Zionists would not accept the Bene Israel as "pure" Jews. There was no consensus on this matter among the Bene Israel, nor were they then clearly informed of the aims and activities of the Zionist Movement. The Board of the Shaar Ha-Rachamim Synagogue, after much debate and insistence upon no discrimination in the Holy Land based on color or on place of origin, voted to express its sympathy toward the Zionist Movement. On the other hand, the *jamat* of the Tifereth Israel Prayer Hall in Jacob Circle supported only the Zionist aims for development of Jewish learning and culture, deferring consideration of Zionist political or national aims.

A Zionist group in Bombay, called the Bombay Zionist Association (B.Z.A.), was not started until 1919-20. It was formed on the initiative of three dedicated young men of the Baghdadi community : Judah J. Gubbay, E.S. Somekh, and J.S. Ezra. Thereafter, Zionist leaders began visiting Bombay. Among them was Immanuel Olswanger who, almost forty years after it was written, learned of Kehimkar's still unpublished manuscript on *The History of the Bene Israel of India*. Olswanger, appreciating its importance, arranged to have it published.[2]

After Olswanger, teachers, most of them from Palestine, came to Bombay where they taught Hebrew as a modern language, giving extra-curricular lessons to the various Jewish youth clubs as well as to adult groups. Classes in Jewish history and for teaching Hebrew songs and folk-dances were also organized. It was not until 1940 that members of the Bene Israel community began to join the Bombay Zionist Association. In 1950 the Zionist Federation of India, consisting of Zionist groups in Bombay, Calcutta, Poona, Ahmedabad and Cochin, was founded. In 1969 a split occurred in the Bombay Zionist Association and a second group, known as the Indian Zionist Organization of Bombay (I.Z.O.), came into being.

Another international Jewish organization, the B'nai Brith,[3] established in Bombay in 1966 a B'nai Brith Lodge of India with a Women's Auxillary. Membership in both the Zionist and the B'nai Brith groups was and is open alike to Baghdadi, Bene Israel, Cochin and foreign Jews : all cooperating and participating together. Many factors contributed toward making this phenomenon possible at this particular juncture in history.

In the late 1930s and early 1940s about 2,000 European Jews, as well as some non-Jews, found refuge in India from Nazi persecution. Some of the refugees had had to come via the Far East. About 1,300 of the European refugees were native to Central Europe. In addition to the Europeans, about 2,000 Iraqi Jews had fled to India from Iraq in 1941 after the oppressive Rashid Ali Revolt there. Most Jewish refugees who came to India during this period were temporary wartime residents, living primarily in Bombay and in Calcutta. However, some individual families went to live in many other parts of India as well, from Kashmir to Madras. The refugees organized a Jewish Relief Association which represented and worked for their common interests. Many of the refugees took up the occupations which they had practised in their native countries, earning a living as physicians, architects, fruit-farming specialists, businessmen, etc. It was the first opportunity for the Jews of India to mingle with large numbers of western Jews. The Indian Jews were thus exposed to new customs and new ideas which changed their own Jewish life almost as intensively as had the contact with the British changed their secular life in the previous century. The peak years of Jewish refugee residence in India were from 1942 to 1946. By 1948 most of the Jewish refugees had left India for the West. Even so, there were still about 200 European Jews living in Bombay alone in 1952.

A refugee from Poland, Hersch Cynowitz, was one of very few refugees who opted to become Indian citizens. Rightly or wrongly, he came to be identified for many years by world Jewry as *the* representative of and spokesman for Indian Jewry.[4] In 1947, when about 500[5] Afghan Jewish refugees had fled to Bombay, en route to settle in Palestine, it was Hersch Cynowitz who organized relief for them in Bombay, sheltering them in temporary huts on Jewish school premises, and arranging for their emigration from

Bombay to Palestine in planes chartered by the Jewish Agency.[6] Before Indian Independence the Bombay Government served as agent for the Central British Indian Government in handling wartime aliens, in camps or in custody. Cynowitz worked through these channels as well. It was through his tireless efforts and influence that flight arrangements were made and certificates granted to hundreds of Jewish wartime refugees and to thousands of Indian Jews, enabling them to reach Palestine, later called Israel. He founded the so-called Palestine Office in India, where he served as the representative of the Jewish Agency vis-a-vis the British India Government. In 1950, the Jewish Agency opened a regular office in Bombay to facilitate emigration to Israel from India. Cynowitz was the Chairman of this Jewish Agency Office. Between 1949 and 1950 he had arranged for 5,000 Indian and Afghan Jews to leave for Israel, on specially chartered planes, without passports, but on official lists of the British Palestine Office which entitled them to receive travel certificates over Cynowitz's signature.

In 1950 Cynowitz became an Indian citizen. Although special examinations are required in order to be enrolled as an Advocate of the High Court of Bombay, in Cynowitz's case his certificate from Poland was deemed to suffice. He not only was an Advocate of the High Court of Bombay but also lectured on Constitutional Law at Bombay University. He had served as Chairman, Honorary Secretary, and (in 1962) President of the Central Jewish Board of Bombay, always representing Indian Jewry at World Zionist Congresses (where he served on the Action Committee), at World Jewish Congresses, etc. Before Cynowitz's participation, Indian Jewry had never been represented at such international gatherings. He was the moving force behind the Bombay Zionist Association and it was he who decided which (if any) other delegates from Bombay were to attend any overseas Zionist conferences. Cynowitz was a good organizer, but at the same time he took advantage of the Bene Israel tendency to fall out among themselves and not cooperate with one another. In 1969, however, an effort was made by some Bombay Jews to free themselves from Cynowitz's rein and under Maurice D. Japheth (a "Baghdadi" Jew — whose grandfather came from Yemen — married to a Bene Israel woman, and very close to the Bene Israel community), the Indian Zionist Organization was founded by those who had split away from the Bombay Zionist Association. Cynowitz still continued to attend World Zionist Congresses as a delegate from the B.Z.A. He died in Jerusalem in 1977.

With the advent of Indian independence on August 15, 1947, there began an intensification of democratization throughout the country, providing new opportunities for the mingling of India's hitherto socially isolated communities. A specified proportion of college seats and of civil service jobs were, as a matter of law, reserved for individuals from deprived, so-called "backward" communities and scheduled castes. Understandably, the Jews of India were not included in this category.

Israel became an independent state on May 14, 1948. Since then, India has not maintained any diplomatic relations with Israel on an ambassadorial level, although on September 17, 1950, it was officially announced that "The Government of India has decided to accord recognition to the Government of Israel". This statement does not indicate whether the recognition is *de jure* or *de facto*. At first the Government of Israel appointed only an Honorary Consul, based in Bombay.[7] But, since early 1953 Israel has continuously maintained an official Israeli Consulate in Bombay. There has been, and still is, a modest amount of commercial activity between Israel and India.

The Zionist Movement embraced Jewish communities the world over. The almost 2,000-year-old constant and universal Jewish longing to return to the homeland of the Jewish people had finally become a reality, a fact which thrilled large numbers of Indian Jews as it thrilled Jews elsewhere, and there was a mass emigration from India to Israel, beginning in the 1950s. There is no doubt that the efforts of Jewish Agency representatives among Indian Jews, their information about Israel, their Hebrew classes and work with youth groups, teaching the ideals and the songs and dances of modern Israel, and explaining her need for pioneers – that all these activities aroused among Indian Jews great enthusiasm to emigrate to the new country, reinforcing their already deeply ingrained religious ideal to return to the Jewish homeland. This emigration almost totally depleted the Cochin Jewish community, and drastically reduced the numbers of Bene Israel remaining in India.[8] Indian Jews left the country of their birth with ambivalent emotions : strong faith in their religion and eagerness to build a new life in Israel; and genuine sadness and regret at leaving India, their beloved home for centuries of unbroken peace and friendship with their non-Jewish neighbours. They were well aware of their close ties to the India which they loved; but, in the end, the emotional, religious pull of Israel proved irresistible. Similar ambivalencies are felt by Jews immigrating to Israel from other democratic countries. The common rationale is that young and small Israel needs their hands and minds and hearts more than do the populous countries in which they were born.

As long ago as 1923, Jacob B. Israel, in a reference to the Zionist Movement, posed a poignant question in *The Israelite* of July-August 1923, Volume VII, Nos.7-8, pp.103-4 :

....for us in India our Muslim neighbours have proved particularly kind. No distinction has ever been shown and help has been rendered even at burials wherever we happened to be few and isolated....Will the Muslims in India be the same to us as they have been, if our brethren in Palestine irritate their brethren there?

In 1943 a conference in Bombay of the All India Muslim League generated some anti-Zionist propaganda. Much later, in June 1951, anti-Jewish posters appeared in Bombay, written in Urdu, English and Marathi, saying : "Muslims, boycott Jewish goods and support the Arab cause!" But this appeal proved to be ineffective. In the 1970s anti-Israel posters were more blatant.

India has a long history of true hospitality to Jews on its soil. In spite of their difference, their insignificant numbers, and their lack of affluence, the Jews of India did, and still do, enjoy the respect of their neighbours and of their government. India's official policy of not maintaining diplomatic relations with Israel and its recently more pronounced pro-Arab policy cannot hide the widespread goodwill toward Israel which is felt and expressed by many Indians from many different strata of the nation's population.

Large scale emigration by Indian Jews to Israel actually began in 1949. Because the pressures of India's over-population are so great, meaningful employment is difficult to find, and opportunities for advancement are usually slow in coming compared to one's chances in more affluent countries. Hence there has been a trend of emigration from India not only by Indian Jews or other Indian minorities, but also by many Hindus. Israel is by no means an affluent country, but it welcomes Jewish immigrants. Even so, it was not only the Bene Israel youths and the poor who flocked to Israel : among those who chose to go to Israel there were also many Bene Israel who were holding good jobs in India – they left largely for idealistic reasons. Later, because so many Bene Israel had already left, more and more among those who had remained in India began to think that they too should leave. A dwindling community, of itself, generates feelings of inadequacy and a lack of self-assurance among those remaining behind.

There is no denying the economic factor as being *one* of the elements motivating Bene Israel emigration. After Indian Independence, some Bene Israel were apprehensive that gradually fewer Government jobs would become available to them, since competitive examinations for such jobs were opened to everyone. Besides, the new avenues of employment and advancement now offered by the private sector seem to have been offset by the beginnings of a new development : according to some respondents, Bene Israel seeking employment were occasionally told by potential employers that they were reluctant to hire Bene Israel because of the likelihood that they too might eventually emigrate, following the example set by so many of their brethren. Anyone with a strong drive for financial success, however, would not have chosen Israel, opting instead for one of the more affluent countries.

The Bene Israel mass exodus from India to Israel involves complicated contexts of situation, underlying all of which there was the vital age-old Jewish ideal of a return to Zion.

The *adult* Bene Israel emigration to Israel from the *rural* areas of the Konkan did not reach significant proportions (i.e. depleting the Bene Israel population from most Konkan villages) until 1968-1973.[9] Before 1968, great numbers of *urban* Bene Israel had already emigrated and settled in Israeli cities and large towns. This partly accounts for the fact that practically none of the rural Bene Israel opted to live in Israel's agricultural settlements, preferring, once in Israel, to live near their relatives and friends who had already become urbanized in India before they came to Israel and subsequently settled in Israel's urban areas.[10]

According to Israeli statistics, as of the end of 1980, a total of 19,500 Jews born in India (and Pakistan) had immigrated to Israel (see below, p.304). Of these, minimally 12,400 were Bene Israel. (Bene Israel in Israel estimate the actual number of Bene Israel immigrants to have been more than 15,000.) For further statistics on immigration to Israel see below, pp.301 — 4.

NOTES

1. Karve : *Maharashtra, Land and Its People*, p.115.
2. Immanuel Olswanger himself was a remarkable scholar. He translated the *Bhagavad-Gita* into Hebrew so beautifully and so faithful to the rhythm of the original Sanskrit that the Hebrew words can be recited in accordance with the traditional Sanskrit chant and rhythm.
3. The B'nai Brith is a Jewish fraternal organization founded in New York in 1843 for the purpose of uniting all Jews regardless of differences among them in dogma, custom and ritual; for inculcating charity, morality and brotherly love; and, at the beginning, barring political and religious discussions. B'nai Brith Lodges were eventually established in European and in other countries. Some B'nai Brith Lodges are today primarily social in function. But, on the whole, the B'nai Brith is active in providing relief for persecuted Jews all over the world; and it functions as a champion and guardian of human rights for Jews, especially through its Anti-Defamation League.
4. Hersch Cynowitz was born in Poland in 1907 and earned a Master of Jurisprudence Degree from Stefan Batori University in Wilno. He fled from the Nazis, arriving in Bombay in 1941. He earned a living there through business and law practice.
5. This figure was given to the author by the late H. Cynowitz. Note, however, that H.G. Reissner puts the figure at 600.
6. On July 22, 1922, when the League of Nations Council confirmed the Palestine Mandate, with Great Britain as the Mandatory Power, the Mandate recognized the Zionist Organization as being "the Jewish Agency" to advise and cooperate with the administration "in such economic, social and other matters as may affect the establishment of the Jewish National Home and the

interests of the Jewish population of Palestine." The Zionist Organization itself served as this agency until the establishment of The Jewish Agency as such, in 1929. When, in 1948, Israel became an independent state, The Jewish Agency relinquished some of its functions to the Government of Israel. Today it concentrates on facilitating immigration, absorption of immigrants, settlement facilities, instruction in farming, youth work, and dissemination of information about Israel.

7. The Honorary Consul was Fritz Pollack, a merchant who, simultaneously with his new duties as Honorary Consul, continued to carry on his own commercial business in Bombay. He also published a very lively periodical called *India and Israel*.

8. After Indian Independence Baghdadi Jews also emigrated from India to Israel; but the majority left India to live in England, U.S.A., or Australia.

9. According to the 1961 Census, there were still living in Kolaba District (which, except for its very few towns, is thoroughly rural) 2,223 Jews (i.e. Bene Israel) among the District's 941,960 Hindus, 63,000 Muslims, and 1,518 Christians.

10. This stands out in contrast to the fact that most Cochin Jews live in rural settlements in Israel. The modern Bene Israel tendency to ignore their village ties (see above, p.158) has manifested itself in Israel as a sort of urban fixation, where almost all Bene Israel (even those who originally tried out life on Israeli *kibbutzim*, i.e. rural collective settlements, and even those Bene Israel farmers who came to Israel directly from rural areas in India) have settled in Israeli towns or in cities in preference to life in a rural community.

Chapter 31
The Jews Remaining in India

In 1948 Bene Israel in India numbered somewhere between 17,500 and 20,000 souls, the Baghdadi Jews about 6,500, and the Cochin Jews about 2,600. Twenty years later, as of 1968, their numbers in India were approximately 13,000, 1,500 and 100 respectively. As of 1978 the towns or cities with considerable numbers of Bene Israel still in residence ranked as follows according to descending order of size in respect of their Bene Israel population: Greater Bombay, Thana, Poona, Ahmedabad, Panvel, Pen, Alibag, Nagpur, Ashtami, Revdanda. No mere listing, however, can convey a proper idea of the situation in an historical perspective. To cite just one example: whereas some 300 Bene Israel families lived in Alibag in former times, the figure in 1978 was less than 20 Bene Israel families. Besides, most of the remaining so-called Bene Israel centers have lost much of their former community vitality as well as numbers of congregants. By 1978 the total number of *all* Jews then remaining in India was estimated at, maximally, 7,000 souls.

Because of the large-scale emigration of Jews, their three once flourishing and distinct communities in India have become too small to be separately viable; and so they came, little by little, to share religious facilities and services, to mix socially, and even to intermarry with each other to some extent.

Of the Bene Israel places of worship mentioned above (pp. 149 and 232), the following have had to close down because of emigration of most of their congregants: the Knesset Israel Synagogue for Tale-Ghosale in Mangaon; the Hesed El Synagogue in Poynad; Shaare Shalom Synagogue in Borlai; Ambepur Synagogue; Bethel Synagogue in Ashtami; Shaar Ha-Tefila Synagogue in Mhasla; Talekhar Synagogue in Post Chorlei; and prayer halls in Satambe, Murud, Shriwardhan, Ajmer and Indore.

In the early 1960s an All India Federation of Synagogues had been established, requiring only very nominal annual dues and leaving full autonomy to each synagogue. It accomplished practically nothing. Only an all-encompassing, properly organized, vital program with well qualified leadership can restore and improve the Jewish content in the lives of India's Jews today.

Several Bene Israel respondents in India nowadays deplore the neglect on the part of many parents in transmitting Jewish knowledge to, and providing a full Jewish life for their own children.

Not only because of the worrisome problem of the slackening pace of Jewish life as such, but also because of the snowballing problem of scarcity of potential marriage partners for the young, Jewish youths were often sent from India (and from other countries as well, but often for different reasons) to Israel before their parents would come. Their first years in Israel were spent in Israeli Youth Villages until their parents arrived, or until they had finished school and had been trained for a job or profession of their own. These youngsters thus got a head start in adjusting to a new life and a new language, improving their chances for a better economic future. But uppermost in the minds of Bene Israel parents still in India was the fact that in Israel their children could now lead a much fuller Jewish life and would have no difficulty in finding suitable Jewish marriage partners. Not only Bene Israel youths from urban backgrounds, but also Bene Israel youths from Konkan villages, under the auspices of the Jewish Agency, came first to dormitories in Bombay for orientation towards life in Israel and to learn about necessary preparations for immigration.

During the earlier years of emigration to Israel (i.e. until about 1965), more Bene Israel boys than girls were leaving for Israel, a fact which, in spite (or rather because) of the modern trend toward love-marriages, actually reinforced the traditional Bene Israel custom of arranged marriages, since the parents were now concerned lest their daughters remaining in India would marry outside of the community because of the growing shortage of available Bene Israel boys. As early as World War I there had been the occasional Bene Israel-Baghdadi marriage. But, on the whole, the Bene Israel and the Baghdadis frowned upon this[1] until very recently. A serious current problem of Bene Israel in India, related to the shortage of marriage partners, is the rise in the number of conversions among Bene Israel girls as a consequence of their marrying outside of the Jewish fold. In the case of previous intermarriages, the Bene Israel wives frequently maintained their Jewishness and brought the children up as Jews. Today, however, the number of conversions far exceeds that of the previous century, even though the Bene Israel were then under very strong Christian missionary influences. On the other hand, however, children of non-Jewish mothers married to Bene Israel fathers have been converting to Judaism in order to facilitate their emigration to Israel as Jews under the Israeli "Law of Return" which entitles any Jew to settle in Israel.

For the Bene Israel remaining in India there is the serious problem of how to care for the now (proportionately) much larger numbers of aged Bene Israel who are left without any family members in India. Today, as always before, there are no Bene Israel beggars on the streets; but needy Bene Israel do call on other Bene Israel for help; and the needy *are* helped, but not really adequately.

Most of the Bene Israel who prefer to remain in India hope to visit Israel at least once in their lifetime. But they want a dynamic Bene Israel community to survive and flourish within India. They hope that their community can be given a new lease on life, continuing in India as do other Jewish communities in other countries. All Bene Israel whether in India, in Israel, or elsewhere in the world – deeply appreciate the hospitality extended to them by India during all their generations.

Actually, in this, as in most respects, at this stage in the history of India's Jews, one need no longer differentiate between the three separate Indian Jewish identities. It is Jewish identity as such which is the focal issue.

There is a very real need for a knowledgable, capable and dynamic person to minister alike to *all* the Indian Jews who remain in India – to the Baghdadis, the Bene Israel, and the Cochin Jews together. Such a person, who could be male or female, an Indian Jew or a foreign Jew, must have all of the following abilities : a sound knowledge of world Jewish history, religion, literature and customs, as well as of the Hebrew language (modern and biblical); familiarity with Israel, past and present; and training and experience in leadership techniques and group dynamics. Bombay would be the center, but there would also be a need to travel (as did the *kajis* of old, but they travelled within a smaller radius) according to a systematic plan, reaching young and old in all the clusters of Jews living in various parts of India; stimulating, guiding and teaching; officiating at rites of passage; even serving as matchmaker where necessary; and conducting an annual all-India camp for Indian Jewish youth. Ideally, the specialist should have competent, salaried assistants, and also other persons qualified to serve as *mohel* and *shohet*. The personnel should be well paid. The position of the "specialist-director" should be a full-time job and the initial contract should be for a three year period.

Properly to design, organize, coordinate and administer such a wide-ranging project cannot be achieved overnight. But the goal is exciting and well worth the time, effort and money. Incomes and funds from the once vital synagogues, and other endowments — Baghdadi, Bene Israel and Cochini — should now be pooled together and put to constructive use in helping to finance this joint venture of revitalizing the Judaism of those Jews who prefer to remain in India.

NOTES

1. Some Bene Israel still refer to a Baghdadi who has married into the family as "that outcaste", or "that Yehudi". It is more common for a Bene Israel boy to marry a Baghdadi girl than vice versa.

Chapter 32
Monument to Bene Israel Ancestors at Navgaon

Formerly a small group of Bene Israel families used to live in Navgaon, near the cemetery where, tradition says, the shipwrecked ancestors of the Bene Israel lie buried. Whenever a visitor came, there used to be someone from these families to show the visitor around and to furnish explanations. But the last Bene Israel Navgaon family has left the place.

At this late hour in their communal history the Bene Israel finally made a concerted effort to construct a monument at Navgaon in memory of their traditional ancestors, lest posterity forget the story. Bene Israel within, as well as outside India supported the project and sent their donations. A committee, under the sponsorship of the Tifereth Israel Synagogue in Bombay, chaired by Shellim Samuel, represented all Bene Israel synagogues and prayer halls in Bombay, Thana, Poona, Tala, Alibag and Revdanda. Their first meeting was held on August 19, 1973.

How the project came into being makes an interesting story: The Government of Maharashtra had offered to build a public water-reservoir in the town of Tala, provided that its citizens would raise Rs.96,000 as counterpart funding toward the costs of its construction. The 50-member Bene Israel congregation of the Knesset Israel Synagogue of Tala managed to raise the astonishing sum of Rs. 16,000—fully one-sixth of all the money which had to be raised by *all* the residents of Tala. To show their own appreciation for this splendid contribution of the Knesset Israel Synagogue congregation, the other residents of Tala wanted to erect "a suitable memorial" in Tala. The Bene Israel congregation, however, offered another suggestion, urging, instead, the erection of a monument to their ancestors at Navgaon.[1] They then addressed letters in that sense to Bene Israel places of worship in India, requesting donations. The letter struck a responsive chord.

The Bene Israel's own fund-raising campaign, with its goal of about Rs. 50,000, was to have ended by December 1974 and construction of the Navgaon Monument to begin in 1975. However, everything lagged behind the original schedule. After the ground-breaking ceremony took place, the target for beginning actual construction of the monument was pushed ahead to mid-1979. In the meantime construction costs went up considerably, and other problems arose also.

The aim of the memorial project was not only that of constructing an impressive monument, but also of providing

a proper road leading up to the cemetery, putting up a proper sign-board and getting the road re-named after the Navgaon Cemetery, properly fencing the cemetery and providing a rest-house near the cemetery. The Committee also proposes to approach the Archaeological Society of the Government of India and enter into an agreement for the preservation of the cemetery and to get it recognized as a monument of historical importance. The Committee also proposes to collect material and sources regarding the landing of the ancestors of the Bene Israels on the shores of the Konkan and to bring out an authentic History of the Bene Israel of the Konkan.[2]

The design for the monument itself was created by the Bene Israel architect, Joshua M. Benjamin of Delhi. (See above pp. 188 and 211).

The design is based on the traditional Jewish symbol, the Shield of David (a six-pointed star),[3] which will be the base of a six-sided pillar about 17 feet high. Appropriate Hebrew, Marathi and English inscriptions will appear on the sides of the pillar to commemorate the landing of the first group of Bene Israels at Navgaon. The construction medium of the structure will be R.C.C. (rich mixture) with rubble infilling, so that the life of the Memorial is long and the cost of maintenance reduced to a minimum. The external surface of the concrete will be shutter finish, the letters will be cast along with the shuttering, so as to get a recessed type effect. The base of the pillar will have six black Kudappa stones on which the donors' names will appear. It is also proposed to construct a compound wall with an iron gate, so that the cemetery can be kept secure from trespassers.[4]

At the time of this writing (1985), although construction of the Bene Israel Navgaon monument itself has been completed, due to lack of funds, the compound wall around the cemetery has not yet been built. The cemetery is still being used for new burials and it is being maintained by the Bene Israel synagogue in Alibag.

NOTES

1. See "Memorial Planned on the Arrival of Bene-Israel in India" in *Shalom*, Special Jewish New Year Issue (c. September) 1973, printed and published by M.D.Japheth for the Indian Zionist Organization of Bombay, p.8.
2. From an article entitled "Memorial to the Ancestors of the Bene-Israel at Navgaon Cemetery" in *Shalom*, Special Jewish New Year (5735) Number, (c. September) 1974, Bombay, p.3.
3. The six-pointed star (formed by positioning two equilateral triangles of the same size, one upside-down over the other) became known as the "Jewish star" or "Magen David" (Shield of David) relatively late in Jewish history. It is not metioned in the earlier rabbinical literature. The form itself is a very ancient symbol, associated with many peoples : it is an important symbol in Hindu philosophy and also appears frequently on Muslim tombs.
4. Quoted from the brochure of a benefit performance of the Marathi drama *Chandne Shimpeet Ja* which took place in Bombay on November 10, 1974. The benefit performance was organized to raise funds for the construction of the Navgaon Monument.

Chapter 33
Demographic Data

Although censuses of Bombay Island were taken as early as 1814/15, and of Bombay in 1833/34 and in 1854, the first significant official censuses in India were taken in Bombay in 1864 and in Calcutta in 1866. Reproduction of the actual detailed count of "Number of Jews of Different Ages Present in Bombay and Its Different Divisions and Sections on the Night of the First of February 1864" can be found below as Table 11. (There were in Bombay City in 1864 1,517 Jewish males and 1,355 Jewish females, making a total of 2,872 Jews.) From *The Indian Census In Perspective*[1] we learn that

> The years 1867-72 were spent in taking a census by the actual counting of heads in as much of the country as was practicable. This series, commonly known as the Census of 1872, was not a synchronous project, nor did it cover all territory possessed or controlled by the British.

The first complete census conducted on a uniform basis throughout India was that of 1881, regularly taken every ten years thereafter.

Beginning in 1911, the Census enlarged its coverage of each province or state as a separate unit and published a separate series for each province or state, as well as on an all-India basis. The censuses contain, as a separate category, tabulations of adherents of "Other Religions".[2] Under this heading one usually finds a column labeled "Jews". The Government of India Census Reports, based on the official surveys made every ten years and covering a great variety of categories of data,[3] unfortunately do not (when and if tabulating Jews) differentiate among the three different Jewish communities of India (i.e. Bene Israel, Cochin and Baghdadi), the sum total of whom has never amounted to more than a very small fraction of one percent of India's total population — even if one allows for the inevitable factor of under-enumeration. One realizes what a considerable factor under-enumeration of Jews must have been in the past (as well as in modern times) simply by comparing the more recent census figures for Indian Jews in specific places of small concentration with the *known* number of actual Indian Jewish residents there at the time concerned. Even so, in each census the overall picture and the orders of magnitude are valid and must be taken seriously.[4] In terms of India's total population, even the most accurate count of India's Jews would alter, if at all, only the *third* digit *after* the decimal point in the percentages noted in the official figures, according to which, in 1961, Jews constituted 0·042 percent of the total population of India.

India's major religions, in order of number of adherents, are Hinduism, Islam, Christianity, Sikhism, Buddhism, Jainism. In addition to these, the 1961 Census, for instance, lists fifty-six "Other Religions and Persuasions" among which Judaism ranks thirteenth in order of relative numbers of adherents. It is a great pity that Jews in India did not follow the example of the Parsi community which, against payment of a fee before the census-taking, made a special arrangement with the local census authorities for extraction, from the primary records, of information about their own community, broken down into social and cultural details, all of which are not published in the census volumes as such but which were included in the original census questionnaires, the replies being made available to interested parties. As an alternative, perhaps a careful study of records of each synagogue and prayer-hall which ever functioned in India might give us a valuable accounting. No definitive study and compilation of population figures of Jews in India as mentioned in the earliest gazetteers, censuses and other types of records has as yet been published. The challenge is to try to make some sort of order out of the welter of figures much of which are unsynchronizable and not comparable. The present chapter will attempt to sort out some coherent information relating to the demography of the Bene Israel.

Concerning the earliest censuses, we note that Hamilton's *Gazetteer of Bombay City* (Volume I, pp.42-3) gives these figures for "1812" probably referring to the 1814-15 Census :

Table 5 : POPULATION OF BOMBAY ISLAND 1812, ACCORDING TO RELIGION

Hindus	103,786
Muslims	27,811
Parsis	13,156
Jews	781
Native Christians	14,454
TOTAL	159,988

Also mentioned for 1812 on Bombay Island were 1,700 Europeans and 3,000 Native Troops. (The latter must have included many Bene Israel.)

The *Bombay Census of 1833* disclosed :

Table 6 : BOMBAY CENSUS OF 1833 ACCORDING TO RELIGION

Hindus and Jains	143,298
Muslims	49,928
Parsis	20,184
Christians (mostly Roman Catholics)	18,376
Jews	2,246
TOTAL	234,032

The Census which Rev. Wilson commissioned, as recorded in his *1838* paper on the Bene Israel, reports for *Bene Israel only* :

Table 7 : BENE ISRAEL POPULATION IN 1838

Location	Number of Bene Israel
English Territories in the Konkan	c. 800
Bombay Island	c. 1,932
Angria Territory	870
Hubshi Territory	444
Bombay Army (including dependents)	c. 1,000[5]
Elsewhere	209
TOTAL	c. 5,255*

* This, according to Rev. Wilson, "falls short of the general native estimate by nearly 3,000"

In an article called "The Census of the Islands of Bombay and Colaba", by Colonel Sykes and published in the *Journal of the Statistics Society of London* in December 1852 (p.12), it was reported that — as of May 1, 1849 — on the Islands of Bombay and Colaba there were 612 Jewish males and 520 Jewish females, making a total of 1,132 Jews out of a total population of 566,119 at the time, the Jews amounting to 0·199 percent of that total population.

Occasional recommendations from within the community for the taking of an exclusively Bene Israel census were forthcoming, particularly during the early 1920s. There were arguments pro and con, some of them voiced in the form of articles in or letters to various Bene Israel journals. Articulate, educated protagonists pointed out how important it was for the community as a whole to cooperate fully in the proposed Bene Israel communal census. They urged — minimally — a census to ascertain the status of literacy among the Bene Israel, arguing that it was essential for the community's progress; and also to find out the number of the community's destitutes and the helpless widows and orphans, in order that help might reach *all* of these people. However, others, some of whom were as articulate and well educated as the protagonists, argued that to take a record of property and of defects would introduce new intra-communal problems causing alienation, hostility and evasion. Indeed, questions about literacy, economic status, infirmities, etc. were already features of the country-wide official decennial censuses, but the prevailing response of the Bene Israel to an intra-communal census was strongly negative, based on the superstitious fear of attracting the evil eye if one were to count one's blessings; also citing the Biblical story of a plague following King David's taking a census (Second Book of Samuel, chapter 24); and a more mundane fear, coupled with distrust and shame, in disclosing to members of the community one's own economic condition, infirmities in the family, etc. They never grasped the true significance of such a confidential community-wide project; nor did they understand its purpose of assessing the actual condition of the community on a purely statistical basis, with an eye toward subsequent design and implementation of measures to improve some of the adverse conditions endemic to the community.

It is appropriate here to mention the four persons who were seriously involved in the collection and/or collation of demographic statistics relating to the Bene Israel. The first, in point of time, was the Rev. John Wilson who arranged for the collection of statistics on Bene Israel population and dispersion (see Appendix 5, p.327). While Kehimkar, in his *History of the Bene-Israel of India*, pp.75-6, does list 1881 Census figures for Jews (extrapolating to arrive at the numbers of the Bene Israel) then living even in very small clusters throughout the subcontinent and in other British territories, the same figures and many more besides were collated by the Rev. J. Henry Lord in Appendix I of his *Jews in India and the Far East* in the form of several demographic tables for the Jewish populations in these areas, comparing the statistics for 1881, 1891 and 1901 — breaking down the data on Jews in Bombay Presidency even to each city ward of Bombay and to each District of the Presidency (See below, Tables 12 a-d and 13 a-e).

Almost half a century after Rev. Lord's work, another outsider, Dr. Hans G. Reissner, a refugee from Germany then residing in Bombay, undertook to make a demographic study of the Jews in India in general and of the Bene Israel in particular. Some of his findings were published in the periodical *India and Israel*, in an article entitled "The Jews of India" Volume 1, No.1, July 1948, pp.12-3; and No.2, August 1948, pp.14-5; as well as in another article, "Indian Jewish Statistics 1837-1941" (Vol. III, No.10, April 1951, pp. 23-5 and pp.46-7). The latter article first appeared in *Jewish Social Studies*, Vol. XII, New York, 1950, pp.349-66. The present author has seen some of Reissner's notes (see above, p.213) and correspondence with various Bene Israel persons and institutions.

Reissner requested, and at least in some cases received, detailed data on the Bene Israel in their respective areas of residence. But, it has been impossible to trace any publication of Reissner's findings in composite, complete form — if indeed he ever did finish the entire project and write it up in full detail. It is, however, a fact that for this project Reissner had the blessings and assistance of the Central Jewish Board of Bombay, as documented in his correspondence with this organization during 1944-45. There probably still were Bene Israel objections raised against questions on financial status and infirmities, because neither of these aspects are covered in Reissner's available notes or published articles.

In his article, "Indian Jewish Statistics 1837-1941", only two of his nine statistical tables carry information for the year 1837,[6] and the only other 19th century date used by Reissner, namely 1881, occurs only in one table. Actually, most of his information deals with the 1940s. His choice of years for the tabulation of each topic which he does discuss is very sporadic and only one table runs through a full series of successive censal years (in this case, from 1901 through 1941). However, Reissner has called attention to several points which bear repeating here:

(a) In 1837 the total Jewish population of the Indian subcontinent was 6,951; in 1941 the total Jewish population of the Indian subcontinent was 22,480 composed as follows:

Table 8 : THE JEWISH POPULATION OF THE INDIAN SUBCONTINENT IN 1837 AND 1941

	1837	1941	
Bene Israel :	5,255	14,805	
Cochin Jews :	1,039	2,000	1,935 in Cochin, Travancore and British Cochin; 65 elsewhere
Baghdadi Jews :	657 (350 in Bombay, 307 in Calcutta)	5,675	2,611 in Calcutta; 2,910 in Bombay; 154 in Poona.

(b) In 1941, of the subcontinent's total Jewish population of 22,480, 19,327 of these lived in British India, and 3,153 in the Princely (Indian) States.

(c) Over the period 1837-1941 the Cochin Jews showed the lowest absolute, as well as relative, increase in numbers. The Baghdadis showed the highest increase. The Bene Israel retained their absolute majority.

(d) "While 90 percent of the total population of India [i.e. the sub-continent, as of 1941] live in villages, 71 percent of the Jewish population are concentrated in six large industrial and commercial cities, viz. Bombay, Calcutta, Karachi, Poona, Ahmedabad, Thana." (Reissner, in *Jewish Social Studies*, Volume XII, p.352)

(e) "There are [as of 1941] probably less than 100 Jewish enterprises that employ an appreciable number of workers, salesmen and clerks." (p.361)

(f) "In the districts of their original settlement in Cochin and in Kolaba, the Jews have remained closer to the soil than Jews ever became in Europe." (p.363)

(g) "An estimate based on local inquiries, as well as on figures in the government census of 1941 for Cochin, shows that 70.43 percent of all the Jews of India are literate. The Cochin Jews have 52.0 percent, the Bene Israel 75.0 percent and the Baghdadis 65.0 percent. This compares with the all-India average of 12 percent but with 78.7 percent for the Parsees in Bombay and Sind provinces." (p.365)

There exist more detailed census data on literacy for Cochin Jews than for the other two Indian Jewish communities. One finds in Reissner's notes (not in his article, "Indian Jewish Statistics 1837-1941") that he had extracted the following additional information on Indian Jewish literacy:

i. In *1891*, for the total population of Bombay Presidency, in regard to literacy, Parsis ranked first, Jains second, and Jews third, except in the Native (Indian) States of the Presidency where Christians ranked third and Jews fourth.
ii. In *1931* these were the *All-India Percentages of Literates in English*: Hindus 1·12 percent, Muslims 0·92 percent, Christians 9·19 percent, Parsis 50·41 percent and Jews 26·36 percent.
iii. In 1946-47 Reissner's own samplings in the Konkan resulted in the following figures for *Literacy Among the Bene Israel*:

Table 9 : LITERACY AMONG THE BENE ISRAEL, 1946-7 *

Place	Heads of families	Whereof Literate
Revdanda	39	34
Ashtami	22	15
Tala	14	7
Virjoli	47	35
Murud	14	12
Borlai Mandle	19	16
Talekar	37	28
Nandgaon	47	43
Mhasle	50	16
Shriwardhan	21	16
TOTAL	310	222

* From Folio 654/3 of the Central Archives for the History of the Jewish People, Jerusalem.

The fourth person to whom we are indebted for his contribution to the study of Indian Jewish statistics is B.J. Israel, whose article "The Jewish Population of Kulaba District of Maharashtra (a demographic study based on Census Reports for 1961 and 1971) appears in his, *The Bene Israel of India : Some Studies*. In this demographic analysis, replete with very detailed tables of statistics, B.J. Israel explains that, during the decades concerned, Kolaba District — an area of 2,712·3 square miles (7,198 square kilometers), mainly rural with but a few towns — the Jewish part of the population was made up entirely of Bene Israel, with no residents from other Jewish communities. Sudhagad Tahsil in 1961 was the subdivision of Kolaba District with the largest Jewish population, but which has the fewest villages linked to traditional Bene Israel surnames.[7] Kolaba District as a whole was the only area in India where the Jewish population was mostly rural in character. Besides, in the decade 1951-61, when India's Jewish population as a whole was declining in numbers, the Jewish population in Kolaba District rose from 1,852 to 2,223 persons, a 20 percent rise. However, the 1971 Census shows a fall in Kolaba District's Jewish population of almost 60 percent — the total number of Jews, all of whom were Bene Israel, then numbering only 850 souls, 546 of whom were living in rural circumstances, and 304 of whom lived in towns of Kolaba District. In 1961 the total population of Kolaba District was 1,058,855; in 1971 its population had risen to 1,263,003. Adherence to the various religions in the District, percentage-wise, was as follows:

Table 10 : RELIGIONS IN KOLABA DISTRICT IN 1961 AND 1971, PERCENTAGE-WISE

	1961	1971
Hindus	88·96%	88·25%
Muslims	5·96%	6·53%
Buddhists	4·36%	4·41%
Jains	0·35%	0·49%
Jews	0·21%	0·07%
Christians	0·14%	0·19%

B.J. Israel says (on p.101 of his book) : "In 1961 this was probaby the only district in the whole of India where the Jewish population (2,223) exceeded the Christian (1,518); in 1971, the Christians (2,436) were almost thrice as many as the Jews (850)."

Besides the statistical contributions of the Rev. Wilson, the Rev. Lord, H.G. Reissner and B.J. Israel, there are the isolated figures which frequently crop up in all sorts of writings about Jews in India. Many of these figures were taken from official censuses, others from personal estimates,[8] or from actual *ad hoc* samplings. Although the present book concentrates on the Bene Israel, all of the tables reproduced below, except Table 20, relate to Indian Jews as a whole rather than to the Bene Israel alone. This is necessary not only for the sake of presenting an overall picture, but also because very few reliable figures are available for the Bene Israel separately. We know, however, that the Bene Israel formed not only the great majority of Indian Jews, but that the Bene Israel themselves were scattered all over the subcontinent even during almost the entire 19th century. The far-flung distribution of Jews all over India is mainly due to the presence of the Bene Israel. Except for the Census of 1872, the three Indian Jewish communities are not differentiated in the published Census Reports[9] and it is therefore impossible to give accurate figures for each Jewish group, especially for Jews living in cities, when the census tabulation enumerates only Jews of all Jewish communities together. However, for Bengal (Calcutta), Quetta and Aden one can assume that most of the Jews were Baghdadis (i.e. Arabic-speaking Jews of various origins).[10] In Cochin and Travencore States and in British Cochin (i.e. those areas which today constitute Kerala) almost every Jew was/is a Cochin Jew. Throughout Bombay Presidency the vast majority of Jews were Bene Israel, while the minority consisted almost entirely of Baghdadi Jews, with but a very few Cochin and European Jews[11] (who lived only in the cities). According to Reissner, the 4,000 or so non-Indian Jewish refugees in the subcontinent — mainly in Bombay and only during the 1940s — were counted by the authorities under a separate category. When dealing with figures for the *rural* areas of the Konkan, one can be sure that *all* the Jews living there were Bene Israel. As for distribution of Jews throughout India, in places other than those mentioned above, wherever there are clusters of Jews,[12] the majority, and in most cases all of them, would be Bene Israel. These considerations must be borne in mind in respect of the tables herein reproduced.

Another complication is due to the fact that certain boundaries of districts, of district-sub-divisions, and even of cities, have been reconstituted sometimes two and three times, especially during the 19th century; and the nomenclature has sometimes, but not always, changed accordingly — so that areas are not consistently comparable for the entire period since census-taking began in India. "Bombay Island" was not the same as "Bombay City", which in turn is not identical with "Greater Bombay". The boundaries of "Kolaba Collectorate" and of "Kolaba District" are not co-extensive although they do contain many of the same areas. British Territories and Feudatory (Native) States are listed separately for pre-independent India, and the States of Independent India are by no means co-extensive with the former States; etc., etc. The term "all India" will be used for convenience throughout, but for pre-independent India it actually included not only what were later Pakistan and Bangladesh, but also included Aden and Burma. If not otherwise indicated, all of the following tables have been compiled by the present writer by collating comparable figures from one or another of the official censuses — either countrywide or local. The few estimates which have been included are acknowledged as such by the use of "c" for *circa*. "Jews" refers to Jews of all kinds, including those of European or other non-Indian origins who had taken up permanent residence in India.

The Rev. Lord's table taken from Appendix IV, pp.56-7 of his *The Jewish Mission Field in the Bombay Diocese* has been selected for reproduction here as part of Table 14 (below) because the areas which it designates can be at least approximately related to (i.e. they either included or formed part of the areas of) the present divisions of India which appear super-imposed upon Table 14 in parentheses, alongside the names of earlier divisions. Also added to Rev. Lord's table by the present author are the comparable Census figures for the years 1901 and 1941. The figures from the Census of 1941 are particularly important because this was the last Census before the partition of the subcontinent and before the beginning of Indian Jewish emigration to Israel. It was also the last All-India Census which divided the subcontinent according to the divisions used by the Rev. Lord; from 1951 onwards, the breakdown into area categories was entirely different, as may be seen in our Table 15.

Until 1950, when Indian Jewish emigration to Israel got under way, any remarkably large increase (going beyond normal range for natural increase), or any large decennial decrease in the Jewish figures for a given area, especially — virtually only — in the case of the Bene Israel, should not be regarded as surprising; in view of Bene Israel history during the past century, the increases and decreases must have been attributable to any one of the following factors which created mobility from one area to another, namely: enlistment and change of station (often with one's family) while in army service; the attraction to cities and towns because of better educational or job opportunities; transfers during government civil service; and transitory employment (such as work on building a railway or during a housing construction boom).

Table 11 : NUMBER OF JEWS OF DIFFERENT AGES PRESENT IN BOMBAY AND ITS DIFFERENT DIVISIONS AND SECTIONS ON THE NIGHT OF THE 1ST FEBRUARY, 1864 : TABLE XLI

[Copied from *Extracts from Reports of the Censuses Held Earlier to the Census of 1871-72*; Office of the Registrar General, India, Ministry of Home Affairs, New Delhi 11; in Census of India 1971's Centenary Monograph Series, No.2.]

			Males according to Ages				
		Males of All Ages	Days 1 to 30	Months 1 to 23	Years 2 to 13	Years 14 to 44	Years 45 & over
	BOMBAY	1,517	2	50	441	829	195
	A Division	74	-	3	15	50	6
	B Ditto	1,154	1	32	331	655	135
	C Ditto	7	-	-	-	4	3
	D. Ditto	1	-	-	-	1	-
	E Ditto	162	-	9	50	73	30
	F Ditto	118	1	6	45	45	21
	Water Division	1	-	-	-	1	-
Division	Section						
A 1	Colaba	5	-	-	1	3	1
2	Fort, Southern	24	-	-	3	18	3
	Fort, Northern	10	-	-	2	6	2
3	Esplanade	35	-	3	9	23	-
B 1	Market	28	-	6	20	2	-
	Mandwee	381	1	16	113	197	54
2	Chukla	12	-	1	3	7	1
	Oomburkharee	346	-	1	74	234	37
3	Dongree	387	-	8	121	215	43
C 1	Dhobeetulao	-	-	-	-	-	-
	Phunuswaree	-	-	-	-	-	-
2	Bhooleshwar	-	-	-	-	-	-
3	Kharatulao	5	-	-	-	4	1
	Koombawara	2	-	-	-	-	2
4	Khetwaree	-	-	-	-	-	-
	Girgaon	-	-	-	-	-	-
D 1	Chaoputee	-	-	-	-	-	-
2	Walkeshwur	1	-	-	-	1	-
3	Mahaluxmee	-	-	-	-	-	-
E 1	Mazagaon	26	-	6	5	3	12
2	Tarwaree	10	-	-	1	8	1
3	Kamatheepoora	119	-	3	42	58	16
4	Parell	7	-	-	2	4	1
5	Sooree	-	-	-	-	-	-
F 1	Seo	5	-	-	2	1	2
2	Mahim	113	1	6	43	44	19
3	Wurlee	-	-	-	-	-	-
	Water Division	1	-	-	-	1	-

(continued)

Table 11 (continued)

		Females of All Ages	Females According to Ages				
			Days 1 - 30	Months 1 - 23	Years 2 - 13	Years 14 - 44	Years 45 & over
BOMBAY		1,355	2	91	431	614	217
A Division		62	-	3	12	34	13
B "		971	1	74	321	463	112
C "		4	-	-	1	-	3
D "		-	-	-	-	-	-
E "		189	1	11	48	97	32
F "		125	-	3	47	18	57
Water Division		4	-	-	2	2	-
Division	Section						
A 1	Colaba	5	-	-	-	5	-
2	Fort, Southern	17	-	-	4	5	8
	Fort, Northern	9	-	-	1	7	1
3	Esplanade	31	-	3	7	17	4
B 1	Market	25	1	9	10	4	1
2	Mandwee	416	-	16	114	217	69
	Chukla	16	-	-	3	11	2
3	Oomburkharee	224	-	8	78	121	17
	Dongree	290	-	41	116	110	23
C 1	Dhobeetulao	-	-	-	-	-	-
	Phunuswaree	-	-	-	-	-	-
2	Bhooleshwur	-	-	-	-	-	-
3	Kharatulao	1	-	-	-	-	1
	Koombarwara	3	-	-	1	-	2
4	Khetwaree	-	-	-	-	-	-
	Girgaon	-	-	-	-	-	-
D 1	Chaoputee	-	-	-	-	-	-
2	Walkeshwur	-	-	-	-	-	-
3	Mahaluxmee	-	-	-	-	-	-
E 1	Mazagaon	36	1	6	9	17	3
2	Tarwaree	5	-	-	3	2	-
3	Kamatheepoora	137	-	5	31	74	27
4	Parell	11	-	-	5	4	2
5	Sooree	-	-	-	-	-	-
F 1	Seo	5	-	-	1	2	2
2	Mahim	120	-	3	46	16	55
3	Wurlee	-	-	-	-	-	-
	Water Division	4	-	-	2	2	-

[Compare these figures with the Rev. Lord's Table for Bombay City of 1881, 1891, and 1901, reproduced below as Table 13d.]

THE JEWS OF THE BOMBAY PRESIDENCY

[The entire contents of these pages 288 through 291 are copied verbatim from Rev. J. H. Lord, *The Jews in India and the Far East;* Appendix I, pp. 2 through 7]

It will be seen from the foregoing that it is in the Presidency of Bombay that by far the larger portion of the Jewish population of India is located.

The 13,919 Jews of the Bombay Presidency are, first of all, distributed over four chief areas as follows :—

1. British Territory, Presidency Proper	9,441
2. " " Sind	428
3. Feudatory States	991
4. Aden	3,059
TOTAL	13,919

The Bombay Presidency Proper — The following gives the Jewish population of each Zillah or District, as shown by the Census enumerations of 1881, 1891 and 1901, respectively :—

Table 12a : THE JEWS OF THE BOMBAY PRESIDENCY PROPER : 1881, 1891 AND 1901

Name of District	1881	1891	1901
Bombay City	3,321	5,021	5,357
Ahmedabad	233	207	256
Kaira	7	9	12
Panch Mahals	7	...	2
Broach	18	23	16
Surat	61	39	9
Thana	892	386	314
Kolaba	2,139	2,422	2,268
Ratnagiri	1	...	2
Kanara	25	12	11
Khandesh	88	99	127
Nasik	101	108	100
Ahmednagar	65	39	20
Poona	619	930	801
Sholapur	94	20	5
Satara	21	82	33
Belgaum	89*	...	2
Dharwar	18	27	106
Bijapur	...	8	...
TOTAL	7,799	9,429	9,441

* The fact that a certain Station will sometimes show a number of Jews present at one census while at a future one they are absent, may sometimes be accounted for by the fact that the Jews were Ben-Israelite soldiers in a regiment, which, at the time of one census, was stationed at one place, and, at the time of another, was removed elsewhere.

SIND—The Jewish population of Sind, it may be noted, is mainly concentrated in the city of Karachi. The following table gives the Jewish population of each District according to the census enumerations of 1881, 1891 and 1901, respectively:—

Table 12b : THE JEWS OF SIND : 1881, 1891 AND 1901

Name of District	1881	1891	1901
Karachi	106	147	381
Hyderabad	31	32	10
Shikarpur	9	27	31
Thar and Parkar	4	...	6
Upper Sind Frontier	3	4	...
TOTAL	153	210	428

ADEN—The numbers of the Jews of Aden according to the Government Census of 1901 are as follows:—

Table 12c : THE JEWS OF ADEN IN 1901

Aden Municipality	2,910
Do. Cantonment	32
Perim Island	9
Shekh Osman Suburb	108
TOTAL, Aden	3,059

FEUDATORY STATES.—The following table gives the Jewish population of each State in 1881, 1891 and 1901, respectively. It will be observed that the Janjira and Bhor States contain the largest numbers of Jews in this Table. They are both contiguous to the Kolaba District, which is the original historic home of the Bene-Israel community, and the Jewish population inhabiting these states may be taken as an extension of that of Kolaba.

Table 12d : THE JEWS OF THE FEUDATORY STATES IN 1881, 1891 AND 1901

Name of State	1881	1891	1901
Catch	19	47	15
Palanpur	1	34	34
Mahi Kantha	5	4	9
Kathiawar	145	105	71
Rewa Kantha	...	6	...
Surat Agency	7	6	11
Janjira	590	599	566
Satara Agency, Bhor State	299	271	284
Do. (other Jaghirs)	...	4	1
Kolhapur } Southern Maratha Jaghirs }	5	6	...
TOTAL	1,071	1,082	991

The Bene Israel in the Twentieth Century

DETAILS OF THE JEWISH POPULATION OF A PORTION OF THE BOMBAY PRESIDENCY

The following tables show the distribution of Jews in the Taluka or Sub-divisions of the three Zillahs or Districts — those of Kolaba, Poona and Thana — in which the Bene-Israel are found dwelling in the largest numbers of any portion of Bombay Presidency, outside of the city of Bombay; and also their distribution in the different Wards or Municipal districts of the Bombay City: —

Table 13a : DETAILS OF JEWISH POPULATION OF KOLABA DISTRICT

Names of Taluka, or Sub-division	Jewish Population, 1891	Jewish Population, 1901
Alibag	790	726
Mangaon	85	74
Roha	413	432
Pen	461	452
Nagothana Petha	76	89
Panvel	521	455
Uran Petha	2	...
Karjat	17	1
Khalapur Petha	57	34
TOTAL	2,422	2,263

Table 13b : DETAILS OF JEWISH POPULATION OF POONA DISTRICT

Names of Sub-division	Jewish Population, 1891	Jewish Population, 1901
Mawal	68	55
Shirur	6	11
Bhimthadi	8	24
Indapur	1	...
Purandar	1	...
Junar	1	4
Haveli	845	707
TOTAL	930	801

Table 13c : DETAILS OF JEWISH POPULATION OF THANA DISTRICT

Names of Sub-division	Jewish Population, 1891	Jewish Population, 1901
Dahanu	5	...
Shahapur	6	1
Kalyan	7	11
Bhiwndi	6	5
Salsette	362	296
Murba		1
TOTAL	386	314

Table 13d : DETAILS OF JEWISH POPULATION OF BOMBAY CITY

City Wards			1881	1891	1901
WARD A	Colaba	Upper	...	4	2
		Middle	...	46	90
		Lower	...	...	...
	Fort Southern		125	262	165
	" Northern		19	109	37
	Esplanade		63	94	87
B	Mandvi		969	751	665
	Chuckla		18	2	1
	Umerkhadi		572	1,027	1,227
	Dongri		387	589	572
C	Market		3	11	13
	Dhobitalao		...	16	2
	Fanaswadi		...	...	...
	Bhuleshwar		...	1	...
	Kharatalao		47	23	19
	Khumbarwada		32	11	3
D	Khetwadi		41	18	21
	Girgaon		...	...	...
	Chaupati		10	7	...
	Walkeshwar		17	39	27
	Mahalaxmi		...	18	17
E	Mazagaon		1	37	43
	Tarwadi		47	263	464
	2nd Nagpada		304	303	406
	Kamatipura		123	185	62
	Tardeo		68	134	41
	Byculla		107	229	381
	1st Nagpada		296	452	374
F	Parel		27	87	76
	Shiwri		...	1	...
	Sion		11	10	25
G	Mahim		3	6	34
	Worlee		25	286	469
Harbour, Docks, Railways, & c			6	...	34
TOTAL			3,321	5,021	5,357

Comparative table of the Jewish Population of the City of Bombay at the five different census enumerations of 1864, 1872, 1881, 1891 and 1901 :

Table 13c : JEWISH POPULATION OF THE CITY OF BOMBAY IN 1864, 1872, 1881, 1891 AND 1901

1864	1872	1881	1891	1901
2872	2669	3321	5021	5357

Table 14 : TOTAL JEWISH POPULATION OF INDIA FOR 1881 AND 1891
[Copied from Rev. Lord's Appendix IV of his *The Jewish Mission Field in the Bombay Diocese*, pp. 56-7, with comparable data for the years 1901 and 1941 added by the present writer.]

Name of Province	BRITISH TERRITORY			
	1881	1891	1901	1941
1. Ajmer (Rajasthan)	94	71		133
2. Assam (Assam)	–	5		9
3. Bengal (West Bengal & Bangladesh)	1,059	1,447	1,939	2,778
4. Berar (Maharashtra)	3	2		9
5. Bombay Presidency (Bombay, Konkan, Gujarat, Karachi, Sind, Aden; eastern half of Maharashtra)	9,023	12,465	12,928	14,471* 1,082*
6. Burma	204	351	685	
7. Central Provinces (Maharashtra & Madhya Pradesh)	63	176		276
8. Coorg (Mysore)	–	–		
9. Madras Presidency (Tamilnadu, Andhra Pradesh, North Kerala)	30	42	45	191
10. North-West Provinces (including Oudh)	101	60		71 80*
11. Panjab (Punjab)	31	27		27
12. Quetta, etc. (Pakistan)	–	23		
13. Andamans				
[Other Provinces]	–	–	251	200
TOTAL, PROVINCES	10,608	14,669	15,848	19,327

* Bombay Province.
** Sind
*** United Provinces.

(continued)

Table 14 (continued)

Name of State or Agency	FEUDATORIES			
	1881	1891	1901	1941
4. Hyderabad (Andhra Pradesh)	47	26		20
5. Baroda (Gujarat)	–	36		47
6. Mysore (Mysore, today **Karnataka**)	1	21		64
7. Kashmir (Jammu & Kashmir)	–	–		11
8. Rajaputana (Rajasthan)	–	15		47
9. Central India (Madhya Pradesh)	38	72		77
10. Bombay States (Maharashtra & Gujarat)	–	1,082	991	948
11. Cochin States (Kerala)	1,249	1,142	1,137	1,528
12. Travancore (Kerala)	97	125	151	371
13. Central Province States (Madhya Pradesh)	–	–		6*
14. Bengal States (West Bengal, Bangladesh)	–	–		5
15. N.W. Province States (Pakistan)	–	–		5
16. Panjab States	–	6		12
17. Shan States (Burma)	–	–		
Other States			101	11
TOTAL, STATES	1,432	2,525	2,380	3,152
TOTAL, INDIA	12,040	17,194	18,228	22,480

* Gwalior

Table 15 : JEWISH POPULATION IN INDIA STATES-WISE FOR 1951, 1961, 1971 and 1981
[Composite : from data of Government of India Censuses of 1951, 1961, 1971 and 1981, prepared by S.B. Isenberg]

Nomenclature : 1951	No. of Jews	States : 1961	No. of Jews	States : 1971	No. of Jews	States : 1981	No. of Jews
Ajmer	—						
Andaman & Nicobar Is.	1						
Assam	—	Andhra Pradesh	13	Andhra Pradesh	12		
Bhopal	66	Assam	—	Assam	5		
Bihar	92	Bihar	14	Bihar	6		
Bilaspur	—						
Bombay	20,135						
Coorg	—						
Delhi	90	Delhi	37[a]	Delhi	4[a]		
		Goa, Daman & Diu	—	Goa, Daman & Diu	1		
		Gujarat	515	Gujarat	431	Gujarat	217
Himachal Pradesh	—						
Hyderabad	16	Jammu & Kashmir	3	Jammu & Kashmir	—		
		Kerala	370	Kerala	112	Kerala	c. 50
Kutch	3						
Madhya Bharat	125						
Madhya Pradesh	228	Madhya Pradesh	219	Madhya Pradesh	46		
Madras	474	Madras	27	Tamilnadu	1		
		Maharashtra	15,851	Maharashtra	5,134[c]	Maharashtra	4,354[e]
Manipur	—	Manipur	—	Manipur	—	Manipur	464
				Meghalaya	6		
Mysore.	162	Mysore	—	Mysore	19		

Demographic Data

P.E.P.S.U.[b]	9	Punjab	—	
Punjab	150	Rajasthan	299	
Rajasthan	—			
Saurashtra	69			
Travancore-Cochin	2,228	(See above Kerala)		(See above Kerala)
Tripura	—			
Uttar Pradesh	34	Uttar Pradesh	14	Uttar Pradesh
Vindhya Pradesh	5			
West Bengal	2,619	West Bengal	1,191	West Bengal	48
				Rest of India	583
TOTAL, ALL-INDIA	26,512		18,553		5,825[d]		5,618

NOTES:

a. This is a case of demonstrable under-enumeration. The number of Indian Jews (inclusive of children) resident in Delhi (State) was about 50 for 1961 and 35 for 1971. There is no need to assume, however, that the degree of under-enumeration was equally large in other places.

b. P.E.P.S.U.: Patiala and East Punjab States Union.

c. In 1971, for Greater Bombay 3,607; Kulaba 850; Thana 293; Pune 328; with a balance of 56 Jews in other parts of Maharashtra.

d. The actual number was closer to 6,000 perhaps even 6,500.

Table 16 : DECENNIAL SUMMARY OF TOTAL JEWISH POPULATION FOR ALL INDIA [a] 1881 - 1981
[Compiled by S. B. Isenberg]

Year of Census	Total Jewish Population	Total Bene Israel Population (* approx.)
1881	12,040	* 7,000
1891	17,194	* 10,000
1901	18,228	
1911	20,980	* 15,000
1921	21,778	
1931	24,081	
1941	22,480[b]	14,805
1951	26,512	* 20,000
1961	18,553	* 16,000
1971	5,825[c]	* 5,215[d]
1981	5,618	

NOTES :

a. Until the 1951 Census, the All-India enumerations included Aden, Burma and what is now Pakistan—for our purposes a feature not wholly irrelevant because roughly one-third of the Jewish population in these areas consisted of Bene Israel in those days.
b. Why this decrease of 1,601 persons between 1931 and 1941?
c. Indian Jewish estimates made all during the 1970s (and even as of 1981) usually put the figure of current total number of Jews remaining in India as "6-7,000".
d. About 500 Baghdadi and 110 Cochin Jews were still living in India in 1971, which would leave a balance of 5,215 Bene Israel in respect of the 1971 Census figure of 5,825 as the total number of Jews in India.

Table 17 : CHRONOLOGICAL SUMMARY OF TOTAL JEWISH POPULATION
FOR BOMBAY, 1814-1971
[Compiled by S.B. Isenberg]

Year of Census	Bombay	Total Number of Jews	Bene Israel[a] (approx.)	Baghdadis (approx.)
1814-15	Bombay Island	781		
1833	Bombay City	2,246	c. 2,000	c. 246
1864	Bombay City	2,872	c. 2,300	
1872	Bombay City	2,669		
1881	Bombay City	3,321	c. 2,407	c. 914
1891	Bombay City & Cantonment	5,021	c. 3,522	c. 1,499
1901	Bombay City & Cantonment	5,357	c. 3,815	c. 1,542
1911				
1921	Greater Bombay	7,698		
1931	Greater Bombay	8,946		
1941	Greater Bombay	10,390	c. 7,480	c. 2,910
1951	Greater Bombay	16,085		
1961	Greater Bombay	6,229		
1971	Greater Bombay	3,607		

NOTE :

a. Reissner explains that he arrived at these figures by adding the total number of Jews returned in the Census for Bombay's wards "A", Nagpada 1 and 2; and Byculla as being all Baghdadi; the Jews in the remaining wards of Bombay he assumed to be Bene Israel. From 1881 to 1941, on the average, there has been a ratio of 28·54 percent Baghdadis to 71·46 percent Bene Israel in Bombay. He ignores here the existence of Cochin Jews in Bombay since 1826.

Table 18 : CHRONOLOGICAL SUMMARY OF TOTAL JEWISH POPULATION
FOR KOLABA DISTRICT 1881-1961

[Compiled by S.B.Isenberg by combining Census figures reproduced by Rev. Lord with those in the 1964 revised edition of the *Kolaba District Gasetteer* on its pages 145 and 1158.]

Year of Census	Jews in Kolaba District[a]			Jews in Janjira State[b]		
	Males	Females	Total	Males	Females	Total
1881			2,139			
1891			2,422			
1901	1,089	1,179	2,268	270	296	566
1911	954	1,087	2,041	310	326	636
1921	834	924	1,758			
1931						
1941						
1951	930	922	1,852			
1961	1,124	1,099	2,223			
1971			850			

NOTE : a. Practically every Jew in Kolaba District was a Bene Israel b. By 1951 Janjira State had been merged with Kolaba District.

H.G. Reissner (in his notes found in Folio 654 at The Central Archives for The History of the Jewish People) condensed the 1941 Census figures for Indian Jews thus:

Table 19 : LOCATION OF INDIAN JEWS ON THE SUBCONTINENT IN 1941

	Total	Males	Females	Baghdadi Jews
Wholly Cochin Jews (Cochin & Travancore States & British Cochin)	1,935	999	936	
Wholly Bene Israel areas	2,564	1,220	1,344	
Bombay	10,849	5,602	5,247	(2,910)
Calcutta	2,611	1,286	1,325	(2,611)
Karachi	1,051	513	538	
Poona	789	387	402	(184)
Ahmedabad	389	193	196	
Thana	306	148	158	
	20,494	10,348	10,146	5,705
Dispersed elsewhere	+1,986	+1,116	+870	
TOTAL NUMBER OF JEWS	22,480	11,464	11,016	

Reissner reckoned that in 1941 there were 14,805 Bene Israel, about 5,705[13] (according to other notes by Reissner) Baghdadis, and about 2,000 Cochin Jews (a total equal to the 1941 Census figure of 22,480 Jews); and that of this total there were in undivided India 21,245 (or 94·5 percent) in the area which became India, and 1,235 (or 5·5 percent) in the area which became Pakistan, not considering the factor of natural increase for the period between 1941 (the census year) and 1947 (the year of partition). Only two Jewish families (a total of eight persons) emigrated from India to Pakistan at the time of partition; and virtually all of Pakistan's Jews eventually left that country for India, U.S.A., U.K., Canada — to the latter countries often via India.

Among H.G. Reissner's notes for 1945-47 (in the same Folio 654) were the following figures for some specific places with Bene Israel population at that time in Kolaba District and Janjira State. The place names (at least) may prove useful some day as additional places in which to try to track down further information on the history and life of Bene Israel — there being in the following list several villages which have no similarity to Bene Israel surnames. These place-names have been marked below in Table 20 by the present writer with asterisks (*).

Table 20 : NUMBER OF BENE ISRAEL RESIDENTS AS OF 1945-1947 IN SOME PLACES OF KOLABA DISTRICT.

Taluka	Place	Males	Females	Total
Alibag	Revdanda	113	100	213
Rohe	Ashtami	17	14	31
,,	* Dar Kaneh	6	6	12

Demographic Data

Taluka	Place	Males	Females	Total
Rohe	* Dolwal	4	1	5
,,	* Damkhadi	3	4	7
,,	* Pui	12	7	19
,,	Rohe	4	6	10
Mangaon	Tala	16	9	25
,,	* Hardi	2	1	3
,,	* Salset	6	5	11
,,	Wali[a]	6	5	11
Rohe	* Virjoli	64	56	120
,,	Ghosale	30	14	44
,,	* Gowalwadi	3	3	6
	TOTAL	286	231	517

NOTE :

a. Although the surname WALKAR (see above, p. 230) does not appear in B. J. Israel's list of Village-linked Bene Israel Surnames, Reissner's inclusion here of WALI, with its eleven Bene Israel residents, indicates that it too could be a Bene Israel Surname-linked village.

Of JANJIRA DISTRICT (STATE)

Place	Males	Females	Total
*Murud	24	23	47
Dande	9	8	17
Borlai Mandle	30	34	64
Korlai	5	3	8
Chorde	20	15	35
Chandgaw	5	7	12
*Chanera	2	3	5
Kokban	6	5	11
*Nhawa	7	3	10
*Parankhar	1	1	2
*Sarsoli	8	5	13
Shrigaw	1	—	1
*Tadgaw	—	2	2
Nandgaon	49	43	92
*Oosrolly	18	15	33
Mhasle	44	42	86
Agerwada	11	6	17
*Gowela	6	11	17
*Kharsai	3	4	7
*Majrona	5	2	7
*Rewli	—	1	1
Shriwardhan	13	14	27
Galsure	5	4	9
Walwati	10	9	19
*Ningdi	3	2	5
*Borlai Panchatan	10	6	16
TOTAL	295	268	553

Table 21a*: RELIGIONS OF BOMBAY STATE ** 1921-1951
PERCENTAGE-WISE

Religion	Number of Persons in 1951	Percentage of each religion in total population at the Census of			
		1951	1941	1931	1921
Hindus	31,785,614	88·40 %	88·18 %	88·72 %	88·78 %
Muslims	2,906,887	8·09	8·47	8·12	7·94
Jains	572,093	1·59	1·51	1·43	1·60
Christians	525,454	1·46	1·40	1·28	1·22
Parsis	97,573	0·27	0·32	0·38	0·40
Sikhs	37,017	0·10	0·03	0·01	-
Jews	20,135	0·06	0·05	0·05	0·05
Buddhists	2,395	0·01	0·01	0·01	0·01
Others	8,982	0·02	0·03		-
TOTAL	35,956,150	100·00	100·00	100·00	100·00

* Found in H.G. Reissner's notes in Folio 654/1 at the Central Archives for the History of the Jewish People.

** The entity Bombay State, as defined at the time of Independence (1947) ceased to exist when, in 1956, in its stead two new states (delineated according to linguistic factors) were created, namely Gujarat and Maharashtra.

Table 21b : JEWISH POPULATION IN BOMBAY STATE 1921-1951 [found among H.G. Reissner's papers, in folio 654/3 at the Central Archives for the History of the Jewish People]

Census Year	Total for Bombay State	Greater Bombay	Bombay Gujarat	Deccan North	Deccan South	Bombay Konkan	District Kolaba	District Poona
1921	11,814	7,698	353	1,027	55	2,681	2,372	870
1931	13,606	8,946	393	1,290	19	2,958	2,579	1,105
1941	15,345	10,849	574	1,272	67	2,583	2,229	1,078
1951	20,135	16,085	642	1,018	31	2,359	1,852	819

More Bene Israel lived — and still live — in what is now Maharashtra than in any other Indian State. Table 22 shows how drastically its Jewish population diminished between 1961 and 1971.

Table 22: JEWISH POPULATION OF MAHARASHTRA STATE 1961 AND 1971
(according to districts)

Area	1961 Census			1971 Census		
	Male	Female	Total	Male	Female	Total
Greater Bombay	6,229	6,137	12,366	1,760	1,847	3,607
Kolaba	1,124	1,099	2,223	432	418	850
Thana	298	310	608	140	153	293
Poona	259	247	506	184	144	328
Nasik	17	13	30	8	8	16
Sholapur	8	8	16	3	3	6
Satara	9	14	23	3	4	7
Nagpur	15	28	43	7	3	10
Dhulia	1	-	1	-	-	-
Jalgaon	6	-	6	-	-	-
Ratnagiri	2	-	-	-	-	-
Ahmadnagar	3	-	3	-	-	-
Aurangabad	-	2	2	4	4	8
Bhir	2	-	2	-	-	-
Bhandara	4	4	8	-	-	-
Wardha	2	2	4	-	-	-
Nanded	3	1	4	8	1	9
TOTAL *	7,982	7,865	15,845	2,549	2,585	5,134

* These figures — obtained from a separate volume on *Maharashtra State Census Statistics* — for the specific areas of Maharashtra do not quite add up to the totals which appear in *1961 Census of India, Vol. I (Social and Cultural Tables)* Part II – C (i), P. 501 which lists "7,983 males, 7,868 females, and 15,851 for the Total Jewish Population" of Maharashtra in 1961. However, the latter volume gives *only the totals* for each state and does not include the figures for each component area within a given state.

The Bene Israel in the Twentieth Century

Finally, we come to data on Indian Jewish emigration to Israel. According to data recorded in Bombay by the Jewish Agency the emigration figures for all Indian Jews leaving for Israel were as follows:

Table 23 : ANNUAL JEWISH EMIGRATION TO ISRAEL, FROM 1948 to 1984

Year	Number	Year	Number	Year	Number	Year	Number
1948	—						
1949	1,055						
1950	1,088						
1951	334	1961	732	1971	1,211	1981	85
1952	—	1962	993	1972	655	1982	97
1953	651	1963	761	1973	561	1983	113
1954	1,533	1964	537	1974	446	1984	156
1955	523	1965	824	1975	474		
1956	292	1966	1,239	1976	345		
1957	969	1967	855	1977	260		
1958	512	1968	2,041	1978	267		
1959	453	1969	1,933	1979	213		
1960	249	1970	1,658	1980	98		

Comparable figures have been published by the Central Bureau of Statistics in Jerusalem, in their report entitled *Immigration to Israel 1948-1972, Part II, Composition by Period of Immigration, Special Series No. 489*, pp. 4-7, and in their subsequent *Special Series* for the years following 1972. One notices a discrepancy between the figures of *emigration from* India to Israel which came from the Bombay Office of the Jewish Agency and the Israeli statistics on *immigration*. The discrepancy can be accounted for by the fact that, beginning with the year 1968, the Israeli statistics distinguish between "Potential Immigrants", i.e. Jews who arrived in Israel on tourist visas and who settled without opting for Israeli citizenship immediately upon arrival in Israel; and "Immigrants", i.e. those entrants who opted for Israeli citizenship. The discrepancy arises because some persons, who emigrated from India on a tourist visa in one year, may have opted for Israeli citizenship in any following year, and therefore would not have been recorded as "Immigrants" in the year of their emigration from India.

Demographic Data

The Israeli statistics are as follows, under the heading "IMMIGRANTS AND TOURISTS SETTLING, BY COUNTRY OF BIRTH":[14]

Table 24: NUMBER OF IMMIGRANTS AND TOURISTS SETTLING IN ISRAEL WHO WERE BORN IN INDIA OR PAKISTAN.

Year	Number of Immigrants	Year	Potential Immigrants	Immigrants	Total
1948	12	1969	96	1,952	2,048
1949	856	1970	121	1,683	1,804
1950	955	1971	90	1,218	1,308
1951	353	1972	79	631	710
1952	50	1973	86	519	605
1953	648	1974	62	414	476
1954	1,511	1975	43	457	500
1955	518	1976	50	334	384
1956	258	1977	51	240	291
1957	951	1978	52	249	310
1958	497	1979	52	178	230
1959	433	1980	103	54	157
1960	514	1981	133	19	152
1961	720	1982	117	31	148
1962	967	1983	161	27	188
1963	740				
1964	513				
1965	845	Total for			
1966	1,206	1969-1983 : 1,296		8,006	9,302
1967	941				
1968	2,017				
Total for 1948-1968 : 15,505					

NUMBER OF JEWISH IMMIGRANTS TO ISRAEL WHO WERE BORN IN INDIA OR PAKISTAN

1948 through 1968 : 15,505
1969 through 1983 : +9,302

TOTAL ·: 24,807 for 1948 through 1983.

In any case, the sum total of the figures given from Bombay (i.e.24,213) for the years 1949 through 1984 is rather close to the total from the Israel Bureau of Statistics (i.e. 24,807) covering the years 1948 through 1983.

Between 1948 and the mid-1950s most of the Cochin Jewish Community and a very large proportion of the Baghdadi Jewish community left India. Proportionate to the size of their community, the percentage of Bene Israel emigrants during those years was smaller than for the other two communities. As a matter of fact, between 1951 and 1953, 150 Bene Israel who had gone to live in Israel were unhappy there with their jobs, housing and living conditions, and they returned to India.[15] Bene Israel emigration from India was at its nadir in 1952.

The Statistical Abstract of Israel 1981, No. 32 (also published by the Israel Central

Bureau of Statistics) in its Table II/24 (on p.58) gives data on *Jews* (in Israel) *by Country of Origin, as of December 31, 1980.* For *Israelis* belonging to families *of Indian or of Pakistani Origin*—taking into account deaths as well as natural increase—there were 19,500 who were born abroad and 16,500 who were born in Israel, making a total of 36,000 Israelis of Indian or of Pakistani origin living in Israel as of the end of 1980.

Table II/25 of the *1981 Statistical Abstract,* on p.59, is entitled *Jews* (in Israel) *Born Abroad, by Country and Age, as of December 31, 1980.* This Table gives the figures for *Jews Born in India and Pakistan* as follows:

Age Group	65+	45–64	30–44	15–29	0–14	Total
Number of Persons	1,300	4,600	6,200	6,200	1,300	19,500

But, the Israel Central Bureau of Statistics never distinguishes between Bene Israel, Baghdadi or Cochin Jews. Without official figures we can be quite sure only of the fact that between 1949 and 1962 about 2,600 Cochin Jews came as immigrants to Israel, leaving only a tiny minority of this community back in India.

As of 1985, counting Indian immigrants together with the children born of these immigrants, it was *estimated* that Cochin Jews in Israel numbered about 3,500; that Indian Baghdadis in Israel numbered about 3,500 to 4,000 persons; and that there were somewhere between 25-28,000 Bene Israel in Israel. In any case, the number of Bene Israel plus their offspring living in Israel today exceeds the Bene Israel population peak in India, reached in the year 1951.

According to the figures of the 1983 Israel Census (i.e. Table 4 : *Jews by Selected Countries of Origin and Place of Birth)* there were living in Israel in 1983 *37,686* Jews who were born in India or in Pakistan or who are the offspring of Jews who were born in India or Pakistan.

The official Government of India 1981 Census records 5,618 Indian Jews remaining in India, all but about 500 of whom are Bene Israel.

In closing our chapter on Indian Jewish demography, it seems that the figures have virtually come full circle. In 1837 (the date of the first known "census" of Indian Jews all together) the total Indian Jewish population numbered 6,951. A Government of India Census peak of 26,512 Jews in India (some say the actual number was closer to 30,000) was reached in 1951. Today (1985) the total number of Indian Jews still in India can be no more than, and very likely has already dipped considerably below the total given for the year 1837.

NOTES

1. *The Indian Census in Perspective,* edited by S.G. Srivastava; Census of India 1971, Series 11, Part I, Chapter 1 : Census Centenary Monograph No. 1.
2. The category "Community" was used instead of "Religion" in the 1941 Census Questionnaire only.
3. Entire volumes are devoted separately to Tables for all of India in respect of Vital Statistics (birth and death rates, age distribution, sex ratio, infirmities), Languages, Migration, Economy (general and household), Housing, Industry, the Scheduled Castes and Tribes (underprivileged, backward communities), and Social and Cultural Aspects. The latter category includes sections on Household Composition, Age and Marital Status, Size of Families, Standard of Education according to Age and Sex, Occupations, Personnel in Each Branch of Science and Technology, Religion, Literacy. There are also monographs on Village and Crafts Surveys, and on Fairs and Festivals.

4. It is in the nature of census-taking that the returns suffer from under-enumeration. The Prefaces to the Government of India Censuses call attention to this aspect. In the case of the data for Indian Jewry it is impossible to venture an estimate as to the likely degree of such under-enumeration. But the Census results as they are, are accurate enough for most purposes, and they do reveal very important information as to *status quo*, change, trends, etc. The most widely varying statements made even today name figures for the peaks of Bene Israel, Cochin and/or Baghdadi populations in India, which go far in excess of the official total Jewish census figure. And, one hears several varying estimates for the number of Jews still remaining in India.

5. As of 1840, it is said that the 19th Regiment of the Bombay Army had more Jews (70-80) than any other corps; that the 4th, 21st and 24th Regiments had from 20-25 Jews each; and that in the remaining corps there were at least 3 and up to 15 Jews in each regiment. (From an article in *The Bombay Times*, as cited in *The Jewish Chronicle* (London), February 6, 1852, p.142.)

6. From the only clue Reissner gives us (i.e. his footnotes 4,5 and 6 on p.350 of his article "Indian Jewish Statistics 1837-1941"), it seems that his source for 1837 was Rev. John Wilson's *The Lands of the Bible*, Volume II (for Cochin Jews p.667, for Bene Israel p. 681, and for Baghdadi Jews p.678); for Baghdadis in Calcutta, W.H. Sykes' "On the Population and Mortality of Calcutta", from the *Quarterly Journal of the Statistical Society of London*, March 1845, p.2; and for Cochin Jews "some private census figures". From 1881 onwards he benefited from official censuses, but he depended largely on his own unsynchronized sample data obtained during the 1940s, and from these he ventured to make estimates. His acknowledged sources of sample data used in this article were;

> government census and, for Janjira and Kolaba, from data supplied by Mr. S. Joseph of Karachi and, for Poona and Thana the secretaries of the local synagogues. The Karachi estimates were supplied by Mr. Rahamim Benjamin and Mr. Gideon Samson. The Calcutta estimate is by Mr. B. V. Jacob. [Footnote 13, p.356]

7. A search for records of the Pant Sachiv of Bhor might afford information about Bene Israel immigration into Sudhagad Tahsil during the 18th and 19th centuries. B.J.Israel explains (in a communication to the present author) that "The Pant Sachiv of Bhor was a Maratha Feudatory Chief who was given his fief in 1698. His territory was in 1948 divided up between Kulaba and Poona Districts, Sudhagad Tahsil coming to Kulaba."(See above, p. 289) for reproduction of Rev. Lord's explanation and *Table-12d* about Feudatory States.

8. For instance, some of the estimates of Rabbi David D'Beth Hillel, Rev. J. Wolff and others are not always credible; and, when given in terms of numbers of families, cannot safely be compared with census figures enumerating individual persons.

9. There have been some local official censuses which did differentiate between Bene Israel, Baghdadi and Cochin Jews (breaking the latter down even into Black and White Jews). The category of "Religion" has been part of every census questionnaire since 1872 with the exception of the Census of 1941 (see above, n. 2) : sect, caste, class, race or nationality in the past have been requested in certain census questionnaires, with significant variation in the form of the question itself. The 1881 Census asked for one's "Caste if Hindu, and Sect for Other Religions". The "Sect" of one's religion was asked for also in the Censuses of 1891, 1911 and 1931, but in no other of the decennial censuses. However, in the published results usually the Jews, being such a tiny minority, have been lumped together simply as "Jews" under the heading "Other Religions"

10. According to Musleah, *On the Banks of the Ganga* (p. 189), before World War II there were about 10,000 Arabic-speaking Jews on the Indian subcontinent. For Reissner's figure, see above, p. 297, Table 17.

11. As of the year 1900 (i.e. long before the era of refugees from Nazi persecutions) there were in Bombay 250 European Jews in residence, most of whom had come from Vienna, Odessa and Roumania. They maintained a separate cemetery and had their own Ashkenazic prayer hall; but for most other Jewish matters they were dependent upon Bombay's Arabic-speaking Jewish community. Some Cochin Jews have resided in Bombay since 1826; their numbers increased until in the 1930s and 40s there were always between 100 and 150 Cochin Jews living in Bombay.

12. The rare exceptions were small clusters of two or three families of Baghdadi Jews usually wherever there were factories and other enterprises owned by Baghdadi industrial magnates. In such places (as Guntur in Andhra Pradesh or in Madras in Tamilnadu) Baghdadis were often employed in managerial or accountancy positions.
13. A discrepancy of 30 persons, compared with Reissner's figures for Baghdadis (as in Table 8).
14. The figures for Table 24 were obtained from the following publications which were entitled thus :

"Israel Central Bureau of Statistics, Ministry of Immigrant Absorption, and Jewish Agency Aliya and Absorption Department : *Immigration to Israel, Part II, Composition by Period of Immigration;* published by the Central Bureau of Statistics, Jerusalem.

Year Concerned	Special Series Number	Date of Publication
1948 – 1972	489	1975
1973	457	1974
1974	503	1976
1975	528	1976
1976	547	1977
1977	580	1978
1978	632	1980
1979	642	1980
1980	672	1981
1981	706	1983
1982	723	1983
1983	747	1984

15. By 1970 all those who had returned to India had either died in India or returned to settle in Israel.

Afterword

The task of writing this account of the Bene Israel community has, indeed, been like trying to put together a complicated jig-saw puzzle of hundreds of tiny component pieces. While much of the puzzle has sorted itself out reasonably clearly, the component parts for one important sector of the picture, namely pre-18th century *documentation,* are missing. Their absence keeps us in the dark about virtually the entire pre-18th century history of the Bene Israel. Obviously, every effort should be made to locate the missing pieces, to find as many of them as may still be there to be found.

Appendix 1
(See above p. 31, note 38)
Garcia De Orta

Any account of the history of Jews in India, and of Bombay in particular, should not omit the story of one Garcia de Orta. It was not until 1934, after the Acts of the Inquisition of Goa were first made available to the public, that the final chapter of this story was revealed.

In 1534 the Portuguese had obtained by treaty with the Sultan of Gujarat, Bahadur Shah, the islands of Bombay together with Bassein and the island of Salsette. In about 1548 the Portuguese Viceroy had given to Garcia de Orta, against payment of an annual quit rent, one of the seven islands which today constitute the city of Bombay. The island was called "Mombayin". (or "Bom Bayia"), meaning "good bay", from which Bombay derives its name, and on which are located the Malabar Hill and Girgaum sections of today's city. The island of Mombayin had been granted to the Portuguese physician, Garcia de Orta, in appreciation of the medical services which he rendered to the Portuguese Captain-Major of the Indian Ocean, to the highly placed Portuguese administrators, and to Catholic prelates (especially in Goa). De Orta had arrived in India in 1534 and had made his home in Goa, although he frequently visited the Bombay area and Ahmednagar. As a physician of high repute, he was several times invited to the court of the Muslim ruler of the Ahmednagar Kingdom, Burhan al-Din Nizam al-Mulk. As a botanical researcher, de Orta spent time on his leased estate in Bombay, cataloguing all the flora of the area, noting any medicinal properties attributed to them by the indigenous people. He was the first European to write on tropical medicine and pharmacology, and attempted a synthesis of Greek, Roman, Arab, and Hindu medical systems. His book, *Coloquios dos Simples e Drogas he Cousas. Medicinias da India,* is written in the form of a dialogue between himself and a fictitious doctor. In 57 chapters *(Coloquios)* he describes with accuracy a vast array of Indian medicinal plants and drugs, tropical diseases, and other botanical, pharmaceutical and medical details. The book was published in 1563 in Goa, in the Portuguese language, dedicated to the Portuguese Viceroy, approved by the Great Inquisitor of Goa, prefaced by the Court Physician of the Viceroy, and graced with an ode written in honor of de Orta composed by the famous Portuguese writer Luis de Camoes. Other editions of de Orta's book were published by Conde de Ficalho in Lisbon in 1891 and 1895. It was translated into English and published by Sir Clemens R. Markham, London, 1913.

De Orta's earlier biographers, no doubt unwittingly, ignored certain facts about the man, considered him a devout Christian, and in some ways even misinterpreted his behaviour. It was not until 1934 that the complete picture unfolded. Dr. Walter Fischel has written a well-researched and significant article on Garcia de Orta in which he proves from the written record of Goa's Inquisition, as well as from reading between the lines of de Orta's book, the *Coloquios,* that de Orta had adhered secretly to Judaism :

This was brought out by the monumental biography, written in 1934, by the

Portuguese scholar Augusta da Silva Carvalho, on the occasion of the 400th anniversary of Garcia de Orta's arrival in India, based on unpublished and hitherto inaccessible *Acts of the Inquisition of Goa,* and in particular on the dramatic confessions of Garcia de Orta's own sister Catarina and her husband Lionel Perez before the Inquisition immediately following the death of Garcia de Orta in 1568.[1]

At the Inquisition, his sister Catarina gave a full account of how her brother Garcia's funeral service had been performed according to Jewish tradition. The testimonies of Catarina and of her husband show that Garcia advocated respect for the Sabbath, strict observance of Yom Kippur, etc; and that his mother, even though she had been converted to Catholicism, had taught her children Mosaic Law. Catarina herself was burned at the stake in Goa in 1569. In the words of Dr. Fischel :

It is obvious that Garcia de Orta .... far from being "a disinterested spectator", was an eye witness of all the manifold manifestations .... of the Portuguese persecution and hunt for apostates, heretics, and New Christians, the destruction of Hindu temples and the burning of their books .... such (his) flattery of religious leaders in a treatise on drugs and medicinal plants seems rather strange and unwarranted but was probably motivated by reasons of expediency, to ascertain the approval of the ecclesiastical authorities for the publication of his work .... In the light of his well-documented Marrano life Garcia de Orta, in his frequent visits to Ahmednagar, in an atmosphere of complete religious tolerance must have enjoyed the exchange of views with the Sultan and the many Muslim, Indian, and European physicians and philosophers, as well as the accessibility of ancient manuscripts for his specific research, housed in the Sultan's huge library.[2]

It can well be assumed that the Goanese authorities were fully aware of Garcia de Orta's Marrano life and had collected ample evidence about this aspect, but were reluctant to make a case against him, probably out of consideration for the prestige, standing and reputation he enjoyed in all Portuguese circles .... Yet, [in 1580] twelve years after Garcia de Orta's death, the Inquisition decided to act, and ordered his mortal remains to be exhumed and burned in an *auto de fé* at Goa. His ashes were carried to Mandobi, where they were cast into the sea as a posthumous punishment for a militant Marrano who had escaped his fate during his lifetime.[3]

Interestingly enough, it was *Portuguese* India which, as late as 1946, issued in Garcia de Orta's honor a Rs.6 postage stamp bearing his portrait.

NOTES

1. Fischel, Walter : "Garcia de Orta : A Militant Marrano in Portuguese India in the 16th Century"; published in the Salo W. Baron Jubilee Volume, American Academy for Jewish Research, *Proceedings,* 1970; pp.115-39. This quotation is from p.127.
    Gerson da Cunha, who wrote in the 1870s and who was one of Garcia de Orta's earliest biographers, states in his *The Origin of Bombay* (p.112) that "Garcia da Orta died a bachelor about 1570". Da Cunha wrote long before access to *The Acts of the Inquisition of Goa* was made available; the latter affords us with the accurate dates, etc.
2. Fischel : op. cit., pp. 132, 133 and 135.
3. Ibid., pp. 130-1.

Appendix 2a
(See above, p. 33)

The Ashtamkar Sanad*

(Quoted from Kehimkar, *History of the Bene-Israel of India*, pp. 81-2)

Be it known to the Dessais, Deshpandeys, Kulkarnies and all the other officers of Taluka Ashtami by this title-deed that Dadawra, son of Nagawra, oilmen, and Mheter (village officer) of the district aforesaid, in reference to the rights and privileges of receiving special honour and precedence, lodged a complaint with Ramchandra Krishna Godbole, the Subedar (chief Judicial officer) of the district of Birwadi; the said officer thereupon called the landlords residing in the said district and asked them to give in writing their opinion as to which of the parties concerned had enjoyed from time immemorial and from generation to generation the rights and privileges of the village officership, and all the honours due to their title. A statement was therefore forwarded by the landlords to the chief officer of the district as follows : — "Looking into the records of Mullik Amber we do not find there a title-deed of the privileges herein-before-mentioned granted to oilman Eswara." He therefore had to pay Ruppees 60 by way of penalty and your rights as Mheters (or village officers) have been confirmed; and title deeds, issued by the chief officer of the district, were granted to you on payment of Ruppees 20 in Nazarana. You then requested the landlords to grant you a title-deed of hereditary rights and privileges confirmed upon you. It being therefore seen *by a reference to the records of Mullik Amber, that the enjoyment of the said rights and privileges of having special honour and precedence has been in the possession of your ancestors for five or seven generations.* [emphasis supplied], your rights as Mheter or village officer have been ratified and granted to you to be enjoyed uninterruptedly from father to son and from generation to generation. Special honours should first be given to the aforesaid Mheters (by all the members of the oil-pressing community). Besides these, you are entitled to be exempted from house tax and cattle tolls, and are authorized to exercise the rights of Mheter or village officer as before, and in perpetuity. Written by the Kulkarni of the district hereinbefore named, signed and sealed.

---

* No date is given by Kehimkar for this *sanad*.

Appendix 2b
(See above, p. 34)

Sanad of 1840 Confirming a Sanad of 1770 Granting Hereditary Kaji Rights to Two Bene Israel Oilmen

(English translation by Kehimkar, *History of the Bene-Israel of India*, pp. 45-46)

A Sanad granted by the Valiant King Yakut-Khan Bahadur, the protector of subjects [the Hubshi King of Janjira].

Be it known from this day to the past, present and future Deshmooks, Deshpandays and Land lords living within the jurisdiction of the chief town of Rajpuri and the palace at Yakutnagar in the Sur year Suma Tisa Arbain Mayaten and Allaff (1240, i.e. 1840 A.D.) that Yacob Elloji and his brothers Saturday oilmen inhabitants of the village Khursai in the district of Mhuslay came in person and handed in a petition to the effect that their hereditary rights as Kajis had been withheld from them for three years although they were in possession of a Sanad granted in the name of their ancestors, Kaji Ebrahim Yacob and Dawud Essub, Shanwar Telis inhabitants of the said Rajpuri, and bearing the date of 17th Shaban of the year Tisa Saben Maya and Allaff i.e. 1170 corresponding to the year 1770 of the Christian Era. This Sanad standing in the names of the two persons aforesaid has been brought and presented before me, and as it has become very old, they have requested me to renew the same and to restore them their rights as Kajis. Having duly considered their Petition, His Maiesty has come to this decision; that the Shanwar Telis hereinbefore-named are legally entitled to enjoy the inheritance of the rights and privileges as Kajis on the said Yacob Elloji and his brothers, and has renewed the Sanad duly sealed. It is hereby proclaimed that all marriage ceremonies, domestic convivialities and funeral rites should be conducted and performed by Kajis agreeably to former rules, and that any caste dispute should be settled by them. It is also proclaimed that the Kajis should be duly honoured and respected as before and that the Kajis living within the jurisdiction of the Hubshi territory should be allowed to hold and enjoy whatever rights and privileges they may have had in their possession before, and that whenever they build a house they should be provided with gratuitous labour (i.e. the labourers employed by them should not ask for any remuneration). Further they should not be obliged to have their Sanad renewed every year. *A copy of this edict should be kept at the Royal Palace* and the original should be kept in the possession of the Kajis for their enjoyment. [Emphasis supplied.]

The hereditary rights of the Kajis should on no account be interfered with and should be continued from father to son and from generation to generation. All should obey this order. This Sanad is granted by Mahomed Ayub Mahomed Jaffer. Witness Yesji Ramaji Naik Kala Afrad-5th Moon of Rabilaval-Date of despatch idem – Signed Tukaji Sadashiv.

Appendix 2c
(See above, p. 34)

Sanad of 1770, Granted by the Peshwa Government

(English translation by Kehimkar, p.46)

This "Deed of Assurance" is granted by Govindarao Mankar and Chimaji Mankar Subedars of the district of Rajpuri to Abraham Kaji and Dawud Kaji Saturday oilmen, residents of the said Rajpuri in the year 1770; your rights as Kajis of Saturday oilmen have been recognized by the Government of Janjira, but they have not been recognized beyond the village of Mahsra by this Government. On being brought to the district of Talagad you have been hindered from exercising your rights as such Kajis, hence all the Saturday oilmen of the said district interceded on your behalf and have requested us to be pleased to allow you to exercise your rights as Kajis, for the performance of their ceremonies has been obstructed. We have therefore been pleased to grant you this deed of title authorising you to come to the district without any hesitation, and to exercise uninterruptedly your rights and privileges as Kajis among the Saturday oilmen. 14th Moon Shaban the first half.

The *new Sanad granted to the ancestors of Kaji Ebrahim Yacob and Dawud Essoob*, Saturday oilmen, residents of the district of Rajpuri, *is dated* the 17th of Shaban Ridanand Tisa Saben Maya and Allaff (1170-*1770 A.D.*), as *the old Sanad granted to them had been lost in a rebellion.*
[Emphasis supplied.]

Appendix 3a
(See above, p. 46)
Discussion as to Date of Samaji Hassaji's Release from Prison-of-war[1]

Various documents relate to the story of Samaji Hassaji and to his establishing the first Bene Israel synagogue.

(a) There is the information from the *Letter of 1768* which, while it does not give the name of the Bene Israel individual who remained in Cochin "for four years mastering our laws and regulations", does provide the information that Bene Israel and Cochin Jewry were not at that time (1768) mutually ignorant of each other and that the Bene Israel must already have been made aware of such an institution as a synagogue.

(b) The relevant portion (i.e. pp.102-103) of the Hebrew account of the Bene Israel by Solomon Reinemann, published in 1884 (see above, p. 81) reads as follows, in a literal English translation:

HISTORY OF THE BENE ISRAEL OF BOMBAY AND HOW THE TORAH CAME TO THEM FROM COCHIN : In the year 1767.[1] Sultan Hyder Ali, King of Mysore, fought with the King of Travancore. He was a mighty king and had subdued most of the land of Malabar .... He was odious to all its inhabitants because he was a fanatic, devout Muslim. He burdened all the towns which he captured under the shadow of his faith. [A prisoner of his] was one of the "Bene Israel"; Samuel Bakoorai[2] was his name; he was commander of 1000 in the British army. Toward him Hyder showed mercy and allowed him to retain the religion of his fathers, saying "Since he has been circumcised and is a believer in the law of Moses, he can be considered as a believer." It was not so with the other prisoners who were non-believers, and therefore they had to be circumcised. He advanced the rank of prisoner Samuel Bakoorai to a commander in war because he was a brave soldier, educated in war tactics and he excelled in the use of European artillery.

At this time Sultan Hyder Ali arrived with his army at the town of Parur (6 hours journey from Cochin town, at the boundary of the King of Cochin). The noble personage, Rav Ezekiel Rahabi, of blessed memory, heard of this and was very concerned about the Black Jews who lived in the town of Parur, and about its synagogue which he had built for them with his money. He feared lest the Sultan would wage war against the King of Cochin and would cross the river and capture the royal town and sack it. He himself was very rich in property and ships. Like him, other White Jews were also very rich. Therefore, he sent his three sons—David, Eliahu and Moshe of blessed memory—and also the venerable great linguist Rav Isaac Sargon accompanied them to meet the Sultan, bearing gifts of gunpowder, guns and white sugar—which was a costly item in India—and precious stones. They asked him not to harm the Black Jews of Parrur and not to begin war against Cochin. The Sultan liked these ambassadors because they were impressive. He had never seen a Jew before. So, he returned to Kanara and did not come to Cochin. He ordered his army not to harm the Jews of Parur and his order restrained them, but the others they raped and pillaged and took their women and daughters into captivity.

Quickly the rumour spread in the Sultan's camp that messengers from the people "Bene Israel" had come before the Sultan, brought gifts to him and found favour with him. Although Samuel was a commander in the army [there], he still was considered to be a prisoner and he longed for his home and his country. He hastened to come before the brothers, the sons of Rahabi, whom he thought were of the Bene Israel community. He fell on his knees before them, as is the custom of the Indians, and pleaded with them to get him out of captivity. He told them that he belonged to the Bene Israel community in Bombay where many of this group lived. The sons of Rahabi knew nothing about them,[3] because in those days they did not know anything outside [their own] region. They were sorry for him and they went a second time to the Sultan to plead for him. The Sultan agreed and released him, and they brought him to Cochin.

BUILDING THE SYNAGOGUE IN BOMBAY: Samuel, in coming to Cochin, marvelled at seeing the House of Prayer, the books in it, the prayer service with all the participants praying, the *Talith* and the *Tefilin*. He examined the Scrolls of the Torah and the later writings on parchment the like of which he had never seen before. He asked: "Who gave them these laws and customs?" When they answered that all this was passed on to them by their forefathers according to the word of Moses, he fell before Ezekiel Rahabi and said: "I beg you to grant me the favour of taking from me all the money which I collected during the days of my captivity[4] as an offering to God dedicated for a House of Prayer. To this Rav Ezekiel replied that there was no need of his money in their [the Cochini] community because they were rich and the synagogue had great wealth without need of his donation. If he wanted to use his money for a holy purpose, it would be best for him to return to his city Bombay and build a synagogue for his brethren and thus to please God. Samuel accepted his advice and returned to his city in a ship which Rav Ezekiel gave to him. The Commander-in-Chief of the [British] Army received him with love and honor. They gave him the honourable title of Commandant, to him and to his descendants after him. I myself saw his son, Sr. David Commandan,[5] a very old rich man with three wives and many sons. He [Samuel] received a pension from the army for life, according to his wartime army service. He built a synagogue in Bombay and returned to Cochin to fetch a Sefer Torah. But he died, and his synagogue remained without a Sefer Torah because his sons did not know what it was and also had never seen a Jew.[6]

(c) A much later Hebrew account (hand-written and unpublished) the "History of the House of Rahabi in Cochin", written by Naphtali E. Roby (Rahabi) in 1939 in Cochin, is very obviously based on Solomon Reinemann's much earlier account about Samaji. Reinemann, however, never uses Samaji's village surname "Divekar", inexplicably calling him, instead, "Samuel Bakoorai". Roby, on the other hand, calls him Samuel Divangar" (close enough to "Divekar"). Reinemann gives the date as 1767; Roby states 1766. Reinemann talks about averting an attack on the Jews of Parur; Roby calls the place "Tirthur" (also a village with Jewish settlement in Malabar). Both Reinemann and Roby give full credit to Cochin Jewry for Samaji's release from captivity and even for the idea of building a Bene Israel synagogue in Bombay. None of this is brought out in Bene Israel accounts. Reinemann was a European Jew married to a daughter of the Rahabi family; Roby was a 20th century member of the Rahabi family.

(d) In 1892 H.S. Kehimkar published a 38-page booklet entitled *A Sketch of the*

History of the Bene-Israel and an Appeal for their Education, the forerunner of Kehimkar's large opus, *The History of the Bene-Israel of India.* In his *Sketch,* Kehimkar has little to say about Samaji Hassaji except that

> Samajee Hassajee (Samuel Ezekiel) Divekar enlisted in about the year 1750, but having rendered good service he was promoted through the several ranks and was made Native Commandant of the 6th Battalion. He served in the Second Mysore War under General Matthews and was taken prisoner by Tipu Saheb and kept in confinement for two or three years. After his release he rejoined his appointment in the Army, and built the first Bene-Israel synagogue in Bombay in 1796. He died in 1797 at Cochin where he had gone to bring scrolls of the law for the synagogue.[7]

In his book *The History of the Bene-Israel of India* Kehimkar adds that

> during the Second Mysore War (1780-1784) several Bene-Israel, who had enlisted in the service of the Honourable Company [the British East India Company], were taken captives by Tipoo's army, and would have been put to the sword had they declared themselves 'Yahudim'. They were released in consequence of Tipoo's mother having begged of her son to spare the lives of the 'Bene-Israel' so much talked of in the *Koran*.[8]

On page 190 of his *History* Kehimkar contradicts his 1750 date for Samaji's army enlistment and says that he enlisted about 1760. Then he goes on to say that

> He [Samaji] was made a Jemedar [see above p. 54, note 13] of a Company in the 6th Battalion on 2nd July 1775, and was subsequently promoted to the rank of Subedar and Subedar Commandant. He was in the Second Mysore War under General Matthews and was taken prisoner and kept as such for some time before he was released .... The records that would throw light on the war services of this able officer can nowhere be traced, with the exception of a warrant issued under date 4th July 1791 at Tellicherry[9] by Major General Abercromby, Commander-in-Chief of His Majesty's and the Honourable Company's forces on the coast of Malabar, appointing him President of a General Court-martial.[10]

And

> Samaji Hassaji built at Bombay a synagogue for the community in 1796, out of gratitude for his miraculous deliverance from the massacre[11] during the Third Mysore War. Some say that the cost of purchasing the site and of building the synagogue was defrayed by himself, while others maintain that it was built after the death of his brother Solomon Hassaji Divekar, also commandant, at the cost of his widow Hannabai.[12]

(e) In 1927 the *Shaar Harachamim Synagogue* itself published a short *account* in Marathi *about Samaji.*[13] In it mention is made of the fact that Samaji's father, Hassaji Divekar, owned land in Janjira, whence he had come to Bombay; that Samaji had enlisted in the British Army when he was 20 years old, in 1750 [as stated in Kehimkar's *Sketch*]; that six of his brothers lost their lives in wars; but that he and his brother Issaji survived; that Samaji, who was then a Commandant, his brother Issaji, and several other Bene Israel soldiers under General Matthews of Bombay, were conquered and taken captive by Tipu

Sultan in 1783. [Hyder Ali had died in December 1782 and was succeeded by his son Tipu Sultan.] Even while they were in prison, Samaji wanted to help his people, the Bene Israel.

> He wanted to build a synagogue and to give religious education to his people .... He was not at all afraid of what would happen to him, but the only thing that he was worried about was the synagogue for the Indian Jews. He said to himself : "If I cannot build the synagogue, then someone else will do so and God will fulfill my wish."

The booklet says that Tipu Sultan's prisoners were given the choice of conversion to Islam, or death; and that they were asked by Tipu during the *darbar* (court session) about their religion; that when Tipu's mother from behind the *purdah* screen heard the reply "Bene Israel", she exclaimed that people who bore a name so honored in the Koran, should not be executed. So their lives were spared but they were kept prisoner until the Treaty of Mangalore was signed in 1784, when they were released.

In this way Samaji Divekar and all his friends came to Bombay safely. They all were very much respected by the English Company. They got all their payments and rewards. Samaji Divekar, even after his 34 years of service, was still strong. He continued his service with the British Company and in the year 1792, in the Third Mysore War, Tipu Sultan was altogether defeated. In 1792, after putting in 42 years of service, Mr. Samaji went on pension and came to Bombay to settle down permanently ....

> He was a very rich man. He was a Commandant and was getting good pay, and always was rewarded in the wars. He purchased the land at Mandvi, Vadgadi. Samuel Street was named after him and the street next to this was named after his brother Issaji .... He started building the synagogue at his own expense. This was finished in the year 1796 .... They selected him as the leader of the community. Till now there was no hand-written Sefer Torah and therefore Samaji Divekar decided to go to Cochin. He took a Sefer Torah from there and was about to leave for Bombay. All of a sudden he fell sick and within two days of illness Samaji Divekar died in Cochin. This was the 14th day of the month of Kislev in the year 1797 ....
>
> He had two wives and only two daughters. When he left for Cochin he told his wives that the whole work of the synagogue should be looked after by his brother's son, David. In this way David took his place and he became the leader of the community ....
>
> On February 23, 1919 the committee and people of Shaar Harachamim Synagogue decided that every year on Yom Kippur the name of Samaji Hassaji Divekar be read during the Memorial Service *(Hazkara)*. On February 21, 1926 the Jamat of the Synagogue decided that the *Hazkara* in the name of Samaji Divekar be read on the day of his death, i.e. the 14th of Kislev.

This account does not mention Samaji's appointment to preside at a court-martial; neither does it mention a visit to Cochin prior to 1797.

(f) *Walter Fischel's* version of the story is similar to Reinemann's. And, Fischel introduces as additional evidence a letter from Isaac Sargon (died in 1788). Originally from Constantinople, Sargon settled in Cochin. He was a well-known Jewish linguist, merchant and diplomat. His first recorded diplomatic mission for the Dutch East India Company occurred in 1766. In a Hebrew letter to Ezekiel Rahabi, Sargon wrote as follows :

> I was honoured by meeting His Excellency the Nawab Hyder Ali Khan, and he talked to me in such a way that he seems to be a good man. His Excellency asked me how you were and I told him that you still feel well. Then His Excellency told me that he wished to see you as a token of gratitude for the medicine which you sent to him previously through his men. I told His Excellency that you are old and that it is hard for you to walk. Then the Nawab asked me how many children you have and I replied that you have three sons. My opinion is that you should send one of your sons or some member of your family, and I'll do whatever I can that His Majesty receives them well.[14]

Fischel goes on to say that Ezekiel Rahabi did send his elder son Elias (Eliahu)—*not David* or *Moshe*— to accompany Isaac Sargon on a mission for the Dutch East India Company to the Nawab. In a footnote Fischel adds that Solomon Reinemann, in his *Travels of Solomon* published in 1884,

> connects the mission of Isaac Sargon to the Nawab with the discovery of the community of Bene Israel in Bombay. It was said that in one of the missions to the Nawab (it is uncertain whether in 1766, or 1775, or at some later date)[15] he (Isaac Sargon) heard about a Jew whose name was Samuel Ezekiel Divekar, who was a captive at the Nawab's camp and who before that was a colonel in the British Army.[16]

Of special significance is Dr. Fischel's parenthetical remark that "it is uncertain whether in 1766, or 1775, or at some later date" there occurred the discovery of prisoner, Samuel Divekar, by a Cochin Jewish mission to the Nawab.

Even if Samaji had been taken prisoner during Hyder Ali's reign, his release might have occurred during Tipu Sultan's reign, since Tipu succeeded to his father Hyder's throne in 1782. B.J.Israel suggests the possibility that Isaac Sargon, together with one or more of Ezekiel Rahabi's sons, had indeed learned of the Bene Israel prisoners at the Nawab's camp; that they did use their good offices to save Bene Israel lives; and that, in order to do so, they might even have approached Tipu through Tipu's mother. Whatever the year of his release, Samaji might well have been inspired by a visit to the Cochin Synagogue, and throughout his subsequent years in army service might have dreamed of building a synagogue for the Bene Israel. Kehimkar specifically says that Samaji built the synagogue "out of gratitude for his miraculous deliverance from the massacre during the Third Mysore War", which need not at all be a reference to Samaji's imprisonment by the enemy, but perhaps to his survival of a terrible defeat in battle

The actual dating of Samaji's imprisonment and of his release from prison still remains a problem. If Samaji's enlistment into the army did indeed take place in 1750 rather than "about 1760", might he not have been taken prisoner by Hyder Ali even in some *pre*-First Mysore War campaign in which Bombay Native Army troops took part, and have been released in 1767 according to the Reinemann story, only to be taken captive once more in 1783 under General Matthews, i.e. during the Second Mysore War? B. J. Israel argues cogently that

> The Bene Israel have a tradition that Divekar was captured in the Second Mysore War at Bednur. The likelihood is that he was taken prisoner there in 1783 when Tipu was the ruler, along with the Bombay contingent under General Matthews. But the matter needs close investigation. If one knows which units of the Bombay Army were engaged in the First Mysore War, and which in the Second Mysore War, and, in each case, which units came from Bombay proper and which were local levies raised in Tellicherry

Samaji's Release from Prison

(which was governed from Bombay), one will be in a better position to check the accuracy of Reinemann, Roby, etc.[17]

With this in mind, B. J. Israel began the search and sent the present author some very pertinent information, prefacing his findings thus :

> Of course, this does not provide any proof of the presence of Samaji Hassaji Divekar in any of these campaigns in which the Bombay Army was engaged in South India, but it does give some indication of the possibilities. I have not yet consulted any detailed histories of the various campaigns, but have thus far relied solely on Sir Patrick Cadell's *History of the Bombay Army*, Longmans, Green and Company, 1938. Appendix I of Cadell's book (from his p.307 et seq.) gives a list of the campaigns in which the Bombay Army was engaged, the localities in which they took place and the units involved.

The details which B. J. Israel excerpted from Cadell's book as being probably relevant to Samaji's army service can be found below.

As regards the question of Samaji's having come to Cochin, he might have accompanied Isaac Sargon immediately upon his release from prison, remaining long enough to have been impressed by their synagogue and Jewish customs. But, the Bene Israel person who had remained in Cochin for four years, according to the Letter of 1768, must have been someone else, probably a Bene Israel *Kaji*, but not Samaji, because he had been on active army service throughout that period and therefore could not have spared time for a long stay among the Cochin Jews. According to the version related in the Shaar Harachamim Synagogue's booklet, Samaji, together with his brothers who were also captives, was released in 1784, and all of them returned directly to Bombay. When in 1791 Samaji served as "president of a General Court-martial" on the coast of Malabar, he might have had an opportunity to be in touch with Cochin Jewry (although the British at that time were not particularly close to the Cochin Jewish settlements). If Samaji's release from prison actually occurred in 1784, another puzzling point is raised, namely the lapse of so many years between the time of his release and the actual construction of the synagogue. The time lag might, however, be accounted for by the fact that until the end of the Third Mysore War (1792) Samaji remained in active army service, having no time to devote to other matters until after 1792.

Appendix 3b
Excerpts from Sir Patrick Cadell's "History of The Bombay Army"
(Longmans Green and Company, 1938)

THE CAMPAIGNS OF THE BOMBAY ARMY IN SOUTH INDIA :

Year	Locality, With Main Engagements	Units
1736-40	Malabar [Tellicherry was governed from Bombay]	Bombay Regiment (European), and Sepoys (local Malabaris).
1747-51	Madras, Cuddalore, Pondicherry, Devicottah (against the French).	European Regiments and Sepoys.
1751	Malabar, Eddikad (fighting with Rajah of Cotiati-Kottayam).	European Regiments, Sepoys and Artillery Company (Native Christians, local Sepoys and allies).
1754-55	Madras, Trichinopoly, Madurai	European Regiment and Sepoys (small contingent).

[There were campaigns in 1759-61, 1760, and 1764, in which, however, only European Regiments were involved.]

Year	Locality, With Main Engagements	Units
1768	Madras, Mangalore *(First Mysore War* 1768-69)	European Regiments and Sepoys [see below, from Cadell's pp.82-84]
1781-84	*Second Mysore War* : Tellicherry Calicut, Tricalore, Ponnani, *Bednur;* capture and defence of Mangalore, Honavar, Cannanore.	European Regiment : 1st, 2nd, 4th, 5th, 8th, 9th, 10th, 11th, 12th Grenadier Companies; 13th, 14th, 15th all Sepoys; Marine Battalions; 2 battalions of Grenadier Companies; Artillery [see below, from Cadell's pp.100 et seq.].

Cadell's "History of the Bombay Army"

Year	Locality with Main Engagements	Units
1790-92	*Third Mysore War :* Dharwar, Tirurangadi, Cannanore, Shimoga, Srirangapatnam	1st and 2nd Battalions, European Regiments; 1st, 2nd, 3rd, 4th, 6*th,* 7th, 8th, 9th, 10th, 11th, 12th *Battalions* (Sepoys) Artillery.
1795	Cochin (Captured in this campaign)	2nd Battalion, Europeans (Flank Companies); 1st Grenadiers and 5th Battalions.

[Note : *Sepoys* are native troops. Bombay Sepoys also took part in cleaning-up operations in Malabar in 1795 and subsequent years, and in the final defeat of Tipu *(Fourth Mysore War)* in 1799.]

The following are the extracts from Cadell referred to in the above Table :

THE FIRST MYSORE WAR (pp.82-84) :
The warfare which lasted throughout this period began with hostilities against Haider Ali in 1768. These were undertaken at the request of the Madras Government which was being hard pressed by Mysore armies. The force available for despatch from Bombay was small enough : 431 of the European Infantry, 80 Artillery cover, and 801 sepoys .... and they captured Mangalore on 1-3-1768.......... They repulsed, moreover, repeated attacks led by Haider's son, Tipu himself, on the 15th and 16th March, the Grenadiers of the Regiment particularly distinguishing themselves by capturing two of the enemies' guns from the centre of their position. The Company's troops at Tellicherry also sought to attack Haider's forces, and on 3rd March an expedition consisting of 189 of the European Infantry, 48 Artillery, Bombay sepoys (drawn from the 1st Battalion, afterwards 108th) [N.B. According to Kehimkar, Samaji Divekar was made Jemadar in the 6th Battalion, p.190], and 225 of the local Nair [a military caste in Malabar] levy attacked Ali Raja, the Moplah [matrilineal Muslims of Malabar] supporter of Haider, at Cannanore .... Major Govan, however, himself returned to Bombay in April with 71 of his men, leaving entirely inadequate garrisons, largely composed of newly enlisted local or 'country' sepoys to hold Mangalore with detachments at Honawar and Fortified Island. (The numbers were 220 Europeans, 400 Bombay sepoys and 600 Country sepoys at Mangalore; 60 Europeans, 400 Bombay sepoys and 300 Country sepoys at Honawar and Fortified Island) .... Early in May Haider appeared in person before Mangalore with his whole army. A too hasty decision to evacuate the place, largely dictated by the Civilian Committee, followed : nor was the withdrawal even well managed. The European Regiment alone lost two officers and thirty-two men killed, and the sepoys were said in the confusion to have fired upon their European comrades. This, however, clearly refers to the Country sepoys. 80 Europeans and 180 sepoys, sick and wounded, were captured by the enemy, with the fieldpieces and stores of the little force. Honawar also fell ....The respite of several months allowed to the Madras Government by the sacrifice of the Bombay soldiers was little used and Haider Ali was able to dictate peace at the gates of Madras in 1769.

THE SECOND MYSORE WAR [pp.100 et seq.];
The Bombay Government's factory and fort at Tellicherry had been closely invested by an army of Haider Ali.......... Humberstone made his way forty miles to Palghatcherry.......... This decisive victory caused Tipu to fall back, and his army shortly afterwards withdrew entirely, the news of Haider Ali's death on the 7th December having been received.

Meanwhile, however, the Bombay Council, in response to Eyre Coote's appeal, and in view of the apparent danger of McLeod and Humberstone, had despatched their whole available force under General Mathews, a Madras Officer who had been brought round in 1780 as second in command to Goddard, and had succeeded the last named on his retirement.......... Relieved of fear for McLeod's safety by the retreat of Tipu, Mathews captured the forts of Rajamundroog, Mirjan, and Honawar, the last on the 6th January 1783.......... Mathews proceeded to capture Cundapore and other forts and he then received orders from the Bombay Council to ascend the Ghats and capture the city of Bednur.........Mathews' advance was astonishingly successful, in spite of the strong fortifications of the Ghats that had to be ascended.........Bednur thus fell on the 28th January 1783.........Mathews was aware of the certainty of a counterstroke and asked for two battalions as a reinforcement which the Bombay Government arranged to send.........Mathews' army was, however, troubled with internal dissensions. The hopes of the troops for a division of the treasure believed to be captured at Bednur were natural enough as the King's troops had received no pay since they left England, while that of the sepoys was in arrears for 16 months.......... After the capture, no distribution of treasure was made.......... Meanwhile Mathews had returned to the coast with a portion of his force to capture Mangalore which fell on the 9th March. Leaving the 2nd, 42nd and the 8th Sepoy Battalion to garrison it, Mathews returned to Bednur where he became aware that an army of over 50,000 men was approaching to attack him against which he could put 1,600 men in the field. Yet he seems to have done nothing to withdraw or even to concentrate his strung-out force. Tipu's blow fell quickly; with an army of 6,000 men he severed the communications of the British force. At Bednur a gallant resistance was made by the garrison of 600 Europeans and 1,000 sepoys......... when further resistance appeared impossible a capitulation was arranged, under which the force was to be allowed free passage to Bombay. These terms were at once broken by Tipu on the grounds that treasure was being removed by individuals. Officers and men were placed in irons, and beyond doubt the senior officers, including Mathews himself, were murdered. A small proportion of the Europeans survived to be released by the peace of 1784, and even then many of them and still more of the sepoys were forcibly detained.......... Their "Black Commandant" (a rank abolished in 1785 but corresponding with the modern Subedar Major) Krishnaji Mugger, a Maratha, is especially praised for his fortitude and zeal..........

The Bombay sepoys who had been taken prisoners by Tipu remained entirely loyal. They refused all temptation and pressure to join Tipu's Army though 2,500 of the prisoners from the Madras Army had done so. On the conclusion of the peace, the surviving Bombay sepoys were marched across to the Madras coast.

Note that the only mention of an engagement by the 6th Battalion—in which battalion Kehimkar says that Samaji "was made a Jemedar of a Company .... on 2nd July 1775"—is found in the above list of excerpts from Cadell not earlier than the Third Mysore War (1790-92). It is to be regretted that Kehimkar and the author of the Shaar

Ha-Rachamim Marathi biography of Samaji did not specify their sources. However, as B. J. Israel has put it :

> Despite the Cochin Chronicles, the Bene Israel tradition (if nothing more) that Samaji Divekar was captured in 1783 and released in 1784 cannot be brushed aside. It fits in with the two definite facts in Kehimkar: Divekar's promotion as Jemadar in 1775 and his serving on a court-martial in 1791.

B. J. Israel went on to say that :

> The campaigns before 1768 can be ignored for our purposes. The first campaign that is relevant is that in 1768. It can be seen from the Cadell extracts that Bombay Sepoys did take part in the First Mysore War against Hyder Ali, and that he did capture 180 sepoys, sick and wounded, at Mangalore in 1768 (not in 1766, as the Cochin document seems to suggest). It is, therefore, just possible that Divekar was captured by Hyder and released on intervention from Cochin, contrary to the Marathi biography and to Kehimkar. But, if he was born in 1740 and enlisted only about 1760 (cf. Kehimkar, p.190.), could he have been an *officer* in the Bombay contingent in 1768? (Kehimkar gives the date of his promotion to the commissioned rank of Jemadar as 2-7-1775, on p.90.) The date of 1783 for capture and of 1784 for release seems more plausible. In any case, if Divekar was indeed captured by Hyder in 1768 and released and taken to Cochin, he must have left from there almost immediately and rejoined his regiment to earn promotion in 1775.

NOTES

1. Reinemann gives this date in numerals, thus : "1767" (p.102, line 4). He does not give its Hebrew equivalent.
2. See below in paragraph (c) of this appendix.
3. If Reinemann is correct on this point, David Ezekiel Rahabi had not as yet (1767) had any contact with any Bene Israel, and presumably had not yet sent any Cochin Jewish teachers to them.
4. This seems to imply that the Sultan was taking advantage of Samaji's superior knowledge of western artillery and that he might have rewarded him financially for this service. Also, Samaji would have received accumulated wages and a compensatory sum which the British paid to their men after release from captivity.
5. The Bene Israel frequently left out the "t" in their pronunciation of the word "Commandant". It also often occurs as "Commadan", without the first "n" *and* without the final "t".
6. Here the word "Jew" means anyone of Jewish faith who was not of the Bene Israel community. The entire above quotation is from Solomon Reinemann's *The Travels of Solomon*. pp. 102-3.
7. Kehimkar : *Sketch*, p.24.
8. Kehimkar : *History*, p.75. This is a recurring theme in accounts about Indian heroes : from the royal ladies gallery, while watching the *durbar* (where law and justice were administered, and some punishments were executed), a royal female intercedes on behalf, or otherwise saves the life, of a convicted man. To cite an example : some relate that the Emperor Aurangzeb's daughter, Zebinessa, in mid-17th Century, saved the Maratha hero Shivaji in this fashion. There is nothing inherently impossible, or even implausible in accepting the historicity of at least some such reports, given the known influence of certain royal ladies.
9. Tellicherry is located about 140 miles north of Cochin and of the area of settlement of Cochin Jews.

10. Kehimkar, op.cit., pp.190-1.
11. According to B. J. Israel, history records no such massacre during the Third Mysore War, but a real massacre of troops did take place in the Second Mysore War. Samaji may have escaped this massacre and still have been taken prisoner. Or, while a prisoner, he may have escaped a massacre of prisoners — Tipu was known to have slaughtered large numbers of prisoners during their captivity.
12. Kehimkar, op.cit., p.255.
13. Mrs. Mary (Shapurkar) Sopher of Beer Sheva has kindly prepared for the present writer a literal translation into English from the original Marathi. This booklet of 16 pages is entitled *Samaji Hassaji Divekar, who Built Gate of Mercy Synagogue in Bombay in 1796* or *Samuel Ezekiel Divekar, Commadan, Mukkadam;* written by Abraham Samson Shapurkar, 2nd Secretary of the Gate of Mercy Synagogue; published by the Gate of Mercy Synagogue, 254 Samuel Street, Mandvi, Bombay, with Samuel Yehudah Chingolkar, 1st Secretary of the Gate of Mercy Synagogue, acting as the publisher; printed by Yashwant Kashinath Padwal. 3544 Parel Road, Byculla, Bombay, 1927. 1,500 copies were printed.
14. Fischel : *Ha-Yehudim B'Hodu* as part of Fischel's chapter on Isaac Sargon. The text of this Hebrew letter appears on p.113 as part of footnote 82. The text, as given here, is a literal English translation.
15. The parentheses are Fischel's.
16. Fischel : op.cit., p.114, a literal English translation of footnote 85.
17. B. J. Israel, in a personal communication to the present author.

Appendix 4
(See above, p.72)

From a "Review of The Travels of Rabbi D. D'Beth Hillel"

Published in *The Oriental Christian Spectator,* volume 4, Number 5, May 1833, Bombay; pp.197-204.

Some of our readers may remember seeing a couple of years ago, a curious looking old man, with a very long face, blear eyes, green spectacles..........labour and profit he had none, poor old man.......... He made many ineffectual efforts to establish himself reputably—and his friends advised, consulted, started him, cheered him on, but he inevitably came back to them again, worse off (at least in apparel), than he was before. To teach Hebrew was one very legitimate means of subsistence, but the difficulty lay in getting the thick-heads in Bombay to learn. He declared he never met with such a set of un-Hebrewish scholars in all his life—it required all his, and a quantity of extra coaxing to make a man face that mysterious language. We believe we are right in saying that the only two attentive and hard working pupils whom he swung the pedagogue's ferula over, were the Venerable the Archdeacon, and the *Rev. J. Wilson* [emphasis supplied]—they soon got possession of all the advice that David had to communicate, and not another pupil would this place produce, though he hunted into every nook and cranny of the Island to see whether such a desirable creature existed. Well, this failing, his friends bethought themselves that one who knew so much of the inside of books, could surely treat their outsides in the same superior way—and book-binding, said they, you may depend upon it, is the line of labour in which David will shine. Books were dribbled out to him rather cautiously at first, notwithstanding, the gay shop, the new materials, the sight of a dozen lusty workmen and Rabbi David himself always in motion, about something or nothing, in one of the most populous parts of Bombay. There was somehow or other always a flaw in his execution. "This book, Mr. David," one would sedately say "is not bound quite so well as I expected."."What, sir, would you have more beautifully lettered, open back, just as good as English binding". "But look here, here are two or three leaves topsyturvy." "Oh never mind that, never mind that, that's nothing, you have only to turn the book over, and it is just as good as it is turned the other way, when you get to that page." There was no resisting this and David went on binding. A European Bookbinder must be the ne plus ultra of the business in Bombay; the bait took.......... The Rabbi and his assistants were all Jews. The Maratho character was Hieroglyphics to them. Our worthy friends of the Society never dreamt of this. "All the sheets are mixed, Sir," said one of the youths, "what are we to do?" "Oh never mind that," said David "it's all the same in the end, they can find out the sheets if they want them." "But the lettering, Sir, we know nothing of these letters." "Never mind that — bind away my boys, only fools like you don't know the letters, those who do, will soon find them out." And bind away they did......... [until finally came the] death blow to all hopes in the book-binding way, and what was the Rabbi to do next.........David set out on his travels from this Presidency.......... And it seems that David had a talent which was hid from the view of most of his Bombay friends, the talent of observation; a Reverend friend at Madras finding it out, has got the Rabbi to display it to some advantage,—so that really although he could never bind a book, he has made one, which is much the most difficult task of the two : and now to speak seriously.......... We were aware that he had many high qualifications. His intellectual powers were of no mean order, but he was hasty in his judgment, and imprudent in his measures—and this we can see much of, in the book which we will now introduce to our readers.......... The Rabbi's account of Bombay will be interesting as the first description of this place given by a Jew.......... Our readers will discover the few sentences in which the Rabbi deals rather roughly with the British Character. We will not quote them—He seems to have been much better pleased with his reception at Madras than at Bombay. We recommend the book to all those who wish to see the curious observations of a clever and well-educated Jew, and we heartily wish the Rabbi success in any of his future speculations.

Appendix 5
(See above, p.74)

From "The Oriental Christian Spectator"
Volume 11, No.1, January 1840, pp.27-36.

ABSTRACT OF AN ACCOUNT OF THE BENI-ISRAEL OF BOMBAY, READ BEFORE THE BOMBAY BRANCH OF THE ROYAL ASIATIC SOCIETY, AT THE ANNIVERSARY MEETING IN NOVEMBER 1838 AND 1839. BY JOHN WILSON, D. D. PRESIDENT OF THE SOCIETY.

HISTORICAL TRADITIONS AND PRESENT RESIDENCE

The Beni-Israel possess no historical document peculiar to themselves; they have no charters granted by native princes, which are often a source of curious information; and their traditions are extremely vague and unsatisfactory. Their ancestors, they say, came to the coasts of India, from a country to the northward, about sixteen hundred years ago. They were in number seven men, and seven women, who were saved from a watery grave, on the occasion of a shipwreck, which took place near Chaul, about thirty miles to the south-east of Bombay. The place where they found a refuge, is named Navagaum. They and their descendants met with considerable favour from the native princes, though they were sometimes forced to conceal their principles. As they increased, they spread themselves among the villages of the Konkan, particularly those near the coast, and lying near the Bankot river, and the road which traverses the country between Panwell, and the Borghat. In this locality, and also in Bombay, in which they began to settle after it came into the possession of the English, their descendants are still to be found. The population of this island amount to about 1932 souls; in the English territories in the Konkan, to about 800; in the districts belonging to the Angria, to 870; in certain villages below the ghat, of the Pant Sachiva, to 209; in the districts of the Habshi, to 444; and in the Bombay army, including women and children, to about 1,000. These numbers, which amount altogether to 5,255, I take principally from a census made under my own direction. They fall short of the general native estimate by nearly 3,000. It is possible that some houses may have been overlooked by the persons sent forth by me to collect information.

PERSONAL APPEARANCE AND DRESS

The Beni-Israel resemble in countenance the Arabian Jews, though they view the name *Yehudi* when applied to them as one of reproach. They are fairer than the other natives of the same rank of life with themselves; but they are not much to be distinguished from them with regard to dress. They have no *shendi* [tuft of hair], like the Hindus; but they preserve a tuft of hair above each of their ears. Their turbans, *angrakhas*,[1] and shoes are like those of the Hindus; and their trousers like those of the Musalmans. Their ornaments are the same as those worn by the middle class of natives in the Maratha country.

HOUSES

The houses of the Beni-Israel do not differ from those of other natives of the same rank.

FOOD

The Beni-Israel do not eat with persons belonging to other communities; but they do not object to drink from vessels belonging to Christians, Musalmans, or Hindus. They ask a blessing from God both before and after their meals, in the Hebrew language.

NAMES

Each of the Beni-Israel, generally speaking, has two names, one derived from a character mentioned in Scripture, and another which has originated in deference to Hindu usage.

The Hebrew names current among the *men* are the following :— Abraham, Isaac, Jacob, Reuben (which is said most to abound), Joseph, Naphtali, Zebulon, Benjamin, Samson, Moshe, Aaron, Eleizer, Phinehas, David, Solomon, Elijah, Hezkiel, Daniel, Sadik, Haim, Shalom, and Nashim. The name Judah, it is to be remarked, is not to be found among them. The Hindu names, by which they are most commonly known among the natives, are Saku, Jitu, Ramu, Bapu, Sawandoba, Tana, Dhonda, Abau, Bandu, Hathu, Dada, Dhamba, Bala, Baba, Vitu, or Yethu, Phakira, Yeshu, Satku, Apa, Bhau, Bapshah, Gauria, Pita, Bawa, Anandia, Kama, Jangu, Aba. Among these, it will be observed, there are only a few which correspond with those of the heathen gods.[2]

Sarah, Rebecca, Rachel, Leah, Saphira, Milchah, Zilchah, Miriam, and Hannah, are the Hebrew names given to the *women*. Esther the favourite Jewish name does not occur among them.[3] The names derived from the Hindus which are found among them, are Balku, Abai, Ama, Yeshi, Zaitu, Tanu, Hasu, Ladi, Baina, Aku, Ranu, Bayewa, Baia, Nanu, Raju, Thaku, Kalabai, Maka, Saku, Gowary, Dudi, Sai, Sama, and Bhiku, Rithu, Wohu, Dhakalu.[4]

The Hebrew names are first conferred on the occasion of circumcision and those of a Hindu origin are first given, agreeably to the convention of each family, about a month after the birth of the individual on whom they are bestowed.[5]

The surnames of the Beni-Israel are generally derived from the villages in which they originally settled.

VERNACULAR LANGUAGE

The vernacular language of the Beni-Israel, is the Marathi. A few of them, however, are able to converse in Gujarathi and Hindustani.

EMPLOYMENT AND PROPERTY

The Beni-Israel resident in the Konkan, principally occupy themselves in agriculture or, in manufacturing oil. (* Hence the Beni-Israel in general are not unfrequently denominated *Teli,* or oilmen.) Those who live in Bombay, with the exception of a few shopkeepers, are artisans, particularly masons and carpenters. A few are blacksmiths, goldsmiths, and tailors. Shoemakers, barbers, and professional washermen are unknown amongst them.[6] Some of them, generally bearing an excellent character as soldiers, are to be found in most of the units of Native Infantry in the Bombay Presidency; and few of them retire from the service, without attaining to rank as native officers. There are not many of them who possess much property. David 'Capitan', their Mukadam, or headman, in Bombay, is believed to possess one or two lakhs[7] of rupees. A considerable number of families are supposed to be worth from 1,000 to 5,000 rupees. Like the Parsis, they do not tolerate professional begging, beyond their own community. The poor are relieved by private charity, or from the funds of the *Masjid,* or synagogue, which are derived from fines and offerings.

POSITION IN NATIVE SOCIETY

In the Company's territories, the Beni-Israel enjoy all the toleration which they can desire. In the district of country belonging to the petty Hindu prince Angria, in which many of them are to be found, they take the same rank as Musalmans. In that belonging to the Habshi, or Musalman Chief of Jiziri, they are viewed as on a point of equality with the agricultural Marathas.[8]

INTERNAL GOVERNMENT OF THEIR COMMUNITY

All questions respecting the cast, and religious discipline of the Beni-Israel, are determined, in a meeting of the adult members of the community in each village, by their Mukadam, or head man, who has a kind of magisterial authority in the community, and the Kazi, who is the president in religious matters, and the conductor of public worship (* Kazis are to be found only in the villages in which a considerable number of the Beni-Israel reside together), and whose duty it is to entertain the complaints which are made to them. The Mukadam and Kazi, have generally the assistance of four *chogale,* or elders, in the superintendence which they exercise, and the judgments which they pronounce. Any of the people present at an investigation, however, may express their sentiments on the subjects under discussion, record their dissent, and, in certain circumstances, procure a new trial. In the administration of justice, they admonish witnesses to speak the truth by their regard to the Torah, or Law; but they seldom exact from them a formal oath.

OBJECTS OF WORSHIP

The Beni-Israel all profess to adore Jehovah, the God of Abraham, of Isaac, and of Jacob. Many of them till lately, however, publicly worshipped, and some of them at the present time secretly worship, the gods of the Hindus, and particularly those who are supposed to be possessed of a malevolent character[9]; and a few of them practise divination, according to the rites of the Hindus. Though they have remained quite distinct from the people among whom they have been so long scattered, we see the applicability to them of the words of Moses, in Deuteronomy xxviii, 64, "Thou shalt serve other gods, which neither thou nor thy fathers have known, even wood and stone."

FOUNDATION OF RELIGIOUS OPINIONS AND PRACTICES

The Beni-Israel have in their synagogues no *Sepher-Torah* or MS. of the law, like the Jews. They admit, however, the divine authority of all the books of the Old Testament.
   It is only lately that they have become familiar with the majority of the names of the inspired writers; and it was not without hesitation that they consented to acknowledge the latter prophets. From the Arabian Jews, they have received the Hebrew Liturgy of the Sephardim, which they partially use in their religious services. A few copies of the

Cochin ritual, printed in Amsterdam about the end of the seventeenth century, are to be formed [found] in their hands. One of their number has a copy of one of the Targums, I believe that of Onkelos, but I do not know that it is turned to any account.

The five books of Moses form the standard of the religious law of the Beni-Israel. Their statutes, however, are but partially regarded. Parchments bearing small passages of Scripture, are sometimes worn on different parts of their bodies. It is understood, that of late they have almost universally abandoned the use of charms, to which the example of the heathen had made them in some degree partial.

CEREMONIES ON THE OCCASION OF BIRTHS, CIRCUMCISION, MARRIAGES, AND DEATHS

When a birth takes place in any village in which the Beni-Israel are not very numerous, they almost all visit the house, and are entertained with sweetmeats or fruits.

Circumcision is performed by the *kazi* on the day appointed by the law of Moses. In connection with it be [he]pronounces the words "Blessed be thou, O Jehovah, our God, the universal King, who sanctifies us by his commandments, and ordains us concerning circumcision." He also invokes the prophet Elijah, and the expected Messiah, using some superstitious ceremonies. The rite is considered as marking the descent of the Beni-Israel from Abraham; but no spiritual meaning is attached to it, except by individuals who may have had intercourse with Christian missionaries. The ceremony is attended by a considerable number of people, who are hospitably entertained, and who invoke the health of the child over the simple juice of the grape. The *kazi* generally receives from eight annas to two rupees for his services. Small presents are sometimes given to the infants.

The marriages of the Beni-Israel generally take place as early in life, as among the Hindus.[10] The arrangements connected with the betrothment, are those of the parents. The ceremonies continue for five, instead of seven, days, as with the ancient Jews; and they are in some respects of heathenish character. On the first day, the bridegroom is restrained from going abroad, is bathed, and gets his hands stained red with the leaves of the *Mendi* (Lawsonia inermis), and the front of his turban ornamented with yellow, or white, paper, cut in the form of the flowers of the *champa* (Michelia champaca), while he is visited by his relatives, who begin to feast and rejoice. On the second day, his neighbours, without distinction, are invited to participate in the hospitality of his father's house; while he is required to have his hair dressed, and to array himself in his best apparel and ornaments. He is then mounted on a horse, and conveyed, with the usual clang and clatter of the natives, to the place of worship, where a part of the marriage prayers is read, and a blessing is pronounced by the *kazi*. From the masjid, he is conveyed, in the same way as when moving towards it, to the house of the bride, where he is received by her father, and seated among the assembled multitude. A dress and ornaments for the bride as expensive as the circumstances of the family will permit, are presented in his name, and by the hands of his father, to the bride, who immediately turns them to use. A couch covered with clean cloth is then produced; and on it the happy pair are seated together. All the visitors stand before them. The *kazi* takes a cup, containing the juice of the grape, which is viewed as a token of the covenant about to be entered into; invokes the blessing of God upon it; and puts it into the hands, first of the bridegroom, and afterwards of the bride, who both drink a little of it, as soon as they have been questioned as to their readiness to enter into the marriage relation, and faithfully to discharge their respective duties. The marriage covenant drawn out in the form usually observed by the Jews, is then produced and read; and after being signed by the individual in whose hand-writing it is, and three other witnesses, it is placed by the bridegroom in the hands of the bride. She holds one end of it, while he holds the other, and declares it to be a legal deed. He then folds it, and gives it into her possession. She disposes of it, by committing it to her father's care. The cup is again tasted; certain passages of the Psalms are read; a ring is placed by the bridegroom on the forefinger of the right hand of the bride; and the religious part of the ceremonies is declared to be closed. The *kazi* blesses the espoused, seated together, and they receive offerings, principally in small sums of money, from their acquaintances. Feasting and rejoicing conclude the labours of the day. Next evening, the bridegroom and bride leave the bride's house,—the former seated on a horse and the latter on a palanquin,—and proceed amidst the firing of squibs and rockets, to the masjid, where they receive a fresh benediction from the kazi, before going to the house of the bridegroom, where they dine along with their assembled friends. Amusement and feasting continue during the two subsequent days.

The marriage covenant is in general rigidly respected, even though adultery is but slightly punished, as by a fine of but one or two rupees. The innocent member of a family, in aggravated cases, is allowed a divorce and the liberty of remarriage. The offending party, in the lax discipline of the community, is seldom prevented from having similar privileges, when he has the means of purchasing them.

Polygamy is practised in a considerable number of families; but there are no instances of a man known as having more than *three* wives. A few individuals keep female slaves as concubines.

Barrenness, as of old, is reckoned a great misfortune; and children are adopted by a written covenant on a failure of issue.

Females are by no means so degraded among the Beni-Israel, as among the Rabbinical Jews; but they are not allowed to go to the masjids for the purpose of worship.[11] The kind treatment which they receive favourably contrasts with that of the Hindu females around them.

The interments of the Beni-Israel quickly follow the death. They bury without coffins in graves three or four feet in depth. The head of the corpse is placed toward the East. They sometimes make offerings to the souls of the deceased of rice, milk and cocoa-nuts, and sprinkle water, mixed with flour, at the time of the interment. And they visit the grave on the third, fifth, and seventh days after it is closed, for the purpose of prayer. They have also an annual ceremony in behalf of the dead, like that of the Hindu *Shraddh*.[12] Their formal mourning for the dead lasts seven days. Some few of them think that there is a purgatory for the reception of souls after death.

DAILY RECKONING OF TIME

The Beni-Israel reckon their day from sunset to sunset. They now denominate their months by the Hebrew names.

WEEKLY SABBATH

The weekly Sabbath is, in some degree, observed by about a third of the population. At six in the morning they assemble for worship in the masjid, where they remain for two or three hours, principally engaged in reciting prayers or parts of the Scriptures after the *Hazzan*, or reader, and practising genuflections. A few of the more devout of their number may be seen in the masjid about mid-day, or about two or three in the afternoon.

The evening service, which commences about six o'clock, is that perhaps which is best attended. It lasts for about two hours, and is frequently concluded by the persons present merely touching with their lips the cup of blessings.

By the greater part of the population, the Sabbath is altogether profaned. A bad example in Bombay is shown by some of the principal men, who are said to spend the day in the audit of their accounts.

MONTHLY FESTIVAL

The day of the new moon is denominated by the Beni-Israel, as by the Jews, *Rosh Hodesh*, or the first of the month; but it is very little observed by them, unless it may happen to fall on the day of the weekly Sabbath. In a few houses, and also in some of the masjids, the prayers and lessons appointed for the day, are read, as they are given in the liturgy of the Sephardim, which they denominate Sidur.[13] On the fifth, sixth, seventh, eighth, ninth, or tenth of the month, when the moon is seen to increase, the readers of the synagogue, and a few other individuals read the *Berchat-ha-Lebana*, the blessing of the moon,—springing on their toes with their faces toward the luminary. This custom, like most of the others connected with their worship, is allowed by the Beni-Israel to have been derived from the Arabian Jews.

ANNUAL FASTS AND FESTIVALS

The annual religious festivals and fasts of the Beni-Israel, I shall mention under the head, and according to the order of the months, beginning with the commencement of the ecclesiastical year, which takes place about the vernal equinox.

1. *Abib* or *Nisan*. The great Jewish festival of the Pesach, or Passover, commences on the fourteenth of this month. It is a curious fact, that the Beni-Israel allow, that their fathers in India, even till a late period, were entirely ignorant of the objects for which it was originally instituted, and the manner in which it should be observed, and that the only regard which they paid to it, was on the eighth day, from its commencement, when they indulged themselves in eating or drinking. At present, particularly in Bombay, about one third of their number imitate, on a small scale, the mode of observance of the Arabian Jews, paying special regard to the two first, and two last days. During eight days, these persons use only unleavened bread, which on the first and second day they mix with herbs. On the first day, they place on their tables, the right foot of a goat roasted, to remind them of the paschal lamb. They do not regard the ancient ordinance in reference to having their loins girded, their shoes on their feet, and their staves in their hands. They use four cups, with the juice of the grape, pretty frequently in the midst of their prayers and readings. One individual in a family holds a bason in his hand into which the contents of a cup are poured in ten portions, corresponding with the ten plagues inflicted upon the Egyptians, which are respectively mentioned as the ceremony proceeds.

The twenty-third of this month, the Beni-Israel denominate *Isru-Hag* ("bind the festival-sacrifice", as in Psalm, cxviii, 27), but for what reason they do not know. It is spent nearly universally by them as a day of rejoicing.[14]

2. *Jyar* or *Zif*. In this month, falls the second passover of the Jews (Numbers ix, 10, 11) observed by those who cannot attend to the first passover. It is never regarded by the Beni-Israel.

3. *Sivan*. The feast of *Shabuoth* (weeks, or Penticost,) commences among the Beni-Israel on the sixth of this month. They partially observe it for two days, as a season of

rejoicing, remaining awake at the masjid during the intervening night, and spending the time principally in reading and praying. They have no ceremonies connected with the produce of their fields, though a very few of them use the ordinary prayers of the Jews which refer to them. They have no aoquaintance with the Rabbinical legends associated with the festival among the Jews,—such as those of the uplifting of Mount Sinai over the head of the Israelites,[15] the crowning of the members of the congregation by 600,000 angels, and the retreat and advance of the people, for twelve miles, on the giving of each commandment.

4. *Thammuz.* The Jews observe the seventeenth of this month *Shiba-esser-Thammuz*, as a day of fasting, in remembrance of the breaking of the tables of the law, and the ceasing of the regular sacrifice; and the Beni-Israel have begun to be their imitators.

5. *Ab.* On the ninth of this month, *Tisha-be-Ab*, the Jews fast, because it is said that the temple was on it first burnt by the Chaldees, and afterwards by the Romans, and because on it God declared, in the time of Moses, that none of those who came out of Egypt should enter the promised land. Some of the Jews of London, who lately opened a correspondence with the Beni-Israel, have exhorted them strictly to observe it, to which, for many years, they had not been disinclined, having been admonished to the same effect by the Cochin Jews.

6. *Elul.* The Beni-Israel observe some customs during this month, and the nine days of the following one preceding the day of atonement, which, as far as I am aware, are peculiar to themselves. Except on the *Rosh Hodesh*, and the weekly Sabbath, they professedly fast with great strictness during the time that the sun is above the horizon.[16] Numbers of them attend the masjid for prayer long before sunrise.

7. *Tisri.* The civil year of the Jews commences on the first of this month, called *Rosh-ha-Shona*. The Beni-Israel universally devote to feasting and rejoicing, the whole day, with the exception of a few hours, during which some of them attend at the masjid, for the purpose of offering up their prayers, and blowing horns and trumpets.[17] Their salutation, when they first meet, is *Tisku le Shanim raboth*, May you survive many years; and the reply is commonly, *Sikateb be sepher haim tobhim*, Let thy name be written in the book of life. Like the Jews, they use honey and sweetmeats at their evening meal. The second day of the year, they spend in the same manner as the first. About three o'clock in the afternoon, some of them repair to the shore, and worship towards the ocean.

On the third of Tisri, the fast of Gedaliah, the son of Ahikam, whose murder is mentioned in the last chapter of 2 Kings, is generally observed by the Beni-Israel, as well as by the Jews.

The fast of the Day of Atonement, or *Kippur*, which takes place on the tenth day, is very strictly regarded by the Beni-Israel. A few families, in deference to some Rabbinical legend, which they have heard from the Arabian, or Cochin, Jews, sacrifice a cock, to which they give the name of the *Kapparah*, or expiation, on the preceding evening. They spend much time, both during the night and day, in confessing their sins, and supplicating the divine mercy, agreeably to the forms of their liturgy.[18] In the course of the night, they offer up prayers to God, for the sovereign of Britain, the Governor of Bombay, and all the authorities of the country. The day following the kippur is distinguished for the exercise of hospitality and charity.

On the fifteenth day of this month, the feast of *Succoth*, or Tabernacles, is celebrated by the Beni-Israel for nine days, being two in excess of the time prescribed in the Old Testament. A booth covered with the branches of the palm, and ornamented with flowers and fruit, is erected in every village near the masjid, in which the people assemble for the purpose of singing some of the Psalms, and receiving the cup of blessing; but their prayers are recited in the usual place. The eighth night, those who attend the tabernacle devote to watching. The two first and the two last days of the festival are those which are most regarded, and during them little secular work is performed.

8. *Bul,* or *Marchesvan.* In this month the Beni-Israel observe neither fast nor festival.

9. *Chisleu.* On the twenty-fifth day commences the festival of *Hanucha,* or Purification of the temple, which lasts for eight days. Few, or none, of the Beni-Israel, illuminate their houses like the Jews. They keep lights burning, however, at the masjid whither, mornings and evenings, they partially repair for worship. A very few of them have some knowledge of the godly zeal of Judas Maccabaeus, which the Jews celebrate at this season.

10. *Thebeth.* On the tenth day, a few of the Beni-Israel fast, in commemoration of the siege of Jerusalem by Nebuchadnezzar the king of Babylon.

11. *Shabath.* This month is not distinguished by any holiday.

12. *Adar.* On the fourteenth day, the Beni-Israel fast, preparatory to the feast of *Purim,* or Lots, which takes place on the following day, and which they partially observe, in imitation of the Arabian and Cochin Jews, as a festival commemorative of the great deliverance wrought through the instrumentality of Esther. They conduct themselves, on this occasion, with more propriety than the Jews in most parts of the world, and few of them are to be seen in a state of intoxication. They do not, like the Jews, repeat the feast of Lots, when the intercalary month *Ve-Adar* happens to occur.

VOLUNTARY FASTS

The Beni-Israel practise occasional voluntary fasts, particularly when they are inclined to make vows.

NEGLECT OF JUBILEE

The Beni-Israel observe no Jubel, or Jubilee.

ARE THEY JEWS OR ISRAELITES?

The brief survey which we have now made of the observances of the Beni-Israel, might appear to warrant the conclusion that they are Jews, unconnected with the descendants of the Rubenites and Gadites, and the half-tribe of Manassah, who were carried captive to Halah, and Habor, and Hara, and Nahar-Gozan, (1 Chron, v, 26) by Pul, king of Assyria, and Tiglath-pelneser, king of Assyria, and unconnected also with the descendants of the ten tribes, who were carried captive to the same and neighbouring places, by Shalmanezer, after the fall of Samaria, in the reign of Hosea (2 Kings, xvi, 6); for they commemorate events with which it is difficult to see how these exiles could be connected, and some of which occurred posterior to the return of the Jews to their own land from Babylon, to which they were removed by Nebuchadnezzer. It is only at first sight, however, that such an inference seems to be authorized. The Beni-Israel most readily admit, that to this adoption of their present practices, they have been led by the example and precepts of the Arabian and Cochin Jews, who from time to time have come to visit them, or to reside in their neighbourhood. The very fact that they required to be instructed by foreigners in the most solemn and interesting ordinances of their religion, as well as in other customs universally observed by the Jews throughout the world, is a presumption that they have been established for many ages in this country, and really belong to the long exiled and 'lost' tribes of Israel. The Jews of Cochin, who say that they came to India immediately after the destruction of the second temple, or according to their own historical notices, in the 68th year of the Christian era (* See Oriental Christian Spectator, September and October, 1839), have all along considered themselves distinct from the Beni-Israel of Bombay of whose circumstances they have from time immemorial[19] been well aware; and the black-Jews of Cochin, descendants of proselytes from among the Hindus and the Jewish families which mixed with them, informed the late Dr. Claudius Buchanan, when he was making inquiries about the Ten Tribes, that it was "commonly believed among them that the great body of the Israelites is to be found in Chaldea;" but "that some few families had migrated into regions more remote, as to Cochin and *Rajapur* in India" (* Christian Researches).[20] The last mentioned place is the district of country, bordering on the Nagotna creek, in which many of the Beni-Israel are even at present settled. The want of MS. *Sepher-Torah*, or Book of the Law, among the Beni-Israel, places them in a situation in which we do not see any congregation of Jews throughout the world. The repudiation, to this day nearly universal among them, of the designation *Jew*, of which no doubt, they would have been proud, had they merited it; and the distinctive appellation of 'Beni-Israel', which they take for themselves; the non-occurrence among them of the favourite Jewish names Judah and Esther; and the predominance of the name Reuben, and other names principally connected with the early history of God's highly-favoured people, appear to me to be circumstances strongly corroborative of the opinion that they are indeed Israelites, a remnant of the posterity of the tribes, which were removed from their homes by the Assyrian kings.

CLAIMS ON CHRISTIAN BENEVOLENCE AND STATE OF EDUCATION

In the view which we have been led to take of the *Beni-Israel, they must be considered as possessed of peculiar interest, even among the seed of Abraham,* connected with whose destinies the most wonderful providences, noticed either by sacred or profane history, have been developed. Amongst us who are Christians, they must be "beloved for the father's sakes"; and it must be our desire and endeavour, that "through our mercy, they may obtain mercy." *Their situation, if properly explained to the Hindus among whom they dwell, might facilitate the illustration of the prophetical testimony to the truth of the Scriptures, which the general ignorance of events which have occurred beyond the bounds of this country, renders it a matter of difficulty for many to understand.* They have never as a body proved averse to Christian education; and they have always been ready to receive and peruse the Bible. [From p.35. Emphases supplied]

About twenty years ago, the American Missionaries who were the first to occupy the field of labour in our neighbourhood, took several of the Beni-Israel into their employment as Marathi teachers; and from about 100 to 140 of their pupils, in different villages near Bombay, were of the children of that community, and till 1836 instructed in the Mission-schools in reading, writing, and accounts. About thirty individuals began the study of Hebrew at Alibag in 1829, but they did not long persevere. (* A good number of youth in Bombay, and in some of the villages on the neighbouring coast, read Hebrew fluently, without, however, being able to understand the meaning. As a help to their studies, I composed and published, in 1832, the "Rudiments of Hebrew Grammar in Marathi," a little work which they gratefully purchased.)

Mr. Sargon, a converted Cochin Jew, instituted for the Madras Jews' Society [21], six schools for their benefit in 1826, which at one time were attended by 165 scholars, and continued in operation for about four years.

The Church of England Missionary Society, has a Hebrew and Marathi school in Bombay, which a few months ago was attended by about 70 or 80 scholars, from which more than the half, however, have been withdrawn, in consequence of some misunderstanding in the Beni-Israel community. The fugitives from this school, and a few others attend a school lately opened by the Mukadam of Bombay.[22]

The Mission of the General Assembly of the Church of Scotland, under arrangements proposed by myself, commenced the work of Christian education among the Beni-Israel in 1837; and 210 pupils, – 159 boys, and 51 girls, – are now receiving instruction in connection with its schools. Of these 19 youth, have entered on a course of superior study in the English Institution in Bombay.[23] The others, with the exception of 14 girls of this place, belong to the villages of Panwell, Alibag, Revadanda, and Ambepur. The Assembly's Committee for the Jews, which has manifested great interest in the situation of the Beni-Israel, will probably soon make arrangements for the regular Christian instruction of the community.

The education of the Beni-Israel, the dissemination among them of the Scriptures, and the addresses of missionaries, are producing visible effects throughout their community. They have already nearly banished from it the idolatry and divination which were formerly practised, and they have done much to awaken in it a spirit of liberal inquiry. I have heard several individuals declare that they could not show reason for refusing to acknowledge that Jesus is indeed the Messiah.[24]

NOTES

1. *Angrakha* (correct spelling = *angarkha*) : A part of male attire, an outer garment or coat.
2. In this list the only specific name of a Hindu deity is Rama (Ramu); some others are only attributes (usually adjectives) by which a given Hindu deity is sometimes also named; for instance, Ananda means "blissful", Kama means "love".
3. The names Judah and Esther are now in use among the Bene Israel. Note that even in Kehimkar's day the name Judah was sometimes used, i.e. Judah Hyam Mhasilkar (see above, p.181)
4. Compare these names with those which Kehimkar gives on p.38 of his *History of the Bene-Israel of India*.
5. The official name-giving ceremony among Hindus does not occur soon after birth: sometimes the ceremony is carried out only several months later.
6. Leather handling, barbering and laundry work are the function of "untouchables" in India.
7. One *lakh* equals one hundred thousand.
8. For "Jiziri", read "Janjira". In strict Muslim states "The People of the Book" (i.e. usually Christians and Jews, but sometimes this also included Parsis and Hindus) were subject to the so-called *jizya* tax (which, for the Moghul Empire in India, the Emperor Akbar abolished); it was forbidden them to lift a hand against a Muslim, even if being attacked; and they were allowed to ride only on donkeys, being forbidden to ride on horses or camels. Either the Muslim potentates of Janjira enforced no such rules, or they did not recognise the Bene Israel as belonging to the Jewish faith, or both.
9. Such as the Goddess of Smallpox, feared by all and petitioned by many non-Hindus as well as by Hindus.
10. As of 1881 this was no longer the case. See above, p.138.
11. At the time when Wilson presented his *Account*, i.e. in 1838 and in 1839 (or even when the *Abstract* of it was printed in *The Oriental Christian Spectator* of January 1840), there seem to have been Bene Israel prayer halls in addition to the first Bene Israel synagogue, because Wilson keeps on referring to *masjids* (in the plural), and the second Bene Israel synagogue was not established until 1840. Perhaps the Bene Israel women were not allowed to pray in the small prayer rooms, but all of the Bene Israel synagogues are built with balconies reserved especially

for the women to offer their prayers. Even those women who were unable to read Hebrew knew parts of the liturgy by heart. But perhaps this was not yet the case in 1839.
12. Jews everywhere say a special prayer, *Kaddish*, at the funeral of any member of the immediate family; and *Kaddish* is supposed to be recited (by the father, eldest son, or husband of the deceased) twice a day for eleven months thereafter. On each death anniversary (according to the Hebrew calendar) *Kaddish* is again recited (on the eve, morning and afternoon) and a candle or oil-lamp (which keeps lit for at least 24 hours) is lit. In order to recite *Kaddish* at least a *minyan* is required to be present. At the time of Wilson's observation, the Bene Israel probably still included in their annual memorial ceremony some features of the Hindu *Shraddha* ceremony. Among Hindus *Shraddha* must be performed by a son or the nearest male kinsman some time between the 10th and 31st day after the cremation of the deceased, in order to assure the proper benefits for the deceased's soul. The male family member who performs the *Shraddha* is thereby constituted as the dead person's heir. The *Shraddha* is also performed as an annual (or otherwise) memorial. The rite includes the offering of balls of rice *(pinda)*, feasting, and gift-giving to Brahmins.
13. This is the Hebrew word for a prayer book. Its literal meaning is "order" or "arrangement" (of prayers.).
14. For Jews in the diaspora this is important as being the last day of Passover.
15. This legend is summarised as follows by Louis Ginzburg in his *The Legends of the Jews* (translated from the German by Paul Radin), published by the Jewish Publication Society of America, Philadelphia, 1911, Volume III, p.92.:

"It was not indeed quite of their own free will that Israel declared themselves ready to accept the Torah, for when the whole nation, in two divisions, men and women, approached Sinai, God lifted up this mountain and held it over the heads of the people like a basket, saying to them : 'If you accept the Torah, it is well, otherwise you will find your grave under this mountain.' They all burst into tears and poured out their heart in contrition before God, and then said : 'All that the Lord hath said, we will do, and be obedient' ."

The element of the deity holding a mountain aloft is reminiscent of a Hindu legend where the god Krishna holds up Mount Govardhan by supporting it with his little finger — in order to protect his worshippers from a deluge sent by a rival god Indra.
16. Kehimkar says that this month of Bene Israel fasting was called by them *Ramadan;* Wilson makes no mention of this.
17. Did they really use trumpets too? Or only the *shofar* (i.e. the ram's horn) of Jewish tradition?
18. Wilson makes no mention of the Bene Israel's unique observances for the Day of Atonement (Yom Kippur) as described by Kehimkar (in his *History*, p.18) and as described by Bene Israel respondents from villages (see above, p.220 – 21).
19. What was Wilson's source for saying that the Cochin Jews were aware of the Bene Israel "from time immemorial"?
20. Buchanan; *Christian Researches in Asia*, p.177 of the 1811 edition.
21. No doubt this is the same group which Rabbi D'Beth Hillel calls the "Madras Jewish Society". The Rabbi wrote that

"About five or six years ago the 'Madras Jewish Society' had established a school amongst them [the Bene Israel] for the purpose of training up their children in the Hebrew language."(p.134)

And again (p.138) he wrote that in the Maratha coastal village of "Panoovellee" [Panvel]

"There are about 30 families of Beni Israel, there is now established a school from the Jews society, for the purpose of teaching their children the Hebrew language."

The Madras Jews Society was probably a wing of the Church of England's London Society for Promoting Christianity Among the Jews.

22. Unfortunately the present writer has been unable to find any further information about the Bene Israel *Mukkadam's* school of 1839 or 1840.
23. See above, p.88, n. 46.
24. Here the Rev. Wilson is perhaps telling only half the truth: according to a few recorded actual incidents, even Bene Israel leaders, when facing Christian missionaries' arguments, admitted that *they* were unable to refute the Christian arguments, but only because they themselves were not learned Jewish scholars, and that Jewish scholars *would* be able to refute the arguments. Cf. Rev. Lord: *The Jewish Mission Field in the Bombay Diocese,* p.14 — as quoted above, p.83.

Appendix 6
(See above, p.81)
Solomon Reinemann on the Bene Israel

LITERAL TRANSLATION, FROM HEBREW INTO ENGLISH OF ALL PAGES ON THE BENE ISRAEL (pp. 99-112) IN *MASA'OT SHELOMO* (TRAVELS OF SOLOMON), BY SOLOMON REINEMANN; EDITED BY WOLFF SCHUR; PUBLISHED IN 1884, PRINTED AT THE GEORG BREG PRESS UNDER P. SMOLENSKIN, VIENNA : pp. 99-102 AND 104-112.

BENE ISRAEL IN GENERAL AND THE TIME OF THEIR COMING TO INDIA (p.99): The group called the Bene Israel were of those exiled by Shalmanezzar, King of Assyria, before the destruction of the First Temple. They had settled in Persia and did not return at the time of the building of the Second Temple..:....... In the year 612 when Ali Ibn Aby Talib fought with Yuzgadar, King of Persia, and took his land from him, there was a time of trouble such as no other, which befell all the inhabitants of the land, even the Bene Israel, for this man Ali persecuted all the lands which he conquered, forced them to change their religion to Islam, and ruled over them by the sword; all those who could escape did so, both Jews and Persians. They came to the city of Abu-Shahar and dwelt there about twenty years. They built small boats and ferries in order to cross over in them to East India, because they had heard that the Indians were pagans and would not only refrain from persecuting them but would refuse to convert others to their religion even if the latter wished to do so. After the Jews and the Parsis finished their work on the boats, they sailed away in them and headed for Bombay. When they reached the island called Gandri Mandir, 5 miles away from Bombay, a storm arose and all their boats were smashed, and only a very few people were saved. [p.100]

When the inhabitants of the place saw the trouble which befell them and heard from their mouths about their escape, and about the threat of forced conversion, they took pity on them and allowed them to remain on these conditions: they should not eat the flesh of cattle which were holy to the inhabitants; they should not speak or write in any language other than Marathi, the language of that land, for a Maratha king then ruled that land from Bombay to Goa, and until this day the Parsis and the Bene Israel speak Marathi for they have forgotten their own tongue. They have written in the books of the Maratha kings [about] all those who were saved from the angry sea, the Persian worshippers of fire separately, and the Bene Israel who worship "Hoda Ya-ak" [one God].[1] Since then the Bene Israel have settled in Bombay and its surroundings and some of them went over into Gujarat and settled there. They are called "Bene Israel" to distinguish them from the rest of the Jews who came later from cities of Persia, Yemen, and Babylon who are called "Yehudi" [Jew].

THEIR CUSTOMS AND THEIR RELIGION : In their dress, food, and all their customs they are like the local inhabitants, only in their faith they are different from them and they do not eat with them. Yet their religion is not the same as the religion of the Jews. They all admit that when they lived in Persia their religious laws were transmitted orally and were observed as the laws of the Torah. But, when they were cast out of their land and they lost in the depths of the sea and along the difficult journey, their elders who were the bearers of the tradition, the remnant no longer knew about their faith and they retained only the custom of circumcision, the Yom Kippur fast, ritual slaughter of animal food, and nothing more than that. On Yom Kippur, observed always on its correct day, since they came to India, they close themselves in their rooms and all day do not speak a word to each other. Each one sits and remains silent. They do not have prayer books, and the prayers which they had by oral tradition were lost during the days of their misfortune.

When they first came to India, they took women of the land to wife, because not every man had brought his wife with him. But they took them as wives only on condition that they would be called 'Bene Israel', would observe the husband's religion, and would not continue to mix with the local women either in eating habits or in worshipping god. In time they multiplied until today their number has risen to 5,000 families, and they do not any longer intermarry with the other people. But, even though their husbands made a condition that their wives give up idols, statues or masks, and though the men do not allow them to bring any picture into the house, nevertheless, the women in their tents,[2] in secret would worship an idol and pray to it like other local women. I myself saw in the year 1846, when I was in the town of Belgaum, that wives of soldiers there, when they lit lamps, would extend the fingers of their hands toward the fire and then kiss them.

They have lived in peace with the people of the place since their coming there. Since the arrival of the British, their status has risen because they made them full citizens and took them into the army; many of them quickly learned English because they had more talent than other Indians for languages and studies. They rose in rank and in importance and now [p.101] many of them are Captains or Majors, and have also reached the status of "Bahadur", which is a very high title in India. Many of them were doctors, military experts, surveyors, and engineers. In these specialities the British have willingly given them responsible positions because they liked and trusted them. In spite of this they did not intermarry with the people of the land and even in time of war they lived alone. They, their wives and their children did not eat the meat slaughtered for the army, and only if one of them performed the duty of the *Shohet*, did they eat of meat.

The *Shohet* was known as a *Kazi*. (* The *Kazi* was also a judge and arbiter. Also today a *Kazi* sits in each court in Bombay and gets paid by the Government.) Among them he was like a teacher and a leader in everything relating to religion. He circumcised their male children, he performed the wedding ceremony which they observed in the fashion of the people of that land. He was the judge, and he preached to the people.

In this way they support the *Shohet* in his work: They will all gather in one house and make a big feast. The important one among them will take a new knife, make sure that it is straight in the eyes of all in the gathering, and call aloud, "Mr. So-and so, this knife is given to you for you to use only this when you slaughter fowl and sheep; from now on you shall be [our] *Kazi*, perform circumcision on our sons, and perform the wedding ceremony according to our custom, the custom of Children of Israel scattered among the nations. The *Kazi*, with face beaming, took the knife and kissed it and said, "In the name of the God of Israel I am prepared to do your bidding." At that very moment he [then] slaughtered an animal right in front of them with that knife—even though it may have been defective—after that he put it in its sheath, and he will not use it for another purpose, because it had been consecrated. This was the duty of the *Kazi*, even if he didn't examine the lungs [of the animal].[3]

Even though before they took non-Jewish wives, now they are very, very careful not to intermarry. If one of them disobeyed [this] law and took a non-Jewish woman, they separated him from the community and kept away from him. They did not invite him to their feasts and functions, and did not attend his functions, because he was considered to be a non-Jew in their eyes until he might wish to return in penitence, which they would accept, if he divorced his non-Jewish wife. For the atonement, all of them would gather, with the *Kazi,* dressed in beautiful garments, at their head. They would go with the sinner to the river; immerse him up to his navel. The *Kazi* filled his hands with little stones the size of nuts, and threw one after another at him until the stones were finished. Then he immersed the sinner three times. He went out of the water and put on clean clothes. The *Kazi* and the people said to him three times: "Your are our brother:" And he returned to his standing as a member of their community.

Even though they do not intermarry with non-Jews, they have adopted much from the people of India. They have come to associate with them, and they have received them. As of now, they circumcise them and teach them to observe the commandments of circumcision, and Yom Kippur—which they do for them for a fee. But they will not marry with them and will not eat with them from one and the same plate, and in all walks of life they keep separate from them. They call them 'Kala Bene Israel' (the black Bene Israel). In this matter [p.102] they act like the Jews of Cochin who also will not marry with the Black Jews there.

[For the remainder of Reinemann's p. 102 and all of p. 103, see Appendix 3a, pp. 314-315]

[p.104] COCHINIS BURNED ALL IDOLS FROM BENE ISRAEL HOUSES IN BOMBAY : At that time Rav Ezekiel Rahabi had died. His son, the venerable and wise Rav David Ezekiel Rahabi, saw that the Bene Israel very much wanted to learn about God and His laws. He hastened to send men from Cochin to Bombay and its surroundings, and to each place where Bene Israel were dispersed, to teach them the Law of Moses and to warn their wives against the idols which they were whoring after, because in secret the women were worshipping the idols of the Maharashtrians, which they had learned to do from their female non-Jewish neighbors. They also sent them *Sifrei-Torah.* The teachers who came there succeeded. After some years Yehudah Ashkenazi, of blessed memory (he was my teacher and my father-in-law[4]) also crossed the sea to the city of Bombay [came to Bombay by sea from Cochin] to take the Bene Israel in hand. He was very successful because he was a handsome man and was skilled in medicine, especially for curing little children. Therefore they paid attention to what he said. He burned the idols from the towns of Panvel and Ravandiran, and from many villages where Bene Israel were living. He taught the women to observe (the rules concerning) the days of menstruation, and to immerse in the *mikveh,* or in a river, or in the sea.[5] Many women did this. They adored him as a holy man. It is now some years since his death and women still light memorial candles in the synagogue in his memory.

TRANSLATION OF THE BIBLE INTO MARATHI BY DR. WILSON AND THE SCHOOLS WHICH HE ESTABLISHED : 'After the darkness, comes the dawn', thus Israel walked in darkness for a long time without the Torah, without the true God, until their eyes were opened to seek knowledge of the Lord. They got rid of the idols, and the Holy Scriptures took their place. Like an angel sent from God, Dr. Wilson appeared among them, and translated all the Holy Scriptures, inclusive of the Prophets, into Marathi, their native tongue, because they still could not understand what they read in Hebrew. All the people hastened to buy the books, and they read them eagerly. He not only did this, but he founded schools for Hebrew and Marathi in Panvel and Bombay. The head teacher in Bombay was my dear friend Sr. Ezekiel Joseph Rajpurkar.[6] The

Bene Israel have named him "Pantatchi" [*Panch* means 'five' in India], meaning to say that he was learned in the Five Books of Moses. He and his brothers Elia and Samuel were the first to get the Bene Israel to adhere in all their ways to Judaism, and to come under the aegis of the Torah. They helped the teachers who had come from Cochin in order to teach them Torah, the customs of the White Jews, and their prayers.

The Lord blessed Ezekiel with a wise son who knew the books of the Torah, the Hebrew language and grammar. He knew four languages: Hebrew, English, Hindustani and Marathi; and he was the head teacher at the school which the Hon. David Sassoon, of blessed memory, founded in Bombay. He was the greatest specialist in the grammar of the holy tongue in all the lands of Persia, India, Yemen and [p.105] Babylon. He also was a wonderful musician, and a charitable and hospitable person. His uncle, Sr. Elia Benjamin, was a *Shohet* and a expert inspector of meat, skillful in his work (I certified his work). He also was *Hazan* in the synagogue. His son, Rav Reuben, followed in his father's footsteps, to instill the love of Torah among his brethren the Bene Israel. After these excellent men had zealously brought the Bene Israel into the service of the God of their forefathers and of His Torah, there was a member of the Bene Israel house of Commandan, Sr. Ezekiel Commandan, the then President of the [Bene] Israel caste and manager of the affairs of his brethren [serving] with wisdom and knowledge, in charity and in fear of the Lord. And then there was the house of Gabai, led by the elderly head of the family, the old Captain, Rav Sr. Eliahu and his son, the most distinguished of the family, the Hon. Sr. Samuel Elia, who at the moment is *Gabbai* of the Great Synagogue. After them, the illustrious doctor, Sr. Daniel, and his son, helped in the good cause, and the elderly Samuel Maestri[7] and his son, and Sr. Haim Gassover.[8] All of these men had one goal: to bring their brethren closer to their religion and their Torah. They achieved their purpose; and even though they could not persuade each and every one of them to live strictly according to the Torah, still, they were successful in burning the idols so that today not an idol nor a graven image will be seen or found in any Bene Israel house. They did succeed in bringing the faith of both the written and the oral Torah to their hearts.

THE DEEDS OF THE SHOHET-INSPECTOR AND RELIGIOUS POET SHELOMO SHURRABI, OF BLESSED MEMORY : The activity of my father-in-law, Judah Ashkenazi, of blessed memory, was great in that place, and his success in his work inspired others to follow him. After him, a light shone in Bombay in the form of that shining star, namely Shelomo Shurrabi, of blessed memory, from Cochin. His ancestors were from Yemen. He came to Bombay not for business reasons, but rather to take souls by his pure language and pleasant voice, for he spoke the language of the place as one of them; and he lavished his money; and by these means he captured the heart of the young men of the Bene Israel and they approached him. Also the women considered him a man of God and they scrupulously followed his teachings.

This was his way: On the eve of the Sabbath and on holidays he invited to dine with him at his house every man or woman who wished to listen to his music. He prepared a generous repast for them. While they sat at the table, he sang hymns for them in the holy tongue, songs for the Sabbath and the holidays, and he translated them into Marathi. Soon everybody knew them and sang them also in their own homes on Sabbath and holidays.[9] In order to keep them from cooking on the day of the Sabbath, for until then they had cooked on the Sabbath, he invited them to eat at his table also during the day, and he gave them warm food which had been prepared on Friday and had been kept warm for the Sabbath-foods pleasant in taste to the *Hacham;* and soon they did likewise in their own homes. Besides this, he concentrated on teaching them to understand the Torah, and on telling them during the meal the stories of Genesis and of the flight from

Egypt, of the parting of the Red Sea, and of the conquest of Canaan, and much more. He explained these to them in clear and simple language which touched the heart, and which, little by little, struck roots of faith in their hearts until they began [p.106] to leave their old customs and they stopped working on Sabbath, and stopped using the *Kazi* as *Shohet*, and also did not go any more to him to perform the marriage ceremony; and respect for the *Kazi* was finished, even unto this day. He no longer held the place of highest honor at feasts and other functions, and they no longer gave him double portion as used to be his due. Another person whom they had elected as President took over his function and the honor.

THE HONOR OF THE PRESIDENT; AND THEIR CUSTOMS AND RELIGIOUS FUNCTIONS : They invite the President, the *Hazan*, and the *Gabbai* to every religious function which they hold. The President sits at the head, and to him is given a double portion. To his right and left sit the *Hazan* and the *Gabbai*, and they receive a larger portion than the other guests. A flask of ready-made, strong wine called 'brandy',[10] imported from Europe, and which is very expensive there, is set before the President; and if he wants to honor one of the guests publicly, he will order a servant, who stands behind his chair, to give a glass of strong wine to whom he choses. Two servants go around the table, one holding a copper vessel, and the other the cups, and they give a cupful to each man, as much as three cups, but no more. And for anyone who does not drink at the function, he will pour his cupful into the flask which he carried in hand.

They all sit on the floor at their banquets, on mats; and four or five persons eat from one copper platter, as do all Indians who do not use pottery dishes. All cooking and eating utensils are of copper [or brass] and they are the property of the synagogue, because many of them do not keep dairy and meat foods separate, so that orthodox observers [*of Kashrut*] would not [otherwise] come to their banquets on religious occasions. Therefore, out of synagogue funds they have purchased the utensils and they are kept there under the care of the *Gabbai*. The person who is giving the banquet requests the use of them and pays something for it. They invite everyone serving in the army to such an occasion, because they consider this a very good deed, to feed soldiers. Sometimes 500 of them are stationed in Bombay and every one of them is invited, because the banquets were held at night when all of them were cleaned up and off duty, and the banquet was held outdoors for they did not have big houses which could hold so many guests.

THEIR FOOD AND THE ORDER OF THEIR EATING : On holidays they eat rice and only a few of them ate wheat bread which their wives baked as unleavened cakes; the meat of fowl and of sheep, but not beef, which they did not slaughter for food because under Indian rule cattle were not allowed to be slaughtered, for they are holy to the Indians and they worship them. They will not eat roasted meat, but cooked as a stew in a pot with many spices. They also add many spices to fish stew and red pepper which they believe has medicinal value. They wash their hands before eating even if it will be only rice that they eat. They do not use [p.107] spoons, knives or forks, but eat only with their hands as do the local non-Jews. They all have tables, chairs and beds of black wood called "shisham". [Schur adds here that this is a kind of ebony wood that comes from the island of Ceylon;[11] that in Bombay all furnishings of rich homes, like tables, chairs and beds, are replete with this wood and they are very beautiful and expensive, for the Indians are great craftsmen in open-work wood-carving, and work of this sort requires much time.] Actually, they make use of these only on Shabbat and on holidays, and on ordinary days they eat and lie on the floor. Even on holidays only the men sit on chairs and not the women, who are considered only as maidservants and do all the housework, grinding and cooking. Even in a rich household you will not find a maidservant, only the man's wife.

SHOHETIM AND HAZANIM : When the *Kazi* ceased to be their teacher and leader and the position was given to the President, from that time they also appointed *Shohetim* for themselves according to Jewish law. Some of them are my pupils whom I taught the ways of proper slaughtering and inspection of the knife according to the Ashkenazic way, and inspection of the lungs according to Rabbi Moshe Isserlis. They also appointed for themselves *Hazanim* who had studied the prayers, and the hymns, and the reading of the Torah with the accents, and grammar, namely the pronunciation of the letters *Bet, Gimmel* and *Dalet* with *dagesh* [the sign for stressing the consonant] (which the Babylonians will not pronounce that way), according to the custom of the town of Cochin. They also will perform the wedding ceremony according to the religion of Moses and Israel. They performed marriage and circumcision in the synagogue, and they ceased the practice of the Levirate (until that time they were observing it); and they did not know about *Halitzah*,[12] only the Levirate. Even today they will take for themselves two or three wives in marriage, even if there are sons from the first wife, and they will all eat together, nowadays only of ritually slaughtered meat. Even the soldiers who come from other places to Bombay, such as those that live in Panvel and in Revada, and also those who do not observe Shabbat, will keep away from meat which has not been properly slaughtered.

TWO GROUPS WITHIN THE BENE ISRAEL : As among all peoples and countries where peace prevails, as long as they are considered to be different from the rest of the people, then when they get together as a whole people, comes the division of ideas that causes them to separate among themselves. Thus it was with the Bene Israel, all of whom desired to be one people walking the same path as the rest of the Jews and to unite with them; and when they had attained this goal of being accepted as full Jews, then the flame of strife and jealousy was kindled among them and disturbed the peace. The House of Commandan and the House of Gabai on the one side, and the family of Pantatshi[13] and the House of Dr. Daniel on the other side, and they split into two groups. Even though the old synagogue was built from the money of Samuel Commandan, anyway Pantatshi's family and the family of Dr. Daniel took it over and they prevented their opponents from entering it [p.108]. Therefore, Sr. Shelomo Shurrabi was stirred to build a new and beautiful synagogue for the members of the group which had been expelled from the old synagogue. When the group that held on to the old synagogue saw the new synagogue of their foe, they were jealous of them and demolished the old synagogue and built a wonderfully splendid synagogue on its site. It did not take long to finish the job because they all contributed their labour gladly. The rich women carried stone and plaster for the builders from 7 in the evening until midnight; and the poor women worked all day at half-wages. Also the artisans took only half their regular fees. The leaders of the people, such as the President and the *Gabbai* supervised the work from dawn until dusk. Now they have two wonderful synagogues, and the quarrels have ceased. For all of this we have to give credit to the Cochinis, because they worked with all their heart to bring our brethren closer to our religion and to our customs, and to make them into [good] Jews. For who proclaimed this to them, that now they will be part of the nation of the children of Israel, they who did not know the scope of their religion and of their

Torah? Half of them had been worshipping idols. [Now they have] houses of prayer like all the Jews have, with separate sections for the women, a *mikveh* with flowing water for the immersion of the women, *succoth*[14] in the midst of the synagogue courtyards, and houses for the use of the *Hazanim, Shohetim,* and *Mohelim*. Above all, our heart rejoices at the sight of the good, well-organized existing schools in which they will teach their children Hebrew and Marathi, writing and arithmetic. All this they now have. Some schools they built for themselves with their own money; others out of government funds. Not only through the reiligious laws did they take to the Jewish way, but in ways of charity and righteousness they tried to rival them [other Jews], and they succeeded. They founded two societies: one was called *'G'milot Hassidim'* [Deeds of Charity], with the aim of supporting the aged and anyone unable to find sustenance for want of money. Many sympathetic people, also from among the British people, joined this society to help it get started. Also Sir Elias, the son of friend Eliezer, of London, who was Hon. District Commissioner in 1858 (and I was there at that time), and after that he was royal adviser in Bombay – he too joined this society and worked toward enlarging it. In 1860, when I went to London, I spoke with him about this society and he promised to speak to Lord Rothschild in London, requesting that he support it. He wrote to me that he did not succeed in enticing the Lord to this good deed. But other men in London did join it. The second society was called *'Hevrat S'farim'* [Book Club] which sought money for the translation into Marathi of the holy writings and prayers for Sabbath, holidays, and High Holidays. The translator was the linguist who knew four languages, Rav Joseph Ezekiel Rajpurkar. These books they sold for the actual cost of the printing and of the paper, and not for more than that.

SABBATH OBSERVANCES, AND THOSE WHO DID NOT OBSERVE THE SABBATH : Although all the Bene Israel really give their heart to the Torah and its commandments, and they willingly observe the commandments, in spite of that, to this day not all of them [p.109] keep the Sabbath and refrain from all work on that day— although they sanctify it—because it is difficult for them to do this in Bombay. There are about 300 households, and they have two synagogues and two *Shohetim,* who do observe the Sabbath. In Panvel there is one synagogue and only 20 households who observe the Sabbath can be found in the synagogue there. In Revandara there is one house of prayer and there are very few Sabbath observers. And there are Bene Israel scattered among the villages as well as soldiers whose number is more than four thousand men, who believe in the Torah and in the commandments but who do not observe the Sabbath and holidays because they cannot do so. Most of them [the Bene Israel] work in the army or for the British Government. Many of them are doctors and clerks. They looked forward to their pension at the time of old age when too weak to work, and they feared that one day per week of service would be deducted; and so they waited until their retirement, and then they began observing the laws and the Sabbath. Also the poor manual laborers refused to lave their work on the Sabbath, saying that if they did not work one day, then they would not have any bread; and, in their eyes, there was no greater shame than to receive free gifts. Therefore their leaders have not succeeded even until today to induce them to observe this commandment, and they were not set apart from the congregation on this account. Also, they showed openly that they sanctified the Sabbath in their words and heart. Those who do observe Sabbath: they return to their houses on Friday at 4 p. m., wash, dress in nice clothes, go to the synagogue to usher in the Sabbath with joy and a good heart, and to recite the *Maariv* [evening] prayer according to the Cochini *minhag* [custom]. After the prayer, the *Hazan* sings Sabbath songs, makes *Kiddush* over raisin wine, drinks his cup, and everyone gets a small glass of wine, and goes home happy. They eat their meal, bread, wine and fruits, and sing holy songs for a long time. In the morning they rise early to go faithfully to synagogue. Only the full Sabbath observers go up for an *Aliyah* [blessings for and reading from the parchment Torah scroll]. Those who do not observe Sabbath according to *halacha*, go home for *Kiddush* and for breakfast; and at 10 o'clock they go to their work, for this is the way of all Indians, that they open the shops and offices at 10 o'clock. This they do on Jewish holidays, except not for the first and second days of Pesach, the first day of Shavuoth, the two days of Rosh Hashonah, Yom Kippur, and the two days of Succoth. On these days the Government gives permission for a day off to soldiers and office workers. Nowadays, like the rest of Jewry, the Bene Israel know the holidays because the teacher Yehudah Ashkenazi, my brother-in-law, wrote and published a calendar of the Jewish holidays for them in Marathi.

THEIR CLOTHING : The Bene Israel are very clean about their bodies and their dress is more beautiful than the dress of other East Indians: They wear very wide trousers ($\frac{1}{2}$ ama), a white shirt down to the navel; over it a long white garment to the knees, made of flax or fine linen imported from Europe, for holidays one made of silk from China. On the head is worn a red or white turban, its rim embroidered with silver thread; and a red kerchief in hand or over the shoulder; [p.110] leather shoes like the Indians wear; and they let side-curls grow on their heads as do the Jews of Poland. The non-Jews of Maharashtra do this also, for they shave their heads and let long locks of hair remain such that everyone who sees a Maharashtrian will say he is a son of Israel. [On this point Schur's footnote says that he never saw such a custom in all of India except among the Parsis.]

The women wear a silk or linen garment which they tie with a cord over their breasts; and from the garment fall fringes down to the wrist; their neck, chest and arms are left bare. Over this garment they wear yet another long garment, which is wrapped around up to their knees; the legs are uncovered. Virgins wear gold nose-rings and they wear gold ornaments on their braids. They go barefoot even on rainy days.

The women of the community stay away from their husbands during menstruation, and the women of the group who pray in the old synagogue are more careful than the others and were more popular among the Cochini men.

All the women remain faithful to their husbands. If a woman is unfaithful and goes astray behind her husband's back, they will pursue her without pity, and if, as a result of adultery she becomes pregnant, they will hit her on her belly until she and the fruit of her womb are both dead.

Men and women follow a very straight path and are trustworthy in their deals, and keep their word; and therefore they are much respected by all the inhabitants of the place. They show charity, and kindness, and love for the stranger. Everyone who comes by they feed as a guest; they also give him money and show him much respect. Every Jew who comes through their town they call "Ḥacham Baba" [wise man] because, since they had not studied the Torah, they thought that every Jew was learned in the Torah and therefore they showed much respect for him.

They educated their sons and daughters as much as they could afford. The boys first learned to read Hebrew and to understand the Five Books of Moses, the *Haftorot*, the prayers, and the psalms for the year round; and after that, writing and the language Marathi in all detail. After that they were sent to school to learn English. After they finished all these subjects, they sent them to higher schools (academies) to study medicine, or surveying, or some other profession for a livelihood. Of this generation, 90-100 are studying some profession for placement in the offices of the British Government in Bombay. But only in Bombay up to Dharwar will they find assignments from the

Government; not so in other districts; although from Bombay to Nagpur many of them are to be found, and also in all of Gujarat and Sind up to Multan on the border of Bombay [Presidency].

In each town or village in which ten Bene Israel live, they get a *Shohet;* and in places where there is no *Shohet,* they eat only fish, vegetables and fruits. In places where they have a cemetery they bury their dead there; where there is no cemetery the Government gives them a burial place, because Jews will not allow a stranger to be buried among them.

[p.111] THEIR LOVE OF THEIR FAITH AND THE TALE OF ONE DOCTOR WHO CHANGED HIS RELIGION : All alike, whether they knew Torah or not, whether they observed Sabbath or not, each and every one was very devout in his faith. In every village, they will not be swayed to convert to another religion. From the day of dispersion from their land—thus they boasted—to this very day no one of them has changed his religion, except for one who did this in the year 1871 in the town of Ratnagiri, 198 miles from Bombay according to British measure. This man was a physician who held a Government position. The senior doctor under whom he worked was a devout Catholic, enticed him to convert, and convinced him. In order to calm his conscience at his betrayal of his brethren, he came to Bombay, and on a Sabbath afternoon sent to the great and learned grammarian Joseph Ezekiel, and to the *Gabbai,* the elderly Sr. Shelomo Elia, and to other wise men, requesting that they gather together to discuss with him matters of religion and belief. They acted upon his request and gathered together, and I, the present writer, was also among them. They deliberated a long time until Rav Joseph Ezekiel won him over with strong arguments from the Holy Scriptures and also from the New Testament. The doctor was very ashamed, and it showed on his face. After some minutes he rose and cried out with a broken heart that he recognizes his perversion and wants with all his heart to return in complete repentance on the following day, in front of everybody.

On the second day I was called to come to the house of the President Ezekiel Commandan, and I found there all the heads of the old congregation, each sitting in his place, and the penitent stood in front of them on his feet, with eyes full of tears. He said in a sobbing voice, "Gentlemen, I have sinned a great sin against God and against you because I left the faith of my fathers which they had received on Mount Sinai, and I chose new gods. I have also brought shame upon you, my brethren, because everyone who sees me will mock you." And he said, "If one person changes his religion, then all others might do so. Indeed I have sinned: God knows that not in rebellion nor out of disloyalty did I do this. But I was enticed by a smooth tongue. Now I make admission and abandon and regret my deed with a broken heart. Any punishment and atonement which you, the President, the Pantatshi, and Sr. Joseph Ezekiel will put upon me as atonement for my crime, I shall accept with love and joy. Please, my brethren, do not cast me off in my sin: Receive me in my repentance and say to me: You are our brother."

When Rav Joseph Ezekiel heard the words of the penitent, he rose to his feet which were trembling and, in a pleading voice, said, "My brothers and friends, I have listened to the story of your servant. This man asks to return from his transgression. According to the law of our Torah it is a good deed for us to receive him, and also according to the commandments of our wise men who said: There is nothing that stands above repentance. It is our duty, and by doing this good deed we shall sanctify the name of our God in the eyes of the nations."

After him the President arose and called out, "My brethren, this man's sin is greater than usual because he abused the name of his God, and caused shame to the whole community of Bene Israel in the eyes of others. A sin as great as he has committed has not been committed amongst us, not even in the early days when we went astray like blind people without a teacher or a leader, without a house of prayer, without Torah, prayer, *talith* or *t'filin*. Even then this sort of thing was not done. And, if now we have *Sifrei Torah* and a synagogue, *Hazanim* and *Shohetim* and *mikvot*, [p.112] and we keep the written and the oral law, and now this man comes to shame our image in the eyes of the inhabitants – his crime is unbearable! In spite of this, permission is granted to *Hacham Baba* (meaning the writer), to the Pantatshi, and to Sr. Joseph Ezekiel to act according to the commandments of our Torah, for you know its laws."

After him, the *Hazan* replies, "It is our duty to receive him even though his crime, of which he is ashamed, is a very serious one."

Then Joseph Ezekiel rose to his feet a second time and said to the penitent, "You should know that the Lord our God of Israel does not want the guilty one to die, but to repent in his way, and to live. Therefore you shall do thus, and be one with us: a) undergo immersion in the water of the *mikveh*; b) you shall be flogged with 40 lashes, and you shall weep, and dedicate yourself to your God that your crime will be wiped away; c) you shall give a sum of money to the synagogue, [an amount] which the President will impose upon you; d) you shall beg forgiveness from all the Jewish people for the shame which you have brought upon them. If you do this, you shall atone for your sin and you shall be one with us." He replied quickly and he accepted all these [stipulations]. We walked him to the synagogue for his immersion and all the people who saw this accompanied us, for they were very happy at this outcome. After the immersion, they flogged him 40 lashes, and he made atonement as was required of him. After that the *Hazan* went up to the platform and blessed the entire assemblage. The penitent and all of them together said three times: "You are our brother!" The penitent gave his thanks and his blessing to all the congregation for having accepted him. He requested to do honor to the distinguished men of the community in the presence of all the congregation, and they walked to his house for the feast which he had prepared for them yet in the morning. Indeed, the President did not favor this. But all of them went to his house, and he gave a feast in honor of the repentance of his guilt. All of us went, and it did our hearts good, and I thanked them for their love and faith. I also spoke words of mild reproof in order to strengthen their heart, their religion, and their faith for the future as well. Happy is the people like that! Happy is the people to whom the Lord is their God!"[15]

NOTES

1. "Hoda" is perhaps the Islamic word for "God": *Khuda*. "Yaak" is perhaps the Marathi word for "one": akh. Note that the words "one God" (in Hebrew) appear in the text in parentheses after "Hoda Ya-ak". It is interesting that this version couples the advent of the Bene Israel to India with the advent of the Parsis. There is no unanimity on the date of the first arrival of the Parsis on the west coast of India. Writers differ on this point: the earliest date suggested is 636 A.D.; the latest estimated date being 936 A.D. Parsis regularly speak Gujarati and not Marathi.
2. Here again we have the Hebrew word for "tent". The present writer has seen only one other reference to tents in connection with the Bene Israel, i.e. in Ezekiel Rahabi's *Letter of 1768*. See above, p.44 and p.48, n.22. Surely this must refer to Bene Israel soldiers who were living *with their families* in military encampments *in tents*.
3. This was another requisite of *Kashrut*.

4. In the foreword to Reinemann's book, his publisher writes that Reinemann had married "a daughter of Cochin, of the Rahabi family". If Reinemann's father-in-law was Yahudah Ashkenazi, then perhaps his mother-in-law was of the Rahabi family.
5. A woman is considered unclean for 7 days from the onset of menstruation (according to Torah); for 14 days according to more onerous *halachic* rules. She must follow this *niddah* (unclean period) by a ritual bath, preferably in a *mikveh*. The *mikveh*, a tank for ritual bathing, must have water deep enough for complete immersion, and the source of the water must be either a natural spring, a river, rain water, or melted snow or ice.
6. In subsequent passages Reinemann refers to him correctly as Joseph Ezekiel, and not Ezekiel Joseph. Reinemann's constant use of the word Senor (Sr.) instead of Mister (Mr.) is probably a carry-over from the days of Portuguese occupation. Reinemann uses the title *Rav* as a general honorific title for a respected and learned Jew.
7. *Maestri* means "artisan" or "carpenter".
8. Gassover is not a Bene Israel name. Could this be Reinemann's incorrect spelling for Garsulkar, or for Ghosalkar?
9. To this day young and old in most Bene Israel families know these songs by heart.
10. Actually, the Hebrew transliteration for this word, as given in the book, is *branry*. This must be a misprint. The Hebrew letter for the sound of *D* (*daleth*) and for *R* (*resh*) are very similar.
11. *Shisham* is the local form for the Indian "Bombay Rosewood" or "Bombay Blackwood". One kind has dark brown timber; the color of the other, which is more costly, is black. Both kinds grow in many parts of India.
12. A ritual where a widow is required to remove the sandal of her deceased husband's brother in order to relieve him of the duty (according to the law of the Levirate, *Deuteronomy* 25 : 5-10) of marrying her if the deceased had had no children. See above, p.102.
13. *Pantatshi* is not a surname. It is the nickname given to Joseph Ezekiel Rajpurkar because he was so knowledgeable about the *Pentateuch*. Therefore, his family was referred to here as "the family of Pantatshi", or "Pantatshi's family".
14. *Succoth* is the plural of the Hebrew word *succah*, meaning "booth". For the week-long holiday of *Succoth*, booths, partially open to the sky, are set up to remind the Jews of their sojourn in the wilderness. Each orthodox family, if possible, puts up its own *succah*. It is required to eat in the *succah*, and some Jews also sleep there.
15. Reinemann: op.cit., pp.99-112; a literal translation from the Hebrew into English, by the present author.

Appendix 7
(See above, pp. 92-3)
The Hebrew-Marathi Haggadoth of the Bene Israel

NOTE : This Appendix has been written in its entirety by B. J. Israel, presenting information *additional to* that which appears in Walter Fischel's introduction to the facsimile edition of the 1846 Hebrew-Marathi *Haggadah of the Bene Israel of India* as published by "The Orphan Hospital Ward of Israel", 673 Broadway, New York, 1968. All the parentheses are those of B. J. Israel, they are not from the original texts of the respective editions. B. J. Israel graciously permitted all of this material to be published in the present volume.

A-1 : ROUGH TRANSLATION OF THE MARATHI TITLE PAGE OF THE 1846 HEBREW-MARATHI HAGGADAH

This had been rendered into the Maharashtra language (Marathi) from 'Leshon Kodesh' or the holy tongue. Behold, this is something new. Nothing like this has happened until now. However, (word not clear) Swami Pandit Hyam Joseph Hallegua who is at present residing in Cochin has brought to light what was so far unknown (to us) with the object that all Bene Israel may understand this version (?) and may be enabled to carry out this beneficial ritual according to God's commandments. For this God will reward them (him).

This book has been prepared (rendered) in the Maharashtra language by worker (?) (the Marathi word is 'sevak' which implies service) Hyam Isaac Galsurkar with the guidance of Pandit Hyam Joseph Hallegua.

The Maharashtra translator and his great friend Ezekiel Joseph Talkar have, with God's favour, joined together for the printing of this book and have published it.

May God have mercy on us all. Amen."

(Here follow quotations from the book of *Proverbs,* chapter 3, verses 1-6.)

This first edition has been reproduced by lithography. The scribe for the Hebrew text is Abraham Judah Gemal and the scribe for the Maharashtra text is Rakhmaji Devji Shimpi (a Hindu of the tailor caste.)

Bombay, year 5606 Jewish Year; year 1843 (a mistake for 1846) Christian Year; Shake 1768 *Parbabunam.*

A-2 : TRANSLATION OF THE MARATHI PREFACE TO THE 1846 EDITION

I make the following entreaty (apology) to the reader of this book. Maharaj, I feel that in reading this book you will find many mistakes in the Maharashtra translation. This is because this book is originally in the 'Leshon Kodesh' or the Holy Tongue in which the Jewish Scriptures or the Torah is written. And it has never before been translated into the Maharashtra language. This is the first version. And I have not the least knowledge of the 'Leshon Kodesh' language. However, with the assistance of Pandit Hyam Joseph

Hallegua who is well versed in the 'Leshon Kodesh' language, and with the aid of the translation into the Maharashtra language of our Torah by the missionary saheb-lok this (translation) has been affected. Now my only request is this : my errors should be excused; I, however, treasure the hope that, by God's grace, some one will come forward from the Bene Israel community and improve this book (translation?) and bring out a second version superior to this.

B. J. ISRAEL'S NOTE : The 1846 edition had, in the Marathi language, instructions regarding preparation for Passover, with illustrations, in all probability taken over from the Cochini version used by Hallegua. These instructions, without the illustrations, and the main features of the *Seder* (without the Hebrew text) were issued in a small booklet also lithographed. Whether this booklet was issued before or after the 1846 version cannot be said. Probably it was issued before, since there would be less occasion to issue it after the full version was available. Perhaps it was part of the preparation for the issue of the full version. The only clue given us is a note at the end which runs as follows: "This small book has been made (written) in the Maharashtra language by Hyam Isaac Garsulkar with the assistance of the revered (the Marathi word is *smaranartha* which might mean 'worshipful') Hyam Joseph Hallegua." Here the translator's name is Garsulkar; in the 1846 edition it is Galsurkar; in the preface to the 1891 version the name is Galsulkar. All three seem to be variants of the same surname.

B-1 : TITLE PAGE OF THE 1874 HAGGADAH
HAGGADAH SHEL PESAH (in Hebrew and Marathi)
or
THE INSTITUTION OF PASSOVER (in Marathi and English)

This book
containing the original Hebrew text and a new Marathi translation, as well as being based on the *Shulḥan Arukh,* the Marathi Haggadah of Rabbi-Hyam (sic, as one word) Joseph Hallegua and Mr. Hyam Isaac Galsulkar and on other works has been prepared by Moses Jacob Talkar and Aaron Daniel Talkar and has been printed at Pune at the printing press of Vithal Sakharam Agnihotri.

This book having been registered according to Act 25 of 1867, all rights in further publication have been reserved by the owners to themselves.

English Year 1874, Jewish Year 5634.

PREFACE
(translated into English from Marathi by B. J. Israel)

It has been a fairly long time since we arrived in India, but up to now we have been very backward in matters of religion, business, industry and education. The reason for this is that, even though we possess the true religious scriptures, we do not give any attention to them and have never striven to act in accordance with their dictates. In this we are like a person who possesses a genuine diamond but does not know its proper use. We give no consideration to the precepts laid down by the various great preceptors who have arisen amongst us and to the manner in which they observed these principles. Nor do we consider how very meticulous they were in their learning and in their religious practice. The chief reason for this failure is that we make no attempt to acquire a knowledge of our original language, Hebrew. From the very few books translated from Hebrew which we see, how much knowledge of religion and learning can we acquire? And how are we to acquire therefrom a love for Hebrew? The number of those who actually practise in all its details the rite which we have set out in this book with a translation in Marathi is so small that we begin to suspect that the version of the Scriptures which they have does not ordain this rite which, in fact, is commanded by God to all Israel. If we refer to the Scriptures we find it clearly laid down that those who fail to observe this rite must be eradicated (*Exodus,* chapter 12, verse 15). Naturally we are bound to say that those who do not observe this rite have no fear of the Lord. As Solomon says in *Proverbs*: the fear of the Lord is the beginning of Wisdom. We however think that the majority of our people are not aware that such a severe punishment is prescribed in our holy Scriptures. With the publication of this book such ignorance is bound to vanish and we hope that in future they will begin to observe this rite.

We have not just reproduced a copy of the Haggadah published by Rabbi Joseph David Hallegua and *Ajjan* Hyam Isaac Galsulkar; we have only followed their arrangement of the book. A comparison of the two books will show that there is a very great difference in the Marathi translation in the direction of greater accuracy. We have introduced new illustrations in as clear a print as was possible. Finally we will be content and our labour will be rewarded if what we have done proves acceptable to our fellow countrymen (literal translation of *deshbandhavas*) and by God's grace they begin to observe this rite.

We are very happy to acknowledge that the printer Anna Balkrishna in the press of Mr. Vithal Sakharam Agnihotri has executed his task very efficiently and enthusiastically. We are very grateful to him.

We are also thankful to Mr. Elijah Solomon Walvatkar who gladly rendered very valuable help as and when called upon in the preparation of this book.

B-2: ROUGH TRANSLATION OF THE TITLE PAGE OF THE 1891 VERSION
THE INSTITUTION OF PASSOVER

This book has been tanslated into Marathi by Elijah Shalom Walwatkar, Head Master of the Elijah (Edward) David Sassoon School, from the new Hebrew *Haggadah* printed in the town of Leghorn (Livorno).

The *Marathi Haggadah* was produced by Rabbi Hyam Joseph Hallegua and the revered Hyam Isaac Galsulkar. The *Shulḥan Aruch* and other books have been consulted (?).

Aaron Joseph Divekar has printed and published (this book) at the Anglo-Jewish and Vernacular Printing Press.

By registering this book, all rights have been reserved by the publisher. Jewish Year 5651; Christian Year 1891 *; price 8 annas.

> (* Dr. Fischel attributes this edition to 1890. Not knowing the Hebrew month of its publication, one cannot be sure from the Hebrew text whether the date should be 1890 or 1891. However, the translation into English from the Marathi does make this clear.)

B-3: TRANSLATION OF THE MARATHI PREFACE TO THE 1891 EDITION

We have few communal workers among our people, and, of these few, still fewer who work with sole regard to the public benefit. Moreover, it is futile for such workers to entertain any hope of encouragement from anyone. Therefore, it is not possible for good and useful books to be published in our community. Some persons wait for a reduction to be made in the price fixed by the publisher. Until this happens, no copies are to be bought. Some persons cannot bear to see a book being brought out by anyone else and so they criticize and ignore it. Naturally there is not the diffusion of religion (religious knowledge?) that there should be. Those who have the necessary knowledge do not have money; those who have the money are ignorant.

The first version of this *Haggadah* has been printed and published by the late revered Hyam Isaac Galsulkar and the late revered Ezekiel Joseph Talkar with the assistance of Rabbi Joseph Hallegua. These gentlemen had published other works as well, such as *Seliḥoth* and *Shirot*. The Jewish Almanac was also issued by Hayamji. Although this gentleman did not have much knowledge of Marathi, he made good use of the knowledge he had. And one may say without contradiction that he strove much in his day to bring our people out of religious darkness into the light.

A second edition of this book was published by the revered Moses Jacob Talkar and the revered Abraham Daniel Talkar with the assistance of some person. Even this edition, with a good deal of information, is a good production, except for the pictures. (NOTE : these were new drawings replacing the figures of the 1846 edition, with women in *sari*, etc. One of them was reproduced to illustrate the article on the Bene Israel in the *Encyclopedia Judaica*.)

For the present edition, there seems no need for pictures. And, as translations of 'hammosi' and 'kiddush' blessings are contained in other books, they have been omitted here. Moreover, whatever additional material is contained in the new *Haggadah*, issued from Leghorn (Livorno), has been included with translation. However, those who do not wish to recite the additional material may omit it without hesitation. (At this point that material is indicated in Hebrew.)

Readers will observe that the portions added greatly exceed those omitted. However, the selection of additional hymns has been made solely by the publisher.

Finally, it is deemed necessary to say only this to the reader. There has been very long delay in carrying out the plan for this publication. Therefore, we have tried to render as much service to our brethren as we could within a short time and with indifferent health. Should there be any shortcomings, we shall be much obliged if they are brought to our notice by the learned.

In this work we have received some help from Mr. Ezekiel Moses Talkar, B.A., and we are very thankful to him. (NOTE : This is the late Prof. E. M. Ezekiel, of the Bene Israel, who was Head Master of one of the Sassoon schools and taught Hebrew for many years at St. Xavier's College, Bombay. The publisher of the 1891 edition of *The Marathi Haggadah*, and the writer of this Preface was Mr. Elijah Solomon Walvatkar.)

C : B. J. ISRAEL'S NOTE ON THE VARIATIONS IN THE INSTRUCTIONS REGARDING PREPARATION FOR PASSOVER IN THE 1846, 1891 AND 1935 VERSIONS

The 1846 version requires that before the 13th day of Nissan there should be a thoroughgoing cleaning of the house and its contents. This is not mentioned in the later versions.

The 1846 version requires all brass and copper utensils and all chinaware to be dipped in hot and cold water; gold, silver and glassware being subjected to *tebila*. The 1891 version explains that the first operation is based on former Cochini practise which is not enjoined in the *Shulḥan Aruch;* though the utensils and chinaware should be cleansed, there is no need to recite the first *berakha* given in the 1846 version, though it is still quoted in full in the later version. The 1935 version merely says that if one cannot have new utensils etc. for Passover, one should clean those in use and dip them in water; reciting the *berakha*. No mention is made of *tebila* for gold, silver and glassware. But the 1891 version alone contains the caution that chinaware used for ordinary occasions cannot be rendered fit for Passover even by dipping in hot water (as allowed in the 1846 version and, presumably, in the 1935 version). Separate ware must be used but, if put aside, can be used for subsequent Passovers.

Both the 1846 and 1891 versions require a piece of leavened bread to be deliberately hidden and then found. The 1935 version says nothing about this, but it alone enjoins complete silence on the part of the searcher. The 1935 version alone requires leavened food required for the night meal after the search and for the meal of the subsequent morning to be kept aside (as do the earlier versions for *hametz*) and it is the unconsumed portion of this food that is to be burned at precisely 10 o'clock in the morning. This version alone says that leaven may be consumed up to 9 o'clock that morning.

According to the two earlier versions, both male and female first-borns have to fast. In 1935 it is only males.

The 1935 version goes into detail about preparations for Passover if it is to commence on the Sabbath. The earlier versions are silent on this point.

The 1891 version alone contains detailed instructions about the wheat to be used for preparing unleavened bread and the procedure for making it. Also, instructions are given about rice and substitute grains for wheat. So also advice is given about diet restrictions during Passover and there is a final "sermon" about the significance of avoiding leavened bread and a warning against pride.

It does not seem that the 1935 version describes the three *matzoh* breads at the Seder, as Cohen, Levi and Israel, nor does it include a requirement to make them differently (i.e. with one, two and three peaks respectively.)

The two later versions seem to lean heavily on the first for the Marathi text, but it appears that there is progressive improvement of the Marathi. It may be interesting to note that in all three versions the word *Pandit* is used for the Hebrew *Hacham*. Is this why the 1846 version refers to Hallegua as "Pandit"? (He was probably known as *Hacham* at the time.)

I have had only a casual glimpse at the 1874 Poona edition and, therefore, do not know to what extent it varied from the 1846 version.

Appendix 8
(See above, p.94)
From The Bene Israel Annual and Year Book, 1919-1920 Volume III
Edited by Rebecca Reuben, Junagadh; pp. 56-80.

BENE ISRAEL PUBLICATIONS

AUTHORS	PUBLICATIONS
	1842
Divekar, Solomon David and Galsoorkar, Haeem Isaac.	हिब्रु सेलिहोथ.
	1846
Galsoorkar, Haeem Isaac and Talkar, Ezekiel Joseph.	चित्रयुक्त हग्गादाचें पुस्तक. (Hebrew and Marathi)
	1853
Galsoorkar, Haeem Isaac and Talkar, Ezekiel Joseph.	हिब्रु शीरोथ.
	1854
Galsoorkar, Haeem Isaac.	इस्राएलांचें पंचांग (तारखेचें पुस्तक.)
	1856
	गरीब लोकांस धर्म करण्याविषयीं बोध. Published by the Bombay Bene Israel Benevolent Society.
	1858
Rajpurkar, Joseph Ezekiel.	प्रायश्चित्ताच्या दिवशीं पापाविषयीं कबूल होणें: Confession of Sins on the Day of Atonement. (Translated from Hebrew.)
	1859
Kehimkar, Haeem Samuel and Kehimkar, Shalom Samuel.	सेफारादीम इस्राएल मंडळीची नित्य त्रैकालिक भजन पद्धति
Rajpurkar, Joseph Ezekiel.	पापाच्या क्षमेसाठी प्रार्थना. Propitiatory Prayers. (Translated from Hebrew.)
	1862
Rajpurkar, Joseph Ezekiel	इस्राएलांचा लग्नविधी. The Jewish Marriage Ceremony (Translated from Hebrew.)

	वर्षप्रतिपदेची प्रार्थना. Prayers for the Jewish New Year's Day. (Translated from Hebrew.)

1864

Rajpurkar, Joseph Ezekiel.	नवसाचि सुटका आणि समुद्रतीरीं करावयाची प्रार्थना Remission of Vows and Prayers offered on the Sea-shore (Translated from Hebrew.)

1865

Kehimkar, Shalom Samuel and Walwatkar, Elijah Shalom.	आमचा गुरु मोशे यानें दिलेलें शास्त्र वाचण्याची रीत व त्याचें स्वर्गारोहण.

1866

Rajpurkar, Joseph Ezekiel.	आन्तीओखोस राजाचा इतिहास अथवा हानुक्याच्या सणाची स्थापना. History of Antiochus Epiphanes or the Institution of the Feast of Dedication. (Translated from Hebrew.)

1867

Divekar, David Haeem and Talkar, Moses Daniel.	इस्राएलांचा जन्मविधी.
Rajpurkar, Joseph Ezekiel.	प्रायश्चित्ताच्या दिवसाची प्रार्थना भाग १ ला. Prayers for the Day of Atonement. Part I. (Translated from Hebrew.)

1868

Ashtamkar, Benjamin Samson.	मोसाए शब्बाथानंतर मागण्याचा आशीर्वाद अथवा इस्राएल लोकांच्या मतांप्रमाणे नवसाची सुटका, आणि मासिक चंद्रदर्शनीं प्रार्थनारूप स्तुति. (Translated from Hebrew.)
Rajpurkar, Joseph Ezekiel.	प्रायश्चित्ताच्या दिवसाची प्रार्थना भाग २ रा. Prayers for the Day of Atonement, Part II. (Translated from Hebrew.)

1869

Divekar, David Haeem.	शलमोनानें केलेल्या गीतांचें कवितेचें पुस्तक.

1870

Bhonkar, Samuel Moses and Talkar, Jacob Daniel.	गुरुजनांचें अर्थशास्त्र अथवा राब्बीनीति शास्त्र. (Translation of Ethics of the Fathers.)
Rajpurkar, Joseph Ezekiel.	सद्गुरुवचनें अथवा नीतिशास्त्र. (Translation of the Ethics of the Fathers.)

1872

Ashtamker, Benjamin Samson.	कोष्टक संग्रह. (Arithmetical tables.) मिशनरी शाळेंतील इंग्रजी दुसऱ्या पुस्तकाचे शब्द. (Words from the English Second Reader used in Missionary School.)

Divekar, David Haeem.	प्रियकान्त व सुशीला (कल्पित गोष्ट).
	छेलबटाऊ व मोहना राणी (नाटक).
Kehimkar, Shalom Samuel.	एस्तेर राणीचा संक्षिप्त वृत्तांत.
	(Translated from the original Hebrew.)

1873

Ashtamkar, Aaron Samson.	काल कर्मणूक अथवा बाळ खेळ भाग १ ला.
Talkar, Ezekiel Samuel (Poona).	इस्राएली विधीचे पुस्तक हिब्रू.

1874

Divekar, David Haeem.	हिंदुस्थानांत आल्यापासून बेने इस्राएल लोकांचा इतिहास.
Navgaokar, Daniel Shelomo.	Flavius Josephus
	किंवा पुरवणीसह इस्राएल लोकांच्या लढाया.
	(Translated from English.)
Penkar, Shalom Joseph (Hazan).	इब्री गीतसंग्रह.
Talkar, Aaron Daniel (Poona) and Talkar, Moses Jocob.	हग्गादा शेल पेसाह अथवा वल्हांडण सणाचें निरुपण. हिब्रू व मराठी.
Talkar, Haeem Joseph and Divekar, David Haeem.	हिंदुस्थानांत आल्यापासून बेने इस्राएल लोकांचा इतिहास.
	(History of the Bene Israel.)
Walwatkar, Elijah Shalom.	सेलिहोथ अथवा पापक्षमेस्तव प्रार्थना, नवसाची सुटका, समुद्रतिरीं करण्याची प्रार्थना व राणीस आशीर्वाद.

1875

Ashtamkar, Benjamin Samson.	इसवी सन १८७५ सालाकरितां बि. सामसनचें नवें पंचांग.

1876

Divekar, David Haeem.	शाहजहान शाहापरी और रोशनजेहेल (उर्दु नाटक)
Rajpurkar, Joseph Ezekiel.	इस्राएली धर्ममतांविषयीं शास्त्रांतील प्रमाणे.
	(Scripture Proofs of Jewish Doctrines.) Published by the Bene Israel Improvement Society.

1877

Ashtamkar, Benjamin Samson.	इस्राएली धर्माच्या मुलांकरितां धर्मसंबंधी व नीतिसंबंधी प्रश्नोत्तरावली
	(Translated from English.)
Daniells, S. and Samuel, R.	राब्बी पेथहचा यांचे प्रवास.
	(Travels of Rabbi Pethachia.)

1878

Kehimkar, Samuel Haeem	आईबापांचें कर्तव्य.
	Parental Duty. (Adapted from I.L. Mocatta's Moral Biblical Gleanings.)
Kurulkar, Samuel Shalome.	"Gooldhusta" (Novel)

Walwatkar, Elijah Shalome	यहुदी व ख्रिस्ती यांच्या धर्मसंबंधी मतभेदा विषयीं विचार.
	(Translation of a course of sermons delivered by Dr. Adler at the Bayswater Synagogue.) Published by the Society for the Diffusion of Religious knowledge among the Israelites.

1879

Ashtamkar, Aaron Samson	काल कर्मणूक अथवा बाळ खेळ भाग २ रा.
Ashtamkar, Benjamin Samson.	मुंबई खात्यांतील सैन्यांत नोकरीस असलेल्या इस्राएल लोकांविषयीं कर्नल वहाब साहेबांचे टिपण. (Translated from Colonel Wahab's Notes.)
	दाक्तर सॅम्युएल जॉनसन यांच्या रॅम्बलर नामें ग्रंथांतील नवरादिनचा मुलगा अलमावलीन याचें वर्णन. (Translated from the "Rambler" of Dr. Samuel Johnson.)
Rajpurkar, Joseph Ezekiel.	इस्राएली धर्माचें खरें स्वरुप म्हणजे इस्राएली धर्माच्या तेरा मूळतत्त्वावर धर्मोपदेश. (The true Aspect of Judaism.)

1880

Kurulkar, Abraham Daniel	किरात भाग १ ला (कादंबरी)
Navgavkar, Solomon Daniel.	बेने इस्राएल लोकांतील ज्ञातिभेदाविषयीं विचार भाग १ ला.
Rajpurkar, Joseph Ezekiel.	इस्राएलांच्या प्राचीन इतिहासांतील गोष्टींचा कालानुक्रम (Chronological outline of Ancient Jewish History)

1881

Ashtamkar, Aaron Samson.	तलमुदांतील आब्राहाम चरित्र.
Ashtamkar, Benjamin Samson.	जिव्हा सामर्थ्य.
Rajpurkar, Joseph Ezekiel.	इब्री पहिलें पुस्तक. Hebrew Primer.

1882

Ashtamkar, Benjamin Samson and Talkar, Enoch Solomon.	कवितावबध्द आब्राहम चरित्र.
Ashtamkar, Benjamin Samson.	पितृभक्ति.
Kehimkar, Samuel Haeem.	इस्राएली धर्माची प्रश्नोत्तरावली. (Translated from English.)
Rajpurkar, Joseph Ezekiel.	इब्री लघु व्याकरण. (Elementary Hebrew Grammar)
Talkar, Aaron Daniel.	पद्यात्मक योसेफ चरित्र

R. Reuben's List of Bene Israel Publications

1883

Ashtamkar, Aaron Samson. — कविताबध्द दाविदराणा चरित्र.

1884

Ashtamkar, Aaron Samson. — दुःखिताश्रुमार्जन.
Ashtamkar, Benjamin Samson. — यहुदी धर्मनिष्टा.
Divekar, David Haeem. — कविताबढ्द मोशे चरित्र.

1885

Ashtamkar, Benjamin Samson. — मद्यपान निषेध.

1886

Divekar, Aaron Jacob. — तलमुद.
(Translation of II. Polano's Selections from the Talmud.)

1887

Ashtamkar, Benjamin Samson. — इस्त्राएली धर्मोपदेश.
(The Jewish Pulpit and Sermons)
इस्त्राएली धर्मांतील नवलाचें वृत्त.
(Curiosities of Judaism.)
तलमुदांतील गोष्टी व म्हणी.
(Sayings and Stories from the Talmud. Translated from the English.)
इश्वर स्तुतीपर गाणी. (इस्त्राएली "सुबोध-प्रकाशक" समाजाचे पुस्तक १ लें.)
इस्त्राएली धर्माविषयीं इस्त्राएल लोकांचे मत; अथवा एका ख्रिस्ती धर्मोपदेशकास उत्तर.
इस्त्राएलांचा विधी.
(A statute unto Israel; containing an account of the Religious Duties of the Israelite, especially elucidating those referring to the Divine Service by Israel Albu.)
मशीहा.
(The Messiah. A Passover Sermon. Translated from the Sermons of the Rev. Benjamin Artom.)

Bamnolkar, Dr. Joseph Benjamin. — Account of the Victoria Jubilee Celebration at Sanand. (Gujarati)

Divekar, Aaron Jacob. — जगविख्यात लोकप्रिय सर मोझस मोन्टीफियर, बारोनेट, यांचे चरित्र.

Ghosalkar, Isaac Solomon. — यरुशालेमेचा प्रवास.
Kehimkar, Haeem Samuel. — इस्त्राएल मुलांकरिता हिब्रु व मराठी गीतें.
Rajpurkar, Joseph Ezekiel. — Ketoneth Yoseph-Handbook of Hebrew Abbreviations, with their explanations in Hebrew and English.

Tarankhopkar, Abraham Samuel.   इब्रीवाचनमार्गदर्शिका.
                                (Guide to Hebrew Reading.)

1888

A'shtamkar, Benjamin Samson.   सुंदर सगुणी.
                                कवितबद्ध शुद्धवासना अथवा नोहाचा भक्तिभाव.

Pezarkar, David Solomon.   ईश्वर स्तुतीपर गाणीं (इस्राएली "सुबोध प्रकाशक"
                                समाजाचे पुस्तक २ रें.)

1889

Ashtamkar, Benjamin Samson.   कविताबद्ध शेमोएलाख्यान.
                                कविताबद्ध आब्राहामाख्यान.
                                येहुदी धर्माविषयीं एक व्याख्यान किंवा एका ख्रिस्ती
                                उपदेशकास उत्तर

Pezarker, David Solomon.   प्रार्थना (इस्राएली "सुबोध प्रकाशक" समाजाचे
                                पुस्तक ३ रें)

Rajpurkar, Joseph Ezekiel.   इस्राएलांतील सेफारादीम मंडळीच्या संप्रदाया-
                                प्रमाणे नित्यांची प्रार्थना.
                                Daily prayers according to the Sephardic Ritual. Hebrew with Marathi Translation.

1890

Aptekar, Solomon Shalom.   कविताबद्ध एस्तेर चरित्र.
Rajpurkar, Joseph Ezekiel   इस्राएलांची पंचोपोषणें.

1891

Ashtamkar, Benjamin Samson.   प्रार्थनेची भाषा हिब्रु होय.
                                Hebrew is the Language of Prayer.
                                (इस्राएली "सुबोधप्रकाशक" समाजाचे पुस्तक
                                ५ वें.)

Bhinjekar, Abraham Reuben.   सृष्टिजन्य अद्भुत चमत्कार.

Shapurkar, Abraham Samson.   Essay on Musketry (Prize Essay.)
                                शांति (इस्राएली 'सुबोधप्रकाशक' समाजाचे पुस्तक
                                ४ थे.)

Talegaonkar, Isaac Abraham.   तलमुद व तलमुदांतील शाळा पद्धति (इस्राएली
                                "सुबोधप्रकाशक" समाजाचे पुस्तक ६ वें.)
                                Translation of Rev. Spier's Talmud and the School System of the Talmud.

Walwatkar, Elijah Shalom.   वल्हांडण सणाचे निरूपण.
                                Institution of Passover. (Translated from Hebrew.)
                                सेलोहोथ पापक्षमेस्तव प्रार्थना.
                                The Propitiatory Prayers. (Hebrew and Marathi.)

1892

Divekar, Aaron Joseph. इस्त्राएली भक्तिमार्ग.
(Morning Service, Prayers before retiring to sleep, and the thirteen chief Principles of the Jewish Faith.)

1893

Ashtamkar, Benjamin Samson. शास्त्रनियमविधीमाला अथवा पद्यात्मक अजहारोथ.
(Translation of Hebrew Azaharoth.)

Bhinjekar, Abraham Reuben and Sankar, Aaron Solomon. सर्वसंग्रह अथवा इस्त्राएली विधींचें पुस्तक, हिब्रु व मराठी उच्चारासह.

Korlekar, David Reuben. इस्त्राएली सुंतेचा विधी आणि सुंतेच्या कायद्याचें निरुपण.
(Translated from English.)

Mazagaonkar, Samuel Solomon. लहरी प्रदर्शन.

1894

Aptekar, Solomon Shalom. दानिएलांचे मानसिक धैर्य.

Ashtamkar, Aaron Samson. कविताबद्धसद्भक्तवात्सल्य किंवा राझी एस्तेर इचें आख्यान.
(इस्त्राएली "सुबोधप्रकाशक" समाजाचे पुस्तक ८ वें.)

Ashtamkar, Benjamin Samson. इस्त्राएली कथा रत्नमाला.
आंग्ल भौमवासी मुख्य गुरु रे./डॉक्टर हर्मन आडलर यांचे चरित्र.
(Life of the Rev. Dr. Hermann Adler Ph. D.)

Bamnolkar, Dr. Joseph Benjamin. The Intoxicating Alkaloids of Tobacco and Indian Hemp. (Gujarati)

Divekar, Uziel Solomon. येशू ख्रिस्त मशीहा आहे काय?

Kharilkar, David Shalom. मराठी लिपीत सेलीहोथ.

Korlekar, David Reuben. शास्त्राध्ययन माला अथवा जीवनमार्ग दर्शिका.
धर्माचरण.

Pezarkar, David Solomon शांति महात्म्य किंबा साधु इयोब यांचें आख्यान.
(इस्त्राएली "सुबोधप्रकाशक" समाजाचें पुस्तक ९ वें.)

1895

Ashtamkar, Benjamin Samson. आंग्ल भूमिनिवासी सर जॉन सायमन क्यू. सी. याचें लघु चरित्र.
(Life of Sir John Simon, Q. C.)

Divekar, Aaron Jacob. अधिक प्रकाश
(Translation of Rabbi Wiess' More Light)

Pezarkar, Samuel Haeem.   मी इस्राएल कां रहावें? (इस्राएली "सुबोध-प्रकाशक" समाजाचें पुस्तक १२ वें.)

Pingle, Jacob Ezekiel. (Neemuch)   Our Travels to Jerusalem.
आमची यरूशलेमची यात्रा.

Shapurkar, Abraham Samson.   ईश्वरी विश्वास महात्म्य किंवा मकाबी वीरांचें शौर्य. (इस्राएली "सुबोधप्रकाशक" समाजाचें पुस्तक १० वें.)

1896

Ashtamkar, Benjamin Samson.   कविताबध्द शिमशोनाख्यान.
कविताबध्द दाविदराणा चरित्र.

Bamnolkar, Dr. Joseph Benjamin   Essay on Primary Education.

Korlekar, David Reuben.   पवित्रशास्त्रनियममाला.
(Book of Precepts : Translated from the Hebrew of Moses Maimonides.)
ईश्वरी नामोच्चार.

Tarankhopkar, Abraham Samuel.   इब्रीवाचनपाटमाला.
Hebrew Course of Reading.

1897

Ashtamkar, Benjamin Samson.   कविताबध्द योनाख्यान.
कविताबध्द एलीशाख्यान.

Awaskar, Isaac Shalom.   कविताबध्द एलीयाहू हन्नाबीचें आख्यान.

Penkar, Joseph David.   संगीत दाविदराणा.

Shapurkar, Abraham Samson.   पवित्र शास्त्राची सत्यता व ईश्वरप्रणीतत्व.
(The Truth and Divinity of the Holy Writ.)

1898

Ashtamkar, Benjamin Samson and Talkar, David Joseph.   कविताबध्द शेलोमोराणाख्यम्न.

Ashtamkar, Benjamin Samson.   साग्र संगीत सहनशीलतेचा कळस अथवा दाविद राजाची अमर्याद शांति (५ अंकी नाटक.)

Divekar, Aaron Jacob.   ख्रिस्ताविषयीं कांहीं विचार.
(English Essay by Rabbi L. Wiess with Marathi Translation by Divekar.)
सार्वत्रिक शांति.
(Essay on the Universal Peace of the Messianic Age.)
धर्म व सदाचरण.
(Translation of Rabbi Straus' Religion and Morals.)
गुरुमोशे यांनी लावून दिलेल्या विधींचें अपूर्व रचितत्व.
(Originality of the Institutions of Moses.)

1899

Aptekar, Solomon Shalom.	संगीत दानिएल (सहा अंकी नाटक.)
Ashtamkar, Benjamin Samson.	प्लेगनिवारणार्थ संगीत ईशाराधना कीर्तन.
Bamnolkar, Dr. Joseph Benjamin.	Sanitary Reform in India. (Gujarati)
Penkar, Joseph David.	कविताबध्द दाविदाख्यान.
	योसेफाख्यान नावांचे नाटकांतील गाणी.

1900

Divekar, Aaron Jacob.	इस्राएली धर्मप्रकाशक पुस्तकमाला. (Hebrew Religion Library.)
Kandlekar, Samuel Moses.	महाराणी एस्तेर चरित्र.
Pezarkar, Elijah Solomon. B.A.	Jews in China and India.

1901

Bamnolkar, Dr. Joseph Benjamin.	Vital Statistics of Ahmedabad.
Rajpurkar, Joseph Ezekiel.	इस्राएलांचे त्रिपर्वोत्साह म्हणजे सुक्कोथ, पेसाह व शाबुओथ.
	Prayers for the three Great Jewish Festivals (Translated from the Hebrew.)

1902

Kurulkar, Elijah Abraham.	संगीत.प्रेमविजया नाटिका.
	पद्यावली (तीन अंकी नाटक.)

1905

Awaskar, Isaac Shalom.	कविताबध्द योसेफाख्यान.
Bhastekar, Solomon Aaron.	पद्यावली संगीत सध्दर्मचिरणप्रभाव अथवा शलोमोसारा.

1906

Aptekar, Solomon Shalom.	संगीत योसेफ (तीन अंकी नाटक.)
Bhastekar, Solomon Aaron.	सगीत एस्तेर अभिमान अथवा गृहरिपुकारस्थान.
Elijah, Dr. Moses. M.D., J.P.	Students' Manual of Materia Medica.
Kasookar, Judah Shalom.	आपली पवित्र भूमि यरूशालेम.

1909

Korlekar, David Reuben.	आपल्या बेने इस्राएल लोकांची सुधारणा.
Vakrulkar, Solomon Moses. B.A.LL.B.	Our Synagogues and their Functions.

1910

Bhastekar, Solomon Aaron.	महासाधू दानिएलाची अमर्याद भक्ति अथवा परमेश्वरानें अर्पिलेली धर्मशक्ति. (पद्यावली)
Ezekiel, B.S., B.A.	The Elementary Hebrew Reader.
Penkar, Joseph David.	कविताबध्द साग्र संगीत महासाधुवर्य योसेफ चरित्र.
Solomon, Joseph E., B.A. LL.B.	धार्मिक व नैतिक शिक्षणाची प्रश्नोत्तरमाला. (A catechism of Religious and Moral Instruction.)

1911

Awaskar, Joseph Haeem.	एस्तेर राणी चरित्र.
Bhinjekar, Abraham Reuben.	शतकावली
	(The Jewish Calendar for one Hundred Years from 5661-5760)
Kharilkar, David Shalom.	मराठी लिपींत हग्गादा शेलपेसाह.
	मराठी लिपींत विधींचें पुस्तक.
Shapurkar, Aaron Reuben	Israelite New Year 5672.

1912

Awaskar, Joseph Haeem.	तिशआबेआबचा हफतारा.
	(Translated from Hebrew.)
	मोशे चरित्र.
Chordekar, Isaac Shadick.	Journal of a Visit to England in 1911.
Penkar, Joseph David.	अबशालोमाचें सिंहासन.
Compiled by the Israelite School Committee.	Children's Devotional Services.

1913

Bamnolkar, Dr. Joseph Benjamin.	Infant Mortality
Kharilkar, David Shalom.	लग्नांत स्त्रियांनीं म्हणण्याचीं गाणीं.
Ramrajkar, Solomon Jacob	शुलहान आरुख हय्ये आदाम (दाथ इस्राएल) इस्राएली धर्माचे नियम-अर्थात व्यवहारशास्त्र भाग १ ला.
	(Translated from English.)
Kharilkar, David Shalom.	हिब्रु व मराठी उच्चारासह सिम्हाथ तोऱ्याचें पुस्तक.
Reuben, Miss Rebecca.	The Bene Israel of Bombay (Cambridge Jewish Publication)
Talegaonkar, Isaac Abraham.	कविताबध्द गुरु मोशे चरित्र अथवा इस्राएलांची मिसर देशांतून सुटका.

1915

Bhinjekar, Abraham Reuben.	पेसाह उर्फ वल्हांडण सण.
	(धर्मोपदेशकमाला नंबर १)
	शाबुओथ. (" २)
Kharilkar, David Shalom.	मराठी लिपींत हिब्रु व मराठी गीतांचें पुस्तक.
Talegaonkar, Isaac Abraham.	शावुओथ सणाप्रीत्यर्थ धर्मोपदेश.

1916

Kasookar, Judah Shalom.	Guide—The Secret Doctrine of the Soul and the Body.
Penkar, Shalom Rahamim (Poona).	सुक्का उर्फ एकी, तिची आवश्यकता व महात्म्य.
Reuben, Miss Rebecca.	शावुओथ.

1917

Bamnolkar, Dr. Joseph Benjamin.	Infant Mortality. (Gujarati)

Borgavkar, M.D., B.A.	A Primer of Hebrew. (Hebrew and English)
Isaac, I.A.	A Short Account of Calcutta Jews, with a short Sketch of the Bene Israels, the Cochin Jews, the Chinese Jews and the Black Jews of Abyssinia. Letters and Speeches.
Mazagaonkar, Samuel Solomon.	बेनेइस्राएल "प्रासंगिक विचार" माला. (Occasional Thoughts.)

1918

Mazagaonkar, Samuel Solomon.	बेनेइस्राएल "प्रासंगिक विचार" माला. (Occasional Thoughts.)
Chordekar, Isaac Shadick.	भक्तिमंत नोहाख्यान. जगाच्या उत्पत्तीचा इतिहास अगर प्रथम पुरुष "आदामाख्यान" समाजास विघातक अशा फोल विचारांची फोड.
Chordekar, Mrs. Milkabai Isaac.	स्त्रियांचा सत्चारिणी धर्म्.

PUBLICATIONS WITH DATES UNKNOWN.

Ashtamkar, Benjamin Samson.
कविताबध्द नोहाख्यान.
तलमुदाचें मराठी भाषांतर.
    with
(Divekar, Shalom Moses.)

Awaskar, Joseph Haeem.
संगीत विषारी सर्प अथवा कर्मफळ नाटक.

Divekar, David Haeem.
गुल व सनोबर भाग दोन.
  सृष्टीतील चमत्कार.
  हिंदुस्थानांत आल्यापासून बेने इस्राएल लोकांचा इतिहास.
(with Talkar, Haeem Joseph.)

Divekar, Shalom Moses.
तलमुदाचें मराठी भाषांतर.
(with Ashtamkar, Shalom Moses.)

Isaac, I.A.
  Judaism.

Kehimkar, Haeem Samuel.
  Sketch History of the Bene Israel and an appeal for their Education.
  गीतांचे पुस्तक.
  Hymn Book.

Kehimkar, Joseph Haeem.
  First Hebrew Reader.

Kharilkar, David Shalom.
    दाविदाच्या गीतांचे पुस्तक.
    मराठी लिपीत पेसाह.

Kurulkar, Abraham Daniel.
    मनमोहिनी (कांदबरी)

Rajpurkar, Joseph Ezekiel.
    Special Prayers for special occasions.
    Child's First Hebrew Book.

Rajpurkar, Moses Elia and Talkar, Moses Daniel.
    पश्चातापाच्या दिवसांत ईश्वर गुणं वर्णनापूर्वीं करण्याची विनंति.
    मोशाच्या शास्त्राचें अपालटत्व.
    Immutability of the Mosaic Law.
    (इस्राएली "सुबोधप्रकाशक" समाजाचे पुस्तक १३ वें.)

R. Reuben's List of Bene Israel Publications

BENE-ISRAEL PERIODICALS

		EDITORS.
सत्य प्रकाश [Satya Prakasha, The Light of Truth]	1877-1881 1881-1885	Ashtamkar, Aaron Samson. Korlekar, David Reuben.
तेरुवा. [T'ruah, The Shofar Call]	1878-1879	Ashtamkar, Benjamin Samson.
इस्राएली धर्मदीप. [Israeli Dharmadip, Lamp of Judaism]	1881-1885 1893-1896	Ashtamkar, Benjamin Samson Mazagaokar, Samuel Solomon.
स्त्री सौंदर्यलतिका. [Stri Saundaryalatika, The Tendril of Female Beauty]	1886	Penkar, Abraham Reuben.
इस्राएली ज्ञानसंग्रह. [Israeli Gyansanghraha Collection of Israeli Knowledge.]	1886	Divekar, Aaron Jacob.
बेने इस्राएल [Bene Israel, The Bene-Israel]	1893-1900	Pezarkar, Abraham Solomon.
इस्राएल [Mitra, Friend]		Kehimkar, Haeem Samuel.
इस्राएल मित्र [Israel Mitra, Friend of Israel]	1898-1899	Bhinjekar, Abraham Reuben.
इस्राएलाश्रम [Israel Ashram, The House of Israel		
The Voice of Sinai.	1904-5	
The Hebrew.	1906-7	I.A. Isaac.
The Jewish Messenger.	1913	
इस्राएल मित्र [Israel Mitra, Friend of Israel (Anglo-Marathi)	1916-(1921) 1916-	Talegaonkar, Isaac Abraham. Aptekar, Jacob Isaac, B. A. LL. B.
इस्राएल [Israel. Israelite (Anglo-Marathi)	1917- [1926-7]	Erulkar, David Solomon, B. A. (Cantab) Bar-at-Law. Jacob B. Israel
Bene Israel Annual and Year Book	1917-	Miss R. Reuben, B. A.
[The Maccabi, Anglo-Marathi]	1947-	

Appendix 9
(See above, pp. 156-8)
B.J. Israel's List of Bene Israel Surnames and Their Village Links

NOTE : The list as presented here combines Appendix 5.I (on pp. 137-145) of B.J. Israel's book *The Bene Israel of India, Some Studies*, together with the population figure for each village according to the *Kolaba District 1961 Census Handbook*.

T.P. = Total population of village according to *Kolaba District 1961 Census Handbook*. (Note that Appendix 5.II (pp.145-152) of B.J. Israel's book presents the population figure for each village as of the 1971 Census Handbook; it also specifies the number assigned to each village according to the official listing.)

* = Names preceded by an asterisk have been singled out for special comment by B.J. Israel in his chapter entitled "Bene Israel Surnames and Their Village Links" of his book *The Bene Israel of India, Some Studies*.

BHUDRUK means "elder" or "larger",
KHURD means "small" (in relation to a place),
TARF means "towards" — all in the Marathi language.

No.	Surname	T. P.	Village	Tahsil (Taluka or Mahal)
1.	Adharnekar	303	Adharne	Pen
2.	Agarwarkar	319	Agarwada	Mhasla
3.	Akshikar	1,723	Akshi	Alibag
4.	Ampurkar	1,473	Ambepur	Alibag
5.	Aptekar	1,620	Apte	Panvel
6A.	* Ashtamkar	7,877	Ashtami (town)	Roha
6B.	* Ashtivkar			
7.	* Ashtekar	136	Ashte	Panvel
		54	Ashte	Pen
8.	* Asrekar	47	Ase	Karjat
9.	Awaskar	2,373	Awas	Alibag
10A.	* Bamnolkar	62	Bamanoli	Alibag
10B.	* Bamanolkar		Bamnoli (uninhabited)	Panvel
			Bamnoli	Mangaon
11.	Barsulkar	271	Barshiv	Murud
12.	Belgaonkar	97	Bedgaon	Mangaon
13.	* Belkar	485	Belkade	Alibag
			Belkhar	Alibag
		728	Belkhar	Roha

368

B. J. Israel's List of Village-Linked Surnames

No.	Surname	T. P.	Village	Tahsil (Taluka or Mahal)
14.	Belulkar	702	Balawali	Pen
15A.	Bhachekar }	1,042	Bhatsai	Roha
15B.	Bhastekar }			
16	Bhalgaonkar	1,203	Bhalagaon	Roha
17.	Bhalkar	352	Bhal	Alibag
18.	Bharjekar	824	Bharje	Sudhagad
19.	Bhinjekar	546	Bhilgikhar	Alibag
20.	* Bhorupkar		Bhorup or Ghera-Sudhagad	Sudhagad
21.	Birwadkar	382	Birwadi	Roha
22.	* Borgawkar	485	Borgaon	Pen
		543	Borgaon Khurd }	Khalapur
		100	Borgaon Bhudruk }	
23.	* Borgharkar	486	Borghar	Alibag
		489	Borghar	Mangaon
24A.	* Borlekar	2,716	Borli	Murud
24B.	* Borlaikar	183	Borle	Shriwardhan
		335	Borle	Mangaon
		378	Borle	Panvel
		56	Borle	Karjat
25.	Chandgaonkar	416	Chandagaon	Roha
26.	Chandrolkar	1,266	Chandore	Mangaon
27.	Charikar	498	Chari	Alibag
28.	Chewoolkar	7,408	Chaul	Alibag
29.	* Chincholkar	754	Chinchawali }	Alibag
		1,236	Chinchoti }	
		517	Chinchawali Tarf Atone }	Roha
		563	Chinchawali Tarf Diwali }	
30.	Chordekar	1,088	Chorde	Murud
31.	Dandekar	15	Dande Tarf Nandgaon	Murud
32A.	* Dandulkar }	578	Dandguri	Shriwardhan
32B.	* Dandgulkar }			
33.	Deulkar	856	Devali	Mangaon
34.	Dhatavkar	920	Dhatav	Roha
35.	Dhokarkar	1,788	Dhokawade	Alibag
36A.	Dighodkar }	505	Dighati	Panvel
36B.	Dighorkar }			
37.	* Divekar	670	Div	Pen
		342	Div	Roha
38.	Dusvikar	1,411	Dushmi Khar Pada	Pen
39A.	* Erulkar }	476	Yeral	Roha
39B.	* Yeralkar }			
40.	Fansapurkar		Fanasapur	Alibag
41A.	Galsulkar }	892	Galsure	Shriwardhan
41B.	Garsulkar }			
41C.	Galsurkar			
42.	* Ghanekar	10	Gan Tarf Parhar	Alibag
		10	Gan Tarf Shrigaon	Alibag

No.	Surname	T. P.	Village	Tahsil (Taluka or Mahal)
43.	Ghosalkar	1,822	Ghosale	Roha
44.	Indapurkar	272	Indapur	Mangaon
45.	*Ivalekar	1,687	Sai (-Ivale)	Mangaon
46.	*Jawalikar	637	Jawali	Pen
		242	Javali	Mangaon
47.	Jhiradkar	1,010	Zirad	Alibag
48.	*Jitekar	1,491	Jite	Pen
		647	Jite	Mangaon
49.	Kamarlekar	1,728	Kamarle	Alibag
50.	*Kandlekar	955	Kandale	Pen
		909	Kandal	Roha
51.	Kanhekar	741	Devakanhe	Roha
52.	Kasookar	638	Kasu	Pen
53.	Kehimkar	1,751	Kihim	Alibag
54.	Khamgaonkar	1,091	Khamgaon	Mhasla
55.	Khamkar	614	Khamb	Roha
56.	*Khanavkar	814	Khandala	Alibag
		307	Khanav	Panvel
		799	Khanaw	Khalapur
57.	Khandalkar	814	Khandal	Alibag
58A.	*Kharilkar }	325	Khar Karavi	Pen
58B.	*Khavilkar	1,154	Kharavali	Mangaon
		341	Kharivali	Khalapur
59A.	*Khulabkar }		Kolaba : Island, Fort	Alibag
59B.	*Kolabkar		(uninhabited)	
59C.	*Khulapkar			
60.	Killekar	1,035	Kille	Roha
61.	Kokbankar	497	Kokban	Roha
62A.	Koladkar }	1,410	Kolad	Roha
62B.	Kolatkar			
63.	Koletkar	586	Koleti	Pen
			Khar Koleti (uninhabited)	Pen
64.	Korlekar	1,624	Korlai	Murud
65.	Kurekar	778	Kude	Mangaon
66.	*Kurgaonkar	1,441	Kudgaon	Shriwardhan
		284	Kudgaon	Mhasla
67.	Kurul	779	Kurul	Alibag
68.	*Malekar	581	Male	Alibag
		490	Mule	Karjat
69.	Malhegharkar	639	Malleghar	Pen
70.	Malyankar	366	Malyan	Alibag
71.	*Mangaonkar	376	Mangaon	Mangaon
		201	Mangaon Bhudrik	Sudhagad
		308	Mangaon Khurd	Sudhagad

B. J. Israel's List of Village-Linked Surnames

No.	Surname	T. P.	Village	Tahsil (Taluka or Mahal)
72.	Mankar	758	Man Tarf Zirad	Alibag
73A.	Mapgaonkar ⎫	703	Mapagaon	Alibag
73B.	Mabgaonkar ⎬			
74.	* Mazgaonkar ⎭	2,058	Majgaon	Murud
		899	Mazgaon	Mangaon
75.	* Medhekar	514	Medhekhar	Alibag
		969	Medhe	Roha
		1,302	Medhe	Mangaon
76A.	Mhaisabkar ⎫		Mhaisbad	Pen
76B.	Mhaisapkar ⎭			
77.	Mhasilkar	3,527	Mhasla	Mhasla
78.	* Morbekar	733	Morbe	Panvel
		2,666	Morba	Mangaon
79.	* Nagavkar	4,702	Nagaon	Alibag
		376	Nagaon	Mangaon
			Nagaon	Sudhagad
			Nagaon	Uran
			Nagaon	Mahad
80.	Nagothenekar	3,611	Nagothana	Roha
81.	Naugharkar		Naukhar (uninhabited)	Pen
			Nigade	Alibag
82.	' Nigadkar	534	Nigade	Pen
		942	Nigadi	Shriwardhan
			Nigade	Alibag
83A.	* Nigrekar	534	Nigade	Pen
83B.	* Ningrekar	942	Nigadi	Shriwardhan
84.	Nowgaonkar	1,952	Navedar-Navagaon	Alibag
85.	Oomerdekar	1,615	Umbarde	Pen
86.	Pabrekar	1,772	Pabhare	Mhasla
87.	* Palkar	3,923	Pali	Sudhagad
		156	Pali Bhudruk	Khalapur
		78	Pali Khurd	Khalapur
88.	Penkar	10,462	Pen (town)	Pen
89.	Pezarkar	575	Pesari	Alibag
90.	Pingle	11	Pingalsai Bhudruk	Roha
		678	Pingalsai Khurd	Roha
91.	Poynadkar	1,202	Poynad	Alibag
92.	Pugavkar	798	Pugaon	Roha
93.	* Ramrajkar	921	Ramraj	Alibag
		158	Ramraj	Pen
94.	Rajpurkar	2,968	Rajpuri	Murud
95.	Rohekar	7,877	Roha (town)	Roha
96.	Sabaskar	1,778	Shahabaj	Alibag
97.	Sagaonkar	240	Sagaon	Alibag
98.	* Saigaonkar	137	Saigaon	Murud
		1,115	Saigaon	Shriwardhan
99.	Saikar	1,492	Sai	Panvel

India's Bene Israel

No.	Surname	T. P.	Village	Tahsil (Taluka or Mahal)
100.	Salavkar	872	Salav	Murud
101.	Sankar	666	Sahan	Alibag
102.	Saralkar	2,116	Saral	Alibag
103.	Sassonkar	1,498	Sasvane	Alibag
104A.	Shapurkar	2,765	Shahapur	Alibag
104B.	Shahapurkar			
105.	*Shirgaonkar	756	Walke (including Shirgaon)	Murud
106.	Shirsekar	402	Sirse	Karjat
107.	Shriwardhankar	10,849	Shriwardhan (town)	Shriwardhan
108.	Sogavkar	689	Sogaon	Alibag
109.	Songavkar	284	Sonagaon	Roha
110.	*Talegaonkar	1,057	Talegaon	Mangaon
		638	Talegaon Tarf Goregaon	Mangaon
111.	*Talhekar	164	Talekhar	Pen
		617	Talekhar	Murud
		4,132	Tala	Mangaon
112.	*Talkar	4,132	Tala	Mangaon
		192	Tale	Murud
		617	Talekhar	Murud
		164	Talekhar	Pen
		252	Tarne Tarf Tale	Mangaon
113.	Tarankhopkar	404	Tarankhop	Pen
114.	Thalkar	3,890	Thal	Alibag
115.	Vadgaonkar	139	Vadgaon	Pen
116A.	*Vadhavkar	255	Vadhav Bhudruk	Alibag
116B.	*Wadhavkar	142	Vadhav Khurd	Alibag
117.	Varsulkar	2,208	Varasoli	Alibag
118A.	Wakrulkar	1,154	Wakrul	Pen
118B.	Wakuralkar			
119.	*Walwatkar	1,088	Walwati	Murud
		1,525	Walvati	Shriwardhan
120.	Wandekar	380	Wande	Murud
121.	Wargharkar	76	Wadghar	Murud
		240	Wadghar	Mangaon
122A.	*Warulkar	1,465	Waral	Mhasla
122B.	*Wahralkar	470	Waral·	Mangaon
123.	*Warvatnekar	542	Waravatne	Mhasla
124.	*Waskar	273	Washi	Roha
		2,193	Washi	Pen
125.	*Wavekar	643	Wave (Nanegaon)	Pen
		142	Wave	Murud
			Wave	Mhasla

B. J. Israel's List of Village-Linked Surnames

SURNAMES ATTRIBUTED TO VILLAGES NOT ENUMERATED IN THE CENSUS HANDBOOK BUT WHICH DO OCCUR IN THE *FRIEND OF ISRAEL* (TARANKHOPKAR) LIST.

No.	Surname	Village	Tehsil (Taluka or Mahal)
126.	* Bandarkar	Bandar	Pen
127.	* Bhonkar	Bhon	Mangaon
128A.	Gadapkar	Gadap	Pen
128B.	Garapkar		
129.	* Gadkar	Gad	Roha
130.	Mazronkar	Mazraona	Janjira State
131.	Mendrekar	Mendhi	Janjira State
132.	Sakshikar	Sakshi	Pen
133.	* Satamkar	Satamba	Roha
134.	Shirkolkar	Shirkol	Sudhagad
135.	Telulkar	Talauli	Alibag

BENE ISRAEL SURNAMES NOT ATTRIBUTABLE TO SPECIFIC VILLAGES

No.	Surname
136.	Bhanekar
137A.	* Doodhkar
137B.	* Dootkar
138.	Dhatawadkar
139.	Malinkar
140.	Nowbaskar
141.	Satarkar
142.	* Yulekar

Glossary and Historical Notes for Indian Terms Used in This Book

AKDA or AKKARA: The traditional wedding ring of the Bene Israel; elongated, covering about one third of the fore-finger.

AKHTANA: Marriage contract (*Ketubah*, in Hebrew).

ANASHI DHAKACHA SAN: Literally "the holiday of the closing of the *anas* (fermentation) pot"; the old Bene Israel traditional holiday of eight days' abstention from eating any leaven, coinciding with Passover.

ANGRIA or ANGREY: A clan of Marathas ruling in the Konkan in the 18th century, with headquarters at Kulaba Fortress.

ANNA: Former coin of Indian currency; 16 *annas* = 1 rupee.

AVABHRTHA SNANA: Hindu expiatory bath; ablution after a sacrificial ceremony.

AYURVEDIC MEDICINE: A Hindu system of medicine.

BAGHDADIS: Used here to mean not only Jews whose ancestors came from Baghdad, but also all other Arabic-speaking Jews.

BAHADUR: Literally "valiant". An Indian title adopted by the British in India as an award for service of distinction in the civil sphere.

BANU ISRAEL: One of the terms for "Jews" used in *The Koran*.

BHAKRI: A coarse, unleavened bread made usually of millet flour; the staple bread of most of Maharashtra.

BHARAT RATNA: Since Independence (1947), the highest civil award in India.

BINDI: Auspicious red dot on forehead of Hindu women (forbidden to widows).

BIRDIACHA ROJA: The Bene Israel name for the Jewish Fast Day on the 9th of Av, commemorating the destruction of the First and Second Temples at Jerusalem.

BOMBAY PRESIDENCY AND STATE: Bombay Presidency was one of the large administrative units into which the British had divided the sub-continent. Within each unit were territories directly administered by the British Government as well as several other areas under the rule of Indian princes whose "Indian or Native States" varied greatly in size and who ruled with varying degrees of sovereignty. "Indian states" comprised about one third of the total area of Bombay Presidency. The Konkan was also part of Bombay Presidency as were today's Gujarat State, Sind (now in Pakistan), and Aden. With Indian Independence in 1947, the "Indian States" and the former British territories of Bombay Presidency merged to form Bombay State. However, in 1960 the entire area was divided according to linguistic considerations and Bombay State as such ceased to exist. The State of Maharashtra came into being as the Marathi-speaking area and includes the Konkan.

BRAHMIN or BRAHMAN: Highest of the four Hindu castes (*varnas*); the Hindu Priestly caste; not to be confused with the Hindu deity *Brahma* or with the neuter noun *Brahman* (the principle of ultimate reality in Hindu philosophy).

CHAPPATI: Unleavened bread of wheat flour; pancake-shaped, roasted briefly.

CHARPOY: A simple bed of four wooden legs and a frame through which is laced a webbing of rope or woven cane which takes the place of a mattress.

CHAVLYA: A kind of Bene Israel "cholent" for the Sabbath meal: i.e. something which could be cooked overnight on a low flame, containing at least one or more of the following ingredients: beans, potatoes, rice or barley.

CHITA: (derived from Sanskrit); funeral pile or pyre.

CHITPAVAN: A *jati* of Maharashtra Brahmins; also known as *Konkanasth*.

CHOGLA: A councillor in Bene Israel synagogue administration; there were usually four or five elders of the community who served as *Choglas* assisting the *Mukkadam* (leader of the community).

CHULA: A small portable stove of metal or clay, typically using wood or cow-dung as fuel.

COLABA: A section of the city of Bombay.

CRIMINAL TRIBES: Certain hereditary groups in various areas of India; traditionally engaged in thieving, murder, etc,; today the Indian Government is trying to rehabilitate them.

CRORE: An Indian numerical unit equal to ten million; written 1,00,00,000.

DACOIT: A robber belonging to an armed gang.

DARFALNICHA SAN: Marathi, meaning "holiday of the closing of the doors"; the Bene Israel traditional name for their Yom Kippur.

DARGAH: The shrine of a Muslim saint; a place of religious resort and prayer.

DECCAN: The plateau in the southern part of India, between the Western and Eastern Ghats.

DESHPANDEY: Hereditary title connected with land administration. Some persons with this title have adopted Deshpande as a surname.

DEVANAGRI SCRIPT: The script used for writing the Sanskrit language as well as for modern Hindi; with relatively minor changes Devanagri is also used for writing some other modern Indian languages, including Marathi.

DEWAN: Chief Minister of an Indian State.

DHOBI: Washerman.

DURBAR: Court of Royalty in India; also an event staged by such a court on special occasions ("holding a Durbar"); or a royal judicial court session.

ELIJAH HANABICHA OORUS or URS: A big fair which the Bene Israel used to hold at Khandala near Navgaon, in honor of the Prophet Elijah.

FAKIR: A Muslim religious mendicant; later the term was also applied to certain Hindu ascetics.

GARUD PURANA: One of eighteen major *puranas* (old chronicles); it is about a thousand years old and is associated with the Hindu god Vishnu.

GHANI: An oil-press; also, that quantity of oil-seeds which is put in at one time to be crushed in the oil-mill *(ghani)*.

GHAT or GHAUT: Literally, a path of descent, a mountain pass, or a landing-place; the mountain ranges paralleling the western and eastern coasts of India.

GHEE or GHI: Clarified butter, an important ingredient in Indian cookery and in Hindu ritual.

GORA: Literally, "light-complexioned"; name of the majority division of the Bene Israel, those with no history of any intermarriage with non-Jews.

GURU: A spiritual teacher (Hindu).

HALDI: Hindi, turmeric.

HAMAZOR: A Parsi custom of ritual salutation, taking the hands of another in one's own and then touching one's head.

HARIJAN: Literally, "child of God"; Mahatma Gandhi used the word to mean the "untouchable castes" of India, i.e. the outcaste groups of the population.

HATH-BOSHI: Marathi, "kissing the hand"; a Bene Israel custom at the close of all synagogue services when each person present takes the hand of each of the other congregants in turn, kissing one's own fingertips after each contact.

HAVALDAR: A native Indian non-commissioned officer, corresponding to a sergeant.

HINDI: Sanskrit-derived and one of the many official Indian languages; the mother-tongue of more than 250 million inhabitants of India.

HINDUSTANI: Popular language of North India; the common, non-classic version of *Urdu* — a form of *Hindi* with admixture of Persian and Arabic words.

HOLICHA SAN: A traditional holiday of the Bene Israel, observed by fasting one day and feasting on the following day—coinciding with the date of Purim.

HOMA SACRIFICE: A fire-offering; oblation prescribed for Hindu ritual occasions.

HOOKAH: A water-pipe for smoking mixtures of tobacco and spices; also known as a "hubble bubble".

HUBSHI: A dynasty of Abyssinian Muslim origin; rulers at Janjira (q.v.), from the end of 15th Century until 1947; also known as *Sidis*.

IRAQI: A term used by the Bene Israel as a synonym for "Baghdadi", and loosely used to refer to all Arabic-speaking Jews.

JAGGERY or JAGRI: Unrefined sugar from palm sap, widely used in India.

JAGIR: A hereditary assignment of land and of its rent as annuity; also the revenues, the district, or its tenure.

JAMAT: The term used to designate the General Assembly of the Bene Israel synagogue congregation.

JANAPADA: Sanskrit: a community, race, nation; a kingdom; the people, subjects.

JANJIRA STATE: The Indian State in the Konkan, ruled by the Hubshis (Sidis) from the end of the 15th century until 1947; included most of today's Murud, Shriwardhan and Mhasla Mahals of Kulaba District.

JARI or ZARI: Indian embroidery with gold or silver thread.

JATI: The term most commonly used in India to refer both to Hindu castes and to Hindu caste sub-divisions; i.e. a group based on common descent (and as such is sometimes used to refer to non-Hindu groups based on race, language or religion).

JAWAN: Hindi, literally "a youth"; a soldier.

JEMEDAR: Native Indian commissioned officer, corresponding to a lieutenant.

KADHI: Meaning "curry", a savoury sauce served with rice or breads; curries can be endlessly varied depending upon the spices used and upon the relative proportions of ingredients.

KAJI or KAZI, KADI: A Muslim term taken over by the Bene Israel to designate their first religious ministers, who also served as judges in both civil and religious matters within the community; the profession of *Kaji* was hereditary.

KALA: Literally, "black"; the term designating that section of the Bene Israel community among whose ancestors have been non-Jews; *Gora* (q.v.) and *Kala* Bene Israel were mutually endogamous.

KARBHARI: Marathi, "a manager"; the equivalent of a Chief Minister in the smaller Indian States, especially in the Deccan.

KAVI SAMMELAN (Sanskrit): An assembly of poets (very popular in various parts of India) who compete with one another in reciting (and often improvising) poetry.

KHADI or KHADDAR: Home-spun, hand-woven cloth popularized in modern India by Mahatma Gandhi originally as a counter to imported mill cloth.

KHAN BAHADUR: A civilian title of distinction in British India.

KHAN SAHIB: A civilian title of distinction in British India.

KHIR: An Indian sweet dish; a milk pudding with rice.

KHIRIACHA SAN: Traditional Bene Israel holiday on the third day of the Jewish New Year.
KIBLAH: The holiest place toward which worshippers face in prayer: i.e. Mecca for Muslims, Mt. Gerizim for Samaritans, Jerusalem for Jews.
KIRTAN: Narration in song; performance by a semi-professional singer (the kirtan-kar) of a programme of devout songs, interspersed with religious stories and moral homilies.
KOLABA or KULABA: A coastal administrative district of Maharashtra State, stretching north-south; the heartland of Bene Israel settlement. Now re-named Raigad.
KONKAN: The coastal strip of Maharashtra which stretches from just north of Bombay to Goa.
KONKANI: A Sanskrit-derived language spoken mainly in the southernmost part of the Konkan and in Goa and the adjoining area of Karnataka.
KORAN or QURAN: The sacred book of Islam.
KSHATRIYA: The second in rank of the four *varnas* (q.v.); the caste of warriors and rulers.
KULKARNI: Indian term designating a village accountant, especially in central and western India; also the name of a *jati* (q.v.)
KUMKUM: Vermilion powder used by Hindu women for making a red spot on their foreheads as a sign of good fortune.
LACCHA: A gold pendant worn by the Hindu wife as a symbol of marriage; the Bene Israel also adopted this custom.
LAKH: An Indian numerical unit equal to one hundred thousand; written 1,00,000.
LAVNI: A ballad, often extemporaneous; very popular in Maharashtra.
LUNGHI: An ankle-length waistcloth, usually woven in a plaid design.
MAHABHARATA: One of the two great Hindu epics (the other being *The Ramayana*).
MAHAL: Term for an administrative unit of a District, in the Konkan.
MAHANT: Literally, "a great one"; term for a Hindu saint.
MAHAR: A very low and ritually unclean Hindu *jati* (q.v.).
MAISTRY: Indian term for a carpenter or other artisan (derived from the Portuguese word *mestre*, a master-workman).
MALABAR: The northern sector of Kerala.
MALAYALAM: A Dravidian language, spoken in Kerala.
MALIDA: The custom peculiar to the Bene Israel of offering a platter of certain foods (the *malida*), accompanied by the recitation of particular prayers in Hebrew, as a ceremonial ritual for thanksgiving, making vows, purification, rites of passage, etc.
MANG: A very low, ritually unclean, Hindu *jati* (q.v.).
MANKARIS: Council of village elders, in Maharashtra; the meaning of *mankari* is "a man entitled to certain honours".
MARATHAS: Non-Brahmin Hindu cultivators, landowners and soldiers from the mountainous areas of Maharashtra who, under Shivaji in the second half of the 17th century, founded a powerful empire.
MARATHI: An Indo-European language, spoken in Maharashtra.
MASJID or MESGAD: A mosque.
M.B.E.: "Member of the British Empire", an honorary award, granted by the British.
MEHNDI: Henna dye made into a paste, traced on hands and feet for wedding decoration; common in India, and used by the Bene Israel.
MHETER: A village officer in Maharashtra.
MOHALLA: Section of an Indian village or town; strictly or mainly inhabited by one

Indian Terms : Glossary and Notes

community or *jati* (q.v.); sometimes just one street, being a communal neighbourhood.

M'SHUHRARIM: Hebrew, "manumitted" or "set free"; the term used for that sector of Cochin Jewry descended from manumitted servants converted to Judaism; also known (by outsiders) as "Brown Jews".

MUKKADAM: The headman of a Maharashtra village, or of a *jati*; the title given by the Bene Israel to the President of a synagogue; a supervisor.

MUSHAIRA (from the Arabic): A literary assembly at which poets recite their poetry, often competing with one another; the Muslim equivalent of the Hindu *Kavi Sammelan*.

M'YUHASIM: Hebrew, "those with pedigree"; the term used to designate that sector of Cochin Jewry, known (to outsiders) as "Malabari" or "Black Jews", who claim descent from the original Jewish community at Cranganore.

NAIK or NAYEK: A native Indian non-commissioned officer, corresponding to a corporal; also, an officer in the 18th century Angria Fleet.

NAVIACHA SAN: The Bene Israel traditional name for the Jewish New Year.

O.B.E.: "Order of the British Empire", an award granted by the British for special service to its empire.

PADMA SHRI: The fourth-highest civil award for national distinction granted by independent India.

PADUKA: Indian word for impressions of feet on stone, attributed to gods or saints and therefore popularly venerated by many Hindus.

PALLU or PALLAV: The most highly decorated end of Indian *sari* (q.v.), worn either hanging over the woman's shoulder or over the head and shoulders.

PANCH: The word for "five" (derived from the Sanskrit) in many Indian languages.

PANCHAYAT: Indian village or communal council-cum-court, traditionally composed of five elders.

PAN SUPARI: *Pan* is the leaf of the piper-betel vine, in which is rolled flaked areca nut (*supari*), a little sugar and shell-lime paste, and sometimes additional ingredients, to form a chewing quid; chewing *pan*, especially after meals, is a common custom throughout India.

PARDESI: The designation given to the separate community of so-called "White Jews" of Cochin, who have descended mostly from Jews who settled in Cochin having come from many different countries.

PINDAREES: Mounted bands of plunderers plaguing central west-India from the late 17th century until crushed by the British in 1817.

PRASADAM (Sanskrit): A little gift (usually food), blessed by having been offered to the deity, and later handed out to each person present, conferring to each person a share in the benefits of the ceremony.

PUJA: Ritual Hindu worship; especially the daily temple worship by a Hindu priest (a *pujari*), or by the head of the house to the household deity.

PURANAS: Sanskrit, "old legends"; an extensive body of Hindu Scriptures containing numerous versions of religious instructions and mythical tales of the gods of the Hindu pantheon; these writings, in their present form, do not go back earlier than the 5th century A.D., and some are much more recent.

PURDAH: Hindustani, "a curtain"; the screening off and the secluding of women from the sight of men; the root of the word *purdah* is Semitic and means "separation".

PURI: A wheat dough made in two layers and deep-fried so that it blows up like a little balloon.

PUTTU: Another name for the red spot *(bindi)* which a Hindu wife puts on her forehead for good luck.
RAMZAN or RAMADAN: The ninth month of the Islamic lunar calendar; for Muslims it is the month of fasting from daybreak until sundown.
RUBAIYAT: Quatrain verse.
SABA'BI ROJA: Traditional Bene Israel name for the Jewish fast-day marking the beginning of Nebuchadnezzar's siege of Jerusalem; on the 10th of the Hebrew month *Tevet*.
SADHU: An Indian (Hindu) ascetic.

SANAD: An Indian official government document or warrant containing a title to land or to an office, or a privilege or authorization for something specific to be done.

SANYASI: Indian term for a very holy Hindu ascetic.

SARDAR or SIRDAR: Hindi, "chief"; the appellation regularly prefixed to the names of males of the Sikh community.
SARDAR BAHADUR: Indian civilian title awarded by the British to distinguished Sikhs.
SARI: Indian women's garment — 5,6 or 9 yards long — draped first around the waist, then across the chest and over the shoulder (with local variations in weave, decorations and style of draping).
SEPOY: A native Indian soldier, employed as a soldier by a European power and disciplined and dressed in European style.
SHAKE: A Hindu era commencing in 78 A.D., still widely used in India today.
SHANWAR: Saturday (in India's Indo-European languages).
SHERRA: A crown of flowers with pendant strings of blossoms hanging over the face; traditionally worn by the Bene Israel bride and groom during certain wedding rituals.
SHILA SAN: Bene Israel joyous holiday on the day after Yom Kippur.
SHIVAJI: b. 1627-d.1680; the founder of the great Maratha Empire.
SHRADH or SHRADHA: Hindu ceremony for departed ancestors, performed by a son or nearest male relative; accompanied by giving gifts and feasts (especially to Brahmins).
SHUKRAWAR: Friday.
SIDI: See *Hubshi*.
SIKH: A follower of the Sikh religion, founded in northern India by Guru Nanak (b. 1469-d. 1538), preaching one god, a casteless society, equality of women with men; the Sikh Holy Book is the *Guru Granth Sahib*, written in the Punjabi language.
SOMWAR: Monday (Sanskrit-derived).
STREE MANDAL: The generic term in India for a women's association.
SUBEDAR: Commissioned rank for Indian soldiers, corresponding to the rank of captain.
SUBJA: *Ocymum pilosum vel basilicum;* a fragrant herb used frequently in the rituals of the Bene Israel as well as of other Indian communities.
SUDRA: The lowest in the hierarchy of the four Hindu *varnas* (q.v); typically *sudras* are engaged in agriculture and menial services.
SWADESHI: Hindi, "of the country", i.e. made in India; the Swadeshi Movement, popularized by Mahatma Gandhi during India's independence struggle, urged the use only of Indian goods and the boycott of foreign goods.
SWARAJ: Hindi, "self-government"; political independence.

Indian Terms : Glossary and Notes

TALI: A special gold pendant, the Hindu symbol of marriage, which is put around the bride's neck as part of the wedding ritual.

TALUKA: Term for an administrative unit of a district in the Konkan (has various shades of meanings in different parts of India).

TEEPA: The red spot worn by Hindu wives on the forehead just above the nose, for good luck.

TEHSIL or TAHSIL: Term for an administrative unit of a District in the Konkan; a *taluka;* has various shades of meanings in different parts of India.

TELI (Marathi): An oil-presser.

THUGGERY: Depredations by gangs of assassin-robbers; originally the "profession" of a ritual sect in Bengal called "Thugs".

TONGA: Hindi; a small, light, two wheeled horse-drawn vehicle, available in India for hire as a taxi.

TULSI or TULASI: *Ocymum sanctum;* a plant sacred to Hindus, usually planted on a special pedestal in courtyards of Hindu homes.

UD: A tree resin with characteristic odour; burned as part of Bene Israel home ritual in memory of departed relatives.

UNTOUCHABLE: Persons who belong to none of the four *varnas* (q.v.) traditionally were considered untouchable by members of the *varna* communities; there are varying degrees of ritual untouchability or uncleanliness: Mahatma Gandhi called India's untouchables "Harijans" (meaning "children of God"); in modern independent India many traditional restrictions regarding untouchability have been disregarded by many Hindus; and India's Constitution has special provisions for uplifting the condition of its depressed classes as well as laws against specific old practises which had been based on the concept of untouchability.

URS or OORUS: The Muslim commemoration of a death anniversary; the *urs* of certain Muslim saints in India is celebrated by a big annual fair.

VAISYA: The third in the Hindu hierarchy of four *varnas* (q.v.); members of this *varna* were traditionally merchants and agriculturalists.

VARNA: Sanskrit, "colour"; the Indian term for the basic divisions of Hindu caste society; there are four *varnas* (in descending hierarchical order: *Brahmin, Kshatriya, Vaisya* and *Sudra*).

VEDAS: The most ancient Hindu holy writings; they consist of hymns; there are four *Vedas* (*Rig, Yajur, Sama* and *Atharva*); the *Vedas* are the foundation of the Hindu religion.

VIDYAPEET: A center of learning.

Glossary and Notes for Jewish Terms Used in This Book

ALEPH: The name of the first letter of the Hebrew alphabet; its literal meaning is "ox"; it also signifies the number "one".

ALIYAH (Hebrew): Literally, "going up"; "immigration to Israel", also, the going up to the reading desk to recite the blessings for, and sometimes also to read from, the *Torah* (q.v.) during synagogue services.

ANTIOCHUS EPIPHANES: King of Syria, 175-164 B.C.; tried to de-nationalize the Jews; desecrated the Jewish Temple in Jerusalem; provoked the Maccabeean Revolt.

ARBITH: The Jewish evening prayer service; also called *Ma'ariv*.

ASHKENAZI (pl. – *im*): Literally "a person from Germany"; nowadays commonly used to include most of western Jewry, and to differentiate their liturgy and customs from those of the Sephardim (q.v.).

AYIN: The 16th letter of the Hebrew alphabet; literally "eye"; it is used in Hebrew to signify the number "70".

BAMAH (Hebrew): an altar, stage, high place.

BET DIN (Hebrew): Literally, "house of law"; Jewish religious court.

B.C.E.: Used by orthodox Jews to denote "Before the Common Era", used by them in place of B.C. (before Christ).

BIBLE: See Old Testament and New Testament.

BIMAH (Hebrew): a pulpit or dais with table for *Torah*-reading in the synagogue.

BRIT MILAH (Hebrew): Jewish ritual circumcision, performed on the 8th day after birth of every Jewish male child (*Genesis* 17 : 10-12).

C.E.: Used by orthodox Jews to denote, "Common Era" instead of A.D.(*Anno Domini*, which is Latin for "in the year of the Lord").

CHRONICLES, Books I & II: Books of the *Old Testament*.

COHEN (pl. COHANIM) (Hebrew): Jews are divided into three hereditary groups of which the highest in rank are the *Cohanim* (priests); next in rank are the Levites; and finally *Kol Yisrael,* all the other Jews. *Cohanim* are believed to be the descendants of Aaron, the brother of Moses. Aaron was the first High Priest of the Jews.

DEUTERONOMY: The fifth of the Five Books of Moses, which together constitute the *Torah; Deuteronomy* contains the laws of Moses.

DIASPORA: The dispersion of Jews scattered throughout the world, beginning with the Roman conquest of Jerusalem in 70 A.D.

ELIJAH, ELIAHU HA-NAVI: Biblical prophet of the 9th century B.C., in the (northern) Kingdom of Israel.

ELLUL: q.v. One of the months of the Jewish Calendar.

EXILARCH OF BAGHDAD: The lay head of the Jewish community of Baghdad and of other diaspora territories under his jurisdiction, during the Middle Ages.

EXODUS (The Book of): The second book of the *Torah*; it deals with the departure of the Jews from Egypt, their wanderings in the desert, and the giving of the Ten Commandments.

Jewish Terms : Glossary and Notes   383

EZEKIEL (The Book of) : Part of the *Old Testament*. The Prophet Ezekiel was among the Jews exiled to Babylonia in 586 B.C.

EZRA : Jewish priest and scribe, 4th or 5th century B.C., who led a group of Jewish exiles from Babylon back to Jerusalem, and who dissolved marriages of Jews with non-Jewish women. The Book of Ezra is part of the Hagiographa, i.e. the last section of the *Old Testament*.

FIRST TEMPLE : Jewish Temple at Jerusalem, built by King Solomon (965-928 B.C.) and destroyed by Babylonian King Nebuchadnezzar (q.v.) in 586 B.C.

GABBAI (Hebrew) : The treasurer of a synagogue.

GAON (pl. GAONIM) : Literally, "genius" or "very learned"; the title given to the heads of the two Babylonian Jewish academies of Sura and Pumbedita (7th-11th centuries A.D.). In the 11th century an academy was established in Palestine and the head of it was also called "Gaon"; and later the title was applied to learned rabbis elswhere as well.

GEDALIAH (the fast of) : A Jewish fast-day in memory of the murder of Gedaliah, who was the Jewish Governor appointed by Babylonian King Nebuchadnezzar (q.v) to govern the remnant of Jews in Palestine whom he did not send into exile.

GENESIS : The first book of the Bible, containing an account of the creation of the universe, and the stories of the patriachs Abraham, Isaac and Jacob, and of Joseph.

GENIZAH (Hebrew, plural GENIZOT) : Literally, "hiding place", "storehouse"; the depository for Jewish sacred books or other objects on which the word "God" is written, and for discarded Jewish ritual objects.

HAFTARAH : Specific portions from the Books of the Prophets (q.v. *Old Testament*) which are read in synagogue each Sabbath and on certain holidays; also popularly called *Maftir*.

HAGGADAH : The book, written partly in Hebrew and partly in Aramaic, which is read from cover to cover at the Passover Seder. It is devoted primarily to explaining the meaning of the Exodus (q.v.) from Egypt.

HAGIOGRAPHA : See below, the definition for *Old Testament*.

HAHAM (Hebrew, pl. HAHAMIM) : Literally "wise"; an honorific title applied to a learned person.

HALACHAH (Hebrew) : Traditional law; civil and ritual Jewish law and custom for which there is no explicit authority in the scriptures, but which is accepted as traditional law.

HALITZAH (Hebrew) : Jewish ritual of removal of the brother-in-law's shoe by the widow of a brother who has died childless, thus releasing the brother-in-law from the obligation of marrying her (as per *Deuteronomy* 25 : 5-10), i.e. Levirate marriage.

HA-MAVDIL (Hebrew) : The prayer recited at the end of the Sabbath, separating the Sabbath from the mundane week ahead.

HOMETZ (Hebrew) : Leavened bread; Jews are not allowed to eat this during the entire week of Passover (q.v. Pesah)

HANUKKAH (Hebrew) : Literally "dedication"; an eight-day Jewish holiday in the Jewish month of Kislev (December) commemorating the victory of Judah Maccabee over Syrian King Antiochus Epiphanes (q.v.); celebrated by the lighting of a special lamp (q.v. Hanukkiah) on each of the eight nights of the holiday, symbolic of the light from a tiny bit of consecrated oil (which, according to tradition, miraculously kept burning in the Temple for eight days) — connected with the rededication of the Temple which had been desecrated by Antiochus Epiphanes.

HANUKKIAH : A Hanukkah lamp consisting of nine holders (for oil or for candles), one light called the *shamesh* being used to ignite the others: one on the first night and, cumulatively, one more on each of the eight nights of Ḥanukkah, until, on the eighth night, all nine are glowing together.

ḤAROSHETH: The mixture (of food ingredients) for the Passover *seder* (q.v.) table, some say to symbolize the mixture for bricks which the Israelite slaves were forced to make in Egypt.

ḤAG HE-ASIF: Jewish Feast of the In-Gathering; q.v. *Succoth*.

HASHKABAH: Jewish prayer for the repose of the dead.

HASKALAH (Hebrew): Literally, "enlightenment, knowledge"; a Jewish movement for spreading European education and culture among Jews (c. 1750-1880).

HAVDALAH (Hebrew): Literally "separation"; the ceremony of bidding farewell to the Sabbath.

HAY: The fifth letter of the Hebrew alphabet; its numerical value is 5.

ḤAZAN: The cantor who chants the liturgy and leads the prayers in a synagogue.

HAZKARAH (Hebrew): Jewish memorial service; also called *yizkor*.

ḤET: The eighth letter of the Hebrew alphabet; its numerical value is 8.

ḤEVRAH KADISHAH (Hebrew): Literally "holy society"; Jewish (voluntary) burial society.

HEYKHAL (Hebrew): Literal meaning "palace" or "temple"; the Ark or cabinet placed in or against the wall of a synagogue toward which the worshippers face, i.e. the wall in the direction of Jerusalem.

HIGH HOLIDAYS (Jewish): *Rosh Hashanah* (q.v.) (the New Year) and *Yom Kippur* (the Day of Atonement). They both occur in the Jewish month of Tishre (September or October), *Rosh Hashanah* being followed ten days later by *Yom Kippur*))

ḤUPAH (Hebrew): A marriage canopy under which the Jewish traditional marriage ceremony must take place. It is usually a richly embroidered cloth raised aloft by four poles being held by four young men. The word is also used as a term for a Jewish wedding as such.

ISAIAH, Book of: One of the *Books of Prophets*, in the *Old Testament*. The prophecies of Isaiah date to c. 740-700 B.C.

ISRAEL: Another name for the Biblical patriarch Jacob; also the name given to the 3rd, and largest, hereditary division of the Jewish people, lower in ritual status than the Cohanim (q.v. Cohen) (priests) and the Levites (q.v.) (temple servants).

ISRAEL, Kingdom of: The Northern Kingdom of Jews, created after the death of King Solomon in 928 B.C., with its capital in Shechem (Samaria); the rest of King Solomon's territory became the Kingdom of Judah.

JUDAH, Kingdom of: After his death in 928 B.C., Solomon's kingdom split into the Kingdom of Judah (the House of David) with its capital in Jerusalem, and the Kingdom of Israel in the North with its capital in Shechem.

JUDGES, Book of: One of the books of *Old Testament* (q.v.); it contains the history of the Israelites from the death of Joshua to the birth of Samuel.

KADDISH: The Jewish Mourner's Prayer, composed solely of praise of God and a plea for peace.

KAPPOROTH: A Jewish ritual performed by swinging a fowl above one's head, saying a specific prayer, and then slaughtering the fowl as an expiation offering; performed on the day before Yom Kippur.

KASHRUT: Observance of Jewish ritual law, especially of the Jewish dietary laws.

KEDUSHAH: Prayer in sanctification of God; it is part of the *amidah* (recited while standing) portion of synagogue service.

KETUBAH: The Jewish marriage contract, which must be in writing and signed by two witnesses.
KIDDUSH: Jewish benediction proclaiming the holiness of the Sabbath or of a Jewish festival.
KINGDOMS OF ISRAEL AND JUDAH: See Israel, Kingdom of; and Judah, Kingdom of.
KINGS, Books I & II: Books of the *Old Testament* which contain the history of Israel from the death of David to that of Jehoshaphat.
KIRYAT SHEMA (Hebrew): The recitation of the *Shema* prayer.
KAMATZ: The name of a Hebrew vowel, pronounced as short *o* or *a*.
KORBAN (Hebrew): Literally, "sacrifice"; the offerings which are prescribed in the *Book of Leviticus*.
KOSHER (Hebrew KASHER, literally, "proper"): Those foods which Jews, according to HALACHAH are allowed to eat.
LEVITES: A hereditary division among the Jews, second to the COHANIM in status; in Biblical days the Levites were Temple servants and administrators.
LEVITICUS, Book of: The third of the Five Books of Moses; it contains the ordinances for sacrifices, sanctuary, purifications, festivals, etc.
LOST (TEN) TRIBES: The inhabitants of the Kingdom of Israel who were deported in 720 B.C. when conquered by the Assyrians.
MA'ARIV: The evening prayer service in Jewish liturgy; also called *Arbith*.
MAIMONIDES: Moses Ben Maimon (also called Rambam); Jewish Talmudist (q.v. Talmud), philosopher, astronomer and physician; born in Cordova, Spain 1135 A.D.; lived in Cairo from 1165 until his death in 1204.
MARRANOS: Jews from Spain and Portugal who had been converted to Christianity under pressure during the days of the Inquisition, but who continued to believe in Judaism and to observe Jewish rituals in secret.
MATZAH (pl. MATZOTH) (Hebrew): The unleavened bread, made according to ritual specifications, to be eaten by Jews during Passover (q. v. Pesasch) when the eating of leavened food is forbidden.
MENORAH: The seven-branched oil lamp used in the Tabernacle and Temple in Biblical days.
MESSIAH (Hebrew M'SHIAH): Literally, "annointed"; the annointed one, the ideal king; embodiment of the Jewish prophetic hope for the future; in Christianity: the Christ.
MEZUZAH (Hebrew): Literal meaning "doorpost". A case containing, on a small piece of handwritten parchment, the verses of the *Shema* (from *Deuteronomy* 6: 4-9 and 5: 13-21 and *Numbers* 15: 37-41). Jews are supposed to affix a Mezuzah on the doorposts to rooms in their homes and other buildings, and on their gates.
MIDRASH: A body of Hebrew writing in exposition or exegesis of the Jewish scriptures.
MIKVEH: Jewish ritual bath, built according to specific requisites, usually but not necessarily near the synagogue; total immersion in the waters of the *Mikveh* being required in all cases of ritual impurity as well as for conversion to Judaism.
MINHAH: The afternoon prayer service in Jewish liturgy.
MINHAG (Hebrew): Custom, usage.
MINYAN: Ten Jewish males 13 years of age or older, as the minimum number required for conducting Jewish congregational prayer.
MOHEL: The person who performs Jewish ritual circumcision.

MONTHS OF THE JEWISH LUNAR CALENDAR in order of their occurrence: *Nissan* (which usually falls in April), *Iyar, Sivan, Tamuz, Av, Ellul, Tishre, Heshvan, Kislev, Tevet, Sh'vat, Adar.*

MOTZEI SHABBAT : The night which begins when Sabbath ends.

MUSAF : Additional offering, in the days of the Temple; in the synagogue service, prayers additional to the main part of the morning and afternoon service.

NASI (Hebrew) : President, chief, prince, head of.

NEBUCHADNEZZAR : King of Babylon who destroyed Jerusalem and its Temple in 597 B. C.

NEHEMIAH, Book of : One of the books of the Hagiographa (see below, the definition for *Old Testament*). Nehemiah was the Jewish governor of Judah, appointed by the Persian ruler Artaxerxes. Nehemiah rebuilt the wall surrounding Jerusalem.

NEW TESTAMENT : The Bible of the Christians consists of both the *Old Testament* and the *New Testament*. The latter deals with Jesus Christ, his teachings and the Apostles. It contains : the *Gospels* and Biographies of Matthew, Mark, Luke and John; the Book of *Acts* of the Apostles; twenty-one *Epistles* (of St. Paul, James, Peter, Judas and John); and the book of *Revelations* (the revelation of St. John about the Apocalypse).

NIDDAH (Hebrew) : Menstrual period; also a menstruating woman.

OLD TESTAMENT : The sacred scriptures of the Jews, the Jewish Bible, known to Jews as the *Tanach*. It consists of the *Torah* or the Five Books of Moses (*Genesis, Exodus, Leviticus, Numbers* and *Deuteronomy*); The Earlier Prophets (Joshua, Judges, 1st and 2nd Books of Samuel, 1st and 2nd Books of Kings), The Later Prophets (Isaiah, Jeremiah, Ezekiel, Hosea, Joel, Amos, Obadiah, Jonah, Micah, Nahum, Habakkuk, Zephania, Hagai, Zachariah, Malachi); and The Hagiographa (Psalms, Proverbs, Job, Song of Songs, Ruth, Lamentations, Ecclesiastes, Esther, Daniel, Ezra, Nehemiah, the 1st and 2nd Books of Chronicles).

PASSOVER : See Pesach.

PENTATEUCH : The *Torah* of the Jews, i.e. the Five Books of Moses : *Genesis, Exodus, Leviticus, Numbers* and *Deuteronomy*.

PESACH (PASSOVER) : The Jewish Holiday in the Jewish month of *Nissan* usually occurring in April, which commemorated the slavery of the Jews in Egypt and their exodus from Egypt; it lasts for 7 days in Israel and 8 days in the diaspora, during which time the eating of all manner of leaven is forbidden.

PIDYAN HA-BEN : Jewish ceremony for the symbolic redemption of a first-born son at the age of one month.

POGROM (Russian) : Destruction, loot, murder and rape by one section of the population against another; raids against defenceless Jews.

PSALMS, Book of : Hymns in praise of God, in the *Old Testament*, most of them attributed to King David.

P'SEELIM (Hebrew) : Idols, graven images.

P'SULIM (Hebrew) : Blemishes, defects, disqualifications.

PURIM : A joyous Jewish Holiday (in the Jewish month of *Adar* which falls in February – March), based on the *Book of Esther* (in the *Old Testament*) commemorating how the Jew Mordecai and his niece Esther saved the Jews of the Persian Empire from destruction at the hands of Haman.

RASHI SCRIPT : This style of Hebrew script was introduced and used by Rabbi Solomonibar Isaac (Rashi), b.1040 – d. 1105, an important Jewish scholar in

France. Rashi script is still being used for commentaries on the *Bible* and *Talmud*.

RAV (Hebrew) : Rabbi, teacher, master, lord; a term of respect applied to learned or otherwise important Jews.

RESPONSA : Decisions and rulings in the form of written replies to written questions (not only about Jewish topics) from diaspora Jews addressed to eminent Jewish rabbis, teachers, scholars or heads of Jewish academies. The corpus of responsal literature had its beginnings in the early 3rd century B.C. and has continued to accumulate through the centuries.

ROSH HASHANAH : The Jewish New Year, which falls on the first day of the Jewish month *Tishre* and which usually occurs in September.

SAADIA GAON : Saadia ben Joseph, the Gaon (head) of the Jewish Academy at Sura (Babylonia); b. 892 – d. 942. Saadia Gaon was a prolific Jewish writer, philosopher and polemicist.

SANDEK : The male adult who holds the infant during Jewish ritual circumcision; the godfather.

SEBAH SHELAMIM : The peace offering (of the Bene Israel) (cf. *Leviticus* 7).

SEBAH TODAH : The thanks offering (of the Bene Israel) (cf. *Leviticus* 3).

SECOND TEMPLE : The Temple of the Jews, in Jerusalem, rebuilt after the return of the exiles from Babylonia (520-515 B.C.); much later it was lavishly rebuilt again by King Herod in 19 B.C.; it was completely destroyed by the Romans in 70 A.D. under the Roman General Titus.

SEDER (Hebrew, pronounced SAY-DER) : Literally "order, arrangement"; the Jewish ceremony on the eve of Passover, recalling the slavery of the Jews in Egypt – through the reading of the entire *Haggadah* while everyone is seated around a festive family dinner table on which have been placed special foods with symbolic meanings.

SEFER TORAH (plural SIFREI TORAH) (Hebrew) : Literally "Book of the *Torah*"; a parchment scroll, on which the Five Books of Moses have been inscribed by hand. When not being read, the scroll is encased in an elaborate covering.

SEPHARDI (plural SEPHARDIM) (Hebrew) : Literally "a person from Spain"; descendants of the Jews who were expelled from Spain and Portugal, wherever in the world they may have settled; they maintain certain customs and portions of Jewish liturgy different from those of the Ashkenazim; the term "Sephardim" has been extended also to all Jews who have adopted the Sephardic synagogue liturgy.

SHABBAT : Sabbath, the 7th day of the Jewish week, a day on which Jews are forbidden to do any manner of work; a day of peace, joy and beauty for the observant Jew, beginning at sundown on Friday and lasting until sundown on Saturday.

SH'LIHIM (plural), SHALIAH (singular) (Hebrew) : Messenger envoy, deputy; this is the term used over the centuries to designate the messengers coming from the Holy Land (Palestine) to collect funds from Jewish communities located all over the Diaspora to support the poor Jews and Jewish institutions located in Palestine.

SHAMASH (Hebrew) : Attendant, caretaker; the sexton of a synagogue; also the name given to the 9th *Hanukkiah* light which is used to ignite all the others.

SHAVUOTH (Hebrew) : Literally "weeks"; the Jewish festival of the harvest of the first fruits; the Pentecost (cf. *Exodus* 34 : 22 and *Deuteronomy* 16 : 10-12).

SHEMA (Hebrew) : Literally "Hear!"; the *Shema* is a passage from *Deuteronomy* 6 : 4-9 which expresses the fundamental tenet of the Jewish faith, beginning with "Hear, O Israel, the Lord thy God, the Lord is One."

SHOFAR : The ram's horn, blown (according to specified notes) at certain points during the synagogue liturgy on *Rosh Hashanah* and at the close of *Yom Kippur*.

SHOHET (plural SHOHATIM) : The Jewish person properly trained and certified to slaughter animals for food strictly according to the laws of *Kashrut*.

SHULHAN ARUH (Hebrew) : Literally, "a prepared table"; authoritative code of Jewish laws, ritual and standards of behaviour, written by Joseph ben Ephraim Caro, b. 1488 – d. 1575.

SH'VAT : The 11th month of the Jewish calendar.

SIMHAT KOHEN : Second Temple custom of rejoicing for the High Priest.

SIMHAT TORAH : Jewish holiday of "Rejoicing over the Law (Torah)". It occurs on the day after the week of the Feast of *Succoth* in the Jewish month of *Tishre*.

S'LIHOTH : The Jewish propitiatory prayers, recited during the month of *Ellul*.

SONG OF SONGS : A book of the *Old Testament*, attributed to King Solomon. It is a love poem often considered as an allegory depicting the relation between God and Israel.

SOPHER (Hebrew) : A writer, author; a Jewish scribe or teacher.

SUCCAH (plural SUCCOTH) (Hebrew) : Literally, "booth"; *Succoth* (also called Tabernacles or *Hag He-Asif*) is the 7-day Jewish festival occurring in the Jewish month of Tishre, commemorating the 40-year wandering of the Jews in the wilderness where they had no permanent habitation. Booths, with roofs of tree fronds, through which the sky can be seen, are constructed next to synagogues and also next to homes of orthodox families where for 7 days religious Jews dwell or at least eat all their meals.

TALITH (plural TALITHOTH) : Prayer shawl worn by Jewish males (after the age of 13), often woven with black or blue stripes at both ends, always with fringes pendant from its four corners. Covering the shoulders, it is worn at morning prayer on week days, and also during the Sabbath and Holy Day prayers.

TALMUD : A compendium of discussions on and additions to the *Mishnah* (the earliest codification of Jewish Oral Law) by generations of scholars and jurists in many Jewish academies, from c.6th – 11th centuries; the "Babylonian Talmud" of the Babylonian Jewish academies of Sura and Pumbedita, and the "Jerusalem (or Palestinian) Talmud" containing discussions etc. of the Palestinian Jewish sages.

TAMUZ : The 4th month of the Jewish calendar.

TASCHLIH : A Jewish propitiatory rite performed on the afternoon of *Rosh Hashanah*, casting one's sins upon the waters by throwing pebbles into a stream or other body of water and reciting appropriate prayers and hymns.

TAV : The last letter of the Hebrew alphabet; its numerical value is 400.

TEBILA (Hebrew) : Immersion, as a Jewish ceremony for purification; it is also one of the requirements for conversion to Judaism.

TEVETH : The 10th month of the Jewish calendar.

T'FILIN (Aramaic) (Hebrew T'FILAH means "prayer") : Phylacteries, i.e. two small leather cube-shaped boxes containing passages from the *Torah* on parchment, one box for the head (just above the forehead), the other for the left arm fastened with leather straps wound around the arm in a specified way, while reciting certain blessings. The tradition is for all Jewish males over the age of 13 to wear the *T'filin* each morning for morning prayers, but not on the Sabbath or Holy Days. The passages contained in the *T'filin* are : *Exodus* 13 : 1-16; *Deuteronomy* 6 : 4-9; and *Deuteronomy* 11 : 13-21.

TISHRI : The 7th month of the Jewish calendar.

TITUS : The Roman general who, after four years of siege, conquered Jerusalem, completely destroyed the Temple and the city as such, and was responsible for the dispersion of the Jews throughout the Roman Empire. He later became Emperor of Rome, from 79 to 81 A.D.

TORAH (plural TOROTH) (Hebrew) : The Five Books of Moses, also called "The Law" by Jews, containing the books of *Genesis, Exodus, Leviticus, Numbers* and *Deuteronomy;* otherwise known as the "Pentateuch".

TRIBES (Jewish) : The Biblical tribes of Jews were descended from, and named after, the 12 sons of the patriarch Jacob, i.e. Reuben, Simeon, Levi, Judah, Dan, Naphtali, Gad, Asher, Issachar, Zebulon, Joseph and Benjamin.

TU B'SHVAT : The 15th day of the month of *Sh'vat;* the Jewish Arbor Day, for planting tree saplings.

TZITZITH (Hebrew) : The long fringes fastened at the four corners of the *Talith* and of the so-called *arba kanfot* (meaning "four corners"); the latter is a short rectangular undergarment with neck-hole and open sides, worn by orthodox Jews every day as a reminder of the duty of the Jew toward the Law.

TZOM (Hebrew) : Fast, fasting.

VA-YITEN-L'HA (Hebrew) : Literally "and may God give thee"; these words begin a series of Biblical blessings which the Bene Israel recite during their *malida* ritual (see glossary of Indian terms, p. 378; sometimes they call the ritual itself "a *Va-Yiten-L'ha*".

YEHUDI (plural YEHUDIM) (Hebrew) : Jew.

YESHIVAH (Hebrew) : Literally "sitting, dwelling, settlement, meeting, session"; a Jewish orthodox high school or rabbinical college, the scholars devoting all their time (and sometimes for a lifetime) to Jewish religious studies, while being supported by donations in money and in kind from other Jews.

YIBUM (Hebrew) : Levirate marriage.

YOM KIPPUR : The Jewish High Holiday of fasting and atonement, on the 10th of *Tishre* (end of September or beginning of October).

Bibliography

A. REFERENCE WORKS

American Jewish Year Book; prepared by the American Jewish Committee and published by them and the Jewish Publication Society of America, Philadelphia, 1953, Volume 54; 420pp.

Bene Israel Annual and Year Book; edited by Rebecca Reuben; Volume I 1917-1918, Bombay; Volume II 1918-1919, Bombay; Volume III 1919-1920, Junagadh.

Bene Israel Conference Reports; The First Bene Israel Conference 1917, compiled and published by Solomon Moses, in English and Marathi, Bombay 1918, v. 160pp.; Education Fund's publication of Reports of Conferences in 1918, 1919, 1920, 1923, 1924, 1927 and 1928.

CENSUSES :

The Census of the Islands of Bombay and Colaba, by Col. Sykes: Journal of the Statistics Society of London, December, 1952.

Census of the Islands of Bombay, February 1864 : Table XLI, "Number of Jews of Different Ages Present in Bombay and its Different Divisions and Sections of the City"; printed for Government at the Education Society's Press, Byculla, Bombay, 1864.

Census of India 1881 : "Jewish Population of India".

Census of India 1891 : "Jewish Population of India".

Census of India 1901 : Volume IX, *Bombay;* Part I, Report by R. E. Enthoven; Chapter III, "Religion and Sect"; Government Central Press, Bombay, 1902.

Census of India 1911 : Volume VII, *Bombay;* Part I, Report by P. J. Mead and C. Laird Macgregor; Chapter III, "Religion and Sect".

Census of India 1921 : Volume VIII, *Bombay Presidency;* Part I, "General Report" by L. J. Sedgwick; Section 11, "Religious Composition of the Population, Judaism", para. 215; Government Central Press, Bombay, 1922.

Census of India 1931 : Volume VIII, *Bombay Presidency;* Part I, "General Report" by A. H. Dracup and H. T. Sorley; Chapter XI, p. 364, para. 13, "Religion" with "Table of Jewish Population and Distribution from 1881 to 1931"; Government Central Press Bombay, 1933.

Census of India 1941 : Volume III, *Bombay Presidency;* and Volume I.

Census of India, Delhi, 1943.

Census of India 1951 : Bombay State.

Census of India 1961 : Volume I, Part II-C (i), "Social and Cultural Tables"; printed by Government of India Press, Simla and published by the Manager of Publications, Delhi, 1965.

A Guide to the 1961 Census Publication Programme : Office of the Registrar

General, India, Ministry of Home Affairs, New Delhi, Government of India Press, 1965, 230pp.

Census of India 1971 :
Census Centenary Monograph Series, published by the office of the Registrar General, India, Ministry of Home Affairs, New Delhi 11.
 No. 1, "Indian Census in Perspective", by S. C. Srivastava, 1972, 416pp.
 No. 2, "Indian Census Through A Hundred Years", by D. Natarajan, with "Excerpts from Reports of the Censuses Held Earlier to the Census of 1871-72"
 Volume I, Part II – C (i) : "Social and Cultural Tables 1971".
 Series 11, Part II – A : "Maharashtra General Population Tables 1971". Part I, Chapters I and II.
District Census Handbook, Kolaba, Census of India, for 1961; also for 1971; published in 1964 and 1973 respectively, by the Director Government Printing and Stationery, Maharashtra State, Bombay.

GAZETTEERS; Government Central Press, Bombay :
 1882, Bombay Presidency, Vol. XIII, Part I : *Poona* and *Thana.*
 1883, Bombay Presidency, Vol. XV, Part I : *Kanara;* Vol. XI, The *Konkan : Kolaba* and *Janjira,* pp. 421-82.
 1884, Bombay Presidency, Vol. XXI.
 1885, Bombay Presidency, Vol. XVIII, Parts II and III : *Deccan* and *Poona.*
 1896, Bombay Presidency, Vol. I, Part II : History of the *Konkan, Dakkan,* and *Southern Maratha Country.*
 1900, Bombay City, Vols. I and II.
 1926, Bombay Presidency, Vol. XI-B : *Kolaba* and *Janjira.*
 1954, Revised Bombay State Gazetteer, Vol. XX, *Poona* and *Thana Districts.*
 1964, Maharashtra State Gazetteer, Kolaba District; the second (revised) edition of the 1883 *Gazetteer on Kolaba District.*
 The original 1883 edition had been "Set up in Linotype Georgian and printed letterpress in India by the Manager, Government Press, Nagpur". Its 1964 edition was published by the Directorate of Printing and Stationery, Maharashtra State.

The Indian Directory, 1905; Thacker, Spink and Company, Calcutta, 1905.

ISRAEL CENTRAL BUREAU OF STATISTICS :
 Israel Central Bureau of Statistics, Ministry of Immigrant Absorption, and Jewish Agency Aliya and Absorption Department : *Immigration to Israel,* Part II, "Composition by Period of Immigration"; published by the Central Bureau of Statistics, Jerusalem.

Year concerned	Special Series Number	Date of Publication
1948-1972	489	1975
1973	457	1974
1974	503	1976
1975	528	1976
1976	547	1977
1977	580	1978
1978	632	1980

Year concerned	Special Series Number	Date of Publication
1979	642	1980
1980	672	1981
1981	706	1983
1982	723	1983
1983	747	1984

Statistical Abstract of Israel 1981, No. 32, Jerusalem, 1981.

Letters of Jews Through the Ages, edited by Frans Kobler; published by the Ararat Publishing Society in conjunction with the East-West Library, London, 1952; Vol. 1.

Statistical Abstract for British India, seventy-second number (18th number of New Series) presented by the Secretary of State for India to Parliament by command of His Majesty's Stationery Office, 1943.

B. BOOKS

ALI, S. Muzafer : *The Geography of the Puranas;* People's Publishing House, New Delhi, 1966; 234pp.

ASHLEY-BROWN, W. (Archdeacon of Bombay, Senior Chaplain Indian Ecclesiastical Establishment) : *On the Bombay Coast and Deccan, the Origin and History of the Bombay Diocese, a Record of 300 Years' Work for Christ in Western India;* Society for Promoting Christian Knowledge, Northumberland Avenue, W.C.2, London, 1937.

ASHTAMKAR, Benjamin Samson : "Preface" to *Colonel Wahab's Notes on the Jews Serving in the Bombay Army* with Ashtamkar's translation into Marathi of Wahab's 12-page English text; Ashtamkar's 3-page Preface is in English; printed at the Education Society's Press, Byculla, Bombay, 1879.

BARON, Salo Wattmayer : *A Social and Religious History of the Jews,* 3 volumes; Columbia University Press, New York, 1937.

BENJAMIN, Israel Joseph : *Un An de Séjour aux Indes Orientales,* 1849-1850; traduit de l'Hebreu par D.L., Alger, Imprimere Typographique de Dubos Freres, Rues Bab. Azoun et Sainte; 1854; 25pp.

(BENJAMIN II, I.J.) : *Eight Years in Asia and Africa, from* 1846-1855; published by the author in Hanover, 1863; 376pp.

BEN ZVI, Itzhak : *The Exiled and the Redeemed, the Strange Jewish 'Tribes' of the Diaspora;* translated from the Hebrew by Isaac A. Abbady; Valentine, Mitchell, and Company Ltd., London, 1958; 334pp.

BETEILLE, André : *Castes : Old and New, Essays in Social Structure and Social Stratification;* Asia Publishing House, Bombay, 1969; 254pp.

BUCHANAN, Rev. Claudius ; *Christian Researches in Asia :* Second Edition published by Samuel T. Armstrong, Cornhill, Boston, 1811 (pp. 171-206); Fifth Edition published by T.Caldwell and W. Davies, the Strand, London, 1812 (pp. 210-49).

CADELL, Sir Patrick : *History of the Bombay Army;* Longmans, Green and Company, Bombay, 1938.

CASPI, Mishael Maswari : "Wedding Customs of the Jews of Cochin According to the Book of Poems and the Songs of Praise"; in *Jewish Tradition in the Diaspora, studies in memory of Professor Walter J. Fischel*, edited by Mishael M. Caspi, Judah L. Magnes Memorial Museum, Berkeley, California, 1981; pp. 231-8.

CHINMULGUND, P.J. and MIRASHI, V.V. (eds.) : *Review of Indological Research in the Last 75 Years;* published by Vinayak S. Chitrao under the joint auspices of M. N. Chitraoshastri Felicitation Committee and Bharatiya Charitrakasha Mandal, Poona, 1967; 845pp.

Chronology of the Past Events of Jews in India, published by Isaac Saddick on behalf of the Israelite Society, 1921, (Bombay?); 14pp., lists 55 "events"; in Marathi.

COHEN, Israel : *The Journal of a Jewish Traveler,* The Bodley Head, J. Lane, London, 1925; 288pp.

DA CUNHA, J. Gerson : *Notes on the History and Antiquities of Cheul and Bassein;* Thacker, Vining and Company, Bombay, 1876; xvi + 262pp.
The Origin of Bombay.

DANIEL, Arthur Judah (Korlekar) : Unpublished manuscript describing his Pilot Training and Apprenticeship (1931) for the Bengal Pilot Service; also the History of the Bengal Pilot Service; 171pp. written in the mid-1950s.

DATTA, B. and SINGH, A. N. : *History of Hindu Mathematics;* Asia Publishing House, Bombay, 1962.

DAVIDSON, Israel : *Thesaurus of Medieval Hebrew Poetry,* Ktav Publishing House Inc., Jerusalem, 1970.

DAVIES, C. Colin : *An Historical Atlas of the Indian Peninsula;* Oxford University Press, second edition, Madras, 1959; 96pp.

D'BETH HILLEL, Rabbi David : *The Travels of Rabbi David D'Beth Hillel : from Jerusalem, through Arabia, Koordistan, Part of Persia, and India to Madras;* printed for the author. Madras, 1832.

DIVEKAR, Ezekiel Solomon : *The Life of Haeem Solomon Kehimkar;* printed by Moshe Avraham Gadkar, Bombay, 1923; 24pp. in Marathi.

DUBOIS, Abbe J.A. : *Hindu Manners, Customs and Ceremonies;* translated from the author's later French manuscript and edited with notes, corrections, and biography by Henry K. Beauchamp; Oxford at the Clarendon Press, 1906, Third Edition, 741pp.; reprinted in 1953.

EGERTON, Lady Francis (Harriet Catherine) : *Journal of a Tour in the Holy Land in May and June 1840*, with lithographic views from original drawings by Lord Francis Egerton; for private circulation only : for the benefit of the Ladies Hibernian Female School Society; London, printed by Harrison and Company, St. Martin's Lane, 1841.

ELIAS, Flower and COOPER, Judith Elias ; *The Jews of Calcutta : the Autobiography of a Community;* Jewish Association of Calcutta, Calcutta, 1974; 243pp.

ELLIOT, Sir H.M. : *The History of India as Told by Its Own Historians : The Muhammadan Period;* the Posthumous Papers of the Late Sir H. M. Elliot, edited by Prof. John Dowson; Susil Gupta (India) Ltd., Calcutta; First Edition 1867; Second Edition 1956; 138pp.

ENTHOVEN, R.E. : *Folklore of the Konkan;* compiled from materials collected by the late A. M. T.Jackson, Indian Civil Service; Cosmo Publications, Delhi; first published in 1915, reprinted in 1976; 92pp. plus 37pp. appendix-glossary.

EZEKIEL, Isaac A. : *Sarmad, Jewish Saint of India;* Radha Soami Satsang, Beas,

Punjab, 1966; printed by N. K. Gossain and Company, Calcutta; 384pp.

EZEKIEL, Moses : *History and Culture of the Bene-Israel in India;* published by the author at J. and J. College of Science, Nadiad, October 4, 1948; 123pp.

FERISHTA, Mahomed Kasim : *History of the Rise of Mahomedan Power in India till the year A.D. 1612,* "translated from the original Persian by John Briggs, to which is added an Account of the Conquest by the Kings of Hyderabad, of those parts of the Madras Provinces denominated The Ceded Districts and Northern Circas; with copious notes, in Four Volumes"; (first edition, London 1829) published by S. Dey from Editions India, reprinted 1966, Calcutta.

FISCHEL, Walter J.:

"The Bible in Persian Translation"; *Harvard Theological Review,* Vol. XLV, No. 1, January 1952; 45pp.

"Bombay in Jewish History in the Light of New Documents from the Indian Archives"; American Academy for Jewish Research, Vol. 38-39 of *Proceedings;* New York, 1972; pp. 119-44.

"David D'Beth Hillel : an Unknown Jewish Traveller in the Middle East and India in the 19th Century"; *Oriens,* Journal of the International Society for Oriental Research, Vol. X, No. 2, edited by E. J. Brill, Leiden, 1957; pp. 240-47.

"Garcia de Orta—a Militant Marrano in Portuguese India in the 16th Century"; *Salo Wittmayer Baron Jubilee Volume,* American Academy for Jewish Research, *Proceeding,* New York, 1970; pp 115-39.

The Haggadah of The Bene Israel of India, a photo-reprint of the 1846 lithographed *Haggadah Shel Pesach* in Marathi and Hebrew; with Introduction and Note by Walter J. Fischel; published by the Orphan Hospital Ward of Israel, 673 Broadway, New York, as Vol. VIII, 1968, part of their series of prints of old Haggadoth.

Ha-Yehudim B'Hodu (in Hebrew) :"The Jews in India. Their Contribution to the Economic and Political Life"; published by the Ben Zvi Institute, The Hebrew University, Jerusalem, 1960; 215pp.

"A Hitherto Unknown Jewish Traveler to India, The Travels of Rabbi David D'Beth Hillel to India (1828-1832)"; from *In the Time of Harvest,* Essays in Honor of Abba Hillel Silver Jubilee, Macmillan Publishing Co., New York, 1963; pp. 170-85.

"The Immigration of Arabian Jews to India in the Eighteenth Century"; American Academy for Jewish Research, *Proceedings,* Vol. XXXII, New York, 1965; pp.1-20.

"The Indian Archives A Source for the History of the Jews of Asia" (from the 16th century on); in the 75th Anniversary Volume of the *Jewish Quarterly Review,* edited by Abraham A. Newman and Solomon Zeitlin, Philadelphia, 1967; pp.193-209.

"Jews and Judaism at the Court of the Moghul Emperors in Medieval India"; American Academy for Jewish Research, *Proceedings,* Vol. 18, New York, 1949; pp. 137-77.

"The Literary Activities of the 'Bene-Israel' in India"; *Jewish Book Annual,* Vol. 29, 1971-72; Jewish Book Council of America, New York.

Unknown Jews in Unknown Lands, The Travels of Rabbi David D'Beth Hillel (1824-1832); edited with an Introduction and Notes by Walter J. Fischel; Ktav Publishing House Inc., New York, 1973; 130pp.

GAIROLA, C.K. : "Western Indian Guilds and International Trade in Ancient India, c.1st-2nd Centuries, A.D."; in the *Journal of the M.S. University of Baroda,* Vol. XIV, No. 1, April 1965; pp. 1-16.

GHURYE, G.S. : *Caste, Class and Occupation;* Popular Book Depot, Bombay, 1961; 356pp.

GIDNEY, Rev. W.T. : *The History of the London Society for Promoting Christianity Among the Jews, from 1809 to 1908;* London Society for Promoting Christianity Among the Jews, 16 Lincoln's Inn Fields, W.C., London, 1908; 672pp.

GIL, Moshe, "The Radhanite Merchants and the Land of Radhān; *Journal of the Economic and Social History of the Orient,* Vol. XVII, Part 3, pp. 299-328; E. J. Brill, Leiden, 1974.

GINZBURG, Louis : *The Legends of the Jews;* translated from the German manuscript by Paul Radin, in five volumes; Jewish Publication Society of America, Philadelphia, 1911.

GOITEIN, Shelomo Dov :

"From Aden to India; Specimens of the Correspondence of India Traders of the Twelfth Century"; *Journal of the Economic and Social History of the Orient,* Vol. XXIII, Part I and II, pp. 43-66; E. J. Brill, editor, Leiden, 1980.

"Jewish India Merchants of the Middle Ages"; *India and Israel,* monthly, Vol. V, No. 12, June 1953, Bombay.

Jews and Arabs, Their Contacts through the Ages, Schocken Books, New york, 3rd edition, 1974.

Letters of Medieval Jewish Traders, translated from the Arabic with Introduction and Notes by S.D. Goitein; Princeton University Press, 1973; 359pp.; especially Chapter V, "The India Traders", pp. 175-229.

A Mediterranean Society, the Jewish Communities of the Arab World as Portrayed in the Documents of the Cairo Geniza; University of California Press, Berkeley and Los Angeles; Vol. I, 1967; Vol. II, 1971.

"Yemenite Jewry and Jewish India Trade" in Hebrew, *Yahdut Teman u-S'har Hodu ha-Yehudi;* published in *Yahdut Teman Pirke Mehkar v'Iyun,* Ben Zvi Institute. Jerusalem, 1976; pp. 47-69.

GRAHAM, Maria : *Journal of a Residence in India,* Longman, London, 1813.

GREENBAUM, Aaron : *Report on India, visited February-March 1966;* for the American Joint Distribution Committee, 10 King George Street, Jerusalem; 37 pp.

GUSSIN, Carl Mark : *The Bene Israel of India : Politics, Religion and Systematic Change;* Ph. D. dissertation, Anthropology Department, Syracuse University, 1972; 214 pp.

HASHIMI, B.A.; "Sarmad : His Life and Quatrains"; *Islamic Culture,* Vol. 7, 1933, pp. 663-72 and Vol. 8, 1934, pp. 92-104; Government Central Press, Hyderabad-Deccan.

HOOPER, J.S.M. : *The Bible in India;* Oxford University Press, Humphrey Milford, London, 1938.

HUDSON, Barbara Johnson, see JOHNSON, Barbara Cottle.

HUSAIN, Sheikh Abrar : *Marriage Customs Among Muslims in India;* Sterling Publishers Pvt. Ltd., Delhi, 1976; 226 pp.

ISENBERG, Shirley Berry :

"The Jews of India : Collating the Data and Suggestions for Further Research";

published in *Jews in India,* edited by Thomas Timberg, Vikas Publishing House Pvt. Ltd., New Delhi, 1986; and Advent Books Inc., New York, 1986,pp. 48-58.

"Paradoxical Outcome of Meeting of Bene Israel and Christian Missionaries in Nineteenth Century India"; published in *Jews in India,* edited by Thomas Timberg, Vikas Publishing House Pvt. Ltd., New Delhi, 1986; and Advent Books Inc., New York, 1986, pp. 348-360.

ISENBERG, Shirley Berry and ISRAEL, Benjamin Jacob : "The Bene Israel", a revision of, with corrections and additions to, Walter J. Fischel's article on the Bene Israel which appeared in the original edition of Keter's *Encyclopaedia Judaica;* 1975/76 *Encyclopaedia Judaica Year Book,* pp. 244-7, and *Encyclopaedia Judaica Decennial Book 1973-1982,* pp. 178-81, Keter Publishing House Jerusalem Ltd.

ISRAEL, Benjamin Jacob:
- "Age of Marriage Among the Bene Israel: Some Statistics of 1881"; in B.J. Israel's *The Bene Israel of India: Some Studies;* Orient Longman Ltd., Bombay, 1984 pp. 167-86.
- *The Bene Israel of India: Some Studies;* Orient Longman Ltd., Bombay, 1984, 248 pp.
- "Bene Israel Surnames and Their Village Links"; in B.J. Israel's *The Bene Israel of India: Some Studies;* pp. 120-66.
- "The Jewish Population of Kulaba District, Maharashtra, India : A Demographic Study Based on Census Reports for 1961 and 1971"; in B. J. Israel's *The Bene Israel of India: Some Studies;* pp. 98-119.
- *The Jews of India,* published by E. Kolet for the Centre for Jewish and Inter-faith Studies, Jewish Welfare Association, New Delhi, 1982, 55 pp.; later incorporated as the introductory Chapter (1) to B. J. Israel's *The Bene Israel of India : Some Studies,* pp. 1-52.
- *Khan Bahadur Jacob Bapuji Israel, A Personal Sketch,* originally published for private circulation by B. J. Israel, Bombay, 1960, printed by G. G. Pathare at the Popular Press Pvt. Ltd., 50 pp.; later incorporated as the final Chapter (7) of B. J. Israel's book *The Bene Israel of India : Some Studies,* pp. 187-242.
- "Religious Evolution Among the Bene Israel of India Since 1750"; in B. J. Israel's *The Bene Israel of India : Some Studies,* pp. 53-87; originally published by B.J. Israel, printed by G. G. Pathare at Popular Press Pvt. Ltd., Bombay, 1963, 22 pp.

JACKSON, Stanley : *The Sasoons;* Heinemann, London, 1968; 304 pp.

JACOB, E. M. (Gadkar) : *"Gate of Mercy" Synagogue, The Religious and Cultural Heritage of the Bene Israels of India,* Book I (photographs) 54 pp.; and Book II, texts and more photographs, 182 pp; published by E. M. Jacob Gadkar, for the Gate of Mercy Synagogue, Bombay, 1984.

JACOBS, Joseph : *Jewish Contribution to Civilization, an Estimate;* Jewish Publication Society, Philadelphia, 1919; 334 pp.

JOHNSON, Barbara Cottle :
- *Shingli or Jewish Cranganore in the Traditions of the Cochin Jews of India* with an Appendix on "The Cochin Jewish Chronicles"; M. A. Thesis, Department of Religion, Smith College, May 1975; 218 pp.
- "The Social Context of Malayalam Songs among the Cochin Jews : Women's Folk Culture and Boundary Maintenance"; a paper delivered at the Association for Jewish Studies Eleventh Annual Conference, Boston, December 1979; 12 pp.

KARVE, Iravati : *Maharashtra, Land and Its People;* Maharashtra State Gazetteers, General Series; printed by the Manager of the Central Press, Bombay and published by the Director of Government Printing, 1968.

KEHIMKAR, Haeem Samuel :
The History of the Bene-Israel of India; written in 1897 but not published until 1937, by the Dayag Press Ltd., Tel Aviv; viii, 290 pp. and 26 pp. of photographs; copyright and editing by Dr. Immanuel Olsvanger, Jerusalem.
A Sketch of the History of the Beni-Israel and An Appeal for Their Education; printed at the Education Society's Press, Byculla, Bombay, 1892; 38 pp.

KOLABKAR, S. J. : *Kolaba Travels Investigations;* printed at the New Diamond Printing Press, Karachi, 1946; 9 pp.

LORD, Rev. J. Henry :
"Bene Israel", an article in *The Encyclopaedia of Religion and Ethics,* edited by James Hastings; T. & T. Clark, Edinburgh, 1909; Vol. II, pp. 469-74.
The Jewish Mission Field in the Bombay Diocese, being a Paper read before the Bombay Diocesan Conference held in March 1893, Bombay; printed at the Education Society's Steam Press, Byculla, 1894; 94 pp.
The Jews in India and the Far East, a reprint of articles contributed to *Church and Synagogue,* with Appendices; printed at the Mission Press, Kolhapur, 1907; 120 pp. plus 17 pp. of appendices.

MAGGID HADASHOTH : see below, WEISEL, N.H.

MAHADEVAN, Meera Jacob (Mendrekar) : *Shulamit,* Arnold Heinemann, New Delhi, 1975, 208pp; translated from the Hindi novel entitled *Apna Ghar* first published in 1961 by Rajkamal Prakashan Pvt., Ltd., Delhi.

MANDELBAUM, David G. : *Society in India;* University of California Press; Berkeley, Los Angeles, London; 1970; in two Volumes.

MC-CRINDLE's Ancient India as Described by Ptolemy, a Facsimile Reprint, edited with an introduction, notes and an additional map by Surendranath Majmudar Sastri; Chuckervertty, Chatterjee and Co., Inc., Calcutta, 1927; xxvii + 431pp.

MODI, Shams ul-ulma Jivanji Jamshedi : "Kiss of Peace among the Bene Israels of Bombay and the Hamazor among the Parsees"; *Journal of the Anthropological Society of Bombay,* Vol. VIII, No. 2, 1907-8; pp. 84-95.

MUJEEB, M. : *The Indian Muslims;* George Allen and Unwin Ltd., London, 1967; 590 pp.

MUSLEAH, Rabbi Ezekiel N. : *On the Banks of the Ganga, the Sojourn of Jews in Calcutta;* Christopher Publishing House, North Quincy, Massachusetts, 1975; 568 pp.

NAINAR, S. Muhammed Husayn : *Arab Geographers' Knowledge of Southern India,* University of Madras, Madras, 1942.

NEUMAN, Stephanie : *The Jews of India, A Study in Majority-Minority Relations ;* M.A. Thesis, Department of Government, New York University, New York, June 1960.

NISSIM, Meyer : "When I Was Mayor of Bombay"; in *India and Israel,* No. 3, p. 14, September 1948; Sanj Vartaman Press, Bombay.

RABINOWITZ, Louis Issac :
Far East Mission, printed by the Eagle Press, Johannesburg, 1952; 223pp.

Jewish Merchant Adventurers, A Study of the Radanites; Edward Goldston, London, 1948; 212pp.

RAHABI, Ezekiel : "Letter of 1768"; published by Naphtali Herz Weisal (Wesseley) in *Ha-Measef,* Koenigsberg and Berlin, 1790; pp. 257-76 of the Third Period Section of Volume 6; in Hebrew.

RANADE, M. G. : *Rise of the Maratha Power and Other Essays,* and TELANG, K. T. : *Gleanings from Maratha Chronicles;* both in one volume published by the University of Bombay, March 1961, 236pp.

REINEMANN, Solomon : *Masa'ot Shelomo B'Eretz Hodu, Burman, V'Sinim* (Travels of Solomon in India, Burma, and China); edited by Wolff Schur; published by Schur in 1884, printed at the Georg Breg Press under P. Smolenskin, Vienna; 204pp.; in Hebrew.

REISSNER, H. G. :
"Indian Jewish Statistics, 1837-1941"; *Jewish Social Studies,* Volume XII, New York, 1950; pp. 349-65.
"The Jews of India"; *India and Israel,* Volume 1, No. 1, July 1948, pp. 12-3; and No. 2, August 1948, pp. 14-5.
"The Ummi Prophet and the Banu Israil of the Qur'an"; *The Muslim World,* a quarterly review of history, culture, religions and the Christian Mission in Islam, edited by Edwin E. Calverly, the Hartford Seminary Foundation, Hartford, 1949; Volume 39, pp. 276-81.
"Yehudai Hodu" (Jews of India); *Yalkut Ha-Mizrach Hatichon,* Jewish Agency, Jerusalem, May-June 1950, pp. 65-79; in Hebrew.

RENFORD, Raymond K.:
"Missionary Records and Indian Ocean Studies", 9 pp. Section VI (Archives and Resources for Study) of the *Documents of the International Conference on Indian Ocean Studies,* Perth, Western Australia, August 1979.
The Non-official British in India to 1920, Oxford University Press, Delhi, 1987; 468pp.

REUBEN, Judge Ezra : *The Housing Problem and the Bene Israels,* Bombay, 1920; 30pp.

REUBEN, Rebecca :
Bene Israel Annual and Year Book, edited by Rebecca Reuben; Volume I : April 1, 1917-March 31, 1918, published in Bombay. Volume II : April 1, 1918-Sept. 24, 1919, published in Bombay. Volume III : Sept. 25, 1919-Sept. 12, 1920, published in Junagadh.
The Bene Israel of Bombay, Cambridge Jewish Publications 4, Cambridge University Press, Cambridge, England, 1913; 20 pp.
"Religious Reorganization"; *The Bene Israel Annual and Year Book,* Volume III; p. xviii.

ROBI, Naphtali : *History of the House of Rahabi in Cochin ;* unpublished, hand-written manuscript, written in 1939, Cochin; 63 pp; in Hebrew.

ROLAND, Joan G. :
"A Decade of Vitality : Bene Israel Communal Development, 1917-1927"; *Jews in India,* edited by Thomas Timberg, Vikas Publishing House Private Ltd., Delhi; and Advent Books Inc., New York, 1986, pp. 285-347.
"The Jews of India : Communal Survival or the End of a Sojourn?"; *Jewish Social Studies,* Volume XLII, No. 1, Winter 1980, New York City; pp. 75-90.
"Modern Bombay Jewry : Bene Israel Communal Activity, 1880-1930"; paper presented at Conference on Jewish Social Studies, Boston, December 1979.

ROTH, Cecil : *The Sassoon Dynasty;* R. Hale Ltd., London, 1941; 280pp.

SAMUEL, Shellim :
"The Succath Shelomo Synagogue, Poona, on the Occasion of its Golden Jubilee, and the Enlightened and Progressive Jewish Community of Poona"; *Shalom*, Special Number on The Jews of Poona, published for the Indian Zionist Organisation of Bombay, mid-1971; pp. 1-8.
A Treatise on the Origin and Early History of the Beni-Israel of Maharashtra State; printed by Iyer and Iyer Pvt. Ltd., Bombay, 1963; 175pp. plus index.

SAPIR, Yaakov Halevi : *Eben Sapir;* L. Silbermann, Lyck, 1866; two volumes in one, Volume II, pp. 35 - 144 on India; in Hebrew.

SASSOON, David Solomon : compiler of *Ohel Dawid*, a Descriptive Catalogue of the Hebrew and Samaritan manuscripts in the Sassoon Library, London; in two volumes; Humphrey Milford, Oxford University Press, London, 1932.

SASTRI, K. A. Nilakanta : *History of India*, published by S. Viswanathan, Madras : Part I, *Ancient India*, 2nd edition, 1953, 330pp; Part II, *Medieval India*, 1st edition, 1950, 355pp; Part III, *Modern India*, 1st edition, 1952, 459pp.

Shaare Rason Synagogue (90 Tantanpura Street, Khadak, Bombay 400 009) *1840-1968, A Brief Retrospect;* published by David Judah Samuel Pugaonkar, Bombay, 1975; 35pp.

SHAPURKAR, Abraham Samson : *Samuel Ezekiel Hassaji (Shmuel Ezekiel Divekar), Commodan Mukkadam;* published by Samuel Yehudah Chincholkar, Byculla, Bombay, 1927; 16pp. printed 1500 copies; in Marathi.

SHARAR, Abdul Halim : *Lucknow : The Last Phase of an Oriental Culture*, translated from the original Urdu and edited by E. S. Harcourt and Fakir Hussain; published by Paul Eleke, London 1975, as part of the Indian Series of Translations Collection of UNESCO; 295pp.

SINCLAIR, W.F. : "Notes of Castes in the Puna and Solapur Districts"; *The Indian Antiquary*, No. 3, Bombay, 1874.

SMITH, George : *Life of John Wilson, D. D., F.R.S., for Fifty Years Philanthropist and Scholar in the East;* John Murray, Albemarle Street, London, 1878; 652pp.

SOOD, Margaret Ann; *The Urban Middle Class Family in India;* Experimental Study Unit Series, Educational Resources Center, New Delhi, 1974; 40pp.

SRINIVAS, M. N. : *Social Change in Modern India*, Allied Publishers, Bombay, 1966; 194pp.

STERNBACH, Ludwik : "Jews in Medieval India as mentioned by Western Travellers"; *Proceedings of the Indian History Congress*, 9th Session, Allahabad, 1960; Bharatiya Vidya Bhavan, Bombay; pp 169-96.

STRIZOWER, Schifra :
"The Bene Israel"; *Journal of the Anthropological Society of Bombay*, Bombay, 1956; pp. 49-58.
"The Bene Israel in Israel"; *Middle Eastern Studies*, Volume 2, No. 2, January 1966, pp. 123-43; Frank Cass and Company Ltd., London.
The Children of Israel : The Bene Israel of Bombay; Pavilion Series, Social Anthropology, Basil Blackwell, Oxford, 1971; xiv, 176pp.
Exotic Jewish Communities; Popular Jewish Library (prepared by the World Jewish Congress); Thomas Yoseloff, London and New York, 1962; 157pp.
"Jews as an Indian Caste"; *The Jewish Journal of Sociology*, Volume I, No. 1, April 1959, pp. 43-57; published on behalf of the World Jewish Congress by William Heinemann Ltd., London.

The Tribal Jews of the Far North East India, a 34 page booklet published by the Beyth Shalom Prayer Hall of the Manipuri Jews of Churachandpur (in Manipur).

TIMBERG, Thomas A. (ed.) . *Jews in India,* Advent Books, Inc., New York, 1986 by special arrangement with Vikas Publishing House Pvt. Ltd., New Delhi, 1986; 373 pp.

VAKRULKAR, Solomon M. : *Our Synagogues and Their Functions;* an address to the Bene-Isreal delivered in Bombay under the auspices of the Bene-Israel Club, Dec. 8, 1907; published by Abraham Reuben Bhinjekar, Bombay, 1909; 24pp.

WALI, Maulavi Abdul, Khan Sahib : "A Sketch of the Life of Sarmad"; *Journal and Proceedings of the Asiatic Society of Bengal,* Volume 20, Article No. 11, pp. 111-22; printed at the Baptist Mission Press, Calcutta, 1925.

WALKAR, Simeon Benjamin : *Rebeka Simeon Benjamin Walkar; Reformer, Educationist, Philanthropist;* translated from Marathi into English by I. A. Isaac, Calcutta, 1925; 146pp.

WEIL, Shalva : *Bene Israel Indian Jews in Lod. Israel : A Study of the Persistence of Ethnicity and Ethnic Identity,* Ph. D. dissertation, Division of Anthropology, University of Sussex, England, 1977; 384pp.

WEINSTEIN, Judah : "Yehudai-Bavel B'Hodu" (Babylonian Jews in India); *Shluchot,* No. 26, Iyar-Sivan, 1951; Jerusalem; pp. 17-9; in Hebrew.

WEISEL (or Wesseley), Naphtali Hertz : in his Hebrew periodical *Ha-Measef,* Koenigsberg and Berlin, 1790 :
   "Ezekiel Rahabi's Letter of 1768"; Volume 6, Third Period, pp. 257-76.
   "Maggid Hadashoth"; Volume 6, Second Period, pp. 129-65.

WILSON, Rev. John :
   "Abstract of an Account of the Beni-Israel of Bombay, Read before the Bombay Branch of the Royal Asiatic Society, at the Anniversary Meeting in November 1838 and 1839"; *The Oriental Christian Spectator,* Volume 11, No. 1, January 1840; pp. 27-36.
   "The Bene Israel of Bombay"; *The Indian Antiquary,* November 1874, pp. 321-3.
   The Bene Israel of Bombay; An Appeal for Their Christian Education; published in Edinburgh 1852, in Bombay 1854, and a second edition in Edinburgh 1865; partially quoted in *The Jewish Chronicle* (London), December 7, 1866, p. 2; the complete text not located.
   Lands of the Bible, in two volumes; William Whyte and Company, Edinburgh, 1847; in 2 volumes, Vol. I has 504pp., Vol. II has 786pp. Volume II : "The Beni-Israel of Bombay" on pp. 667-78 and "The Jews at Cochin" on pp. 678-82.

WOLFE, Rev. Joseph :
   Researches and Missionary Labours Among the Jews, Mahomedans and Other Sects; James Nisbet and Company, London, second edition 1835; 531pp.
   Travels and Adventures of the Rev. Joseph Wolff, D.D.,LL.D.; Saunders, Otley and Company, West London, 1861.

Wonderful Testimonies (Pla'ot Aydot) : the Old Testament in Hebrew with four different word-by-word English translations placed beneath the Hebrew text (translation no. 1 is the King James Authorized version); in five volumes; published by Pandita Ramabai; printed by Aaron Jacob Divekar at the Mukti Mission Press, Kedgaon, 1910-11.

YAARI, Abraham: *Hebrew Printing in the East (Ha-Dfus Ha-Ivri B'Arzot Ha-mizrah)*, Part II "India and Baghdad"; Special Supplement to *Kriyat Sepher*, Volume XVII, pp. 9-99; Jerusalem at the University Press, 1940; in Hebrew.

YULE, Col. Henry and BURNELL, A.C. : *Hobson-Jobson*, A Glossary of Colloquial Anglo-Indian Words and Phrases, and of Kindred Terms, Etymological, Historical, Geographical and Discursive; (originally published in 1903) second edition edited by William Crooke; Munshiram Manoharlal, Oriental Publishers and Booksellers, Delhi, February 1968; 1021pp.

ZALIZAR, Gerry : "The Road to Wakrul" (Ha-Derech l'Wakrul); in *Gesher* Quarterly, 9th year, (35)2, 1963, pp. 118-21; published by the Israel Branch of the World Jewish Congress; in Hebrew.

C. PERIODICALS

And Ye Shall Teach Them : in English, 1959-1961; a Bulletin published occasionally for the educational, social, cultural and religious uplift of the Bene Israel community of India; edited by Baruch B. Benjamin, New Delhi.

Bene-Israel Review : in English and Marathi, 1925-26, Bombay.

Friend of Israel : in English and Marathi, 1916-1921, Bombay.

India and Israel : English monthly, 1948-53; edited by F. W. Pollack, Bombay.

The Israelite : in English and Marathi, 1917-27; editors : 1917-22, David S. Erulkar; 1923-1926, I.J. Samson; 1926-1927, Khan Bahadur Jacob B. Israel, Bombay.

The Israelite School Bulletin : 1927 —

The Jewish Chronicle (London) : English weekly, London.

The Jewish Tribune : English monthly journal, edited by Joseph Sargon, 1930-1941; Bombay.

Lamp of Judaism: in Marathi and some English; a social, religious and literary journal; edited by Benjamin Samson Ashtamkar 1881-85, and by Samuel Solomon Mazagaonkar 1893-96.

Nofeth : Marathi monthly journal for Jewish children; was published for $3\frac{1}{2}$ years, edited by Rebecca Reuben.

The Oriental Christian Spectator: English monthly journal of Christian missionaries; mostly printed at the American Mission Press, Bombay; edited by Rev. John Wilson; 1830-1863.

Shalom : in English, two to three times a year; edited, printed and published by M.D. Japheth for the Indian Zionist Organization of Bombay, 1969-1974.

Index

Abraham (Patriarch) : 229
Abraham, A.S. : 211
Abraham, D. & Sons : 182, 207 n.4
Abraham, David (Cheulkar) : 210, 211
Abraham, Shalom : 251, 265
Abridgement : 74, 75
Abroad : 188, 258, 266, 304
Absentee : 216, 217
Abstract (Rev. Wilson's) : 74, 81, 88 n.39, 110 n.23
Abyssinian : 25, 26, 30 n.33
Academic, Academy : 20, 28 n.1, 242 n.6
Accomplishment (see Achievement) : 246
Account (of The Beni-Israel, by Wilson) : 74, 75, 81, 88 n.37 and n.40
Accounts :
    Antisemitic : 335
    Bookkeeping : 151, 152, 163
    Viceroy : 239
Achievement : 185, 194, 211, 245, 260
Activities : 261, 263, 264, 266, 268, 271
Actor, Actress : 210, 225
Adaptation : 6, 15, 117, 118, 127, 129, 177
Address (see Road, Speech) : 151, 243, 245, 255 n.9
Aden : 21, 59, 60, 63 n.5, 98, 145 n.22, 284, 285, 289 Table 12c
Administer, Administration : 59, 62, 151, 176, 178, 190 n.4, 199, 224, 233, 234, 235, 244, 248, 253 n.1, 254 n.3, 276, 309
Admiral : 34, 210
Admission : 258, 260, 261, 264, 265
Adoption : 115, 129, 139, 176, 177, 331
Adult : 61, 132, 181, 234, 236, 263, 266, 269, 272
Adultery : 62, 108 n.6, 139, 331, 346
Advancement : 271, 272
Advertisement : 239
Advocate (see Law) : 247, 270
Affluence (see Wealth) : 148, 150, 160, 267 n.5, 271, 272
Affiliation : 237
Afghanistan, Afghans : 9, 24, 186, 187, 269, 270

Age Group, Age of Consent : 137, 138, 142, 213, 228, 279, 286-7 Table 11, 304, 304 n.3
Aged : 275
Agent, Agency : 186, 187, 207 n.4, 270
Agerwada : 222 n.1
Aggarwal, Kashiram : 242 n.8 and n.9
Agitation : 247
Agra : 32 n. 47, 186, 190
Agree : 237
Agriculture (see Farmer) : 200, 216, 222, 273, 328, 329
Ahmedabad : 15 n.17, 37, 59, 149, 176, 181, 183-185, 188, 190, 191 n.8 and n.9, 209, 210, 222, 243, 247, 250, 266, 269, 274, 282
Ahmednagar (Sultanate, District) : 25, 26, 33, 36, 86 n.24, 182, 208, 309, 310
Al Idrisi : 9, 23, 28 n.9
Aims : 269
Airforce : 212 n.4
Aitz Haim (Hayyim) Prayer Hall : 149, 150, 170, 171, 237 n.1
Ajmer : 37, 59, 176, 184, 185, 188, 189, 274
Akaba : 7, 8, 9
Akbar, Emperor : 26, 27, 32 n.47, 41, 42, 47 n.4, 186
Akhtana : 136
Akkara, Akda : 135, 136, 145 n.23
Al-Balkhi, Rabbi Hiwi : 20
Al-Biruni : 20, 23, 28 n.11
Al-Kazwini : 23, 122
Al-Mas'udi : 9
Alcoholic : 125 n.21, 161
Aleppo : 44, 48 n.20, 98
Alexander The Great : 20, 89 n.49
Ali, S. Muzafer : 9, 16 n.42
Alibag : 3, 10, 13, 26, 27, 37 n.4, 60, 66, 70, 106, 149, 153 n.3, 158, 170, 173, 175 n.6, 213, 216, 274, 277, 278, 336
Alienation : 233, 270
Aliyah : 152, 346
All India Federation of Synagogues : 274
All India Israelite League : x, 208, 239, 243-246, 250, 255 n.9, 268
All India Muslim League : 246 n.1, 248, 271

403

Allies : 187, 243
Alphabet : 142, 143 n.4, 155
Altar : 6, 71, 116, 123 n.12
Alumni : 263
Ambassador : 270
Amba River : 216
Ambepur : 10, 149, 150, 213, 274, 336
Amber, Malik (Mullik) : 33, 311
Ambition : 258, 268
Ambivalence : 250, 271
America(n) U.S.A. : 65, 79, 94, 95, 108 n.6(9), 150, 215, 226, 227, 229, 235, 236, 237, 241 n.6, 257, 258, 266, 335
American Jewish Joint Distribution Committee : 261, 262 n.11
American Jewish Year Book : 230 n.4
American Mission : 65, 77, 79, 95
Amidah : 100
Amulet : 127, 143 n.4
Analysis, Analytic : 51, 138, 283
Anashi Dhakacha San : 4, 5
Ancestor, Forefather : 3, 4, 6, 8, 9, 10, 11, 22, 23, 35, 40, 41, 52, 53, 60, 98, 104, 111, 112, 116, 118, 120, 122, 126 n.29, 128, 152 n.1, 155, 158, 169, 216, 220, 221, 244, 246, 264, 277-278, 311, 312, 342
Ancillary Services : 60, 163, 178, 189
"And Ye Shall Teach Them" : 239
Anderson, Prof. B. : xi
Andheri : 225
Anglican (see Church of England) : 73, 82, 90 n.68
Anglicisation : 233
Anglo-Indian : 249, 250
Anglo-Jewish and Vernacular Press : 92, 352
Anglo-Jewish Association, London : 100, 102, 103, 109 n.6(10) and 109 n.10, 169, 171-172 n.4, 233, 259
Angrey (Angria) : 26, 32 n.50, 34, 37 n.4 and n.6, 50, 51, 52, 91, 155, 280 Table 7, 327, 329
Animal : 114, 116, 219, 340
Animist : 257
Ankle(t) : 143 n.4, 166
Anniversary : 142
Anthology : 211
Anthropology, Anthropologist : vii, x, xi, xii, 15-16 n.33, 53 n.1, 104, 146 n.34, 231 n.11, 268
Anti-Defamation League : 272 n.3
Anti-Semitism : viii, ix, xiii n.4, 190, 271
Antiochus Epiphanes : 6, 118
Apathy : 151
"Apna Ghar" : 240
Appeal : 82, 188, 271

Appreciate : 275
Apprentice(ship),Training : 102, 161, 193, 200, 255 n.18
Aptekar, Dr. Segula : 210
Aptekar, Solomon Shalom : 238
Arab : 7, 20, 24, 30 n.25, 72, 177, 271, 309
Arabia : 7, 8, 9, 69, 76, 98, 99
Arabian or Arabic-Speaking Jews : 7, 43, 66, 67, 68, 70, 71, 72, 73, 74, 77, 78, 79, 84, 86 n.11 and n.19, 93, 98, 99, 102, 103, 108 n.6 (2) and (7); 109 n.6 (13), (14) and (15); 182, 207 n.8, 267 n.2, 284, 305 n.10 and n.11, 327, 329, 332, 333, 334
Arabian Sea : xiii n.6, 21
Arabic language : 7, 11, 14 n.9, 19, 20, 21, 28 n.3 and n.11, 43, 66, 73, 76, 98, 101, 103, 191 n.7, 207 n.8
Araki Hacohen, Elazar Ben Mari Aharon Saadiya : 96 n.3
Aramaic : 19
Arbith (Ma'ariv) : 109 n.6
Archaeology, Excavation : viii, 8, 9, 72, 123 n.12, 277
Architect : 184, 188, 199, 211, 269, 278
Archives, Records (see Research) : viii, 3, 21, 25, 27, 34, 38-39 n.19, 39 n.20, 51, 74, 86 n.24, 152, 159 n.12, 207 n.7, 222 n.1, 231 n.11
Areca Nut : 115, 174
Argument : 70, 71, 76, 102, 227, 281
Arithmetic : 66, 335, 345
Ark : 63, 130, 136, 148, 179, 188
Armenians : 36
Army, (see Military, Native Troops, Soldier) : 46, 52, 54 n.13, 60, 69, 138, 161, 162, 169, 176, 178, 185, 194, 199, 210, 212 n.4, 243, 280, 285, 314, 315, 316, 317, 318, 327, 340, 343, 344, 345
Aromatic : 113
Arrest : 249
Art, Arts, Artist : 91, 93, 95, 206, 211, 257, 258
Article : 74, 92, 94, 95, 122, 170, 181, 200, 208, 214, 239, 250, 255 n.18, 257, 281, 282, 283, 305 n.6, 309
Artisan, (see Craftsman) : 91, 161, 163, 176, 178, 184, 185, 191 n.7, 200, 328, 344
Aryan : 104, 110 n.16, 137
Ascetic : 123 n.4
Asher (Tribe of) : 8, 9, 16 n.37
Ashkenazi (Jews) : 41, 79, 90 n.56, 111, 117, 118, 138, 188, 304 n.11, 344
Ashkenazi, Judah David : 45, 341, 342, 346
Ashley-Brown, W. : 90 n.70
Ashtami : 33, 37 n.2, 47 n.13, 60, 68, 149, 158, 213, 219, 222 n.1, 274, 283

Index 405

Ashtamkar : 12, 33, 47 n.13, 51, 91, 93, 96 n.1, and n.11, 158, 159 n.9, 213, 311
Asia : 72, 81, 186
Assam : xiii n.7, 146 n.33
Assembly : 250 .
Assimilation : 104, 106, 168, 199
Assistance : 77, 100, 102, 282
Assistant : 183, 275
Association : 233, 263, 264, 266
Assyria : 8
Atonement (see Yom Kippur) : 4, 5, 125 n.25, 333, 347
Atrocity : 244
Attendance : 66, 237 n.7, 259, 261
Attitude : 101, 110 n.26, 169, 265
Auction : 62, 64 n.15
Aundh : 208, 212 n.1
Aunt : 228
Aurangzeb (Emperor) : 27, 186
Auspices : 275
Auspicious : 111, 114, 115, 117, 124 n.15, 132, 134, 138, 143 n.4 and n.6, 144 n.12 and n.19, 148, 168 n.2
Australia : 190, 273 n.8
Authenticity : 40
Author, Writer : 9, 19, 36, 40, 52, 74, 94, 96 n.11, 97 n.12 and n.13, 208, 209, 210, 211, 238, 240, 241 n.1
Autonomy : 234, 274
Auxiliary : 269
Average : 282
Aviation : 181, 199
Awards : 181, 209, 210, 211, 212 n.3 and n.7, 240, 259
Ayurvedic : 230

Babulbund Cemetery : 182
Baby : 128, 130, 131, 144 n.7, 180, 184, 223 n.11
Babylon, Babylonian : 6, 7, 28 n.1, 71, 89 n.49, 118, 334
Bachelor : 187, 188, 258 B.A.
Background : 103, 188, 275
Backward(ness) : 150, 223 n.8, 235, 270, 304 n.3
Bactria, Balkhi, or Valhi : 20, 28 n.9
Baghdad : 19, 20, 21, 36, 45, 59, 93, 98, 99, 102, 231 n.4, 235
Baghdadi Jewish · viii, x, 36, 38 n.19, 61, 64 n.10, 69, 70, 71, 84, 92, 93, 95, 96 n.3, 98, 99, 100, 101, 102, 103, 107, 108 n.6, 109 n.6 and n.11, 110 n.26, 119, 127, 145 n.21, 148, 149, 150, 152, 152 n.1, 153 n.7, 175 n.2, 178, 179, 181, 182, 183, 187, 190 n.4 and n.7, 194, 200, 205, 211, 225, 226, 234, 235, 236, 240, 245, 260, 261, 264, 265, 266, 267 n.5, 269, 270, 273 n.8, 274, 275, 276, 282 Table 8, 284, 296 Table 16 n.d, 297 Table 17, 298, 303, 304, 305 n.9, 306 n.12 and n.13
Bahadur : 51, 54 n.13, 162, 181, 184, 188, 208, 211, 340
Bahmani Kingdom : 25, 30 n.33
Balcony, Gallery (women's) : 121, 148, 180, 236
Ballads : 91, 223 n.8
Bamnolkar, Dr. Joseph Benjamin : 184, 243
Bandra : 194, 225, 226, 232
Bangladesh : 177, 285
Bangle : 128, 129, 130, 131, 132, 133, 134, 137, 140, 144 n.19, 166
Banihal Pass : 21
Bank, Banker : 151, 154, 184, 186, 205, 245
Bankot : 51, 327
Bankruptcy : 205
Banu Israel : 7, 25, 154
Baptism : 71, 79, 82
Baptist Church : 84
Bar : 265
Bar (& Bat) Mitzvah : 132, 181, 188, 236, 307
Barber : 131
Barkoot : 60, 63 n.10
Baroda : 37, 183, 184, 193, 209
Baron, Salo W : 28 n.2
Barren : 138, 331
Barter : 51
Basra : 14 n.9, 77
Bassein : 9, 24, 31 n.40, 32 n.47, 42, 173, 309
Bath, Bathe (see Mikveh) : 5, 119, 125 n. 24, 128, 131, 132, 134, 140, 141, 142, 144 n.18, 148, 219, 220, 223 n.9, 227, 330
Bay : 36, 309
Beach : 36
Bead : 132, 145 n25
Beard : 72, 167
Bed : 265, 266
Bednur : 318, 322
Bedroll : 219
Beef : 53, 104, 167, 343
Beer Sheva : 171 n.1
Beggar : 223 n.8, 275; Begging : 329
Behaviour : 227
Beheaded : 186
Belgaum : 176, 185
Belief : 235
Bells : 219
Ben Yiju, Abraham : 22, 29 n.17 and n.19
Ben Zvi, Isaac : xiii n.5, 87 n.33

Bene Israel (appellation) : 7, 49, 53 n.3, 124 n.14, 154
Bene Israel Annual and Year Book : 94, 97 n.12, 209, 238
Bene Israel Benevolent Society : 100, 139, 170, 244
Bene Israel Conference, The : x, xiii n.9, 163 n.3, 181, 184, 191 n.8, 206, 208, 225, 226, 227, 239, 243-246, 246 n.2, 250, 255 n.9, 258, 262 n.5, 268
Bene Israel Cooperative Banking Society : 205, 245
Bene Israel Education Fund : 214, 244, 245
Bene Israel Home for Orphans and Destitutes : 152, 205, 224, 234, 245
Bene Israel Kullianechhu Sabha : 139
Bene Israel Prayer Hall Poona : 179, 181
Bene Israel Review : 231 n.14, 239
Bene Israel Youth Convention : 263
"Bene Israelite" (publication) : 95, 194
Benefit : 252, 262, 278 n.4
Bengal : 65, 85 n.1, 90 n.57, 163 n.6, 177, 223 n.8, 253, 256 n. 18, 284
Benjamin, Baruch B. : 188, 239
Benjamin, Dr. E. 210, 212 n.3
Benjamin, Israel Joseph, (same as J.J. Benjamin) : 61, 63 no.10
Benjamin, Dr. Joseph (Bamnolkar) : 184, 191 n.8, 247
Benjamin, Joshua M. : 188, 191 n.19, 210, 278
Benjamin, Khan Bahadur Solomon : 184
Benjamin, S.M. : 252
Benjamin, Sybil : 261
Berar Sultanate : 25
Besant, Dr. Annie : 250
Best, Dr. Eliezer Moses, : 185, 210
Best, Mr. and Mrs. Ralph : 185
Bet Din : 188, 243
Beteille, Dr. Andre : 53 n.1
Betel (see Pan Supari) : 129, 130, 132, 145 n.26, 174
Bethel Synagogue, Ashtami : 149, 213, 274
Beth El Synagogue, Panvel : 149, 174
Beth El Synagogue, Revdanda : 149, 152
Beth Ha-Elohim Synagogue, Pen : 149
Betrothal : 133, 144 n.14, 330
Bhagavad-Gita : 272 n.2
Bhakri : 167, 218
Bhargekar : 223 n.6
Bhiwadi : 173
Bhonkar : Banduji : 83; Solomon Aaron : 179
Bhor : 176, 216
Bhorupkar : 223 n.6
Bible, Books of, Biblical : 3, 4, 5, 6, 7, 9, 10, 12, 14 n.6, 15 n.16 and n.20, 16 n.37 and n.38, 20, 42, 47 n.5, 53, 60, 68, 69, 72, 76, 80, 85, 88 n.49, 91, 92, 93, 96 n.2, 110 n. 26, 112, 114, 117, 123 n.12, 130, 131, 154, 158 n.1, 208, 227, 229, 238, 240, 241 n.3 and n.6, 275, 277, 281, 335, 341; Names : 31 n.38, 154, 158 n.1, 328
Bibliography : x, 82
Bicycle : 215
Bid(ding) : 63, 150, 152, 153 n.3
Bidar Sultanate : 25
Bier : 140, 141
Bigamy (see Polygamy) : 138, 244
Bigotry : 72, 80, 103, 230
Bihar : 209
Bijapur (see also Vijapur) : 25, 26
Bimah : 150, 185, 188, 265
Biography : xiii n.8, 51, 72, 79, 221, 230, 309, 310 n.1, 323
Birdiacha (San or Roja) : 4, 118
Birth (see Childbirth), Born : 10, 72, 200, 216, 239, 243, 271, 272, 303 Table 24, 304, 304 n.3, 330; Register: 158 n.1, 184
Black Jews (see Kala Israel and Malabari Jews) : Bene Israel: 67, 71, 86 n.19 and n.23, 101, 107; Cochini: 40, 41, 42, 106, 107, 232, 305 n.9, 314
Blessing : 71, 111, 114, 121, 131, 135, 136, 142, 143, 150, 218, 229, 234, 265, 281, 282, 332
Blood : 133, 213, 221, 222 n.3
Blouse : 131
B'nai Brith : 269, 272 n.3
Boat : (see Ship and Shipwreck) : 49, 128
Boaz, Tuvia : 43, 48 n.24
Body : 134
Bohra : 146 n.34
Bombay : viii, x, xii, 3, 10, 15 n.17, 23, 24, 25, 31 n.38 and n.40, 32 n.45 and n.50, 34, 35, 36, 38-39 n.19, 42, 43, 44, 45, 46, 47 n.14, 48 n.29, 49, 50, 51, 52, 53, 54 n.8, 55 n.15, 59, 60, 63 n.10, 65, 66, 67, 68, 69, 70, 71, 72, 73, 74, 75, 76, 77, 78, 79, 81, 82, 84, 85 n.1, 86 n.24, 88 n.35, n.41 and n.44, 89 n.54, 92, 93, 94, 98, 99, 100, 101, 102, 103, 105, 107, 109 n.6(12) and n.11, 110 n.26, 113, 119, 122, 123 n.8, 125 n.24, 126 n.29, 128, 138, 139, 146 n.34, 149, 150, 152, 152 n.1, 157, 158 n.5, 160, 161, 162, 163, 165, 170, 171 n.1, 173, 174, 178, 179, 180, 183, 185, 187, 188, 189, 190, 193, 194, 199, 200, 201-203 Table 2, 204, 205, 208, 209, 210, 211, 214, 215, 216, 218, 220, 221, 222, Chapter 24 *passim* 224-230, 234, 235, 236, 238, 239, 241 n.1, 243, 244, 245, 247, 249, 251, 252, 253 n.2, 260, 261, 263, 264, 266, 268, 269, 270, 271, 275, 277, 279, 280, 282, 284, 286-287

Table 11, 297 Table 17, 300, 301 Table 22, 305 n.11, 314, 315, 316, 317, 318, 320, 321, 322, 325, 326, 327, 328, 329, 332, 336, 341, 342, 343, 345, 347; Bombay Fort : 68; Bombay City : x, 279, 291 Table 13d, 297 Table 17; Bombay Government : 257, 265, 270; Greater Bombay : 30 n.25, 225, 266, 274, 284, 297 Table 17; Bombay Island : 42, 279, 280 Table 5, 281, 284, 297 Table 17, 309; Bombay Municipality : 259.

Bombay Army : 156, 163 n.4 and 6, 164 n.8, 280 Table 7, 305 n.5, 319, 320

"Bombay Chronicle, The" : 250, 251, 255 n.10

Bombay Diocese : 84

Bombay Electric Supply and Tramways Company : 226

Bombay Hebrew Publishing and Printing Press : 92

Bombay Missionary Union : 79, 82, 86 n.24, 162

Bombay Presidency : 17 n.52, 43, 47 n.15, 51, 63 n.5, 73, 75, 87 n. 26, 115, 171 n.2, 178, 226, 251, 255 n.13 and n. 16, 281, 283, 284, 288-289 Tables 12 a,b,c and d; 290-291 Tables 13 a,b,c,d,e; 292, 328, 347; Bombay President : 43, 99

Bombay Province : 255 n.16, 259, 292 n.*

Bombay State : 210, 300 Tables 21 a and b

Bombay Times : 305 n.5

Bombay University : xi, 72, 74, 77, 84, 87 n.26 and n.27, 88 n.41 and n.46, 93, 94, 102, 108 n.6, 169, 180, 208, 209, 211, 258, 265, 270

Bombay Zionist Association : 266, 269, 270

Book (see Writings), Text : 3, 22, 45, 68, 69, 72, 73, 75, 81, 82, 84, 91, 92, 93, 94, 99, 150, 181, 205, 238, 240, 263, 264, 309, 310, 315, 325, 345; Binder : 60; Prayer : 227, 236

Booth : 15 n.19

Borgavkar, John Joseph : 190 n.4

Borgawkar, M.D. : 250

Borlai : 213, 283; Panchaton : 222 n.1; Synagogue : 149

Borrow : 236

Botanist, Botany : 31 n.38, 123 n.12, 309

Boundaries : 284

Boy (see Male) : 65, 66, 80, 129, 131, 133, 152, 175, 184, 200, 205, 218, 227, 236, 255 n.11, 257, 258, 346

Boycott : 244, 251, 252, 271

Brahmin : 13 n.2, 16 n.45 and n.48, 27, 29 n.19, 56 n.21, 86 n.9, 104, 123 n.12, 130, 141, 144 n.10, 158 n.3, 159 n.12, 169, 223 n.8, 237 n.4, 241 n.3, 247, 260; Chitpavan : 32 n.49, 123 n.4

Brandy : 162

Brass : 165, 221

Bread : 167; Unleavened : 218

Break : 140, 141

Breast : 128, 140

Bride : 60, 132, 133, 134, 135, 136, 137, 145 n.23, n.25 and n.26, 146 n.28, 218, 222, 229, 265, 267 n.5, 330, 331

Bridegroom (see Groom) : 229, 330

Briggs, John : 37 n.3

Brit Milah (see Circumcision) : 41, 185, 215, 231 n.15

Britain, British, The British (see England, English) : 94, 152, 169, 188, 193, 199, 229, 253, 253 n.1, 264, 319-323, 326, 333, 345; British East India Co. : 85 n.2, 316; Universities : 258; Viceroy : 239

British Rule, Raj (Government), (see Army) : 10, 11, 31 n.40, 32 n.45, 36, 37 n.4, 38 n.10, 42, 43, 46, 51, 54 n.13, 56 n.19, 59, 61, 65, 100, 104, 109 n.6(9), 160, 162, 178, 183, 185, 186, 243, 247, 248, 250, 251, 252, 253, 253 n.1, 254 n.2 and n.3, 255 n.9 and n.13, 270, 279, 282, 347; Army, Forces, Military : 25, 50, 174, 177, 188, 258, 315; Territories : 280 Table 7, 281.

Broach : 24, 183, 193

Brother : 46, 52, 133, 136, 142, 208, 214, 216, 226, 227, 228, 251, 265, 316, 319; Brother-in-law : 102, 139

Brown Jews : 40

Bubonic Plague : 194

Buchanan, Rev. Claudius : 41, 42, 47 n.9 and n.10, 60, 63 n.6, 335

Buddhism, Buddhist : 228, 251, 279, 284 Table 10

Buffalo : 217

Buffam, Rev. C.J. : 84

Building, Build : 46, 59, 71, 148, 151, 170, 178, 179, 181, 184, 185, 189, 215, 220, 233, 234, 236, 237 n.1, 245, 258, 260, 261, 285, 344; Construction : 188; Building Fund : 102

Bulletin (Board) : 189, 234, 239, 262 n.9

Bullock (see Ox) : 51, 114, 218, 220, 257

Burial (Mounds) (see Cemetery) : 3, 8, 13-14 n.3, 16 n.33, 36, 39 n.19, 43, 46, 53, 62, 69, 73, 99, 100, 102, 105, 108 n.6(7), 109 n.15, 122, 123 n.5, 124 n.14, 139, 140, 141, 142, 147 n.38, 157, 173, 184, 187, 194, 243, 244, 271, 277, 278; Burial Society : 139

Burma : xiii n.7, 32 n.50, 59, 285

Bus : 174, 226, 230 n.4; Stop : 216

Business (see Commerce) : 52, 154, 161, 178, 182, 191 n.9, 193, 205, 215, 220, 252, 260, 269,

272 n.4, 273 n.7, 345;
Buy : 236
Byculla : 47 n.14, 149, 220, 224, 225, 232, 233, 236, 265

Cadell, Sir Patrick : 163 n.4 and n.6, 164 n.8, 319, 320-322
Cairo (see Geniza) : 2, 21, 23, 24, 29 n.17 and n.19
Calcutta : viii, xiii n.8, 63 n.10(b), 69, 70, 73, 96 n.3, 101, 103, 108 n.6, 185, 189, 190, 193 n.3, 204, 209, 236, 252, 255 n.17, 266, 269, 279, 282, 284, 305 n.6
Calendar, Year : 35, 38 n.13, 48 n.26, 122, 125 n.23, 142, 221, 346
Caliphate : 19, 20, 21
Cambay : 9
Camp : 266, 270, 275
Camphor : 140
Canada : 198
Cannanore : 49, 67, 85 n.9
Cantonment : 173, 182, 183, 191 n.8, 193; Bombay : 297 Table 17; Poona : 179
Cap : 129, 131, 166, 214, 249
Capital : 43, 178, 185, 186, 189, 205, 232
Captive, — ity, Capture (see Prison) : 6, 8, 26, 315, 316, 318
Career (see Employment) : 93, 162, 163, 180, 181, 182, 185, 206 n.1, 211, 252, 253
Carey Library, Serampore : 73, 86 n.24
Carpenter, Carpentry : 43, 53, 160, 161, 163, 174, 178, 189, 200, 204, 220, 245, 328
Cart (see Bullock Cart) : 160, 257
Casey : 85 n.2
Cash, Money : 160, 216, 218, 219, 226, 230 n.1
Caspi, Mishael M. : 92, 96 n.7
Caste : ix, xii n.1, 7, 9, 10, 11, 12, 13 n.2, 14 n.4, 16 n.48, 25, 29 n.19, 31 n.39, 50, 51, 53, 55 n.16, 62, 63 n.2, 66, 76, 86 n.9, Chapter 9 passim 98-110, 114, 132, 143, 146 n.34, 155, 156, 160, 162, 163, 166, 199, 206 n.1, 237 n.4, 243, 248, 249, 270, 312, 342; Definition of : 16-17 n.48, 110 n.18
Catalogue : 238, 309
Catechism : 66, 82
Catherine of Braganza : 43
Catholicism : 25, 31 n.37 and n.38, 65, 69, 79, 84, 144 n.10, 226, 309
Cattle : 27, 52, 115, 160, 165, 311; Feed : 51; Toll : 10
Celebration : 162, 219, 228, 265
Cemetery and Markers (see Burial) : 13 — 14

n.3, 28 n.13, 35, 36, 37, 38 n.9, n.13 and n.19; 39 n.20, 43, 46, 47 n.17, 53, 69, 99, 100, 103, 105, 115, 134, 140, 141, 147 n.39, 152, 174, 180, 181, 182, 183, 184, 185, 186, 187, 188, 190 n.6, 205, 234, 246, 266, 277, 305 n.11, 347
Census (see Population) : ix, xiii n.3, 7, 54 n.1, 63 n.4, 80, 105, 138, 173, 175 n.2 and n.6, 177, 195 n.1, 200, 216, 223 n.7, 244, 245, 251, 259, 273 n.9, Chapter 33 passim 279-306, 327
Center for Jewish and Inter-Faith Studies : 189
Central Archives for The History of The Jewish People, Jerusalem : 38-39 n.19 and n.20, 152, 200, 207 n.7, 213, 222 n.1, 283, 298, 300
Central Bureau of Statistics (Israel) : 302
Central India : 231 n.10
Central Jewish Board of Bombay : 152, 178, 266, 270, 282
Central Jewish Board of India : 266
Ceremony (see Ritual) : 8, 10, 61, 62, 67, 81, 102, 105, 111, 112, 113, 114, 115, 117, Chapter 11 passim 127-147, 170, 188, 189, 227, 228, 229, 247, 265, 330
Certificate : 102, 137, 263, 270
Chair : 112, 130, 135, 148, 166, 343
Chairman : 171, 174, 226, 252, 270
Chaldea : 42
Challenge : 246
Chamber of Commerce : 252
Chandgaon : 213, 217, 222 n.1
Chanera : 213, 222 n.1
Change : xii, 155, 161, 194, 248, 254 n.3, 259, 260, 264, 285, 305 n.4
Chant : 131, 188, 218, 234, 265, 272 n.2
Chaplain : 85 n.2
Chappati : 167
Charcoal : 165
Charity, Alms : 5, 102, 115, 116, 139, 142, 187, 192 n.7, 193, 224, 234, 262 n.11, 263, 272 n.3, 329, 345, 346
Charlemagne' 20
Charles II, England : 43
Charms : 69, 84, 330
Charpoy (see Cot) : 166
Charrikar, Aaron Solomon : 183
Charter : 85 n.2, Plane : 270
Chastity : 105
Cheruman Perumal : 41, 47 n.8
Cheul, Chaul : 6, 23, 24, 25, 26, 30 n.25; 31 n.34, n.38, n.40 and n.41;32 n.43 and n.46, 37 n.6, 42, 48 n.21, 122, 144 n.10, 237 n.4; Cheulkar : 24, 26, 156, 211

Chicken : 62, 160, 217, 220, 223 n.11
Chicken-pox : 132
Child, Children, Childhood : 11, 22, 45, 59, 60, 65, 66, 67, 68, 70, 77, 80, 84, 103, 105, 116, 119, 125 n.21, 128, 129, 130, 131, 132, 133, 136, 138, 144 n.7 and n.10, 150, 167, 174, 176, 177, 179, 181, 184, 185, 187, 188, 193, 199, 209, 210, 211, 212 n.2, 214, 216, 218, 220, 221, 223 n.9, 225, 226, 227, 228, 229, 234, 236, 239, 259, 260, 261, 263, 264, 274, 275, 304, 310
Childless : 102, 138, 139; Child Marriage : 136; Offspring : 107
Childbirth, Delivery (see Birth) : 116, 128, 129, 131, 145 n.19
China : xiii n.7, 19, 20, 23, 42, 85
Chincholkar, Hyem Shlomo : 212 n.6
Chitpavan : 13 n.2, 32 n.49, 123 n.4, 247
Chogla (see Councillors) : 61, 62, 64 n.12, 153 n.3, 329
Choice : 271, 272
Cholera : 162, 195 n.3
Chorde : 213, 222 n.1; Post : 149, 274
Chorpuri : 182
Christian, Christianity : vii, xiii n.7, 3, 6, 17 n.48, 19, 23, 25, 27, 29 n.17, 32 n.46, 35, 50, 56 n.21, 62, Chapter 7 *passim* 65-90, 92, 93, 94, 99, 104, 108 n.6(1), 115, 116, 121, 122, 144 n.10, 147 n.37, 159 n.12, 179, 186, 206 n.1, 226, 229, 230, 241 n.3 and n.6, 243, 247, 249, 251, 275, 279, 283, 284, 309, 335
Chronicles : 27; Book of : 131; Cochin Malabari and Pardesi : 40, 41, 46 n.1, 323
Church: 86
Church Missionary Society, London : 86 n.24
Church of England (Mission) : 65, 69
Church of Scotland (see Scottish Mission) : 71, 74, 76, 82, 336; General Assembly : 7
Churrikar : Aaron : 33, 34; Abraham David : 178
Cincinnati : xiv n.10, 236.
Cinema (see Films) : 208, 210, 226
Circumcision (see Brit Milah) : 3, 23, 41, 49, 50, 60, 67, 68, 87 n.35, 92, 109 n.6(12), 112, 116, 130, 148, 184, 185, 314, 328, 330, 340, 344
Circumambulation : 116, 123 n.12, 144 n.10; Circuit : 12
Citizen(ship) : 189, 211, 269, 270, 277, 302
Citron : 120, 130
City (see Urban) : 43, 52, 101, 105, 135, 156, 158, 160, 161, 165, 166, 186, 200, 211, 228, 237, 264, 272, 273 n.10, 274, 281, 282, 284, 285

Civil(ian) (Service) : ix, 59, 65, 73, 151, 161, 163, 170, 176, 177, 182, 199, 205, 209, 211, 212 n.2 and n.3, 221, 251, 253 n.1, 270, 285.
Class, (see Middle Class) : 104, 107, 131, 136 138, 141, 160, 165, 166, 175, 178, 179, 194, 206, 225, 227, 235, 236, 241 n.3, 244, 246, 249, 251, 260, 261, 264, 305 n.9; School Classes, lessons : 80, 174, 181, 187, 188, 260, 261, 263, 269, 271
Clay (Earthen) : 100, 140, 141, 142, 165
Clean(ing) : 221
Clerk : 100, 103, 161, 163, 177, 179, 183, 191 n.7 and n.9, 199, 200, 205, 206, 207 n.3, 234, 236, 245, 246, 253 n.1, 282, 345
Climate (see Monsoon) : 139, 178
Clothing (see Dress), Cloth : viii, ix, 73, 101, 119, 121, 128, 130, 133, 134, 140, 141, 142, 166, 200, 206, 220, 227, 249, 261, 346
Club : 263, 264, 266, 269
Clues (see Research) : 34, 51, 213
Cluster : 275, 281, 284, 306 n.12
Coast : 3, 13, 22, 24, 26, 40, 43, 50, 67, 74, 128, 158, 176, 215, 268
Cochin : xiii n.4, 10, 11, 31 n.38, 41, 42, 44, 45, 48 n.20 and n.25, 49, 64 n.10, 67, 67 n.11 and n.18, 68, 70, 79, 93, 95, 108 n.1, 269, 284, 314, 315, 316, 317, 319, 335, 341
Cochin Chronicles : 40, 41, 323
Cochin Jew, Cochin Jewish, Cochini : vii, viii, x, 19, 22, 23, 35, 37, 38 n.14, Chapter 4 *passim* 40-48, 50, Chapter 6 *passim* 59-64, 69, 71, 74, 81, 85 n.9, n.11 and n. 23, 91, 92, 96 n.2, 98, 99, 100, 101, 103, 104, 105, 106, 107, 110 n.22, 113, 114, 117, 121, 122, 123 n.8, 125 n.22, 135, 136, 137, 145 n.21, 148, 151, 154, 169, 174, 184, 187, 188, 204, 231 n.11, 232, 235, 240, 253 n.1, 266, 271, 274, 275, 276, 279, 282, 283, 296 Table 16 n.d, 297 Table 17 n.a, 298, 304, 305 n.6, n.9 and n.11, 314, 315, 318, 319, 323 330, 333, 334, 335, 341, 342, 344, 345, 346, 351, 353
Cock : 130, 131
Coconut : 36, 51, 52, 120, 125 n.25, 128, 129, 130, 131, 132, 133, 135, 140, 143 n.1 and n.6, 144 n.13, 165, 174, 331; Oil : 218, 221
Coffin : 140, 141, 147 n.37 and n.38, 331
Cohen (pl. Cohanim) : 6, 60, 67, 89 n.53, 93, 100, 144 n 8, 234, 354
Cohen, Israel : 231 n.6
Cohesive : 193, 194
Coin : 129, 132, 143 n.4, 144 n.13
Colaba (Kulaba) : 47 n.14, 224, 281
Collector : 183, 184, 208; Collectorate : 284

College : 71, 76, 77, 87 n.27, 88 n.46, 93, 180, 182, 185, 209, 210, 230, 235, 236, 238, 258, 259, 266, 270, 353
Colony : 42
Color (see Skin) : 101, 104, 249, 269
Commadan, Dada Commadan, Daood Captaan Comma(n)dant : 34, 46, 51, 59, 62, 63 n.1, 70, 193, 210, 234, 245, 314, 315, 316, 317, 323 n.5, 342, 344
Commandment (see Ten Commandments) : 7, 44
Commentaries : 93
Commerce, Commercial (see Business) : 43, 207 n.4, 245, 252, 254 n.2, 270, 273 n.7, 282
Commission(ed)(er) : 54 n.13, 199, 244, 253
Committee : 77, 170, 171, 188, 234, 235, 236, 244, 252, 264,
Communications (see Post & Telegraph, Railway, Shipping) : 20, 183, 208
Communal, Community : vii, viii, ix, x, xi, 6, 7, 10, 11, 21, 22, 23, 24, 25, 27, 36, 40, 43, 45, 46, 49, 51, 52, 53, 70, 72, 74, 79, 80, 81, 82, 83, 84, 85, 92, 93, 95, 98, 99, 101, 102, 103, 104, 107, 111, 112, 137, 143, 148, 150, 151, 155, 160, 162, 164 n.8, 166, 169, 171, 174, 176, 177, 180, 181, 182, 185, 186, 187, 188, 190 n.3, 193, 194, 199, 204, 205, 206, 208, 215, 224, 225, 226, 227, 228, 230, 231 n.11, 233, 234, 235, 236, 237, 238, 243, 244, 245, 246, 247, 248, 249, 250, 251, 253 n.2, 255 n.9, 256 n.19, 258, 259, 260, 261, 264, 265, 266, 267 n.2, 268, 270, 271, 274, 275, 277, 279, 281, 283, 284, 303, 304 n.2 and n.3; Center : 232
Commute : 180, 233
Comparable, Comparative : 284, 285, 291 Table 13e, 292 Table 14, 302
Compass (points of) : 123 n.12
Competition : 22, 174, 217, 264, 272
Complication : 284
Composer, Composition : 91
Comptroller : 189, 210, 252
Concession : 42
Concubine : 11, 12, 59, 105, 331
Conduct : 235; Services 179, 188, 236
Conference : 230, 243, 266, 270, 271
Confidence : 193, 227, 245, 281
Confirmation : 236
Congregant, Congregation : 21, 22, 42, 59, 60, 62, 81, 82, 100, 101, 119, 120, 121, 148, 150, 151, 173, 174, 177, 179, 180, 181, 183, 184, 185, 187, 188, 189, 191 n.8 and n.11, 213, 215, 218, 219, 223 n.12, 224, 226, 232, 233, 234, 235, 236, 237, 243, 245, 263, 266, 274, 277, 348; Congregational : 65

Congress : 251; Indian National : 248
Conquest : 24, 110 n.16, 118
Consensus : 247, 268
Consent : 228
Conservative Judaism (Movement) : 153 n.8, 179, 194, 205, 220, 230, 231 n.5, 234, 235, 239
Constitution(al) : 16 n.48, 152, 244, 246 n.1, 248, 249, 255 n.9
Construction : 59, 122, 148, 160, 174, 178, 187, 189, 211, 261, 277, 278 n.4, 285
Consul(ate) : 270, 273 n.7
Consultant : 187
Contact : Chapter 4 passim 40-48, 71
Contract : 136, 137, 275
Contractor : 59, 160, 161, 163, 174, 194, 199, 245
Contribution (see Donation) : 78, 148, 169, 263, 283, 284
Controversial, Controversy : 79, 95, 239
Convent : 177, 229
Convention : Youth : 263
Conversion, Convert (see Proselytizing) : to Christianity : xiii n.7, 25, 31 n.37 and n.38, 41, 50, 62, 65, 67, 69, 70, 72, 76, 79, 80, 81, 82, 83, 84, 89 n.53 and n.54, 95, 101, 107, 229, 241 n.3, 275, 310, 335, 347; to Hinduism : 13 n.2; to Islam : 14 n.9, 24, 62, 65, 95, 186, 317; to Judaism : 11, 12, 17 n.50, 30 n.19, 40, 53, 83, 87 n.33, 101, 105, 107, 151, 233, 246
Cooked, Cooking : 130, 165, 166, 167, 205, 218, 219, 227, 344, 261; Utensils : 221, 234
Cooper, Judith Elias : xiii n.8
Cooperate, Cooperation, Cooperative : 99, 182, 193, 227, 228, 249, 269, 270; Banking Society : 245; Credit Society : 205, 243, 245; Housing : 226, 244
Copper Vessels, 129, 132, 140, 165, 343; Cochin Copper Plates : 47 n.8
Copyright : xi
Corporation (of Bombay) : 254 n.2
Corpse : 141
Correspondence : 83, 213, 281, 282; Courses : 262
Cosmopolitan : 230
Cost : 245, 278
Cot : 129, 134, 140, 141, 147 n.36
Cottage : 264
Council of Indian Jewry : 266
Councilor, Counsel : 104, 247, 253-254 n.2; Provincial Council : 250.
Country : 269, 270, 271, 274, 275, 298, 303, 304
Course : 261, 262; Manual Training : 175; Teacher Training : 218
Court (Dispute) : 10, 29 n.17, 62, 188, 191, 209,

Index

239, 243, 245, 247, 254 n.3, 270; Darbar : 317; Martial : 316, 319, 323; Royal : 27, 91, 186, 309
Cousin : 22, 145-146 n.28; Cross Cousin Marriage : 133
Cow : 217, 220, 221
Cow-dung : 141, 142, 147 n.40, 165, 218
Cradle : 131
Crafts, Craftsman (see Artisan) : 160, 191 n.7, 194, 199, 200, 245, 304 n.3
Cranganore : xiii n.4 and n.5, 9, 23, 40, 46 n.3, 47 n.8
Credit (see Cooperative Credit Society) : 243
Creed : 249
Cremate : 13 n.2, 123 n.5, 141
Cricket : 211
Crisis : 117
Crop : 160
Crore : 255 n.12
Crowded : 226, 227, 228
Crown : 134, 136
Cultivation, Cultivator (see Farmer) : 16 n.48, 31 n.40, 115, 131, 166, 217, 223 n.8
Cultural, Culture : xii, 59, 80, 178, 187, 189, 199, 206, 224, 227, 231 n.5, 239, 263, 269, 280, 304 n.3
Curds : 143 n.4
Curriculum : 234
Curry, Khadi : 121, 125 n.26
Custom (see Ritual) : viii, 7, 8, 43, 51, 70, 87 n.32, 95, 99, 107, 111, 115, 116, 117, 121, 122, 122 n.1, 125 n.25, 127, 132, 135, 141, 143, 144 n.12, n.13, n.18 and n.19, 145 n.23 and n.24, 166, 187, 219, 220, 221, 228, 230, 233, 267 n.5, 269, 272 n.3, 275, 319, 344, 345, 353; Dept. : 176, 199
Cynowitz, Hersch : 269, 270, 272 n.4

Da Cunha, Gerson : 24, 30 n.28, 32 n.43, 32 n.46, 310 n.1
Dacoits : 52
Dudar : 225
Dadawra : 33, 37 n.1, 311
Daman : 31 n.40
Damascus : 98, 145 n.22
Damkhadi : 222 n.1
Dance : 120, 150, 219, 261, 269, 271
Danda-Rajpuri : 26, 31 n.41, 42, 156; Dande : 222 n.1
Dandekar : 26; Solomon Benjamin : 183; Joseph Solomon : 183; Reuben David : 184, 211
Danger : 112

Daniel (Biblical) : 238
Daniel, Dr. Sr. : 342, 344
Daniel, Arthur Judah (Korlekar) : 252, 255 n.18
Danish : 43, 49, 65
Dara Shikoh : 186
Darbar : 317
Darfalnicha San : 4, 5
Dargah : 115
Daskroi : 183
Data : Chapter 2 *passim* 19-32, 73, 200, 216, 269, 281, 282, 292, 294, 301
Date : 3, 4, 8, 24, 27, 33, 34, 35, 36, 38 n.13, 41, 45, 46, 62, 65, 79, 91, 92, 94, 96 n.2, 97 n.12, 122, 122 n.1, 142, 144 n.12, 157, 158, 173, 189, 213, 223 n.12, 282.
Daughter : 22, 38 n.17, 43, 69, 81, 99, 103, 131, 133, 139, 142, 144 n.7, 146 n.34, 225, 241 n.6, 259, 275, 315, 317, 346; daughter-in-law : 138
David, Biblical King : 278 n.3, 281; Star of David : 278
David (Daud) Commadan (See Commadan) : 317
David, Joseph : 174
David, Dr. Rachailbai : 184
David, Reuben (Dandekar) : 184, 210, 211
Davidson, Israel : 145 n.22
Dawn : 119
Day of Atonement (see Yom Kippur) : 268
D'Beth Hillel (Rabbi David) : 60, 63 n.9, 72, 73, 74, 75, 87 n.28, n.31, n.32, n.33 and n. 35, 98, 99, 144 n.14, 173, 178, 305 n.8, 325-326
De Orta, Garcia : 31 n.38, 309-310
DePaiva, Mosseh Pereyra : 43
De Sola Pool : Prayer Book : 188
Dean : 185, 209; Med. College : 210
Death, Dead, Deceased, Die : 10, 27, 33, 36, 43, 46, 55 n.16, 73, 77, 81, 84, 98, 99, 102, 123 n.4, 132, 134, 138, 139-142, 150, 169, 170, 171, 181, 190, 194, 200, 212 n.5, 214, 222 n.2, 239, 243, 260, 270, 304, 304 n.3, 306 n.15, 310, 310 n.1, 316, 317, 330, 331; Anniversary : 114, 123 n.5, 142; Register : 184
Debate : 263, 264, 268
Debt : 136, 200, 236
Deccan : 14 n.9, 17 n.52, 25, 50, 56 n20, 166, 174, 182, 212 n.1
Decennial : 281
Decision : 228
Decline : 283, 301
Decoration : 133, 166, 211
Decrease : 285; Decline : 283; Diminish : 301
Dedication : 171, 232, 261, 269

412 *India's Bene Israel*

Deesa : 183, 189
Defect : 281
Defence : 50, 83, 211; Akademy : 210
Defile : 166, 206 n.1
Defunct : 266
Degree : 171, 242 n.6, 258
Deity : 114, 115, 116, 124 n.15, 125 n.25, 129, 143 n.4, 154, 227, 237 n.4; Goddess : 131, 144 n.9
Delegate : 270
Delhi, New Delhi : 15 n.17, 24, 32 n.47, 37, 176, 185-189, 190, 211, 233, 239, 266, 278
Delhi Jewish Welfare Association : 187, 188
Delhi Symphony Orchestra : 189, 210
Delivery (see Childbirth) : 127-128
Democracy, Democratic : 16 n.48, 250, 270, 271
Demography (see Statistics or Population) : 213, 222 n.1, Chapter 33 *passim* 279-306
Demonstration : 177
Denomination : 261, 266
Dependent : 204, 213, 265, 280; Adj. : 51, 82
Descendant, Descent (see Progeny) : 6, 10, 33, 40, 44, 49, 53, 59, 62, 87 n.33, 101, 102, 107, 108 n.1, 110 n.18, 174, 315, 327; Offspring : 105, 106
Deshastas : 86 n.9
Destitute : 178, 234, 281
Destroy, Destruction : 4, 6, 8, 42, 69, 118
Detail : 75, 79, 238, 240, 282
Deteriorization : 193
Deuteronomy, Book of : 3, 5, 14 n.6, 102, 113, 165, 329
Devanagri : 14 n.9, 35, 92, 93, 97 n.12
Development : 80, 248
Devotion : 75
Dew Kaneh : 222 n.1
Dewan : 208, 212 n.1
Dhanduka : 183
Dharwar : 37
Dhulia : 162
Diary, Journal : 38 n.18, 54 n.10, 69, 70, 72, 73, 74, 79, 255 n.18
Diaspora, Dispersal : viii, 5, 6, 17, 20, 28 n.1, 42, 61, 186, 337 n.14
Dichotomy : 229
Dictionary : 88 n.41, 115, 124 n.18, 125 n.19, 212 n.1
Dietary (see Food) : 53, 104, 124 n.13, 129, 167
Differ, Differentiate : 51, 101, 103, 104, 114, 143, 179, 189, 221, 238, 271, 275, 279, 284
Dighorkar, Reuben Hyam : 184
Dinner Party, Dine : 105, 128, 129, 137, 142

Diploma : 209, 230
Diplomat : 187, 270, 271, 317
Director : 43, 209, 210, 252, 276
Directory : 244; Directory of Villages & Towns of Kolaba District : 159 n.12
Disciple : 186
Discipline : 103
Discord : 151, 185
Discovery (of Bene Israel) : 3, 8, 10, 21, 75, 101, 112, 115, 117, 122 n.1
Discrepancy : 302, 305 n.13
Discrimination : ix, 16 n.48, 100, 105, 127, 177, 206, 252, 265, 269
Discussion : 76, 78, 234, 235, 239, 244, 263, 272 n.3
Disease : 114, 125 n.25, 132, 133, 144 n.10, 222 n.2, 237 n.4, 257, 309
Dish : 111
Dispensary : 84, 184, 217, 243, 261, 263
Dispersion (see Diaspora) : 7, 10, 42, 51, 67, 176, 281
Dispute : 10, 52, 62, 181, 312
Dissa : 36
Dissertation (Ph. D) : 63 n.15, 110 n.26, 124 n.15, 125 n.24, 145 n.20 and n.27, 231 n.11, 239
Distance : 176, 224, 226
Distinction : Chapter 21 *passim* 208-212, 264; Difference : 107, 199
Distribution : 76, 112, 114, 121, 130, 132, 136, 284, 290
District (see by name of each) : 281, 301
Distrust : 249, 281
Diu : 31 n.38
Diva Borlai : 26
Divekar : Aaron Jacob : 92, 238, 241 n.3; Aaron Joseph : 352; David Haeem : 97 n.13; E. S. Divekar : 171; Issaji Divekar : 59, 225, 316, 317; Samuel Ezekiel (see Samaji Hassaji) : 46, 59, 60, 225, 314-319, 322, 323; Solomon David : 94
Divide, Divisiveness : 119, 194; Division : 284, 285, 286-287
Divination : 336
Divorce : 55 n.16, 101, 108 n.6(9), 110 n.26, 138, 139, 146 n.34, 245, 331, 341
Docks : 207 n.4
Doctor (see Medicine, Physician) : 81, 184, 189, 206 n.1, 209, 214, 221, 257, 340, 345
Doctrine : 66
Document(ation) : 21, 24, 27, Chapter 3 *passim* 33-39, 40, 43, 44, 46, 48 n.25, 49, 50, 51, 71, 74, 76, 82, 104, 137, 152, 158 n.1, 187, 231 n.11, 256 n.19, 267, 282, 307, 310

Dolwal : 222 n.1
Domestic Science : 261
Dongakherry (Dongri) : 225
Donation, Donor, Contribution, Subsidy, Charity : 5, 76, 78, 102, 109 n.6(10) and n.10, 116, 122, 136, 142, 148, 150, 151, 169, 172 n.5, 174, 179, 180, 181, 188, 219, 224, 234, 236, 260, 261, 264, 277, 278
Doodkar : 52, 155
Door : 129, 222 n.3; Doorpost : 165
Dormitory : 170, 180, 275
Dowry : 139
Draftsman : 161
Drama : 261, 278 n.4
Dravidian : 110 n.16
Dream : 243
Dress, Clothing, Costume : viii, 5, 67, 72, 166, 185, 227, 233, 327
Drink, Drunk (see Liquor, Alcoholism, Temperance) : 118, 161, 162, 200, 218, 219
Driver : 160, 207 n.3
Drown : 3, 24, 60
Drugs : 253
Du Bois, Abbe J. A. 115, 124 n.16
Dues, 234, 274
Durham University : 183
Dutch : 40, 43, 47 n.18, 49, 108 n.1, 253 n.1; Dutch East India Company : 43, 44, 317
Duty : 234, 253
Dyers : 179, 190 n.2
Dynamic(s) : 233, 275
Dynasty : 25, 27, 42

Ear(ring) : 131, 166; Locks : 167
Earning : 73, 169, 170, 174, 193, 199, 200, 229, 269
Earth : 140, 141, 147 n.38
East Africa : 14 n.9, 16 n.35
East India Company British : 43, 47 n.15, 50, 60, 85 n.2, 156, 162, 163 n.7, 316, 329
East India Company, Dutch (see Dutch East India Company)
Eat (see Food) : 100, 118, 150, 167, 179; Eating Stalls : 103
Ecology : 208
Economy, Economic : 42, 105, 162, 193, 208, 243, 271, 274, 281, 304 n.3
Edinburgh : 82, 86 n.24, 89 n.51
Editor, Edition : 69, 73, 88 n.39, 92, 93, 94, 97 n.12, 170, 182, 208, 209, 210, 239, 240, 253, 268
Education, Educated : 7, 53, 59, 60, 61, 76, 77, 78, 79, 80, 81, 82, 83, 85 n.3, 91, 93, 100, 103, 105, 109 n.6(9), 116, 120, 150, 151, 161, 162, 166, 169, 170, 171, 174, 178, 179, 180, 184, 185, 187, 190, 193, 194, 199, 205, 206 n.1, 208, 218, 219, 221, 222, 224, 228, 230, 231 n.5, 233, 234, 235, 236, 239, 242 n.6, 243, 246, 252, Chapter 28 *passim* 257-262, 268, 281, 285, 304 n.3, 316, 317, 335, 346; Fund : 214, 244, 245; Primary : 170; Secondary : 185, 258, 259
Egypt, Egyptian : 6, 41, 67, 121, 186
Ehrenfels, Prof. Umar Rolf Von : 104
Eighteenth Century : Chapter 5 *passim* 49-56
Eilat, Etzion Geber : 8, 9
Elders, Aged, Elderly : 61, 67, 70, 71, 105, 138, 161, 185, 190 n.3, 214, 215, 225, 227, 329, 345,
Election : 181, 247, 248, 250, 254 n.2
Electrician, Electricity : 174, 176, 199, 214, 217
Elephant : 27
Elias, Flower and Cooper, Judith Elias : xiii n.8
Elijah, the Prophet : 6, 8, 101, 111, 112, 113, 115,116, 117, 118, 121, 128, 131, 134, 148, 229, 230, 231 n.15, 330; Chair : 111, 130, 148
Elite : 182, 261
"Eliyahu Ha-Navi" : 111, 112, 113, 114, 124 n.14
Elliot and Dowson : 16 n.40, 41; 28 n.11; 30 n.22, 23, 24
Elloji Nagawkar, Shahir : 91, 95 n.1
Emancipation (see Enlightenment) : 206, 231, n.5
Emigration : viii, ix, 107, 150, 179, 182, 183, 190, 205, 213, 215, 216, 218, 221, 222, 224, 226, 230, 237, 241, 243, 245, 260, 264, Chapter 30 *passim* 268-273, 274, 275, 285, 298, 301-302 Table 23, 303
Emotion : 227, 229, 271
Empathy : 81
Empire : 185
Employment, Employer, Job, (see Occupations, Government of India, Earnings) : 34, 61, 77, 100, 160, 161, 166, 170, 174, 176, 178, 182, 183, 184, 185, 187, 189, 191 n.9, 194, 199, 200, 204, 205, 217, 232, 235, 250, 252, 253 n.1, 271, 272, 282, 285; Placement : 346
Encyclopaedia : Hastings : 84; Judaica : 353
Endogamy : xii n.1, 10, 16 n.48, 46 n.2, 49, 55 n.16, 103, 264
Endowment : 59, 170, 235, 265, 276
Enemy : 50, 95
Engagement, Espousal, Betrothal : 133, 228
Engineer(ing) : 161, 181, 184, 199, 210, 212 n.3, 212 n.6, 340
England, English (see Britain, British) : xi, 31 n.38, 42, 43, 50, 69, 72, 73, 77, 78, 83, 95, 103,

108 n.1, 155, 162, 166, 182, 183, 235, 247, 248, 252, 253, 255 n.11 and n.18, 259, 273 n.8, 327, 335

English (Language) : x, xi, xii n.1, 33, 34, 35, 37 n.3, 40, 44, 70, 72, 73, 74, 80, 81, 88 n.41 and n. 48, 92, 94, 96 n.11, 97, 97 n.12 and n.14, 99, 103, 115, 122, 148, 153 n.3, 169, 170, 171 n.1, 175, 181, 182, 191 n.7, 194, 206, 209, 211, 227, 230, 231 n.11, 233, 238, 240, 241, 241 n.3, 242 n.8 and n.9, 245, 259, 262, 263, 264, 271, 278, 283, 309, 340, 342, 346; English Medium : 185, 222, 260, 261

Enlightenment, Emancipation : 80, 137, 168, 169, 176, 206, 206 n.1, 231 n.5

Enlist(ment) : 50, 51, 156, 162, 163, 169, 174, 285

Enterprise, Enterprising : 102, 161, 193, 227, 253, 264, 268, 282, 306 n.12

Entertain : 263, 264

Enumeration : 284, 289, 291, 296 Table 16 n.a; Under-enumeration : 279, 295 Table 15 n.a

Epic : 227

Epidemic : 131

Eppstein, Rev. J. M. : 79

Equality : 251

Error : 70, 74

Erulkar : Family : 189; Dr. Abraham Benjamin : 183, 184; Dr. Abraham Solomon : 184, 209, 249, 250, 251, 252, 254-255 n.8; David Solomon : 32 n.50, 183, 184, 209, 239, 243, 244, 246, 247, 252, 253, 254, 255 n.3, n.7 and n.8, 256 n.19, 268; Issac Ellis : 184; Dr. Sol : 254 n.7; Dr. Solomon Abraham : 183.

Estate : 139, 151, 230 n.1, 234

Esther : 91, 120, 238, 334; Book of : 5, 97 n.11, 120

Estimate : 63 n.4, 272, 282, 284, 285, 296 Table 16 n.c,, 304, 305 n.4, n.6 and n.8

Ethics : 12, 235

Ethiopia or Abyssinia : 24

Ethnic, Ethnicity : 50, 61, 64 n.15, 80; Ethnography : 213

Etymology : 238

Eurasian : 258

Europe, European : 6, 19, 20, 21, 22, 25, 29 n.17, 40, 55 n.16, 63 n.10, 67, 69, 70, 78, 81, 101, 108 n.1 and n.6(9), 109 n.11, 150, 158 n.2, 159 n.7, 162, 167, 186, 205, 215, 225, 226, 236, 244, 246 n.4, 250, 252, 253, 257, 258, 265, 269, 272 n.3, 280, 284, 285, 305 n.11, 309, 310, 314, 315, 320, 321, 322, 343

Evaluation : 81

Even Sapir : 90 n.61

Evidence : 137

Evil eye : 70, 125 n.25, 127, 132, 143 n.4, 144 n.10 and n.13, 146 n.30, 147 n.41, 281

Examination : 72, 88 n.41, 167, 180, 244, 261, 270, 272

Examiner : 84, 93

Excavation (see Archaeology) : 9, 36, 123 n.12

Excellence : 208

Excommunication : 30 n.19, 62, 105, 185, 230, 244

Execution, Executed : 27, 186, 317

Executive : 151, 209, 247

Exilarch of Baghdad : 20, 29 n.17

Exodus : Book of : 3, 5, 6, 67, 85 n.1, 121, 123 n.12, 222 n.3; to Israel : 237, 272

Exogamy : 40

Expel : 7, 344

Expenses : 70, 131, 139, 152, 177, 260

Experience : 275

Expiation : 125 n.24 and n.25

Extant : 157, 158

Extended Family (see Family) : 138, 146 n.28 and n.29, 177

Eye(s) : 49, 117, 281

Ezekiel, Book of : 131

Ezekiel : E.M: 265; Isaac A. : 238, 242 n.7 and 9; Dr. Jacob : 251; Joseph : 4; M.S(?) Ezekiel : 249; Moses : 37 n.2, 97 n.13 and n.14, 110 n.19, 156, 240, 265; Nissim : 211, 240, 266; Rahamim J. : 249; Sarah Sampson : 180, 190

Ezra, Sir Alwyn : 254 n.2

Ezra, J.S. : 269

Ezra (Prophet) : 6, 89 n.49

Face : 49, 135, 140

Facilities : 234, 274

Faction, Factionalism : 59, 60, 150, 151, 152, 176, 243, 260

Factor, Factory : 9, 25, 29 n.17, 43, 47 n.16, 48 n.18, 178, 200, 206, 322

Failure : 78

Fair, Oorus : 112, 113, 118, 123 n.5, 160, 304 n.3

Faith : 3, 61, 65, 115, 168, 176, 187, 215, 230, 271, 347; Faithful : 219

Fakir : 115, 186

Family : 10, 11, 12, 13, 22, 26, 27, 34, 40, 41, 42, 43, 44, 46, 52, 59, 66, 68, 70, 73, 77, 81, 84, 92, 93, 98, 99, 100, 102, 128, 130, 131, 133, 134, 135, 136, 137, 138, 139, 141, 142, 146 n.34, 153 n.3, 155, 156, 158, 160, 162, 166, 170, 173, 174, 175, 176, 177, 178, 181, 182, 183,

Index   415

184, 185, 187, 188, 189, 190, 194, 199, 200, 207 n.3, 212 n.2, 213, 214, 218, 219, 222, 223 n.8, 224, 227, 228, 229, 233, 238, 241, 245, 258, 260, 261, 266, 269, 274, 275, 277, 281, 285, 298, 304, 304 n.3, 305 n.8, 306 n.12; Joint : 138, 177, 205, 216, 217, 219, 220, 221, 228; Nuclear :154, 155, 177, 228

Famine : 194, 253

Fan : 135

Far East : 269

Farmer, Farming, Cultivator : 3, 34, 148, 160, 166, 200, 208, 219, 220, 237, 269, 273 n.6 and n.10

Fasting : 4, 5, 68, 116, 117, 118, 119, 120, 121, 125 n.22, 142, 151, 219, 221, 227, 249, 250, 332, 333, 334, 340

Fat (see Obesity) : 70

Father : 44, 46, 93, 95, 129, 130, 133, 135, 136, 138, 142, 155, 170, 190, 199, 200, 220, 221, 226, 228, 233, 275, 311, 312, 330

Fear : 281

Feast, Banquet : 4, 5, 10, 15 n.19, 68, 114, 129, 130, 131, 134, 136, 137, 142, 144 n.8, 167, 170, 177, 219, 223 n.11, 229, 331, 343, 348

Federation : 243

Federation of Indian Jewish Youth : 266

Fee (see Tuition) : 10, 51, 61, 62, 63, 128, 130, 151, 169, 180, 181, 184, 233, 234, 260, 279, 344

Fellow : 209

Fellowship : 264

Female : 3, 66, 77, 81, 95, 121, 125 n.25, 129, 130, 133, 134, 137, 138, 140, 151, 155, 166, 175, 180, 234, 241 n.3, 257, 275, 279, 281, 287 Table 11; 297 Table 18; 298 Table 19; 299 Table 20; 301 Table 22; 331

Fence (see Wall) : 277

Ferishta, Mahomed Kasim : 37 n.3

Fertility, Fruitfulness : 130, 132, 134, 135

Fertilizer : 51

Festival, Festive : 5, 112, 113, 135, 153 n.3, 219, 220, 221, 227, 250, 256 n.19, 264, 304 n.3, 332-334

Feudatory States : 284; 289 Table 12d

Field : 52

Fight : Forces : 50; Political : 247

Films : 199, 208, 210, 211, 226, 240

Finances, Financial : 59, 62, 100, 102, 138, 151, 153 n.7, 165, 169, 181, 182, 185, 193, 194, 199, 235, 266, 272, 276, 282; Aid : 236; Ministry : 187

Fines : 62, 329

Finger : 117, 122, 136

Fire, Firewood : 130, 134, 167, 213, 215, 218

Fireworks : 136, 331

First-Born : 121, 144 n.8, 238

Fischel, Prof. Walter J. : ix, x, xiv n.15 and n.16; 27, 32 n.47 and 48, 43, 47 n.16, 48 n.19, 49, 50, 51, 53 n.2, n.3 and n.5; 54 n.7, n.9, n.10, n.11 and n.12; 72, 73, 74, 87 n.31, n.34 and n.35; 92, 93, 96 n.10, 97 n.13 and n.14; 99, 108 n.4, 186, 238, 317, 350, 352

Fish : 3, 167, 343

Fission, Divisiveness, Schism (See Friction, Split) : 189, 194, 264, 344

Fitter : 206

Five, Fifth : 114, 128, 129, 132, 133, 134, 143 n.4, 145 n.26, 330, 342

Flag : 47 n.16

Flat : 165, 220

Flee : 26, 269

Fleet : 34, 51, 210

Flexibility : 233

Floor : 119, 142, 147 n.40, 215, 219, 343, 344

Flower, Flora, Foliage : 114, 115, 128, 131, 134, 140, 153 n.3, 219, 309

Food, Feeding, Diet, Cooking : 3, 15 n.12, 17 n.50, 48 n.26, 52, 53, 62, 104, 105, 108 n.6(8), 110 n.15, 111, 115, 120, 121, 124 n.13 and n.15, 124-5 n. 18, 125 n.26, 130, 132, 133, 134, 167, 215, 217, 218, 221, 227, 233, 261, 328, 340, 343

Folk(lore), Folkways : viii, 91, 112, 115, 125 n.20, 127, 138, 141, 143 n.4, 147 n.10 and n.13, 227, 230, 231 n.11, 240; Dance : 261, 269; Songs : 96 n.2, 229, 256 n.19

Foot, Feet : 132, 134, 136, 140, 141, 145 n.23, 148, 153 n.3, 214

Footnote : x, xii, 81, 82, 91, 127, 238

Footprint : 112, 123 n.4

Forearm : 134

Forefather (see Ancestor) : 45, 60, 122, 244

Forefinger : 133, 134, 145 n.23

Foreign, Foreigner : xiii, 11, 21, 22, 23, 24, 27, 30 n.19, 35, 40, 53, 70, 151, 156, 187, 188, 220, 249, 255 n.11, 269, 275

Foreman : 200

Forgiveness : 119

Fort, Fortress : 25, 26, 31 n.41, 35, 36, 47 n.14, 51, 68, 70, 149, 174, 254 n.2, 322

Fortune : 52

Foundation, Founders : 149, 151, 180, 181, 189, 193, 232, 235, 263, 266, 269

Fowl, Cock, Hen : 104, 119, 125 n.25, 130, 144 n.10 and n.13, 167, 177, 343; Liver and Gizzard : 114, 116, 131

Fragrance, Aroma : 113, 114, 123 n.12

France, French : 19, 23, 47 n.5, 186, 261;

Franks : 20
Franchise : 248
Free (Gratis) : 66, 76, 77, 184, 237, 243, 261, 263; Freeship : 260; Free Will Offering : 116
Free Church of Scotland : 71, 79, 82, 89 n.54, 93; Free General Assembly : 88 n.46
Free Mason : 181, 208, 264, 267 n.4
Freedom : 186, 249, 250; Freedom Fighter Tilak : 181, 247
Friction : 185, 189
Friday : 121, 125 n.26, 218, 233, 236
Friend, Friendly, Friendship : 83, 101, 129, 139, 142, 173, 174, 178, 186, 187, 188, 193, 219, 229, 237, 263, 271, 272
"Friend of Israel" (Israel Mitra) : 95, 156, 239
Frontispiece : xiv n.10, 92, 96 n.6
Fruit, Fruitfulness : 113, 114, 115, 116, 128, 129, 143 n.4, 174, 269, 330
Fuel : 165, 166, 167, 218
Function (see Dinner Party) : 62, 63, 148, 152, 167, 180, 194, 234, 237, 264; Govt. : 189
Fund, Fund-Raising (see Donation) : 14 n.3, 62, 78, 102, 122, 139, 148, 150, 152, 169, 170, 179, 184, 187, 188, 190 n.3, 193, 194, 234, 235, 243, 244, 245, 258, 260, 263, 264, 276, 277, 278, 278 n.4, 329; Chit : 205; Education : 214, 224
Fundamentalist : 95
Funeral (see Death) : 61, 63, 141, 181, 310, 312
Furniture : 160, 165, 200, 343

Gabai (House of) : 342, 344
Gabbai (see Treasurer) : 61, 62, 63, 342, 343, 347
Gadkar : Daniel Elijah Benjamin : 181; Elijah Benjamin : 181, 190 n.4; E. M. Jacob : 240
Gairola, C.K. : 17 n.51
Galilee : 6, 8, 12, 14 n.6, 167
Gallery : 121, 135, 179
Galsure : 222 n.1
Galsurkar, Haeem Isaac : 94, 350, 351, 352, 353
Gambling : 162
Games : 132, 136, 137
Gandhi, Mahatma : 183, 184, 209, 212 n.5, 249, 250, 252, 254 n.5, n.7 and n.8
Gangli : 27
Gaon : 19, 20, 28 n.1, 29 n.17
Garland : 134, 219
Gate of Mercy Synagogue (Bombay) : 14 n.3, 240
Gazetteer : ix, 185, 280; *Bombay Presidency 1882-1883* : 17 n.52, 25, 26, 32 n.42 and n.46, 40 n.52, 139, 144 n.10, 161, 163 n.1 and n.2, 173, 175 n.2, 207 n.8; *Bombay Presidency 1884-1885* : 61, 62, 131, 141, 144 n.11, 160, 161, 166, 182, 190 n.6, 191 n.13; *Bombay City 1900* : 36, 54 n.15; *Revised Bombay State 1954* : 165, 178; *Revised Kolaba District 1964* : 159 n.12; *Maharashtra State 1964* : 55 n.16, 166
Genealogy : 27, 52, 154, 189, 223 n.8
General Assembly : Scottish : 77, 88 n.46, 336; Synagogue : 104, 151
Generation : 33, 34, 43, 52, 53, 65, 94, 105, 107, 120, 150, 156, 158, 170, 177, 180, 194, 215, 217, 219, 221, 228, 235, 236, 275
Genesis, Book of : 3, 16 n.37, 85 n.1, 102, 113, 342
Geniza : 21, 24, 28 n.13, 29 n.17 and n.19
Gentleman : 72
Geography : 9, 16 n.40 and n.42, 19, 23, 30 n.25
Gerizim : 78
German : Jews (see Ashkenazi) : 50, 69, 79, 90 n.56, 103; Germany : 281; Language : 40
Ghani (see Oil-Press) : 218
Ghat : 178, 327; Police : 173, 174
Ghee : 115, 124 n.18, 143 n.4
Ghetto : 231 n.5
Ghosale : 173, 219, 221, 222 n.1, 232
Ghosalkar : Daniel : 162; Isaac Solomon : 122
Ghosalkar Prayer Hall Poona : 179
Ghost : 125 n.25, 144 n.10
Ghurye, Dr. G.S. : 14 n.4
Gidney, W.T. : 79, 90 n.55
Gift (see Present) : 43, 131, 134, 136, 188, 234
Gil, Moshe : 19, 28 n.6 and n.7
Girl : 65, 66, 68, 77, 80, 129, 131, 132, 133, 175, 180, 205, 206 n.1, 218, 226, 227, 236, 241 n.3, 257, 258, 261, 263, 336
Gizzard : 114, 116, 131
Glass : 165; Bangles : 128, 134, 136, 144 n.19; 166; Beads : 132, 145 n.25; Drinking Glass : 120, 121, 135, 145 n.24
Goa : xiii n.6; 25, 26, 31 n.38 and n.40, 42, 47 n.16, 48 n.21, 56 n.19, 101, 176, 309, 310
Goal : 258, 266
Goat : 62, 114, 144 n.10, 177, 221, 222 n.3; Liver : 142
Goblet, Wine-glass : 135, 136, 233
Goddess : 131, 132, 144 n.9 and n.10, 237 n.4
Godfather, Sandek : 130, 148
Goitein, Shelomo Dov : 17, 21, 22, 24, 28 n.14, n.15, and n.16; 29 n.17, n.18 and n.19, 30 n.21

and n. 27
Golconda Sultanate : 25
Gold : 131, 134, 135, 136, 166, 229; Beads : 132; Embroidery : 129; Gold Medal : 210, 211; Goldsmith : 220
Golden Jubilee : 180
Goodman, Paul : xiv n.10, 171
Goods : 252, 253, 271
Goodwill : 271
Gora : 15 n.21, 104, 105, 106, 107, 110 n.23 and n.26, 144 n.17, 228, 264; Jehudi : 67
Gospel : 65, 68, 71, 79
Govardhana : 17 n.51
Government : 36, 169, 174, 176, 184, 186, 187, 199, 205, 245, 248, 249, 257, 258, 263, 264, 265, 271, 272, 347; British : 10, 250, 252, 345, 346; Internal : 329; State : 189
Government of India : 174, 177, 188, 189, 195 n.3, 209, 211, 248, 259, 260, 270, 272, 277, 279, 304, 305 n.4; British : 137, 169, 171 n.3; Employ : 184, 187, 191 n.7 and n.9, 192 n.20, 194, 199; Service : 205, 206, 208
Governor : 49, 247, 268, 333
Gowalwadi, Gowala : 222 n.1
Grace : 167, 168, 227
Grades (School), Marks : 260, 261
Graduate, Graduation : 163, 169, 236, 242 n.6, 257; Post : 258
Graham, Maria : 36, 38 n.18, 54 n.8, 55 n.15
Grain : 52, 134
Grammar : 75, 76, 80, 209, 342, 344
Grandparent(s) : 60, 131, 155, 215, 228
Grant : 36, 159, 181, 231 n.11
Grape Juice : 62, 105, 121, 135, 140, 233, 330
Grass : 141
Grave (see Burial, Cemetery) : 35, 36, 115, 116, 122, 140, 141, 142, 174, 186, 246
Greece, Greek : 20, 88 n.46, 241 n.3 and n.6, 309
Green : 128, 134, 137, 144 n.19
Greeting : 126 n.28
Grinding : 134, 166; Stone : 165
Groom : 132, 133, 134, 135, 136, 137, 145 n.24 and n.26, 229, 267 n.5
Gryn, Rabbi Hugo : 236
Gubbay, Judah J. : 269
Guest : 62, 130, 133, 134, 136, 167, 168, 219, 220, 227, 237, 343, 346
Guide : 44, 45, 80, 252, 275; Boy & Girl Scouts : 263
Guild : 17 n.51
Gujarat, Gujarati : xiii n.6, 9, 17 n.52, 21, 24, 37, 40, 41, 42, 44, 87 n.32, 88 n.42, 126 n.29, 146 n.34, 149, 176, 182, 183-185, 205, 208,
220, 221, 230 n.2, 255 n.16 , 300 Table 21a, n.**; 309, 328; University : 184
Gupta Period : 12
Guru : 237 n.4
Gussin, Carl Mark : 124 n.15, 125 n.24
Gym : 199

Habitation (see Settlement) : 42
Haham, Hahamim : 44, 45, 59, 108 n.6 (3), 161, 342, 346, 348
Haeems, H.D. : 97 n.16
Haffkine, Dr. Waldemar Mordecai Wolff : 194, 195 n.3; Haffkine Institute : 195 n.3
Haftarah : 108 n.6, 235
Hag He-asif : 4, 5
Haggadah ; 92, 93, 96 n.9, 121, 350-354
Haifa : 231 n.15
Hair : 116, 125 n.21, 128, 131, 134, 135, 142, 166, 167, 261, 346
Halacha, Halaha, Halahic : 80, 100, 101, 102, 107, 110 n.26, 139, 150, 167, 176, 188, 215, 220, 226, 230 n.4, 265, 346
Haldi : 134, 219
Halevi, Jaakov Sapir ; 90 n.61
Halitzah : 102, 139, 344
Hallegua : 48 n.20; Hyam Joseph : 350, 351, 352; Joseph David : 352, 353
Halliday, S. : 45
Haman : 120
Hamavdil (see Havdala)
Hamburg : 236
Ha-Me'asef : 41, 47 n.6 and n.7, 48 n.24
Hamilton : 280
Hand : 119, 121, 122, 126 n.28, 134, 141, 167, 214, 221, 222 n.3, 249, 343
Handa : 140
Handicrafts : 199
Handkerchief : 116, 119, 132, 136, 140, 145 n.23
Handwriting : 60, 213, 254 n.4
Hanukah, Hannukiah (see Chanukah) : 6, 118, 120, 264, 334
Harbor : 47 n.14, 84
Hardi : 173, 222 n.1
Harosheth : 121
Harassment : 42, 257
Harvest ; 5, 15 n.19, 52, 125 n.25, 217, 218
Hashkabah (see Memorial Prayer) : 115, 116, 120, 134, 142
Hashmi, B.A. : 242 n.9
Haskalah : 206
Hassaji (see Samaji) : 314-319

Hastings Encyclopaedia of Religion and Ethics : 24
Hath Boshi : 121
Havdala, Hamavdil : 121, 123 n.12, 233
Hazan : 7, 60, 61, 62, 64 n.14, 71, 92, 100, 106, 108 n.6(3), 109 n.6(15), 110 n.22, 114, 122, 123 n.8, 130, 131, 133, 134, 135, 136, 140, 141, 148, 151, 167, 171 n.1, 179, 180, 181, 184, 188, 215, 218, 219, 224, 232, 235, 331, 342, 343, 344, 345, 348
Hazkara (see Memorial Prayer or Hashkabah) : 317
Head : 122, 134, 135, 141, 142, 166, 167, 279; Family : 213, 283 Table 9; Household : 214
Headmaster, Headmistress : 93, 108 n.6, 225, 259, 260, 261, 265, 352, 353
Headquarters : 10, 26, 43, 178
Health : 116, 167, 210
Heartland : 27, 41
Heathen : 45, 66, 72, 79, 101
Hebrath Beth Yakob Prayer Hall : 179
Hebrew (Language) : 3, 4, 5, 10, 13 n.3 and n.5, 19, 21, 28 n.13, 35, 36, 38 n.13 and n.14, 40, 41, 43, 44, 45, 47 n.5, n.7 and n.17, 48 n.22, n.24, n.26 and n.27, 49, 60, 61, 62, 64 n.10, n.12 and n.14, 67, 68, 69, 72, 73, 75, 76, 77, 80, 81, 84, 85, 87 n.27 and n.29, 88 n.41, n.46 and n.48, 90 n.61, 91, 92, 93, 94, 95, 96 n.3, 99, 102, 108 n.6, 113, 116, 117, 121, 123 n.8, 124 n.14, 130, 133, 135, 136, 137, 139, 140, 142, 148, 150, 152 n.2, 153 n.10, 154, 155, 157, 158 n.1, 159 n.6, 169, 170, 174, 175, 179, 180, 181, 183, 184, 185, 187, 191 n.7, 205, 207 n.8, 214, 215, 218, 220, 221, 223 n.12, 227, 234, 235, 236, 237 n.6, 238, 239, 241 n.3, 256 n.19, 259, 261, 262, 263, 265, 269, 271, 275, 278, 314, 315, 317, 325, 328, 335, 341, 342, 345, 346, 350, 351, 353
"The Hebrew" and "The Voice of Sinai" : 108 n.6, 109 n.6
Hebrew Union College : 236, 241 n.6
Hebrew University : 152, 241
Hebron : 78
Hegemony (see Rule) : 42
Heir : 139
Heller, Rabbi Bernard : 236, 266
Help(er) (see Assistance) : 117, 178, 194, 217, 220, 228, 258, 263, 275; Helpless : 281
Henna (see Mehndi) : 132
Hereditary : 10, 16 n.48, 27, 33, 34, 59, 61, 62, 133, 311, 312
Heritage : 239
Hesed El Synagogue, Poynad : 149, 274
Hevrah Kedushah : 139, 152, 243, 245

Heykhal : 148, 153 n.11, 188
Hierarchy : 34, 51, 104, 160, 194
High Priest : (see Cohen) : 5
High School : 66, 88 n.46
Hind : 19, 23
Hindi : 14 n.9, 67, 124 n.18, 208, 211, 240, 241 n.3, 249, 278 n.3
Hindu : ix, xii n.1, 3, 5, 10, 12, 16 n.48, 17-18 n.52, 20, 25, 27, 29 n.17, 31 n.39, 36, 50, 51, 55 n.15 and n.16, 62, 66, 67, 69, 75, 76, 77, 79, 84, 85 n.9, 87 n.32, 91, 94, 98, 102, 103, 104, 107, 109 n.15, 110 n.18, 114, 115, 116, 122, 123 n.4, n.5 and n.12, 124 n.13 and n.15, 125 n.24, 126 n.28, 127, 128, 129, 130, 131, 132, 133, 134, 136, 137, 138, 139, 140, 141, 143, 143 n.1, n.4 and n.6, 144 n.9, n.10, n.12, n.13, n.14 and n.18, 145 n.19 and n.25, 146 n.30, 147 n.40, 154, 155, 159 n.3 and n.12, 160, 161, 166, 167, 168, 168 n.2, 173, 174, 177, 179, 185, 186, 187, 193, 199, 206 n.1, 216, 217, 219, 220, 221, 223 n.11, 225, 227, 228, 229, 231 n.10, 237 n.4, 241 n.3, 247, 250, 251, 256 n.19, 257, 261, 263, 265, 267 n.5, 271, 278 n.3, 279, 283, 284 Table 10, 305 n.9, 309, 310, 327, 328, 329, 330, 331, 335; Marriage Act : 228
Hindu Ideas, Hinduism : 13 n.2, 15 n.18, 16 n.45, 51, 55 n.15, 87 n.32, 102, 124 n.13 and n.18
Hindustani : 4, 5, 14 n.9, 49, 73, 84, 85 n.9, 88 n.42, 89 n.52, 91, 100, 101, 117, 118, 229, 231 n.11, 328, 342
Hire : 160, 205, 217, 218, 220, 265, 272
History, Historian, Historical : vii, viii, ix, x, xi, xii, 8, 11, Chapter 2 *passim* 19-32, 23, 26, 27, 37 n.7, 40, 43, 44, 51, 52, 53, 60, 75, 80, 89 n.52, 96 n.2, 97 n.13, 101, 104, 107, 109 n.6(9), 110 n.16, 112, 152, 156, 158, 180, 183, 187, 213, 215, 231 n.11, 240, 244, 246, 248, 253, 262, 265, 268, 269, 271, 274, 275, 277, 278, 278 n.3, 285, 298, 307, 316, 319, 320-323, 328
Holi : 5
Holicha san : 4, 5
Holidays : Bene Israel : 4, 5, 6, 15 n.11 and n.12, 61, 91, 92, 93, 105, 113, 117, 118, 120, 122, n.1, 123 n.7, 169, 177, 179, 182, 185, 186, 187, 188, 189, 215, 218, 220, 224, 226, 232, 264, 342, 344, 345, 346; Hindu : 5, 223 n.11; Indian : 123 n.7
Holy : 89 n.49, 105, 143 n.4, 237 n.4; Writings : 148
Holy Land (see Palestine) : 72, 76, 77, 78, 88 n.44, 89 n.49, 98, 113, 122, 152 n.1, 268, 269
Home (see House) : 52, 92, 100, 111, 116, 128, 130, 134, 141, 142, 144 n.18, 147 n.40, 160,

Chapter 15 *passim* 165-168, 176, 178, 179, 185, 199, 200, 206, 218, 219, 220, 222, 226, 227, 228, 229, 233, 238, 260, 261, 309, 343; Land : 268, 270, 271

Home Rule (Movement) : 184, 247, 250, 254 n.3

Honan, China : xiii n.7, 85

Honey : 130, 143 n.4, 333

Honor(s) : 10, 162, 167, 219, 237 n.4, 244, 260, 265, 311, 343; Honorary : 62, 209

Hooghly River : 252, 255 n.17

Hookah : 144 n.8

Hooper, J.S.M. : 241 n.6

Horoscope : 144 n.12

Horse, Horseback : 112, 133, 135, 136, 174, 330, 331

Hospital : 36, 161, 183, 185, 188, 194, 209, 210, 252, 265

Hospitality : 227, 271, 275

Hostel (see Dormitory) : 180, 243

Hostility : 253

House, (see Home) : 10, 12, 68, 69, 76, 77, 99, 119, 121, 134, 135, 136, 141, 160, 165, 168, 173, 174, 179, 183, 214, 216, 217, 221, 225, 229, 257, 328, 331; Household : 120, 121, 131, 133, 138, 140, 145 n.28, 146 n.29, 166, 176, 158 n.12, 165, 185, 214, 218, 220, 228, 230, 304 n.3; Housing : 178, 226, 227, 243, 244, 285, 303

Hubli : 37

Hubshi, Habshi (see Sidi) : 25, 34, 280 Table 7, 312, 327

Hudson (see Johnson)

Human Rights : 189

Humanities : 206

Humayun Road : 186

Hupah : 135

Husain, Sheikh Abra : 146 n.34

Husband : 128, 131, 132, 136, 138, 139, 142, 146 n.34, 160, 166, 176, 185, 218, 221, 228, 230, 310, 346

Huzoor Paga Girls High School, Poona (now, High School for Indian Girls) : 180, 182

Hyam, Khan Bahadur Dr. Judah : 181, 188, 189, 245

Hyams, Abigail (Moses) : 180

Hyder (Haider) Ali : 314, 317, 318, 321, 323

Hymn : 233, 256 n.19, 342, 344

Ibn Ezra : 20, 28 n.8

Ibn Khurdadhbe : 19, 20, 28 n.3

I.C.S. (Indian Civil Service) : 182, 209

Ideals : 233, 271, 272

Identity, Identification : 80, 151, 156, 177, 269, 275

Idol, Idolatry, Image : 41, 44, 48 n.26, 67, 68, 69, 78, 87 n.32, 219, 336, 340, 341, 342, 345

Ignorance : 83, 150, 229

Ill(ness) : 46, 117, 132, 171, 260

Illegitimacy : 102; Illicit : 107

Illiteracy : 7, 80, 120, 121, 206 n.1, 213

Illustrations : 93, 352, 353

Image (see Idol) : 219, 229

Immersion : 146 n.30, 219, 348

Immigrant, Immigration : 53, 104, 122, 200, 232, 271, 272, 273 n.6, 275, 302, 303, 304

Implement(ation) : 220, 227, 235, 244, 257, 281

Imprint : 214, 221, 222 n.3

Improvement : 208, 214, 244, 245, 274, 281

Impurity (see Purity) : 101, 102, 103, 104

Incense : 5, 113, 124 n.14, 134, 145 n.21, 147 n.41

Income : 52, 59, 62, 63, 148, 150, 152, 170, 171 n.4, 180, 200, 204, 205, 234, 235, 237, 276

Increase : (Natural) : 285, 298, 304

Independence, Independent : 77, 101, 107, 150, 184, 189, 199, 200, 211, 216, 239, 243, Chapter 27 *passim* 247-252, 268, 270, 271, 273 n.6 and n.8, 285, 300 Table 21a, n.**

India (Independent) : 162, 199, 270, 271, 285, 294 Table 15

Indian, an : 252

"India and Israel" : 195 n.2, 273 n.7, 287

"Indian Census in Perspective" : 279, 304 n.1

Indian Civil Service : 182, 209

Indian Home Rule League : 184, 247, 250

Indian Medical Council : 255 n.8

Indian National Congress (see Congress) : 184, 246 n.1, 247, 248, 255 n.16

Indianization : 252

Indifference : 151, 169, 233

Indigenous : 17 n.52, 22, 23, 26, 65, 110 n.16, 117, 231 n.10, 309

Individuals : 176, 181, 186, 187, 194, Chapter 21 *passim* 208-212, 227, 233, 245, 247, 252, 253 n.1, 264, 266, 268, 269, 270

Indore : 59, 176, 184, 185, 191 n.12, 274

Indus River : 9, 21; Civilization : 16 n.43

Industry : 164 n.8, 174, 184, 200, 208, 252, 253, 282, 304 n.3, 306 n.12

Infant : 3, 211, 227

Infantry (see Army) : 162, 173, 174

Infirm(ity) : 139, 281, 282, 304 n.3

Inflation : 162

Influence : Chapter 6 *passim* 59-64, Chapter 7 *passim* 65-90, 107, 114, 118, 143, 166, 209, 219, 227, 233, 236, 249, 265, 270, 275
Information : 81, 239, 258, 266, 268, 279, 280, 282, 283
Inheritance : 139
Initiative : 194, 205, 232, 269
Innovation : 194, 235
Inoculation (see Vaccination) : 194
Inquisition : 25, 31 n.37 and n.38, 47 n.18, 152 n.1, 309, 310, 310 n.1
Inscription : 17 n.51, 30 n.25, 35, 36, 38 n.13, 46, 47 n.17, 122, 155, 157, 181, 278
Insight : 235
Inspector : 169, 170, 184, 185, 188
Inspiration : 236
Institution : 71, 79, 82, 102, 152, 158, 180, 181, 194, 199, 207 n.4, 230, 233, 234, 239, 240, 245, 266, 281
Instruction : 42, 66, 76, 77, 82, 221, 234, 273 n.6; Medium of : 260, 261
Insurance : Life : 235
Intellectual, Intelligent : 120, 161, 181, 200, 206
Interdine : 105
Intermarriage : 12, 17 n.48, 22, 50, 64 n.10, 89 n.49, 101, 102, 103, 105, 107, 108 n.6(1), 109 n.6(14), 124 n.14, 161, 225, 228, 264, 274, 275, 340, 341
Internal, Intra-Communal : 185, 194, 205
International : 261, 269, 270, 352; Conferences : 266
International Labour Organization : 209, 252, 253
International Organization of Industrial Employers : 252
Interpreter, Interpretation : 60, 214; Mis- : 69
Interview : xi, 215
Intimacy : 74, 103, 184, 237
Intolerance : 27, 230
Intrigue : 194
Introduction : 78, 92
Invest : 62, 151, 234
Investigation : 67
Invitation : 63, 137, 167, 237, 268, 309
Invocation, Invoke : 111, 112, 113, 120, 121, 128, 130, 131, 134, 229
Iqatpuri : 176
Iraqi (see Baghdadi) : viii, 98, 269
Irrigation : 160, 217
Isaac (Patriarch) : 229
Isaac, Eliahu Hai : 184
Isaac, I.A. : 230
Isaacs, Rufus Daniel, Lord Reading : 255 n.11

Isaiah, Book of : 131
Isenberg, Artur : xi
Isenberg, Shirley B. : 90 n.72, 292, 294, 296, 297
Islam, Islamic (see Muslim) : 7, 8, 20, 22, 24, 62, 104, 123 n.4, 125 n.23, 126 n.29, 143 n.4, 146 n.34, 154, 186, 230 n.2, 279, 317
Island : 3, 42, 43, 47 n.14, 50
Isolation : 82, 148, 176, 215, 219, 222, 270, 271, 275
Israel (the Land of, the Country) : vii, 88 n.41, 92, 93, 110 n.26, 145 n.22 and n.27, 150, 159 n.6, 177, 179, 184, 185, 190, 205, 213, 215, 216, 218, 221, 222, 224, 230, 231 n.15, 237 n.6, 241, 243, 260, 268, 270, 271, 272, 273 n.6, n.8 and n.10, 274, 285, 301-302 Table 23, 303, 304, 306 n.15
"Israel" (Magazine) : 170
Israel, Benjamin J. : ix, x-xi, xiv n.18, 13, 14 n.9, 25, 34, 35, 36, 38 n.13, 45, 48 n.28, 50, 80, 90 n.59, 93, 95, 96 n.11, 97 n.15, 138, 143, 146 n.32, 156, 157, 158, 190 n.6, 210, 212 n.2, 214, 216, 240, 267 n.4, 283, 284, 318, 319, 323, 324 n.17, 350-354
Israel, Hyam S. : 212 n.3
Israel, Jacob Bapuji : 208, 212 n.2, 230, 239, 243, 244, 245, 246, 246 n.1, 249, 257, 271
Israel, Richard : 236
Israel, Samuel : 210
Israel, Shalom Bapuji : 181, 208, 212 n.3, 249
Israel, Solomon Jacob : 212 n.3
Israel Alley, Mohalla : 174, 175 n.3, 178
"Israel Ashram" : 95
Israel Central Bureau of Statistics : 302, 303, 306 n.14
"Israel Mitra" : 95
Israel Mohalla : 46, 224, 225, 258
Israel National Phonoteque Archives : 231 n.11
"Israeli Dharmadeep" : 95
"Israeli Gyan Sanghara" : 95
"The Israelite" : 8, 15 n.28, n.29 and n.31, 32 n.50, 83, 156, 207 n.2, 208, 209, 230, 231 n.13, 237 n.5, 239, 240, 243, 245, 246 n.5 and n.7, 248, 250, 255 n.9, n.10 and n.14, 257, 262 n.1, n.2, n.3 and n.4, 265, 268, 271
Israelite Brotherhood : 263
Israelite Press : 182
The Israelite School (see Sir Elli Kadoorie School) : 77, 100, 102, 109 n.6(10), 149, 150, 152, Chapter 16 *passim* 169-172, 193, 209, 233, 234, 235, 242 n.6, 243, 245, 258, 259, 260, 262 n.9, 263, 264
Israelites : 42, 75, 76, 334
Issaji (see Divekar) : 59

Index 421

Jabalpur : 37, 176, 185
Jacket : 166
Jackson, Stanley : 102, 109 n.8
Jacob (Patriarch) : 229
Jacob Circle : 225, 232, 259, 269
Jacob (Gadkar) : E.M. : 153 n.11, 240
Jacob, Jessica : 211
Jacob, Dr. Sarah : 209
Jacobabad (Baluchistan) : 124 n.14
Jacobs, Joseph : 28 n.3
Jagir : 27
Jain : 27, 76, 79, 228, 243, 251, 279, 283, 284 Table 10
Jaipur : 191 n.11; Medical College : 209
Jama Masjid : 186
Jamat (General Assembly) : 61, 62, 64 n.12, 104, 269, 317
Janjira, Jiziri : 17 n.52, 25, 26, 27, 31 n.35, n.40 and n.41, 34, 42, 46, 95, 131, 160, 161, 208, 222 n.1, 297 Table 18, 299 Table 20, 312, 313, 316, 329, 336 n.8
Japheth, Maurice D. : 270, 278 n.1
Jarrett, Mr. : 67
Jati : xii n.1, 12, 16 n.48, 17 n.52, 104, 110 n.18, 137, 145 n.25, 220
Jawan : 173
Jealousy : 151, 161
Jemedar : 51, 54 n.13, 316, 322, 323
Jeremiah, Prophet : 268
Jerusalem : 5, 7, 67, 72, 73, 78, 88 n.49, 97 n.11, 108 n.6(6), 111, 118, 122, 123 n.4, 140, 148, 151, 152 n.2, 189, 243, 268, 270, 302
The Jerusalem Center for Anthropological Studies : xi
Jesus Christ : 69, 71, 73, 76, 77, 82, 84, 123 n.4, 336
Jew, Jewish, Jewry : vii, xii-xiii n.2, xiii n.5 and n.7; xiv n.10, 3, 4, 5, 6, 8, 10, 11, 12, 17 n.48, 20, 21, 22, 23, 24, 26, 27, 35, 36, 41, 43, 44, 47 n.16, 48 n.26, 49, 50, 53, 54 n.13, 56 n.21, 60, 64 n.11, 67, 68, 69, 70, 73, 74, 76, 77, 78, 79, 80, 81, 82, 83, 84, 86 n.24, 87 n.32, 88 n.40 and n.49, 89 n.51, 90 n.62 and n.72, 92, 93, 94, 95, 98, 99, 101, 102, 103, 104, 107, 108 n.1 and n.6(1) and (7), 109 n.11, 110 n.26, 111, 112, 113, 117, 118, 119, 122, 124 n.13 and n.14, 125 n.23, n.24 and n.25, 127, 130, 133, 139, 141, 142, 143, 143 n.4, 144 n.12 and n.18, 145 n.24, 150, 151, 152 n.1, 153 n.5, 154, 158 n.1 and n.2, 159 n.7, 167, 168, 170, 174, 175, 175 n.5 and n.6, 176, 177, 178, 179, 181, 182, 185, 186, 187, 188, 189, 191 n.12, 194, 200, 201-203, 205, 206 n.1, 209, 211, 212 n.6, 214, 215, 216, 218, 219, 220, 221, 222 n.3, 224, 225, 227, 228, 229, 230 n.4, 231 n.11, 233, 234, 235, 238, 239, 246 n.4, 247, 248, 249, 250, 251, 252, 255 n.9, n.11 and n.13, 257, 258, 260, 261, 262, 263, 264, 265, 266, 268, 269, 270, 271, 272 n.3, 274, 275, 278 n.3, Chapter 33 *passim* 279-306, 318, 319, 326, 333, 344, 345
Jewel, Jeweler, Jewelry : 42, 133, 136, 142, 144 n.19, 142, 166, 186; Bangles : 128, 129, 133, 134, 137, 140, 141, 144 n.19, 145; Laccha; 133, 135, 137, 141, 145 n.23
Jewish Agency : 270, 271, 272, 272 n.6, 275; 301-302 Table 23
Jewish Association of Delhi : 186, 187
Jewish Association of Calcutta : 266
"The Jewish Chronicle" (London) : ix, 82, 103, 124 n.14, 161, 163 n.5, 305 n.5
Jewish Club Bombay : 266
Jewish Communities : vii, viii, ix, xiii n.5
Jewish Cooperative Credit Society, Ltd. : 245
Jewish Cultural Ass'n. : 266
"Jewish Encyclopaedia" (Funk & Wagnall) : 4, 109 n.7
Jewish Nationalist Party : 238, 250, 251
Jewish Relief Association : 269
Jewish Religious Union : 209, 230, 232, 235, 236, 241 n.1, 263; Youth Wing : 266
Jewish Theological Seminary of America : 236
Jhelum River : 20, 28 n.10
"The Jewish Tribune" : 152 n.1
Jhirad, Dr. Jerusha : 181, 209, 211, 235, 263
Jhiradkar : 10, 13; Hyam Samuel : 184; Joseph Solomon : 179, 181
Jinna, Mohamed Ali : 177, 247, 254 n.3
Job (see Employment) : 103, 160, 179, 186, 194, 199, 205, 220, 221, 222, 226, 261, 270, 271, 272, 274, 276, 285, 303
Johnson, Dr. Barbara Cottle : 40, 46 n.2 and n.3, 85 n.7, 231 n.1
Join (see Unite) : 266, 269
Joint Family (see Family)
Joseph (Patriarch) : 229, 238
Joshi, Mrs. : 261
Journal (see Diary) : ix, 36, 41, 70, 95, 138, 152 n.1, 208, 209, 230, 281
Journalism : ix, 199, 240; Journalist : 211, 238
"Journal of Commerce & Shipping Telegraph" : 253
Journey : 72, 218
Jubalpur : 37, 176, 185
Judah, Dr. Rachel : 188
Judah Hyam Prayer Hall : 181, 185, 188, 189, 232,
Judah Magnes Museum : 105
Judaica : 179, 189, 238

422 India's Bene Israel

Judaism (see Revival of) : vii, viii, xiii n.7, 10, 11, 12, 27, 28 n.1, 41, 44, 45, 46, 53, 59, 60, 65, 80, 83, 84, 87 n.33, 95, 100, 101, 104, 107, 111, 112, 138, 148, 150, 185, 186, 229, 230, 231 n.5, 233, 236, 239, 242 n.6, 275, 276, 279, 309

Judge, Judicial : 11, 62, 107, 181, 183, 208, 209, 239, 254 n.3, 340

Junagad : 208

Jungle : 26, 214

Jussay, Prof. P.M. : 231 n.11

Justice : 94, 253, 329; Lord Chief : 255 n.11

Kabbalah : 153 n.2

Kadavambakkam Synagogue : 232

Kaddish : 108 n.6, 141, 142, 233

Kadoorie, Sir Elly (School) : 152, 209, 214, 260, 261, 262 n.10, 264

Kaifeng : xiii n.7, 85, 90 n.72

Kaji, Kadi, Kazi : 10, 12, 13, 34, 35, 37 n.6, 45, 48 n.23, 50, 51, 52, 55 n.15, 61, 62, 110 n.22, 114, 117, 130, 133, 134, 136, 140, 141, 142, 145 n.6, 167, 184, 275, 312, 313, 319, 329, 330, 331, 340, 341, 343, 344

Kala Israel : 15 n.21, 67, 101, 104, 105, 107, 110 n.19, n23 and n.26; 144 n.17, 179, 228, 264, 341

Kalbadevi : 251

Kalina : 225

Kalyan : 173, 174

Kamateepura : 36, 105

Kamerlekar, Rotanbai Joseph : 180

Kamti : 36

Kandahar : 28 n.9

Kanheri : 30 n.25

Kapadvanj : 183

Kapporoth : 119, 125 n.25, 333

Karachi : 59, 83, 150, 174, 177-178, 179, 187, 204, 208, 214, 244, 246, 282

Karbhari : 208, 212 n.1

Karchund : 216

Karjat : 173

Karnataka (Mysore State) : 37, 48 n.21, 176, 185, 255 n.16

Karsulkar, S.S. : 260

Karve, Dr. Iravati : 24, 30 n.30, 55 n.16, 268, 272 n.1

Karwar : 31 n.40, 185

Kashmir : 20, 28 n.8, 123 n.4, 186, 269

Kashrut : 17 n.50, 100, 104, 110 n.15, 167, 343

Kathiawar : 183

Kehim : 3, 173, 190

Kehimkar (other than H.S.) : Abraham Aaron :
Judge 183, 209; Joseph Samuel : 169; Samuel ; 170; Samuel Jacob : 169, 171 n.1

Kehimkar, Haeem Samuel : ix, xiii-xiv n.10, 3, 4, 5, 6, 7, 8, 9, 10, 14 n.10, 15 n.13, n.15, n.19 and n.22, 16 n.44, and n.46, 22, 32 n.45, 33, 34, 36, 37 n.6, 38 n.19, 45, 48 n.30, 50, 52, 53 n.4, 54 n.14, 55 n.17, 56 n.24 and n.25, 59, 63 n.3, 69, 75, 80, 86 n.13, 90 n.60, 91, 95, 95 n.1, 99, 100, 103, 104, 105, 107, 108 n.2, 109 n.9, n.14 and n.15, 110 n.20 and n.24, 111, 113, 115, 116, 117, 118, 119, 120, 121, 122, 123 n.5 and n.9, 125 n.26, 127, 128, 129, 130, 131, 132, 133, 134, 135, 136, 137, 139, 140, 141, 142, 143 n.2, n.3, n.4 and n.5, 144 n.8, n.9, n.12, n.13, n.15, n.17 and n.18, 145 n.21 and n.26, 149, 150, 151, 153 n.7 and n.9, 166, 167, Chapter 16 passim 169-172, 183, 235, 240, 245, 246 n.6, 257, 267 n.3, 268, 269, 281, 311, 312, 313, 315, 316, 318, 321, 322

Kerala : vii, viii, xiii n.5, 9, 24, 29-30 n.19, 43, 64 n.12, 67, 95 n.2, 146 n.33, 206 n.1, 231 n.11, 257, 284

Ketubah : 10, 31 n.38, 136, 137, 330, 331

Khadak : 149

Khadi : 249

Khalapur : 223 n.6

Khan Bahadur : 54 n.13, 181, 184, 188, 208, 211

Khan Sahib : 211, 212 n.6

Khandala : 112, 113, 116

Khandesh : 208

Khar : 225

Kharilkar, Simeon Jacob : 92

Kharsai : 222 n.1

Kher, Dr. B.G. : 260

Khiriacha San ; 4, 5, 15 n.19

Khoja : 17 n.52, 146 n.34, 224, 230 n.2

Khorasan : 186

Kibbutz : 88 n.41, 273 n.10

Kiblah : 78, 89 n.49

Kiddush, Kedushah (see Blessing) : 17 n.50, 63, 108 n.6, 136, 218, 233, 346, 353

Killekar : 181

Kindergarten : 261

Kindness : 227

Kindil : 113, 123 n.8

King : 71, 135, 136, 185, 255 n.9; Solomon : 9

Kingdom of Israel : 6, 8, 88 n.49, 111, 154

Kingdom of Judah : 6, 7, 154

Kin(ship) : 155, 220, 228, 229

Kippur (see Yom Kippur) : 333

Kirki : 189

Kirtan, Kirtankar : 91, 95-96 n.2, 208, 238, 240, 263

Index 423

Kiss : 119, 121, 122, 129, 136, 214
Kitchen : 165, 217
Knesset Eliyahu Synagogue, Bombay : 149
Knesset Israel Synagogue, Tala-Ghosale : 149, 274, 277
Knowledge : 93, 94, 107, 151, 242 n.6, 258, 274, 275
Kobler, Franz : 23, 30 n.26
Koder, Satu : 266
Kokban : 213, 222 n.1
Kolaba, Kulaba, Colaba : 26, 32 n.44, 36, 37 n.6 and n.7, 47 n.14, 204 Table 3, 222 n.1, 281, 284; District : xiii n.6, 17 n.52, 25, 31 n.35 and n.41, 37 n.4, 42, 56 n.19, 65, 93, 105-106, 115, 138, 149, 158, 160, 173, 179, 207 n.8, 213, 214, 215, 216, 232, 237 n.4, 273 n.9, 283, 284, 290 Table 13 a, 297 Table 18, 299 Table 20
Kolabakar, S.J. : 26, 37 n.7, 153 n.5, 213, 214, 222 n.1, 232,
Kolet, Ezra : 187, 189, 210, 266
Koletkar, David Eliezer : 181
Kolhapur : 31 n.40, 182
Konkan : viii, ix, xiii n.6, xiv n.11, 3, 7, 8, 10, 11, 12, 13, 13 n.2, 14 n.7, 17 n.52, 22, 23, 24, 25, 26, 27, 30 n.19, 31 n.38 and n.41, 33, 35, 36-37, 41, 42, 43, 44, 45, 48 n.21 and n.22, 49, 50, 52, 53 n.4, 56 n.19, 59, 60, 65, 67, 71, 80, 84, 85, 93, 95 n.2, 112, 115, 116, 120, 123 n.4, 124 n.18, 125 n.20 and n.25, 128, 138, 143 n.1, and n.4, 146 n.34, 148, 152, 154, 156, 158, 168, 169, Chapter 17 *passim* 173-175, 175 n.6, 176, 177, 182, 185, 189, 212 n.2, 219, 220, 221, 222, 222 n.1, 237, 268, 272, 275, 278, 280, 283, 284, 327
Konkani : 52, 56 n.19
Koran, Quran : 7, 25, 125 n.18, 162, 316, 317
Korban Nedaba, Free-Will (Voluntary) Offering : 116
Korban Neder, Vow Offering : 116
Korban Neser : 116
Korban Tehara : 116
Korlai : 222 n.1
Korlekar : 185, 252
Kosher : 12, 17 n.50, 48 n.26, 60, 62, 100, 102, 215
Krishna : 94, 137
Kshatriya : 16 n.48
Kulaba (see Kolaba)
Kunbi : 166, 243
Kurla : 225, 232
Kutch : 24, 183
Kuzari Kingdom : 87 n.33

Laborer, Labour : 53, 160, 199, 207 n.3, 209, 211, 217, 252, 312, 345; Landless : 223 n.8
Laccha : 132, 136, 137, 141, 145 n.23, and n.25
Ladies, Lady : 77, 137, 233, 234, 235, 258
Lahore : 32 n.47, 186
Lakh : 255 n.12
Lamb, Sheep : 114, 177, 214, 222 n.3, 343; Pascal : 332
Lamp, Light : 55 n.16, 115, 120, 121, 128, 130, 140, 142, 150, 166, 188, 214, 217, 218, 227, 231 n.7, 264
"Lamp of Judaism" : 194
Land, Landlord : 27, 33, 34, 46, 52, 100, 148, 160, 173, 174, 183, 184, 186, 187, 214, 216, 217, 218, 220, 237, 246, 264, 282, 311; Landless : 16 n.48, 223 n.8
Language : 35, 67, 68, 69, 70, 73, 75, 76, 80, 91, 93, 94, 101, 102, 136, 150, 159 n.12, 176, 181, 206, 228, 233, 234, 235, 241 n.6, 260, 261, 269, 274, 304 n.3, 309, 328, 340, 342; Mother Tongue : 207 n.8, 216
Lap : 116, 128, 129, 130, 136, 145 n.26
Latin : 171 n.3
Lavni : 91
Law, Legal, (see Advocate, Court) : 23, 44, 62, 83, 102, 108 n.6(9), 110 n.26, 137, 139, 151, 161, 181, 185, 186, 199, 209, 216, 222, 228, 239, 245, 247, 254 n.3, 255 n.11, 257, 258, 270, 272 n.4; Jewish : 7, 60, 69, 71, 80, 89 n.49, 93, 275, 310, 314, 341
Leader, Leadership : 62, 99, 151, 167, 193, 194, 205, 227, 230, 234, 237, 246, 250, 267, 268, 269, 274, 275, 344
League of Nations : 252, 272 n.6
Learning (see Scholarship) : 107, 160, 185, 269
Leave : 271
Leaven : 120
Lectures : 91, 94, 170, 175, 188, 235, 236, 257, 263, 264, 270
Legend : 13 n.2, 45
Leisure ; 200
Lesson : 76, 180, 234, 269
Letter : 21, 22, 23, 24, 28 n.13, n.14 and n.15, 29 n.16, 30 n.26, 49-50, 70, 78, 88 n.48, 104, 105-106, 108 n.6, 139, 253, 277, 281, 317-318; Alphabet : 35, 91, 92, 117, 142, 155; Letter from M.K. Gandhi : 245 n.5; Letter to E.S. Montague : 248-249; Letter from Ezekiel Rahabi in 1768 : 38 n.14, 40, 43, 44, 45, 48 n.24, 59, 67, 75, 81, 117, 314; Letter from Rev. John Wilson : 77, 88 n.47
Levirate : 102, 110 n.26, 139, 344
Levite, Levy : 6, 60, 67, 93, 354

Leviticus, Book of : 3, 5, 6, 98, 111, 114, 116, 131, 144 n.7, 145 n.21
Liberal, Liberation : 101, 151, 230, 235, 236, 239, 241 n.3, 257; Liberty : 249
Libraries : xi, 73, 74, 86 n.24, 89 n.51, 170, 179, 181, 189, 209, 231 n.11, 235, 241 n.2, 256 n.19, 263, 310
License : 137
Lid : 140, 141
Life-Cycle (see Rites of Passage) : Chapter 11 passim 127-147, 167, 229
Life-History : 215-222
Life-Style : viii; 100, 103, Chapter 10 passim 111-126, 176, 177, 194, 199, Chapter 23 passim 224-231, 269, 274-275
Light, (see Lamp) : 62, 120, 150, 217, 264
Lingua France : 19, 186
Linguistics : 71, 231 n.11; 300 Table 21a n.**, 317
Liquor (see Alcoholism, Temperance) : 161, 167
List : 270
Literacy, Literate : 169, 191 n.7, 206 n.1, 213, 217, 219, 220, 281, 282, 283 Table 9, 304 n.5
Literature, Literary, Writings : ix, xiv n.16, 6, 79, 80, 88 n.43, 89 n.49, 91, 92, 93, 97 n.13, 185, 211, 217, 236, 257, 275, 278 n.3
Lithograph : 89 n.52, 92, 93, 94, 96 n.3
Litigation : 245
Liturgy : (see Prayer) : 3, 7, 10, 60, 61, 92, 93, 111, 113, 114, 135, 136, 218, 329
Liver : 114, 116, 142
Livelihood, a Living : 170, 174, 200, 229, 247, 260, 269
Livorno (Leghorn) : 93
Loan : 205
Lobbying : 137
Local : 65, 67, 121, 127, 132, 133, 136, 137, 143, 150, 154, 162, 167, 237, 247, 282, 285, 305 n.9
Lok : 49
Lonavla : 36, 182
London : 32 n.50, 79, 84, 86 n.24, 188, 190, 209, 235, 252, 256 n.19, 259, 260, 305 n.5 and n.6, 333
London Society for Promoting Christianity Among Jews : 67, 79, 85 n.8, 90 n.55, 110 n.23
Lord, Rev. J. Henry : x, xiv n.13, 7, 9, 15 n.25, 24, 30 n.25, 32 n.43, 82, 83, 84, 90 n.62, 99, 109 n.11, 112, 115, 121, 123 n.6 and n.12, 124 n.14, n.17 and n.18, 125 n.27, 156, 182, 191 n.8, 233, 281, 284, 285; Lord's Tables : 288-291 Table 12 a through 12 e, 292-293 Table 14, 297 Table 18

Love : 60, 72, 135, 171, 228, 249, 268, 271, 272 n.3, 275
Loyal(ty) : 80, 161, 243, 250, 255 n.9
Lullaby : 96 n.2, 131, 229
Lunghi : 140

"Maccabi", Maccabeean Fellowship : 91, 118, 239, 264, 266; Judas Maccabeus : 334
Madai : Moses Elia : 106; Moshe & Jacob : 184
Madhya Pradesh : 37, 176, 185
Madras : 50, 67, 68, 72, 73, 98, 211, 269, 306 n.12, 321, 322, 326; Presidency : 73; Province : 185
Madras Jews Society : 68, 335
Madras University : 104
Magazine : 170, 257
Magen Avraham Synagogue, Ahmedabad : 149, 184
Magen Avoth Synagogue, Alibag : 149, 153 n.3, 173, 175 n.1
Magen David Synagogue, Bombay : 36, 149, 265
Magen Hassidim Synagogue : 232, 234
Magen Shalom Synagogue, Karachi : 150, 177
Maggid Hadashoth : 40, 41, 42, 44, 47 n.6
Magic, Magician : 70, 144 n.10
Magistrate : 184, 208, 209, 247
Mahabharata, The : 20
Mahadevan, Meera Mendrekar : xii n.2, 211, 212 n.5, 240
Mahal : 216, 223 n.5
Maharashtra, Maharashtrian : xii, xiii n.6, xiv n:11, 9, 13 n.2, 14 n.7, 15 n.33, 24, 31 n.39, 36, 48 n.21, 49, 53, 55 n.16, 56 n.19, 87 n.26, 137, 146 n.34, 155, 158, 176, 178, 184, 206, 223 n.7, 247, 255 n.16, 268, 277, 283, 300 Table 21 a n.**; 301 Table 22, 341, 346, 350
Mahi Kanta : 183
Mahim : 47 n.14, 128, 225
Maimonides, Moses : 23, 24, 223 n.12
Maimounda : 267 n.2
Mainland : 43, 50
Maintenance : 36, 122, 148, 151, 152, 180, 182, 229, 234, 237, 251, 275, 278
Maistry : 245
Major General : 199, 210
Majority : 107, 160, 234, 243, 248, 250, 258, 273 n.8, 282, 284; Major : 279
Majrona : 222 n.1
Malabar : 22, 23, 29 n.17, 36, 41, 43, 52, 74, 121, 122, 319; Malabari Jews : 40, 41, 46

Index   425

n.2, 47 n.11, 56 n.21, 85-86 n.9, 107, 232, 314, 315, 317
Malabar Hill : 224, 309
Malaria : 214, 222 n.2
Malayalam : 95-96 n.2, 231 n.11
Male : 3, 76, 81, 105, 121, 125 n.25, 130, 131, 133, 134, 137, 138, 139, 140, 142, 144, n.7, 154, 162, 166, 175, 201-203, 214, 217, 228, 241 n.3, 257, 258, 279, 281; 286 Table 11; 297 Table 18; 298 Table 19, 299 Table 20; 301 Table 22
Malida : 6, 111, 112, 113, 114, 115, 116, 117, 120, 124 n.15, 124-125 n.18, 128, 130, 131, 134, 142, 230
Malik Amber : 26, 33, 37 n.2, 47 n.13
Man, Men : 91, 105, 116, 134, 138, 140, 166, 167, 194, 199, 200, 208, 214, 223 n.9, 228, 234, 236, 244, 245, 258, 266, 342
Manager, Management : 62, 102, 205, 208, 210, 212 n.1, 234, 245, 260, 306 n.12
Manchester Mill : 205
Mandate : 272-273 n.6
Mandvi, Mandobi : 46, 149, 224, 310, 317
Mangalore : 22, 29 n.17, 189, 321, 322
Mangaon Taluka, Mangaonkar : 27, 42, 223 n.6, 274
Mango : 52, 134, 138, 174
Manipuri Jews : xiii n.7
Mankari, Headman : 62, 145 n.26
Manual Training : 175
Manufacture : 249, 253
Manumission : 40
Manuscript : ix, 10, 20, 81, 89 n.49, 245, 255 n.18, 269, 310
Maow : 36
Map : 11, 13, 42, 199, 214
Maratha(s) (Maharattas) : 18 n.52, 26, 27, 31 n.39, n.40 and n.41; 34, 35, 38 n.10, 42, 44, 49, 50, 56 n.20, 85 n.9, 87 n.35, 131, 159 n.12, 164 n.8, 166, 322, 327, 329
Marathi : 4, 5, 13 n.3, 14 n.9, 15 n.12, 35, 36, 38 n.13, 49, 52, 56 n.19, 64 n.12, 65, 68, 72, 75, 76, 77, 80, 82, 84, 85 n.1, 88 n.41 and n.42, 91, 92, 93, 94, 95, 96 n.2, n.6 and n.11, 97 n.12, 99, 100, 103, 115, 117, 118, 121, 130, 131, 134, 139, 140, 142, 152, 153 n.3, 156, 169, 170, 171, 171 n.1, 175, 176, 177, 178, 181, 183, 206, 207 n.8, 208, 209, 216, 219, 220, 227, 229, 230, 231 n.11, 235, 238, 239, 241 n.3, 241-242 n.6, 245, 256 n.19, 259, 261, 263, 271, 278, 278 n.4, 316, 328, 335, 341, 342, 345, 346, 350, 351, 352, 354
Marine, Navy (see Merchant Marine, Naik) : 50, 54 n.8, 55 n.15, 209, 210, 252

Marker : 35, 38 n.9, 141, 142
Market : 217
Marrano : 25, 31 n.38, 35, 310
Marriage, Married (see Wedding) : 10, 12, 22, 29 n.19, 31 n.38, 55 n.16, 81, 83, 95, 102, 103, 105, 106, 107, 108 n.6(1), 110 n.18 and n.26, 123 n.8, 131, 132-139, 144 n.12, n.14, n.15, and n.16, 145 n.25 and n.27, 146 n.34, 152 n.1, 155, 166, 177, 181, 184, 190, 199, 200, 213, 217, 218, 221, 225, 228, 229, 239, 243, 245, 265, 267 n.5, 270, 274, 275, 276 n.1, 304 n.3, 312, 330, 331, 343, 344; Cross-Cousin Marriage: 101 n.14, 133, 134, 136, 144 n.16; Re-Marriage : 102, 108 n.6(9), 133
Masjid (Synagogue) : 329, 331, 333; Mesgad : 60, 63 n.8
Mason (see Free Mason) : 174, 178, 206, 245, 328; Construction : 160
Master : of Arts (M.A.) : 210, 258; Weaving Master : 103
Mat : 219
Matchmaker : 133, 275
Matheran : 264
Matriculation : 72, 87 n.27, 170, 171 n.2, 180, 209, 258, 261
Matrilineal : 29 n.19, 146 n.33, 257
Matrimony : 245
Matthews, General : 316, 318, 322
Matunga : 47 n.14, 225
Matzah, Matzoth (see Unleavened) : 93, 218
Mayor : 180, 225, 247, 253-254 n.2; Bombay : 208, 266
Mazgaon : 170, 224, 225, 258, 259, 260; Dock : 210
Mazgaonkar, S.S. : 239, 249
M.B.E. : 209, 210, 211, 212 n.3
McCrindle, J.W. : 30 n.25
Meal : 114, 118, 119, 120, 121, 134, 141, 142, 167, 221, 261, 342, 346
Measles : 132
Meat : 60, 100, 104, 114, 167, 177, 215, 227, 340, 343
"Mebasser" : 239
Mechanics, Mechanical : 163, 176, 199, 200, 206, 261
Medicine, Medical (see Doctor, Physician) : 31 n.38, 84, 102, 161, 163, 181, 183, 185, 195, 199, 208, 209, 210, 217, 230, 235, 261, 263, 309, 341, 346
Medieval, Middle Ages : 23, 30 n.31, 145 n.22, 231 n.11
Mediterranean : 21, 29 n.17
Meeting : 62, 63, 68, 79, 104, 151, 188, 233, 234, 243, 244, 252, 263

Mehndi : 132, 134, 137, 145 n.20, 228, 229, 330
Melody : 188, 229
Member, Membership : 61, 151, 152, 181, 234, 235, 236, 237, 237 n.3, n.6 and n.7, 252, 264, 266, 269, 287; Fee : 233
Memoir : 51, 81
Memorandum : 246 n.1, 250, 251
Memorial Monument : 277, 278, 278 n.1 and n.2
Memorial Prayer, (see Hashkabah) : 115, 134, 142, 181, 188, 189
Menasseh, Shimshon : 88 n.41
Menorah : 148
Menstruation, Menses : 132, 234, 257, 341, 346
Mentality : 104, 245
Mercenary : 25
Merchant (see Trader) : 7, 11, 12, 17, 19, 20, 21, 22, 23, 24, 26, 28 n.13, 29 n.17, 30 n.19, 31 n.38, 32 n.47, 35, 40, 42, 43, 47 n.11, 52, 59, 65, 77, 81, 85 n.2, 98, 99, 108 n.1, 160, 179, 186, 191 n.7, 193, 273 n.7, 317
Merchant Marine : 199, 210, 252, 256 n.18 and n.19
Merit : 162, 211, 259, 260
Messiah : 64 n.10, 67, 71, 73, 75, 76, 77, 82, 97 n.11, 112, 268, 336
Metal : 143 n.4
Meyuhasim : 40
Mezuzah : 14 n.6, 165, 175 n.1, 214, 227, 237 n.6
Mhasilkar : 213; Khan Bahadur Dr. Judah Hyam :181, 188, 189
Mhasla (Mahal) : 31 n.35, 149, 208, 213, 222 n.1, 274, 283
Mhawa : 213, 222 n.1
Mheter : 33, 37 n.2, 311
Microfilm : 86 n.24
Middle ages : 7, 19, 22, 40, 60, 96 n.2
Middle Class (see Class) : 121, 136, 160, 327
Middle East : 6, 177
"Middle India" or "Second India" : 24
Midrash : 10
Midwife : 128, 199, 230
Migrate : 42, 187
Mikhail Joseph : 89 n.53
Mikveh : 144 n.18, 148, 233, 341, 345, 348
Military (see Native Troops) : ix, 25, 27, 50, 51, 59, 60, 73, 93, 109 n.6(9), 162, 163, 170, 173, 174, 176, 177, 178, 179, 193, 199, 205, 209, 212 n.3, 221, 244
Milk : 100, 115, 128, 130, 131, 133, 143 n.4, 155, 160, 167, 221
Mills : 51, 102, 103, 134, 164 n.9, 182, 184, 191 n.9, 205, 217, 218, 232, 253

Minha : 109 n.6
Minhag Cochin : 109 n.6, 345
Minister : 235, 236, 275
Ministry, Minister : Commerce : 252, 253 n.1; Finance : 187, 189; Irrigation and Power : 188; Posts and Telegraph : 187; Shipping and Transport : 187, 189, 210; Works and Housing : 188, 211
Minneapolis : 188
Minority : xii n.2, 177, 189, 193, 194, 243, 246 n.1, 248, 250, 254 n.2, 271, 284, 304, 305 n.9
Minyan : 102, 114, 130, 141, 142, 148, 180, 185, 188, 223 n.12, 224, 237, 265
Mir, Ezra : 211
Mis'ar Bin Muhalhil : 23
Mishnah : 116, 124 n.14
Misinterpretation : 69, 80, 104
Missionaries & Missions (see Lord, Rev. J. H. and Wilson, Rev. John) : ix, xiii n.7, 3, 6, 25, 43, 49, Chapter 7 *passim* 65-90, 91, 93, 94, 95, 99, 148, 161, 166, 169, 170, 174, 177, 185, 214, 229, 238, 241 n.3, 275, 330, 335
Mitchell, Dr. J. M. : 93
Mizoram : xiii n.7
Mizrach (see Shivti) : 152 n.2
Mobile Creches : xiii n.2, 211, 212 n.5
Mobility : 52, 189, 190, 285
Mocatta Library : 85 n.7
Mocha : 253
Modern : 53, 73, 154, 155, 166, 177, 199, 217, 219, 220, 225, 228, 229, 230, 233, 236, 257, 261, 263, 269, 271, 275, 279
Modi, Shams ul ulma Jivanji Jamshedi : 122, 126 n.29
Moens, Adriaan : 49, 53 n.3
Moghul, Mongol : 14 n.9, 24, 25, 26, 27, 32 n.47, 40, 41, 42, 44, 47 n.4, n.13 and n.16, 48 n.21, 54 n.13, 186, 193
Mohammed, the Prophet : 6, 7, 123 n.4
Mohammedan(s) (see Muslim(s)) : 36, 37 n.3, 50, 161, 248, 250
Mohel, Circumciser : 60, 61, 130, 177, 180, 275, 340, 345
Mokha, Mocha : 40, 41
Mombayin : 309
Money (see Cash) : 62, 63, 73, 151, 170, 226, 230 n.4, 247
Money-Lender : 52, 186
Monopoly : 186, 193
Monsoon : 52, 167, 178, 214, 215, 217
Montagu, Edwin Samuel : 248, 249, 255 n.15
Month (Hebrew) : 15 n.9, 113, 116, 117, 118, 120, 121, 125 n.22, 128, 223 n. 12, 331, 332, 333, 334

Index   427

Monthly (Journal) : 94, 239
Monument : 181, Chapter 32 *passim* 277-278
Moon : 116, 221, 223 n.12, 332
Morals, Morality : 59, 66, 69, 75, 91, 151, 228, 233, 235, 258, 263, 272 n.3; Immorality : 193
Morocco : 31 n.38, 267 n.2
Mortar and Pestle : 165
Moses (Biblical) : 44, 71, 229
Moses, Dr. Elijah (Rajpurkar) : 208, 225, 247, 253-254 n.2, 266; Mrs. : 180
Mosque : 23, 174, 186
Mother : 48 n.20, 119, 129, 130, 131, 132, 133, 142, 144 n.7, 190, 225, 227, 228, 229, 275, 310, 317, 318; Mother-in law : 136, 138, 146 n.29
Mother Tongue (see Language) : 207 n.8, 216, 219

Motivation : 271
Motzei Shabbat : 114
Moulder : 206
Mound : 3, 8, 35
Mount Gerizim : 88 n.49
Mourner, Mourning : 4, 6, 140, 141, 142, 233, 331
Moustache : 167
M'shuḥrarim : 40, 46 n.2
Muhammed of Ghazni : 28 n.11

Mukkadam : 59, 61, 62, 63 n.2, 64 n.12, 193, 329, 336
Mukti Mission, Kedgaon : 241, n.3; Press : 238
Müller, F. Max : 9, 16 n.35 and n. 39
Mullik, Amber : 33, 311
Mulnaji : 10
Multan : 177
Municipal(ity) : 174, 178, 181, 184, 208, 209, 226, 247, 253-254 n.2, 259, 260
Murud, Mahal : 10, 13, 31 n.35, 149, 213, 222 n.1, 232, 274, 283
Musaf : 108 n.6
Musajee : 34, 35, 154
Music : 91, 133, 134, 135, 136, 138, 199, 229, 231 n.11, 342; Violinist : 210
Musleah, Rabbi Ezekiel : xiii n.8; 236, 305 n.10
Muslim(s), Mohammedan : 3, 7, 11, 12, 13 n.3, 14 n.9, 17 n.48, 19, 21, 23, 24, 26, 27, 28 n.9, 29 n.17, 31 n.34 and n.40, 32 n.46, 35, 36, 45, 50, 51, 53, 53 n.4, 54 n.13, 55 n.15, 56 n.20, 63 n.2, 64 n.12, 66, 69, 76, 77, 79, 104, 114, 115, 116, 118, 119, 121, 123 n.4, n.5 and n.12, 124 n.14, 125 n.18, 127, 131, 134, 135, 138, 139, 141, 143, 144 n.10, 146 n.28, n.30 and n.34, 147 n.39, 150, 154, 159 n.12, 160, 162, 166, 168 n.5, 173, 174, 179, 186, 187, 193, 206 n.1, 216, 217, 219, 220, 224, 225, 243, 246 n.1, 247, 249, 250, 251, 256 n.19, 261, 263, 271, 278 n.3, 283, 284 Table 10; 310, 314, 327, 328

Muslim League : 246 n.1, 247, 248
Mutiny 1857 : 162
Myrtle : 120, 131, 147 n.41
Mysore (see Karnataka) : 37, 44, 46, 314; Wars : 51, 154, 316, 317, 318, 319, 320, 322, 323
Mystic : 145 n.22, 186, 238
Mythological : 208

Nablus : 78, 88 n.49
Nagaonkar : 251
Nagavkar : Shalom Benjamin : 210
Nagawra : 33, 37 n.1, 311
Nagpada : 224, 225, 263
Nagpur : 36, 176, 185, 241 n.6, 274, 347
Naik, Nayek : 34, 37 n.6, 54 n.13
Nair : 29 n.19, 30 n.19
Najara, Israel ben Moses : 135, 145 n.22
Name, Appelation (see Term) : 4, 45, 49, 53 n.3 and n.4, 67, 74, 78, 79, 83, 89 n.53, 95, 116, 117, 118, 130, 138, 142, Chapter 13 *passim* 154-159, 166, 175 n.3, 182, 189, 213, 215, 219, 223 n.10, 225, 228, 229, 260, 284, 285, 298, 327, 335
Nana Peth : 178
Nandgaon : Synagogue : 149, 213, 222 n.1, 283 Table 9
Nasi : 43, 47 n.17, 67, 70
Nation, Nationality, Nationlist : 178, 209, 243, 247, 248, 249, 250, 251, 252, 269, 272 n.6, 305 n.9
National Book Trust : 210
National Defence Academy : 210
National(U.S.A.) Federation of Temple Sisterhoods : 236
Nativ, Rabbi Elisha : 236
Native Place, Native(s) : 23, 49, 50, 66, 67, 70, 75, 76, 98, 155, 176, 193, 194, 219, 221, 252, 268, 269, 283, 284
Native Troops, Native Army (see Regiment, Sepoy) : 25, 38 n.10, 46, 50, 51, 67, 69, 99, 101, 138, 161, 162, 164 n.8, 280, 318, 329; Bombay Army : 163 n.4 and n.6
Naturalist : 210
Naturalization : 268
Navgaon : 3, 6, 8, 9, 16 n.33, 23, 32 n.50, 35, 38 n.13, 60, 112, 244, 246, 277-278, 327
Navgaonkar : 180, 182

Naviacha San or Roja : 4, 5; Roja : 118
Navsari : 193
Navy (see Marine) : 34, 50, 51, 199, 210, 212 n.4
Nawab (of Janjira) : 25, 27
Nazi : 209, 269, 272 n.4, 305 n.11
Nazirite (see Korban Neser) : 116, 125 n.21
Nebuchadnezzar : 118, 334
Necklace : 132, 145 n.25
Neder (see Vow) : 114, 116, 117
Need(y) : 102, 170, 235, 261, 262 n.10, 266, 275;
Neglect : 274
Nehemiah : 6, 131
Nehemiah Mota : 114
Neighbor, Neighborhood : 12, 20, 50, 53, 104, 115, 118, 119, 129, 134, 139, 143, 144 n.10 and n.13, 153 n.7, 162, 166, 168, 168 n.5, 174, 179, 182, 215, 219, 220, 221, 224, 225, 226, 227, 229, 233, 237, 258, 260, 263, 264, 265, 271
Nesbit : Rev. R. : 93
New Delhi (see Delhi) : 37, 181, 185, 232, 237
New Synagogue : 149
New Testament : 68, 75, 76, 82, 238, 241 n.6, 347
New Year (see Rosh Hashanah) : 62
New Zealand : 190
Newlywed : 136, 145 n.25
Newspaper : 182, 187, 249, 254 n.7, 263, 266
Night : 170
Nigudshet : 173, 219
Ningdi : 222 n.1
Nissim, Meyer : 253-254 n.2, 266
Nizam Shahi Dynasty : 33
Noar Memorial Hall : 180
Nofeth : 209, 239
Nomination, Nominee : 247, 248, 254 n.2
Non-cooperation : 249
Non-Indian ; 252, 253
Non-Jew(ish) : 78, 81, 105, 107, 110 n.15, 119, 143, 158, 176, 181, 182, 183, 189, 215, 225, 229, 231 n.1 and n.4, 233, 237, 239, 240, 260, 269, 271, 275
Non-Sectarian : 224
Non-Violence : 249
Noorbagh : 225
North(ern Country) : 3, 8, 9, 12, 24, 25, 67, 225; Kingdom : 111, 154
North India : 42, 43, 186, 231 n.10
Nose : 49, 131
Nose-Ring : 131, 132, 133, 141, 166, 346
Notes, Notice : xii, 71, 82, 93, 200, 213, 239, 281, 283, 298, 300 Table 21a n.*
Novel : 240, 241

Nuclear Family : 155, 176, 228
Numbers, Book of : 5, 15 n.19, 116
Numerals, Numbers (see Population) : 20, 35, 59, 118; Numerology : 143 n.4
Nurse, Nursing : 175, 184, 199, 206 n.1

O.B.E. : 211, 212 n.3
Obesity : 49, 70
Objection : 69, 103, 282
Observance, Observer, Observation (see Ritual) : 5, 10, 51, 52, 53, 60, 66, 73, 74, 75, 81, 103, 118, 150, 169, 215, 219, 226, 230, 345
Occupations, Employment : 11, 12, 17 n.51 and n.52, 34, 43, 44, 50, 51, 52, 53, 55 n.15, 56 n.21 and n.23, 59, 79, 103, 105, 110 n.18, Chapter 14 *passim* 160-164, 166, 189, 191 n.7, Chapter 20 *passim* 199-207, 213, 221, 242 n.6, 269, 304 n.3
Offerings (see Malida) : 6, 7, 8, 63, 111, 112, 113, 114, 115, 116, 117, 124 n.14 and n.15, 125 n.25, 145 n.21, 229, 230, 329
Office, Official : 43, 45, 51, 73, 100, 161, 163, 164 n.9, 177, 178, 182, 189, 200, 206, 216, 234, 245, 247, 251, 252, 270, 271, 279, 281, 284, 285, 304, 305 n.4, n.6 and n.9, 346
Officer : 33, 46, 51, 62, 103, 104, 151, 162, 199, 205, 212 n.4, 233, 234, 252, 263, 311, 316, 322, 323
Ohel David Synagogue, Poona : 150, 153 n.7, 157, 179, 181, 190 n.4
Oil-Lamp (see Lamp) : 55 n.16, 115, 120, 188, 218, 227, 231 n.7
Oil-Press(ing) and Selling, Oilman (see Ghani, Oil) : 3, 8, 11, 12, 14 n.4, 17 n.51 and n.52, 27, 33, 34, 44, 51, 53, 55 n.16, 55-56 n.18, 124 n.14, 160, 165, 173, 174, 189, 193, 215, 217, 218, 220, 221, 222, 311, 312, 328
Old (see Elder) : 81, 229, 261, 275
Old Students Union : 263
Old Testament : 49, 68, 75, 76, 82, 84, 85 n.1, 89 n.49, 93, 116, 229, 235, 238, 241 n.6, 329
Olsvanger, Dr. Immanuel : ix, 91, 95, 167, 168 n.4, 269, 272 n.2
Oomerdekar : 150, 174
Oorus (Urs) : 112, 118, 123 n.5
Oosrolly : 222 n.1
Ophir : 9, 16 n.35 and n.38
Opinion : 248, 253, 268
Opportunity : 45, 178, 269, 271, 285
Opposition : 170, 209, 252, 253, 260, 268
Oppression (see Discrimination) : 41
Or L'Israel Synagogue, Nandgaon : 149

Ordained : 236
Order of British India (O.B.I.) : 54 n.13, 162
Ordinance : 170, 178
Organization, Organize (see Society) : 77, 94, 193, 206, 224, 237 n.6, 246, 263, 264, 266, 269, 270, 274, 276; Reorganization : 162
Organization for Rehabilitation Through Training (see O.R.T.)
"The Oriental Christian Spectator" : 65, 68, 70, 72, 74, 76, 78, 79, 85 n.4, 86 n.18, 88 n.38, n.39 and n.45, 89 n.51 and n.52, 90 n.57, 325, 327
Origin, Theories of Origin : viii, x, Chapter 1 passim 3-18, 20, 26, 66, 74, 80, 92, 93, 94, 104, 107, 109 n.6, 152, 158, 177, 194, 207 n.8, 224, 269, 284, 304
Orissa : 209
Ornament (see Jewelry) : 141, 166, 327
Orphan, Orphanage : 139, 152, 205, 224, 234, 243, 281
O.R.T. Organization for Rehabilitation Through Training : 174, 175 n.5, 261
Orthodox : 63, 80, 83, 92, 95, 98, 100, 101, 102, 107, 109 n.11, 110 n.15, 121, 125 n.25, 146 n.34, 188, 206, 220, 223 n.12, 229, 231 n.5, 233, 234, 236, 237, 343
Outcaste : 16 n.48, 101, 168 n.5, 206 n.1
Outing : 263, 264
Overseas : 270
Own, Ownership : 43, 46, 92, 148, 160, 165, 173, 200, 214, 216, 217, 220, 225, 233, 237 n.1, 264
Ox(en), Ox-Cart : 217, 218, 219

Padma Shri Award : 181, 209, 210, 211, 212 n.7
Pakistan : 150, 177, 178, 187, 210, 247, 272, 285, 298, 303 Table 24, 304
Palace : 34, 229, 312
Palanquin : 133, 136
Palestine, Holy land : 8, 9, 23, 29 n.17, 77, 84, 177, 243, 245, 268, 269, 270, 271, 272-273 n.6
Pali : 60, 216, 217
Palkar : 223 n.6
Palm : 105, 120, 174
Pamphlet : 181, 214, 226, 239
Pan (Supari) : 129, 233, 144 n.8, 168
Panchaitan : 26; Borlai : 222 n.1
Panchgani : 36, 182
Panchvi : 129, 143 n.4
Pandit : 241 n.3, 354; Pandita : 241 n.6
Pandita Ramabai : 238, 241 n.3 and n.6

Pant Sachiv : 305 n.7, 327
Pantatshi : 342, 344, 347, 348, 349 n.13
Panther : 214
Panvel : 10, 11, 60, 68, 70, 84, 149, 173, 174, 175 n.4 and n.6, 214, 215, 222 n.3, 223 n.4, 274, 327, 336, 341, 344, 345
Parali : 215-219
Parankhar : 213, 222 n.1
Parchment : 165
Pardesi Jews (White) : 40, 41, 42, 43, 44, 46 n.1, 48 n.20, 59, 107
Parel : 36, 47 n.14, 225, 226, 232
Parents : 77, 128, 130, 131, 133, 134, 136, 142, 158 n.1, 193, 218, 221, 222, 226, 227, 228, 236, 257, 259, 261, 274, 275, 330
Paris : 191 n.19
Parliament : Act of : 85 n.2
Parsee, Parsi : 23, 32 n.47, 54 n.13, 55 n.15, 76, 77, 79, 98, 99, 121, 122, 126 n.29, 138, 144 n.10, 159 n.12, 166, 179, 182, 193, 194, 195 n.1, 205, 225, 243, 245, 247, 249, 251, 256 n.19, 279, 282, 283, 329, 339, 346, 348 n.1
Participant, Participation) : 229, 247, 264, 268, 269, 270
Partition : 99, 177, 187, 247, 285, 298
Partner : 274, 275
Party (see Social Gathering) : 128, 129, 137
Parur : 314, 315
Passover (see Pesach) : 4, 6, 15 n.20, 92-93, 112, 118, 120, 121, 165, 167, 214, 218, 219, 221, 222 n.3, 250, 264, 267 n.2, 350-354; Pascal Lamb : 332
Passport : 270
Patapatanam : 185
Pathan : xiii n.7
Patience : 227
Patients : 265
Patna : 209
Patriarch : 229
Patrilocal : 138
Patriotism (see Loyalty) : 268
Patron : 91, 112, 115, 169
Pattern : 194, 215, 228, 229, 264
Pay, Payment : 189, 246, 250, 260, 276, 317
Peace : 116, 183, 243, 271
Peak : 90 n.71, 195 n.1, 269, 304
Pedagogy : 261
Peddle : 218
Peer : 252
Pen : 35, 37 n.4, 84, 149, 173, 175 n.6, 190, 213, 214, 216, 218, 223 n.4, 274
Peninsula : 47 n.14
Penkar : Ezekiel Benjamin : 92; Hyam Ezekiel :

92; Joseph David : 208, 240; J.M. : 184; Shalom Joseph : 92, 135; Solomon Samson : 181
Pennsylvania : 190
Pension(er) (see Retirement) : 178, 206, 315, 317, 345
Pentateuch, Five Books of Moses : 69, 235, 330
Percentage : 251, 260, 279, 283, 300 Table 21a, 303
Periodicals, Journals : 72, 94, 95, 97 n.12, 108 n.6, 161, 162, 181, 200, 238, 239, 281, 366-367
Persecution : 6, 8, 42, 126 n.29, 151, 193, 269, 272 n.3
Persia, Persian : 6, 8, 9, 14 n.9, 21, 23, 24, 37 n.3, 73, 76, 88 n.42, 89 n.52, 98, 101, 115, 122, 126 n.29, 145 n.22, 171 n.3, 177, 186, 193, 242 n.8 and n.9, 339
Personality : 181, 240
Perth, Australia : 190
Pesach (see Passover) : 4, 332
Peshawar : 177
Peshwa(s) : 27, 32 n.49, 34, 42, 91, 164 n.8, 178, 313
Petition : 36, 99, 100, 137, 249
Pezarkar : A.D. : 169; Abraham Solomon : 96 n.11; David Solomon : 94, 96 n.11; Samuel Haeem : 96 n.11
Pharaoh : 250
Pharmacology : 309
Philadelphia : 188
Philanthropy : 207 n.4, 230
Philips Ltd. : 210
Philosophy, Philosopher : 71, 186, 210, 278 n.3, 310
Photograph(s) : 39 n.20, 95, 181, 227, 240
Physical Characteristics : ix, xiii n.7, 15-16 n.33, 49, 101, 104, 110 n.16, 258
Physical Culture (see Gym) : 244
Physician (see Doctor) : 184, 209, 235, 250, 263, 269, 309, 310, 347
Picketing : 251
Picnic, Outing : 263, 267 n.2
Picture : 166, 227
Pidyan Ha-Ben : 144 n.8, 215
Pilgrimage, Pilgrim : 26, 108 n.6 (6), 116, 122, 231 n.15
Pillar : 278
Pilot : Air : 190, 199; Shipping : 252, 255 n.18
Pindaree : 52, 56 n.20
Pinglay, Daphne Samuel : 175 n.4; Pingle : 155
Pioneer : 208, 257, 271
Pir : 115
Pirate : 26
Pizmon : 113, 114

Plague : 194, 195 n.3, 281
Plan : 248
Plane : 270
P'Laot Aydot : 238
Platter (Malida), Dish : 111, 114, 115, 116, 124 n.14, 131, 134, 167
Plays (see Drama) : 188, 208, 227, 238, 240
Plumbing : 233
Plunder : 52, 173
Poem, Poet, Poetry : 91, 135, 145 n.22, 186, 211, 240, 242 n.9, 342
Pogrom : 244, 246 n.4
Pola : 219
Poland : 269, 270
Police : 34, 174, 177, 178, 184, 208, 211, 252; Special Ghat : 173
Policy ; 243, 260, 271
Polite : 227
Politics, Political : 151, 194, 243, 247, 248, 251, 253 n.1, 255 n.9, 257, 269, 272 n.3
Pollack, Fritz : 273 n.7
Pollution, Unclean : 16 n.48, 110 n.15, 144 n.7, 234
Polygyny (see Bigamy) : 59, 138, 228, 243, 244, 245, 331
Poona (Pune) : 15 n.17, 31 n.40, 37, 37 n.4, 40, 41, 42, 44, 59, 69, 70, 92, 93, 100, 101, 102, 105, 108 n.6(5), 109 n.6(12), 137, 138, 149, 150, 153 n.7, 165, 166, 170, 173, 176, 177, 178-183, 185, 188, 189, 190, 190 n.1, n.4 and n.7, 194, 204 Table 3, 206, 212 n.4, 233, 244, 245, 246, 257, 264, 266, 269, 274, 277, 282; District : 178, 216, 241 n.3, 290 Table 13b
Poona Jewish Benevolent Association (Welfare) : 179, 190 n.3
Poona Jewish Reading Room and Library : 181
Poor (see Poverty) : 100, 121, 125 n.25, 133, 136, 139, 162, 165, 166, 167, 175 n.18, 179, 184, 193, 199, 233, 234, 243, 258, 259, 260, 261, 263, 264, 266, 271, 344
Popular(ity) : 239, 259, 260
Population (Figures) (see Demography) : vii, viii, x, xiii n.3, 32 n.46, 40, 44, 50, 52, 54 n.8, 55 n.15, 59, 63 n.10, 70, 74, 87-88 n.35, 90 n.71, 98, 101, 173, 174, 175, 175 n.6, 176, 177, 182, 185, 186, 187, 188, 189, 190-191 n.7, 191 n.8 and n.9, 195 n.1, 203, 205, 216, 219, 224, 225, 232, 250, 251, 258, 260, 266, 271, 272, 273 n.6, 274, Chapter 33 *passim* 279-306, 327
Pork : 167, 168 n.5
Port, Seaport : 6, 7, 8, 9, 11, 13, 23, 24, 25, 26, 34, 42, 52, 156, 173, 177, 252, 255 n.17
Portion : 68, 235
Portrait : 95, 240, 310

Index

Portuguese : 21, 25, 26, 27, 31 n.34, n.36, n.38, n.40 and n.43; 36, 42, 43, 46 n.1, n.16 and n.18; 53, 55 n.15, 65, 101, 103, 108 n.1, 110 n.18, 174, 309
Possessions : 3, 52
Post and Telegraph : 161, 176, 187, 199, 216; Postmaster : 19, 210
Poster : 271
Pot (see Utensil) : 140, 141, 142, 221
Potential (Immigrant) : 302
Poverty (Poor) : 52, 169, 194, 211, 245
Poynad : 149, 213, 274
Prantej : 183
Prasadam : 114, 124 n.15, 125 n.18
Prasangik Vichar : 239
Prayer, Prayer Hall : 3, 10, 21, 49, 67, 69, 71, 91, 92, 93, 112, 113, 115, 117, 118, 119, 121, 123 n.12, 124 n.14, 125 n.18, 135, 141, 142, 143, 167, 173, 185, 189, 191 n.12, 215, 221, 223 n.12, 235, 243, 268, 332, 344, 345; Books : 227, 236, 237 n.6; Hall : 7, 36, 52, 60, 100, 105, 108 n.5, 109 n.6, 149, 150, 170, 177, 179, 181, 183, 187, 188, 214, 218, 224, 226, 232, 233, 234, 237, 274, 277, 280
Preacher : 60, 68, 70, 71, 79, 91, 151
Precept : 229, 244
Preface : 93
Pregnancy : 127-128, 145 n.19, 346
Prejudice : 67, 70, 76, 101, 104, 265
Premises : 170, 180, 187, 232, 234, 236, 265; School : 269
Present (see Gift) : 129, 133, 144 n.10, 145 n.26
Preservation : 193, 219, 266
President : xiii n.9, 72, 170, 171, 174, 181, 184, 188, 189, 209, 210, 211, 241 n.1, 245, 247, 251, 252, 254 n.2, 255 n.8, 264, 266, 270, 316, 319, 343, 344, 348; Address : 191 n.8, 206, 225, 226, 243, 255 n.9, 258
Price : 76
Priest (see Cohen) : 4, 5, 6, 10, 11; 27, 60, 67, 84, 120, 234; Hindu : 16 n.48, 237 n.4; Parsi : 126 n.29
Prince of Wales : 249
Princely States : 212 n.1, 216, 282; Princess : 95
Principal : 185, 199, 209, 235, 236, 259, 260
Printing, Press : ix, 65, 73, 74, 88 n.41, 91, 92, 93, 94, 96 n.5, 109 n.13, 161, 182, 238, 241 n.3 and n.6; 345; Reprint : 109(6), 239
Priority : 259
Prison(er) 44, 46, 81, 314, 315, 316, 318, 319
Pristine : 4, 21, 75, 88 n.40, 117
Privacy, Private : 138, 148, 163, 167, 178, 193, 224, 226, 227, 234, 239, 260, 272, 305 n.6

Privilege (see Kaji) : 25, 33, 34, 45, 51, 194, 243, 250, 311
Prize : 103
Problem : 228, 246, 274, 275, 287
Procession : 135, 136, 141
Produce, Product, : 52, 216, 218, 249
Profession(al) (see Occupations) : 63, 109 n.6(9), 183, 191 n.7 and n.9, 194, 195, 199, 205, 206, 206 n.1, 222, 228, 257, 266, 274, 346
Professor : 209, 211, 265
Profit : 216, 253
Progeny (see Descendant) : 12, 22, 105
Program : 77, 263, 267, 274
Progress, Progressive : 77, 137, 176, 193, 194, 230, 236, 258, 281
Prohibit(ion) : 161, 167, 184
Project : 72, 226, 267, 276, 279, 281, 282
Prolific : 240
Promotion : 102, 162
Propaganda : 271
Property : 62, 140, 146 n.28, 179, 189, 200, 234, 237, 281, 314, 329, 343
Prophecy, Prophets : 68, 71, 75, 89 n.49, 101, 329
Proportion : 193, 199, 253 n.1, 258, 259, 260, 270, 272, 275, 303
Proselytization (see Conversion) : 12, 17 n.50, 65, 69, 72, 77, 78, 82, 83, 84, 101, 226
Prosper : 193
Prostitute, Prostitution : 39 n.19, 109 n.11, 162, 211, 257
Protect : 227, 253
Protestant : 25, 65, 79, 84
Provident Fund : 187
Provinces : 255 n.16, 279, 282
Psalms, (Book of) : 85 n.1, 113, 125 n.25, 130, 140, 142, 240, 268, 331, 332, 333
Ptolemy : 30 n.25
Puberty : 132, 144 n.14
Public : 36, 59, 163, 167, 174, 178, 210, 224, 227, 231 n.4, 234, 247, 253, 277
Publication, Publish : 65, 69, 72, 73, 74, 75, 79, 80, 81, 82, 83, 88 n.41, 91, 92, 93, 94, 95, 97 n.12 and n.13, 109 n.6(9), 150, 152 n.1, 170, 181, 189, 214, Chapter 25 *passim* 238-242, 244, 245, 266, 269, 273 n.7, 279, 280, 281, 282, 284, 302, 309, 346, 352-353, 355-367
Pui : 222 n.1
Puja : 115; Pujari : 237 n.4
Pulpit : 236
Pumbedita : 20
Pune (see Poona)
Punjab : 21

Pupils, Students : 66, 72, 76, 80, 82, 103, 177, 229, 257, 260, 261, 262 n.10, 265, 336, 344
Puranas : 16 n.36 and n.42
Purao, Mrs. : 261
Purchase : 100, 148, 183, 184, 226
Purdah : 317
Pure, Purity, Impurity (see Purification) : 101, 102, 103, 107, 108 n.6(1), 110 n.26, 133, 141, 194, 265, 268
Purification : 108 n.6(4), 116, 131, 141, 142, 145 n.19, 147 n.40
Purim : 4, 5, 120, 188, 334

Qualify : 171, 199, 215, 236, 237, 259, 262, 263, 275
Quality : 170
Quarrel, Argument : 161, 227, 228, 234, 244, 264, 344
Quatrain : 238, 239, 242 n.9
Queen : 136
Questionnaire, Question : 43, 280, 282, 304 n.2, 305 n.9
Quetta : 59, 177, 284
Quotation : xi
Quran (see Koran)

Rabban, Joseph : 41, 44, 47 n.8
Rabban, Simcha (Simon) : 40, 41, 47 n.4
Rabbi, Rabbinical (see D'beth Hillel) : 20, 23, 28 n.1, 61, 68, 69, 72, 73, 76, 80, 83, 84, 87 n.32, 88 n.43, 108 n.6(9), 110 n.26, 124 n.15, 151, 236, 237 n.3, 266, 278 n.3, 331, 333
Rabinowitz, Louis Isaac : 21, 28 n.4 and n.11, 222 n.3
Race, Racial : 248, 249
Rachel's Tomb : 122
Radha : 137
Radhān, District of : 19
Radhānite(s) : 19, 20, 21, 28 n.4 and n.5
Rahabi, David (of Bene Israel Tradition) : 3, 4, 8, 10, 11, 12, 13, 14 n.9, 24, 44, 45, 48 n.26, 75, 112, 113, 117, 118, 122 n.1
Rahabi Family, House of : 81, 253 n.1; Ezekiel I : 48 n.20; David I (1646 – 1726) : 44; Ezekiel II (1694 – 1771) : 43, 44, 48 n.20 and n.24, 49, 53 n.3, 59, 67, 75, 81, 117, 314, 315, 317, 318, 341; David Ezekiel (1721-1791) : 44 45, 48 n.23, n.27 and n.31, 314, 315, 323 n.3; Eliahu : 314, 315, 318; Moshe : 314, 315; David Baruch (1790-1862) : 45; David Hyam (19th century) : 48 n.29; Naphtali (see Roby): 20th century
Raigad District (see Kolaba) : xiii n.6
Railway (see Station Master) : 174, 176, 177, 178, 182, 183, 185, 186, 187, 191 n.11, 199, 221, 231 n.4, 285
Rain (see Monsoon) : 220
Raj (British) : 247
Raja Kelkar Museum : 181
Rajasthan : 37, 176, 185, 191 n.11
Rajkot : 37, 183, 222
Rajpuri : 13, 31 n.41, 51, 312, 313; Rajapoor : 42, 49, 70, 335
Rajpurkar (Family) : 10, 13, 26, 34, 348; Ezekiel Jospeh : 93, 169, 171 n.1, 341; Joseph Ezekiel : 92, 93, 108 n.6, 265, 345, 347
Ramraj : 52, 170
Ramzan, Ramadan : 117, 118, 119, 337 n.16
Ranade, M.G. : 85 n.9
Ranadive, Lee : 16 n.33
Rangoon : 209, 252
Rank, Title, Status (see Hierarchy) : 12, 16 n.48, 34, 37 n.6, 51, 62, 101, 102, 103, 104, 105, 114, 162, 163 n.6, 166, 199, 209, 212 n.3, 223 n.8, 228; Army : 54 n.13
Rao, Madurai Narasimha : xii n.2
Rapprochement : 103
Rashi Script : 41, 47 n.5
Rastha Peth : 178, 179, 181
Ratnagiri : xiii n.6, 347
Rav : 214
Read, Reader : 10, 61, 62, 63, 66, 67, 74, 101, 104, 105, 106, 120, 121, 169, 175, 209, 218, 234, 235, 335; Reading Room : 263
Reading (Lord) : 250, 255 n.11
Rebellion : 34
Reception : 135, 224, 265
Recitation : 113, 114, 265
Reclamation : 47 n.14
Recognition : 270
Recommendation : 70, 243, 244, 281
Record(s) (see Research) : 22, 25, 27, 28, 32 n.50, 43, 50, 79, 86 n.24, 152, 156, 159 n.12, 185, 206, 216, 217, 279, 280, 301, 302, 304, 316
Recruit : 50, 51
Reference : 263
Reform(s) : 216, 230, 235, 237, 246 n.1, 248, 249
Reform Judaism : 95, 150, 176, 220, 231 n.5, 234, 236, 241 n.1, 242 n.6
Refugee : 178, 187, 193, 269, 270, 281, 284, 305 n.11

Regiment : 10, 67, 85 n.3 and n.9, 162, 169, 182, 199, 288, 305 n.5; European : 320, 321

Registration, Register : 109 n.6(12), 137, 155, 184, 191 n.8, 234, 243

Rehabilitation : 178, 261

Reinemann, Solomon : 48 n.26, 81, 90 n.61, 110 n.23, 123 n.8, 126 n.29, 314, 315, 317, 318, 323 n.1, n.3 and n.4, 339-349

Reinstatement : 81, 83

Reissner, H.G. : 7, 15 n.26, 38 n.19, 145, 157, 162, 182, 185, 190 n.7, 191 n.9, 200, 201, 202, 203, 207 n.7, 213, 222 n.1, 272 n.5, 281, 282-283, 284, 298 Table 19, 299 Table 20, 300 Table 21a, 305 n.6, n.10 and n.13

Relative(s), Relation(ships) : 22, 100, 101, 107, 120, 125 n.18, 129, 133, 136, 139, 142, 178, 194, 199, 215, 218, 227, 228, 237, Chapter 29 *passim* 263-267, 270, 271, 272

Release : 46

Relief, Rehabilitation : 151, 262 n.11, 269, 272 n.3

Religion, Faith (see Conversion, Religious Revival) : vii, ix, 3, 5, 13 n.7, 24, 41, 49, 50, 51, 53, 59, 60, 61, 65, 66, 68, 71, 72, 73, 77, 80, 82, 83, 91, 94, 95 n.2, 111, 121, 124 n.15, 127, 139, 148, 150, 151, 154, 158 n.1, 160, 167, 170, 174, 179, 181, 183, 184, 186, 187, 189, 193, 199, 205, 208, 218, 219, 220, 221, 227, 228, 230, 231 n.5, 233, 235, 236, 237, 238, 239, 243, 244, 249, 251, 261, 263, 266, 271, 274, 275, 279, 280, 283, 300, 304 n.2 and n.3, 305 n.9, 314, 329, 344

Religious Controversies : 79

Religious Revival : 4, 10, 15 n.15, 23, 44, 45, 46, 48 n.26, 60, 74, 76, 96 n.2, 107, 110 n.22, 112, 115, 117, 118, 119, 120, 127, 131, 133, 137, 143, 150, 154, 167, 168, 169

Remaining : 271, Chapter 31 *passim* 274-276

Remarriage : 108 n.6(9), 133, 138, 141, 267 n.5, 331; Widow : 55 n.16, 102, 139, 151, 146 n.34

Remnant (see Vestige) : 74, 78, 80, 266

Renford, Dr. Raymond K. : xi, 85 n.2, 86 n.24

Rent : 27, 148, 165, 170, 180, 184, 186, 200, 216, 217, 220, 224, 233, 234, 237, 263, 264, 265, 267 n.5, 309

Repentance : 347; Penitent : 348

Report : 49, 65, 66, 67, 68, 79, 235, 246 n.2, 262 n.5, 279, 302; Census : 283, 284

Representative, Representation : 189, 234, 237, 248, 249, 250, 251, 252, 253-254 n.2, 266, 269, 270, 271

Republic Day : 211

Research, Records, Clues, Archives : vii, viii, xi, xii, xii n.2, 9, 15 n.33, 26, 27, 29 n.17, 32 n.50, 34, 38 n.19, 46, 47 n.16, 50, 71, 79, 85 n.9, 86 n.24, 95, 95-96 n.2, 97 n.13, 156, 158, 158 n.1, 159 n.12, 209, 210, 214, 231 n.11, 240, 244, 267, 298, 309, 310

Reserve : 250, 270

Reservoir : 277

Residence (Resident) : 17 n.52, 21, 23, 27, 50, 55 n.16, 150, 156, 157, 173, 174, 178, 182, 183, 184, 187, 190 n.7, 215, 219, 220, 222 n.1, 224, 225, 227, 236, 246, 268, 269, 274, 279, 281, 282, 283, 285, 299 Table 20, 305 n.11; Inhabitant : 221

Resignation : 171

Resolutions : 243, 244, 245, 250, 255 n.9, 258

Resource(s) : 182, 193, 266

Respect : 60, 116, 154, 166, 189, 219, 220, 221, 227, 228, 234, 237, 252, 271, 343

Responsa : 19

Respondent : x, xi, 42, 83, 105, 118, 128, 132, 143 n.4, 217, 223 n.10, 227, 229, 257, 272, 274

Responsibility : 169, 194, 228

Rest : 3, 218

Resurrection : 141

Retirement (see Pension) : 60, 170, 173, 174, 179, 182, 184, 189, 209, 260, 261, 345

Return : 303; Law of : 275

Reuben (Tribe of) : 8

Reuben : 328, 335; David Ezra : 182, 209; Judge Ezra : 208, 226,; Judah : 211; M.R. Reuben : 212 n.3

Reuben, Rebecca : 80, 90 n.58, 94, 97 n.13 and n.14, 112, 123 n.3, 155, 158, 182, 209, 233, 237 n.2, 238, 239, 257, 259, 260, 263

Revdanda : 10, 26, 32 n.43 and n.46, 45, 60, 68, 70, 105, 106, 150, 158, 222 n.1, 274, 277, 283 Table 9, 336, 341, 344, 345; Synagogue : 149, 152, 213

Rewa Kanta : 183

Reward : 248

Rewli : 222 n.1

Rhone River : 19, 28 n.5

Rice : 52, 114, 115, 123 n.11, 125 n.25, 128, 131, 132, 133, 134, 142, 160, 165, 166, 214, 217, 218, 229, 253, 343

Rich (see Wealthy) : 69, 98, 121, 133, 160, 162, 166, 167, 259, 314, 317, 343, 344, 345

Ride : 100, 119, 133, 135, 215, 233

Right(s) : 33, 34, 45, 51, 243, 250, 253, 272 n.3, 311, 312, 313

Ring (see Earring) : 135, 136, 145 n.23, 331; Nose : 131, 132-133

Riot : 177, 249

Ritual, Custom, Rites of Passage (see Ceremony, Observance) : 5, 6, 7, 10, 52, 62, 69, 83, 92,

101, 111, 112, 115, 119, 121, 122 n.1, 123 n.12, 125 n.24 and n.25, Chapter 11 *passim* 127-147, 148, 154, 167, 177, 206, 218, 224, 226, 228, 229, 230, 233, 234, 237 n.4, 272 n.3, 275, 344
River : 216, 217, 223 n.9
Road (see Street) : 36, 37, 105, 208, 215, 218, 225, 236, 266, 277; Addresses of Bene Israel Places of Worship : 232; Highway : 216
Robenji Isaji Nawgaonkar : 91, 95 n.1
Robinson, T., Archdeacon of Madras : 73
Roby (Rahabi), Naphtali : 44, 45, 48 n.25 and n.26, 119, 315
Rock : 12
Rodef Shalom Synagogue : 232, 233, 234, 236, 237, 237 n.1
Roha (Rohe) Ashtami : 11, 70, 158, 222 n.1; Creek : 219
Roha (Rohe) Taluka : 37 n.4, 42, 47 n.13, 158, 215-216, 217, 222 n.1, 232
Rohekar, S. David : 188
Roja : 4, 118
Roland, Prof. Joan G. : ix, x, xi, 246, 246 n.8
Role : 249
Roof : 136, 165, 214, 220, 227
Room : 128, 219, 165, 185, 200, 217, 218, 227, 233, 234; Reading : 263
Roots : 213
Rose Water : 140
Rosh Hashanah, New Year : 4, 15 n.17, 119, 121, 125 n.22, 153 n.10, 165, 218, 221, 333
Rote : 185
Roth, Cecil : 99, 108 n.3
Royal Asiatic Society Bombay Branch : 72, 74, 88 n.37, 327
Royal Family : 71, 268
Rubaiyat : 186, 238
Rubins, Dr. Jack and Tamara : xi
Rudiments of Hebrew Grammar in Marathi : 75, 76
Rulers, Rule : 12, 25, 26, 27, 51, 91, 151, 178, 185, 186, 208, 228
Rupee : 60, 145 n.26, 161
Rural (see Village) : ix, 51, 52, 141, 146 n.34, 148, 162, 168, 207 n.3, 208, 214, 215, 221, 222 n.1, 228, 237, 272, 273 n.9 and n.10, 283, 284
Russia, Russian : 151, 186

Sababi, Roja : 118
Sabbath, Shabbat : 3, 24, 41, 44, 49, 68, 75, 92, 100, 105, 108 n.6(2), 111, 114, 115, 118, 121, 123 n.10 and n.12, 124 n.15, 135, 140, 142, 150, 151, 168, 169, 170, 175, 187, 188, 215, 218, 219, 223 n.12, 226, 227, 229, 233, 235, 310, 331, 332, 342, 345, 347
Sachar, Abram L. : 112, 122 n.2
Sacred : 132, 145 n.22
Sacrifice : 114, 116, 119, 124 n.14, 125 n.25, 130, 144 n.10, 171, 214, 222 n.3, 249, 261
Sadar Bazaar : 186
Sadikali, Sheikh : 124 n.14
Safed : 72, 78, 145 n.22
Saffron : 115, 125 n.26, 145 n.25
Sahitya Akademi : 240
Sai : 84
Saimur (Simylla, Chaul) : 23, 30 n.25
Saint : 112, 114; Christain : 144 n.10; Hindu : 116, 123 n.4; Muslim : 115, 123 n.5, 125 n.18; Saint John's Ambulance Brigade : 251; Saint Joseph's School : 261; Saint Mary's School : 261; Saint Xavier's College, School : 87 n.27, 261, 265
Salary : 60, 62, 103, 148, 205, 206, 234, 236, 237 n.3, 245, 259, 260, 275
Sale (see Sell) : 218
Salsette : 25, 31 n.40, 42, 173, 309
Salshet : 173, 219, 222 n.1
Salt Tax : 218, 250
Samaji Hassaji, Samuel (see Divekar, S. E.) : 59, 60, 61, 67, 81, 314, 315, 316, 317, 318, 319, 323 n.4; Samuel St. : 46, 317
Samaritans : 38 n.16, 78, 88-89 n.49
Samson : Benjamin A. : 210; B. J. : 249; D. J. : 6, 8, 15 n.33, 249; E. D. : 212 n.3; I. J. : 239, 245, 249, 250, 252, 255 n.15; Major General Jonathan Reuben : 199, 210; Captain J.S. : 265; Sarah Ezekiel : 180
Samuel, Flora : 260, 261
Samuel, Jacob : 70, 71, 86 n.19 n.20 and n.23
Samuel, Shellim : ix, xiv n.11, 6, 8, 15 n.33, 16 n.34, 37 n.5, 42, 55 n.18, 175 n.7, 180, 191 n.8 and n.10, 240, 266, 277
San : 4, 118
Sanad : 12, 33, 34, 37 n.2, 45, 47 n.13, 49, 51, 53 n.3, 159 n.9, 311, 312, 313
Sandals : 166
Sandalwood : 115
Sanitation : 214, 226, 230; Plumbing : 233
Sanskrit : ix, 9, 14 n.7, 101, 171 n.3, 184, 241 n.3, 260, 272 n.2; Sanskritization : 146 n.34
Santa Cruz : 225, 226
Sanyasi : 123 n.5
Sargon, Abraham : 45, 79
Sargon : Isaac : 67, 314, 317, 319; Isaac Elias : 152 n.1
Sargon, Joseph : 79, 152 n.1

Index 435

Sargon, Michael : 45, 49, 67, 68, 69, 79, 85 n.9, 86 n.11, 99, 152 n.1, 169, 335
Sari : 116, 128, 131, 134, 137, 166, 200, 353
Sarmad : 186, 191 n.17, 238, 239, 242 n.8
Sarsoli : 213, 222 n.1
Sartorius, J.A. : 43, 49, 53 n.3
Sarul : 10
Sassoon, David Solomon : 36, 38 n.16, 48 n.31, 59, 77, 93, 99, 100, 102, 103, 153 n.7, 167, 179, 264, 342, 352
Sassoon Family : 93, 99, 102, 103, 108 n.6, 109 n.6(10), 149, 164 n.9, 171 n.4, 178, 179, 182, 190 n.4, 194, 205, 214, 225, 226, 236, 253-254 n.2, 261, 265, 266
Sastri, K. A. Nilakanta : 30 n.31
Satambe : 173, 213, 219, 222 n.1, 232, 274
Satamkar, Daniel Abraham : 207 n.4
Satamkar(s) : 213
Satara : 37, 176, 182
Saturday (see Sabbath) : 3, 115, 121, 169; Oilmen : 51, 313
"Satya Prakash" (Bene Israel Periodical) : 95
Saurashtra : 184
Scandal : 162, 193
Scatter : 42, 44, 177, 180, 193, 215, 222, 284
Scheduled (Castes & Tribes) : 223 n.8, 270, 304 n.3
Schism : 71, 193
Schloss, David : 103
Scholar, Scholarship (see Learning) : ix, 9, 20, 23, 25, 28, 33, 45, 61, 72, 73, 81, 82, 93, 102, 103, 108 n.6, 193, 206, 236, 240, 242 n.6, 259, 260, 263, 272 n.2, 335, 337 n.6
School : 65, 66, 67, 68, 70, 71, 77, 80, 81, 82, 88 n.46, 93, 97 n.11, 102, 103, 108 n.6, 109 n.6(10), 117, 150, 152, 163, Chapter 16 passim 169-172, 174, 176, 177, 178, 185, 188, 193, 199, 200, 205, 214, 225, 229, 234, 235, 236, Chapter 28 passim 257-262, 263, 264, 265, 269, 274, 335, 341, 345, 352, 353; High, Secondary : 66, 180, 185, 209, 216, 217, 218, 219, 220, 260
Schur, Wolf : 81, 90 n.61
Science : 258
Scindia Steam Navigation Co. : 209, 252, 253
Scottish Presbyterian Mission (see Church of Scotland) : 65, 70, 71, 77, 79, 87 n.29, 88 n.46, 95, 336
Scouting : 263
Scribe : 123 n.8
Script : 159 n.12; Devanagri : 14 n. 9, 35, 92, 93, 97 n.12, Hebrew : 93; Rashi : 41
Scriptures (see Bible, Old & New Testament) : 7, 10, 60, 65, 66, 75, 76, 80, 84, 129, 130, 336, 341
Scroll (see Torah) : 3, 46, 60, 63 n.10, 120, 316
Sea : xiii n.6, 7, 8, 9, 21, 22, 50, 116, 128, 136, 143 n.1, 146 n.30, 173, 215, 253, 255 n.11, 310
Search : 46
Seats : 250, 251, 270
Sebah Offerings : 116
Secretary, Secretariat : 171, 184, 188, 189, 199, 210, 211, 247, 250, 252, 261, 270; Secretary of State : 248
Sect : 77, 104, 188
Sectarianism : 254 n.2
Secular : 61, 65, 76, 78, 80, 145 n.22, 150, 160, 161, 205, 219, 222, 247, 258, 269
Security : 206, 247, 250, 254 n.3, 258; Insecurity 194
Seder : 121, 351, 354
Sedition : 254 n.3
Seed : 217
Sefer Torah (see Scroll, Torah) : 60, 63, 64 n.10, 69, 108 n.6(3) and (5), 179, 236, 329, 335, 341
Segregation : 104, 132, 144 n.7, 229; Segmentation : 110 n.18
Self Assurance, Confidence : 206, 271
Self Help : 194
Self-Interest : 151
Self Reliant : 227
Self Sacrifice : 171, 261
Seller, Sell : 17 n.52, 51, 63, 200, 217, 220, 237; Salesman : 282
Semah, Jacob : 99
Seminar : 266
Sengupta, Padmini : 241 n.3
Separatism, Separate (see Split) : 103, 144 n.7, 182, 224, 228, 233, 236, 251, 257, 258, 264, 274, 275, 279, 284, 285, 304 n.3, 305 n.11
Sephardi(c) : 60, 90 n.56, 111, 117, 118, 127, 153 n.2, 188, 329, 332
Sepoy : 54 n.13, 67, 85 n.9, 163 n.6, 182, 320, 321, 322
Serampur (Bengal), Serampore : 65, 73, 85 n.1, 86 n.24, 241 n.6
Sermon : 61, 79, 91, 150, 170, 235
Servant : 6, 11, 12, 40, 71, 104, 108 n.6(7), 166, 207 n.3, 227, 262 n.10, 343, 344
Service : Civil, Government : 163, 170, 176, 182, 189, 205, 245, 248, 252, 258; Military : 50, 93, 162, 244; Prayer : 43, 60, 61, 62, 92, 98, 100, 121, 142, 150, 173, 174, 177, 181, 185, 186, 189, 218, 232, 234, 235, 236, 237, 244, 263, 265, 274

Sesame : 14 n.4, 51, 55 n.16, 220
Settle, Settler, Settlement : 6, 22, 24, 25, 26, 41, 43, 46, 50, 51, 53, 78, 100, 154, 173, 174, 176, 177, 178, 179, 183, 184, 185, 187, 193, 216, 222, 224, 232, 268, 269, 272, 273 n.6 and n.10, 275, 282, 303, 306 n.15, 315
Seventeenth Century : 154
Sewing : 166; Needlework : 263
Sex : 22, 105, 213, 227, 257, 263, 304 n.3
Sexton : 61, 104
Shaar Ha-Rahamim Synagogue : 46, 138, 149, 152, 153 n.11, 230 n.1, 234, 235, 240, 245, 263, 268, 316, 317, 319, 322-323
Shaar Ha-Shamayim Synagogue, Thana : 149, 174
Shaar Ha-Tefilah Synagogue, Mhasla : 149, 213, 274
Shaarei Rason Synagogue : 48 n.29, 60, 61, 91, 138, 149, 151, 152, 263
Shaarei Shalom Synagogue, Borlai : 149, 274
Shabbat (see Sabbath) : 41, 44, 344; Motzei 114
Shah Jehan, Emperor : 186
Shahaji : 86 n.9
Shahapur : 13
Shahapurkar : 10, 13; Benjamin David : 235; Mary (Sopher) : 171 n.1
Shake Era : 35, 38 n.13
"Shalom" : 175 n.4 and n.7, 191 n.10, 278 n.1 and n.2
Shamash (see Sexton) : 61, 62, 104, 121, 140, 148, 167, 184
Shame : 281
Shanwar Teli : 3, 14 n.4, 25, 49, 159 n.12, 160, 189, 312
Sharar, Abdul Halim : 124 n.18
Share : 274
Shave : 116, 131, 134, 142, 167
Shavuoth : 5, 118, 135, 332
Shawl : 134, 135
Shed : 160, 165, 217
Sheep : 343
Sheet (see Cloth) : 129, 133, 140
Shellim, D.S. : 254 n.2
Shelter : 234, 269
Shema : 3, 5, 10, 14 n.6, 44, 49, 64 n.10, 67, 75, 113, 117, 131, 140, 141, 142, 167
Shemini Atzereth : 218
Sherra (Crown) : 134, 136
Shia : 50, 146 n.34, 230 n.2
Shigaon : 213, 222 n.1
Shiksan Prasarak Mandali College (now Sir Parashuram Bhau College) : 180

Shila San : 4, 5, 15 n.12 and n.16, 120
Shingli : 23, 46 n.3
Shipping, Ship, Ship Building : 3, 9, 25, 34, 43, 49, 52, 69, 102, 160, 182, 189, 207 n.4, 209, 210, 252, 253
Shipwreck : 4, 7, 8, 12, 13 n.2, 23, 60, 112, 126 n.29, 128, 169, 277
"Shirei R'nanot" : 92, 135
Shirkolkar, Joel Samuel : 122
Shirt : 166
Shitla Devi : 131, 144 n.9 and n.10
Shivaji : 26, 27, 31 n.40, 35, 86 n.9
Shivti (see Mizrach) : 152 n.2
Shoe : 102, 142, 166, 167, 168
Shofar : 119, 151, 153 n.10
Shohet, Shohatim : 60, 61, 62, 64 n.10, 106, 110 n.22, 177, 180, 181, 275, 340, 342, 343, 344, 345, 347, 348
Sholapur : 37, 182
Shop, Shopkeepr : 160, 166, 200, 220, 328
Shorthand : 261
Shraddh : 331
Shrine : 134, 186, 227
Shrivardhan Mahal or Town : 31 n.35, 70, 208, 213, 222 n.1, 232, 274; 283 Table 9
Shroud : 140, 142
"Shulamit" : 241
Shulhan Arukh : 351, 352, 353
Shurrabi, Shelomo Salem : 60, 92, 151, 174, 342, 344
Sibling : 144 n.16, 154, 254, 220
Sidi (Hubshi) : 25, 26, 27, 31 n.35, n.40 and n.41; 33, 34, 50, 52, 159 n.12
Signature : 255 n.15, 270
Sikh : 54 n.13, 177, 187, 228, 249, 251, 279
Silence : 116, 142
Silk : 166
Silliman (Seleman) (Solomon) : Jacob: 38 n.17, 68, 69, 70, 98, 99, 108 n.6; Sharhanabai Haruna : 38 n.17
Silver : 129, 132, 134, 135, 166, 233, 236
Simhat Kohen : 4, 5
Simhat Torah : 120, 135, 218
Simonsen, D. : 28 n.5
Sin : 100, 119, 125 n.24, 347
Sinclair, W.F. : 179
Sind : 14 n.9, 19, 20, 21, 23, 210, 255 n.16, 282, 289 Table 12b, 347
Sir Elly Kadoori School (see Israelite School) : 214, 233, 260, 261, 264
Sir Jacob Sassoon School : 260, 261, 264, 265; High : 214
Sirdar Bahadur : 51, 54 n.13, 162

Sister : 77, 119, 132, 133, 136, 142, 216, 227, 228, 234, 263, 310; -hood : 233, 236; -in-law : 170

"Sketch of the History of the Bene Israel and an Appeal for Their Education," by H. S. Kekimkar. 170

Skill : 200

Skin (see Physical Characteristics) : 40, 49, 67, 101, 104, 110 n.16, 128, 186

Skirt Ceremony : 132

Slaughter, Ritual (see Shoḥet) : 53, 62, 104, 167, 177, 215, 340, 344

Slave : 22, 29 n.17 and n.19, 30 n.33, 40, 331

Sleep : 227

Sleeve : 166

S'lichot : 117, 118, 119, 125 n.22

Slum : 211

Smallpox : 115, 131, 144 n.9 and n.10; Goddess Mata : 132

Smith, George : 72, 74, 76, 77, 79, 86 n.25, 87 n.30, 89 n.50, n.53 and n.54

Social Gatherings, Socializing : 101, 104, 107, 111, 162, 178, 179, 181, 182, 183, 187, 188, 193, 199, 206, 224, 231 n.5, 233, 234, 239, 243, 246, 264, 266, 272 n.3 and n.6, 274, 280, 304 n.3

Social Service, Social Welfare, Social Work : 180, 184, 199, 230, 259, 263

Social Structure & Status, Sociology : 51, 199, 206, 213, 227, 230, 236, 243, 245, 263, 264, 270, 280

Societies : Aryan Ladies Ass'n. Poona : 137; Bene Israel Benevolent : 139; Bene Israel Kullianechhu Sabha : 139; Burial, Bene Israel Hevra Kedusha : 139, 152, 243, 245; Bene Israel Cooperative (Banking) Credit : 205, 243, 245; Subodh Prakash Samaj : 91, 94, 96 n.11; Zoological Society : 181

Society of Saint John the Evangelist, S.S.J.E. : 84, 90 n.68

Soldier (see Army) : 44, 50, 69, 152, 154, 161, 173, 183, 187, 268, 288, 314, 316, 328, 343, 344, 346

Solo : 91

Solomon (King) : 9, 16 n.36 and n.43; Kingdom : 111

Solomon : David J. : 242 n.6; Dr. Esther : 184; Dr. Jacob E. (Warsulkar) : 184, 247, 249, 250, 251; Moses Jacob : 186, 191 n.11

Somalia : 30 n.32

Somekh, E.S. : 269

Son : 50, 97 n.16, 100, 130, 138, 139, 141, 142, 144 n.7, 146 n.29, 170, 177, 183, 186, 190, 199, 200, 226, 231 n.15, 257, 311, 312, 315, 318, 346

Song, Sing : 69, 91, 92, 94, 95 n.1, 95-96 n.2, 120, 130, 132, 134, 135, 136, 145 n.22, 186, 187, 219, 229, 231 n.11, 233, 261, 269, 271, 342, 345

Sood, Margaret Ann : 137, 146 n.31, 227-228, 231 n.8

Sopara, Sopora ; 9, 23

Sopher : 61; Mary : 171 n.1

Sophistication : 161, 266

Soul, (see Spirit) : 120, 123 n.12

Source : 80, 93

South India : 133, 156, 231 n.10

South Indian Jews Association : 266

Spain : 152 n.1

Speech, Oration (see Address) : 22b, 245, 254 n.3

Spelling : 41, 158

Spice : 25, 52, 123 n.12, 125 n.26, 343

Spinster : 199, 267 n.5

Spirit, Spiritual : 134, 140, 144 n.10, 145 n.22, 151, 235

Split (see Faction) : 111, 194, 232, 243, 269, 270

Spokesman : 269

Sports : 181, 210, 211, 263, 264; Gym : 199; Maccabeean Sports Club : 266

Srinivas, Prof. M.N. : 146 n.34

Stability : 228

Standard : 261; School : 260

Star : 278 n.3; of David : 278

State : 279, 284, 285, 294 Table 14, 300 Tables 21 a and b , 301 Table 22

"The Statesman" (Calcutta) : 109 n.6

Station : 176; Master : 183, 186, 191 n.11

Statistics (see Population) : 79, 89 n.54, 137, 138, 139, 144 n.15, 205, 255 n.13, 272, 281, 282, 283, 284, 301 Table 22 n.*; 302-304, 305 n.6

Status (see Rank) : 12, 22, 51, 61, 104, 105, 107, 126 n.28, 146 n.34, 160, 194, 205, 236, 237 n.4, 250, 281, 282, 305 n.4; Strata : 251

Steam : 160, 174, 253; Steamship Co. : 252

Steinschneider, Moritz : 28 n.8

Stigma : 105

Stone : 35, 100, 278

Stool : 129, 130, 133, 134, 165

Store Room, Storage : 52, 166, 167, 217

Story : 46, 91, 121, 238, 240

Stove : 165, 218

Stratification : 205, 206; Strata : 271

Stree Mandal : 180, 209, 263

Street (see Road) : 72, 77, 225, 275, 317
Streetcar (see Tramway) : 226
"Stri Soundharyalatika", Bene Israel Publication : 95
Strizower, Schifra : ix, x, xiv n.12, 11, 16 n.47, 35, 38 n.11 and n.12, 44, 48 n.25, 50, 54 n.6, 85 n.9, 103, 104, 105, 109 n.12 and n.13, 110 n.21, 205, 225, 228, 230 n.3, 231 n.9, 267 n.1 and n;3
Struggle (National) : Chapter 27 passim 247-256
Students (see Pupils) : 66, 68, 76, 77, 90 n.54, 169, 180, 187, 236, 244, 258, 259, 260, 261, 264, 266
Studies, Study : 183, 184, 213, 234, 237 n.6, 247, 258, 261, 280, 283, 287, 336, 340
Subcaste : 155
Subcontinent : 27, 72, 162, 177, 186, 187, 247, 281, 282, 284, 285, 298 Table 19, 305 n.10
Subedar : 51, 54 n.13, 316
Subodh Prakash Samaj : 91, 94, 96 n.11
Subja : 114, 123 n.12, 131, 134, 140, 142
Subsidy : 260
Suburb ; 225, 260
Succath Shelomo Synagogue, Poona : 149, 179, 180, 181, 182
Success Successful : 77, 78, 174, 182, 185, 199, 224, 228, 243, 244, 246, 265, 272; Successor : 260
Succoth : 5, 120, 135, 218, 333, 345
Sudhagad : 215-216, 223 n.6, 283
Sudra : 3, 16 n.48
Sufism : 186
Sugar : 115, 120, 131, 133, 134, 136, 140, 143 n.4, 218, 253
Sultanates : 14 n.9, 27, 46; Ahmednagar : 25; Bijapur : 26; Delhi : 24
Sun : 130
Sunni : 50, 146 n.34
Superintendent : 93, 178, 184, 185, 205, 209, 210
Superstition : 103, 127, 143, 144 n.9 and n.13, 220, 223 n.11, 281
Supervisor : 174
Support : 248, 260, 271
Supremacy, Superior : 102, 103, 104, 252
Sura : 20
Surat : 37, 42, 43, 45, 47 n.16 and n.17, 49, 50, 59, 98, 99, 108 n.1, 183, 184, 193
Surgeon : 183; Veterinary : 181
Surnames : 17 n.48, 24, 26, 27, 30 n.29, 35, 62, 92, 153 n.4, Chapter 13 passim 154-159, 214, 215, 216, 223 n.6, 283, 298, 299 Table 20, 328 368-373

Surparaka : 9, 16 n.36, 23
Surplus : 218
Surveys, Surveyors : 213, 216, 223 n.7, 279, 340, 346
Survivor, Survival : 3, 112
Surya River : 9
Swadeshi : 249, 251
Swaraj : 249
Sweets : 15 n.12, 115, 116, 120, 124-125 n.18, 127, 330, 333
Swing : 229, 231 n.10
Sykes, Col. : 281, 305 n.6
Symbol, Symbolic : 121, 129, 130, 135, 141, 249, 278, 278 n.3
Sympathy : 269
Symphony (Delhi) : 189, 210
Synagogue : 7, 23, 27, 32 n.47 and n.51, 36, 42, 43, 44, 45, 46, 46 n.1, 48 n.29, 59, 60, 61, 62, 63, 64 n.11, n.12, n.13 and n.15, 69, 70, 71, 73, 91, 98, 99, 100, 101, 102, 104, 105, 106, 107, 108 n.6(7), 109 n.6(13), 110 n.19 and n.22, 113, 116, 119, 120, 121, 122, 123 n.10, 130, 131, 132, 133, 134, 135, 136, 140, 141, 142, Chapter 12 passim 148-153, 157, 167, 170, 171, 173, 174, 177, 178, 179, 181, 183, 184, 185, 186, 187, 188, 205, 206, 213, 215, 218, 219, 220, 222 n.1 and n.3, 223 n.4 and n.12, 224, 225, 226, 230 n.1, Chapter 24 passim 232-237, 239, 240, 244, 263, 264, 265, 266, 267 n.5, 274, 276, 277, 278, 280, 314, 315, 316, 317, 318, 319, 329, 342, 343, 344, 345, 348
Syria, Syrian : 7, 19, 23

Tabernacles : 5, 15 n.19, 120
Tables, Statistics (see pp. xviii-xix for Titles and Pages for each Table) : 79, 90 n.57; Religions in British Districts of Bombay Presidency from 1921 Census : 251; Israelite School Attendance 1921-1927 : 259
Tabulation : 279, 282, 284, 304 n.3
Tadgaon : 213, 222 n.1
Taj Mahal : 186
Tala, in Mangaon Taluka : 27, 149, 173, 283
Tale-Ghosale, Tala : 149, 150, 213, 222 n.1, 274 277; 283 Table 9
Talekhar Synagogue : 149, 213, 222 n.1, 274; 283 Table 9
Talgaonkar, Isaac Abraham : 96-97 n.11
Tali : 145 n.25
Talith, Talesim : 71, 105, 121, 135, 140, 237 n.6 315, 348
Talk : 221

Talkar : 27; Aaron Daniel : 181, 247, 351; Abraham Benjamin : 83; Bahais Joseph : 94, 97 n.13; Daniel Rahamim : 181; Ezekiel Joseph : 350, 353; Ezekiel Moses : 353; Ezekiel Samuel : 92; Haeem Joseph : 97 n.13; Moses Daniel : 95, 97 n.14; Moses Jacob : 351, 353; Samson Joseph : 211; Shelomo Abraham : 27

Talmud : 7, 10, 47 n.5, 93, 95, 97 n.11, 116, 167, 206, 231 n.4, 239

Taluka : 42, 149, 174, 214, 216, 217, 223 n.5, 368-373

Tamhankar, D.V. : 254 n.3

Tamil : 87 n.32

Tana (see Thana) : 22, 23, 24

Tanjore : 86 n.9

Tank (Water) : 122, 217

Tarankhopkar, Abraham Samuel : 156

Taschlich : 119, 125 n.24 and n.25

Tax : 10, 186, 237, 250, 311

Tea : 119, 120, 218

Teacher, Teach : 10, 35, 44, 45, 59, 60, 61, 65, 66, 67, 68, 72, 73, 77, 79, 80, 91, 93, 98, 101, 117, 150, 151, 152, 161, 169, 170, 171 n.1, 174, 179, 180, 181, 184, 187, 199, 205, 209, 214, 232, 234, 235, 236, 239, 241 n.3, 257, 259, 260, 261, 262, 263, 265, 269, 271, 275, 310, 323 n.3, 325, 335, 340, 341, 342, 344, 353; Training : 218

Tebila : 219, 353

Technical : 205, 261, 304 n.3

Teenagers : 260, 263

Tefilin : 14 n.6, 121, 237 n.6, 315, 348

Tehsil, Tahsil : 216, 223 n.5, 368-373

Telegraph (see Posts & Telegraph) : 161; 216

Telephone : 216

Teli, Til, Tili : 14 n.4, 17 n.52, 49, 55 n.16, 160, 173, 205, 312, 328

Tellicherry : 43, 67, 316, 318, 320, 322, 323 n.9

Tembi : 174

Temperance : 161, 162, 163 n.3, 244, 251

Temperature : 52

Temple in Jerusalem : 4, 5, 6, 7, 8, 12, 14 n.6, 69, 88 n.49, 111, 118, 120, 145 n.21 and n.24

Temple (Hindu) : 132, 144 n.10, 159 n.12, 186, 310

Ten Commandments : 66, 70, 75

Ten Lost Tribes of Israel : viii, 8, 74, 154

Tenant : 148, 216, 237

Tenement : 227

Tenet : 235

Tent : 44, 88 n.22, 133-134, 135, 340, 348 n.2

Term (see Name) : xi, 11, 16 n.48

Territories : 279, 280, 281, 284

Text : 41, 91, 93, 96 n.2, 122, 140, 237 n.6, 238, 240

Thakur : 217, 223 n.8

Thale, Thalkar : 219, 220

Thana (see Tana) : District : 9, 144 n.10, 149, 173, 174, 175, 208, 290 Table 13c; Town : 22, 23, 24, 149, 175, 175 n.6 and n.7, 180, 194, 204, 274, 277, 282

Thanksgiving : 113, 116, 130, 230

Thapar, Prof. Romila : 110 n.16

Thatch : 165, 214, 220

Theology : 70, 71

Theories (see Origin) : Chapter 1 *passim* 3-18, 73, 80, 112

Theosophist : 184

Thesis : 40, 125 n.24

Threshold : 133

Tiberias : 78

Ticket : 226, 230 n.4

Tie, Tying : 132, 136, 140, 145 n.25, 146 n.30

Tifereth Israel Prayer Hall : 100, 108 n.5, 149, 232, 269, 277

Tigris River : 19, 98

Tilak, Lokamanya Bal Gangadhar : 181, 247, 254 n.3

Tiles : 168

Timberg, Dr. Thomas : xiv n.17

"Times of India" : 211

Tinning : 121, 165, 221

Tipu Sultan : 316, 317, 318, 321, 322

Tirthur : 315

"Tirukkural" of Tiruvallavar : 87 n.32

Tisha B'av : 118

Title (see Rank) : 62, 72, 92, 93, 96 n.11, 208, 211, 228, 244

Titus : 6

Tobias, Moses (Tuvia, Moshe) : 43, 47 n.16 and n.17

Toddy : 105, 162

Tolerance : 248, 310

Tolkovsky, Paul : 268

Tombstone, Tomb, Marker (see Burial, Cemetery) : 35, 36, 38 n.13, 43, 115, 116, 122, 134, 141, 155, 157, 158 n.5, 173, 183, 185, 186, 278 n.3

Tonga : 84, 174

Torah (Scroll) : 3, 7, 14 n.6, 23, 41, 44, 46, 48 n.26, 60, 61, 62, 63, 64 n.10 and n.15, 71, 88 n.49, 101, 105, 106, 120, 123 n.10, 136, 142, 143 n.4, 148, 150, 174, 179, 188, 224, 234, 235, 237 n.6, 265, 314, 315, 317, 329, 342, 344, 345, 346, 347

Touch (see Untouchable) : 5, 119, 122, 141, 165

Tourist : 187, 214, 302, 303 Table 24
Towns : 35, 44, 49, 51, 70, 156, 158, 160, 161, Chapter 17 *passim* 173-175, 176, 182, 216, 221, 237, 272, 273 n.10, 274, 277, 283, 285
Tract : 65, 94
Trader, Trade(s) (see Merchant, Commerce) : 6, 7, 9, 11, 19, 20, 21, 22, 23, 24, 25, 26, 28 n.13, 31 n.34, 50, 51, 52, 65, 102, 160, 170, 173, 174, 177, 179, 186, 187, 193, 230 n.2, 252, 253
Tradition : Chapter 1 *passim* 3-18, 13 n.2, 21, 23, 26, 33, 35, 41, 42, 44, 45, 51, 61, 70, 75, 95, n.2, 98, 100, 103, 105, 112, 117, 135, 137, 156, 157, 168, 183, 185, 188, 189, 193, 205, 207 n.3, 213, 215, 217, 220, 227, 228, 229, 230, 231 n.11, 233, 264, 275, 277, 278, 283, 310, 318, 323, 327; Pristine : 4, 21, 117
Train (see Railway) : 231 n.4
Training : 235, 236, 245, 259, 261, 274, 275
Tramway : 226, 230 n.4
Transfer : 285
Transition : 82
Translation : xi, xiii n.5, 28 n.4, 29 n.16, 33, 34, 37, 37 n.3, 40, 44, 63 n.10, 65, 72, 76, 80, 81, 83, 84, 85 n.1, 87 n.32, 88 n.48, 91, 92, 93, 94, 96 n.11, 97 n.12 and n.14, 122, 135, 157, 169, 170, 171, 227, 231 n.11, 238, 239, 240, 241, 241 n.3, 242 n.8, 272 n.2, 312, 313, 314, 339, 341, 342, 345, 350, 351, 352, 353
Transliteration : 92, 93
Transport, Conveyance : 174, 200, 206, 210, 226, 230 n.4, 253
Travancore : 86 n.9, 282, 284, 314
Travels, Traveller : ix, 7, 10, 13, 17 n.50, 20, 23, 24, 28 n.13, 30 n.25, 37 n.7, 52, 53 n.5, 69, 72, 73, 76, 78, 81, 87 n.31, 90 n.61, 108 n.6(1), 177, 184, 214, 218, 224, 230 n.4, 270, 275
Treasury, Treasurer (see Gabbai) : 148, 171, 184, 234
Treatise : 83
Tree : 113, 114, 116, 118, 123 n.7, 138, 165, 214
Trespass : 278
Trial : 254 n.3, 329
Tribe (see Ten Lost Tribes) : 8, 9, 223 n.8
Tribunal : 245
Trip : 77
Trousers : 50, 166
"T'ruah" Bene Israel Periodical : 95
Trustee, Trust : 151, 152, 181, 185, 234, 236, 265, 346
Tu B'Shvat : 113, 116, 118
Tuition : 242 n.6, 260, 261
Tulasi : 123 n.12
Tunis : 22

Turban : 50, 134, 135, 166, 330, 346
Turks, Turkey : 24, 152 n.1
Turmeric, Haldi : 128, 129, 134
Turner ; 206
Type, Typing : 35, 261
Typhus : 214
Tzitzith : 121, 140

Ud : 134
Umbilical Cord : 128
Umbrella : 135
Umerkhadi : 84, 149, 170, 224, 225
Umpire : Cricket : 211; Wrestling : 210
Uncle : 226, 228
Unclean, Defiling (see Pollution) : 15 n.18, 109 n.15, 144 n.7, 166
Under-Enumeration : 279, 295 n.a; 305 n.4
Understand(ing) : 234, 235
Union of American Hebrew Congregations : 236
Union of Orthodox Jewish Congregations of America : 235, 239
Unique : 111, 136, 160, 168, 229
Unison : 113
Unite, Unify, Unity : 99, 132, 194, 227, 244, 246, 249, 250, 251
United Kingdom: : 298
United Nations : 187, 189
United States of America, U.S.A. (see America) : 73, 236, 272 n.3, 273 n.8, 298
United Synagogues of India : 237 n.6
University : 74, 88 n.41, 171, 183, 184, 206, 208, 209, 244, 258, 259
Unleavened Bread (Matzah) : 165, 218
Unmarried : 138, 139, 216, 228
Untouchable (see Defiling) : 5, 15 n.48, 51, 62, 104, 109 n.15, 119, 249
Uplift : 206, 239, 241 n.3
Urban, Cities : ix, 7, 100, 107, 135, 146 n.34, 148, 158, 162, 173, 193, 194, 199, 205, 211, 229, 233, 272, 275, 275 n.10
Urdu : 14 n.9, 101, 124 n.18, 208, 242 n.8, 271
U.S.A. (see America, United States)
Utensils, Vessels : 100, 105, 108 n.6(8), 110 n.15 and n.19, 121, 140, 148, 152, 165, 234, 343

Vacation : 214, 220, 222
Vaccination : 131, 195 n.3
Vaishya : 16 n.48
Vakrulkar, Solomon M. : 62, 64 n.13, 107, 110 n.25

Van Dort, Leopold Emanuel Jacob : 41
Varhad Jumbulpada : 217
Varna : 16 n.48, 104
Va Yiten L'ḥa : 113, 121, 124 n.14
Vedas, Vedic : 16 n.36, 144 n.10
Vegetarian : 114, 215
Vegetables : 220
Venice : 19
Venkoji : 86 n.9
Verandah : 153 n.3, 165, 167, 179, 214
Verbatim : xi, xii, 239
Verdict : 62
Vernacular : 92, 103, 154
Verse : 113, 114, 130, 131, 215, 238, 240
Version : 41
Vessels (see Utensils) : 143 n.4
Vestige, Vestigial, Remnant : 10, 53, 72, 75, 78, 156, 228
Veterinary : 181, 210
Vice : 161
Vice-Admiral : 210
Vice-Chancellor : 72
Vice-President : 188, 266
Viceroy, Viceroyalty : 26, 210, 239, 250, 255 n.11, 309
Victim : 244
Victor Sassoon Trust : 236
Vienna : 81, 305 n.11
Vijapur (Bijapur) : 44, 48 n.21, 49
Vile Parle : 225
Villa : 178
Village, Villager : 3, 10, 11, 17 n.49, 26, 27, 33, 43, 51, 53, 55 n.16, 59, 61, 63 n.2, 66, 68, 84, 105, 112, 115, 125 n.25, 133, 141, 144 n.10, 148, 153 n.4, 154, 155, 156, 158, 159 n.8 and n.12, 160, 161, 165, 166, 169, 173, 178, 189, 190, 194, 200, 205, 207 n.3, Chapter 22 *passim* 213-223, 237, 272, 273 n.10, 274, 275, 282, 283, 299-300 Table 20, 304 n.3, 311, 327, 328, 329, 330, 335, 341, 345, 347; Village-linked surnames : 368-373
Vilna : 72
Violinist : 189, 210
Viramgam : 221
Virgin : 134, 135, 138
Virjole (Satambe) : 213, 222 n.1, 232; 283 Table 9
Visa : 302
Vishnu : 123 n.12
Visit, Visitor : 5, 41, 45, 81, 120, 158, 160, 215, 260, 269, 275, 277
Vital Sakharam Agnihotri : 92, 351, 352
Vital, Vitality : 233, 274, 276

Vocation (see Occupation) : 51, 150; Training : 175
Volume : 238, 241 n.2, 280, 304 n.3
Volunteer : 69, 141, 263, 334
Vote : 250, 269
Vow(s), Votive, Neder : 8, 10, 62, 111, 112, 114, 115, 116, 124 n.14, 125 n.21, 130, 144 n.10, 145 n.19, 151, 167, 231 n.15

Wadhwan : 183
Wages : 62, 161, 200, 217
Wakrul : 214, 215, 223 n.4
Wali : 173, 219, 299 Table 20 n.a
Walk : 224, 226, 233
Walkar, Rebecca and Simeon : 230, 231 n.12, 299
Wall (see Fence) : 99, 100, 130, 165, 182, 187, 188, 190 n.6, 221, 222 n.3, 227, 244, 278
Waluk (near Pen) : 190
Walwatkar, Elijah Shalom:93, 352, 353; Walwati : 70, 222 n.1
Wandering Jew : 11, 12, 190
Wanowarie : 182
War(s) (see World War) : 26, 27, 42, 50, 51, 54 n.14, 56 n.20, 154, 189, 269, 270
Ward : 281, 290, 291 Table 13 d
Wargharkar : Abraham Shalom : 182; Benjamin J. : x, 156; Shalom Bapuji Israel : 182
Wash(ing) : 122, 123 n.12, 136, 140, 141, 142, 168, 343; Clothes : 166
Water : 119, 122, 123 n.12, 125 n.24, 128, 129, 131, 140, 142, 160, 166, 214, 217, 231 n.7, 277; Shore : 333
Water Buffalo : 217
Wealth, Wealthy (see Rich) : 24, 52, 100, 101, 116, 174, 177, 178, 193, 207 n.4, 224, 234, 253, 260, 264, 265
Weaving : 49; Master : 103
Wedding (see Marriage) : 43, 92, 96 n.2, 116, 132-138, 188, 228, 229, 265; Double : 133, 144 n.14
Weil, Dr. Shalva : 38 n.9, 64 n.15, 110 n.26, 145 n.20 and n.27
Weisel (Weseley), Naphtali Hertz : 41, 47 n.6
Welfare (see Societies) : 77, 78, 148, 187
Well : 78, 122, 160, 166, 217
Wellington, New Zealand : 190
The West, Western(ized) : 95, 100, 103, 119, 130, 140, 141, 150, 153 n.8, 155, 159 n.7, 166, 167, 187, 194, 199, 200, 206, 225, 229, 233, 243, 248, 261, 267 n.5, 269

Wheat : 114, 115, 134, 166, 343
White Cloth, Sheet : 119, 124 n.14, 129, 130, 133, 140, 220
White Collar : 194
White Jews (see Gora, Pardesi) : Baghdadi : 68, 70, 99; Bene Israel : 67, 110 n.19; Cochin : 40, 59, 86 n.11 and n.23, 105, 106, 107, 110 n.16, 305 n.9, 314, 342
Whitewash : 119, 121, 165, 221
Widow : 102, 132, 138, 140, 141, 168 n.2, 228, 241 n.3, 243, 265, 267 n.5, 281; Remarriage : 55 n.16, 108 n.6(9), 133, 139, 146 n.34, 151
Widower : 138, 139, 167 n.5
Wife, Wives : 29 n.19, 44, 59, 69, 77, 83, 101, 111, 122 n.1, 131, 136, 138, 139, 142, 146 n.29 and n.34, 160, 162, 166, 181, 185, 199, 216, 217, 218, 220, 222, 228, 236, 275, 315, 317, 331, 340, 341, 344
Will : 183
Willow : 120
Wilson College : 76, 87 n.27, 88 n.46, 169
Wilson High School : 88 n.46
Wilson, Isabella Dennistown : 77
Wilson, Rev. Dr. John : x, 3, 7, 13 n.1, 15 n.27, 22, 63 n.4, 71, 72, 73, 74, 75, 76, 77, 78, 79, 80, 81, 82, 84, 87 n.29, 88 n.36 through n.48; 89 n.53 and n.54; 93, 110 n.23, 115, 120, 148, 169, 280, 281, 284, 305 n.6, 325, 327, 341
Wilson, Margaret Bayne : 77
Window : 214
Winds (seasonal) : 7
Wine : 112, 133, 134, 135, 142, 145 n.23 and n.24; 233, 343, 345
Winnowing Fan : 228
Wisdom : 240
Witchcraft : 70
Witness : 136, 137, 146 n.34
Wolff, Rev. Joseph : 69, 70, 73, 79, 86 n.15, n.16 and n.17, 178, 305 n.8
Woman, Women : xii n.2, 10, 22, 59, 77, 80, 91, 95 n.2, 102, 103, 105, 107, 108 n.6(9), 116, 119, 121, 127, 128, 131, 132, 133, 134, 136, 137, 138, 139, 140, 141, 143 n.4, 144 n.10, 145 n.25, 146 n.34, 154, 155, 166, 167, 168 n.2, 180, 188, 194, 199, 200, 208, 209, 214, 223 n.9 and n.11, 227, 229, 231 n.11, 234, 235, 236, 240, 241 n.3, 244, 259, 263, 266, 269, 270, 315, 340, 341, 342, 344, 346, 353; Balcony : 135, 148, 179
"Wonderful Testimonies" : 238, 241 n.2
Wood, Wooden : 36, 165, 188, 231 n.10, 343
Work, Worker : 3, 68, 100, 142, 160, 161, 176, 178, 184, 188, 199, 200, 205, 206, 218, 220, 228, 233, 244, 249, 269, 282

Workshop : 150, 170, 193, 200
World : 238, 239, 240, 262 n.11, 269, 270, 272 n.3
World Council of Synagogues : 235, 237 n.6, 239
World Jewish Congress : 189
World Union for Progressive Judaism : 235, 236
World War : I : 207 n.4, 243, 275; II : 182, 187, 191 n.18, 199, 205, 209, 210, 212 n.3, 266, 305 n.10
Worli : 47 n.14, 261
Worship : 52, 63, 67, 70, 99, 105, 115, 127, 132, 150, 173, 179, 182, 185, 187, 188, 222 n.1, 227, 229, 230, Chapter 24 *passim* 232-237, 264, 265, 274, 331, 333
Wrestling : 210
Writings, Write, Writer (see Literature, Publication) : 4, 7, 10, 20, 23, 71, 72, 74, 75, 79, 81, 82, 83, 91, 93, 94, 104, 170, 175, 181, 186, 206, 208, 211, 214, 218, 220, 238, 240, 248, 255 n.18, 256 n.19, 268, 284, 301, 335, 345, 346

Yaari, Abraham : 96 n.5 and n.8, 238
Year : 208, 279, 282
Yehezkiel, Abraham Solomon David Hai : 92
Yehudi, Yehudim, Yahud : 7, 49, 67, 173, 245, 276 n.1, 316, 327
Yellapur : 185
Yemen, Yemenite : 6, 7, 22, 23, 40, 60, 61, 63 n.10, 77, 92, 93, 98, 99, 135, 145 n.22, 236, 270, 342
Yeshiva : 19
Yibum : 102
Yiju, Abraham : 22, 29 n.17 and n.19
Yom Kippur (Day of Atonement) : 4, 5, 15 n.12, 41, 67, 119, 120, 121, 125 n.26, 153 n.10, 218, 219, 220, 221, 223 n.12, 268, 310, 333, 340
"Yonati Ziv Yifatayh" : 135
Young, Youth : 81, 83, 160, 180, 228, 235, 236, 237 n.7, 244, 257, 258, 261, 263, 266, 268, 269, 271, 273 n.6, 274, 275
Young Men's Hebrew Association, Poona : 181
Young Men and Women's Hebrew Association, Bombay : 236, 266
Young Men's Jewish Debating Club : 263

Zalizar, Gary : 214, 215, 223 n.4
Zebah Todah, Thanks Offering : 116
Zebulon (Tribe of) : 8, 9, 16 n.37

Zionism, Zionist : 239, 263, 268, 269, 270, 271, 272-273 n.6
Zirad : 13

Zoo Ahmedabad : 184, 185, 210; Zoological Society : 181
Zoroastrian (see Parsi) : 122

950　　　　　　　　　　92-332
Is4　　　Isenberg, Shirley Berry
　　　　　India's Bene Israel

950　　　　　　　　　92-332
Is4　　　Isenberg, Shirley Berry
　　　　　India's Bene Israel

FAIRMOUNT TEMPLE LIBRARY

93 97